For Gerard Gardner,
from Vilhjalmur Stefansson

9 December 1948

ARCTIC MANUAL

By
VILHJALMUR STEFANSSON

My Life with the Eskimo, 1913

Anthropological Papers (American Museum of Natural History), 1914

The Friendly Arctic, 1921

Hunters of the Great North, 1922

The Northward Course of Empire, 1922

The Adventure of Wrangel Island, 1925

My Life with the Eskimos (abridged), 1927

The Standardization of Error, 1927

Adventures in Error, 1936

The Three Voyages of Martin Frobisher, 1938
(With collaboration of Eloise McCaskill)

Unsolved Mysteries of the Arctic, 1938

Iceland: The First American Republic, 1939

The Problem of Meighen Island, 1939

Ultima Thule, 1940

Greenland, 1942

The Friendly Arctic (new edition), 1943

BOOKS FOR YOUNGER READERS
(In collaboration with Violet Irwin)

Kak, the Copper Eskimo, 1924

The Shaman's Revenge, 1925

The Mountain of Jade, 1926

(In collaboration with Julia Schwartz)
Northward Ho!, 1925

ARCTIC MANUAL

By

VILHJALMUR STEFANSSON

Prepared under direction of the
Chief of the Air Corps

UNITED STATES ARMY

*With a special Introduction
and Index*

NEW YORK
THE MACMILLAN COMPANY
1945

Reprinted March, 1945

TABLE OF CONTENTS

TABLE OF CONTENTS

INTRODUCTION

This Manual was written for the Air Corps of the United States Army, but the reasons for it go back to civilian flying, indeed to the first job of ordinary commercial air transport between North America and Asia. They go back also to Alaska's first Arctic airplane tragedy.

The summer of 1929 the ship·*Nanuk*, commanded by the veteran Arctic navigator Olaf Swenson, had gone up through Bering Strait and west along the north coast of Siberia under a fur-trading agreement with the Moscow government. The season had proved difficult, and they were forced to winter near North Cape—now Cape Schmidt. This was awkward, for the pay roll of the crew was heavy and mounting costs would eat into the profits. It struck Swenson that flying was perhaps by then so far developed in Alaska that he could arrange by radio to carry unwanted men to railhead or steamer and send them home. He thought, too, that fur prices were likely to drop, and that the sooner the cargo were marketed the larger the return; so he desired also to ship out his furs by air.

Then as now the aviation capital of Alaska was Fairbanks, and there the Territory's most famous aeronautical pioneer, Carl Ben Eielson,* had organized a company that would handle practically any sort of flying. By radio he agreed with Swenson to take on what appears to have been the first job of routine commercial air traffic between the continents of North America and Asia. The tariff for Bering Strait and Siberia would be the same per mile as within Alaska.

The agreement made, Eielson proceeded by way of Nome and East Cape to the *Nanuk*, picked up those of her crew that were being sent out, and delivered them to Nome. On the second trip, to begin the fur transport, he and his mechanic Earl Borland took off from Teller, Alaska, crossed

---

* In polar work Eielson had to his credit more important "firsts" than any other pilot: among them, he was first to descend with skis on the pack of the Arctic Sea far from shore, and first to cross the Arctic by airplane (as distinct from flying part way in and back again). He was the first pilot to fly in the Antarctic and was the first in the history of aviation to be at the controls when new land was discovered. All this had been under command of Sir Hubert Wilkins. On his own, he had carried the first U.S. air mail in Alaska and had organized at Fairbanks the pioneer company which, in amalgamation with other companies, was later to form the nucleus of the Alaska system of Pan American Airways.

Bering Strait in bad weather, and were seen flying northwest over some villages on the north Siberian coast. The plane was not seen from other villages farther west, and the day passed without its reaching Swenson's base.

There were several days of little concern, for Eielson had been through many things supposed to be far more difficult and dangerous than this routine trip. At first it was thought he would come in to the *Nanuk* after a while, flying a repaired plane; then that he would walk in, somewhat as he and Wilkins had done in 1927 when they had been forced to abandon their plane on the drifting pack eighty miles north of Alaska. But when a week had passed there was real concern, which spread to Ben's innumerable friends and admirers in Canada, the United States, and, indeed, throughout the world.

Then developed gradually the Eielson Search. We should like to dwell upon the helpfulness and unselfishness that brought volunteer flyers from Canada, the States, and the Soviet Union, and upon how the need for Soviet help occasioned what were (so far as we know) the first official communications from the Government of the United States to the Government of the Soviet Union—from William E. Borah, as Chairman of the Senate's Committee on Foreign Relations, and from Ray Lyman Wilbur, as Secretary of the Interior in charge of Alaska.

What we dwell on here is how and why the need for an Arctic Manual appeared when flyers of the three countries, some of them among the most experienced of northern pilots, turned out to be, with a number of striking exceptions, nearly as helpless when on the ground as they were competent while in the air.

When the Eielson Search took on large proportions, the general supervision was placed in the hands of Alfred Lomen, who had been living at Nome more than a quarter of a century, and who was experienced in travel by air, dog sledge, and reindeer team on the shores and prairies of northwestern Alaska and in the marginal forest.

Those who do not know Alaska may think that such experience as that of Alfred Lomen brings with it, of necessity, a knowledge of cold-weather technique which will give safety and comfort with a minimum of equipment under the most rigorous conditions of an Arctic winter. But Mr. Lomen was fully aware that this is not the case—for instance, the essential art of building snowhouses and using them is unknown not only to the white men of Alaska but also to the Alaska

Eskimos and those of Siberia, to whom the real snowhouse technique, most important of all cold-weather methods for safety and comfort, developed by the Eskimos of northern Canada, had never penetrated.

The flyers who gathered around Bering Strait were on the average not merely good pilots but also good mechanics, able to service their planes under primitive conditions; but many of them were so little prepared to take care of themselves on the ground that it appeared likely they would lose their lives after a safe forced landing, if it took place in a country without fuel and where the direction and distance of local inhabitants might be unknown.

There was at Nome a man, August Masik, who had learned the building of snowhouses, and the general technique of comfortable and safe Arctic living, some years before in Banks and Victoria islands when a member of our third expedition, and also when he lived as a trapper with the Victoria Island people, who (with their neighbors immediately to the east) are the greatest masters of cold-weather method in the world. Lomen employed Masik to demonstrate snowhouse building to the flyers and to instruct them in some of the other fundamentals of cold-weather procedure.

About three months after the disappearance of Eielson and Borland their plane was discovered from the air by Eielson's friend Joe Crosson—who, by the way, was destined to become Eielson's successor in the affection of Alaskans and in the flight leadership of Alaska. Signs in the snow were read to indicate that the wing tip of Eielson's plane had touched the ground when he was banking for a turn, doubtless intending to go back for the night to a village they had just passed. The engine had been hurled to a great distance from the plane, and so had the bodies, which it took a long search to discover beneath the drifts.

When found, the bodies were first placed on Soviet planes and carried to the *Nanuk;* thence Crosson took them back to Alaska. A Soviet plane accompanied them to Fairbanks as a guard of honor; and one of the Soviet flyers accompanied the body of Eielson to Hatton, North Dakota, for the funeral.

The occasion was sad; but this cooperation of flyers from Canada, the United States, and the Soviet Union through several months of Arctic midwinter in a work of humanity was a happy beginning of an association which has developed with increasing mutual respect and affection between the air pioneers of our three countries. This frontier comradeship was to prove an entering wedge of friendship which has made smooth and effective the grand-scale cooperation by way of Bering Strait that has been such a striking fact and such an important factor of the present war.

As said, the Eielson Search left at Nome, and particularly with its family of outstanding pioneers, Alfred Lomen and his brothers Carl and Ralph, the feeling that something had to be done to remove the disparity between air and ground techniques. They decided that perhaps the first thing should be to write a textbook of Arctic procedure which would place in the hands of northern flyers, and others who go North, the fundamentals of comfort and safety in the North. Along this line Alfred Lomen wrote me a letter which, though flattering, we place here verbatim, for it explains, as nothing else can, the genesis of our Manual:

LOMEN REINDEER CORPORATION

Nome, Alaska, February 28, 1930

Mr. Vilhjalmur Stefansson,
Explorers Club, New York City.

My dear Stef:

Our corporation has had much to do with furnishing fur clothing to Arctic and Antarctic expeditions, including the Byrd-Floyd Bennett North Pole flight, the Amundsen-Maud North Pole expedition, the Wilkins expedition and the Byrd Antarctic expedition. This winter we have been in charge of the Aviation Corporation Eielson-Borland Relief Expedition, and have supplied the pilots with the necessary fur clothing for their flight to Siberia and sojourn there.

Our experience has brought forcibly to our attention the fact that there is at this time a great need for a manual that can be used by fliers and travelers in the Arctic and the Antarctic, one that will contain instructions on the following subjects living on the ice and on the land, finding one's way, caring for one's self, building shelters, procuring game, wearing Arctic clothing and caring for same, et cetera. From now on there will be more and more flying in the extreme north and south, and this text would serve as a "bible" for the pioneers.

We feel that there is but one person qualified to write such a book, and that person is Vilhjalmur Stefansson. Such a manual coming from him could not be questioned; it would be absolutely authoritative. His experience and keen observations in the Arctic have qualified him for this task above all others.

We therefore take the liberty of calling this matter to your attention, in the hope that it will bear fruit. While you have been long absent from the North, it is evident that your heart is still in the Arctic to which you have given the best years of your life. Through your writings and lectures the world is beginning to know the Arctic as it really is.

Your vision of importing reindeer into Canada is soon to be realized, as our drive, in which you have taken such an interest and have so materially assisted, is well organized and under way. The drive is a greater undertaking than appears on paper, but we are confident that we will be successful in delivering our herd of 3,000 deer, plus the increase en route, to the Kittigasuit Peninsula, there to be received by the Canadian Government.

With kindest personal regards, in which my father joins me, I am

Sincerely yours,
(Signed) ALFRED J. LOMEN

For various reasons nothing happened about a manual until three men came together in Washington: Carl Lomen; Major General George E. Leach, Chief of the National Guard Bureau of the War Department; and the Honorable Ross A. Collins, of the House Committee on Appropriations. Carl, as said, had been impressed by the same things that impressed his brother Alfred in the search for Eielson; General Leach and Mr. Collins thought there might be a war coming which would carry our troops to spheres of operations where they would need an Arctic technique and a knowledge of Arctic conditions—basic not merely to individual comfort and safety but to the success of operations in which they might be engaged. These men interested, among others, the Secretary of War, the Honorable George H. Dern, the Deputy Chief of Staff, Major General Hugh A. Drum, and the Chief of the Air Corps, Brigadier General (later Major General) Oscar Westover. An item covering the purchase of information about the Arctic was inserted into an Army appropriation bill; the administration of this sum was turned over to General Westover, and my research organization and I were employed on April 2, 1935, to make a report on living and operating conditions in the Arctic.

At this stage our library contained perhaps 10,000 books, pamphlets, and manuscripts relating to the Arctic and Subarctic, and there was a small staff which had grown up with the library. In view of the needs of the job now assigned to us, we gradually expanded the library by another 5,000 or so titles during three years while working out a report of nearly two million words. (That number of words does not mean much unless you are a writer of books, or a publisher; so we mention that in length the report was equal to about five of those thick novels, like *Anthony Adverse* and *Gone with the Wind*. It was about five times as long as my own longest book, *The Friendly Arctic*, which has 812 pages.)

Most of this huge report has little to do with our present Manual, but a section is directly concerned. For it had been agreed that in addition to a work of general information about the North there should be the suggested manual or handbook which would try to give in reasonably small compass those underlying facts and principles which would be

xi

most useful to a man who wanted to travel or live in the Arctic, whether under conditions of peace or war, but with special reference to the needs of the Army.

Now arose the question of form. Should this manual be as condensed as possible, giving brief and snappy directions for specific things to do under specified conditions? Such a book would be intended for carrying in the pocket; when you got into trouble you would pull it out and thumb it in quest of a solution for whatever predicament you might be in. Or should the book, on the other hand, undertake to explain things at such length, and so clearly and interestingly, that a man would remember what he had read, would understand it? Then, instead of carrying a small manual in a pocket, he would carry with him a still more portable memory and would have such a grasp of fundamentals that he could devise the appropriate solution for any problem which might arise.

General Westover, who had now become Chief of the Air Corps, considered this matter of format so important that he carried it up to the Chief of Staff, who was then General Malin Craig. I never talked with General Craig about it, but I was called in by the Deputy Chief of Staff, Major General George S. Simonds, who said they had decided that the manual should be written in a topical form, with a narrative trend similar to that of my published books, such as *Hunters of the Great North* or *The Friendly Arctic*, and with an attempt at such lucidity and human interest that the work might be read for pleasure, or at least without mental distress, by anyone who was interested—as anyone would almost necessarily be if he thought of going North. Later, said the General, I might be employed to make an abridgment suitable for carrying in a pocket.

After the tragic death of General Westover in an airplane accident, our work went forward under the direction of his successor, now General H. H. Arnold, commanding the Air Forces, but then Chief of the Air Corps. A new arrangement was made. We would divide up the rather inchoate mass of the two-million-word report into four "Guide Books"—of Alaska, Arctic Canada, Greenland, and Arctic Siberia—ranging in length from 1,100 to 2,500 typewritten pages each; and then there would be the present Arctic Manual, which was to be in conception and form on the lines prescribed by the Chief of Staff, as above told.

By 1939 war had descended upon Europe as well as Asia; clouds were gathering above the United States. There was much to do in Washington, and General Arnold, had he so desired, could not have spared the time to be with us in New York a day every month or two, watching and counseling as General Westover had done. Colonel H. H. C. Richards took charge and remained in close touch until he was sent to the Philippines. Colonel (now Brigadier General) R. C. Candee then took over, and we worked closely with him until we delivered the manuscript of the Arctic Manual to the War Department on August 8, 1940.

It had been my understanding that, if the book was to be printed, I should be asked to get it ready for the press, meaning a further editing, with perhaps an introduction and certainly an index. But the first thing I knew a printed copy was on my desk.

It had also been my understanding that, if a pocket manual was to be produced by condensation from the 536 pages of the original publication, then the condensing would be done by me. However, a ready-printed condensed version came along, now available as the Army's TM-240, 74 pages. I was surprised; but when I read it I was not so disappointed, for, though familiar with the material, since it is largely derived from my own experience, I am not a bit sure that I could have condensed it so well.

A pocket manual, such as TM-240, to consult when you are already in trouble, does not conflict with a larger book designed to be read at leisure before you go into the field, or to be read in the field during times of quiet. Then there are many who go North in other service than that of the War Department, and many again who, without thought of northern journeys, would like to view the Arctic from a distance, as they might want to learn about conditions of the tropics without going there.

Accordingly, the War Department has granted the request of The Macmillan Company for ordinary commercial publication of the Arctic Manual.

VILHJALMUR STEFANSSON

November 3, 1943

ACKNOWLEDGMENTS

Since 1935 and throughout the preparation of the various manuscripts referred to in the Introduction, we have had the sympathetic and active cooperation of officers of the United States Army and members of various government departments in Washington. Those we called on are too numerous for mention, and so are professional colleagues at home and abroad who replied at length to lengthy questions and sometimes to questionnaires.

Most of the research work naturally was done by our staff; but the preparation of the Manual was so combined with that of the far more voluminous Guide Books that we cannot single out for mention any of the various contributors.

But like all except the first two of the fourteen books which carry my name on their title pages, those published in 1913 and 1914, the Arctic Manual owes more to Olive R. Wilcox than to any other collaborator.

VILHJALMUR STEFANSSON

ERRATA

Page 3, line 9: For Hypoboreans read Hyperboreans

Page 12, line 4 of 3rd pgf.: For North Devon read Devon

Page 23, line 2 from bottom: For manify read magnify

Page 66, lines 11 and 20: For *Papanin* read Papanin

Page 112, line 16: For Nuskagak read Nushagak

Page 124, lines 11 and 12: For Insect Life on the West Coast of America read Insect Life on the Western Arctic Coast of America.

Page 216, line 14 from bottom: For dazed read adzed

Page 460, line 10: For (scaredest) read "scaredest"

Page 487, line 1: For to do you handling read to do your handling

Page 534, line 12 of 2nd pgf.: For Kushkokwim read Kuskokwim

A serious mistake occurs near the bottom of page 225: "It proved that on the average their requirements were supplied by about 1⅓ lb. of lean and ½ lb. of fat." These are figures which have been used in several things published about the Russell Sage tests, and we cannot as we write discover the original source of the mistake, but the statement is incompatible with other things which seem beyond reasonable doubt. For instance:

Dr. Clarence W. Lieb was the clinician at the Russell Sage tests. He published in the *Journal of the American Medical Association* for July 6, 1929, an article "The Effects on Human Beings of a Twelve Months' Exclusive Meat Diet" in which he has two statements about the relation between lean and fat throughout the year in an exclusive meat diet as observed upon myself and my former companion in the North, Karsten Andersen. Speaking in terms of weight, Dr. Lieb says:

"The diets on which these two experimental subjects have been for the past year have not been particularly high protein diets, being but 30 or 40 per cent above the average protein intake. Their protein intake amounted to between 100 and 140 Gm. a day. The remaining calories were derived from fat which was equal to about three fourths or four fifths of their caloric intake."

Speaking in terms of calories, Dr. Lieb says: "Stefansson averaged about 2,650 calories a day, 2,100 calories consisting of fat and 550 of protein. Andersen averaged about 2,620 calories a day, 2,110 calories consisting of fat and 510 of protein. Carbohydrate in the meat varied between 20 and 50 calories a day."

The standard pemmican, as used by explorers of the plains,

and by the Hudson's Bay Company and other fur traders for more than two hundred years, and as described by a number of authorities, usually contained by weight thoroughly desiccated lean 50 percent, rendered suet 50 percent; but the composition is said to have varied at times in the direction of more lean, so that the ratio might be as 5 of desiccated lean to 4 of rendered fat. This would fit in approximately with Dr. Lieb's statement that between three fourths and four fifths of the calories were derived from fat in the exclusive carnivorous diet of the Russell Sage tests at Bellevue Hospital, New York, which would be the same, calorically speaking, as an exclusive pemmican diet, since the only ingredients of the standard pemmican (as opposed to the holiday or flavored pemmican) were lean and fat.

Now we are told by scientists connected with the packing industry that between five and six pounds of fresh lean (undried) are required to make one pound of thoroughly desiccated lean, as used for pemmican. Our statement at the bottom of page 225 should then have been to the effect that the proper ratio between lean and fat in pemmican will be such that a pound cake contains the desiccated equivalent of about 3 pounds of fresh (undried) lean beef, the other half-pound being fat rendered from beef suet. This would fit in with the usual "half fat and half dried lean" description of the pemmican that the explorers and traders of the plains used to make from buffalo meat.

But according to the chemists of the Russell Sage trials, as quoted by Dr. Lieb, when he speaks in calories, Karsten Andersen and I derived about twenty percent of our calories from protein. This fits in reasonably with the statement found in the authorities that the buffalo pemmican usually was half dried lean and half fat, though it sometimes was made in the ratio of five parts of dried lean to four parts of rendered fat.

It is to be emphasized that no preparation is rightly called a pemmican if it contains carbohydrates, other than those of the meat itself, in any material quantity. This means that custom does sanction calling it pemmican, although sugar or dried fruit has been introduced to flavor the dish, but not if the intention is to employ carbohydrates as a material food element, for supposed improvement of dietetic values. In the case of such material addition of carbohydrates you have a new food, which may or may not be a better food than pemmican, but which is then no longer pemmican—it wants a name of its own.

CHAPTER 1

HISTORICAL BACKGROUND

SECTION I

GENERAL

To sketch a historical background for the Arctic, by listing expeditions and evaluating achievements, is beyond our scope; to do so would contribute little to the effectiveness of this Manual, the purpose of which is to present to Air Corps troops a broad and general view of the living and working conditions which they will meet in the North and which differ so greatly from those to which most of them have been accustomed. But we feel we must at least outline the theories and beliefs which, from the time of the Greeks, have influenced thought and action with regard to the northern regions of the world. For many of these beliefs have been found both untrue and dangerous to the believer. We consider that the best way to learn how to protect oneself against the possible harmful effect of some theories still held by many is to have a grasp of all the more important ones and to understand rationally how and why some have been found correct while others have been found not merely incorrect but harmful.

SECTION II

THE CLASSIC VIEW

Powerful later in molding thought on the Arctic, the philosophical doctrines of symmetry came to Europe apparently by way of the Greeks and likely through the Pythagorean school around 500 B. C., if not earlier.

As applied to the earth, and then to the climates and their results, one of the main lines of argument was:

The earth is a heavenly body; the heavenly bodies are perfect; the most perfect shape is a sphere; the earth is

1

therefore spherical. The heat of the noonday comes from the sun (which, at an early Greek stage, was believed to be only a short distance up in the sky). It was considered that the lands of Greek civilization happened to lie at the right distance from the sun. It was sometimes unpleasantly warm or unpleasantly cold in Greece, but the average wasn't bad.

But if you went south from the Greek world, your approach to the sun would bring greater and greater heat. Finally you would come to the limit of human or animal endurance; beyond that you would die. Right under the sun, and for some distance on either side, the rocks would be red hot and the water, if any, boiling. This was the Burning Zone, the Torrid Zone.

Similarly, going north from the Greek world and getting too far from the sun, you would arrive where the cold was no longer endurable; beyond that you would freeze to death. This was the Frozen Zone, the Frigid Zone.

Said the Greeks: "Just as part of the world is uninhabitable underneath the sun because of the burning, so is it uninhabitable too far from the sun because of the freezing."

Through the doctrine of symmetry the Greeks felt it evident that there must be another livable, temperate zone south of the burning tropics and beyond this another frozen zone. That plants and animals existed south of the tropics was considered anything between very probable and certain; but it would remain a question of theory. For northern man could never cross the tropics south; men of the south, if any, could never cross them north.

Under this general view, which held sway from, say, 400 B. C. to after 1400 A. D., people of the north temperate zone were like rats in a revolving cage, free to move east and west, but imprisoned by a wall of flame to the south and of ice to the north. It was always theoretically possible to go around the earth east or west, and many thinkers took it for granted that someone sometime would do it. But that anyone ever would go around the earth south and north was absurd beyond discussion.

CONTRARY VIEWS

This, in outline, was the Doctrine of the Five Zones—two of them livable, three of them lifeless. It was what might be called the orthodox scientific view, corresponding, for instance, to the modern evolutionary concept in biology or to the Copernican theory in astronomy. There were many popular beliefs in contradiction, as, for instance, among the Greeks the idea that there were to the north the Rhipaean Mountains, from which cold winds blew, and beyond them a warm country, the land of the Hypoboreans, with golden fruit on the trees, unipeds, perpetual or protracted youth, a paradise beyond the cold. Such views the philosophers, scientists of their day, treated as folklore.

There were in circulation, too, from remote time stories that journeys had been done which would necessarily involve crossing the tropics, as, for instance, tales that the Egyptians had circumnavigated Africa. These were considered folklore. They were "obviously untrue"—they could not be true because the burning tropics could not have been crossed. The flaming zone was "known" to be such a short distance to the south from the Mediterranean that the length of the journey and the size of Africa, as described, became absurdities.

SECTION III

THE 1400–1845 VIEW

Those who like to personify revolutionary ideas and great deeds almost necessarily claim that Prince Henry the Navigator, beyond dispute a great man, was one of the greatest geniuses of all time. The argument runs that achievements like those of Columbus and Magellan are second rate, for they were only doing what thoughtful men in nearly or quite every century for 2,000 years had maintained that somebody would some time do. But Henry did what the same thoughtful men for the same length of time had "known" nobody could ever do.

Prince Henry of Portugal, and those who worked with him during the beginning of the fifteenth century, got the idea

3

somehow that the "burning tropics" might not be burning hot, that they might be crossable. Ship after ship of theirs went south, farther and farther along the west coast of Africa, many returning with what we now call an alibi, an explanation that they had gone so far that further progress would have been suicidal. But most of them returned, and others were therefore sent, until finally in 1471 Fernandez and Estesves went so far that the sun stood above their masts at noon. They returned to Portugal with the report that it had been no hotter right below the equator at sea than it sometimes is on shore in Portugal.

This final overthrow of the burning tropics came eleven years after Prince Henry's death, but was in continuation of the research which he started. It was scarcely more than routine thereafter for Diaz to reach the Cape of Good Hope in 1486 and for Da Gama to sail around it in 1497 to the Indies.

In the late fifteenth and in the sixteenth century voyages across the tropics grew common, both for reaching the south temperate zone and for circumnavigating Africa and South America. Fabulous and grotesque beliefs about the tropics were now too frequently checked against reality and began to decrease. They have decreased steadily since, until there is today among most temperate zone people almost as rational an attitude toward the tropics as there is toward home countries. Besides, many of our civilization now live in the tropics. Common sense has therefore had sway for a long time over the whole region that extends between the northern and southern polar zones.

The conquest of the polar districts, whether by actual travel or in the thought of our people, has been in comparison with the tropics a slow matter.

At one time it was the Greek orthodox view that to the north of them lay, extending east and west through what we now think of as the middle territories of the Soviet Union, a line beyond which no human or animal life could go because of the cold. Farther west this line was at one time considered to pass just north of the north tip of Scotland.

4

LIFE BOUNDARY MOVES NORTH

But some time before 795 A. D. the Irish discovered Iceland; by that date they were living in Iceland the year round. This pushed the southern boundary of the region of universal death some 600 miles north of Scotland.

Between the tenth and twelfth centuries the Icelanders (of Norse and Irish descent) who colonized Greenland, went up along its west coast at least 20 miles north of Upernivik, where their most northerly runic monument has been found. They probably reached Smith Sound, according to Rasmussen's conclusions from Smith Sound Eskimo studies, which were confirmed later archaeologically.

The Upernivik monument is more than 350 miles north of the north tip of the Arctic Circle; the Smith Sound archaeological finds are some 200 miles north of Upernivik, nearly 600 miles beyond the Circle. Besides, either by the Dutch in 1596 or earlier, Europeans reached Spitsbergen, which through the spectacular development of the whale, seal and walrus "fisheries," was soon cultivated by large fleets. The seas roundabout were known well north of the north tip of the Svalbard archipelago, to nearly or quite 1,000 miles beyond the Circle. The realm of frozen death was shrinking.

To the student of the history of European thought, it is striking about the northward movement of the white race on the Atlantic that the great pioneers, the Irish, Norwegians, Icelanders and Greenlanders, were unaware of the theoretical northward limit of human and animal life which had been set by Greek cosmography. But later explorers, who had been indoctrinated by southern philosophy, particularly those of the eighteenth and nineteenth centuries, believed consistently that there was somewhere a northern limit; and were uniformly surprised, startled and bewildered when they discovered at least some life wherever they went. But they usually "knew" that at their farthest north they had been at the farthest outpost of life; and that beyond all would be dead.

EXPLORATION MOTIVES IN 15TH CENTURY WERE COMMERCIAL

However, during the revival of exploration which followed Columbus, trade motives were supreme, or the desire to spread Christianity. It was therefore as pleasing as it was surprising to find life far north, for this implied resources and even riches. So explorers received compensation for their voyages, glory upon their return, in proportion to how they reported either discoveries of wealth or the prospect of such discovery. Particularly was it advantageous to report or make seem probable the existence of people—traders would later profit by them and priests convert them. Greatest of all desires was the finding of a near seaway to the wealth of "the Indies."

Swayed by a compelling desire, Europe changed its thinking after Columbus. The earth remained spherical. European countries were north of the tropics; so were the Indies. In consequence, the shortest route between Europe and the Indies must lie northwest, northeast or north.

Wish being parent of thought, it was assumed following Columbus that if there were an Arctic ocean it would be crossable. The view persisted for centuries.

Those explorers were now most readily believed who made the most favorable reports and indulged in the rosiest speculations. Their attitude persisted, although somewhat on the decline, until there came a full stop through the tragedy of Sir John Franklin. Two ships, great for that time, sailed in 1845 with 129 men, some of them from the "best" families of England. Not one of them ever came back. For years the place and manner of their loss was unknown. When knowledge came it showed that not only had they starved to death but that they had eaten each other—when some were already dead of hunger their comrades ate them and then also died.

SECTION IV

THE VIEW SINCE 1845

The shock to the world of the Franklin tragedy put a full stop to that hopeful commercial era of northward exploration which began with Columbus.

There were two elements in the changing attitude following 1845:

One was the change from the commercial motive toward a sporting one; particularly there developed an analogy to mountain climbing. Because wall maps are customarily suspended with the north side up, there grew the idea of the North Pole as the top of the world. The "attainment of the Pole" held the same lure that the topmost peak of Mount Everest has for alpinists. There were subsidiary reasons for the analogy between the Pole and the top of a mountain. Both were thought of as snow-covered or ice-covered. The North Pole was assumed to be in the center of a vast ice cap and to be, as a result, the hardest point in the Northern Hemisphere to reach. Therefore, whoever attained it would be the first in history to reach the equivalent of the top of the world's supermountain—with corresponding views about the South Pole and its attainment.

The other element in the changing attitude following 1845 was that the reports of travelers now tended more to the exaggeration of dangers and difficulties than to the exaggeration of the ease and safety of travel. Those were hereafter more readily believed who emphasized or magnified difficulties. Consciously or not, the ambition of the explorer was no longer to be a pioneer but rather to be a hero. Finally this was sublimated into a desire to secure and report scientific results, usually with background and trimmings of heroism and sacrifice.

This attitude toward the North, with its blending of sport and heroism, has persisted. There is a further blending in that many of the classic Greek theories are now much in evidence. The resulting point of view, a combination of folklore, heroism, and sport, is familiar to all of us from the narratives of explorers and from our schoolbooks; it has become a part of our accepted knowledge.

The following chapters are intended to present to the reader the Arctic as it really is. As best we can we shall strip from it the exaggeration of its dangers and difficulties. Then we shall attempt showing how to deal with such dangers and difficulties as are real.

CHAPTER 2

PHYSICAL GEOGRAPHY

SECTION I

LAND: TOPOGRAPHY

First of the northern subdivisions we consider Greenland; for it is at once most like what all Arctic lands were believed to be and most unlike what they really are.

GREENLAND

In the sense of land differentiated from ice, Greenland is considered to be low in its center, with mountain ranges along both western and eastern coasts. The western range averages perhaps 7,000 feet, running to 8,840 feet at Camp Watkins; the eastern reaches heights of 9,000 to 11,000 feet, with the probable maximum at Mount Forel, 11,500 feet.

Glaciers have filled the central land depression, flowing east from the western range and west from the eastern, till the basin is more than filled—has a flattened dome outline, somewhat higher in places than any but the extreme peaks of the eastern range.

At stations 300 to 400 miles inland from the east and west coasts respectively, measurements have been made by echo-sounding which show such ice thicknesses as 8,800 feet where the surface of the ice is 9,800 feet above sea level.

Greenland is, then, for practical purposes a turtle-backed island continent, 600 to 800 miles wide generally and more than 1,600 miles long, with a maximum height of the turtle-back which is probably around 10,000 feet and with few if any passes across from east to west that are less than 7,000 feet high. The "divide" from which the ice slopes east and west,

8

is an irregularly curved line running generally north and south somewhat farther east than the middle of the ice dome.

The coasts are the most rugged in the whole Northern Hemisphere, well beyond the Norwegian or even the Icelandic. Every valley is a path for seaward glacial flow, although the glaciers may not reach the sea. In a few cases it is more than 100 miles from the coast to the nearest land ice. If this be remembered, a topographic map of Greenland, such as published by the Geodaetisk Institut, Copenhagen, gives the rest of the description—except that we should describe the ice slopes.

Because Greenland is the one northern land heavily glaciated we reserve for the Guide Book of Greenland a detailed discussion not only of the Inland Ice and its technique but also of crevasses and the technique of ascending and descending a crevassed slope. However, we place here a few notes on glacier slopes. (See also Section IV, Chapter 11, of this volume.)

At distances reported to vary between 15 and 100 miles from the seaward edge of the ice its flow towards the coast is speedy enough to form crevasses. Some authorities say that these become more numerous the closer you are to the seaward edge; others say they are most numerous where the slope is steepest. In any case, crevasses are usually numerous near the seaward edge and are numerous on all steep gradients. It has been reported frequently by parties ascending glaciers that after passing a belt of crevasses another belt free from crevasses is traversed and then a second and later other belts.

The crevassed belt is wider back of a valley through which the glacier is going to flow than back of higher coastal land that tends to obstruct the flow. Crevasses extend farthest inland behind those fjords which have the most rapid ice flow—gaps in the coastal mountains which are the widest and deepest gates for the exit of the Inland Ice.

WIDTH OF CREVASSES

The reported gaping width of a crevasse at the top varies from less than 10 feet to more than 60. That narrow crevasses are seldom reported is because a narrow gap will be bridged over by snow which usually is strong enough to support men and dogs, and which might support taxiing airplanes but of course not a tractor.

Crevasses are both produced and widened by flow motion of the ice; they are further widened in spring and summer. For the direct sun, the warmth of the air and the action of running water unite in turning them practically into valleys toward the end of the warm season. Each of these valleys will naturally fill with snow the following winter, whereupon they cease to be crevasses from the point of view of travelers— the snow will be packed so hard that there would be no danger to sledges or taxiing airplanes and no source of catastrophe, although perhaps of difficulty, to a heavy tractor.

Crevasses are usually at right angles to the direction of ice flow and seldom extend more than part way across a valley, so that each in its turn can be gotten around by zigzagging right and left.

Because of the crevasses and their "treacherous" covering of snow, it is dangerous to sledge or walk up or down in winter, since you and your team, tractor, or taxiing airplane may fall through without warning and to a depth which would normally be fatal for men and animals—the like even more probably true for tractor or plane, except that a plane likely would hang suspended by its wings.

TRAVEL PRECAUTIONS

In climbing or descending a glacier, men should be roped together alpinist-fashion, the distance between them being greater than the greatest width of a crevasse that can be bridged by drifting snow. There is, however, no agreement on how wide such crevasses could be. Probably a distance of 20 feet between men advancing at right angles to the crevasses would be sufficient. For like safety purposes dog teams can follow each other with the harness of the leading dog of one team attached by a rope to the sledge next preceding. It should not happen on the ascent of a glacier that more than one dog team falls into a crevasse, where they would be suspended each in his own harness. The danger is considerably greater descending a glacier slope, for if a leading team falls through it will be difficult for the teams and men behind to hold back. What you do is turn the teams sideways and upset the sledges to stop them from sliding.

In summer the crevasses are not hidden, for the snow has been melted away, but they nevertheless form a very serious handicap in going up or down.

EXTENT OF SNOWFREE LAND

No doubt because of a combination of high mountains and a heavier precipitation, there is comparatively little snowfree coastal land near the south tip of Greenland; it is correspondingly true that because of small elevation and light precipitation there is a large section of mainly snowfree land at the north tip of Greenland, Peary Land. The widest sections of territory free from snow in summer are at distances between 200 and 500 miles northward from Cape Farewell along the west coast of Greenland (between about Latitudes 63° and 68° N.) and on the east coast at and north of Scoresby Sound (between Latitudes 70° and 74° N.). These and the wide glacier-exempt stretches of Peary Land have been known for a long time.

In recent years we have found that the Peary Land snowfree areas are even larger than believed and that there are "surprisingly large" icefree lands in northeast Greenland. Elsewhere on these coasts there are narrow snowfree coastal strips broken here and there by glaciers which reach the sea. On the west coast there is one long stretch practically without snowfree coastal land which extends from about 74° N. Lat. to about 77°.

Around 1920 it was estimated that 84 percent of Greenland was covered by ice; but each new exploration usually shows "unexpected" snowfree land, and it seems in 1940 that the iced parts of Greenland will prove to be not over 80 percent. This will mean that every summer there is more snowless country in Greenland than in Great Britain and Ireland combined, or more than in the New England states, with New York, New Jersey, Delaware, and Maryland added.

11

GLACIERS

We have described for Greenland a proper ice cap. There is no real ice cap in any other Arctic land; there are glaciers in some of them, but only if they are mountainous. Roughly the height of mountains required for glaciation varies inversely with the precipitation. Latitude does not seem to be an important factor in glaciation when you are once north of 60°.

As we said about Greenland, the section we now treat, Arctic Canada, Alaska, and Siberia, are fully covered in the respective Guide Books and we give here the briefest sketch only.

CANADA

As we go west and southwest from Greenland the glaciers decrease rapidly. The biggest ones, no doubt, are in Ellesmere Island, which is rugged; but it is possible that glaciers equalling them are to be found in Heiberg Island. North Devon has smaller glaciers and Baffin Island still smaller. There are no proper glaciers, but at most an occasional snowbank hidden from the sun in a deep ravine, when you go westward through the island tier to which Baffin Island belongs—Somerset, Prince of Wales, King William, Victoria, and Banks. It may be that some of these do not have even a small snowbank left anywhere toward the end of summer.

In the tier west from Devon—Cornwallis, Bathurst, Melville, and Prince Patrick—there are somewhat more numerous snowbanks that persist, for these islands are more rugged. In Melville Island, properly mountainous although the highest peaks may not be more than 4,000 feet, the name glacier has been applied to a few large snowbanks, particularly back of Liddon Gulf and Murray Inlet. No one has been in Prince Patrick Island during the summer to tell whether it has persisting snowbanks—likely there would be a few of considerable size, though hardly to be called glaciers.

In the tier west of southern Ellesmere—Amund Ringnes, Ellef Ringnes, Isachsen, Lougheed, Borden, and Brock—there are snowbanks at the end of summer but almost certainly none as large as those of Melville.

12

There remains a small island at 80° N., 100° W., Meighen. This was reported by Stefansson to have, when viewed from the sea, a flattened dome skyline of such a kind that he thought it might have an ice cap—if you would name as a cap a shield 15 or 20 miles in its greatest diameter. There is, however, a chance that this island has, in proportion to area, the largest amount of land ice found anywhere between Greenland and the Beaufort Sea.

There are no mountains in continental Arctic Canada, and therefore few or no persistent snowbanks, until you come to the very northwest, Yukon Territory, where a few small glaciers have been reported in that territory's real mountains. However, the permanent snow in Arctic Yukon is almost certainly much less than 10 percent of the permanent snow in the non-Arctic part of the same territory. On the whole Yukon is a mountainous region with peaks running up to 8,000 feet.

The greater part of mainland Arctic Canada, outside Yukon Territory, is prairie land.

ARCTIC ALASKA

In Arctic Alaska the Brooks Range separates the waters flowing southward into the Yukon, or westward into Bering Sea from those flowing northward into the Arctic Ocean. Although spoken of as a unit, this range consists of many individual mountain groups—the De Long, Baird, Schwatka, Melville, and Endicott toward the south; the Franklin, Romanzof, Shublik, and Sadlerochit groups toward the north.

Compared with other Alaska ranges, the Brooks is relatively low, with a few peaks between 7,000 and 10,000 feet high.

In the range, west of the meridian 150°, Smith and Mertie report that while glaciers were formerly extensive they are uncommon now. Leffingwell found near meridian 146° that there were no proper glaciers in the 5,000- or 6,000-foot mountains visible from the coast, but that there were glaciers of some size a little farther south where peaks run up toward 10,000 feet.

Although the height of the peaks and ridges makes them formidable barriers to travel, there are many gaps at lower elevations—both east-west and north-south—by which passage of the mountains can be made with reasonable facility.

13

COASTAL PRAIRIE

North of the Brooks Range is a triangular prairie. It is only 15 or 20 miles wide, from the sea to the rugged foothills, at the Alaska-Canada boundary; it reaches a 200-mile north-south width abreast of Barrow, and disappears near Lisburne. You find most portions of this prairie so level, when you are near the sea and east of Barrow, that it is difficult or impossible for the unaided eye to judge which way it slopes; but if you follow a river inland you notice readily that the territory along it is getting higher and higher. First you are in rolling prairie and then you get into proper foothills. But west of Barrow, although not quite at Barrow itself, the land tends to increase in altitude more rapidly and perceptibly from the coast.

NORTH COAST OF ALASKA SINKING

In attempting to utilize the north coast of Alaska for any sort of supply depots, or bases of operations, it must be taken into consideration that this coast is sinking rapidly.

So long as the sea ice remains in winter and spring, nothing happens to the injury of the islands off the north coast; but when the ice goes away, as it does nearly every summer, and when a gale comes from the open sea, the waves will undermine the cliffs of the islands at a great rate, so that the coastline sometimes recedes as much as a hundred yards in a single summer. An instance of how coastal islands disappear is Flaxman. When the early whalers came to the eastern north coast of Alaska in 1889 this island was probably some 8 or 10 miles long. Thirty years later it was no more than half that length, having also narrowed correspondingly.

What happens to north coast islands is happening to that coast itself, especially where unprotected by off-shore isles and reefs.

SIBERIA

Generally speaking, the coast of Arctic Siberia resembles that of Alaska, although mountains come near the coast at places which are less regular. The mountains are not far inland between Cape Dezhnev (East Cape) and Serdzekamen. Thence westward to and around Kolyuchin Bay the land is low, but mountains are not far from the coast at the western edge of the bay. Then comes lowland extending for several hundred miles to Cape Severny. From there the low plain is rather narrow, and high land is visible when you look south from the coast till you approach the Kuvet River; then, after a narrow patch of lowland, you find it high inland again to Cape Shelagski. Back of Chaun Bay there is a good deal of lowland, the practically joint valleys of several rivers. High land is usually visible toward the interior west of that bay till you come to the eastern edge of the Kolyma.

The mountains begin to recede from the coast once the Kolyma is approached; and also to decrease in height. In central Siberia lowland, forest or prairie, is found in the drainage basins of the western tributaries of the Kolyma, and in those of the eastern and western tributaries of the Indigirka. The mountains do not approach the sea closely again until the Yana is reached. The highest land in this district is Tomuskaya Mountains, east of the Indigirka, which taper off into Alazeya Plateau.

West of the Yana, the mountains once more recede to considerable or great distances from the coast; the land is mainly prairie with great northward-flowing rivers—the Lena, the Yenisei and the Ob, and several others of less length and smaller drainage basins. Along these rivers the evergreen forests stretch far north beyond the Arctic Circle— more than four hundred miles on the Yenisei to tidewater on the Lena. The Ural Mountains constitute the only high break in this country.

No glaciers are found in the vast extent of mainland Arctic Siberia. Some large areas are also free of persisting snow-banks, as we described for Arctic Canada. Where there are mountains, chiefly in the northeast, descriptions apply such as those we used from Leffingwell for the Canning River district of Arctic Alaska.

With the exception of Wrangel, the islands of the eastern Asiatic section of the Soviet Arctic are comparatively low and none of them contain permanent snow. Herald Island

15

is almost a solid mass of granite, nearly or quite 1,000 feet high. Wrangel has a mountainous plateau traversed by two longitudinal ridges and several deep-cut valleys. The highest point is about 2,500 feet, but no glaciers are found. The New Siberian Islands, which lie a considerable distance west of Wrangel have greatest heights between 1,000 and 1,200 feet.

Proceeding westward we find the first glaciated areas at Severnaya Zemlya. Approximately 45 percent of the entire area of this island group is covered with ice fields from which glaciers descend to the coast. The interior has plateaus 1,300 to 2,000 feet high. Novaya Zemlya is an island in two main parts. Its northern section, running down to approximately 75° N. Lat., is largely covered with ice, with average altitude of nearly 2,000 feet, the highest peak reaching an elevation of some 3,000 feet. The highest sectors of a mountain range, which stretches from north to south, are in the central portion of the island, where the glaciers begin to disappear. In this section the highest elevation is 3,350 feet. The land south of 72° N. Lat. is generally low and flat.

The reason why the highest part of this island has little ice is considered to be that as you go south along the island you get away from the ice-making, because precipitation-encouraging, influence of the warm ocean current that sweeps east and northeast around the north of the Scandinavian peninsula and of Novaya Zemlya.

Vaigach and Kolguev Islands, south and southwest of Novaya Zemlya respectively, have no glaciers and no permanent snow. Most of Vaigach is swampy and filled with lakes, but there are two ranges of hills stretching from one end of the island to the other which reach an elevation of 300 feet in the center. The northwestern part of Kolguev Island attains 425 feet but the southeastern section is flat, only a few or a few dozen feet above sea level.

In the northernmost and westernmost section of the Soviet Arctic lie the group of islands known as Franz Josef Land. They are mainly ice-covered plateaus, rarely more than 1,000 feet high with the exception of Cape Tirol, on Viner Neishtadt

Island, which is near 3,000 feet. Frequently the snow line comes down to 300 feet, the only bare area of considerable size being on Alexandra Land.

Many shores of these islands are ice covered; but where there is no ice they exhibit a terrace formation with elevations ranging from 100 to 400 feet.

SVALBARD ARCHIPELAGO

Between Novaya Zemlya (Soviet territory) and Greenland (Danish) lies the Norwegian Svalbard archipelago.

The chief island, Spitsbergen, is a much dissected plateau with many deep fjords penetrating far inland. Small plains are found in the north and west. Sharp peaks rise to 4,960 feet in Horn Sunds Tinder in the south, 3,450 feet in Mount Monaco on Prince Charles Foreland and 4,770 feet in Mount Eidsvoll in the northwest. In the middle and east the mountains are flat-topped and seldom over 2,000 feet; Mount Newton, 5,445 feet, in New Friesland, is the loftiest peak in the archipelago.

Glaciers fill the valleys except in the southern interior where they have receded; they generally reach the sea, often along broad fronts, but give rise to no large icebergs. An ice covering over New Friesland is the nearest approach to an ice sheet in the Svalbard group. Barents and Edge Islands have glaciers only on the east. The Wiche islands have no large glaciers, but North-East Land and Giles (Gillis) Land are each covered with a dome of ice that almost envelops them. Prince Charles Foreland has numerous glaciers.

Isolated Bear Island, a part of administrative Svalbard therefore remote from (south of) the Spitsbergen group, rises to 1,630 feet in Mount Misery. The northern part is a plain at an elevation of about 150 feet. There are no glaciers.

ARCTIC LAKES

For travel purposes it is to be remembered that land which is described as flat will usually have from 40 percent to 60 percent of its surface represented by lakes of various sizes. Most of them are shallow and some of them so shallow that a man can wade across by a lake's greatest diameter that may be one or even several miles. This shallowness of lakes is important to remember in connection with pontoon or flying-boat descents; but it is equally to be remembered that if the keel of your pontoon or boat were to touch lake bottom it would be, in nine cases out of ten, soft and slippery mud. For below the water of shoal lakes the "eternal frost" will thaw for several feet, although on the prairie between the lakes it will thaw only as many inches.

In rolling Arctic country there will be fewer lakes than on the flat lands, although a considerably larger number than we expect on such a terrain in other zones. It is only in very rugged districts, practically mountainous, that the proportion of lakes to the rest of the country is about the same in the Arctic as we would expect in temperate zone or tropics.

When the land is flat and the lakes most numerous, some of the lakes will have no outlet; many of these will connect one lake with another by sluggish streams. In rolling country, lakes are connected with each other, or not, about as they would be in the temperate zone; and the same, of course, is true for what few lakes there are in rugged country.

The proportion of rocky land is less in the Arctic than in the other zones. The chief reasons are, no doubt, those of erosion. Because of the permanent frost that prevents underground drainage, land is seldom dry enough to permit winds blowing it away. Because the rainfall is light there is little water erosion, except the described breaking of coasts by the sea.

GROUND FROST AND GROUND THAW—GENERAL PRINCIPLES

Ground frost is related to several of the Arctic and sub-Arctic problems with which this Manual deals. It has an important bearing on European-American community life in the North, and is of perhaps even greater importance in connection with road construction, aviation, the use of tractors, etc. We place here our chief disscussion of the problem and refer back to it later when we deal with the topics in which it plays a part.

A light on the interplay of ground frost and ground thaw comes from studies of water at sea and in lakes.

If at a given very low temperature you have at sea five inches of young ice forming the first 24 hours after a lead opens, then 4 inches may be added the second 24 hours, three inches during the third twenty-four, and so on; until after say 2 weeks the daily increase of thickening is a fraction of an inch, and continues decreasing.

This is on the assumption that no snow has fallen. Should there fall a blanket of snow, the speed of freezing decreases immediately. It is probable that under an average snow blanketing a foot thick the entire freezing of an Arctic winter would not produce more than 6 or 7 feet of ice. A heavier blanketing would keep the ice still thinner.

Sea ice gets crusted on top with salt, is never slippery, and therefore always has a certain snow covering, so that freezing in one year to a thickness of more than nine feet probably never occurs. (By breaking and superimposition, sea ice under pressure may become 200 feet thick.) Fresh water ice is glare, large patches remain uncovered with snow, and there the thickness of freezing may be as much as 15 feet.

But the principle is always the same—you arrive finally at a point where the thickness of the ice itself gives so much insulation from the weather that no more water congeals on the under side of the ice. Its maximum thickness has been attained.

On land in the sub-Arctic districts, where there is no permanent ground frost, nine feet may be the maximum depth to which the winter frost of any year penetrates. This would be where the ground is swept clear of snow by the wind. There are few such places, only those without vegetation and with a smooth surface.

But for reasons upon which geologists do not as yet agree there is permanent ground frost in nearly the whole Arctic and in a considerable part of the north temperate zone.

LAND BENEATH A GLACIER USUALLY OR ALWAYS UNFROZEN

A theory for ground frost which no longer appears tenable is that it is a "relic of the Ice Age." For, logically, the frost goes down to that point where a balance is reached between the earth's interior heat and the chill that has penetrated down into the crust from the atmosphere. Now if you have, above the topmost layer of proper earth, a layer of ice perhaps thousands of feet thick, such as there now is in interior Greenland, then you would think that the point at which a frost line balance was reached between the atmospheric cold and the earth's interior heat might be very near the underside of the ice. Recently this has been proved true in at least a considerable number of special cases. Where glaciers are retreating, pits have been sunk into the earth and it has been found, in most if not all cases, that the earth beneath the glacier had been unfrozen.

According to recent geological findings, there were great areas of land in the Far North not glaciated during recent Ice Ages, no doubt for the same reason (elsewhere explained) that keeps northernmost Greenland free of permanent snow. The northern plain of Alaska has always been free of glaciation, so far as geologists have yet discovered. When the front of the ice was perhaps as far south as New York City the winters must have been long and intensely cold on the nearly snow free prairies south from Point Barrow. That was the time, no doubt, and those were the circumstances under which the frost penetrated so deep that even today the north Alaska ground frost line, balanced against the interior heat of the earth, is several hundred feet down.

Ideas on the geographic extension of frozen subsoil are being altered in recent years. Textbooks are still in use which would indicate that perhaps a third of all British North America, continental and insular, had frost beneath the surface. Railway construction engineers have pointed out, however, that they encountered permanent frost at one or more points on the north shore of Lake Superior while the more northerly right-of-way of the Canadian National back of Superior encountered still more frost. There are, near the southern limits, islands of frozen ground surrounded by large areas without frost. As you go north the situation changes and you have islands of thawed ground in a generally frozen district. It would appear a conservative guess, if you allow for both types of islands, that 50 percent of all British North America has permanent ground frost. A likelier guess is 55 percent.

Generally speaking, frost goes well south in British North America, chiefly east of the Red River of the north. In the prairie provinces the southern limit of frost runs north-westerly so that it is most southerly in Manitoba, intermediate in Saskatchewan, and farthest north in Alberta where the limit of sporadic occurrance is probably not far from Lesser Slave Lake. It may be equally far north in British Columbia. In Alaska there seems permanent ground frost in all land north of the Brooks Range. The Yukon drainage basin is mainly frozen. South of the Alaska range divide much land is unfrozen.

GROUND FROST IN SOUTHERN ALASKA

Ground frost has been reported from the Cook Inlet-Susitna district where there are islands of frozen subsoil. Where there is thick moss, ice is not infrequently found within 40 inches or less of the surface, but elsewhere its presence that near the surface is exceptional. Ice is common within 3 feet or less of the surface between Montana and Willow Creeks and was found within about a foot of the surface along the banks of the Susitna River, near the mouth of Willow Creek, in August.

GROUND FROST IN SIBERIA

Perhaps because heavily ice-covered in glacial times, there is "surprisingly" little ground frost in northern European Russia. But the Soviets, mainly in Siberia, have a far larger total area of frozen ground than does North America. There, as with us, the known limits of the ground frost are being moved farther and farther south the more complete the exploration. An approximation of the southern boundary was made in 1939 by Professor George B. Cressey, of Syracuse University. He considers that on the Pacific side the permanent frost occupies the northern half of the Kamchatka Peninsula as well as all land to the north. West of the Okhotsk Sea the frozen ground pretty well follows the coast south until you are abreast of Sakhalin Island. Then the frost trends inland; somewhat west of Khabarovsk a tongue of it extends a little farther south than that city, or about to the latitude of northern Lake Superior. West of there the frost in some places goes a little south of 50° until you are abreast of (south of) Lake Baikal. Then it trends northwesterly, keeping mostly to the east of the Yenisei River, and runs northward to about 65° N. Lat., where it crosses the Yenisei and trends westerly, coming to an end, or practically so, on the shores of the eastern White Sea. Altogether, he estimates that permanently frozen ground underlies 3,728,900 square miles of Soviet territory.

PROBABLE TOTAL FROZEN AREA

Northern hemisphere lands underlain by "eternal" ground frost may have a total area equal to not much less than that of continental North America from the Rio Grande north.

DEPTH TO GROUND FROST

Specific figures on the depth at which ground frost begins were used for named localities and described conditions in southern Alaska because this Manual is more likely to be used in Alaska than elsewhere. Speaking generally, we may say that frost islands are discovered usually at a depth of from 7 to 11 feet near the southern limit of their range. Around Great Slave Lake, Canada, the frost may be discoverable at 3 feet. In the forest just north of Great Bear Lake or on the lower Mackenzie, as around Fort Macpherson, there is practically no thawed ground—all that thaws out in several weeks of weather so warm that people complain about it is the leaves, branches, and muck. North of the forest, however, where the sun gets more direct play, the thaw will be deeper again; so that even a hundred miles north of the treeline the thaw may go 2 or 3 feet down, especially on southward slopes that are sandy. A similar slope if covered with swampy meadow will thaw to 8 or 10 inches. Level land on the north coast of Canada and Alaska is thawed in August to depths of between 6 inches and a foot. The like is true for prairie in the islands to the north of Canada.

SPECIAL CAUSES OF THAW

Geologists have reported thawed ground extending to an indefinite depth in some parts of Alaska where frozen ground is nearby. It may be that in at least some cases the observers did not realize a special factor—that Arctic rivers, and even lakes, will remove permanent frost from the ground for a considerable distance. The ocean does the same. On the north coast of Alaska, where the sea is advancing upon the land, the thaw produced by the sea will on a gravelly coast precede the advance of the water, according to different reports, from a hundred feet to a hundred yards. Where the sea coast is muck or ground ice the thaw does not precede the advance of the sea—the frozen outbanks are thawed and sloughed away by the direct attack of the waves.

THICKNESS OF GROUND FROST

In some Arctic districts shafts have been sunk more than 200 feet without going through the permanent frost. The whole subject has been so little studied it is scarcely worth speculating what the maximum depth of ground frost may be.

With regard to the bearing of ground frost upon the location of towns which expect to carry on in a more or less typical "civilized" way, the important point is to study the exceptions to the rule. Northern lands are not everywhere permanently frozen. (See section I, chapter 7.)

SECTION II

SEA: TIDES, CURRENTS, ETC.

The Arctic "Ocean," with its 5,000,000 or so square miles, is tiny when compared with a real ocean. It is, say, one-thirteenth the size of the Pacific; it is not over one-seventh as large as the Atlantic, from which it is a gulf. It does look like an ocean on Mercator charts, which manify it grotesquely. Viewed in true proportion, as on a globe, the Polar

Sea is a mediterranean that separates Eurasia from North America somewhat as a smaller mediterranean separates Europe from Africa.

This relatively small north polar basin has on its margins a continental shelf, wide in most places when compared with shelves in the rest of the world, and, indeed, conspicuously narrow only toward Alaska.

By ordinary definition, continental shelves have upon them water 200 meters (656 feet) or less in depth; the Arctic shelf, while it is still a true one in the sense that eventually it is going to descend rapidly to great depths, is likely to have on it water of 300, 400, or even 500 meters, as we shall see when we come to a description of particular segments.

Nor is the polar sea uniformly surrounded by a shelf of even these greater depths. There are still deeper openings, or gates. For instance, in Baffin Bay we have depths falling below 6,000 feet; in the Greenland Sea they fall to twice that depth; Barents Sea (sometimes thought of as a gulf of the Greenland Sea) is shallow, not often below 1,600 feet and frequently much shoaler. Beaufort Sea is even deeper than the Greenland Sea.

DEPTHS

The Arctic deep sea basin probably covers a large part of the still unsounded area. The depths found during Nansen's *Fram* expedition (1893–96) range between 9,840 and 12,628 feet. Peary got 8,997 feet without bottom near the North Pole in 1909. Stefansson during his 1913–18 expedition got 4,546 feet without bottom at various points in the eastern Beaufort Sea, and Storkerson of the same expedition, farther west in the same sea, found 9,726 feet without bottom. In 1925 Amundsen-Ellsworth recorded 12,300 feet at 87°43′ N. and 10°21′ W. The deepest sounding of the polar basin, 17,843 feet was taken by Wilkins in 1927 at 77°45′ N., 175° W. Papanin sounded 14,038 feet near the North Pole in 1937. The Soviet ship *Sedov* reported in 1939 a sounding of 16,990 feet without bottom near 86°30′ N., 39° E. Other soundings in the vicinity showed depths exceeding 16,400 feet. Soviet scientists consider there is indication of a basin across the

Arctic connecting their deep soundings on the Eurasian side with that of Wilkins on the Alaska side.

SEA TEMPERATURES AND SALINITIES

It was discovered during the *Fram* expedition of 1893–1896 that the Polar Sea is covered by a layer 500 to 650 feet thick, of cold water with temperatures between 32° F. and 28.6° F.[1] and with a comparatively low salinity owing to the admixture of fresh water—river water and products of rain, melted snow, and melted sea ice freshened through aging. Then comes a layer, some 2,000 or 2,500 feet, of warmer and saltier water, with temperatures above 32°. This is Atlantic water which is carried into the Arctic basin by the tentacles of the Gulf Stream reaching northward, perhaps chiefly along the west coast of Spitsbergen. Below this there is again colder water, probably filling the whole basin to the bottom, with temperatures between 32° and 30.6° and salinity about the same as that of the warm middle layer. This cold deep layer is taken to originate in the northern part of the Norwegian Sea, north-northeast of Jan Mayen.

From Soviet press reports in advance of publication of the scientific results of the Papanin expedition, it would appear that its oceanographer, Shirshov, found within a few miles of the North Pole ocean layers which differed by temperatures and salinities about as Nansen had found them to differ some hundreds of miles to the south (in the direction of Siberia). One press statement has it that: "* * * from the surface to the depth of 200 meters, the temperature of the water is below zero [Centigrade], and from 200 to 800 meters it rises to 1.7° above zero [35° F.] This warm water is of Atlantic origin * * *. Beginning with 800 meters, and down to the very bottom, the temperature again falls gradually. The salt content in the water also depends on the depth—the highest content was found at depths of 200–800 meters."

---

[1] The *Sedov* reported throughout its 1937–40 drift higher air temperatures and thinner ice than encountered by the *Fram* in the same vicinity, and a drift more rapid than that of the *Fram* which they connected with the thinner ice. Some scientists consider that this may indicate a warming of the whole polar basin—which, if real, may be a short or a long cycle.

PACK ICE

Even toward the end of summer, two-thirds of the Arctic Sea is covered by drifting pack ice, formed by the freezing of surface layers during autumn, winter, and spring. The pack is in motion during all seasons of the year, floes breaking up and drifting about through the effect of wind and current, with leads of water opening and closing between the various floes. Ice to average thickness of 7 feet, and not more than 10 feet, will form through freezing in one year; ice 2 or 3 years old may be 2 or 3 feet thicker. Pressure due to currents and wind may cause piled or raftered ice to a maximum thickness of 150 or 200 feet. These extreme heapings up are never found far from land but occur chiefly at or near what is called the flaw, or floe, where the landfast shore ice meets the moving pack with resulting pressure such that ridges may pile up that have peaks 60 or 70 feet above sea level. Far from land the ridges probably do not exceed 35 or 40 feet in height.

It is not possible to calculate accurately how deep a ridge goes below sea level from how high its peak rises above it; for the ridge is pyramid or A-shaped, with its wide base submerged.

Ice fields are most level when they have been made by uniform freezing and have never been broken by pressure. In that case, if of this year's information, they have no surface inequalities except snowdrifts; if two or more seasons old, they have relief sculptured by rain, by flowing thaw water, and by sun.

PLANES CAN DESCEND UPON SEA ICE

We know from reports by the Papanin North Pole expedition that even the biggest land planes can descend with safety upon such strong, level fields as are found pretty much all over the Polar Sea in winter; for the transport pilots which delivered the Papanin group and their ten tons of supplies at the North Pole in 1937 made, between latitudes 85° N. and 90° N., about twenty different landings with heavily loaded, half loaded and light four-engined airplanes, nearly the largest then in existence, every descent followed by a successful take-off.

ICEBERGS

Icebergs have only local occurrence because, as said, there are few Arctic lands except Greenland and North-East Land that have glaciers sufficiently large and active to produce real bergs. Usually, a berg is found in a more southerly location than its point of origin, for the water movement tends to be southward.

In the heart of the Arctic Ocean icebergs are never seen. Around North-East Land, Franz Josef Land and Novaya Zemlya they are occasional. In both the East Greenland current and the Labrador current they are frequent. Melville Bay is notorious for its bergs. Of course, we are all familiar with the bergs, originating in Greenland, which in spring menace the Atlantic shipping lanes. On the Siberian coast bergs are rare—a few small ones about Northern Land.

CURRENTS

The tendency of the light surface layers of the Arctic Sea, with their low salinity, is to spread outwards, a movement which is helped by the prevailing winds and the overflow necessary from a constricted basin to which the inflow of river water is considerable, with evaporation slight. Within the polar basin the surface waters are sweeping across from Alaska and Siberia toward Spitsbergen and Greenland. Most of these waters, and the ice they carry, find their way southward into the Barents and Greenland Seas by the east Spitsbergen and east Greenland currents that flow southward along these coasts and tend to block them with streams of pack ice. Some of the polar water escapes through Smith Sound and other channels west of Greenland and feeds the Labrador current along the west of Davis Strait and the coast of Labrador. Lastly, some moves westward through the Beaufort Sea and merges again in the great transpolar drift, except a little which flows southward on the western side of Bering Strait. Thus the current off the north coast of Alaska is considered to be prevailingly westward.

But there is some evidence of a gigantic eddy north of Alaska and west of the Canadian islands, so that ice 200 or more miles north from Alaska would be moving east or northeast; then it would curve around and move south and southwest along Borden, Prince Patrick and Banks Island; and then, as said, west along Alaska.

Through McClure Strait and Melville Sound the ice moves easterly toward the Atlantic.

Much of what we have just given on drifts is from the De Long, Nansen, Peary, and Stefansson expeditions. Recent studies of Arctic drift have been chiefly by Soviet expeditions.

The Papanin group of four was established by planes in a base camp at the North Pole in May 1937, to drift with their floe encampment and conduct scientific investigations meanwhile. The direction of the drift was as expected—towards the gap between Iceland and Greenland. By February 1938, when they were taken off their floe by icebreakers, the party had drifted to a point off the East Greenland coast between King Oscar Fjord and Scoresby Sound. The average rate of drift was more than three miles per day, which exceeded most predictions; in the vicinity of the Pole the drift was two to three miles per day, as against a drift rate which had been estimated commonly at from half a mile to a mile and a half.

The *Sedov*, Captain Constantine Badigin, repeated during 1937–1940 the drift of the *Fram* more than forty years earlier. As mentioned, their drift was more rapid than the *Fram's*; the course of their drift was also considerably more northerly.

In relation to the Arctic, there is a fundamental difference between the Atlantic and the Pacific, although they are similar in that each has a great stream of warm water flowing northward. No matter how hard it tries, the Pacific Japan Current is unable to reach the Polar Sea. It is fenced out by the chain of the Aleutian Islands and by Bering Strait, where Alaska and Siberia almost lock horns. The Strait is 56 miles across, only about double the width of the channel between Great Britain and France; and besides being narrow and shallow it has two islands in the middle. The Japan Current, therefore, instead of reaching the Alaskan Arctic with its warmth, spends its heat upon the air of the North Pacific, with only a little and practically imperceptible amount of slightly warmed water finding its way to the north coast of Alaska.

In the Atlantic the condition is different. The waters warmed by the Gulf Stream spread northward through the wide and deep gap between Norway and Greenland splitting on Iceland with such effect that, although Arctic in name and sub-Arctic in latitude, it is temperate in weather. Nor does the Gulf Stream stop at Iceland. Its water creep north into the polar ocean and melt away the ice that otherwise would be there, so that Scotch, Norwegian, and other whalers and sealers were wont to cruise in an ordinary season more than seven hundred miles closer to the Pole on the Atlantic side than the American whalers were able to on the Pacific side.

REGION OF INACCESSIBILITY

From this it results that the center of the pack is not the North Pole, as commonly assumed, but rather that spot or region in the Polar Sea which is most difficult to reach. This approximate center has been determined by taking the farthest point attained on any meridian by all ships of which we have record. A line connecting these points bounds what is known as the area of maximum inaccessibility. Within this area the point most difficult to reach, considering attack from all sides, was determined to lie approximately at 83°50' N. Lat., 160° W. Long. This point has been called the Pole of Inaccessibility or Ice Pole.

TIDES

In most of the Arctic, tides, properly speaking, are insignificant—ranging, for instance, from 18 inches on certain parts of the north Alaska coast down to 8 inches in Coronation Gulf.

On most parts of the north Atlantic seaboard a cake of ice that is aground during summer in shallow water has during most of the day a peculiar mushroom-like appearance; for high tide is only a matter of an hour or two, and at all other times these cakes are lying aground with the water around them considerably lower than it was at the moment of high tide. In such places an experienced navigator can tell by glancing at a cake of ice whether it is afloat or aground. If it is afloat he can tell from the freeboard of the ice whether his ship will have plenty of water under her keel.

However, in that part of the Arctic Sea which is north of the Pacific even grounded cakes may present an appearance of being afloat; for there has been insufficient rise or fall of tide to give them undercut edges of the kind found in the east. There is practically no tide in many parts of this region—a tide of only a few inches.

But there is, at certain times, a so-called "storm tide." It seems that when a strong southwest or west wind begins to blow around and north or northeast of Bering Strait it produces a wave or swell that moves eastward and reaches the Colville delta or Herschel Island possibly 8 to 12 hours ahead of the storm itself. This rise of water that presages a strong sou'wester may sometimes amount to as much as five feet; in advance of a moderate southwest wind the rise may be a foot or two. There is a corresponding fall with or before a northeast wind. These two are, on the north coast of Alaska, the directions of the main winds.

LIFE IN THE POLAR SEA

A principle of oceanography recognized for some decades is that the amount of animal life per unit of ocean water is least at the equator and, on the average, increases toward the poles.

But it has been argued that when you come to where there is ice in the sea, or at least when you come to where the ice is thick and continuous, the principle will break down because the ice covering shuts out oxygen needed for animal life, because light will be insufficient for the biological processes of those plants upon which the animal life ultimately depends, and for a variety of other reasons. This position was until recently taken by most if not all scientists and by many explorers, as well as by laymen.

The contrary position was taken that even if the principle of *increasing* life with increasing distance from the equator did fail to hold all the way to the North Pole, still some life, both vegetable and animal, might extend to the Pole and to every other section of the northern sea.

We consider this under the heads of logic and of experience:

Plankton, floating organisms generally, are helpless to direct their own movement and are borne along by currents. It follows that these organisms drift with the currents that sweep the polar sea. Shrimps and other larger organisms live on the smaller plankton. These, too, are carried involuntarily by the polar currents. The floating and the weakly swimming organisms in turn provide food for the strong swimmers, fish and seals: for there is no reason for assuming that fish and seals will not try to go wherever food is plentiful.

That life may be stifled by the ice covering is difficult to believe when we remember that the floes of the Polar Sea are continually breaking up, with narrow or wide leads of open water between the broken floes. The ice cakes, too, float along as well as break up, so the water that was yesterday covered by an extensive floe may be open today.

The argument that Arctic sea water may lack oxygen is further weakened when we remember that the power of water to hold oxygen in solution increases with decrease of temperature. It is known from observation that fish die from strifling through the mere warming up of the water in which they swim; it has never been more than a theoretical conclusion that they might stifle through lack of oxygen if their chill water were thickly ice-covered for long periods. That they do not so stifle we really know, for lakes in sub-Arctic and Arctic Canada and Siberia that have ice thicknesses of ten or more feet (sometimes 15 or 20 feet) remain good fishing lakes throughout the year; the fish caught in them when the thickest ice is pierced are in apparently healthy condition and usually fat, either normally or beyond average.

Many explorers (even ones who believed in the "lifelessness" of the Polar Sea) have sighted occasional seals far from land. That these explorers did not see more seals was likely enough through not expecting to find animal life in these regions and therefore not looking for it. Stefansson, who was looking for game because he fed both men and dogs by hunting, found no diminution in seal life as he went farther from land. Papanin reported from the vicinity of the North Pole that a net raised from a depth of 3,280 feet (1,000 m.) fairly teemed with diverse molluscs, larvae, medusae, and crustacea.

In the leads at the Pole crustaceans were moving sluggishly near the surface; seals were swimming about and gulping them down.

The number of seals, from the human point of view the most reliable and valuable of Arctic food mammals, varies in different parts of the ocean. This seems to depend neither on latitude nor on distance from shore, but obviously depends on the mobility of the ice. Wherever there are strong currents, and consequent broken ice, for instance north of Alaska in Lat. 73° or 74° N., seals are abundant though it is far from shore. In areas where the ice is sluggish and consequently very thick and little broken, a scarcity of seals is to be expected. Stefansson found one such region north of Borden Island, where seals were not absent but comparatively rare.

There will be in the Arctic sea, then, certain "ice deserts." On coming to them the traveler, whose main reliance for food and fuel is upon seals, will face a problem similar to that of one who, in crossing an unknown continent in tropical or temperate regions, finds himself entering a desert produced by lack of rain. Such a traveler overland would have to depend upon his judgment. He might avoid the desert by skirting it; he might turn back, giving up his journey for the time being; or he might make a dash across, hoping that his resources would take him to the farther side of the hostile area. Just such a problem one would have to face in ice travel on coming to a region where an eddy existed and where massed ice had evidently persisted for years.

SECTION III

ICE: GLOSSARY

We give below a glossary of ice terms, somewhat expanded by description:

Young Ice has formed so recently that it is not strong enough for a man to walk on. We have most frequent occasion to refer to this in connection with leads.

Old Ice is from last year, or from two or three years ago. Its pressure ridges and hummocks are still fairly angular.

Paleocrystic Ice is several years old; some of it may be dozens of years old. The rains and thaws have rounded the fracture angles so that you have the general but small-scale appearance of a rolling prairie.

Shore Ice (Landfast Ice) is that ice which at one edge touches and adheres to the beach, the other edge meeting the pack. Some of the shore ice is sometimes aground, especially because the pressure of the pack has crushed it up in the fall and early winter, piling it into ridges that draw a lot of water.

The *Flaw* is where the landfast shore ice meets the moving pack.

The *Pack* is ice, of considerable extent and thickness, which is in constant motion or which is thought of as being so.

The *Shore Lead* is open water that appears when the pack moves a little away from the shore ice. If you think of the pack as still being somewhere in the offing, you speak of a shore lead even when the water is so wide that no ice can be seen from the flaw or from shore. Only in summer, or after an offshore gale so strong that you want to describe it as having produced summer-like ocean conditions, do you speak of the water outside the flaw as "the sea" or "the open sea."

A *Field* is a large coherent mass of pack ice several miles in area.

A *Floe* is smaller than a field, say acres or scores of them, instead of miles, in area.

A *Cake* is smaller than a floe, say from piano size upward. Smaller ice is called chunks, fragments.

Mush or *Brash* is what its name fairly well implies, small chunks mixed with the finely ground result of pressure between larger bodies of ice.

A *Hole* is an irregular opening in sea ice, square yards, square rods, or acres in extent.

A *Crack* is a break in ice so narrow you can step or jump over it and manage to cross fairly readily with dog teams and sledges.

A *Lane* is a crack too wide to jump across but so narrow that emergency methods frequently suffice for crossing. For instance, you get men and dogs on a cake of ice, use it for a raft and paddle across; or, by man power, you work an oblong cake crosswise in the lane so that it forms a bridge. This defines *lane* as used by sledge travelers. A sailor in a ship uses the same word to mean a passage through ice wide enough for his ship.

A *Lead* is a crack wider than a lane, from dozens of yards to several miles in width.

Pressure Ice is ice which has been broken under stress of wind or current and piled up into ridges or hummocks.

A *Hummock* is a pile of pressure ice not thought of as being particularly long.

A *Pressure Ridge* is a long hummock or a linear series of hummocks of broken ice.

Sky map.—Reflection of the terrain in clouds. Water is represented in the sky as black; snow as white; ice more or less mottled according to amount of snow covering and character of the ice itself; land as black if snowless and mottled in various ways according to snow and vegetation; pink may show in the sky from "pink snow"; yellow or brown from faded vegetation.

Ice blink; land sky; water sky.—These are portions of the sky map as described above.

Needle Ice.—Ice formed by the freezing of fresh water will in spring separate into crystals each having the length of what was the full vertical thickness of the ice when it lay horizontal. These crystals will slide past each other in such a way that ice 2 or 3 feet thick will give way under the weight of a man. The tops of the crystals are so sharp that they tear the feet of dogs and rapidly wear out the boots of men on spring journeys. (It is debated whether fresh ice that was originally salt will break into needles.)

Slush, when spoken of in winter at sea, has a special meaning which is bound up with a process not widely known, that

34

of the elimination of salt from brine by freezing. The process is the clearer in its stages the colder the weather.

Assume a temperature of −40° F. and an open lead. During the night ice forms so thick that next morning men and dogs can travel over it. If the intense frost continues a second day, without snowfall or drifting snow, the new ice will be fairly hard, although there may be on top of it a slight tendency to slush because it has been "steaming"— moisture has been evaporating and condensing again.

Assume, then, for the third day a quiet fall of snow, blanketing the lead and its eight or 10-inch ice as if with an eiderdown quilt. While the snowfall continues the weather will be warm (slightly below freezing). You may now reasonably suppose that the slush which you find under the snow is the result of the warm weather. However, if during the following day or two the temperature drops to around −50° (about the coldest you ever would expect at sea) and stays there, you will discover that underneath the snow the ice which covers the lead seems if anything more slushy than it was during the warm spell.

The explanation is: The freezing point of the most condensed brine is around 0° F. Your 12-inch ice has, then, on its lower side ordinary sea water at, say, 27° warmer than the freezing point of the very saltiest water. On its upper side it has brine, above that is snow and above the snow is an air temperature 50° colder than the point at which the brine freezes. This intense cold, however, does not get access to the brine nearly so effectively from above through 10 inches of comparatively nonconducting snow as the 27° temperature does from below through the 12-inch ice that is a comparatively good conductor. So the brine between the snow and the thin ice may be kept well above its freezing temperature through several days of the severest cold snap.

Fresh sea ice is produced by the continuation of the process described for the formation of slush, which results in the elimination of salt from the ice.

In the first stage, described above, when a lead freezes over, you will notice that sledges pull very hard. This is because there is a crust of salt on top of the ice, indicating the elimination process which appears to be mechanical, something like squeezing water out of a sponge. Another figure of speech is that the ice is like a honeycomb; where the ice of comparatively fresh water corresponds to the wax and the globules of concentrated brine to the honey. Throughout the winter this process continues with every cold snap, more salt being forced each time out of the ice.

When the sea ice was first formed it was salty, although not quite so salty as the water from which it was made. In April, and even in May, ice formed the previous October is still too salty for ordinary cooking uses. But in June and July, when it rains and the snow melts, with little rivulets trickling here and there over the ice, the salt crust is washed away. The saltiness of the ice now has disappeared, or at least that degree of it which is perceptible to the palate. The following year this ice is the potential source of the purest cooking or drinking water. It is fresher than any river although doubtless containing more salt than does rain or snow.

Most of the *snow on sea ice,* except that it has a little salt mixed with it, is much like snow on land. You have drifts in lees. There are no glare spots on sea ice because it is sticky; but you do have large areas sometimes where there are just a few inches of snow, and this beaten hard by the wind. Only toward spring does the snow at sea become a serious handicap to travel afoot. It then becomes *granular, mushy,* and you and your sledge sink into it as if the drifts were bins of wheat.

The *Ice Cap* was once believed to be for the Arctic, and really is for the Antarctic, an ice sheet of great thickness with its center at or near the pole and extending with fair uniformity in all directions. The ancients believed that the lands near both poles, if any, would be covered with thick ice; and that the sea, if there were a sea, would be frozen to the bottom. This frozen sea of the Arctic was at one time supposed by Mediterranean philosophers to extend well towards Scotland; later it was supposed to have its margin just north of Iceland. Such an ice cap has never existed in the Arctic; or at least not during the last several thousand years.

Inland Ice is a term used only for Greenland, where it is also used interchangeably with ice cap. The ice cap of the Antarctic and the inland ice of Greenland are considered to be snow accumulations, which through age and compression have turned to ice.

A *Glacier* is in Greenland a stream of ice flowing slowly away from the inland ice through a valley or over the top of a ridge. When this glacier reaches the sea it breaks off and forms icebergs. Outside Greenland, glaciers of the Arctic are about like those of Switzerland or of the State of Washington.

Icebergs, then, are large blocks of ice which have broken off from the edges of glaciers as they reach the sea. Some bergs are many hundreds of feet thick and several square miles in area.

An *Ice Foot* is for glaciers extending to the sea what shore ice is for sea ice.

A *Crevasse* is a crack in land ice produced by its unequal flowing motion. In sea ice we do not speak of crevasses, merely of cracks or crevices.

Section I

GENERAL

The torrid averages warmest of the zones, but the earth's greatest heat is not found there. The Antarctic averages coldest, but does not contain the coldest spot. The north temperate zone holds the records both for extreme heat and for extreme cold. The hottest known place on earth, with a recorded 136° in the shade, is Azizia, Tripolitania, more than 600 miles north of the northern edge of the torrid zone. In the New World the hottest place is Death Valley, California, about 900 miles north of the Tropic of Cancer, with a recorded 134°. The coldest known spot is Oimekon, Siberia, more than 200 miles south of the Arctic Circle. Both hottest and coldest places are on low ground.

It is now believed that temperatures colder than those on the earth are not reachable above the earth. For instance, the U. S. Army-National Geographic balloon ascent over South Dakota by Stevens and Anderson found its coldest temperature in the twelfth mile altitude, 81° below zero. This is thirteen ° less cold than the Verkhoyansk observation taken at 328 feet above sea level. During the rise from the twelfth to the thirteenth mile the temperatures above South Dakota grew less cold, −68° at the highest altitude reached.

The zone of the most intense cold above the earth is considered to be farthest from the earth at the poles, nearest at the equator.

There is a belief, too, that a far more intense cold may be recorded on high lands that are extensive—on high plateaus—than on mountain peaks of the same latitude. "Ground" level temperatures from —80° to —85° have been observed on the Inland Ice of Greenland at 9,000 and 10,000 feet 200 and 300 miles from the sea. It is thus much colder on high Arctic plateaus than at the same land in the free air, and somewhat colder than at any free air level; but not as cold, apparently, as in certain low, forested areas of the North Temperate Zone.

The lowest mean temperatures of the northern half of the earth are doubtless those of the Inland Ice, probably around 70° or 80° N. Lat. and near or just east of the median line of Greenland. So that although Oimekon, in the temperate zone, is the Pole of Cold Intensity, some spot in Greenland is the Pole of Mean Cold.

Coasts do not run to extremes like interiors. Point Barrow, Alaska, for instance, goes from —56° to 76°, a range of 132°. The range on Arctic islands, other than practically continental Greenland, is on their coasts similar to that of Point Barrow; but the range is greater in their interiors, if they are large. On the pack ice the range is least of all. At the North Pole it probably runs from about —55° to 45°, a spread of about 100°.

The northern polar zone, with which this work mainly deals, has great intensities of heat and cold, though it does not quite reach extremes. The hottest record, under Weather Bureau conditions, is at Fort Yukon, Alaska, a few miles north of the Arctic Circle—100° in the shade. The coldest is Verkhoyansk, Siberia, about 50 miles north of the Arctic Circle—94° below zero.[2]

---

[2] The lowest temperature so far actually recorded under weather bureau conditions anywhere in the world is at Verkhoyansk; but during the first 10 years of the recently begun regular observations at Oimekon that place averaged considerably lower. It is therefore generally agreed that Oimekon, 300 miles southeast of Verkhoyansk and 200 miles south of the Arctic Circle, will establish some time a record lower than Verkhoyansk. (It is believed by

Fort Yukon may have the greatest individual temperature range of the American Arctic, from 100° to —71°, or 171°. The probable American Arctic range will be approximated by using Good Hope, Canada, as if it were an Arctic post though it is perhaps 25 miles south of the Circle; its minimum is lower than that of any known Alaskan or Canadian Arctic spot, —79°. The gap from that figure to Fort Yukon's 100° F. is 179°, the (as said) probable American Arctic range.

The Old World Arctic individual range is from 96° to —94° at Verkhoyansk, 190°. The temperature range of the north temperate zone is about 225°. The United States comes in between with a range of around 200° (from Riverside, Wyoming, --66°, to Death Valley, California, 134°).

Section II

TEMPERATURES

a. Summer

As said, the maximum temperatures recorded within the Arctic Circle under weather bureau precautions and conditions is 100° in the shade. While this record has been made only once, and in only one place, temperatures of 95° have been recorded at numerous times in many places. Heat of 85° to 90° may be expected most anywhere, no matter how far north, if the following conditions can be met: land low, snowclad mountains remote, distance from the sea more than 100 miles.

The crucial thing for determining Arctic summer temperature is local delivery of heat direct from the sun, or rather of light—not the arrival of heat from a distance through currents of air or water. In fact, the extreme Arctic summer temperatures have been recorded, nearly or quite all of them, in places notably removed from warm ocean current influence.

At the top of the earth's atmosphere the sun delivers on June 22 a little more heat each 24 hours at the North Pole than at the equator; the amount computed to reach sea level

some that —90° should be accepted as a "corrected" reading for Verkhoyansk.)

40

is at the Pole about 3 percent or 4 percent less than at the equator.

The degree to which light is converted into heat depends mainly on the color of the surface struck by the rays. On most Arctic lands most of them strike a dark surface; for winter snowfall is light and the snow tends to be swept by wind into gullies or piled in the lee of hills. Grass, which is yellowish or brown, sticks up through the snow; there is sand and dust on the snow; rocks project in some places. When these and similar things are taken together with the large areas that are practically bare, you have, even in early spring, much opportunity for the sun's rays to be converted into heat, instead of being reflected as light.

PERCENTAGES OF SNOWFREE LAND

The little snow there is disappears rapidly from 80 percent to 90 percent of the land. This land is then a vast radiator to melt snowdrifts and to create hot weather. Accordingly, all snow, except a few banks in gullies, will disappear every summer from all land in the Arctic, except from mountains and from lowlands so near mountains that glaciers can slide that far before being melted. Roughly this means that in late August 80 percent of all land north of the Arctic Circle is free of snow. Most of the snowclad, 20 percent, is in Greenland. That country, as said, because of a combination of mountains and precipitation, is estimated to be from 80 percent permanently snow-covered; however, one of the largest areas of ice-free land is found at the north tip—Peary Land, which is 1,500 miles north of the relatively ice-covered south tip of Greenland.

In midsummer, temperature differences between night and day are in the Arctic small compared with those of tropics or temperate zone. For the sun, though not so efficient when low, is nevertheless shining at midnight and delivering some heat.

High northern temperatures, found, as said, only on low lands far from the sea, are likely to be more distressing to people than the same temperatures farther south, for three chief reasons:

41

1. In those parts of the Arctic where temperatures run high, all the land is a swamp. The heat is therefore very humid.
2. The sun does not set and you do not have at night that relief from its heat to which you are accustomed nearer the equator.
3. Mosquitoes, sandflies, and other biting pests compel you to dress heavily in the Arctic, no matter what the heat, as against your ability farther south to dress lightly or even to go partly naked.

The possible extremes of Arctic heat, and the possible attendant discomfort, were so graphically described by Lieutenant Frederick Schwatka, United States Army, from his Yukon River expedition of 1883, that we cannot do better than quote him. He was traversing that short stretch of the river which, in the vicinity of Fort Yukon, lies within the Arctic Circle. It has been found since that this district has more intense summer heat than any temperate zone portion of Alaska. Lieutenant Schwatka says that July 29, 1883, "* * * was an exceedingly hot, blistering day on the river and almost unbearable on the raft * * * Here, within the limited part of the Yukon River in and near the arctic zone, our greatest discomforts were the blistering heat and dense swarms of gnats and mosquitoes that met us at every turn."

SUMMER TEMPERATURES AT SEA

Sverdrup, depending mainly upon the observations taken by the *Fram* and *Maud* expeditions, says that as spring advances the temperature of the polar sea area rises until 0° C. (32° F.) has been reached and the melting of the snow cover and the top layer of the ice commences. During the melting the temperature on the surface remains at freezing, and that of the air just above can never deviate far from this norm. Therefore temperature fluctuations are slight during the summer months.

This does not mean, however, that you might not feel uncomfortably warm if dressed in an ordinary dark business suit and walking around on the sea ice. Melting is rapid wherever the sun can find a dark spot.

Elsewhere we have referred to the experience of travelers on the northern pack with the disagreeable amount of melting that occurs during summer. There have been climatologists, however, who maintained that north of 85° there would be negligible melting of the snow, or of the ice, since no land would be anywhere near to create local heat. This failed of confirmation by the Papanin expedition which started its drift from about 90° North in late May, 1937, and was moving south (toward the Atlantic) through latitudes 89° and 88° during June. For that month Fedorov says: "Summer brought us an abundance of water. All the surface snow melted, as did likewise the top layer of ice. Large puddles of fresh water covered the surface of the ice floe   *   *   *"

On June 11, while the party was still north of 88° and apparently during the same heat wave which produced the melting described above, Papanin, the leader of the party, noted in his diary: "At midnight the weather became calm. On the sky not a single small cloud. The sun warmed our black tent to 24° [75.2° F.]. There's the North Pole for you!"

Even allowing for the attraction which the black tent would have for the sun's rays, it is apparent that in summer there is a wide spread between the almost constant freezing temperature of the ice surface and the temperature of the air 2 or 3 feet above it.

This becomes the more evident when we read in press dispatches such things as what Captain Badigin said about temperatures on the *Sedov* at 85°32′ N. Lat., 61°50′ E. Long. He reported on July 24, 1939: "Summer weather has set in after the rains. The thermometer now registers 25° to 27° C. [77° to 80.6° F.], and the hummocky ice, once so grim, is becoming transformed into wretched mounds of melting snow. Numerous little lakes, more than 300 meters in length and about half a meter deep, have formed on the surrounding ice. Taking advantage of the warm weather and the appearance of lakes, the crew has gone in for a new form of recreation, cruising around in their canoes."

There appears no doubt that Captain Badigin is here wanting to tell us about what seemed great warmth in view of his situation out on the polar sea. However, there is probably some mistake, or the necessity for a qualification, about the 77° and 80.6° temperatures. Surely the thermometer which registered that high must have been in the direct rays of the sun (in view of how near the ice was to give a countervailing chill).

Or did the newspapers lose a decimal point when setting up the type for this dispatch—were the readings perhaps 2.5° C. and 2.7° C.? That would be 36.5° F. and 36.9° F. In that case the temperature was probably taken on the regular weather bureau scheme of having a thermometer shelter about four feet above the ice where the instruments were protected from direct "radiation" of the ice from below but where all four sides of the cage were open to the winds, though not to the sun, in a manner that permitted free circulation around the thermometer of air that had been chilled by the ice in the vicinity.

When thermometers register 36° or 37° F. under the conditions described you would be uncomfortably hot while reading them if you were in the direct rays of the sun while doing so and were clad in an ordinary business suit of dark color. Under those conditions, too, you would have on top the sea ice towards the end of July lakes of the size and depth which Badigin describes.

GENERALIZATION ON HEAT AND COLD

What you do with extremes of heat and cold differs fundamentally. In the main you endure the heat; in the main you protect yourself from the cold.

Our discussion of warm weather and extreme heat needs little development. The users of this Manual are experienced in dealing with heat. Besides, there is less use explaining how to endure what you have to endure than how to avoid what you can avoid. The section on warm weather and its technique is therefore brief, while that on winter, its conditions, and methods will occupy the main part of our book.

b. Winter

As said, the most intense cold yet reliably recorded on the earth's surface is —90° or —94° F. (about 125° below freezing). Temperatures approaching this are likeliest where a lowland far from the sea is surrounded by mountains—that, for instance, is the condition at the coldest spot in the United States, Riverside, near the Montana-Wyoming line, which is the same distance north of the equator as Milan, Italy, and Portland, Oregon. The Arctic's coldest place, Verkhoyansk, is similarly on lowland surrounded by mountains, and that is likewise true of the world's cold pole, Oimekon. (See discussion *ante*.) All these record-holding localities have it in common, too, that they are remote from the sea and its influences. All have hot summers and are forested.

SEACOAST MINIMA

There is probably no place on any seacoast in the Arctic which can show as low a minimum as Riverside, Wyoming. For instance, the lowest yet recorded by the Weather Bureau at Point Barrow, Alaska, over 300 miles north of the Arctic Circle, is —56°. The lowest on the north coast of Canada is —52° at Herschel Island, 200 miles north of the Arctic Circle.

That even narrow seas in the midst of a great deal of land have a marked effect on the temperature appears to be shown by such experiences in the Smith Sound region of Greenland as those of Commander Donald MacMillan and Dr. Noel Humphreys, MacMillan reported —37° as the low-est of the winter 1934–35. These records were taken some 500 miles farther north than the north tip of Alaska and some 800 miles north of the Arctic Circle. There is no known warm sea current nearer than 800 or 900 miles east, on the other side of 9,000-foot-high Greenland; so it is really ice water (water around 30° F.) that warms up the Smith Sound region—and most of it is water frozen over in midwinter, so there must be considerable radiation through sea ice.

At sea, no matter how far north you are, the temperatures are likely to be those of the coasts; so that we can safely assume a weather bureau thermometer at standard elevation on an ice floe at the mathematical north pole would in a hundred years fail, by something like five or ten degrees, to record a temperature as low as the minimum for Wyoming. The coldest Nansen ever recorded, while drifting three successive winters at distances of 500 to 1,000 miles north of the Circle, was —54°.

VARIATION IN COLD WITH ALTITUDE

That valleys are colder than hills during the chilliest parts of a northern winter is, of course, because cold air is heavier than warm, thus flowing down slopes into valleys and pockets. The like is why airplanes which take off from low ground in intensely cold weather usually find themselves flying at considerably warmer temperatures even a few hundred feet up, and much warmer at half a mile up.

The change between hill and valley is striking when you travel afoot at temperatures of —50° or lower. On climbing a hill you feel as if you were going upstairs into a warm room; when you descend a slope it is like going down into a chilly cellar. The same is, of course, the reason why the midsummer frosts which kill grain in the temperate zone take their quickest and heaviest toll in low places.

We have pointed out, *ante,* that this reasoning does not apply to extensive plateaus.

c. *Physical Effects of Cold*

In later chapters we discuss the effects of cold on instruments, tools, and other paraphernalia, with suggestions for dealing with the problems created. Here we consider some of the effects of cold on the natural surroundings.

Perhaps the most conspicuous effect of cold on air is to dry it. A demonstration under practically laboratory conditions occurs whenever you open in cold weather a European-type door that leads out from a heated room. At temperatures like —50° outside and 70° inside, and even with the air of the house fairly dry (as when no cooking is going on), you observe a cloud of steam rushing in along the floor. This thins as you go upward and somewhere around the middle of the door it ceases to be noticeable to the occupants of the room. Persons outside get the reverse effect. They see a cloud of steam rushing out from the upper half of the door, densest at the top. The air is being dried in both cases. Along the floor the damp air of the house is chilled, producing moisture that starts settling toward the floor and which, if the conditions are just right, will strike the floor as hoar frost. The air escaping from the upper half of the door is dried when it gets out, the vapor again appearing first as a fog and later turning to silver particles[3] that flutter to the ground, once more assuming the conditions for observation are just right.

Air at −50° is no doubt considerably drier than any that can be found at 100° over a tropical desert. However, the drying of a wet piece of cloth would be retarded several hundred, if not several thousand, percent by the 150° drop, through the moisture turning almost instantly to ice. It will take several days for a wet cotton handkershief to dry in still air at −50°.

Probably the drying of the air is the chief, though not sole, reason for several of the astmospheric phenomena described just hereafter.

At temperatures in the −30° to −60° range there are various extreme phenomena of sight and sound. Your hand, though apparently dry when you pull it from a mitten, will steam at −60° almost as would at room temperature a cloth soaked in boiling water. Mosture from a dry face or dry hands will cloud spectacles, field glasses, sextants. The moist eye produces more pronounced clouding and frosting of instruments; the breath is still worse, of course. We treat this subject in detail elsewhere but mention here that clouding of surfaces can be avoided or lessened in various common-sense ways.

For the same reason bodies of ice-cold water at low temperatures will steam as if they were boiling. Clouds will rise from flooded rivers, or from leads at sea, that resemble the smoke of a forest fire. Animals and power vehicles leave "fog tails" or "fog trails" behind. At −60° or colder there is a trail in the air behind running caribou or behind a speeding airplane, as if a smoke screen were being laid. An extreme

---

[3] "First as fog and later turning to silver particles" is, perhaps, questionable. It has been maintained that there is direct passage from gas to solid at very low temperatures. It has also been claimed, however, that liquid particles of extremely small size may long persist in very cold, still air. We do not attempt deciding these points.

report is that a reindeer, probably as dry as it could normally be, was invisible from its own steam at 10 feet. This report is from near the Siberian pole of cold, presumably at a temperature lower than −80°.

A reindeer or a horse can be invisible through its own fog, of course, only from one side—the side toward which its moisture is slowly drifting.

VISIBILITY AT LOW TEMPERATURES

Visibility is the greater the colder the air, providing it is not interfered with by condensing moisture. At −50° you can see comparatively small objects two or three times as far away as at 50°, and remote things, such as mountains, acquire neither the purplish appearance which we associate with distance nor the blurred outlines, so that judging distance is not merely impossible to a man unused to cold weather but even to one who is used to it. For instance, after seven winters of Arctic experience Stefansson mistook for a small hill a mile away what proved to be a mountain 20 miles away. He walked toward it for several hours and it constantly seemed about as far from him as when he started, until perhaps within the last hour or so.

Flyers who took part in the International Polar Year expeditions of 1933 have said that they could see as clearly at 50 miles in the Arctic as they could at 10 miles in the Dutch East Indies.

NOISES AT LOW TEMPERATURES

The powers of hearing, or rather facilities for it, are increased more than those of sight. Under ideal conditions, with a temperature of −60° to −80°, you can overhear an ordinary conversation at distances from half a mile to a mile. You can hear a man stamping his feet on the ground at 2 miles, and at 10 to 12 miles you can hear the barking of dogs or the chopping of wood with an axe.

d. Special Aviation Problems

The icing of wings of airplanes in very cold weather may be due in part at least to atmospheric content as well as to air temperature, since some flyers have never experienced it at all while others have been brought down by it. There is seldom icing at 28° to 32°, though it has been reported within this temperature range both from Alaska and the States. There is probably little or none at temperatures above 35°. Icing conditions of the rime type have been reported from temperatures as low as −40°. According to American and Canadian Arctic testimony, the worst icing range there is between 15° and 25°.

FROST ON WINGS, ETC.

A condition which, in Alaska, may trouble in several kinds of weather is the deposit of frost or rime (as opposed to ice) on the wings, changing their contour. This frost is frequently seen on planes that stand overnight, even in perfectly clear weather, and it is standard Alaska practice to sweep wings, propellers, and other parts clean of frost before taking off in the morning. If the plane is left standing for any length of time during the day, frost is likely to gather again, necessitating further sweeping. In extreme and infrequent cases frost in quantity enough to bother has been known to collect while the plane was taxiing down the runway for a take-off.

As said, this frost accumulation may occur at almost any time when temperatures are low, no matter how clear the air may be—it is, in fact, said to be of more frequent occurrence on clear days than on days of light fog.

Temperature inversions occur in winter frequently. There are more of them and they are more pronounced as the cold becomes more intense. Apart from being slightly guilty of reasoning in a circle, we may say that temperature inversions are greatest in coldest weather and that the most intense cold at ground levels is the result of temperature inversion.

As said, temperature inversions depend on cold air being heavier than warm. Air dries as it chills and to that extent it must be lightened on chilling, since moisture is heavy; but evidently the increase in weight per cubic volume due to chill is greater than the decrease in weight due to elimination of moisture. You have, then, usually in temperature inversion air near the ground which is both extremely heavy and extremely dry.

These inversions are most pronounced on the calmest days. When there is a wind, the air is churned up; and if the wind is at all strong the inversion disappears completely for all practical purposes. The greatest inversions undoubtedly occur in those topographic configurations which produce the greatest cold. They occur, therefore, oftenest at considerable distances from the sea and are most pronounced where a low land is surrounded by high mountains. There is said to be an ideal configuration of this sort at the pole of cold, Oimekon, Siberia.

Examples of temperature inversions:

Alaska, Circle Hot Springs, ground —49° F.; 2,000 feet up, 30° F.

Canada, northeastern coast, ground —49° F.; 1,000 feet up, —7.6° F.

Canada, Mackenzie district, ground —60° F.; 1,500 feet up, —25° F.

Temperature inversions become noticeable in a rise of 50 feet or less. There is likely to be no pronounced temperature difference between the 1,000- and 1,500-foot levels and 2,000 to 2,500 feet. That there may be no appreciable difference for 6,000 feet is the experience of W. E. Gilbert, who was trying to get out of a freak cold condition. The ground temperature at Fort Norman, lower Mackenzie River, in January 1934, was —72°. In the air it grew warmer up to 1,500 feet, where it was —47°. The air remained at about —47° from 1,500 to 6,000 feet.

Further special aviation problems are discussed below under Fogs.

Section III

WINDS AND GALES

Nansen said that it was an outstanding conclusion from his studies that the Arctic, taken as a whole, is less stormy than perhaps any other region of equal size in the world. He gives maximum wind velocity for 3 years at sea, 100 miles and more from land, as 50 m. p. h. De Long, after drifting far from land for more than a year in the *Jeannette* north of eastern Siberia, said it was strange how seldom the wind blows and how gently it blows when it does. Stefansson considers he has never seen more than a 50-mile wind when more than 50 miles from shore.

However, these are winds measured only 10 or 20 feet above ice-surface level at sea. The observations of Harald U. Sverdrup with balloons would indicate somewhat stronger winds aloft.

CONFLICTING VIEWS

Statements are frequent in print that howling gales are numerous, or even that gales blow steadily for weeks on end. Sometimes these statements generalize that "the Arctic" is a region of gales. The words "Arctic storm," "Arctic blizzard" convey terrifying impressions to most.

What such travelers have meant when they said that the Arctic was stormy can be interpreted that they observed strong gales where they happened to be and did not realize they were local.

Stefansson considers that a reconciliation of the statements may be found by such things as comparing his experience far at sea on sledge journeys with his experience at Langton Bay (between Cape Bathurst and Cape Parry).

On a typical occasion he was traveling from inland north toward Langton Bay. When he was still 8 or 10 miles from the coast, a perfect calm changed to gentle breezes at his back. The wind continued increasing as he approached the escarpment of the 1,500- to 2,000-foot plateau which is here 3 miles back from the sea. On beginning the descent, the gale was terrific. The land was bare except that here and there patches of snow had been pounded till they were like glare ice. Pieces of slate were torn from the cliffs as he descended a ravine and these went spinning down ahead of him. As he traversed the mile of flat land between the foot of the escarpment and the base camp of his expedition on the Langton Bay sandspit, the cartwheels of slate kept overtaking and passing him. Going north beyond the camp, along the land which runs toward Cape Parry, he found the wind steadily decreasing. In 3 or 4 miles it was a gentle breeze again. Looking back he could not see the cliffs for snowdrift, although the weather was otherwise clear.

SEA ICE ROCK STREWN BY LOCAL GALES

So much slate was torn from the cliffs during the winter that in the spring when the snow began to melt, sledge travelers had to keep well out on the sea ice, a mile or two from shore, along stretches between Horton River and Langton Bay—the whole surface of the ice near land was black with a layer of slate.

Through several years spent in the vicinity of Langton Bay, and through interviewing natives, Stefansson found that the gales of the type described begin to blow soon after the freeze-up, or as soon as there is a pronounced difference in temperature between land and sea, the land being colder. Apparently there are currents of light, warm air rising over the water and the cold heavy air pours like an invisible Niagara off the plateau escarpment to fill the space being vacated by the rising warm currents.

This local wind keeps ice from forming near the beach; any crust that forms being broken and carried out to sea. The winds continue increasing toward midwinter; for the temperature discrepancy between sea and land keeps growing more pronounced. But some day this local offshore gale will be interrupted by a storm of considerable area and strength blowing from the northwest. This brings the pack into Franklin Bay. If then cold weather follows, everything freezes solid.

The warm water of the bay is now insulated from the air by so much ice and snow that the conspicuous difference of temperature between the plateau and the sea margin no longer holds. The violent locally generated gales are over for the year, though there may continue some of the same processes on a milder scale.

These Langton Bay gales are narrowly local. Broader, but still in a sense local, are the gales from the Mackenzie mouth westward along the coast. They are about as bad as the worst blizzards of North Dakota but are more frequent. Storms deserving the name of blizzard probably occur on an average two or three times a month at Herschel Island, frequently lasting several days each. Three days is not an uncommon duration.

LOCAL STORM AREAS

Our general statement, then, follows Nansen, that the Arctic as a whole is not a windy place. We qualify by saying that there are regions of intense local storms, usually where high land faces the open sea. The most conspicuous case of that relation is Greenland. While the center of the Greenlandic inland ice is probably on the average quiet, the coasts are probably the windiest regions of the northern hemisphere. However, it is found that gale violence does not usually extend more than 10 or 15 miles out to seaward.

With the exceptions well in mind, a general understanding of world weather furnishes a grasp of the situation in the Arctic. From a map showing contours, and with the knowledge of the seas in the vicinities of land, you can, in a general way, forecast Arctic weather as to storminess—you can tell when you are about to enter a region where local gales are to be expected.

There are a score of practical applications, one of them illustrated by the experience of Storkerson of the third Stefansson expedition. He once camped at a certain place for a week in a continuous and terrific winter gale and finally returned from a surveying journey only to realize, years later, that if he had advanced perhaps half a dozen miles he would have been in good weather. This slip prevented the expedition from completing the mapping of Victoria Island.

Another sample practical dodge is to avoid a gale by getting right up close to the cliff that produces the wind. If the cliff is high and fairly precipitous you will be in a position analogous to going behind the waterfall at Niagara. Niagara water cascades out only a few feet or yards, however; a Greenland gale, it is said, may not strike the lowland for as much as 2 or 3 miles beyond the escarpment over which it is cascading.

Section IV

PRECIPITATION

It is difficult to measure Arctic snowfall because the snow is usually dry and fluffy and is driven about a good deal by even the lightest winds. There is no doubt, however, that on the average Arctic precipitation is very light. It is estimated that, if the snow of winter be added to the rain of summer, the result would be about 8 inches of water, certainly not more than 10, on most parts of the Arctic lowlands of Canada and Alaska. The Siberian lowlands may be even drier. We have, therefore, the apparent paradox that the average snowfall of the Arctic is much less than that of Scotland or Iowa. A further seeming paradox is that, although some parts of the Arctic have an annual precipitation so light that it would bring about desert conditions in any state of the union, the ground is nevertheless a swamp in practically any part of the Arctic that is not rocky.

The reasons why these are no more than seeming paradoxes are chiefly two—that evaporation in the Arctic is very slow and that in most parts there is no underground drainage. Both these subjects are treated elsewhere in this Manual.

FACTORS CAUSING PRECIPITATION

Whether moisture from the atmosphere is precipitated depends mainly on two factors: on how much moisture there is in the air and on what the factors are that bring the air to the condensation point.

In a country like Iceland one sees frequent and vivid examples of the role played by mountains. In few countries is there a more abrupt rise from the sea, but still there are often low coastal stretches. The air moving in from the sea across these will be perfectly translucent; when it strikes the mountains you see that the precipitation gradient is related to the slope of the mountain, for you note slight evidence of precipitation low down on the slopes, more and more as your eye travels upward, till the higher part of the mountain is concealed from you by a cloud that soon starts delivering rain or snow.

No doubt it is for a reason of this sort that the winds are able to deposit on Greenland snow enough to maintain the Inland Ice. If Greenland were a low country, many of these winds would no doubt sweep all the way across it without producing rain or snow. In this we have a large part of the explanation of why Peary Land in the north of Greenland is mainly snow-free toward the end of each summer. The same reasoning explains why most of the islands north of Canada have no glaciers, or negligible ones, and why the glaciers we do find are in the easterly part of the archipelago. They do not have flowing over them air that starts out with a higher degree of moisture but they do have mountains that are good at capturing moisture.

Most of the Arctic has the heaviest precipitation in the spring. On the north coast of Alaska from which, as said, it is so difficult to get instrumental verification, we have, nevertheless, a consensus among observers that more snow falls during April, May, and the first part of June, than during the remaining $9\frac{1}{2}$ months. It rains a good deal in summer, so that if the rain were snow it is possible that the summer precipitation would impress observers as much as does that of the spring. Fall is inclined to be cloudy, and snowfalls are frequent but average light in comparison with spring. From November to March, inclusive, the precipitation is light.

In their frequency and denseness fogs run somewhat like the snowfalls. Both are heavy in spring. The summer rains may approximate in water content the spring snows, but the fogs of summer are markedly lighter and fewer than those of spring. In autumn both fogs and snowfalls are frequent, but neither of them as heavy as in spring. In winter, fogs as well as snows are few, the fogs, however, relatively even fewer than the snows.

These general remarks on fog must not be understood to contradict what is said elsewhere specifically about *local* fogs.

The above on seasonal variation of precipitation, based directly on the north coast of Alaska, is broadly applicable to the Arctic coasts of America and Eurasia and, with modification indicated hereafter, to the islands. A separate statement is required for the interior of the Polar Sea. Here we depend

55

mainly on Nansen (1893–96); for the only studies which cover the field, and perhaps even more adequately, are those of the *Sedov* (1937–40), which have not yet been published.

Nansen, whose observations for 3 years were in the main at least 500 miles north from the north shores of the Eurasian mainland, found that the variation of snow precipitation by seasons was similar to what we have described for Alaska, with a chief difference in that the winter season, the one from the decrease of the autumn snows to the increase of the spring snows, was somewhat longer than on the Alaska coast. The heaviness of the spring snows, in comparison with the other seasons, is perhaps less marked near the center of the pack than it is near the pack margins and on the mainland shores. The decrease of snow in winter is, on the other hand, more marked in the pack than on the coasts.

Most striking of the differences between the central pack and the Arctic coasts is the decrease in winter fogs. We cannot say for the coasts more than that fogs are few in winter. Nansen says for the pack outright that there are no fogs through the 4 months December–March, inclusive. This does not mean, of course, that the sky is never overcast, for it sometimes is; although that condition is also more rare than on the coasts.

Section V

FOG

a. General

Generally speaking, the central area of the polar sea, where the floating ice is heavy, is considered to be not very foggy— its interior less foggy than its margins and the margins less foggy than the region of looser ice farther south. No doubt there are least fogs in midwinter (the period from December to March or April); Nansen considered you might fairly say that there is no fog near the center of the Arctic pack from December to March, inclusive. In spring fogs apparently occur occasionally; the summer months, particularly July, are worst, and then the fogs become fewer as autumn advances.

COASTAL FOGS

Arctic lands are, generally, warmer than the seas in summer, colder than the seas in winter. Accordingly, it is in summer a warm land wind which produces a fog at sea; in winter it is a cold land wind that produces it. In reverse case, during summer it is the comparative chill of the sea wind that makes fog on the land, while during winter it is its comparative warmth.

A vacillation of the winds, therefore, produces a fog belt more or less parallel to the shore, covering a strip of land and a strip of bordering ocean. Where a peninsula juts out into the sea the entire peninsula, unless very wide, will have the disagreeable coastal climate, though not as pronounced along the median line of a widish peninsula as along its shores. Similarly, a bay of cold water is often foggy in summer, for some land wind will be blowing across it at nearly any time. The shore to the lee of the bay will be foggy.

The rule, to which there are exceptions, is that coastal fogs are fewest in winter, the longest season of the year; next in order of fewness is midsummer; then comes autumn; their greatest frequency is in spring.

It would seem that in midwinter, when the land is coldest, a land wind would most quickly produce a fog at sea. This would be the case if the sea were unfrozen, and is true whenever a gale or other factor has taken away the ice or prevented its forming. But ordinarily the sea near land is covered with such thick ice in winter that a land wind does not produce much of a sea fog.

Similarly the ice covering of the sea prevents a sea wind from producing spectacular land fogs in winter.

We turn now from winter to spring, the season foggiest upon Arctic coasts. The sea is then likely to be very much colder than the land. There have been during winter temperatures as low as —50° at sea and some of this vastly below-freezing chill must have been stored in the ice, to be liberated gradually. On shore the sun that is melting the snow is already fairly high and it is shining for a good deal more

57

than half of the 24-hour period. It has begun its thawing by striking dark objects. The heat that radiates from these initial dark areas soon melts the neighboring snow and creates more dark areas which in their turn become radiators.

It may be thought that the chill to which the sea has been exposed in winter, and some of which has been stored, will have been playing with even greater forces upon the land, with storage of chill resulting there also. This has only slight practical truth; for there are two conditions which make chill storage by the land negligible and make ineffective what there is of it.

To begin with, the land is during winter partly snow-covered. This blanket of insulation protects whatever lies beneath it from a good deal of the effect of the winter chill. The cold that does penetrate the snow is then met by a second insulator, not so good as snow but a whole lot better than ice—frozen earth in some places, rock in others. Accordingly, the penetration of winter cold is not very deep. It has been considered that it will not go through more than 9 or at most 12 feet of earth.

However, the ground is frozen for a depth which in places has been found to exceed 300 feet. There is, then, a vast amount of chill in storage. Accordingly, the second factor is the important one, for it prevents the escape of chill that has been stored.

When the land begins to steam in spring under the heat of the sun its very steaming has a cooling effect upon the ground itself, somewhat as perspiration and evaporation from the human skin cools the body, so that thaw is thereby hindered from deep penetration. When the thaw has made its way down several inches the thawed layer becomes and remains an insulator which prevents any such effective upward escape of chill as would materially change the weather.

SIX-FOOT TEMPERATURE RANGE AT FORT YUKON

For illustration, take conditions observed through a vertical height of less than 6 feet in the garden of the Hudson Stuck Memorial Hospital at Fort Yukon. In July 1918, the shelter holding the weather bureau thermometer was standing in the potato patch about 4 feet above the ground. Within this shelter, of wood painted white to evade heating by the sun, with sides of slats to admit the wind freely, but with a floor of boards to shut out direct radiation upward from the black soil of the garden—under these conditions the thermometer registered on various days varying temperatures between 80° and 95°. A few inches below the surface of the ground were potatoes growing towards maturity which was to be only a week or two later than that of similar potatoes in Vermont. Less than a foot below the growing plants was the upper limit of "eternally" frozen soil.

We had, then, in that garden a heat range from the freezing point a foot below the potatoes to 95° 5 feet above them. Twenty or thirty feet farther down there was, no doubt, a temperature which is ordinary for those depths in the Arctic, around 10° F.

The ground, then, does not release much of its stored chill because its top layers imprison the chill; sea ice releases its chill readily, some of it to the ocean waters beneath, some to the air. Sea water releases its stored chill readily both through being a good conductor and through being constantly churned up by winds and currents so that colder layers farther down are brought to the surface.

The amount of warmth generated ashore during, say, 20 hours of continuous May sunshine is tremendous; and this during the period when the sea ice is still at least somewhat below even the freezing point of ordinary sea water, which is 3° or 4° below the freezing point of our Fahrenheit thermometer scale (around 27° or 29°). Naturally, then, the sea winds will produce land fog. Similarly, land winds in spring create sea fogs.

When the temperature is, say, 50° or 60° in the shade, the fog caused by a sea wind would be densest somewhere between 5 and 10 miles inward from the shore, while its farthest extension inland would not be much beyond 20 miles. Most of these summer fogs are low, whether on land near the sea or at sea near the land. For instance, on the sea off the north coast of Alaska, whaling captains often could see each other, crow's-nest to crow's-nest, when sailors on deck could not see from ship to ship. Inexperienced aviators might remain grounded for days under such conditions, not suspecting that moderate hills, and even a hundred-foot mast, would show above the fog.

The Arctic islands are, of course, subject to the same conditions that produce mainland coastal fogs—with variations according to the size of the island and in some cases in relation to other circumstances.

In summer even small islands like Lougheed (30 miles by 10 miles) generate enough heat for the creation of local fogs upon them; but hardly any fog of consequence at sea is produced by so small a radiant body of land.

An island like Banks (medium-sized for the Arctic—150 miles wide and nearly twice that long), gets away from being wholly oceanic and coastal. Western local sea fogs rolling inland have their summer limit commonly around 20 miles from the beach, and similarly for the south limit from the north coast and the north limit from the south coast, so that nearly half the land surface will be reasonably fogless during the summer. Much of central Victoria, example of a large island, was reported by Eskimos to Stefansson as comparatively fog-free—probably a true report, since it fits with theory verified elsewhere.

A case worth noting for its application generally is that the 10- to 20-mile Prince of Wales Strait, between Victoria and Banks, is not wide enough to chill east winds enough so they can generate a pronounced fog when they move west into Banks. This wind really comes from Victoria Island, where it has been warmed, and produces fog on the strait (as would a westerly or Banks Island wind); but this fog is not carried very far inland usually—and, as said, little or no true land fog is generated.

BELTS AND TIMES OF POOR SPRING VISIBILITY

The Canadian Archipelago has, at such lines as the one which joins the seaward promontories of Borden and Meighen Islands, spring and early summer belts of almost continuously bad visibility—the fogs and snows of spring merge into the fogs and snows of autumn, with not a very appreciable slacking between. But you don't have to go far southeastward into the Archipelago to note an amelioration in midsummer.

The above-mentioned line drawn from Meighen Island southwest, touching western Borden and Prince Patrick, runs through a belt which has probably the worst visibility in the Arctic between May and November, for the descriptions of the only travelers who have been there, McClintock, Mecham, Isachsen, and Stefansson, agree in portraying worse conditions in this respect than have been reported by travelers from anywhere else.

Not only are fogs in this region about the most frequent in the Arctic but also about the most complicated in their sources. For we have here three fog-producing factors in a rare combination—the islands in summer generating heat, the sea ice remaining motionless between the islands either far into or throughout the summer, and the sea to the northwest lying partly open, with a great deal of mobile ice. On most coasts you have only two of these three factors, the land and the open sea. There is, however, an almost equally complicated situation in Greenland where you have at a corresponding season the heat-generating coastal strip lying between the cold open sea and the still colder Inland Ice.

b. Special Aviation Problems

We now describe some of the special forms of fog that may be encountered in the Arctic, a majority of them produced by low temperatures.

Water smoke lies over flooded rivers; you normally have to fly at least 500 feet high to keep clear. It looks like the smoke of a small forest fire and does not spread any great distance.

On land a possible source of water smoke is unfrozen lakes. Most lakes freeze over so early in the fall that the weather is not cold enough yet to produce smoke; but Great Bear Lake (and possibly some other Arctic lakes or lakes on the margin of the Arctic) is so deep that it may have open water as much as two months after the freezing of small ponds. Under such conditions water smoke may rise in quantity, though probably not to a great height.

A still more rare source of water smoke is springs that come from a hillside too warm for quick freezing. These need not be warm springs in the proper sense of the word. Of course, warm and hot springs produce, in ratio to their size, very conspicuous smoke. For instance, in Iceland, where boiling springs during summer distinctly give the impression of steam, the same springs in winter will give the impression of smoke, even though the temperature which enables them to do so is little, if at all, below Fahrenheit zero. An instance is in the naming of the capital city, Reykjavik, *Smoky Bay*. It will not occur to anyone to speak of Smoky Bay who has seen Reykjavik only in summer; it is a most natural description to those who have seen the bay on a cold and clear day in winter.

Water smoke is most conspicuous at sea. True, the lowest sea temperatures of the air are only around —55° while land temperatures may drop in Canada and Alaska to —70° and —80°, in Siberia to 90° below, when a flooded region would give off in proportion to its area a far greater amount of smoke than possible at sea. However, some rivers never flood; the rest do so only at considerable intervals. But sea ice is constantly breaking, forming leads and holes through the pull and push caused by either the motion of the water beneath the floes or that of the air above them. Accordingly, you practically always have water smoke visible in some direction when you are traveling over the Polar Sea in clear midwinter weather.

Since flyers have apparently determined that river smoke seldom goes much above 500 feet it may be that lead smoke does not go higher; but to sledge travelers the impression is strong that it does rise to a thousand or more feet. However, the columns of smoke often have a flattened top, as do smoke columns on land that are derived from a forest or prairie fire—a kind of ceiling.

One striking difference between sea ice and fresh-water ice is in relation to water smoke.

Practically as soon as a river or lake is frozen over it ceases to have smoke-producing power. If you examine the surface of fresh-water ice, even if no more than an inch or two thick, you will find it dry. As we have explained in another connection, young salt water ice is damp or wet. To begin with, its own consistency is mushy, or wetly granular, as contrasted with the glass-like appearance and behavior of fresh ice.

The slush on top young sea ice is nearly always at a temperature lower than the freezing point of the sea (27° or 28° F.); but even if it is as cold as just a few degrees above Fahrenheit zero, it is still a lot warmer than air of −40° or −50°. So long as it is wet in consistency it evidently has more power of releasing particles of itself into the air. At any rate, leads will continue to steam and produce smoke long after they are frozen over. During the first day, when the thickness of the mushy ice is perhaps only 2 or 3 inches, the smoking is almost as conspicuous as that of open water. On the second day it is less conspicuous. It does not wholly disappear, if conditions of a chill and clear atmosphere are right, until the ice is so thick that it is no longer damp on top. This thickness is probably somewhere between 8 and 12 inches.

Human-animal fog is of the same nature as the invisible perspiration discussed in Chapter 9. Your normally moist (apparently dry) hand will show as much steam at −60° in calm clear weather as a towel wrung in boiling water shows in a room at 60°. Transfer this standard to other sources of "steam" and you have the basic idea of human-animal fog.

Alaskan and Canadian flyers report that in the early morning, before and around sunrise, with a ground temperature of −50° to −65°, fog is usually or always noticeable over villages. The steam (together with smoke in some cases) make a "ceiling" at a few hundred feet. The fog will disappear if the sun develops heat or if a wind comes up. Flyers, knowing the condition to be local and temporary, take off from within these local fogs and are, of course, almost immediately out of them.

At Fairbanks this fog sometimes extends a half mile or more beyond the limits of the town. When you fly directly above that town nothing is usually obscured, visibility is perfect—you see the town clearly through its fog. But flying at an angle the town is blurred or hidden.

Flyers can pick up a town by the fog bank over it. Finding such a fog bank and shooting for it, you will come either upon a town or upon open water. But the reverse may happen—you may not be able to see a local fog that hides a town. One danger then is that you may think yourself off your course when you are not. For instance, you may plan to identify a river by a town in a certain position on it. If you do not see the town, in apparently perfect weather, you may think yourself on the wrong river.

The houses in one edge of a village are usually visible, for the air will have some movement and the windward side of the town will be exposed. Similarly, an entire band of caribou or reindeer is seldom hidden—you will see at least a few animals at one edge of the herd.

FOG TAILS

On some days Arctic planes will leave a fog tail 15 to 20 miles long that hangs still (straight) in the air, or may become wavy. One flyer setting out after another whose machine has disappeared from view can track the pilot to his destination by following the tail that is hanging in the air. Canadians have reported fog tails 18 miles long in the lower Mackenzie.

Although "spicule fog" appears to be a widely accepted term, it is a bad one. To begin with, what you see, as described below, looks more like a snowfall than a fog—it is as if snow were forming before your eyes and then slowly falling. Perhaps some term could be devised on the idea of "frost flakes."

Dr. Ralph L. Belknap, leader of the Michigan-Pan American Airways Expedition, reported spicule fogs from the Greenland Inland Ice. He gives the conditions under which they occur:

Because of the relatively low air temperatures over the interior of Greenland, the relative humidity is invariably high (i. e., the precipitation point is not far off). When condensation occurs it is most often in the form of ice spicules. Especially during the early morning hours, when the temperature was less than 10° F. the air, although cloudless, contained many small glistening particles falling slowly in the nearly motionless air. If there is a slight air movement, the particles have a tendency to collect and adhere to the lee side of obstructions.

On the Inland Ice these particles sometimes were in quantity sufficient to obscure objects usually plainly visible. Such "fogs" develop in periods of low temperature, high humidity, and calm to light winds. Dr. Belknap believes the fog effect is confined to a zone of limited vertical extent (a few hundred feet).

Spicule fogs pronounced enough to be dangerous to airplanes are apparently very rare in all those parts of the Arctic where flying has been developed extensively—are seemingly more frequent on the Inland Ice than anywhere else. It is an indication of how rare the condition is in that there are no reports of trouble from all the flying yet done in Arctic Canada, according to the information of one of the most experienced of Canadian flyers, W. E. Gilbert. Only two Alaska cases are known to Pacific Alaska Airways; but they were serious, producing a heavy coating of frost on the wings just after the take-off or just before the landing so that planes came down out of control.

"BLACK FOG"

Reported as a hazardous fog is the "black bank" which Canadian flyers have found in March low over the ice of the frozen sea in the Mackenzie River to Cape Parry district. It is most particularly dangerous where the coast is flat, and is more noticeable on overcast days. Flying along a flat coast, say in the Baillie Island neighborhood, if you are strange to the country, you might imagine you were approaching an area of high coastline, the low fog resembling a high cliff.

SECTION VI

BAROMETRIC PRESSURES

The following statement on barometric pressures within the Arctic regions is based upon the work of Dr. Harald U. Sverdrup, an explorer of note, a leading authority on Arctic climatology, chief of scientific staff of the *Maud* expedition, now Director of the Scripps Institution of Oceanography, La Jolla, California. No long series of climatological observations has been carried out in the polar regions but Dr. Sverdrup has collated all the available material. His conclusions are based largely upon observations in the Arctic sea made during the *Fram* expedition in 1893–96 and the *Maud* in 1922–24. To these have been added data from various Arctic expeditions of the last century.

Barometer studies of probable great importance were carried out systematically by the *Papanin* expedition which began its drift at the North Pole late in May 1937, and closed its observations near the east coast of Greenland north of Scoresby Sound in February 1938. Longer continued and systematic were the observations of the *Sedov* which drifted between October 23, 1937, and January 16, 1940, westward north of Asia, generally parallel to the track of the *Fram*, although most of the time north of it. The *Sedov* expedition results, however, are more likely to amplify than to alter those of the *Fram*. So perhaps it is most from the *Papanin* results that we may anticipate changes in the view presented by Sverdrup.

We now summarize and paraphrase what Sverdrup has said on Arctic barometric pressures in his two main publications, Volume II of the *Norwegian North Polar Expedition with the Maud 1918–25, Scientific Results,* Norway, 1933, and in Band II Teil K of the Köppen-Graz-Geiger, *Handbuch der Klimatologie,* Berlin, 1935:

In winter (January) the Atlantic side of the polar sea is under the influence of a low-pressure trough, extending from Iceland toward Cape Chelyuskin, Siberia. On the Siberian-American side the pressure distribution shows a saddle point between the low-pressure sections south of Spitzbergen and over Bering Sea; another saddle point is found between the high-pressure regions over Siberia and Canada-Alaska. Between these high-pressure regions there appears a disturbing zone, within which deep winter cyclones are formed. These, moving in a northeasterly direction, later turn around and reach the Canadian archipelago from the northwest.

In the spring (April), high pressure predominates over the greater part of the polar sea and the Canadian archipelago. During this time of the year the disturbances are much smaller than in winter.

In the summer (July), the pressure differences are very small over the entire region, the disturbances are frequent, but slight. The direction of the wind indicates higher air pressure over the northern part of the archipelago, but this is not borne out by the observations of pressure. All differences are, however, slight.

In the fall (October), a transition to winter pressure distribution takes place, with a saddle point north of Bering Strait. From this month onward strong disturbances again occur.

As in lower latitudes, the greatest number of disturbances occurs in the winter, when the air pressure is generally high. The mean monthly fluctuations of air pressure are here, as elsewhere, greater in winter than in summer.

CHAPTER 4

LIGHT IN POLAR REGIONS

SECTION I

GENERAL

A practical way of discriminating between daylight and darkness is to say that it is not dark so long as a man of normal sight can read ordinary print out of doors. By this definition you would have at the North Pole (at 90° N. Lat.) each year something around seven months of daylight and five of darkness.

We may also consider defining as dark that period when no daylight can be seen anywhere in the sky. On that definition you would have at the earth's pole about eight months of daylight and four of darkness.

It is never pitch dark inside either of the polar circles except where you find a sea without ice, as to the north and northeast of Iceland. In summer, when land in the Arctic usually is black, brown, or green, there is perpetually either sunlight or twilight. In winter, when direct and indirect sunlight are both absent much of each day, the ground is usually white, with a snow covering which so reflects and magnifies whatever light gets to it that, even at maximum darkness, you could probably see a dark-clad man on a white field at least 100 yards away. Maximum darkness will occur when the sky is densely overcast, when there is no twilight, when there is no moon in the sky, and when there are no northern lights behind the clouds. The stars by themselves, then, succeed in transmitting enough light through the densest clouds so that when this is reflected by the snow it prevents that type of pitch darkness with which we are familiar in the nonpolar zones.

Because of the shape of the earth, its relation to the sun, and refraction, there is some daylight at any given moment over about 66 percent of the earth's surface. This means that you would at either pole see daylight, from first trace in spring to last trace in fall, continuously for about two-thirds of the year. There is most daylight per year in the polar zones, intermediate in the temperate, least within the tropics. For refraction increases with decrease in temperature; and while polar zones do not have the most intense cold they do have the lowest average yearly temperature.

The main reasons why there is more effective light in the polar zones than people from outside them expect, are the following:

Air transmits light more easily when it is dry. Chilling the air dries it. The air over the polar zones during winter, therefore, transmits light more perfectly than we are used to even in deserts.

The Arctic is mostly sea, lake, or swamp. Accordingly, less dust escapes into the air than we are used to, and dust-free air transmits light better.

There is not as yet in the Arctic any considerable pollution of the air by the smokes of industry or even by those of numerous dwellings. Forest fires are rare, and volcanic dust has less chance than in most places, although there is a certain amount of vulcanism on the fringes of the Arctic in two sectors—Iceland and the Aleutian Islands. The absence of these smokes contributes further to the clarity of Arctic air.

The sun stays above the horizon for something more than half each year, because of refraction. After sinking below the horizon in the autumn and before attaining it in the spring, there is a twilight brighter through the above-described clarities of the air and which is increased in effectiveness by reflection from the snow.

As said, the stars, least considerable of the sources of light, succeed in delivering a higher percentage of their total product in the Arctic than in the temperate zone or tropics. What they do deliver is increased, perhaps doubled, by reflection from the snow, so that we might say that the Arctic stars give light between two and three times as effective as that of the stars of other zones.

The same increased quantities of delivery and the same multiplication by reflection applies, naturally, to the moon. A rough check has been made with a number of polar travelers, both Arctic and Antarctic, who agree that on a cold, clear midwinter night you get more useful light from half a moon on a snowy landscape than from a full moon shining on a green landscape.

With a clear sky, you can see a mountain range as far by the light of stars and half a moon as you could by sunlight. Several Arctic pilots have written agreeing that you can land an airplane about as safely with half an Arctic moon as with daylight. Some informants have said that, while there is not with half a moon quite as much light as you would ideally want for landing, you are for compensation free from the glare that sometimes interferes with snow landings during full daylight.

Some experienced flyers disagree that the light of half a moon is adequate for safe landings, and feel that moonlight really sufficient is available only for the two or three nights at the immediate full. These flyers, however, are all from Alaska, all have their main experience in the Yukon valley, not on the prairie north of the Brooks Range or on the Arctic coast. This brings out an important thing—that clumps of forest scattered here and there about an otherwise snowy landscape detract from the total reflecting effectiveness more than you would expect. For one thing the moon is usually at a slant so that the trees not only absorb the light which strikes them directly but also throw a shadow over some more of the landscape. Then there are like shadows thrown by rocks and cutbanks while cliffs are usually dark because they are steep. Mountain slopes are not on the average as effective with moonlight as are horizontal landscapes.

A considerably higher percentage of the moon's light is available for human use in northern Alaska than in southern Texas. For in Texas the moon sets every night both while it gives little or no light around the new and when it gives maximum light around the full. At Barrow the moon does not rise at all when it is new; but it does not set at all when it is full. Barrow people lose no light from missing the moon that has no light to give; they gain a lot from never losing sight of the full moon.

The moon at its full stays above the horizon only between one and two full days at the Arctic Circle. At the North Pole it rises just a little before it is half full; then it stays in the sky through the full until it is a little less than half. If you figure a lunar month at 28 days, you have the moon visible for about 15 and invisible about 13.

A special aid to visibility in the Arctic night is the aurora borealis. At its brightest it may give as much light as the full moon—some say more. However, the auroral is the least dependable of the lights—you never know when it is going to come or fade. But it is at times very useful, sometimes aiding materially throughout the whole night. (When we say "whole night" we are speaking, of course, of latitudes south of 84° N., for below that parallel there is some daylight in the sky even on December 22.)

An advantage of moonlight over sunlight, connected with the absence of glare, is that it throws more sharply defined shadows or appears to do so; and shadows give an airman his one possibility of telling the difference between a level and a rough snow or ice surface when he is coming down for a landing. It is, therefore, a serious defect of auroral light that it never comes from a single focus, like moonlight, and seldom even from a small part of the sky—more often from several points of the compass and occasionally from nearly or quite all of them. Coming from several directions, the aurora throws no clear shadow; if it is very bright it may interfere so much with the moon's power of making well-defined shadows that, for airplane landings at least, the increase of light through the aurora is more of a hindrance than a help.

Section II

SPECIAL CHARACTERISTICS

For the period when the sun is above the horizon the Arctic light requires only a few special comments:

Sunlight reflected from water produces quick and violent sunburn. For like reasons sunburns are quickly produced by the glare of Arctic snow. For protection, dark veils are sometimes worn.

When the sun is well above the horizon and the sky uniformly though not densely overcast you have the maximum of eyestrain and tendency to snowblindness, as well as the most difficult of all light conditions from the point of view of a traveler, whether walking or flying.[4] On sea ice, or on land uniformly snow-covered, you are literally unable to see anything that is white. For invisibility you don't have to have snow-whiteness, exactly matching the landscape. For instance, a polar bear, in reality yellowish white, may be invisible as he approaches you, except that you see his black nose and will, with that for a key, be able to notice his eyes and perhaps his claws or other dark spots and even a faint outline of his body. Under the conditions where a bear is invisible a hundred yards off, a blue fox might be visible at a mile or more.

We discuss in chapter 11, "Travel," how these conditions may lead to your walking over a precipice or stepping into a crevasse, and we deal there with the precautions that should be taken.

We couple with our general statements on light a group of phenomena pronounced in the Arctic and important for winter travel—water sky, land sky.

We have from the temperate zones and tropics some examples which prepare for the more clear-cut phenomena of polar regions. For instance, when the clouds are just right, you can see the lights of a city reflected in them at great distances, particularly on prairies. In the mountains, even in the tropics, you may, when the clouds are just right, see white patches in the sky surrounded by dark. The white ones are the reflections of glaciers, the dark are over the snow-free parts of the mountains.

The most perfect example of these phenomena, as well as their most useful manifestation to a traveler, is met with when sledge parties traverse the polar sea far from land—nearer

---

[4] Apparently snowblindness is not contracted by pilots while aloft.

land the same phenomena are present, but in some cases so confused as not to be useful.

Far at sea, then, on a day completely and uniformly overcast, and with clouds at fairly high levels, you have above you a real map of your surroundings. The higher the clouds the greater the area of sea pictured in the sky.

Cloud areas below which level ice is uniformly covered with snow will be a uniform white on your sky map. Broken surfaces with many pressure ridges can themselves never be quite uniformly white and are, therefore, represented above by a slightly mottled appearance. One kind of ice surface, the paleocrystic, has been converted by many summers of rains and thaws into a small-scale equivalent of an undulating prairie. The hollows are choked with snow, the hills that have been swept free of snow are blue in appearance, because, as elsewhere explained, old ice is always fresh and glare. Paleocrystic floes are, then, reflected in the sky by round, oval, or at least not angular, dark patches in a matrix of white.

The sky map shows leads in their full variety of manifestations. Those which are several weeks or months old are smoothly snow covered and are therefore shown by the clouds more uniformly white than any other ice; and so you will discover long ribbons in the sky representing them cleanly. Other leads have ice from one to several days old, and they are represented by sky ribbons of various degrees of darkness. Those leads in which the water is still unfrozen are shown the darkest of all, practically black.

The experienced sea traveler has definite views on every type of ice. Looking into the sky he recognizes those he wants most to avoid, those which are most desirable, and all the intermediate grades. This may be of importance to his strategy. In Chapter 11, Section III, we tell how the traveler chooses and varies his route according to the sky map.

A special type of sky coloring begins to appear in spring when temperatures start running from —20° in the late night to 20° in the late afternoon. The traveler over the northern sea will then begin to notice a general pinkish tinge in large patches of his sky map, most pronounced in certain places and sometimes giving a definite pattern to the sky. This shows him that the tiny plant known as "pink snow" has begun to develop. (See also chapter 6.)

When you approach land in winter or early spring you see first a general darkening of the sky. This is not as pronounced as if caused by open water. There are certain patterns in the sky map now which you recognize as showing land formations, and there is an amber or yellow tinge due to the bleached grass which sticks up here and there through the snow. If there are in the land sky a few patches as dark as over water, you know they are sandy or rock stretches—at any rate land where the wind has swept all the snow away.

A modification of land sky is sometimes found at sea in that strong offshore winds have carried dust and fragments of rock out upon the ice. There will then be belts and tongues of gradually fading darkness stretching out in the sky map from the denser drabness of the land.

Next after its supreme usefulness to a sledge traveler comes the usefulness of the sky map to the navigator of a ship in broken ice. Looking ahead (always presupposing a suitably cloudy day) you can see where the ice presses against the sea coast and where it does not; you see the leads and open patches and you form some idea of the character of what ice there is.

A flyer passing over the northern sea, having a wider horizon, does not need the map quite so badly as other travelers, but even to him it will be useful. His method of interpreting the map will, of course, have to be a little different since he is likely to be near the clouds and will therefore have a different perspective.

LOW FLYING FOR USE OF SKY MAP

Wilkins, who got accustomed to using the sky map as a traveler afoot on the northern pack, makes a suggestion for a novice in Arctic sea flying. If he is below the clouds and close to them he can make practically no use of the reflected map. In practice on such occasions Wilkins goes down as low as he can safely; for the lower you are the more accurately and easily you can read the map.

In making this suggestion, Wilkins has in mind chiefly the problems of landing. If you are flying a craft with wheels or skis and want to make a landing, or think you may need to do so, you will select from the sky map patches that are uniformly white—not mottled or peppered to indicate the rolling, glare paleocrystic ice or recently fractured ice of whatever age. If in a flying boat, you look for uniform black patches that show open waters free or nearly free of drifting ice fragments; if none is seen in the map then, alternatively, you seek a uniformly white patch and make a snow landing.

CHAPTER 5

ANIMAL LIFE

SECTION I

WILD ANIMALS

This chapter does not pretend to give a complete list of the animal life found in the Arctic, nor to give all of the scientific facts that would be necessary in a zoology volume. It does list those animals which are important in the economy of the Arctic hunter, with brief discussions of the outstanding characteristics of each.

The so-called Barren Ground caribou is found winter and summer on the north coast of the most northerly islands in the world, with the exception of Peary Land, from which they seem to have been exterminated by wolves, and certain small islands which they never seem to have reached—no doubt from inability to traverse the sea, ice-covered or not, that separates these from other lands. Its range extends south at all seasons down into the forests of both the Old and New Worlds. Among islands seemingly never reached are the Franz Josef group and Jan Mayen. They may never have reached Wrangel Island and the tiny islands discovered by the De Long expedition—Henrietta, Bennett, etc.

Estimating the numbers of caribou is so difficult that guessing is perhaps a better wording. Those of Arctic and sub-Arctic Canada have been estimated at all figures from one to twenty million, with five million perhaps a reasonable guess. In Alaska there might be from one-fifth to one-third as many as in Canada. In the Soviet Union there are not as many as you would expect; or, rather, the small estimates are due to the occupation of what were the wild ranges by the domestic animals, under the name of reindeer. Perhaps in spite of all the vastness of northern Siberia there may not be as many wild caribou there as in Canada.

Caribou and reindeer are of one species. We have said of reindeer that they vary from the smallest, which are represented by certain breeds of Lapland, to the largest, which are probably the Tungus—with the biggest Tungus animal at least twice as heavy as the smallest Lapp. The range is probably somewhat smaller with a wild caribou. They are tiniest in northern Ellesmere Island and northern Greenland, the Peary Caribou. They grow on the average larger as you pass southward and southwestward through the Canadian archipelago. They are apparently somewhat larger in northwestern Arctic Canada than in northeastern. Perhaps largest of all are those which spend part of the time in the forest and part on the prairie in central and northern Alaska.

Then we have the question of whether there is a difference between prairie or "barren ground" caribou and woodland caribou. There is no doubt that those prairie caribou that go into the forest mingle with the forest varieties, which may account for the gradually increasing size from the Peary caribou south and southwest—assuming that the woodland caribou is "naturally" the larger.

It is not possible to say what are the boundaries between woodland and prairie caribou—unless by agreeing that there are not any, or that they are somewhere in the Arctic or sub-Arctic forests. The southward limits of the woodland caribou are found in the United States—in Maine, Minnesota, Idaho, and Washington.

MIGRATIONS

In certain parts caribou movements are to an extent seasonal and have somewhat the character of a real migration, though not so strictly as we used to believe. Nor are the directions as regularly north and south as those of properly migrating birds.

On the Canadian Arctic mainland and Victoria and King William Islands there is a fairly regular movement southward in the fall and northward in the spring, but not all of the caribou move out of Victoria Island in the fall and a few within the island appear to move north. On the Canadian mainland south of Cape Parry, in the autumn of 1911, Stefansson found that the caribou moved south around the earliest snowfall but started moving north again well before Christmas—thus were moving north during a period when the cold was increasing, and would continue to increase for another two months. In Banks Islands, so far as there is a movement, it appears to be south in the spring and north in the autumn—certainly Stefansson found caribou more numerous in the northern than southern end of Banks Island in the years 1914–17. M'Clure reported the Banks caribou behaving just that way a half century earlier; for they were numerous around the Bay of Mercy in midwinter.

There is no sure way of telling when "migrating" caribou will arrive or just where they will pass. One thing that is known to affect the direction of migration is the freezing of a lake—if caribou arrive before it freezes the herd will split to right or left or else the whole of it will be deflected to one side; if they arrive at a lake well frozen they make straight across. They might also be delayed by the late freezing of a body of water—hardly by a river, perhaps by a lake or a bay, certainly by a wide stretch of sea. Thus the time of arrival, if the herd does arrive, may be varied a month or two by early and late falls; the "migration track" may be deflected 50 or 100 miles by unfrozen lakes; or movement may be in effect stopped—in the sense that a herd does not arrive at all one year in a district to which they usually come.

A second factor that tends to direct caribou movement, whether they are a "migrating" or simply a grazing herd, is the direction of the wind—they tend to feed and to move up into the wind, but do not always do so.

The reasons for deflection and delay by unfrozen lakes is obvious; the reasons for control by wind are perhaps two: that caribou depend upon their sense of smell for warning against their chief enemy, the wolf; and that in a blizzard their eyes will be kept reasonably free of snow by the wind while they are facing it, but are going to be filled with eddying snow if they turn away, particularly if they do so while grazing.

We have spoken thus far of a herd of caribou as if this

78

were a natural and inevitable formation. It is nothing of the sort. Caribou do tend to be gregarious. But one year they will be found in a certain district in bands few of which are above a hundred, while in the same district perhaps two or three times a century they are in a single herd as large as a million. We take a hypothetical case for illustration.

Suppose, for instance, that there are a half million caribou in Victoria Island which "intend" to move south but are delayed perhaps a month by storms and open water from crossing Dolphin and Union Straits and Coronation Gulf to the mainland. Assume that there are 250,000 caribou feeding on the mainland west of Coronation Gulf and another 250,000 on the mainland east of the Coppermine. It might be that the mainland half million would be restrained from moving south by prevailing northerly winds into which they face, or by some other natural condition.

If both these quarter millions begin moving south about when the half million are crossing from Victoria Island, you still do not have your million in one continuous herd unless something happens that focuses all three groups to a point. This could be that the bands east of the Coppermine are deflected westward by a series of occasions when they strike a lake in such a way that it "appears to them more logical" to turn west for the detour and that the bands west of the Coppermine are similarly deflected eastward; or perhaps these two deflections might result from a southeasterly wind west of the Coppermine and a southwesterly one east of it.

We have just dealt in a lot of ifs; that is correct, for it takes a lot of ifs to explain the two well-known facts that usually caribou are found in bands of only a few hundred or at most a few thousands, but that once or twice in each human generation there is a credible report of incredible moving swarms.

HERDS OF A MILLION CARIBOU

There was, for instance, the case reported by members of the second Stefansson expedition, that a herd, which required four days to pass, moved south across the headwaters of the Dease the fall of 1911. First there was a day of scores of bands ranging from dozens to hundreds. Then there were 2 days of a moving ribbon of caribou four miles wide that practically covered the land from sight. Last was a fourth day of scattered bands. According to report these animals sometimes trotted or galloped, sometimes walked, and sometimes stopped to graze, and sometimes lay down. The estimate was that a resulting average speed was that of a slow walk, say a mile and a half or 2 miles per hour. The herd must have been several hundred thousands and may have been a million. It was comparable in numbers to the great buffalo herds of the Dakota-Kansas region a hundred years ago.

Caribou movements are similar, with the irregularities of them similar, in the Old World.

That grasses are a preferred caribou food in summer but lichens in winter may be a key, or at least one of the keys, to the "migrations." It has been found with domestic caribou, named reindeer, that they have a good memory for localities, amounting to a "homing" instinct for districts in which they have lived. An animal that can remember its home can presumably remember the kind of food it ate in a given district. This seemed to Stefansson the probable explanation of the southward movement in Banks Island toward the end of winter and the northward movement toward the end of summer. For it appeared that grasses were the chief vegetation in southern Banks Island; grasses were the prevailing vegetation also in northern Banks Island, but there seemed to be more lichens up there, and this (perhaps) enticed the caribou north in the fall.

The suggested Banks Island explanation does not argue against a southward movement on the mainland of Canada in autumn, if it be thought that the animals "plan" to go all the way to the forest; since it is probably true that there are more lichens available in the northern forest margin than on the prairie just to the north of it, which is primarily a grass land.

So far as we can generalize, the continental movements are, on the average, seasonal, more likely to be south than otherwise in the autumn and more likely to be northward in the spring. But on the islands, with the chief exception of Victoria and King William, many of the movements are not seasonal and those which are seasonal, such as Banks Island, may be the reverse of the movements of migratory birds—may be north in fall and south in spring.

Shed horns are the most reliable indication of caribou movement. The old bulls shed them around midwinter, younger bulls later in the winter, and cows not until spring. Thus the age and sex groups leave behind clues to their seasonal movements that can be read hundreds of years later. Stefansson found the shed horns of old bulls, indicating midwinter residence, on Isachsen Island and on the other Canadian islands in the same latitude (77° to 80°) discovered by his third expedition. He saw animals there both fall and spring, accounting for two more seasons and virtually proving that they were there the year around.

Among the northern caribou in the New World the smallest are found in Greenland and generally to the northeastward. The largest, southwestward in Alaska, weigh up to 400 pounds. Approximately speaking, some of the caribou near the Endicott Mountains of Alaska are twice as large as the Peary caribou of northern Greeland.

Roughly, there is a similar variation in color. The Peary caribou are lightest and the Alaskan darkest. There are no albino species of caribou and albinism must be very rare. Stefansson never saw a white, partly white, or spotted animal in tens of thousands of caribou during ten years in the Arctic, though he frequently studied large herds through field glasses.

The fatness schedule for caribou varies slightly by districts—by climate. Generally a bull more than four years old has practically no fat at the end of the rutting season, which may be some time in October. There is no appreciable fattening through November and December—even the bone marrow contains little fat. In January the marrow has considerable fat, and fat begins to show behind the eyes and around kidneys and intestines. The increase in fat is continuous through February, the coldest month of the year, and through March and April, still at a slow rate; there is a rapid fat increase through May, June, and July until by middle or late August a bull of 400 pounds live weight may have more than 75 pounds of fat (suet). About half the total fat is in a slab along the back which extends forward along the neck and down behind along the haunches. The thickest parts are just a little forward of the tail, but not straight in front of it—2 or 3 inches to either side. Careless hunters sometimes describe this slab as being four inches thick but it is probably seldom thicker than 2¾ inches. In butchering it is Eskimo and forest Indian custom to remove or, as they say, skin off the slab of fat, which may weigh 35 pounds, and more in extreme cases.

A bull of 2- or 3-year age gets fat along about the same cycle as an older bull, except keeping a month or so behind in schedule. In proportion to total body weight, the younger the bull the less fat.

The fatness schedule for cows is nearly opposite to that of bulls. True, a cow as well as a bull is fat in the autumn; but in winter she loses fat gradually during the time that the bull is gaining it gradually. Proportionately even fatness of mature bulls and mature cows may occur somewhere around February or March. Thereafter the bulls are fatter in proportion to total weight. The cow does not lose all her fat until at the calving season, which may be in April. Indeed, she is likely to be thinnest somewhat after that, in late April or in May.

The fat cycle for the domestic animal, the reindeer, is about the same as for the caribou, except that steers have a cycle that resembles that of the cow. Probably steers have more fat in proportion to body weight than bulls.

It is the view of Eskimos, and of whites who live on an exclusive meat diet, that the lean tastes better in proportion to how fat the animal is. This view is strongly held only by those who do not use seasoning in their food—who use no salt, pepper, onions, and the like. Those who use seasoning judge meat from a somewhat different point of view—are likely to prefer a cow or a young bull when those who do not use seasoning prefer the meat of an old bull.

Among caribou, bulls never get very old, probably not older than 6 or 7 years. This is because of the speed ratio between ages and sexes. When a wolf pursues caribou he catches the slowest runner—the animal that drops behind. Big and fat bulls are slow for those reasons and additionally slow in the fall through carrying heavy antlers. If a caribou calf lives to be 2 or 3 days old it is not likely to be killed by a wolf until it is 5, 6, or 7 years old, the males being killed somewhat younger than the females, for the reasons given. Practically no caribou attain an age of 9 or 10 years. They do not closely approach a time when they might die of age. The causes of death among them, in order of increasing frequency, are accident, human hunters, wolves.

There are few if any things manufactured that can equal caribou skin for clothing. They are at their best from mid-July to about the middle of September, depending on age and sex and on the purpose for which the skin is wanted. Later than September the hair begins to get brittle, and eventually loose; spring it is so very loose that the skin is practically worthless for clothing. The hide is then at its thinnest, ideal for parchment—to make Eskimo-style windows. During June and July the caribou have a more or less patchy appearance, due to bunches of loose, faded old hair remaining in places. Summer skins are often badly perforated by a species of botfly. (See more detailed discussion of use of skins for clothing in chapter 9; for description of damage by botflies, see Sec. IV, this chapter.)

In many districts the natives live for long periods almost exclusively on caribou. Eskimos and experienced whites can pick out from a herd the fat caribou by observing the shape of the horns. This is merely the ability to distinguish between the sexes and ages in a herd at the different seasons.

MUSK OXEN

There is no logical reason for calling this polar animal musk ox. The origin of the name is obscure. It may have been some early English navigator who was a better sailor than zoologist and misidentified him with the musk deer of Asia. Or possibly he was more of a trader than a scientist and wanted to convey the impression that he had discovered a new commercial source of the costly perfume of our ancestors—a trick with many parallels in early exploration.

Scientists gave the beast a fairly descriptive name, *ovibos* or sheep-cow. This is what he is to the casual observer—a cow (or bull) with a coat of wool. Sverdrup, having eaten the meat and drunk the milk through several years "without ever detecting the flavour of musk from which they are supposed to derive their name," calls them polar oxen. Other travelers refer to them as cattle, among these the most famous British explorers of the eighteenth and nineteenth centuries, the men who discovered and mapped the chief lands where this beast has been found. Stefansson has suggested popular use of the technical name, ovibos.

In times geologically recent the musk ox ranged at least to Kentucky in the New World and correspondingly far south in the Old. There is apparently no record that live animals were sighted in the Old World by Europeans or by natives whose tradition has been preserved, even in northern Siberia. Two hundred years ago they ranged halfway south along the western side of Hudson Bay, into the edge of the forest. During the nineteenth century they came nearly or quite down to the north shore of Great Slave Lake. In the decade 1860–70 what was apparently the last band of them was killed in Alaska, inland south from Barrow. None have been reported by Europeans between Barrow and the Mackenzie River. In the early Hudson's Bay Company period, a hundred years ago, they came approximately as far west as the east bank of the Mackenzie. When American whalers wintered at Langton Bay, around the turn of the century, musk ox were killed just a little to the southeast.

When Stefansson was there around 1910 a few were still surviving north of Bear Lake and west of the Coppermine. Today live animals are found on the Canadian mainland only in the northeastern part, chiefly around a game sanctuary created for them on the Thelon River west of Chesterfield Inlet, where they are variously estimated at from 300 or 400 to 1,000—these being the supposed totals both at the sanctuary and in all outlying districts. All killings have been prohibited for some years past, but there are doubtless surreptitious ones.

In Banks Island there were thousands of musk oxen around 1850, when the first British explorers were there—the bones are now scattered over that island somewhat as buffalo bones were on a Dakota prairie; but the last living animals were killed either in the first or second decade of the twentieth century. There may still be a few along the northern edge of Victoria Island, with none in King William, and probably none in Somerset and Prince of Wales Islands. There are a few score in Prince Patrick, perhaps 4,000 in Melville, doubtless several hundred in Bathurst. It is anybody's guess how many there are in Heiberg and Ellesmere Islands; but they are probably the richest musk ox territories in proportion to area—with perhaps the exception of Melville. Peary found them at the north tip of Greenland, in Peary Land—apparently no more than a few hundred. It used to be thought that northeastern Greenland, from Peary Land to Scoresby Sound, would have only another few hundred; but following 1930 reports of Norwegian hunters would seem to indicate that the hundreds of the estimates should be replaced by thousands, with 10,000 a probable outside limit.

In 1934, Dr. R. M. Anderson, chief biologist of the National Museum, Ottawa, gave 500 as an estimate of living musk oxen in mainland Canada and 13,000 for all Canada—therefore 12,500 for the Canadian Arctic islands.

The usual explanation for the shrinkage of the musk ox range from the central United States northward to Arctic Canada, and the like in the Old World, is that they belong in a cold country and that they followed northward the retreat of the ice at the close of the last Ice Age. However, these animals have lived to a normal old age without special care for their health in zoological gardens of New York, London, and other cities, feeding on clover hay and other things not particularly similar to their present northern food which is in the main sedges, grasses, and small bushes in places like Melville Island.

A more likely explanation of the disappearance of the musk ox in ages past would seem to be that the rule which now holds has always held—that the permanent ranges of hunting man and of the musk ox never overlap.

The musk ox has a perfect defense against all northern predatory animals except the grizzly bear, which has been successful in killing them in Alaska during the recent domestication experiments. Wolves they do not fear at all, nor do wolves attack them unless they find an animal by itself, which seldom happens except with very old beasts that have "lost the instinct of the herd," and are wandering by themselves. When attacked they form in a circle or group with the biggest animals on the outside, standing shoulder to shoulder with heads out. A thrust of their horns or a blow of their feet is dangerous; but perhaps the deciding factor is the heavy wool around the neck which would fill the mouth of a wolf and prevent his teeth from doing harm.

But this perfect defense against wolves is the reverse of defense against hunting man. Bows, arrows, and spears were no doubt invented 20,000, 30,000, or 40,000 years ago. Ever since those days nearly every band of musk oxen has in effect committed suicide by not fleeing but standing up against man to fight.

It seems probable that the newest bones of the musk oxen from the United States are not older than the oldest Folsom points and other weapons of North American man 15,000 or 20,000 years ago. It was probably Folsom man and contemporaries, or possibly their predecessors, who began exterminating the musk oxen from the northern United States and then from southern Canada 10,000 to 30,000 years ago.

Musk oxen are in chief grass eaters. They are, therefore, to be found in the grassiest country which, other things being equal, is also the most nearly level and the lowest. If born on an island, such as Melville, they will almost certainly die there—as against caribou, which move through hundreds of miles, swim rivers, lakes, and even an arm of the sea, and travel freely over ice, whether salt water or fresh.

Anyone who has herded ordinary cattle knows that they tend to rove in search of pasture. Musk oxen here differ squarely. They fill their paunches with the vegetation nearest them and when satiated they lie down. After 2 or 3 hours of rest they get up again, commence feeding in their immediate vicinity, and lie down a second time when no longer hungry. They do not move on the average more than 2 or 3 miles a month. In their march they crop the grass down fairly close and browse on shrubs, moving chiefly in one direction until they come to a patch devoid of vegetation. They then march till they come to the nearest meadow where they stop and resume their systematic slow progress at the rate of a few rods a day.

Musk oxen are peculiar among animals in that they seldom attack, neither do they usually flee. Occasionally a frightened herd will run away, in which case they are more difficult to overtake than caribou. But commonly when alarmed they will run to the top of the nearest small knoll and make a defensive formation (circle, square, triangle, irregular) with the big animals outside and the calves in the center. If danger is approaching from one side only, they may form in two or three lines, with the biggest animals in the front rank and the smallest in the rear. Their central idea is defense, though they may charge upon occasion. Two animals may charge together but a whole band has probably never been reported to charge in a body. Usually they charge singly, each one making a short rush of from 10 to 15 yards, then whirling, running back to the herd, facing about once more and backing into line.

The live weight of grown males perhaps averages 700 pounds. Very large and very fat males perhaps go to 900— that estimate is occasionally seen.

The musk oxen fat cycle does not differ nearly as much as with caribou by sex or by age groups. Generally both males and females are least fat in midsummer, but they are seldom as skinny as caribou get, except in case of extreme age. They begin to increase their fat around the freeze-up, gain steadily through the winter, and are fattest in late winter. As the season warms they begin to lose. It has been assumed rather than proved that this is for two discomfort reasons—they are too warm in their extremely heavy coat of combined hair and wool, and they are uncomfortable through carrying around a heavy matted fleece that is frequently soaking wet, first from spring snows melting and later from rains.

The musk ox furnishes meat which is practically indistinguishable from beef; it is also a possible source of milk supply. (See further discussion below in Section II of this chapter; also in Chapter 8.)

The entire body of the musk ox is covered with long, straggling, stiff black hair, in nature similar to the mane of a horse. In the roots of this hair grows wool. The wool is shed every spring but the hair is never shed. Through the autumn and early winter the wool gradually thickens and by spring it bulges out all over the body, especially on the shoulders. In April and May the wool is shed. They are short-legged animals and when you have a side view of them at the shedding season frequently the legs cannot be seen at all for the curtain of wool that hangs to the ground. The wool drags in long tags after the animals as they walk, and wisps of it can be picked up from the ground.

NORTHERN MOUNTAIN SHEEP

The white sheep probably never ranged east of the Mackenzie, although they are said to be still fairly common in the mountains on the west side of the river from Fort Norman to the west side of the delta. The Endicott Mountains, or that branch of the Brooks Range which runs northwest from the western edge of the Mackenzie delta, are about 12 miles from the coast at Herschel Island, and 75 or 100 miles from the coast of the Colville, the largest river flowing into the Arctic in Northern Alaska. Sheep were formerly numerous on the heads of nearly all the rivers on the Arctic side of this mountain divide, at least as far west as the Colville. Before whalers started wintering at Herschel Island, in 1889, they were not much hunted, since caribou were plentiful; but when the caribou were almost exterminated the Eskimos gradually occupied one mountain valley after another until the sheep became too scarce to be an adequate food supply. It was no doubt in a similar way that sheep had earlier been nearly or quite exterminated from the Brooks Range west of the Colville.

Although the rocky slopes where the sheep feed look pretty barren, they manage to find enough to eat. The stomachs usually contain grass, sometimes moss. The natives say the sheep do not browse on willows, although they often descend in summer to where the willows are. In winter they usually keep to the higher ridges where the snow is less deep, feeding through the snow which they push aside with the nose. In summer they sometimes go up on the ice-capped mountains when mosquitoes get very bad on the lower ranges, but they come down again toward evening for food.

88

Sheep are singularly unsuspicious of danger from above, although they are continually on the alert for enemies from below. Their eyesight is keen, the scent and hearing acute, and it is difficult to approach them from below. The hunter therefore endeavors to work around some adjoining ridge or to ascend some creek valley and approach from above. In this manner natives sometimes get within 15 or 20 yards and kill several out of a band.

The habitat of mountain sheep prevents hunters from using them as a side line to other game; those who hunt sheep must depend on them more or less exclusively for the time being.

Eskimo mountain sheep hunters make their clothing, tents, and snowshoe lashings of sheepskin. Their families subsist almost entirely on its meat. Although the outer hair is brittle, only the ends of the hairs break off, so that a garment of mountain sheep may be warm a full winter, sometimes longer.

WOLVES

The typical Arctic wolf is light tawny-yellowish in color, with a few black hairs intermingled along the median line of the back. The usual Eskimo belief is that light wolves are old wolves, but dark females have been seen with white cubs.

Wolves prey on caribou, on small beasts, and on birds. They are usually found where caribou are found. They range along the northern sections of both the Old and New Worlds beyond the treeline, on the polar islands, and have been reported, though in small numbers, from the northern part of Greenland.

Since they follow the caribou, wolves occasionally go south into the forests or north out on the ice; they seem to prefer the prairie between the treeline and the polar shore.

In the polar regions of both the New and Old Worlds wolves aggregate tens of thousands.

The wolf pack, as described in fiction and in news dispatches, does not exist. Stefansson has for years traced every yarn of this nature in the press, whether from Roumania, Siberia, Canada, or wherever, and in each case the story of the sleigh pursued by wolves (where the parents throw one child out to save the others, or the husband his bride), the farmhouse attacked by them, and so on, were proved without foundation. Interested in learning why such dispatches were carried, he was told that wolf stories were expected by newspapers every so often and were always believed if the locale was sufficiently far away. Many newspapers pay space rates, or used to, on whatever they print.

Others, notably E. W. Nelson, former Chief of the United States Biological Survey, have traced numerous wolf pack stories, always finding them either inventions or based on a misunderstanding. Stanley P. Young, chief of predatory and rodent control of the Survey, is carrying forward the work of Nelson, with similar results.

As will appear below under Psychology of Wolves, the pack stories are alien to their nature. The largest band you will ever see is perhaps 8 or 10, a single family of parents and partly-grown cubs. Apart from these family groups, wolves hunt singly or at most in pairs.

As said, wolves are the chief enemies of the caribou. In the northern islands, in every season except summer, caribou furnish 99 percent of their food, mostly old animals, with a few very young calves. As explained already, young adult caribou are too fleet for them, and musk oxen have perfected a defense. Wolves may follow herds of musk oxen, but they get only beasts almost dying of old age, a very few calves, and some cripples—chiefly animals that break a leg. With caribou they occasionally resort to the strategem of two wolves working simultaneously on one deer, one pursuing and the other trying to head off their prey. Foxes are snapped up as appetizers.

It is a common belief that seal blubber is no bait for wolves, that they will not eat it. This may, however, be just superstition; for Stefansson came upon a wolf who was eating a seal he had just killed—no doubt having surprised him asleep at his hole.

It is probable that wolves cannot kill polar bears and that they never try. In any case, the meat is so strange to them that while they will gnaw meatless bones of musk oxen, and dry hides, they will leave untouched caches of bear meat, either because they don't get the idea that bear is food or else (more probably) for the reason given under Food Prejudices of Dogs—in Chapter 12, Section IV.

Wolves are also the enemies of sledge dogs, and so strong and fleet is a wolf that he can carry off (according to report and belief) a dog that weighs almost as much as he does.

It would seem reasonable that wolves would not be afraid of any living thing they find; for practically their only danger arises from failure to find something. They can run faster than all the animals that are more powerful and they are more powerful than any animal (if there is one) that can run faster. This would make it seem probable that a wolf would run frankly up to any creature he sees—he has a right to believe that if the animal is dangerous he will be able to avoid it easily. But the northern wolf shows no such self-confidence. Singly or in pairs they will circle to within 150 yards, but a strange scent (that of man, for instance) sends them loping away. A family party, especially if the cubs are well grown, will occasionally approach a little closer.

Although wolf furnishes a palatable and wholesome meat, it is not an important source of food supply for hunters. The beast is wary and you seldom get a shot. Then the cartridge which kills a wolf, yielding less than 100 pounds of meat, might better have been used on a caribou giving several hundred pounds. However, it has been a rule of traveling parties of the Stefansson expeditions who were living by hunting to shoot wolves upon opportunity. No smaller animals are shot, the food return per cartridge being too small.

Eskimos use wolf fur for trimming and, if it is of the fashionable shade. they prize it even more highly than wolverine. These skins must be well furred, with the hair black-tipped. When cut into strips it should show: first a dense layer of fur next the skin, then a band of whitish fur, and last a peripheral band of black. These strips are used for a sort of aureole around a hood; less desirable pieces trim sieeves of coats and are used as pendants.

FOXES

The white fox is found almost everywhere along the Arctic coast but seldom goes far inland in any numbers.

In summer most or all white foxes are on land, having their young, living on birds and small animals. In winter 90 percent of them leave the islands and the mainland, going north rather than south. What they mostly do is to leave the land for the sea ice where they subsist on remnants of seals that have been killed and not completely devoured by polar bears.

Foxes have been reported as small as 5½ pounds. The usual weights are 8 to 14 pounds.

Foxes that go to sea, as above, live exclusively on seals that are provided for them by the polar bears—see below in our bear discussion. Along shores they live on the carcasses of such dead whales as they find. Those foxes that go inland to brush or forest country live on rabbits, ptarmigan, and other birds. When they are all ashore in summer they live on lemmings, eggs, and nesting birds chiefly.

It is not definitely known whether foxes will abandon a seal when they have had one feed. Likely they do, for that is how they behave on land. When a hunting fox is particularly successful with lemming, for instance, it will kill one after another of these and bury each, seemingly with an idea of coming back—an idea which is probably never carried out, for it is likely that if a fox eats a buried lemming it will be one which it has discovered that was killed by another fox.

Foxes will sometimes break into food caches but losses from their thieving are on the whole slight.

Much has been said about their wisdom, but in the north they are (depending on your point of view) stupid or trustful. A fox that sees you is very likely to come up to examine you more closely. If he finds your trail, he may follow it till he catches up with you. He is one of the most easily trapped of fur animals.

The flesh of foxes has been compared in taste to that of rabbit by Hearne, and to young kid by Lyon. Eskimos frequently eat it, and so do a few whites who are not swayed by the customary European food taboo.

The white fox is the staple fur of the Arctic coast, a medium of exchange in many districts. In summer the skins are bluish-gray, maltese color on back, head dusky mixed with silvery white, belly dirtyish yellow. Skins rarely become "prime" (pure white with long hair) before December, and the hair usually begins to get loose by the last of March.

The blue fox coloration of the white fox is rare east of western Alaska—about one blue for each hundred white (the blue and the white are color phases of the same animal). By selection under domestication blue foxes have been evolved that breed true to color.

The red fox (with its variations through rufus, cross, silvery-grey and black) is rare north of the northern limit of trees—it is a forest animal of little consequence as a potential source of food.

BEARS

Classifications of the numerous species and subspecies of bears, some of them based on technical characters which cannot be readily recognized by the layman, are often confusing and misleading. For purposes of simplicity we here consider the northern bears under two main groups—the polar bear and the grizzly. The polar bear we discuss in more detail, since the others are likely to have little importance for the users of this Manual.

The polar bear (*Thalarctos maritimus*) is of a uniform white or yellowish white color, with a dense oily fur that nearly covers the soles of the feet. It is probably the largest of all bears, though this distinction is disputed by those who claim the honor for the big brown Alaska bear (Kodiak bear). The heaviest weight of record is 1,600 pounds for a male.

The white bear is a circumpolar cosmopolitan, inhabiting every part of the Arctic Sea in the Old World as well as the New. They are found on the adjoining land but seldom very far from sea ice—except in connection with hibernation. (See below.) In winter they may appear anywhere along the coast, but in summer their occurrence depends largely upon the nearness of pack ice. Along the Arctic coast of Alaska, east of Point Barrow, they are not very abundant, nor on the coast east and west of the Mackenzie Delta. Numbers are annually killed near Cape Bathurst. They are abundant around Cape Parry and the southern end of Banks Island, but very rarely pass through Dolphin and Union Strait into Coronation Gulf. Occasionally they follow the shore line of Hudson Bay as far south as James Bay; on the Atlantic side they have been taken in Ungava and along the Labrador

93

coast; they may be found on any Greenland coast; and similarly for the Soviet sector of the Arctic. They are in plenty on island shores in such groups at Spitsbergen and Franz Josef. Generally they are numerous where two conditions meet—many seals and much ice that is frequently broken to show open water between.

In most land bears both sexes hibernate. In polar (sea) bears only the female hibernates and seemingly only when she is to have young. Usually they go inland for this purpose, sometimes 20 or more miles. A few perhaps hibernate on the sea ice, on paleocrystic floes—that is inferred from such things as a visit of a mother bear with the small cubs to the Soviet drifting camp when it was right near the North Pole. The young are born around midwinter, usually two but never more than that, and are incredibly small and helpless. Only after 3 or so months is the mother able to leave the hibernating place with them.

"Hibernating" is the word for the Eskimo idea of what the polar bears do, but that may be just from analogy to grizzlies with which they are familiar. Possibly there is no real hibernation. Stefansson has picked up many stories of polar bears being discovered in their dens but never one of their being in a stupor, as grizzlies frequently are when so discovered.

The seal is practically the one food of the polar bear. It is disputed whether they stalk and kill walrus; if so, their prey would be only the very young. Occasionally polar bears eat from a whale carcass if they happen upon one on a beach, and they are said to eat the eggs of birds when they find them on an Arctic shore. These items, however, form so small and merely incidental a part of their diet that it is still practically true that the polar bear lives exclusively on seals. These they hunt indefatigably, stalking them with patience and skill and moving when the time comes to pounce with speed and lithesomeness that grizzly and black bears do not approach.

We said when discussing the white fox that most of them spend their winters at sea and that they depend for their food on the polar bear. To a limited extent bears also provide sea gulls with food; the important difference is that the foxes would starve to death except for the bears but that

94

the gulls are able to take care of themselves by feeding in the leads—mainly on shrimps.

The food habits of the polar bear, as attested by those who have studied them on the sea ice far from land, are difficult to reconcile with the ordinary theories of the dietitian who says that protein is required to renew body tissue—that fat serves as a fuel but not as a body builder. For the bears eat chiefly fat, or seem to.

When a bear kills an ordinary seal he usually gets an animal weighing anything below 200 pounds—he may get a 600- or 800-pound bearded seal. A number of cases are on record where a traveler has come along after a bear killed and fed from a seal but where as yet the foxes and sea gulls had made no inroads. If there were several bears together, as, for instance, a mother with two yearling cubs, nearly or quite the whole seal may have been eaten. But if only one bear was concerned he usually eats only blubber and what skin there is that covers the blubber he eats. In some cases he has eaten in this way about a third or a quarter of the hide, but that is practically the only protein, although there is of course a little blood in the fresh blubber. There is no evidence that the bear has sucked blood—anyhow, it is probably more folklore than natural history that carnivorous animals suck blood. We have, then, in the bear a feeder who apparently consumes no more protein than what is practically inseparable from the fat he wants.

There may be, however, an explanation in the behavior of the bear subsequent to his meal. He then walks off a few or a few dozen yards, lies down and goes to sleep. When he wakes up he apparently still has a feeling of satiation; at any rate, he pays no attention to the seal carcass but walks off in some other direction. It may be that while he slept all the lean and fat, along with the entrails, everything except the bones, has been eaten by foxes, by sea gulls or by them together. But since it may also be that whatever he did not eat himself is still there, it seems clear that he goes off because he has no desire for or interest in food.

But this bear may have poor hunting luck the next few days. He sniffs the air wherever he goes. In 2 or 3 days he may find himself passing to leeward of the remains of a seal, more likely one killed by another bear than by himself. Now he is hungry, goes up the wind, and eats whatever he finds. If there is lean still on the seal he eats that, and now has to eat bones with the lean for the whole is frozen into one equally hard mass. If nothing is there except the bones he will eat those, even the head. It may be this feeding on lean and bones that predisposes him to making an exclusive meal of blubber when next he gets a seal.

As the bear travels, one, two or more foxes are following along behind him, sometimes close up, sometimes far behind. They may even run around him and ahead of him—they are playful and unconcerned, treating the bear as they sometimes do a man on shore. When the bear secures a seal the foxes stand at a not very respectful distance, perhaps occasionally dashing in, hoping to get a mouthful. Ordinarily the bear keeps them at bay as long as he is feeding, sometimes with an occasional blow of his paw—that misses, or else there is a dead fox. If the season is winter the foxes eat everything that the bear leaves except the bones—their small teeth seem unequal to at least the harder bones.

If the season is spring or autumn it may happen that both foxes and sea gulls are waiting for the leavings of the bear; the gulls do not follow the bears as they travel, but they have good eyesight and come from afar when they see him eating. They flutter around, or they settle on hummocks or on the water of a lead. When the bear goes off for his sleep they come nearer but are in the main kept at bay by the foxes. However, towards the end of their feast different foxes may drag parts of the seal away. Then a gull may have a chance, either at the main carcass or at a fragment that a fox has dropped.

During the summer when the foxes are on land, the sea gulls will have an opportunity to eat on the average three-quarters of every seal that is killed by a polar bear—to eat all the bear leaves. It is, as said, only for short periods in spring and autumn that fox and gull cooperate on the scavenging. For just as there are few or no foxes at sea in midsummer so are there few or no sea gulls there in midwinter—almost certainly none; for they have not been re- ·

ported from the midwinter period, and we think we know that they could not live at sea during the coldest month.

Polar bears are successful chiefly in securing seals that are basking on the ice or swimming in open leads between floes. As explained in Chapter 13, only man is able to secure seals that are living in their holes under old floes of great extent. Since polar bears are powerless to break through heavy old ice, they will never be found in such areas. The absence of polar bears from a locality does not, then, mean that seals also are absent, although such reasoning has been common by writers on the Arctic.

DANGEROUS TO MEN AND DOGS

On shore polar bears are ordinarily timid animals, afraid of men, and afraid of wolves and dogs. But far from shore they have no enemy to fear. Besides their own kind they are familiar on the pack ice with only three living things—the seals on which they live, the white foxes which they unintentionally provide with food, but which never come near enough to be caught themselves, and the gulls which cry out loudly and flutter about them at their meals. When a bear sees men or dogs lying on the ice and moving a little, he apparently mistakes them for seals and is likely to stalk them and eventually pounce on them as if they were seals. (See also chapter 13.)

Occasionally bears will stalk a man who is upright. Stefansson once had a narrow escape when he himself was stalking a polar bear among some ice hummocks. He knew there was a bear in the vicinity and was searching for h'm in some rough ice when he heard a slight noise behind him and realized that the bear was stalking him, with only about 20 yards to go. There was just time to fire the decisive shot. The reason Stefansson had not seen the bear's approach was that it had not occurred to h'm to look back over his own trail; he was so used to hunting bears that the possibility of one of them assuming his own role and hunting him had been left out of consideration. A good hunter, like a good detective, should leave nothing out of consideration.

A 4-year-old polar bear will produce in meat the equivalent of four seals, and scarcity of ammunition may in emergency make him the most economical source of food. However, bear meat has a fundamental defect. It has nothing to do with taste, toughness, or wholesomeness but lies in the stringy nature of the meat of any but the youngest. (See chapter 8.) Thus other meats are usually preferred when ammunition and other game animals are plentiful.

Polar bear skins are utilized for clothing to some extent. As discussed more fully in Chapter 9, the skins are strong but heavy, and not warm for the weight.

In utilizing whole bears in time of need the Stefansson parties scraped hair from the skin for fuel, and fed the skins to the dogs. It may be well not to eat bear livers or feed them to dogs, for some of them may be unwholesome.

Barren Ground Grizzly (*Ursus richardsoni Swainson*) is called by the western Eskimos *aklak,* by the Copper Eskimos *akshak*. The term "Barren Ground" is applied also to a number of other subspecies.

Formerly more widespread, these grizzlies are now said to be found in Canada, only in a restricted area from the Mackenzie eastward some distance beyond the Coppermine; in northern Alaska they do not appear to be very common on the north side of the Endicott Mountains, and seldom, if ever, come out on the coastal plains. In size they are medium compared with other grizzlies; color variable from yellowish to grizzly brown, with smooth foreclaws of medium length. Their diet is miscellaneous—largely vegetarian although sometimes including ground squirrels (spermophiles) and lemmings. Like all grizzlies they are shy and wary, seeking to be let alone by man, but dangerous if wounded and at bay.

Alaska Brown Bear, or Kodiak Bear. In many works of reference this is credited with being the largest carnivorous animal living in the world today. But, as said, other authorities would confer this honor upon the polar bear. A number of specimens have weighed from 1,200 to 1,500 pounds; the largest of record was 1,656 pounds. The color is relatively uniform, from light creamy brown to rich blackish brown, with little or no silver-tipping, and with short stout curved claws. These bears inhabit the islands and the Pacific coast of Alaska, from the Alaska Peninsula nearly or quite to British Columbia. Their diet consists chiefly of grass, roots, and berries, but in addition they eat field mice. Along the beaches they may eat dead fish, whale, or seal that has been cast up on the shore.

Although provided with a fighting equipment second to none on the continent, these, like their Arctic land cousins, try to live peacefully and inoffensively. Like other grizzlies, whenever they discover the sign of a human being, whether they see or smell his footprints, or see him or get his wind, they immediately use every means in their power to get out of the way.

Almost as tame as shooting musk oxen is shooting grizzly bears. They are dull of sight and not very quick of hearing, and once a hunter sees them there is small chance for the bear. A wounded grizzly, however, is a difficult beast to deal with. They appear even more tenacious of life than polar bears. Natives warn you that if you must shoot them you should do so from a hill, for then a wounded bear has more difficulty charging.

The meat of both the Barren Ground and the Kodiak bear (or, indeed, of any bear) can be used to supplement the food supply. Likewise the skins can be utilized, if necessary, though, as with any bear skin, they are not warm for the weight. If circumstances warrant it, most hunters would prefer to keep the skin of a Kodiak bear, for instance, for a trophy. However, they make excellent bedding and are used by Eskimos as doors for houses.

SEALS

The order Pinnipedia to which seals, sea lions, and walrus belong, is large, with several families under which there are numerous subspecies. Although several of these species extend into the sub-Arctic and Arctic, we consider here only the ones which play a part in the instructions given in this Manual. If you should happen to be in a vicinity where members of a different species are found (for instance, the large *Phoca groenlandica,* which is numerous in the seas around Greenland), you would deal with them in the same fashion and make use of their meat and skins in much the same way as you would those which we have described.

Erignathus barbatus; bearded seal; ugrug. Rare along the north coast of Alaska east of Point Barrow, although fairly common south and west of Point Barrow. Rare at Herschel Island, Baillie Islands, and Franklin Bay; numerous around Cape Lyons, abundant in Dolphin and Union Strait; in Asia, they range eastward from the Okhotsk Sea to the coast of Alaska; also found along the coasts of southern Greenland and of Iceland. Average weight 500 to 600 pounds.

Phoca hispida; hair seal—this classification includes several sub-species. Distributed throughout entire Arctic regions; they are found along coasts of Greenland and Labrador; fairly common everywhere along the coast from Bering Sea east to Coronation Gulf; along coasts of the Soviet Arctic, and are particularly numerous in the Barents and Kara Seas; they are also found in the polar sea at all distances from land and have been sighted in the vicinity of the North Pole. Average weight 125 to 175 pounds. Dr. R. M. Anderson reports a very large male shot at Cape Parry, December 12, 1910, measured 65 inches in length and greatest girth 54 inches, weight about 200 pounds.

Callorhinus alascanus; Alaska fur seal. Occurrence of the species in the Arctic Ocean is only casual. It is included in this list because we have suggested the possible use of its skin as a substitute for the skin of the hair seal or of caribou for Eskimo-type clothing.

Phoca hispida (called by Eskimos *natsik*) and *Erignathus barbatus* (called by Eskimos *ugrug*) are, then the seals that are likely to be of chief importance to the users of this Manual, the seals on which so many of the methods outlined hereafter are based. Where we speak of "seals," "seal skin," etc., throughout this volume, it is always the small hair seal that is meant; the bearded seal, or ugrug, which has its particular excellences, is specified as such.

HOW TO RECOGNIZE SIGNS OF SEALS

A man inexperienced in woodcraft may walk through a forest without seeing any sign of moose when signs will be patent to the hunter or guide who knows the woods and the ways of animals. So a man who does not realize the presence of seals unless he sees their heads bobbing about in the water of an open lead might make a long journey over the polar ice and still retain his original conviction that food animals are absent. There may be on the sea ice inconspicuous signs of seals, as clear in their meaning when once noted as bear tracks in snow. How to recognize these signs is described below (in chapter 13 we tell of hunting methods).

The presence or absence of seals has nothing to do with latitude, as such, but mainly with the mobility of the ice. In any region where we have violent ice movement and consequently much open water, we have a large number of seals. Food they can find everywhere, but in certain places they lack easy opportunity for coming up to breathe.

During the summer seals congregate in regions of open water, deserting those where the ice lies but slightly broken. Then in the autumn, when young ice forms, they make for themselves breathing holes which they use all winter. If this young ice remains stationary, the seal remains stationary with it. If it floats in any direction he travels along, for his life depends upon his never going far from his breathing hole as long as the ice around it remains unbroken. If it does break and if leads are formed, he may do a certain amount of winter traveling along them, but this traveling ceases when the first hard frost forms new ice over the new leads.

AREAS FROM WHICH SEALS ARE ABSENT

From the point of view of seal life, there are in the polar mediterranean certain desert areas, as described *ante*. We repeat here: These desert areas are caused by the sluggishness or absence of currents, as deserts on land are caused by lack of rainfall and porousness of soil. And just as land deserts are restricted in area, so are the sea deserts. The experienced overland traveler crossing a new continent would know, or at least suspect, when he was entering a desert. It would then be a matter of judgment whether he was to turn back and give up his journey or whether he should attempt skirting the desert or making a dash across it. So it is when the ice traveler who depends on game for subsistence comes to one of these sea deserts. The signs are in the thickness

101

and evident age of the ice, in the fewness of the leads and of other signs of motion, and in the absence or rarity of seal traces on such patches of young ice as may be visible.

The younger the seal the more delectable the meat. Its lean and fat make together a diet upon which whole groups of Eskimos live in good health to a normal old age. Some whites do not like the meat at first, because it differs considerably from any meat with which they are familiar; but you gradually get to like it, and the longer you live on it the better you like it. You may be dreadfully tired of seal after three weeks, or even three months, but few are tired of it after three years. It is a complete diet—contains more than enough of all the vitamins, as well as calcium, iron, etc.

In addition to giving lean and fat for food, the seal furnishes fat for fuel. Many thousands of Eskimos have no other fuel in winter, and it does them very well. They burn the fat in stone lamps that, when properly tended, do not smoke or smell.

Besides food and fuel, the seal furnishes clothing. The Eskimos use water boots in summer that are made entirely of seal skin (uppers from one species, soles from another). In winter they use caribou skin boots which in some cases have sealskin soles. Raincoats are made of sealskin and so are mittens intended to be used in handling fish nets or anything that is wet. Coats and trousers for winter may be made of sealskin but this is seldom done except when caribou is scarce. (For description of sealskin garments see chapter 9.)

Sealskins furnish material for boats. The small seals are used for kayaks and the big (bearded) seals for umiaks—see chapter 12.

When a seal has been skinned by the method described in chapter 13, the resulting bag makes the *pok* which is used for a seal-oil container and which will hold the fat of about four seals. The same sort of bag may also be inflated by blowing and then forms a float with a buoyancy of two or three hundred pounds. Occasionally, instead of using canvas to convert a sledge into a boat, you might fasten three or four of these inflated poks to the sides of the sledge, making a sort of life raft. This Eskimo method is satisfactory in warm weather; but not in winter, because the water which splashes over the sledge turns into an ice coating difficult to remove.

The *Encyclopaedia Britannica* says of the walrus (*Odobaenus rosmarus*) that it is a "large marine mammal allied to the seals. Characterized by the prolongation, in both sexes, of the upper canine teeth into tusks, which may reach a length of 2 feet, the adult walrus measures some 10 or 11 feet and is a heavy-built animal. * * *

"The walrus inhabits the northern circumpolar region in small herds. It prefers the coastal portion or ice-floes and feeds largely on bivalve molluscs which it digs up from the bottom of the sea with its tusks. Normally inoffensive and affectionate, when attacked the walrus can use its tusks with terrible effect, and the herd usually combine against an enemy. * * * The Pacific walrus, with longer and more slender tusks, has been separated as *O. obesus*. Like the Atlantic form, its numbers have been much reduced within recent years. * * *"

The reduction in numbers is notable around the Svalbard archipelago, where walrus, formerly plentiful, are now rarely seen. Between Greenland and the Canadian islands the reduction, though considerable, is not so pronounced. Comparatively, there has been little reduction, although noticeable, in Bering Sea and north of it. Northeastward from Bering Strait the walrus does not go in any numbers around Point Barrow, for it, unlike the seal, is unable to gnaw breathing holes in the ice, and therefore must keep out of waters where ice fields are extensive and little broken. For the same reason the walrus does not go in any considerable numbers west of Cape Schmidt (formerly North Cape) and Wrangel Island.

Walrus hide is sometimes used for covering the large Eskimo boat, the umiak, but is not considered as good as either the bearded seal or white whale, though more convenient than the bearded seal in that it is larger so that fewer skins are required for a single boat—perhaps three or four walrus hides for a 40-foot boat against six to nine bearded sealskins. Walrus is used also for boot soles, but seldom unless the hide has been employed for at least a year as a umiak cover;

otherwise it stretches unevenly and the boot goes out of shape. Walrus hides are used extensively for the cover of depots to keep the rain out and under some circumstances for roofs of houses. They are used for floor coverings beneath bedding.

At present the ivory from the tusks has some commercial value. Formerly it was used for harpoon points and other parts of harpoons, and sometimes in the construction of arrows and spears. It was used for bag and other handles and carved into toys. This carving has lately been developed along commercial lines. Eskimo carvings of various sorts are sold to tourists who visit Alaska and also by curio dealers in Seattle and other Pacific coast cities.

The first known commerce between Europe and North America, during the four centuries before Columbus, dealt partly in walrus ivory and walrus "ropes." These ropes were favored in Europe all the way to the Mediterranean. It is still an important use of the hide to convert it into a thong perhaps a quarter of an inch wide. This is done in one of two ways: You skin the animal, dry the skin, wet it again, make a hole near the center of the hide and cut round and round till the margins are reached. Another way is to make the thong when you skin the animal, or else to skin it by the casing method, in either event cutting round and round the body, spirally.

As in many other things, the competitors with walrus thong are from the hides of the white whale and the bearded seal, if a stout "rope" is required. When more slender and less strong ones are needed as, for instance, snow shoe babiche, it will be cut from the small variety of seal or from land animals, such as the caribou.

ALASKA GAME LAWS

The killing of all walrus in the territory of Alaska, except by natives for food or clothing, by miners and explorers in need of food, or for scientific specimens to be taken under permit issued by the Secretary of Commerce, is prohibited.

Walrus are likely to play a small part in the kind of economy outlined in this Manual. However, the meat is palatable and, as said, the skins are strong and useful. See chapters 9 and 12.

The idea that walrus meat, as such, is "strong" derives mainly from a reason applicable both to walrus and whales. These are very large warm-blooded animals, difficult to cut up in the place where killed. The towing ashore may take from one to several hours. If a steer were not cut up until several hours after being killed the meat would taste strong; but, knowing beef, we would realize that the fault was in the handling, not in the meat itself. However, white men, unfamiliar with walrus and whale meat, sometimes attribute to the animals themselves the strong taste which comes, as indicated, from a long decomposition period that has intervened between the killing and the cutting up.

WHALES

Of the many species of whales, we list the ones common to Arctic waters.

Of the Greenland whale, *Balaena mysticetus,* the *Encyclopaedia Britannica* says: "Head enormous, one-third the total length; rostrum greatly arched, providing room for exceptionally long baleen, up to 15 feet. Arctic, circumpolar, and formerly abundant off Spitsbergen, both sides of Greenland and the North Pacific to Beaufort sea, but reduced by whaling to the verge of extinction." This is one of the largest of sea mammals, reaching a length of from 50 to 60 feet. American whalers call it the Bowhead.

The waters around Spitsbergen are a good illustration of the above-mentioned reduction of numbers. According to Scoresby, no fewer than 57,500 Greenland whales were killed in this region between 1669 and 1775. During the same period reckless extermination of seals also took place. Now the Greenland whale has practically disappeared in the vicinity of the Svalbard archipelago in consequence of the havoc made by the early whalers.

American whaling north of Bering Strait was what it was called, "Yankee" whaling; if by Yankee we mean New Englander. On account of laws considered unfavorable, some of the vessels sailed at different times under the flags of Hawaii, when it was an independent country, of Chile, and of other nations; but most of the men and most of the money were from New England chiefly—rather from New Bedford than from Nantucket, for Nantucket featured sperm whaling, which was non-Arctic.

Whaling north of Bering Strait, although not east of Barrow nor west of Wrangel, had considerable proportions before the War between the States. What is said to have been the last action of that struggle was a Confederate attack upon the northern (Arctic Alaska) whaling fleet, with a heavy loss of ships and cargoes, though not of men.

The industry spread east beyond Barrow definitely when there was a first wintering of an American whaler at Herschel Island, just west of the Mackenzie delta, in 1889. Ten to fifteen ships sometimes wintered at Herschel Island; occasionally more than 500 but never a thousand men. Other wintering places were farther east, chiefly the Baillie Islands off Cape Bathurst and Langton Bay in the southeast corner of Franklin Bay. The voyages were typically for three years.

The maximum catch per voyage was probably between 60 and 70 whales. Only the "bone" (baleen) was taken, with enough flesh of one or two whales to give the crew fresh meat, and to feed Eskimos who were employed as well as dogs belonging to whalers and to Eskimos. Bone ran a maximum of a little over 2,000 pounds per whale, with the average probably around 1,000 pounds. A high price for bone, although not the highest, was $4.50 the pound. At that rate a big whale would bring $9,000. In conversation one hears of "a ten-thousand-dollar whale."

According to information gathered at Herschel Island in 1908–12 by Dr. R. M. Anderson, the largest catches of the entire history of Yankee whaling east of Barrow were 69 whales by Captain Smith, steamer *Narwhal,* 1893–95; 67 whales by Captain Norwood, steamer *Balaena,* 1893–95; 64 by Captain Bodfish, steamer *Beluga,* also 1893–95.

Commercial whaling ceased abruptly about 1906, for three reasons which came along nearly together. Women's corsets ceased being fashionable; buggy whips ceased being used; a substitute was invented, called featherbone. In 1 or 2 years the price of whalebone dropped to 40 cents and even 20 cents a pound; practically there was no market.

In Arctic waters the industry has never been revived as oil whaling; oil whaling developments, tremendous in their way, have been in the Antarctic.

In prehistoric times the taking of the bowhead by primitive hunters seems to have been extensive, for signs of whaling are found at various points on the north coast of the Old World. In the New World whaling was carried on as far northeast as Cape Kellett, Banks Island, and perhaps nearly 200 miles east of Cape Parry on the mainland. In historic times, however, there has been no native whaling from Banks Island nor from farther east than Cape Bathurst on the mainland side. After the coming of the American whaling fleet, natives did not compete with the Yankees farther east than Point Barrow. They did give effective competition from Barrow to Bering Strait, the chief centers being Cape Smythe village, now Barrow Post Office, and Point Hope.

Natives and resident whites still like to take a few whales each year, both for human food and for dog feed, but this now only on the coast from Barrow to Hope.

A small whale, which may be a different species or a young bowhead, was favored as a food animal, not because it was easier to handle but because the meat was considered to taste better. This whale is a scientific problem as yet, and is, therefore known only by its Eskimo name, *ingutok* or *inyutok*. The usual Eskimo and local white view is that they are a small species. Some believe, however, that they are yearling and 2-year-old bowheads.

White whale or beluga, *Delphinapterus leucas,* kilaluak: Adult milk-white all over, young dark slate color, becoming gradually paler for several years until it attains its growth. While it is said at times to attain a length of 20 feet, its ordinary length is nearer 10 or 12 feet. The white whale is a circumpolar species, limited to the extreme northern coasts of the Old and New Worlds. Plentiful along the coast of Alaska, especially in Bering Sea and the Arctic Ocean, it also ascends the Yukon for a long distance. It is found along the Atlantic coast south to the St. Lawrence River.

In the Alaskan and west Canadian Arctic the white whale was as important as the seal, although not farther east than

Cape Bathurst. They came in schools during early summer. Unlike the bowhead, which was hunted from umiaks, the white whales were pursued and harpooned from kayaks. With a bowhead whale two or three inflated seal skins, each with a buoyancy of 200 or 300 pounds, were attached to each harpoon; and the thing was to follow the whale and get more and more harpoons into him, until it took so much exertion for him to dive and submerge all the floats that he was worn out, whereupon he was dispatched with a lance. The white whales, walrus-size or smaller, required only one harpoon and a single float. Indeed, they were sometimes killed outright with spears. In recent years they have been shot with rifles, but they usually or always sink. Therefore they must be harpooned at the same time as they are shot, so that the rifle is no great advantage. The vulnerable point for rifle shooting is the brain, or the spine at the base of the brain, preferably the latter.

The great killings of the white whale were made by driving them into shoal waters. Scores of kayaks would paddle out to sea when the watchers from the land reported a school on its way. They would get outside the whales, form a line, and with a great shouting and splashing of paddles would advance abreast, shepherding the whales to a bay or other shoal place where they could be dispatched.

The meat and blubber were used as with seal or walrus. The hide was in some districts considered even better than the bearded seal for boot soles and umiak covers. The leather is said to be excellent for various commercial uses, as, for instance, belting.

Prior to 1936, whaling in Alaska waters was unrestricted. On May 1, 1936, an act was passed to give effect to the convention concluded at Geneva on September 24, 1931, and subsequently ratified by the United States and 25 other countries for the regulation of whaling.

The narwhal, *Monodon monoceros*: "Adult greyish-white, with leopard-like spots, sometimes whitish when old, young unspotted; teeth unlike those of any other animal, reduced * * * to a single upper pair. * * * Arctic, rarely reaching Britain. Large numbers of narwhals are

killed by the Esquimaux in certain parts of Greenland
* * *." They are very rare in or absent from Canadian
waters west of Baffin Bay, as from Alaskan and eastern
Siberian seas.

It is likely to be chiefly by accident that the users of this
Manual will have occasion to utilize whales. However, when
one has been killed or if it is found dead on the beach, it is
a source of a large supply of food and fuel.

As an alternative to cannibalism or death from hunger,
whales that have lain dead on Arctic beaches as long as 4
years have been eaten. By that time, however, all the lean
has decayed away; the blubber has largely dried out; what
remains has become somewhat like felt in texture, and the
interstices have been filled with products of the dashing surf
and spray, among them salt and iodine. Stefansson and his
party of a half dozen Eskimos, when without "solid" food
for a few days, tried eating this sort of blubber. Some of
them did eat it and kept it down, others found it worse than
nothing because it made them ill.

A whale that has been on the beach only a year does not
taste stronger than venison and game birds do that are
fashionably eaten. Both lean and fat are at that stage
nourishing and nonpoisonous.

The idea that people die of "ptomaine poisoning" from
eating "rotten whale" has been checked by Stefansson in
a half dozen cases where serious illness or death was reported. In only one of these cases was there a possible connection with decayed whale. All other deaths were from
eating fresh whale. The most serious case, where several
Eskimos died within a day or two, was from eating a white
whale so fresh that the flesh was still warm when it was
cut up and put in the cooking pots—the cooking was
Eskimo-style, probably to what we call medium done. Whatever killed the people was, therefore, present in the flesh of
the living or at least the still warm animal, and had nothing
to do with any of the foodborne poisons which are ordinarily thought of as "ptomaines."

A stranded whale can be a source of great quantities of
food indirectly. If a party is marooned, they can camp

at some distance from the whale and set armed watchers by the whale who shoot polar bears, foxes (and possibly a rare wolf) when they come in to feed on the carcass.

SECTION II

DOMESTIC ANIMALS

Reindeer is the same animal as caribou, only domestic. They vary in size by subspecies, as caribou do. About the smallest are certain Lapp varieties from Scandinavia; about the largest are from the Tungus section of Siberia.

All the original reindeer breeding stock of Alaska came from Siberia. Most of the imports were of a rather small variety from the northeast, the Chukchi peninsula; but there were also some Tungus deer. When export from Siberia was no longer permitted by Russia, some effort was made to increase the size of Alaska reindeer by crossing with caribou bulls of large variety secured from the Yukon valley.

Large herds of reindeer are found in Alaska (see below) and in Siberia from the Chukchi peninsula west to the Kolyma and beyond. They are also numerous in northwestern Siberia, northern Russia, and in Finnish, Swedish, and Norwegian Lapland. Herds have recently been introduced in Canada from Alaska by the Canadian Government.

True albinism, while not common among reindeer, does occur but seems to be unknown among caribou. Spotted and white deer, which are not true albinos, occur frequently in Alaskan herds but are seldom if ever found among caribou. This usually gives a ready way of detecting that item of movie faking which represents domestic reindeer as wild caribou. The character may be used safely in airplane or other scouting or census taking where it is necessary to discriminate between wild and domestic animals; for you would seldom have a reindeer band of any considerable size without one or more white and spotted animals, while you would not expect even one spotted or white among a thousand caribou. (Still, it must be remembered that reindeer sometimes stray and get mixed with caribou herds; you would have to make at least a mental allowance for this possibility.)

By the last decade of the nineteenth century the native

caribou of northwestern Alaska had been slaughtered to such an extent that it was feared by some the Eskimos would suffer from a food shortage. Through the efforts of a missionary, Dr. Sheldon Jackson, 1,280 reindeer were introduced into Alaska from Siberia for the purpose of building up a permanent food supply for the Eskimos. The introduction period was eleven years, 1892–1902.

From these small beginnings there grew up an extensive stock industry in Alaska, so that it was estimated in 1930 that there were in the Territory a total of 1,000,000 animals, some of these in herds owned by whites (individuals, corporations), others in Eskimo herds which were under the supervision of the United States Government.

Then there developed a controversy, which we do not go into here, centering largely on whether the reindeer industry should be permitted to operate as it had in the past (with some herds under white ownership and others native-owned) or whether it should be maintained and developed exclusively by and for the benefit of the natives. The problem was complicated by many factors, and there was no doubt considerable misunderstanding on both sides. Whatever the merits of the opposing viewpoints, there was the unfortunate result that during the period of uncertainty, about from 1928 to 1940, many herds were neglected—some animals running wild and mixing with the caribou, while many others, instead of being tended as formerly, were killed by the Eskimos without regard to need or economic value. With the herds untended, depredations by wolves were heavy. Now, however, as indicated below, the industry seems on the way to being stabilized through control by the Department of the Interior. It is hoped to develop a plan through which the deterioration process may be changed to one of increase.

By the Act of September 1, 1937, Seventy-fifth Congress, Public, No. 413, ownership of reindeer was vested exclusively in natives (Aleuts and Eskimos, chiefly), the United States Government to take over and pay for herds of non-native-owned deer.

During the period 1937–40, while negotiations were going on, estimates of the number of nonnative deer differed—the white owners claiming about 500,000, the Congressional Com-

mittee about 180,000. By 1940 everyone concerned agreed
that there were considerably fewer deer than had been seen
the summer 1938.

On June 24, 1940, the Secretary of the Interior reported
that the reindeer-acquisition program had been completed.
The number of reindeer purchased by the Government from
white owners amounted to 82,538, with not more than 1,000
animals remaining which would have to be obtained by con-
demnation proceedings.

RANGE

The chief grazing areas for the formerly white-owned part
of the reindeer industry, are, from north to south, on the
Noatak River around Kotzebue; on the Kobuk River around
Kobuk; on the Selawik and Buckland Rivers; throughout
Seward Peninsula; on the Unalakleet River; on St. Michael's
Island and the lower Yukon; on Nunivak Island; on the
lower Kuskokwim, including Goodnews Bay; on the Nuskagak
River; on the Wood River which flows into Nushagak Bay;
on Alaska Peninsula in the Aleutian Range; on one Aleutian
island, Umnak. A few native-owned herds also graze in the
named areas. There are one or two on the Aleutian chain.

From this listing it appears that the largest and in some
ways the best reindeer grazing section of Alaska was solely
in the hands of natives—the vast triangular coastal plain that
has a northern apex at Point Barrow and a southern base
along the north slopes of the Brooks Range. South of that
Range there is a little reindeer country, mainly in the slopes
of the mountains; down lower, towards the Yukon River, the
land is too forested. Along the Bering shore sea breezes do
not keep the forest quite so effectively at bay as they do north
of the Brooks Range so that prairie lands, the best reindeer
pastures, are not as extensive eastward from this western sea
as they are southward from the polar shores.

By our listing, above, it is seen that of the Bering mainland
grazing the whites controlled about half, natives the other
half. Of the two big islands of Bering Sea we have said
Nunivak was under the white owners; this was balanced by
St. Lawrence Island, exclusively native.

112

In December 1929 the Canadian Government purchased from the Lomen Reindeer Corporation in Alaska a herd of 3,197 reindeer, to furnish the nucleus for reindeer raising in the Dominion's northern territories. Then began the great reindeer drive, lasting 5 years, 3 months, until the band of deer was finally delivered in March, 1935, at the Mackenzie delta. During the period of the trek there were considerable losses from wolves and other causes, which were only partially offset by natural increase; the herd numbered 2,109 animals upon arrival at their Canadian range.

By the 1939 count the herd at the Mackenzie delta numbered 4,146. A band of 900 which was separated from the main herd and driven eastward in December 1938 has been established in the Anderson valley under native management; there was a satisfactory fawn crop, with the August 1939 round-up showing 1,196 animals.

The reindeer constitute an important source of food supply for civil or military populations in Alaska. They are equally important as a source of material for clothing. All that is said elsewhere in this Manual concerning the use of caribou for food and of caribou skins for clothing and other equipment applies equally to the meat and skins of reindeer.

Reindeer support themselves, whether winter or summer, on the vegetation of the Arctic prairies and can discover food here and there in any but the most densely forested areas. If their meat is needed for a large body of men, a herd of them could be driven on the hoof and butchered where most convenient. Winter butchering on snow is a clean process in cold countries. Once the carcass is frozen it can be handled like cordwood. Even if it gets muddy or dirty you can wash it off, for it is as hard as granite from the freezing.

The reindeer has further value as a draft animal, and is used extensively for this purpose among the reindeer-owning peoples of the Old World.

At present little use is made in Alaska of reindeer as draft animals, but there was a rather extensive utilization for several years around 1918. Reindeer are less expensive to use than dogs but it is more work to tend them, so that gradually the Eskimo reindeer owners shifted back to dog driving.

With the increase in the number of dogs came an increase in the amount of meat needed to feed them and a resulting slaughter of thousands of deer to provide dog feed. It is said, for instance, that during 1 year the people of a single Alaska village, Deering, killed more than 5,000 reindeer to feed their dogs. Thus we have another factor in the mentioned numerical decline of Alaska reindeer.

For a detailed discussion of the use of reindeer as pack and draft animals, see Section V, Chapter 12.

MUSK OXEN

Attempts to domesticate musk oxen have been made by the United States Government, in Alaska, by the Norwegian Government, in Spitsbergen, and by an Icelandic private company, in Iceland. The Soviet Government has announced its intention to make the experiment also.

The chief reasons for domestication are that musk oxen give meat like beef and wool like sheep. They need no barn to shelter them, no hay to feed them, or protection from enemies except humans (in Alaska also from grizzly bears). Apart from possible attack from micro-organisms, it would appear they would do well indefinitely far south, for they are long-lived in zoological gardens. But the central argument for their use is that they are capable of turning into food and clothing far northern vegetation which no other animal uses.

Reindeer, an ancient domestic animal, attempts to confine itself to lichens and browse in winter, although they eat grasses, sedges, etc., if they have to; in summer they prefer grass. There is estimated to be in the Arctic at least 10 times as much grass food as lichen food, so that when you have stocked those lands with as many reindeer as the lichens will support, 90 percent of the grass still remains to be used.

The Icelandic experiments have gone badly in that all the animals have caught diseases, no doubt from other domestic animals, and have died. The United States experiment appears in a fair way of success.

When a band of 34 musk oxen were brought by the United States Government from Greenland to Alaska some years ago for experimental purposes, they were first kept in the vicinity of Fairbanks, where they had no difficulty with the climate and were found able to protect themselves from all enemies except the brown (Kodiak) bear. The bear depredations, however, were serious and in 1936 the herd (31 in all) was moved to Nunivak Island, where there are no bears. Here they have been thriving, increasing satisfactorily. In March 1940 the Nunivak herd numbered 70 animals.

Studies on the wool of this domesticated group made by the University of Alaska have confirmed the results attained by the University of Leeds on the wool of undomesticated animals. There have been like studies by or under the supervision of departments of the United States Government.

Several observers have said that you cannot tell the meat from beef by color, taste, or odor, and only by the shape of bones, if any are included in the piece you are eating—the musk ox bones being unusually stout in proportion to length. The milk has a taste similar to cow's milk and is in quantity per animal about three or four times that of reindeer milk, which latter is used in the Scandinavian countries for butter and cheese as well as for drinking purposes.

DOGS

Lieutenant Schwatka tells that he used to be annoyed by having people ask him constantly, "How big is an Eskimo dog?" He finally developed a bright, effective reply: "An Eskimo dog is about the size of a rock." On the Schwatka analogy, the answer to "What does an Eskimo dog look like" is in Pennsylvania that he is like a Pennsylvania dog, in Ohio that he is like an Ohio dog. For the usual come-back, "What, then, is an Eskimo dog?" The reply would be that it is any dog owned by an Eskimo.

These three replies cover the situation at least for the twentieth century. For the eighteenth they are probably not far astray. Eskimo dogs have long been mongrels; but it seems there may have been a time, before European influence reached America, when there was approximately a single breed. Judging by what is still fairly typical in the more isolated districts, these dogs were probably from 40 to 60 pounds in weight for males, well-furred, with rather sharp noses and tails well curled up on their backs. That they were of uniform color seems doubtful.

Certain common views of Eskimo dogs are vulnerable. The claim that they descend from the northern wolf is particularly fragile. For that wolf runs from 100 to 120 pounds or more, double the probable size of the Eskimo dog; the wolf drags his tail, and is of a uniform color pattern—darkest on the shoulders, lightening downward as well as back. The Eskimo dog, whatever his color may have been, was almost certainly not wolflike, since this color is rare now among dogs belonging to Eskimos and is usually found where it is known that the father or some not very remote ancestor was a wolf.

Saying that the Eskimo dog is not derived from wolves is, of course, very different from denying that there may have been now and then a wolf strain joining what was primarily a dog stock.

About the sole analogy that really holds between wolves and Eskimo dogs is that neither barks—both howl. Perhaps the wolf-dog idea started from this similarity.

From southern North America the European horse spread more rapidly than the Europeans themselves. Similarly the European dog outstripped his master across northern Canada and Alaska. These European forebears were of several breeds, for they came to America with explorers and colonists of practically every nationality from Spain and Italy to Norway and Russia. By the time their descendants reached widely separated parts of the American Arctic there had developed a wide variation in size and appearance. The difference would then be further accentuated by admixture with whatever may have been the original Eskimo dog. To illustrate:

A frequent query is regarding the difference between huskies and malamutes. For the answer, bear in mind what has been said about the mixture of the hypothetical original Eskimo dog with European and perhaps Asiatic stocks. The rest of the explanation is linguistic.

The Hudson's Bay Company's servants used to speak of the Eskimos as Huskies. A husky dog is, therefore, an Eskimo dog. This designation spread from northeastern North America, where the Hudson's Bay Company is strong.

When the gold rush reached Bering Sea the stampeders found near the mouth of the Yukon a group of Eskimos called Malligmiut, meaning "the people of the place where the waves are high," which no doubt signified that these people had lived or were living near some flats where breakers roar in from an open sea. The dogs purchased from them were naturally Malligmiut dogs. In the careless pronunciation and spelling of the miners this became Malamute.

There have been people in northeastern North America whose minds saw clearly the picture of an Eskimo dog which they, following the Hudson's Bay Company, called husky. Similar clarity of mental vision developed the malamute idea in western Alaska. But naturally the dogs in northeastern America and western Alaska were not the product of exactly the same mixtures. On the law of chances they were bound to differ.

When dog breeders go to work, each selecting for survival those traits which fit his picture, there will develop among the followers of the husky conception one type and among the followers of the malamute conception another type. Eventually these will become "pure breeds"—perhaps they are "pure" by now.

Naturally certain dog types, if mixed with the hypothetical Eskimo stock, would disappear by selection. A greyhound admixture would so disappear, for they could not stand the climate and would freeze or would be killed by their owners because useless.

Being ordinarily a small, well-furred mongrel, the "Eskimo dog" gives good results for heavy work when crossed with mastiffs. There have been crosses with Newfoundland, but these do not seem quite so good. The mastiff, pure, has two chief draw-backs—his fur is not good enough nor are his feet. The Newfoundland dog may do for fur but his feet are not good. Half-breeds from both, with the Eskimo mongrel, usually have both good fur and sound feet.

Perhaps the best cross, whether with bigger or smaller dogs, is the wolf. There appears to be no reason to think that the product is undesirable temperamentally. Testimony that they are vicious probably comes, in most cases, from people who, knowing there was a wolf strain, were afraid of the

117

pups and brought them up accordingly. Stefansson testifies that he had two dogs known to be half wolf and that in temperament and all other qualities they were about the finest he ever had. They were particularly gentle and gave minimum trouble in fighting with other dogs, although they were powerful and in a fight nearly or quite always victorious. He does not exactly credit the gentleness to the wolf blood. The temperament of these dogs was probably in large part the result of their having been brought up as well-treated house dogs.

Though not so strongly of the opinion now, Stefansson expressed in *The Friendly Arctic* the view that the white man's dog, of whatever kind, seems to have more "character" than the Eskimo mongrel. The latter (he then felt) will stop pulling when he gets tired but the white man's dog seems to have a sense of duty and, especially when he is well treated, will continue working hard though his stomach be empty and his legs tired. This view may have geen a generalization on the basis of too few observations but is at least worth considering.

For a discussion of the care of dogs, methods of harnessing, etc., see Chapter 12.

Section III

FISH

On a number of sub-Arctic rivers, particularly in Alaska, the run of salmon and other fish gives the main food supply of the year to natives and could do so to whites if they were willing to live on them. For it has been established that a diet consisting exclusively of fish and water is quite as healthful as a diet exclusively of mammal flesh and water. In both cases you avoid every kind of deficiency disease and maintain good general health, whether in hot weather or cold. (See Section II, Chapter 8, and Section I, Chapter 10.)

However, in Alaska it will only be in emergencies that white men depend mainly on fish. So a discussion does not appear called for beyond what we have under fishing methods in Chapter 13.

On the Arctic mainland coast of North America and Asia

fishing is less cultivated by the natives, but that does not always mean that fish are less numerous. It may mean instead that the people have never developed a fish culture or that other supplies of food are more easily obtained and better liked—as walrus, seals, caribou.

White men have found both on the Alaska and Canadian Arctic coasts that when they are told by natives that certain localities are good for fish, the information is usually correct; but when they are told that certain localities have no fish, there is little correspondence between the information and the fact. For instance, Stefansson camped once for several weeks at the mouth of the Ikpikpuk River in Smith Bay, eastward from Barrow, and never put out nets or made other attempt to fish because the natives with whom he was said they knew there were no fish. Just as the party was about to move—had to move for other reasons—they discovered that this was an excellent fishing locality. Usually it is worth while to shove a net out from the beach wherever you happen to be, in the manner described in Chapter 13.

The fish caught in nets near shore are usually small, of the white-fish type, locally known as herring, or perhaps salmon trout. There are known to be cod in the Beaufort Sea and east as far as Cape Parry. Only a few have been caught, but those in nets pushed out from the beach. The habits of the cod are such as rarely to bring him inshore, so that a few having been secured may indicate a great wealth outside.

As an indication of what may be expected on Arctic coasts and in the lower reaches of rivers that flow into the Arctic, we give a synopsis of notes on fish and fishing made on the second Stefansson expedition, 1908–12, by its second in command, Dr. R. M. Anderson, now biologist of the National Museum, Ottawa.

Catostomus catostomus (Forster). Long-nosed Sucker. Milluiak—name given by Eskimos of northern Alaska and the Mackenzie delta. Miluk—milk; milluiak—he milks, or sucks.

Found commonly in parts of the Mackenzie delta; not valued very highly as a food fish by the Eskimos, and used only for dog food when other fish are obtainable.

Argyrosomus tullibee (Richardson). Tullibee. Toolaby. It is probably the species known to the Mackenzie Eskimos as pikoktok.

This fish is taken commonly in branches of the east side of Mackenzie delta; large numbers were caught in nets set under the ice of a large lake south of Langton Bay. It resembles somewhat another fish called the Anarkhlirk. The Anarkhlirk is much more highly regarded by the Eskimos than is the pikoktok, because the former species is usually fatter. The pikoktok is usually without much fat, and the flesh is rather coarse and tasteless.

Leucichthys lucidus (Richardson). Great Bear Lake Herring. Kaktak (pl. Kaktat), the name given by all Eskimos from northern Alaska east to Cape Bathurst.

The most common food fish, found almost everywhere along the coast, and for some distance up into the larger rivers. Anderson found the species common as far east as Coronation Gulf. It is generally taken in gill-nets, during the whole summer, but in early spring at the time when the ice-sea opens up into cracks (early in June, and later), large numbers are caught with hooks through holes or cracks, or from the edge of floating or grounded ice-cakes near shore. This fish is the species commonly spoken of as "whitefish" by white men and English-speaking natives along the Arctic coast.

Clupea pallasii Cuvier and Valenciennes. California Herring.

Great numbers come into the Cape Bathurst sandspit during the latter part of August. Only occasional stragglers appear during the middle of the month. On August 3d, 1911, one end of a 200-foot sweep-net was run out from the beach with a dory, and drew in about 13 barrels of Herring (about 3,000 fish) at one sweep. A very few *Leucichthys lucidus* were taken in this haul. Three days later, at the same place, two hauls brought in about a barrel and a half of Herring and about two barrels of "Whitefish." The Herring were very fat, one Herring being as satisfying as two much larger "Whitefish." The Baillie Islands Eskimos say that the Herring were never caught here before the white men came (a little over 20 years ago), and think that the Herring followed the white men in. The explanation seems to be that the Herring schools came in only periodically, and not often close inshore, while the Eskimos did not use long seines, confining their fishing operations to short gill-nets along the beach.

Stenodus mackenzii (Richardson). Inconnu. Connie. Asjhiurok, commonly called Shi (shee) by Mackenzie River Eskimos.

Common in the Mackenzie River, Great Slave Lake, and up the Slave River as far as the Grand Rapids at Fort Smith, 60° N. Lat. Found in brackish and salt water as far west as Herschel Island, on the east side of the delta, to Toker Point.

Large numbers are caught in gill-nets in brackish water at Shingle Point, Mackenzie Bay, in July and August, but the flesh is rather soft and flabby at that season. Eskimos catch many with barbless hooks through the ice on the east mainland side of Richard Island in October, November, and December. The Connies are fat and firm of flesh at that season. Not many are caught in midwinter, but they bite better again after the sun comes back, later in the winter. The average weight here is 8 or 10 pounds, but a specimen taken at Fort McPherson, Peel River, weighed nearly 50 pounds.

Salvelinus malma (Walbaum). Salmon Trout. Ekkallukpik, name given by Eskimos from northern Alaska to Coronation Gulf.

Found in most of the larger streams where the water is clear. Not so common in salt water, but quite frequently taken at Herschel Island, Cape Bathurst, and Langton Bay. While seining some pools in the Hula-hula River, in the foothills of the Endicott Mountains, Alaska, together with the common form, the party caught a large number of what may be a dark phase of this variable species, or perhaps another species. The common form seen near the coast has back, dull grayish green; sides, pale silvery green, with numerous round, pale pink spots; and belly, silvery white. The others had back, very dark olive, almost black, with very faint, small, obscure, pinkish spots, some irregular, some comma-shaped, etc.; sides, bright olive-green, with brilliant vermilion spots; belly, bright vermilion, sometimes inclined to crimson, slightly paler along median line, and fading to salmon color on breast and throat; pectoral and ventral fins with anterior border white. Females were duller colored, belly pink or rosy, sometimes with a yellowish tint, and the lower jaws were less strongly hooked; most of the fish were spawning at that time (September 11, 1908), the large yellow eggs being about the size of No. 1 shot. These brilliantly colored Trout were seen only in the Hula-hula River.

Cristivomer namavcush (Walbaum). Lake Trout. Kaluakpuk, Mackenzie River Eskimo name for fish brought from the Eskimo Lakes. Also called Sinayoriak by Mackenzie River and Baillie Islands people. Ishiumut, Coronation Gulf Eskimo name.

Found in most large inland lakes from Alaska to Coronation Gulf. At Great Bear Lake the people claim that they are often taken of 40 pounds' weight, and occasionally run to 60 pounds. They are taken on set-hooks, or by "jigging" through the ice, or in nets.

Thymallus signifer (Richardson). Arctic Grayling. Sulukpaurak (Alaskan Eskimo), or Sulukpauyak (Mackenzie River Eskimo).

The Grayling was observed in the Hula-hula and Chandlar rivers, Alaska, in the Horton River and its tributaries, and in the Dease River. It was not observed in the delta of the Mackenzie River, as the water seems to be too turbid, but several were seen in the Mackenzie at Fort Providence, where the river water is quite clear. The Grayling is commonly called Bluefish on the Mackenzie.

Usmereus dentex Steindachner. Arctic Smelt. Very rarely taken along the Arctic coast.

Esox lucius Linnaeus. Pike. Jackfish. Shiulik, name given by Eskimos from northern Alaska to Cape Bathurst. Found abundantly in the Mackenzie delta and other rivers, also in lakes as far east as Coronation Gulf.

Platichthys stellatus (Pallas). Starry Flounder. Small Flounders were occasionally taken in nets at Langton Bay only; they did not appear to be very common.

Microgadus proximus (Girard). Tomcod. Ogak (pl. Okat), by Eskimos as far east as Coronation Gulf.

At Toker Point, on the east side of the mouth of the Mackenzie River, the species is apparently rare. Locally, common in Liverpool Bay. Tomcod are very abundant in certain spots near the eastern end of Langton Bay, and very easily hooked through the ice all winter with almost any kind of hook. In Coronation Gulf they are common in certain localities. The Copper Eskimos catch them with a very large, barbless, gafflike hook which is "jigged" up and down. On the shank of the hook, 2 or 3 inches above the point, small bangles of white bone are suspended. When the fish come to nibble at these swinging bangles, the hook is jerked sharply up, usually catching the fish in the throat. A species of Rock Cod, growing to 18 inches in length, is occasionally caught in the Tomcod fishing place at Langton Bay, and is called Ugavik. The Rock Cod was not observed elsewhere.

Oncocottus hexacornis (Richardson). Six-horned Bullhead. Kanaiyuk is the Eskimo name for the Sculpin from northern Alaska to Coronation Gulf.

This Sculpin was described from specimens collected at the mouth of Tree River near the Coppermine. Sculpins or Bullheads are found almost everywhere along the Arctic coast, but are only occasionally eaten by the Eskimos, at times when other fish are scarce. They are quite common as far up the Mackenzie delta as Kittigaryuit. They are frequently taken on hooks while fishing in salt water for Tomcod and other fish. The common, universally distributed species is dull drab-colored, paler below. In Langton Bay there is another species, averaging a little larger, and lighter colored, mottled with yellowish.

Lota Maculosa (Le Soeur). Ling. Loche. Known as Titallirk by the Eskimos from northern Alaska to Cape Bathurst.

It is probably the favorite food fish of all these Eskimos, and is universally distributed in fresh and brackish waters, but seems nowhere to be taken in very large numbers. The very large, fatty liver is considered the best portion for food. It is caught both in gill nets and on set hooks on the bottom.

INSECTS; PARASITES AND PESTS

In comparison with temperate zones and tropics the Arctic has few species of insects but some of these in great numbers. It is the general belief that most of them survive the winter as eggs that hatch in spring, but some at least derive from hibernation, of which we give some account. We quote, paraphrase, and condense from Frits Johansen, who was entomologist of the third Stefansson expedition, when he had an opportunity for study in Arctic Alaska and in Arctic mainland Canada as far east as the Coppermine district. He had previously worked upon the insects of the northern east coast of Greenland. We quote from his Insect Life on the West Coast of America, Ottawa, 1921:

"Insects are scarce along the Alaskan Arctic coast after October and are found only under stones and driftwood, or by digging in the frozen tundra or cutting holes in the fresh-water ice * * *.

"The main objective of the hibernating insects is to find, before the snow and frost come, some place where the spring water can best be avoided. They therefore take every advantage of cover, especially of those places likely to become free of snow in the early spring. In this, not all are successful, but they are more likely to be found, during the winter, on such exposed localities than on lower ones that have a better vegetation. An exception is, however, formed by certain larvae, such as large diptera, e. g., tipulidae, which hibernate down in the ground until the medium surrounding them thaws. Aquatic insects and larvae that inhabit water all through the year endeavour to bore themselves into the mud and, failing this, are killed, and hibernate only as eggs when the water freezes to the bottom.

"* * * Most hibernating insects can withstand temperatures down to 50° below, and the mortality may be ascribed rather to factors in the life-cycle of each particular insect than to the cold.

"In the fresh waters of northern Alaska insects and larvae are abundant, even in winter, as compared with those on land. * * * In a pond only 4 feet deep, on which the ice was 10 inches thick on October 9, many copepods, *Limnocalanus johanseni* Marsh, ostracods, and other minute animals, and a number of midge larvae were found. Ponds such as this would, of course, freeze to the bottom later in the winter."

Among the organisms which Johansen concluded were hibernating successfully in lakes that froze to the bottom were: Aquatic diptera—larvae (especially tipulids and muscids); dytiscid—beetles; trichoptera—larvae and perlid larvae; mosquitoes—females, a few (*Aëdes* sp.); various midge larvae; and hydrachnid mites.

Johansen concludes that various insects pass the winter at various stages of development. He lists them as: imago, larva, nymphs, and pupa. Bees and wasps may hibernate as queens.

We shall dwell mainly upon those insects that affect human life conspicuously in the Arctic, whether directly or indirectly, and have no more than a brief sketch of the rest.

One insect in flight has been reported farther north than any land in the world; for Peary saw a bumblebee about a half a mile north from the north coast of Greenland when he was returning to it in spring from a sledge journey by which he had attempted to reach the North Pole. A butterfly was reported by the De Long expedition fluttering over the sea ice in spring some 20 miles from the nearest tiny island, several hundred miles north from the mainland coast of Siberia, and nearly a thousand miles north of the Arctic Circle. This insect was captured, sent to the Smithsonian Institution and receipted for; but was then lost. There has been much search for it, including that by a European entomologist who came to America a few years ago on purpose. The mystery apparently cannot be solved. However, the Soviet Government now has a scientific station on the De Long Islands. Perhaps they have already captured butterflies there, some of which would probably be of the same kind as De Long's capture.

Among the insects which are not pests and which are found in the most northerly islands in the world are, besides the two mentioned, house flies and beetles. There is a considerable number of other insects.

LICE

It is generally considered that there are two main kinds of human lice, those of the head and those of the body. In many Eskimo communities there are lice; but the communities vary conspicuously, which is known to the Eskimos and often reported to great distances. For instance, it is commonly said throughout Alaska that the lousiest natives are in the delta of the Yukon, the fish eaters.

Apparently there were some communities from which all human lice were completely absent. Amundsen reports for King William Island that in 2 years they found only one lousy individual and this (strangely, says Amundsen) was an old woman who had been employed as seamstress on his ship.

Generally speaking, then, you are in some danger of getting lice when traveling through Eskimo communities, though certainly not in more danger than if you were doing social work in a big American city.

Apart from methods of handling lice which readily occur to anyone, since they are more or less traditional with us, there are some special suggestions for the Arctic.

Freezing probably does not kill even the grown lice. It certainly does not kill the nit. What you do, then, is to hang up an infested garment for an hour in the cold, till the live lice are numb; then you beat it like a carpet and the lice fall out. Now wear the garment long enough for some of the nits to develop into lice, and repeat the freezing and beating. In this way lice may be completely eliminated from a garment in a few days.

FLEAS

There are apparently no fleas in the Arctic. None have been found on foxes or wolves, and if there are any in your party they probably came in with your own men or dogs. Fleas are seldom or never a problem in northern work.

Mosquitoes and sandflies are more of a problem, so far as numbers are concerned, in the Arctic than in the tropics. There probably are 10 times as many mosquitoes per square mile over at least two-thirds of the land north of the tree line as the highest average anywhere attained for even a small area in the tropics. However, these northern pests do not kill unless by actually sucking blood. Perhaps there is a small degree of direct poisoning as well; but still you have the main consolation that they do not infect the victim with disease, certainly not with malaria or yellow fever.

MOSQUITOES

It is estimated that the number of species of mosquitoes in Arctic and sub-Arctic regions approaches 30; of these 4 or 5 are decidedly important in Alaska and northern Canada. The principal ones are *Aedes punctor, A. communis, A. aldrichi,* and *A. stimulans.* Practically all of the species which are pestiferous and annoying pass the winter in the egg stage.

The mosquito season starts early. Stefansson reports for the north shore of Great Bear Lake, which is about under the Arctic Circle, that the first mosquitoes appeared the first week in May (1911). Throughout the Arctic the most severe annoyance is usually experienced from about the middle of June to the middle of July, although some of the mosquitoes persist through the summer until the heavy frosts of the fall—which, in the Bear Lake woods may be any time in September.

The chief reason why mosquitoes are worse in the Arctic than anywhere else appears to be the slight variation in heat between midnight and midday, giving, when the warm weather sets in, ideal incubation conditions.

These special conditions of Arctic summer temperature produce on insects an effect that has startled travelers. In temperate zone districts, such as the Adirondacks, the young of the mosquito are likely to be killed by a night chill, for the long hours of darkness permit a great drop in temperature as compared with the noonday. The Arctic mosquito has, on the contrary, at birth and during early life a suitable temperature both at midnight and at midday. This decreases the infant mortality to a minimum and accounts for the clouds of mosquitoes which make the summer wretched.

The second reason why the North is a mosquito paradise will be the incredible number of tiny lakes. Wherever a deer or other beast has trod is a little puddle or hole, ideal for the growing mosquito. The roughness of the ground forms other puddles. The water remains in these because of the permanent ground frost a few inches or a foot or two down, far enough away not to chill materially the water in which the mosquitoes are hatching and growing, near enough so the water cannot percolate down to leave the young mosquito high and dry.

If night chills are the greatest cause of infant mortality among mosquitoes in the temperate zone, desiccation is perhaps next. From desiccation also they are safe in the Arctic.

Though perhaps not impossible, it is difficult to exaggerate by words the number of mosquitoes you find in suitable Arctic localities. Stefansson vouches for it that on numerous occasions he had to make repeated attempts before he could take sight on caribou with a rifle. He would brush the mosquitoes from front and rear sights; before he could get a bead there were insects on at least one of the sights and sometimes on both. Seton, speaking of mosquitoes north of Great Slave Lake, has said that they settle so thick on short-haired parts of animals that you cannot tell the color of the skin.

You are wholly free from mosquitoes only at sea. On the great northern lakes they may trouble you a little even far from land, but only in case your vessel leaves shore in a high wind which keeps the plague under cover and then gets a calm out in the lake so that they can leave their hiding places and begin flying around. Stefansson has reported thousands of mosquitoes on the sheltered side of a boat-sail far from shore. Traveling in the middle of one of the great northern rivers, such as the Yukon or Mackenzie, you are reasonably free; but you are attacked the moment your boat approaches the land.

In good-sized towns, such as Nome or Fairbanks, you have little trouble in among the houses. A fairly extensive area that is drained will also have few. On a shore you are not bothered when the wind is from seaward or lakeward; right on the Arctic shore, with a land wind, the mosquitoes bite you. Chilly winds from the sea have a certain dampening effect on mosquitoes for a few miles inland; but frequently mosquitoes are pretty bad within half a mile of the beach, even with a sea wind.

The mosquito is a great enemy to many northern animals.

Probably most of the birds are nearly or quite immune. Except for biting around the eyes, they don't bother materially musk oxen or grizzly bears, because of the thick fur; the polar bear is usually out of reach at sea during the fly season. They do annoy foxes and wolves. Dogs of Eskimo and white owners are frequently so bitten that there is a running sore around each eye, and perhaps other parts of the body where the hair is short. You can keep mosquitoes away from eye sores by an ointment, but only if all dogs are tied—loose dogs will lick almost any preparation from each other.

Caribou find the mosquitoes intolerable and dash about vainly trying to be rid of them. In a few places, such as among the rugged hills south of Coronation Gulf, snowdrifts persist in the shade well into the mosquito season; there you will find caribou lying on the snow, getting some protection.

Animals and men not used to mosquitoes swell with their bites. Stefansson reports for a half-mastiff which came from San Francisco, and which had perhaps seldom or never been bitten, that his eyes were completely closed the first year by the swelling, that there was noticeable swelling the second year, and that the third year no swelling was noticeable. The same reactions would probably be typical for humans if they permitted themselves to be sufficiently bitten.

The Eskimos had no adequate way of protection from mosquitoes. For coolness they used in summer clothes which were nearly worn out, hairless, and full of holes. Through the holes the mosquitoes would enter and bite. The skin tents would not exclude mosquitoes, and they tried smudges, even though they really knew, as we do, that mosquitoes can stand more smoke than people. Still, it was sort of half tolerable lying close to the ground breathing fresh air where it came under the edge of the tent, with the interior above filled by smoke.

As a result of the mosquito torture, the second most coveted thing when the Stefansson party visited the Coronation Gulf Eskimos (Stone Age people who had never before seen Europeans) was mosquito netting. (What they coveted most was needles.)

For mosquito protection you need, first, clothes all over your body through which they cannot sting. This means reasonably heavy garments, no matter how hot it is, and accounts in part for the frequent statement of whites that they have suffered more from heat in the Arctic than anywhere else. You wear leggings on your ankles, gauntlet gloves on your hands, and a sombrero hat to keep the mosquito netting away from your face. The net should have an elastic which grips the crown. Then the material comes out over the brim and is tucked inside of your coat collar. Having it hanging down like a sort of cape is no good—the mosquitoes crawl up under in great numbers.

It is therefore important when you go North to provide yourself with summer garments which have a maximum of insect resistance (bite-proofness) with a minimum of warmth. You must also have fly netting and the means of using it—suitable broad-brimmed hats to keep the netting away from your face by day; suitable arrangements for bed nets to use at night; fly net for windows in tents, etc. Ordinary mosquito netting is not good enough in the Arctic, for the meshes spread. Use bobbinet or something of the sort.

For complete peace at night you should have double protection. First you camp in a tent which has ventilating windows equipped with mosquito netting. Then you sleep under a bed net.

The Stefansson parties used to have a sort of combination tent and bed net for emergencies. This was an A-shaped roof of water-shedding material at least a foot longer than the user (say, 7½ feet for a 6-footer) and about 4 feet wide. From this would hang down mosquito netting on all sides. Mosquito netting tears easily if you try to tuck it under bedding, and so you would have at the lower edge of the netting wall a light cloth, say, a foot of it, to tuck in under the bedding all around.

Smokers have a problem, and so do those who chew and spit. With a wide-brimmed sombrero to hold the net away, you could smoke a cigarette inside the net; but you would have to lift your veil every time you handle the cigarette, and mosquitoes would get in. Pipe smokers will try a long-stem pipe, smoking it through a small hole in the net. Unless the hole is a tight fit, mosquitoes will crawl in along the stem.

Fly "dope" may be some good, but few bother with it for long in the North, except people who live in towns and do not have much trouble with mosquitoes anyway. Still, if you have a favorite dope that has worked in New Jersey or in the tropics, you might as well take it along and try it in the Arctic.

SANDFLIES, MIDGES, "NO-SEE-UMS"

After the mosquitoes have been going awhile there develops a pest in some respects worse; these have many names and vary in size and in other respects. Known variously as sandflies, punkies, midges, or "no-see-ums," they are members of the family *Chironomidae* and of the genus *Culicoides*. They are bad in the forest and go farther out on the Arctic prairie than do the blackflies (see below). They are found in numbers large enough to be a pest only on the mainland, although they do occur on Arctic islands.

The breeding habits of the northern species have not been worked out; they probably breed in decaying vegetable matter along streams and around the margin of ponds. They may also breed in rot holes in trees. Some people are very susceptible to the bites and show marked reaction when attacked.

This group of insects are active throughout the summer, their season in many places starting later than that of the mosquito and tending to persist further into the autumn. It is said by some that their annoyance is confined largely to periods when there is little or no breeze. Stefansson's experience is that they will stand a considerable breeze, but that they quiet down upon any chill—mosquitoes bother you at night as well as in the day; midges are worst at noon and in the afternoon, slacking off as the evening cools.

These insects are persistent bloodsuckers, and they are so small that they can go through ordinary screens or head nets. Vanderlip says that in northeastern Siberia he found the only thing which kept them out was 30-mesh wire which he had brought with him for screening gold.

131

The worst of all with midges or sandflies is that they crawl around on your body like fleas and may bite you anywhere. Here came in what Stefansson found to be the third keenest desire of the Stone Age Eskimos whom he met in 1910 near Coronation Gulf—when they found out that the cotton underwear carried for summer use by the white men was so tightly elastic at the ankles and wrists that it prevented sandflies from crawling under, they became almost as eager to get such underwear as to secure mosquito netting.

The bite of the mosquito merely itches. The bite of the sandfly both hurts and itches.

The third of the major pests, from both the human and animal point of view, is the bulldog, sometimes called moosefly, deerfly, horsefly. These look like overgrown houseflies and bite as if you were being lanced with a surgical instrument, drawing blood that trickles. They are about only on hot days, but are then not restrained by a considerable wind—they can fly almost or quite as fast as a horse can run. You keep them out with mosquito netting and other mosquito precautions. Like sandflies, they stop troubling you toward sundown and are little bother on a cool day.

Black flies, or buffalo gnats as they are sometimes called, are bad pests in certain sub-Arctic and Arctic areas. They are at their worst well within the forest; near the northern edge of the forest their numbers decrease so that they do not constitute a real pest; and they do not go much out on the prairie.

These flies, of the family *Simuliidae,* spend their larval and pupal stages in the water of rapid streams. Several of the species attack man and animals. These begin to appear early in the summer and become most abundant and vicious during the first half of the season, after which they gradually decline. Some people are very susceptible to their bites and may be incapacitated for days after being exposed to a severe attack, the face and arms being badly swollen and some systemic effect in evidence.

BLUEBOTTLES

An insect which bothers though it does not attack is the bluebottle. You find them ready to deposit larvae on meat everywhere on the continental mainland and in several of the larger islands. They are, for instance, troublesome in Victoria Island—in the interior, however, rather than on the coast.

BOTFLIES

A pest which indirectly affects the Eskimos and northern whites who live by hunting, and owners of reindeer herds, is the botfly or warble fly (Oedemagena Tarandi). It is a beelike insect of yellowish orange coloration and is one of several parasites that plague caribou.

The fly's season of activity is about 3 months, late June to some time in September. They lay their eggs on the fine, woolly hairs which constitute the under-down of the reindeer or caribou coat. Eggs hatch in 6 to 7 days and the young larvae start boring through the skin, causing dermatitis and abscesses fatal to from 1 to 2 percent of a herd. It is not until the end of October that the holes through the skin attain any size; by February the encysted grubs are about the size and appearance of a white navy bean. The larvae grow progressively and evenly in size until May when they begin to emerge. The chief time of emergence is June.

Reindeer skin is very thin at this season, and the larvae make large openings as they work their way out. Even after the wound has healed, the skin is not strong in these spots. Skins of caribou killed in midsummer are thus likely to have a sieve-like character.

It has been found simple to extract the larvae by squeezing the skin, which causes the reindeer little pain and the operation is quickly done. Theoretically, if all warble flies were thus squeezed out and destroyed, there should be no flies left to attack the animals. Unfortunately, warbles are able to travel considerable distances, and seem to have the power of following animals and catching up with a herd. (It is contended by some that a warble is the swiftest of all flying creatures, insects, or birds. This is hard to prove; for if an insect so small were traveling so fast it would be invisible ordinarily.)

For a number of years the St. Lawrence island reindeer herds were reported free from warbles, although these deer were derived from the same sources as the other Alaska herds.

It was considered that they had been transported from the mainland to the island after all the grubs had left their backs and before egg-laying had started.

The reindeer herd on Nunivak Island was transported after the grub emergence. A letter from Carl Lomen dated August 1, 1940, reports that for many years there were no grubs on this island and that in consequence this herd produced the prize hides of the north. A few years ago, some warble flies were reported—presumably they were blown over from Nelson Island or brought over by some ship or boat—but the herd as a whole is "practically free" from these parasites even now.

A measure of success in warble-control was reported by one owner. After most of the grubs had left the reindeer, about July 1, he drove his herd as far away as possible from the point where the grubs had fallen, the idea being that when the flies emerged from the pupal cases they would not find any reindeer to attack; and, as they only live for a few days, they would soon die. It is thought that the distance which reindeer must be driven should be not less than 15 miles, but the point has not been settled. Lomen has conducted some experiments along this line and agrees, both on theory and on the distance a herd should be driven.

TAPEWORM

Of internal parasites found in the Arctic the most serious, economically, are tapeworms. Many reindeer herds suffer, with a resulting financial loss.

The tapeworm is conveyed to the reindeer by dogs. On St. Lawrence Island, where reindeer dogs have never been used, the herds are said to be free from tapeworm cysts. So far, the only effective control has been in the prevention and cure of them in the dog carriers. No means of prevention in reindeer is known.

Dr. Victor J. Levine, consultant for the United States Public Health Service in Alaska, states that in six summer investigations he has not found Eskimos who had tapeworm.

134

CHAPTER 6

VEGETATION

Section I

VARIETY

Markham, in his *Life of McClintock*, says that there had been at that time (1908) identified from the Arctic 250 species of mosses, 330 of lichens, and 760 of flowering plants. Thus in species the flowering plants outnumber the nonflowering. In tonnage the preponderance of the flowering is still greater. There would be on the average north of the tree line at least 10 tons of flowering plants for every ton of mosses and lichens combined. More likely the ratio in tonnage would be a hundred to one. There is perhaps no island in the Arctic of the size of Puerto Rico or larger in which flowering plants do not literally outweigh the nonflowering. In large islands, like Victoria, they probably outnumber them also in species.

It should be remembered, further, that not merely are the volume and weight of flowering plants at any given moment greater than those of the nonflowering but that the flowering grow more rapidly.

Among the most northerly of the flowering plants, the following have been cited by various authorities, many of them found within a few hundred yards of the north coasts of the most northerly islands: bluegrass, timothy, goldenrod, dandelion, buttercup, poppy, primrose, anemone, alpine chickweed, purple saxifrage, heather, arnica, ferns, shinleaf, bluebell, rhododendron, cranberry, curlewberry, and catspaw.

We mention incidentally and merely as a curiosity the "pink snow" (usually *Sparella nivalis*) which is found at distances as much as 20 miles from shore, and therefore perhaps at any distance from land—microscopic plants growing in snowbanks. You cannot see the coloring of the snow when you pick up a little of it in a spoon or, indeed, when you stand close to a snowdrift. But go a few yards away, perhaps best 30 or 40, and get the right slant of the sun. Then you see a pink or even red coloring to the drifts, varying and the colors shading into each other. This coloring of the snow eventually proceeds so far that at its height, which is naturally while most of the snow has not as yet turned to water, the hue of the snowbanks is on a cloudy day reflected in the skies, giving them a pink tinge.

Section II

GROWTH

In *The Northward Course of Empire,* 1922, Stefansson has the estimate that (excluding lakes and the Inland Ice of Greenland) vegetation edible to the Arctic grazing animals between the tree line on the continents and the most northerly shores of the most northerly islands averages per square mile of land surface about as abundant as the vegetation edible to cattle and sheep which is found on those tropic- and temperate-zone lands which are used for stock because they cannot be irrigated and have a rainfall insufficient for cereals and other economic crops.

Grass does not usually grow tall on the Arctic islands. Lieutenant Mecham, however, around 1850, spoke of meadows in Melville Island "resembling English meadows"; and, be it remembered, Melville is well north of the middle of the Canadian Arctic archipelago. Such great islands as Victoria, Baffin, and large parts of Greenland are considerably hotter in summer because larger. Remember, too, that few islands in the polar sea are more remote than Melville from those popular explain-alls, the Gulf Stream and the Japan Current.

The perpetual light and the considerable warmth may, in the case of some plants at least (among them wheat and tuberoses), produce a growth per week of the order of twice as rapid as the maximum tropical—which, if you think of the plant as growing during sunlight, means the same growth per hour in tropics and Arctic, the double Arctic

136

growth being due to the double number of hours of sunlight per calendar day.

Section III

USES

A considerable use of Arctic vegetation as food or medicine might have been made by explorers during the period when it was believed that scurvy resulted from lack of vegetable elements in the diet. That such use was seldom made actually was due to the firm but ill-advised confidence with the explorers had in lime juice as a specific. On a few expeditions one form of green vegetation or another was eaten in connection with the lime juice and always with good results. However, as more fully developed elsewhere, the only expeditions which ever were completely free from scurvy were those which had considerable amounts of fresh animal food in their diet. Now that we understand that complete protection from scurvy is derived from such things as steaks and roasts as easily as from citrous fruits and onions, we have lost the greater part of our motive for eating northern vegetation.

In saying that fresh meat will prevent scurvy as adequately as fresh vegetables we do not mean to say anything about the comparative percentages of Vitamin C, by weight or otherwise, in carnivorous and herbivorous diets. What we do mean is that since an all-meat diet appears to contain twice as much Vitamin C as needed for optimum health, there can be no more danger of scurvy on a fresh all-meat diet than there is on a fresh all-vegetable diet. It is a case of enough being as good as a feast.

The greens that explorers did in fact use against scurvy was most often sorrel, or plants which they thought resembled it. This was because the antiscorbutic virtue of lime juice was supposed to depend on its acid content. Probably an equal benefit would have been received from eating many nonsour local green things that were succulent enough to be readily swallowed.

Berries that are more or less relished by whites and by some Eskimos are found in the Canadian archipelago as far north as Melville Island, and correspondingly elsewhere. The most northerly of these is the Eskimos paunrat (Crowberry, *Empetrum nigrum* Linn.), watery, of little food value, and, as said, of no significance as scurvy preventive to people already on an antiscorbutic meat diet, though doubtless useful if your party had scurvy from some other diet and you were unable to get fresh meat.

The most northerly berry of significance in the Eskimo economy, and correspondingly available to Europeans, is the salmon berry (Cloudberry, *Rubus Chamaemarus* Linn.). This is yellow in color and looks somewhat like a raspberry, grows somewhat like a strawberry, and is found in numerous places well north of the Arctic Circle. It may be in such abundance that patches of ground look yellow at a distance. This berry tastes agreeable to the average European, delicate rather than pungent in flavor. They can be gathered by the bushel and no doubt preserved for winter in any of the ordinary European ways, or they could be frozen by a quick-freezing process. The whalers used to freeze them at Herchel Island by placing in the natural cold storage houses where they kept their caribou meat. Moreover, frozen on their stalks, many of them can be found still in position during the winter, and even into early spring you can sometimes pick them. Eskimos preserve them in oil—chiefly in western Alaska. In some districts, for instance, Coronation Gulf, they were not eaten, fresh or preserved.

When you come to the edge of the woods, many of the accustomed Temperate Zone berries appear. Currants and cranberries are the chief of these.

In the forest, as in the Yukon, wild strawberries are found and domestic ones may be cultivated.

Indeed, something like half of the ordinary berries of the northern United States can be cultivated successfully in districts like those bordering the Yukon in Alaska and the lower Mackenzie well toward the polar sea in Canada. Reports are available from the United States and Canadian governments and, more recently, from the Arctic Institute of the U. S. S. R.

EDIBLE ROOT

One northern root is used extensively and regularly by some Eskimos and in famines or minor emergencies by others.

This is a species of knotweed—either *Polygonum bistortum* (Tourn.) L., *Polygonum viviparum* L., or *Polygonum fugax* Small. The root is called by the Eskimos by some variant of the word *masu*. In western Alaska and some other places large bags of these roots are kept for winter, soaked in oil, usually seal or white whale.

The chief objection to *masu* is that they are constipating. Western Alaskans recognize the oil in which they are preserved as counteracting this—they say that *masu* are not good to eat by themselves. In Coronation Gulf, where they are seldom eaten except during times of scarcity, there usually is no oil available at the time. So the constipating effect is much feared. The fact that ordinary constipation was rare or unknown among these people made them the more reluctant to face it in connection with hunger.

PLANTS USED FOR WICKS

It is of use to a traveling party to know such things as what makes a good wick for an Eskimo seal oil lamp. The best answer is that most anything serves, if it is dry and finely shredded or not too finely powdered. The use of decayed wood, pussy willow fuzz, moss, and so on for this purpose is discussed in Chapter 7.

As an Arctic prairie fuel,[5] most valuable is the resinous *Cassiope tetragona*. This is a species of white heather, varying in height from 3 to 10 inches. An important element in what might be called polarcraft (by analogy with plainscraft, woodscraft) is to learn during the summer to recognize locations where this heather will grow. Then during the winter you can go with some confidence to places covered with several feet of snow, dig down and find your fuel. A description of the method of using heather is given in Chapter 7.

Willows, tall enough to shelter a camp or for their stems to be of much use as fuel or for house building, are found only on a few of the larger islands, chiefly Victoria Island and Greenland, but perhaps also on Jan Mayen.

However, in many of the Arctic islands the willows are of

---

[5] In Chapter 7 there is a detailed discussion of Arctic fuels and how to utilize them. Here we mention only those which are of vegetable origin.

considerable value for fuel when you take the roots along with the stems. In many places, even in midwinter, you can find these readily where the snow has been swept from the tops and slopes of hills. Watch as you travel by sledge and pick up those you see; by camp time you likely will have enough for cooking supper and breakfast.

BRUSH

We have mentioned heather and willow for the northern islands. When you get to the mainland there are few rivers which do not contain, a half dozen miles or so from the sea, willows with which you deal as you would with any brush. (These "willows" are true willows as well as alders and other species.)

TREES

The first plant thought of as a tree which you meet coming from the north is in some places the cottonwood. However, this is of botanical rather than practical interest, for such cottonwood clumps are nearly always small. The first "important" tree is, therefore, usually the white spruce, then the black spruce, then cottonwood. After that the number of species increases rapidly.

NORTHERN LIMIT

It was formerly considered that trees became smaller gradually as you went farther and farther north. The actual northward limit is not always arrived at in any gradual way, however. In a sheltered bend the forest belt along a river may be up against a ridge so that in say half a mile you walk from tall and graceful trees up a steep slope to where the trees end abruptly and beyond which there are none—going straight north from there you would reach none until you crossed the polar sea and attained a corresponding climatic situation in Siberia.

The white spruce may be found growing as tall within a dozen miles of the tree line as that species grows even a thousand miles farther south. White spruces, 40 feet high, have been reported within 40 yards of the tree line.

CHAPTER 7

SHELTER, HEAT, AND LIGHT

SECTION 1

"CIVILIZED" ARCTIC COMMUNITIES

When structures of considerable magnitude and of "civilized" type are being erected in the Arctic, the principles and procedures generally will have to be in the main those which we are used to farther south.

The site must be carefully selected. Here the meandering habit of rivers and the cutting of a shore line become important. Especially when there is considerable ground ice, but on the average in any case, an Arctic river will cut its banks more rapidly than you are used to farther south. Fortunately the laws of this process are well understood by geographers and geologists. If you are locating a civil or military establishment on a river you had better choose a place where the stream is meandering away from rather than toward your side, and where that process seems likely to continue for at least a few decades. True enough, the river may get so far away that it will no longer keep the ground thawed for you; but on the whole, that is better than having it undercut and destroy your construction and pipe lines.

Earth that is solid, and gravel, hold the footings referred to below. No footings are possible in swampy tundra and the entire foundation must be on a mat.

Of rare occurrence but important locally is the thaw that comes from volcanic sources. It might well be worth while

141

to consider the advisability of locating military establishments in the vicinity of hot springs.

Hangars must be located with relation to prevailing winds.
A line drawn from the hangar to a nearby village should be
at right angles to the likely drift of air on a cold day; for the
steam created by the life processes of animals and the housekeeping of people (cooking, etc.) may blanket with fog several square miles of low country to leeward of a village when
temperatures run to −60° or −70°. At the present airport
at Fairbanks, human-animal fog has at times obscured the
landing field, with resulting damage to planes.

For deep excavation, if there is plenty of time, you can get
good results without the ordinary hot point and other such
thawing processes used by northern miners.

Natural summer thawing goes only a few inches down on
most land while it is in its native condition. For instance, a
meadow in the Arctic, partly because of a layer of damp vegetation, is cooled by the evaporation of the water somewhat as
the human skin is by the evaporation of perspiration. Moreover, sunlight is not nearly so fully converted into heat when
it strikes the dead grass of last year, light yellow in color, as
when it strikes black soil.

Stefansson found in his archaeological excavations that
in a country where the thaw of a whole summer would not
go down more than 8 or 10 inches he could get in 1 day 3 to
5 inches thaw by removing at the first operation, from the
entire area to be excavated, the sod and all that was thawed,
and then removing each morning the thaw of the previous
day. In that way a 300-inch (25-foot) thawing could be
secured by a 100-day summer operation in a district that
normally would thaw only a foot. If it is known, then, that
an excavation for a large building is going to be needed next
year, the work could be done cheaply if carried through the
whole summer, or any necessary part of it, this year.

One of the difficulties with modern structures in the Arctic
is that, through the removal of grass and the keeping of most
earth surfaces bare and black through traffic, thaws begin
to go much deeper down into the ground than they used to.
Accordingly, corner posts and similar things that are placed

in earth frozen as hard as concrete, say in August of the year of building, may be standing in thawed and soggy ground in August a year or two later.

To insure foundations that won't heave with frost action you need a mat footing, with a very much larger surface at the bottom of the footing than is customary in the States. Very large buildings need an entire mat foundation. (For a full discussion of ground frost see Section I, Chapter 2.)

As implied in Chapter 2, the important exceptions to the rule of permanent Arctic ground frost are connected with unfrozen waters, those of the polar sea, of rivers, and lakes.

From the point of view of sinking wells to supply water the year round, and for the laying of water mains which are to be of 12-month use each year, it is crucial to study for the intended locality the character of the ground thaw.

On the north coast of Alaska you are likely to reach unfrozen ground at a 20- or 30-foot depth 50 feet from the shore line. The permanent value of this, however, is negligible, for in most parts the sea is cutting away the land at such a rate that it would be only a few years till a system of water mains, for instance, laid in such ground would have to be moved or abandoned. Generally speaking, the importance of ground thaw along the Arctic sea is, therefore, negative—in the sense that if you want an excavation, as for permanent cold storage perhaps, you had better be careful that it is made far enough from the sea.

The thaw may extend as far from lakes, on the average, as it does from the sea—perhaps farther, since their waters are warmer. The shore lines of lakes are usually almost stationary, so that the ground thaw can there be utilized for water supply by wells and for burying permanent mains. Near some lakes the thaw comes near or to the surface.

The best understood situation with regard to the removal of ground frost by rivers is in the case of the Snake which enters the sea by the town of Nome, Alaska. A few miles back, where the valley is about a mile wide, it seems that practically anywhere in the valley you strike permanently thawed ground at about 30 feet down. Where there are willows, the thawed ground comes nearest the surface, of course, because

143

in a generally open country these willows catch a lot of snow and hold it as a blanketing, giving every opportunity for the ground water to thaw the soil and to keep it thawed.

Here the meandering habit of rivers becomes important. Fortunately the laws of this process are well understood by geographers and geologists. If you are locating a civil or military establishment on a river, you had better choose a place where the stream is meandering away from rather than toward your side, and where that process seems likely to continue for at least a few decades. True enough, the river may get so far away that it will no longer keep the ground thawed for you; but, on the whole, that is better than having it undercut and destroy your construction.

For reasons already stated or implied, it is most important that after the laying of your water mains (see below) or the sinking of your wells you shall keep for the ground the same protection which it had and, if possible, increase the protection. This means that you must not destroy bushes. If possible, you should plant more willows, or perhaps white spruce or cottonwoods, to extend the area that holds the snow. If this fails, or if it is considered too costly and slow, you could attain, at least in windy places, the same result with snow fences built and used on the principles well known to the railways which traverse the prairies of the United States and Canada.

The laying of water mains naturally has problems connected with ground temperatures. At or near the surface these temperatures become the same as those of the weather and may accordingly be −60° in the forested parts of the sub-Arctic and −50° near certain of the northern coasts. What might be spoken of as the indigenous temperature of the ground itself is probably around 10°—at least that is the temperature 40 feet down at Cape Smythe (Barrow), Alaska; similar figures are given for the underground coal mining operations in Spitsbergen.

It would appear, then, that in winter cold decreases as you go down and that it might be advisable to have mains deep. However, the depth at which you attain 10 above zero is so great, and that temperature itself so cold, that the situation is academic. Mains, in practice, will have to be near the surface on all sites where ground frost is permanent. They should be well insulated. This is sometimes accomplished by having a smaller pipe inside a larger one, with an air space around, or there may be some form of insulator packing around the pipe itself, whether or not it is surrounded by a larger pipe. It is important to keep running large quantities of water through a main when temperatures are low.

Hydraulic miners, working at low temperatures, have comparatively little trouble because of the rapidity with which the water passes through their pipes, a warmth slightly above freezing then sufficing to neutralize the chill that reaches the outside of the pipes.

In some cases the problem of freezing water mains has been solved by running through the same tunnel or large pipe both the water lines and steam lines from a central heating plant.

There are various applications of heat and electricity to water systems. These can be borrowed practically unchanged, for use in the very coldest Arctic and sub-Arctic localities, from the practice of such cities as Winnipeg, which occasionally have temperatures of $-50°$. True enough, one of the principles in Winnipeg is to bury mains at something like seven or nine feet, the limit of frost, since the ground is not permanently frozen. Apart from this, Winnipeg deals with winter temperatures under natural conditions practically identical with those of the Arctic. And, of course, cities like Fairbanks have had a long enough experience to develop a suitable technique through methods of trial and error.

NOME, ALASKA, WATER SYSTEM

A statement on the water system of Nome, Alaska, has been furnished by Carl J. Lomen:

"Nome has water mains for general use and a separate system for the fire department of the city.

"The water for household use is piped from Moonlight Springs in a wooden pipe line of some 16 inches in diameter—wooden staves banded with iron. The pipe line ends at D Street, and from there the pipe lines are of iron and only a few inches in diameter. The mains are less than three feet below the surface. The exposed pipes leading into the homes are of $\frac{1}{2}$ and 1 inch diameter.

145

"The pipes are not insulated by packing, though they are laid in a wooden gutter, the top of which is about even with the surface of the street. The mains * * * could not be protected against frost even though sunk deeper because of perpetual frost to bedrock.

"During October, when low freezing temperatures may be expected, the custom has been to open all faucets and permit the water to run continuously. This continues until an exceptionally cold snap freezes the entire system. Many householders are so anxious to keep a flow of water going that they permit the pipe lines to freeze each year, and (because of bursting) many lengths have to be replaced next spring. Following the freeze the watermen come into their own and for some 6 or 7 months river or spring water is delivered to the homes in large water tanks on bobs drawn by horses. From tank to ditches the transfer is in 5-gallon cans.

"In the spring the water company send out their gangs, who thaw out the town pipes. They use long iron points through which they pass steam. It requires several weeks' work.

"The fire-department mains are a bit deeper and, as I recall, are also iron pipes with a square box covering. This system is drained in the fall of the year and kept clear all winter. When a fire alarm comes in—during the winter season—the engine at the fire house commences pumping to fill the water mains. The 'Chemical' rushes to the fire to hold the flames in check until the mains are filled and sufficient pressure is secured to reach the fire with water. As soon as the fire has been extinguished, the firemen again drain the system, thaw and reassemble the hose, and make everything ready for the next call. It depends upon the distance the fire is located from the fire pump as to the length of time which will elapse from the sound of the alarm to the play of the water—from five to fifteen minutes."

CONTROLLING ROOM TEMPERATURE BY GRAVITY

It might be worth while to experiment with adapting to buildings of European-American type a principle used by the Eskimos, that of entering a room from below instead of from the side.

Where you desire to maintain within a building a 60° temperature against —60° outside, there is a sudden and rapid interchange of the inner and outer atmospheres when you open an ordinary door perhaps 7 feet high and 3 or 4 feet wide. Through the pronounced difference in gravitational values, quantities of the chilled air rush in along the floor, in appearance a dense cloud of steam, and equal quantities of the heated air, also steamlike in appearance, rush out through the upper half of the opening.

If instead of a vertical door in the side of your room you had a horizontal door (a trap door) of the same dimensions in the floor, you could have it constantly open and less cold would enter in an hour (by diffusion of gases) than enters in a minute through the side door. There would also be full relief from violent changes of temperatures.

It might seem that this problem would be still better worth facing in shops than in dwellings. Assume, for instance, you desire to maintain a constant 40° temperature in a hangar or workshop for repairing airplanes. If you open at —60° a side door big enough to admit a plane, you will not merely drop the interior temperature very low but there may occur such chilling of metals already in the shop that when you raise the temperature again by the use of fuel there will be sweating of metal surface. This may produce rust; perhaps water may gather in some hidden place, so that when the machine or instrument is later taken outdoors freezing up may prevent its proper operation.

If, instead of entering through a side door, the plane were to come in by ramp or elevator from below, there would be no great change in temperature within the hangar, certainly not enough to produce sweating on metal things already there.

This argument of sweating applies, of course, only to what is already in the shop or hangar when the door is opened. It cannot apply to the machine just brought in, which will be iced all over, later becoming wet when the ice thaws.

The sweating of metals as they pass from cold to warm is one of the most serious of Arctic problems. Every effort should, therefore, be made to devise procedures by which all instruments and machines can be repaired and serviced out of doors, or in sheds which differ from the outer air in little except that they keep out the wind.

For the Arctic summer there is no special problem about living in average temperate zone style, except that in small villages you must be especially careful with mosquito protection.

MOSQUITO PRECAUTIONS

This will be on the same style as used farther south. Where there is trouble with sand flies you need for windows and screen doors a mesh considerably finer than for mosquitoes, say each mesh only one quarter as large.

HEAT RELIEF

During the short period of intense heat in certain inland districts, it may be well to make provision for cooling off in basement rooms. Where the walls of these are up against the earth, and if the walls are of material that is a good conductor, you have a cooling of the air by the coolness of the walls. This is particularly important in hospitals.

NATURAL COLD-STORAGE ROOMS

In connection with an establishment of considerable size, such as military posts, arrangements could probably be made for natural cold storage of food products by a system more reliable, as well as less expensive, than the artificial. The chill you need, say 10°, is supplied by the permanently frozen ground.

When white men construct storehouses in the Arctic, as, for instance, the American whalers at Herschel Island, they commonly begin with a fundamental error—the storage chamber is cut into the side of a hill and they enter the cold room through a door in the front wall. Then you have a reversal of what we discussed for winter—each time the door is opened in summer the cold air from inside flows out through the lower half and the warm air from outdoors flows in through the upper half.

Probably the first Alaska use of the right principle by whites was at Cape Smythe. This came about through accident. The Army expedition of 1881–83, under Lieutenant Ray, sank a shaft for earth temperatures. After they moved out and the house and all other property they left came under the charge of Mr. Charles D. Brower, he enlarged the bottom of the shaft into a chamber, which had a year-round temperature of about 10° F.

Since warm air is light and cold air heavy, and the shaft to the storage chamber vertical, you can enter and leave this Barrow storehouse a number of times on the hottest day without materially changing its temperature. Men, if necessary, can work down in it all day without closing any trap or other door.

If the cold-storage chamber is to be part of a building proper, the subcellar idea is what you use. The storage chamber would then be entered by a stair from the cellar just as the cellar itself is entered by a stair from the ground floor.

GROUND ICE AN ADVANTAGE

If you are choosing between localities for building a civilian town or military post in Alaska, the Geological Survey may be able to tell you from previous surveys that the land near one of them contains ground ice. This can be an advantage, for in such places storage chambers can be excavated with little more trouble than if they were being hewed from an iceberg.

SHORING UNNECESSARY

Whether cold rooms are hewn or thawed out from ice or frozen earth, there is no shoring necessary, unless possibly in rock of poor quality. Mud that would be semiliquid when thawed makes ideal storage walls when frozen.

SECTION II

CAMPS

a. Houses

The principal type of emergency house discussed is of earth and wood, but the fundamental principles of this type apply to the others. Some of the principles are:

The wall framework leans in slightly so that the earth hugs it through force of gravity. Walls and roof should be so thick that no appreciable heat gets out except through openings deliberately left for ventilation. All the fresh air, then, enters through the ventilating system, which is gravitational and therefore completely automatic. In practice this means that you enter the house from below through a permanently open trap-door which is also the ventilational air intake.

GRAVITATIONAL VENTILATION

There is always some ventilation by diffusion of gases through any opening into a chamber, but the amount of fresh air which enters through a trap door in the floor, no matter how large, is in the main determined by the amount of air that can escape upward from the house. Therefore, you control the effectiveness of a large intake by varying the size of a small exit in the roof.

With this type of house, as with others, you should remember the general principle that when in doubt as to a building site in treeless country, avoid a lee. This goes against the grain with most temperate zone people—they try to find a shelter or to build one. In the Arctic (as more fully stated elsewhere) it is frequently a matter of life and death to avoid lees. This is one of the reasons why Indians of the northern fringe of the forest, habituated to woodlands, and conservative, are perhaps the worst possible companions when you go out upon the Arctic prairie. The propensity for camping in a lee accounts for much of the trouble, hardship, and loss of life among early and recent travelers who have used Indian companions. (See more detailed discussion under Tents, later in this chapter; also Section V, Chapter 10.)

Wood and earth are the best local materials when you can get them, and it is possible to get them in many parts of the Arctic.

On a coast, where driftwood is obtainable, you erect four posts at what are to be the corners of your house. These need crotches. Simplest is to find trees with roots on them, whereupon your posts are four stumps with the roots up. You make them stand by digging holes for them in the ground, which can usually be done even with the most primitive tools. You may have to use some ingenuity, however, as, for instance, making several successive fires. You thaw the ground a few inches each time, scrape away the thawed ground with the ashes, repeating until the hole is deep enough.

This is the primitive way, used when you have no modern appliances. Alaskan and Siberian miners use "points." You make steam in some kind of a boiler and run from it a hose which terminates in a metal pipe through which the steam emerges at or near the tip. With this type of gear you can thaw a small hole, not much bigger than to fit your post; if you use the method of successive fires you thaw out a basin that is deep enough, stick your post in the middle of it and pack around with the thawed earth which, of course, will soon freeze if the weather is cold. If the weather is not yet cold the post has to stand through some factor of rigidity introduced in the construction of the house.

If the post hole is of medium size, as usual with Eskimos when a house is built in thawed ground (near open water), you wedge or fill in with whatever under the circumstances seems most suitable, perhaps slivers of wood or stone. If it is necessary to use earth which depends for its supporting power on being frozen, then, after dampening it, if necessary, you will have to make sure that it is covered by enough more earth so that a thaw (caused by the house being warmed during occupancy) does not loosen it.

The posts firmly planted, you lay four logs across to make the tops of your four walls. The rest of the wood part of your walls will be up-and-down sticks, perhaps logs split in half and propped up, leaning in just enough so that loose earth thrown against them will not fall away.

You now determine, according to materials on hand, what kind of roof to have. The most common Eskimo type is also one of the best. In a square of from 3 to 5 feet you plant in the center of your house four posts so much taller than the corner posts that the slope will be considerable, anything from 15° to 30°. At the top you connect these posts by four logs, as in the case of the walls. The square between—3' x 3', 4' x 4', or larger—is going to be your skylight. A particularly strong rafter runs from each corner of the window frame to each corner of the wall. The other rafters will rest one end on the wall beams, the other on the window beams, or on the main or corner rafters.

The next thing is to determine where your door is to be; for, before you pile earth on the walls, you must dig a trench, not necessarily more than 3 feet wide, and bridge it over with wood where it is to go under the wall. The outside entrance to the alleyway should be 10 or more feet away from the house so that the down slope shall not be too steep. Walls and roofing of the alleyway can be as flimsy as you please so long as they keep the wind out. The outermost door need not be weathertight, for even if a little snow drifts in during a blizzard this will not go far into the alleyway and is easy to shovel out.

You now shovel or pile loose earth or broken sod against the framework so that the walls will be perhaps 4 or 5 feet thick at the bottom, and perhaps 12 or 18 inches thick at the house eaves. (Eskimos usually have the walls only from 3 to 5 feet high, which greatly simplifies the heating problem—the house is, even so, fairly high inside at the center, perhaps 7 or 8 feet.) Your rafters will be covered with earth to a thickness of anything between 3 and 6 inches. Should it be impossible to find rafters strong enough to hold that load, you can perhaps make out by going inland and finding some tall grass, moss, or other fluffy vegetation. With 2 or 3 inches of dead grass or moss on the roof you need merely enough earth on top of that to hold it down and for windproofing—say, 2 inches.

In the comparative warmth of early and late winter, when temperatures go above zero F., you will have to depend for daylight entirely on your top window, which may be made of thin white cloth, if you have any, of a thin skin made transparent by rotting the hair away (i. e., parchment), or of the intestines of large animals slit lengthwise and the strips sewn together after the inner membranes have been removed.

In midwinter, when temperatures seldom go above zero F., you can use an ice window. This would melt if it were in the roof and has to be in a wall. If your building looks forward to such a window, you will have left a space for it, somewhat as for a narrow doorway, with a temporary covering until the weather gets cold enough. Then you cut ice for your window from the surface of some pond or fresh-water stream. If you use salt-water ice, you get somewhat less light, for it is milky rather than glassy.

If the occupants of the house are scientifically-minded, they get some amusement and a little extra light by applying the principle of lenses, curving the surfaces of the ice window panes.

To an extent, the ice window is self-protecting. If the weather outside is too warm, or the house overheated from inside, melting will take place. The thicker the window the more quickly it begins to melt; as it thins, chill from the outside gets increased play until finally thawing stops before a hole is melted. Only if it is warm both outdoors and in will a hole form. To prevent that you put out your fire or protect your window from inside warmth by skins or blanketing, thus giving play to the cold locally stored in the earth around the window. If that fails, you just have to get a slab of ice for a new pane after the warm spell is over.

METHODS OF SECURING ICE WINDOW PANES

You secure ice that is right for windows in a number of ways. Fresh ice is more translucent than salt, so river or lake ice is normally used. If you know in the autumn that you are going to spend a long time at a given place, it is well to cut ice from a lake when it is about 2 inches thick, dividing this into a number of panes, either of the right size or of excess size so that they can be cut down later. You stack these up with slivers of wood or other protection between the layers; otherwise they might freeze together. Then you store them where a thaw is not likely to reach—perhaps you cover them with a pile of skins or with moss and then snow.

Even in midwinter you can usually find thin ice. Look for a stream that was frozen over at a high level, the water then sinking away from the ice. This is common on many small rivers.

Another way of getting a window pane is to chop a hole in river or lake ice that is a little bit bigger than your intended window. Remove all ice fragments and snow, so that perfect ice will form, and then wait until the gap so artificially made has frozen over. When the ice is of the thickness you desire you remove it by sawing or by gentle chipping along the edges.

If thin ice is hard to find, thick ice will serve. Sometimes you start with windows 12 or fifteen inches thick, but that does not last long if they are near the cooking apparatus which melts the inside and keeps on melting until a point is reached where the outer cold balances the inner heat.

We suggested above that windows could be made with lens surfaces. This can be done by chiseling as a sculptor chisels marble. It can also be done, of course, by melting, as with a piece of iron or sliver of rock that you alternately stick in the fire and apply to the ice. In a similar way, a heavy block of ice can be thinned down as desired for a window.

The floor of the house can be just earth, as it frequently was in pioneer sod houses of the western United States prairies. It can be covered with sawdust shavings or a brush matting. But in most cases you would follow the commonest Eskimo fashion by splitting logs and laying them with the round backs down, adzing or whittling the flat surfaces so that, if not smooth, they shall at least be without slivers. These logs can then, if desired, be covered, or parts of the floor at least, with skins or whatever you have. However, you will use for a proper floor cover only rawhides without hair. Skins with hair on them will cover those parts of the floor only where men sit down or where they sleep.

Some Eskimos do not use anywhere a door that can be closed, not even at the outer entrance of the alleyway. Their dependence on gravity control of the balance between outer and inner air is in those cases complete. If you have a door, it must not, of course, be weather-tight; for ventilation depends on it. (See below.)

Usually it is advisable to build a house on ground level. Under special circumstances, as when you build in the side of a hill, the dwelling may be partly a dugout.

In either case the entrance should be through a tunnel dug 3 or 4 feet deeper than floor level. Eskimos frequently have such alleyways 20 or 30 feet long, sometimes with alcoves. Either with or without alcoves, they are useful for storage, for dogs to sleep in, etc. Sometimes one of the alcoves is an auxiliary kitchen—you may think cooking everything within doors would overheat the house; or you may be in a hurry, and then a bonfire in the outer kitchen will serve for quick boiling or roasting.

As said, the outer door of your alleyway must not be weather-tight; it need not be closed at all. The rest may be walled and roofed as high as you please, but where you stoop to get in under the wall the tunnel is necessarily low. Passing that constriction, you stand up inside the house in such a way that to inmates you are visible above the waist. This means that in the floor there is an entrance, always open, say 3 or 4 feet wide and running 5 or 6 feet into the house.

To have the alleyway extend thus indoors is sometimes convenient. When the weather is —50° outside it may be anything from —20° to 20° at the bottom of your entrance when the interior of your house, 5 to 8 feet higher, is 60° or 80°. This means that you have a cold storage chamber right indoors. A piece of meat down there, suitably protected from dogs, will remain frozen and fresh for days—indeed, until the weather outdoors becomes so warm, say around zero, that the heat of the house is able to crowd down into the entrance and produce a thaw at alley floor depth.

Ventilation should be of the Eskimo gravity type. In the roof, just to one side of its peak, you have a wooden chimney made of a hollow log, of boards, or something of the kind, and from 5 to 10 inches in diameter, according to how big your house is and how much fuel you burn. For increasing house temperatures you decrease this opening by sticking something into it, as a wad of skins or a mitten. To decrease indoor warmth you increase the size of your ventilator opening. The flow rate of the warm air up through th's top ventilator determines the rate at which cold air can enter from the bottom, through the trap door.

With the cold air entering by a floor opening of, say, 15 or 20 square feet area, and the warm air leaving by a roof ventilator of less than a square foot in cross section, you can have no draft or air motion that is readily perceptible in the room. The cold air just wells up slowly through the trap and spreads evenly over the floor—unless something within the house is in violent motion, stirring up the air, as, for instance, people

155

dancing. But go on top the roof, hold your hand a foot above the ventilator chimney and you feel so strong a draft that it seems to press your hand upwards.

Ordinarily house temperatures vary so with elevation that you can regulate body temperature by the level which you occupy. For instance, when you stand in a house the air around your shoes might be at 40° F., around your waist at 50°, and just above your head 60°. Stefansson says that he never measured this gradation in a wooden house but that he did measure corresponding gradations in a snowhouse. At any rate, it is common practice in this type of house to cool off by lying down on the floor. (Eskimos frequently keep wooden houses at 80° to 100° F. temperature as measured, say, 1 foot below the peak of the roof.)

When material is available (perhaps gasoline tins) out of which a stove and stovepipe can be constructed, a stove is much better than an open fireplace when the fuel to be burned is wood or coal. In many cases, however, the traveler is forced to depend on fireplaces.

FIREPLACES OF EUROPEAN TYPE

There are two main types of fireplace, the Eskimo-Indian and the European. The European need not be described in detail, since its principles are well understood. You make that fireplace in one wall of your house. If it is used, you may safely forget nearly everything that has been said about ventilation; for the fireplaces takes care of it in one way though spoiling it in another. A chief drawback of a European fireplace is that it provides too much ventilation, so that at —40° or —50° it is extremely difficult to keep a house comfortable. The fire does not throw enough heat into the room to counterbalance the cold that is pulled in with the air which replaces the current that goes up the chimney.

FIREPLACES OF ESKIMO TYPE

In spite of drawbacks, which will appear, the Eskimo type of fireplace is better for cold weather use than a European, though a stove is better than either. This fireplace is in the center of the house. It can be just a spot on the earthen

156

floor, but stones are advisable both for convenience while the fire is burning and to absorb and preserve warmth. While a fire on this central hearth is going, you have to remove the window covering at the peak of your roof. Even so, in very cold weather a central fireplace keeps the house warmer than a European wall hearth; for it sucks in no more cold air than the European while throwing out heat not merely in one but in all directions.

When the cooking is over, or when the heating of the house has been accomplished, you throw out of doors the least smoking embers and cover the roof aperture in a hurry so as to imprison as much heat as possible.

Stefansson has described living in a house so heated in northern interior Alaska. They were comfortable all day and all night as a result of cooking just two meals, breakfast and supper, on an Eskimo central fireplace. Heat for the rest of the time was furnished by the gradual cooling of the stones of the fireplace.

Another plan is to do your cooking in a specially constructed shelter out of doors and to heat loose stones during the cooking. When the food is brought in, you also roll into the house half a dozen of these toasted small boulders. They radiate warmth for hours. A house may be fairly comfortable with two heatings, morning and evening, though commonly there are more—partly for amusement and busy work.

DANGERS OF CHARCOAL

There is a temptation for Europeans, because of inherited ideas, to try to improve on the Eskimo method by developing practically a smokeless charcoal to burn on the central fireplace. This is all right if you are very cautious about monoxide poisoning, with which we deal in Section V, Chapter 10.

If there is more animal oil than you need for food, burning it Eskimo fashion is, if you really know how, a better way of heating and cooking than the use of wood, even where suitable firewood is abundant. There is the drawback to oil lamp cooking that pots are slow in boiling; but the advantage that the lamps give light as well as heat. With proper trimming there is no odor and no smoke, if you burn fresh fat. There

157

will be an odor from fermented fat, but it is not unpleasant to those used to it—a few Europeans like it from the start, most will not notice it after they have been in the house ten minutes, and nearly all will eventually get to like it insofar as they smell it at all. (The method of burning fat is described in Section III of this Chapter.)

It is not necessary to describe other houses in detail if the principles of the usual earth-and-wood coastal Eskimo house are fully understood. You simply adapt yourself to the materials obtainable and to the conditions. In one case, for instance, near the center of Melville Island, the third Stefansson expedition could find no stones, bones, or other materials that would support a heavy roof, nor was there anything available as a framework to support earthen walls. They, accordingly, dug themselves into a hill and sewed skins together for a roof. The skins were light enough to be supported by some bamboo poles and similar things which they had on their sledges. The campers spread several layers of skins over the initial layer, but the total weight was, of course, much less than even the thinnest useful earth covering.

In order that the roof should not cave in under weight of snow during the winter, they selected for the house site the top of a hill so that there would be no lee anywhere in which snow could accumulate. The house roof had to be nearly flat, for if there had been an A-pitch to it this would have produced a lee, making inevitable a heavy snow accumulation on one side, if not both. They erected no other structure anywhere near, allowed no sledges to stand about, and were so successful with the various precautions against snowdrifts (elsewhere described) that the weak ridgepole never suffered a breaking strain.

On most Arctic coasts something can be found to support heavy walls and roofs—rib and shoulder bones of whales, etc. In such cases the buildings have to be small or have to be divided into many separate compartments.

Generally a party arriving on an Arctic seacoast without house-building material or fuel of its own should, if it has to winter, do so on the coast. For game is likely to be more abundant there than inland—seals and polar bears. One of the above types of house will then be used.

158

But should there be a reason for leaving the coast, as, for instance, absence of sea game and the likelihood of land game or of superior fishing from lakes or rivers inland, the chances are that the best camp to build would be of the Eskimo hemispherical house type, with a framework of willows. (It is customary for northern travelers to call "willow" anything not a cottonwood or a spruce.)

Willows descend almost to the sea along many northerly continental rivers and will be found as driftwood north of their growth limit along the lower courses and deltas. Tall willows are rare on Arctic islands, however. There are willows suitable for houses of the type about to be described on some of the rivers in the southern half of Victoria Island and in southern Greenland; there may be on Novaya Zemlya. Probably all other northern islands are lacking in suitable willows.

A willow framework is not strong enough to sustain a drift of snow. Therefore you must build your house either in so extensive a stretch of willows that there is no drifting snow where you are, or else in an exposed location where there are no rocks, cliffs, or other things behind which snowdrifts may form.

SHAPE

For maximum interior space with given materials, for strength, ease of heating, and for some other advantages, your willow house should be dome-shaped. If necessary it may be a sort of oval dome—one diameter considerably longer than its transverse diameter.

FRAMEWORK

For a 10-foot diameter you take a pair of willows each from 7 to 9 feet long, plant their big ends 10 feet apart and bend them toward each other, lashing the overlaps together with twine, thong, roots, or strips of bark. Take a second pair, place, bend and lash them similarly and so that they cross the first pair at right angles. Where they cross you fasten them together. Parallel to one of the pairs, some 15 or 20 inches away, you place similar pairs similarly bent and lashed. At right angles to these again you put in successive

159

pairs of willows until you have made the equivalent of an inverted basket, in most or all cases lashing the willows wherever they cross each other. (Especially in small houses the framework need not be as regular as here described.)

COVERING

The willow frame is not strong enough to support a covering of earth. You therefore use skins or fabrics and provide warmth on the air-space principle by using grass or moss outside. If there are no skins or fabrics you can manage just with moss and grass, but the meshes of your framework must then be small.

The skins covering your inverted basket may overlap more or less shingle-fashion, with a cap skin at the center of the dome; or the covering may be of skins that have been sewn together. If cloth is used, and if many kinds are available, prefer the one that is most nearly airproof.

Outside of the tent covering you put grass or moss enough to make a thickness of 2 or 3 inches and outside that a second covering. You next bank with snow. It may be advisable to shovel a certain amount of snow all over the house, including the center of the roof, for the willows are amply strong enough to support this although not strong enough to support a deep snowdrift.

WINDBREAK

If the house is built on the open prairie, provide a windbreak, as described under Tents. The snow that falls on a house protected by such a windbreak settles lightly and not in quantity to produce a cave-in.

DOOR

As to shape, size, location, and manner of closing, the door of the dome house is like that of the dome tent, described hereafter.

WINDOW

The windows are about as already described for earth-and-wood houses—if of ice they are low down in the wall, if of skin they are high up in the roof.

HEATING

We said that the usual and best fuel for heating Eskimo houses on a coast is animal fat. This is practically never obtainable inland, where you almost necessarily heat by either of two methods, both already described—the central fireplace below a central window, the covering of which can be removed; or stones heated outside and rolled in.

b. Snowhouses

The Eskimos seemingly have at least one fundamental discovery to their credit. They are the only people, whether of ancient or modern times, who have succeeded in building a dome without the use of scaffolding during construction.

It has been claimed that the Eskimos have been able to dispense with scaffolding because the blocks of snow are sticky, clinging as if with mucilage. But, in fact, the second block of a snowhouse, and every block after that, stands because it has been placed in such a position that it cannot fall without first breaking. Give blocks considerable time and they do begin to adhere to each other; but touch them immediately after they have been set in place and you find that disengaging them requires merely overcoming the force of gravity.

MISUSE OF WORD IGLU (IGLOO)

There is a doubly unfortunate practice in our books and speech to use the Eskimo word *iglu* (*igloo*) for a special type of house which we suppose to be or think of as being peculiar to the Eskimo. The first trouble is that we are then making a narrow, specific use of one of the broadest terms possible; for in the Eskimo language, which is one from east Greenland through Canada and Alaska to eastern Siberia, iglu means a temporary or permanent shelter for man or beast. To an Eskimo a railway station, cathedral, farmhouse, and cow barn are iglus. (There are districts, or it is claimed that there are, where the word is slightly narrowed; but even then only to meaning a temporary or permanent shelter for human beings, as opposed to animals.)

A second difficulty with our use of iglu is that a writer will call an iglu that type of Eskimo house with which he is most familiar. If he has been in northwesterly Greenland he tells you that an iglu is a house of earth with a framework of bone or stone. If he has been in King William Island he tells that an iglu is a house of snow. From Alaska he will tell you that an iglu is a house of wood and earth.

Not understanding the language, travelers from Alaska and Greenland will argue this as a linguistic point, saying that an iglu is not a snowhouse at all. Similarly, a traveler from the central district, unless a good linguist, will come back supporting the popular view that an iglu is indeed a snowhouse. And each can prove himself linguistically right by questioning Eskimos, who will point to either a snowhouse or an earthen house and call it an iglu. What they overlook is that the same Eskimo would also speak of the White House in Washington and the Empire State Building in New York as iglus.

CORRECT USE OF IGLU

In a district where only one house type is in use, iglu is employed normally; the word may even be used locally in usual speech for whatever type is more common than another. But no one who desires to be precise will do so—they will use specific words like our skyscraper, church, or cottage. An example of correct Eskimo use, taken from the Mackenzie dialect, is *tupermik iglukaktok*—he has a tent (tupek) for a dwelling; *apujamik iglukaktok*—he has a snowhouse for a dwelling. In Coronation Gulf, where snowhouses are in winter the regular thing, you will often hear them spoken of as iglus. However, in spring and autumn when some people are in tents and some in snowhouses the language will be more specific. The name there for a snowhouse is *ini*. The second of the above sentences will, then, be *inimik iglukaktok*—he lives in a snowhouse.

In this Manual, accordingly, we never use the word "iglu." In fact, we shall use only two Eskimo words, and them because they are specific names for peculiar things of Eskimo invention and because they have been taken into our language in their correct Eskimo meaning. These words are "kayak," a

162

small, covered-over skin boat; and "umiak," a large dory-type open, skin boat.

There are several theories of how the Eskimos developed the snow house, none of them with sufficient probability over the others to be worth detailing except in an extended theoretical work.

Though the dome snow house was probably an Eskimo invention, it was never universal among them. It seems likely that more than half of the Eskimos of a hundred years ago either had never heard of a dome snow house or knew of it only by such remote hearsay that it was either unreal or disbelieved in. A remaining 25 percent knew of the snow house by fairly definite hearsay concerning use by groups not very remote. Another 5 percent or 10 percent knew how to build snow houses but used them only in emergencies. The remaining 15 percent or 20 percent lived in snow houses during the intensely cold part of each winter, when temperatures averaged lower than zero F. and seldom went above 10°.

Geographically the domed snow house is unknown, except recently through hearsay and through photographs and movies, to approximately 1,500 Eskimos who live in northeastern Siberia, to about 7,000 in southern, western, and northern Alaska, to about 17,000 in Greenland, and to a few hundred in Labrador. Several hundred Canadian Eskimos around the mouth of the Mackenzie, who now do not use them, are descendants of people who a generation ago employed snow houses in traveling, though they lived in other houses.

At the margins of the snow-house area there are, then, transition belts where people know how to build snow houses but seldom use them. The builders there are not such experts nor do they make proper use of the snow dwellings—they have forgotten, or have never understood, the technique of comfortable snow house living. These transition groups are, as said, in the west, the Mackenzie Eskimos. In the northeast are the only people of Greenland who have snow houses. They are a transition group in the sense that they normally live in other dwellings, that they make snow houses rather badly and do not seem to be really comfortable in them—at least not in comparison with the true snow house dwellers. The southeastern transition group is on the Ungava peninsula between Hudson Bay and the Atlantic. Apparently there is not a real transition group at that southeasterly corner of Eskimo territory which is west of Hudson Bay—even the most southerly people there are rather good at snow-house building and use.

THE REGULAR SNOW HOUSE DISTRICTS

The Mackenzie transition belt extended east as far as Cape Bathurst, or even Cape Parry. East of Parry has been, for nearly or quite a century, a belt from 100 to 200 miles wide that was not, properly speaking, inhabited. Then, at or before reaching Cape Bexley, you come to the real snow-house dwellers who, excepting their summer tents, have no housing other than of snow. Snow continues the winter house northeastward into Victoria and the other inhabited islands and eastward along the mainland coast to the Hudson Bay district and Baffin Island, with some use of snow houses in Ungava east of the Bay.

The true snow house people, those with whom domed snow dwellings are standard and not a makeshift, are at present less than 10,000 in number—perhaps only 7,000 or 8,000. Two hundred years ago when the Eskimo population may have been 100,000 to 200,000, the ratio of snow house dwellers to the rest was probably not very different from what it is now.

Approach toward perfection in dome snow house building varies with districts. Obviously it must vary also with individuals.

Some of the poorest dome houses are the ones best known through pictures. As said, the Eskimos of northwest Greenland use snow houses merely as emergency dwellings or when traveling, but these are the group who have been most frequently visited by explorers—this because, since the beginning days of photography, attainment of the Pole has been a chief northern endeavor and it was realized early that Smith Sound is one of the most favorable gateways to the Pole.

The Cape York or Smith Sound snow house is frequently not merely irregular in shape, showing lack of individual skill or knowledge of principles in the builder, but is even of nearly conical rather than dome shape, which shows that the community lacks a fundamental grasp of principles. For a house that departs notably from a perfect dome shape will necessarily begin to cave in soon after it is finished.

The Cape York house, therefore, is necessarily built of fairly strong (hard) snow blocks, for otherwise caving would be immediate and disastrous. Even when the blocks are strong the house cannot be very large because the strain toward cave-in increases rapidly with the size of that area which does not conform to dome principles.

Approximately speaking, snow houses improve architecturally as you go west or southwest from northwestern Greenland into the Canadian archipelago and to the North American mainland until they approach nearest perfection between King William Island and Coronation Gulf. In that locality, when snow is nearly perfect and the community's best craftsmen are working together, a dome can be erected for assembly purposes which is 18 or 20 feet in diameter and 9 to 11 feet high (the builders, toward the last, standing on temporary snow platforms). Such houses are occasionally without sign of cave-in a week or even two weeks later. There seems no evidence available of how far after that the settling can continue without an inward bulge appearing. (See below on Building a Dome Snow House.)

A practical inference from the above is that a traveler cannot expect natives to build dome snow houses for him except in a limited part of the Eskimo territories. An American Boy Scout is more likely to have ideas on how to go about it than is the average Eskimo boy of Alaska, Siberia, or Greenland partly because the Scout has read more and partly because he thinks it would be great fun to build a snow house; while the eastern or western Eskimo, if he has heard of snow houses at all, thinks of them as unfashionable and hence inferior.

Eskimo children build play houses of snow throughout nearly the entire Eskimo world but, outside of the dome areas, these are about like the play houses of children anywhere—in Vermont, Montana, or Norway.

Makeshift snow houses, not much better than children's, are made by grown people. For instance, when a hunter of northern Alaska is forced to sleep out, perhaps through losing his way on a hunt, he builds a coffin-like box. This may be 4 feet wide, 7 feet long, and the walls erected by laying the blocks as if they were sods in the wall of a sod house. Or the blocks may be put on edge, in which case they should be very heavy, say 30 by 20 inches, with a thickness of 8 to 12 inches as against the 4- to 6-inch thickness of blocks used by dome builders. When the walls are high enough, perhaps only 2 or 3 feet, the Alaskan makes an A-roof by leaning together pairs of blocks that stand on opposite walls. The gable ends he fills in roughly, then chinks all crevices with soft snow, cuts a hole in one of the walls big enough to crawl through, shoves in through this hole a block which he is going to use for a door, crawls in himself, closes the door, and makes afterward one or more tiny holes for ventilation.

A chief difficulty of these houses is that they usually get so warm from the occupant's body heat that snow melts on his clothes, making him wet. There are numerous cases of Alaska Eskimos having difficulty in getting home from one of these camps, even during clear weather; for their clothes, being wet, freeze stiff and are difficult to walk in. Besides, wet clothes, if you don't watch them carefully when they are freezing, will wrinkle up, perhaps leaving a bare wrist between sleeve and mitten, or, worse still, the trouser legs may pull out where they meet the socks. Then a wet garment, frozen or not, is less warm than a dry garment.

A type of snow house built in places like northern Alaska has a framework of wood, somewhat as described for earth-and-wood houses. The snow is then used as the earth is used. Such houses are generally made very large, the idea frequently being to pitch a tent inside them, which makes a cosy camp. Practically any kind of tent is good if it is pitched inside one of these barnlike structures.

BUILDING A DOME SNOW HOUSE

There is such infinite variety in the conditions under which snow houses could and should be built, and in the manner and expedients of building them, that nothing but practice leads anywhere near perfection. What should be done is to build a lot of snow houses just for practice, starting under nearly ideal conditions. When you become skilled you will gradually extend the application of the principles and technique to as much variety of conditions as you can find.

Suitable building snow for dome houses takes a lot of finding even at the right time of year on good terrain.

In the very early fall, while thaws still alternate with frosts, there is seldom any use trying to build a snow house—you then use tents. A little later, when thaws have ceased but temperatures still run as mild as only 10° or 20° below freezing, tents continue preferable and you would not use a snow house except in an extreme emergency. For even the heat from the bodies of the occupants would melt holes in the roof and the snow would be so damp in any case that it would be nearly impossible to keep your clothing dry.

Since the finding of suitable snow if of some difficulty under the best of conditions, it is well when traveling to begin watching for suitable drifts as camp time approaches. It has been the practice of the Stefansson expeditions to camp as much as an hour before the time planned if the party found itself crossing a drift that seemed particularly good. It happened on other occasons that they had to keep traveling for 2 or 3 hours past the intended camp time before finding a suitable bank.

The nearly perfect conditions for snow-house building are: That the terrain shall be level enough to permit strong sweeps of wind, yet with snags or other inequalities that will accumulate drifts 4 feet or more in depth. The winds that made the drift should have been strong rather than violent and the drift should have been made only a few days ago. However, a drift made yesterday by a terrific gale may be just right for house building, though a week or two hence it may have settled into such hardness that building is difficult.

Terrific blasts continued for several days or weeks, with the snow then lying for some time, will make practically the equivalent of ice, so that you have to hack or chop your blocks out of the bank instead of cutting them. They are then heavy, likely to break, difficult to shape, slippery on the wall, and are such good conductors that the dwelling erected is going to be a poor insulator from the cold.

Under other conditions snow that lies for some time, instead of becoming a solid block of ice becomes a mass of ice granules, the so-called sugar snow, granular snow. In extreme cases you can't cut this snow into blocks at all—it is almost as if you were dealing with a bin of wheat. Under medium conditions, the blocks you cut are fragile. If they are strong enough to handle, and you get your house built, you have a poor one, for not only are the grains icy, and therefore good conductors, but the blocks are also likely to be so overporous that the wind comes right through. This last can be remedied to an extent by heavy outside banking, as described below.

The snows of early winter, except in areas of particularly strong winds, are so soft even in the best drifts that the blocks crumble in handling. When they are just strong enough to handle you can get your house up, but it would soon begin to cave in; for the lower tier of blocks would be compressed gradually by the weight of those higher up. That destroys the dome shape; and when any part of a snow dome changes from its spherical curvature to flat, the next stage is bulging in—which leads to an eventual full cave-in. This process is seldom rapid enough for you to see the motion; but it may be so rapid that views a quarter of an hour apart show a noticeable difference.

The third Stefansson expedition reports taking such chances with soft snow as the following: When a house settled enough during the first 4 hours of occupancy that an inward bulge began to appear, they slept the night and got away 7 or 8 hours later with the sag of the roof still about 3 feet from the floor of what had been a 7-foot house. In practice he sometimes slowed a sag by using a T-shaped post for support where the sag first appeared—a rod with a board across the top. A pillar of snow blocks could have been used.

Building a dome with snow is simpler than with masonry, for stone is intractable and has to be shaped according to mathematical calculation; snow is tractable. Place each block in its approximate position, lean it gradually against the block that next precedes it, and, by trial and error, snip off piece after piece, or scrape where necessary, until the block settles comfortably into position. (See detailed description of method of building below.)

The equipment needed for building a snow house is: A rod or cane 3 or 4 feet long and one-quarter to, at most, 1 inch in diameter, for testing consistency of snow; a knife with a blade 14 to 20 inches long for cutting blocks, a shovel for piling soft snow on the completed house; a ball of string and two wooden pegs for determining the shape and size of the house when you are new at building—later you will judge by eye.

With four men building, one usually cuts the blocks, a second carries them to the builder, a third (inside the circle) does the building, a fourth (outside the circle) follows the builder to chink crevices. If two men are building, one would work inside the circle and the other outside. In such case a number of blocks would be cut by both and placed inside the intended circle of the house wall before the erection begins. When one man builds, and if the snow permits vertical cutting of blocks (see below), he gets most of the blocks needed from the floor; otherwise he has to crawl out through a temporary door in the wall to get them.

Select a snowbank 4 feet or more deep and of uniform consistency. Determine the surface hardness by your footprints. If the foot (softly shod in Eskimo boot or moccasin) makes no mark, the snow is too hard; if the foot sinks so that its entire outline is visible, the snow is too soft. If you see a faint outline (just enough so that another person could follow your trail), you assume the drift is suitable but you give it a further test.

Drive the testing rod down into the snowbank with a steady shove. If it sinks with even pressure, the snow is the proper consistency. If varying pressure is needed, the snow is in layers and not good, though possibly usable by an expert builder. The novice should whenever possible find nearly perfect snow, for a defective block may bring his nearly finished structure down like a house of cards.

We have described a drift permitting the cutting of vertical blocks, a great convenience especially when the builder has no assistant. If the snow has uniform consistency to four or more inches down but then begins to show stratification, it is still all right for horizontal cutting. In fact, a house can be built of uniform 4-inch snow lying directly on the ground; but then you are likely to be troubled with grass or pebbles, and the blocks are seldom very good.

When you find in one place a drift of suitable depth but unsatisfactory consistency, and shallow snow of better consistency elsewhere, it usually pays to carry the good blocks even 20 or 30 yards to the snowdrift rather than to build a house on shallow snow. If you must build on shallow, your house will have to be of larger diameter than otherwise needed, for it must be of a certain height and must keep to its hemispherical shape.

If you build right on earth, especially if it be on gravel, you must cover every part of the floor with at least 5 inches of snow; for the ground "radiates" cold. Try to see that the snow used for this purpose is not granular—if granular, it permits a draft up from the ground.

Building blocks should be domino-shaped, from 20 to 40 inches long, from 12 to 20 inches wide. If your snow is both tough and light you can have the blocks large. When you first cut blocks they are any thickness from 4 inches up; if the block is too thick you trim it down so that when it is finished it is 4, 5 or 6 inches thick, according to your desire.

According to their size and the density of the snow, the blocks will weigh from fifty to a hundred pounds and must be strong enough to stand not only their own weight when propped up on edge or carried around, but, if they are intended for the lower tiers of the house, must be capable of supporting the weight of 200 to 500 pounds of other blocks resting upon them.

You build the house preferably on a level part of a drift where the snow is three or more feet deep. In any case you either find a level spot or devise some common-sense way of overcoming inequalities or a slope. One way of handling a slope is to build the first tier as described below and then shave it off in such a way that the top of your wall is horizontal. This might mean cutting the blocks down to practically nothing along the uphill side. It may seem a waste of labor to build a full lower tier just to cut much of it away, but in practice doing so is easiest. Of course, as we shall have frequent occasion to remark or imply, you will be able to modify or even break many of the rules (including this one) when you become really expert.

The first step toward cutting blocks vertically is to dig a pit in your snowbank which, according to your tools and the circumstances, may be of any shape provided one side of it turns out to be straight, of a length equal to the blocks wanted, and as deep as you want them wide. You might keep in mind a block of standard size when cut, say, 36 inches long by 18 inches deep by 4 to 6 inches wide.

To produce your first block you hold the knife vertically and make a cut parallel to and 4 to 6 inches from the side of the straight 36-inch side of the pit, its depth the full length of your knife blade. At both sides of the pit you cut downwards; 18 inches below the surface of the drift you slice with the knife horizontally, undercutting the block.

Now you reinsert the blade of the knife into the lengthwise cut and pry by pulling the handle toward you gently. The block will come out full size and of fairly regular shape, even though in case of a 14-inch knife blade there were 4 inches at the lower side uncut.

You pull the block away to where you can handle it and, if there are any notable roughnesses, you slice them off with the knife. Should a corner break, destroying the rectangular shape of the block, you restore it to rectangular by shortening it that much with a cut of your blade. If the break would necessitate a shortening to less than 20 inches, you discard the block and cut a new one. For, unless you are very skillful, short blocks are more bother than they are worth.

If the blocks are obtained by vertical cutting, it is usually best, when they are placed in the wall of the house, to have uppermost the edge that was the surface of the snowdrift.

When the quality of the drift is not up to vertical block standards, you must cut horizontally. You start with the pit as before, only it need not now be more than 6 or 8 inches deep. The 36-inch cut is now 18 inches away from the face of your pit. When three cuts have described an 18- by 36-

171

inch quadrangle, you undercut say 6 inches below the drift's surface. This block is not going to come loose as easily as in the vertical case, especially if your knife blade is less than 18 inches long. You therefore move the knife back and forth several times so as to widen the cut, and then very gently you kick with your foot into the cut at various points cn the block. Of course, if the snow is really good, one sharp kick will bring the block out. Usually what you have to do with your foot is something like pecking at a block of ice to make it crack along a given line.

When the final kick loosens the block it sinks down a fraction of an inch, because of the undercutting. You now put your knife aside and slip your mittened hands under the edge of the block at points about 8 or 10 inches from either end. If the snow is very fragile, you can help by using one of your feet at the middle of the block so as to have three points of pressure in lifting it up.

When this block, a good deal thicker than you want it and of somewhat irregular shape, is on edge you slice down what was the underside of it until you have the domino shape desired, about 36″ x 18″ x 5 ″, if the snow is of good quality but somewhat thicker if it is soft. Houses have been built of snow so fragile that the blocks had to be 8 inches thick. This would be comparatively new-fallen snow which had not been pounded by wind into a sufficiently hard drift and had not had time to settle.

GROUND PLAN

The easest house to build is circular in ground plan; but for camping purposes a somewhat better shape is oval, the plan being to have the bed platform in the smaller end and the entrance in the larger one.

For a beginner planning to make a house of 10-foot diameter the sample way is to describe a circle with a 5-foot string and two pegs. Even if the house is to be egg-shaped, this is a good way to start, for you have the big end of the house follow the circle approximately.

The larger the diameter of the house the more you promote ease of building by keeping to the circular form. If you intend a house of 15-foot diameter or more, even the most skill-ful builder is practically forced to conform to a circle. Houses that big are seldom used for dwellings or even for 1-night camps, since they have to be so high that before the lower half of the interior, where the people are, gets warm enough for them the heat has accumulated just below the roof suffi-cient to melt a hole and escape.

A house of 10-foot diameter is comfortably large for 4 sleepers, snug for 5. You have the bed platform in the small end when the house is oval because you sleep with your heads toward the big end—your body being broader at the shoulders.

When there are more in the party than can be accommo-dated in a house of 10- or 12-foot diameter, you can either build 2 houses and use them separately or you can build 2 houses right against each other and when they are finished cut a door in the walls between, so as to make a 2-room dwell-ing. Three- or four-room houses are sometimes constructed in this way. In fact, there is no limit to the extension on cluster principles.

When skillful, you can build one house first and then build the second against it in such a way that if both hemispheres were complete they would intersect to an extent of 2 or 3 feet. Then you build the third house either against the first or second.

SETTING UP THE FIRST BLOCKS

With the finished dome house in your mind's eye, you set the first block on edge as a domino might be on a table. With your knife you then slightly undercut the inner bottom margin so as to make the block lean toward you—at a very small angle if the house is to be a big one; at a greater angle if it is to be small. The second block leans against the end of the first so that a pressure from the outside would not push one over without pushing both over. In similar manner the other blocks are erected until the first circle is complete.

It will be seen that once you have the first block standing on edge it is a simple matter to prop all the other blocks up by leaning one against the other. The nature of snow is such that when a block has been in place for 5 or 10 minutes in frosty weather it is cemented to its adjoining block and to the snow below at all points of contact and can be moved only by exerting a breaking force.

When the first tier is finished, you can start the second tier any place. From a point three or so blocks away from where you intend to begin the second tier make a diagonal cut, removing the upper quarter of one block, the upper half of the next, and about three-quarters of the third, bringing the cut almost down to ground level. Then take a block of ordinary size and put it in the niche so that its right-hand end rests against the end of the whole block that is next to the right. (The assumption here is that the builder is right-handed. Left-handed you would do these things in reverse.)

Once the second tier is started, build it to the left, leaning each block against the one previously set up, so that the walls rise in a spiral. Since you are building a dome-shaped house, the blocks of the second tier lean in more sharply than those of the first tier.

There is no change in method as the house approaches completion but, of course, the higher up the blocks are the more they lean in. If you lean each carefully against the one set up before it, no block can fall unless one or the other breaks. If the blocks are set up at all carefully and are of passable quality this will never happen.

There will be crevices everywhere between the blocks, some narrow and some wide. These are filled in with soft snow from the outside. It is done gently, for the wall is fragile at first. If the crevice is particularly large, you stick in first a slice of a discarded block and then tamp in soft snow around its edges.

When the wall gets three tiers high it becomes difficult for the man outside to hand blocks in over it. The builder then cuts a hole in the wall and blocks are shoved in to him.

Completing the dome looks difficult. Actually it is easy. If you take two dominoes and place them end to end so that they are nearly in a straight line, you will find it difficult to make them stand by leaning against each other. But the same two dominoes, leaning against each other at a sharp angle, will stand easily, supporting each other. The like is true of snow blocks—more so, for they meet on comparatively extensive surface while dominoes meet only on corners. Near the roof your circle is small compared with the ground tier. The blocks, therefore, meet at so sharp an angle that you can lean them together pronouncedly. They then support each other well.

When the house is all but completed, the builder finds in the center of the dome above his head a little irregular open space where the blocks do not quite meet. With experienced eye he decides how to enlarge this hole so as to make it big enough for the block he wants to put in it. With his knife he snips off projecting corners and now has above him an opening of regular shape. He next takes up a snow block, trims it so that, for easy handling, it is a little thinner than the average. It is, too, somewhat larger than necessary. This block the builder sets on end and lifts vertically through the hole, so that a person outside can see his two arms sticking up. He now allows the block to take a horizontal position in his hands and lowers it gently down upon the opening so as to cover it like a lid. The block is then trimmed down to size and slips into place.

When all cracks and crevices have been filled, and the builder has, as well, filled in the hole through which blocks were passed to him, the men on the outside throw shovelfuls of soft snow up on the dome. None sticks except what fills the outer part of the crevices that have been chinked, from inside by the builder or from outside by his assistants. Sliding down the sides the soft snow forms an embankment all along the bottom of the wall. Eventually, when the shoveling stops, the snow piled at the bottom makes the walls there perhaps 3 feet thick. Two feet up the banking is only 8 or 10 inches thick. The roof is in thickness only the 4 inches or so of the original blocks.

DOOR

What is to be the final door is made by collaboration of the builder within and his assistants without, and can be at any point except that, usually, it should not be where the temporary door was. For the original block of the lower tier has there been cut away and replaced, warmly but otherwise inadequately.

Inside an 11-foot house the builder lays off 7 feet for the bed platform. In the remaining 3 feet he digs a trench toward the door, 3 or 4 feet wide and 3 or 4 feet deep (if the drift on which the house stands is that deep). The men outside have dug a matching trench. They know where to dig for the builder has poked his knife out through the wall at a point that is going to be centrally over the door. The door is, then, where the inner and outer trench diggers meet under the wall.

No single block of the ground tier needs to span the trench, for it has taken about an hour to build the house and long before now the various blocks have coalesced so that the house is practically a one-piece structure.

RELATION OF DOOR TO WIND

In a 1-night camp you often have the door to leeward, but for a semipermanent camp it is best to have it at right angles to the prevailing winds. Then at the end of your alleyway you make a turn in the trench, like an elbow joint in a stovepipe, and have this open to leeward. Still more practical is to have a kind of T-joint trench at the end of your alleyway. Then you can open one end and close the other as the winds change, and have an open door to leeward with minimum trouble.

Some Esk'mos have the bottom of a snow house door at ground level, not applying those principles of thermodynamics which many of them use in the earth-and-wood houses described *ante*. However, if the camp is to be more than temporary they usually build up inside a platform or bench of snow blocks on which to sleep. This is frequently higher than the top of the door, giving part of the effect you get if you have the entrance by way of a trench.

If you are building a 1-night camp, very likely when the door is finished nothing further is done. But if the weather is bad, or threatening, and particularly if the camp is to be occupied for more than 1 day, a shed will be built over the trench outside the house. This is so small and therefore so easy to build that no directions for it are needed by men who have been able to erect the main snow house.

The main factor in the control of temperature of snow-house interiors in very cold weather (for reasons given below) is that the top of the door should be at least 18 inches lower than the bed platform, on which the occupants sit or lie. Usually there are about enough broken blocks inside a house when construction ends to build up this platform 6 or 8 inches, which means the top of the door should be at least 12 inches below the surface of the drift on which you build. This is why the drift should be at least 4 feet deep; it is not easy to crawl in through a door which is less than 3 feet high.

If the drift is so shallow that the above ends cannot be attained, and if you want maximum warmth in what amounts to the living quarters of your house, you must build up the bed platform correspondingly. Should this in turn be impossible, you are driven to the expedient of closing the door after the men have all come in, and may even have to open and close it as they go in and out. You use for this closure a block of snow just a little bigger than the door opening and beveled so as to fit snugly.

VENTILATION

Since, no matter how the house is heated, ventilation is necessary, you usually put a ventilating hole in the roof. Its diameter follows conditions of external temperature, abundance of fuel, and whether people are awake or asleep.

By trial you find that, when neither CO nor CO_2 is being generated by a fire, a snow house is adequately ventilated by diffusion if it has been constructed as just indicated and if there is constantly open a door with an aperture of from 5 to 8 square feet. When fuel of any sort is being burned there should be additional ventilation through a hole at the top of the dome. If this is a mere aperture, the escape of warm air melts the snow and gradually enlarges the ventilator. For this reason you should carry a sort of wooden stovepipe to insert in the roof. (Metal does not serve, for the warm air heats it through and that melts the snow which touches the metal.) When no ventilation except from the door is needed, you fill this chimney with a wad of something or other. With wadding, too, regulate the size of the aperture according to desire. Common practice is to stick two mittens up into the chimney to block it completely, pulling out one or both as ventilation is needed.

When a strong wind blows, gusts of it, and even swirls of snow, will enter through the door unless there is an alleyway as described. With such an alleyway the ventilation through the door is regular irrespective of winds. The cold, fresh air from outside wells up from the door below into the house as fast as, and no faster than, is necessary to replace the warm air passing out through the ventilator at the top.

If the house is of fairly soft snow, no banking is ordinarily thought necessary unless fuel is very scarce or lacking. But if the snow is hard, and particularly if it tends to be granular, then banking is something between moderately helpful and nearly essential. The best way for thorough banking is to erect a tier of average-sized blocks around the house in a circle that is broken only by the doorway. These blocks should lean inward considerably and should be 18 inches or 2 feet away from the house. The space between them and the house is shoveled full of snow; more is shoveled on top of that so the house is banked, but less and less thickly, for a total of 4 or 5 feet up.

Strong winds are rare out on the sea ice, at least when you are more than 50 miles from shore. Nearer shore and on land there are some districts where violent gales may cut your snow walls, largely by a sandblast effect. The danger line is near the ground.

Banking for this protection must naturally be according to circumstances. Perhaps with the pick-axe you carry for making a road through rough ice, or with an ice chisel, you can cut blocks of ice and build something like a stone wall of them to windward; perhaps you can get water and pour over the windward snow banking of your house; perhaps there are pieces of driftwood that can be used, sods, willows, grass that is held in place by something or other. Or you may have a piece of canvas that can be spread over the windward side of the house. (A canvas spread over the top of the dome may cause too much melting, but there is no corresponding danger for the lower part of the wall.)

PLATFORM INSIDE THE HOUSE

The house is now complete outside, with banking for warmth and protection against cutting winds. You will find on the floor, as we have said, fragments of blocks that were unsound and broke in handling, and other blocks which, for one reason or another, the builder did not use. Out of these you make a platform a foot or so high and covering about two-thirds of the floor space. This is the bed platform which provides your sleeping quarters. It serves to elevate you still further above the top of the door.

Over the bed platform you now spread a layer of caribou or other skins, with the hair side down. The hair side, if snowy, need not be brushed off, for it is against the snow and nothing will thaw; but the skin side, being upward is going to be warm and so must be brushed or wiped clean of all snow. On top of this is placed, hair up, another snow-free skin. Then come sleeping bags or blankets. The two layers of furs are put down not so much to protect you from cold as to protect the snow beneath from heat. The interior of the house is going to be warm presently and people are going to sit around on the bed platform and later are going to sleep on it. If the insulation were not practically complete, heat enough from the cooking and from the bodies would penetrate through the bedding to melt the snow and make the bedclothes wet.

When the temperature of the air outside, and consequently of the snow floor and walls of a newbuilt house, is zero F. or lower, a double layer of deerskins will prevent any thaw underneath the bedding, the snow there remaining as dry as sand in a desert. When the weather is above zero F., or at least when it is above 10° F., you will use tents in place of snowhouses. The procedure for them is described later.

HEATING

When the platform has been covered and the bedding, cooking gear, and other things have been brought in, a fire

179

is lighted—alcohol lamp, blue-flame (primus) kerosene stove, seal lamp, or whatever. If there is fire enough, it will thaw the walls, but that is what you intend it to do. If fuel allows, bring the temperature up to as high as 80° F.; meantime keep poking roof and walls gently with your fingers to keep track of the process of thawing. This, of course, is most rapid in the roof, for the hot air accumulates against it; usually the lowest tier of blocks, near the floor, does not thaw at all.

GLAZING

The thawing proceeds without dripping, because dry snow is the best sort of blotter and soaks water into itself as fast as it forms. When the inner layer of the roof approaches slushiness and the walls are damp to a less degree, either put out the fire or make a large hole in the roof, or both, and allow the house to freeze. This glazes it inside with a film of ice, giving it strength, with the further advantage that, if you rub against it, scarcely anything will adhere to your clothing. From the dry walls before the glazing you would get your shoulder white at a touch, with a good deal of snow perhaps falling on the bed.

We think of this heating to the slush point and subsequent cooling as mainly to produce an ice glazing; but it has an incidental further benefit. Those snow layers of the dome structure which directly touch the air within the house are no longer of their former intense cold, same as that of the outer air, but now hold a chill which is only a little below the freezing point. Consequently the dome no longer "radiates" into the house the chill that it did formerly. The snow over two-thirds of the floor is still at its outdoors temperature; but it is powerless to chill your room because it is held prisoner underneath the skins that have been spread over the bed platform. The only part of the house that still remains at nearly outdoors temperature and in contact with the air is the floor in front of the bed platform. If this is of gravel, as sometimes occurs when you have to build in a shallow drift on a sand bar, there is a tremendous amount of cold "radiated" upward, so you had better do something about it—at a minimum, spread over it some soft snow. Frozen earth chills the room a good deal more than snow; so does ice if it is very thick.

POSSIBLE MELTING OF ICE FLOORS

But if you build a snow house on ice only a foot or two thick, you may have a reverse situation; then the comparative warmth of the water is conducted through the ice, meeting the comparative warmth of even the floor levels of the house at a temperature that may produce thawing. This you can counteract by spreading snow over the ice, thus protecting it from the warmth of the house; whereupon the warmth of the ocean beneath ceases being adequate to produce melting.

This said melting is of course much more likely to take place on salt ice than on fresh; for, as discussed already, there is likely to be a crust of salt on top of sea ice, and this will turn into brine at temperatures well below the freezing point of fresh water.

The house, when well glazed, is so strong that without taking special care any number of men could climb on top of it. However, it is well to remember that the strength of snow houses is somewhat like that of eggs—they are difficult to cave in with pressure but easy to crack with a blow.

INTERIOR TEMPERATURE

The heating of snowhouse interiors, like ventilation, has a prime relation to gravity. When the temperature outdoors is —50° F. some such temperatures as the following will be recorded within doors when you are burning enough fuel to keep the room as warm as can be done safely—i. e., without danger of melting holes in the roof:

> —45° on the floor of the alleyway, just outside the door.
> —40° just above the floor and just in front of the edge of the bed platform.
> 0° on a level with the top of the door.
> 20° right on the bed platform.

40° at the level of your shoulders when you sit on the platform.

60° just above your head, about a foot below the highest point of the dome.

By mere gravity it ought to be still warmer nearer the dome; but the snow sort of radiates chill, and if you raise the thermometer to within 3 or 4 inches of the snow it may not read quite so high as it would 6 or 8 inches lower down.

The crucial temperature is in the highest air layers, which touch the roof; for they melt the snow unless that effect is checked by penetration of chill from outside. When the weather is —50° and when the highest point of the dome is between 2 and 3 inches thick, with the innermost quarter of an inch ice, a temperature of 60° can be maintained indefinitely without melting.

Temperatures around —50° are rare in the Arctic winter and it is, therefore, rare that you can keep your interior around 60°. Typically you have to be content with 40° or 45° a foot below the dome.

With temperatures from —10° to —40° you usually find that (with the "latent cold" already neutralized, as above) you can keep the full-size door open all night and sleep at a temperature in which it freezes a bit right where you lie. But if you drive a peg into the wall a little above your head and hang a fountain pen from it the ink will probably not be frozen in the morning—which means that the frost during this night has not gone more than a foot or 18 inches above the bed platform.

At temperatures approaching —50° you usually decrease the size of the door opening. The simplest way is to close the aperture with a snow block of the right size, out of which you cut a smaller door—one nevertheless big enough so that by crouching down you can crawl out if necessary. For the door is kept open not merely for ventilation but also in order that you may pass easily and quickly in and out. Sample emergencies which may arise are: A dog fight, which must be stopped immediately to prevent injury to dogs; the approach of a polar bear; break-up of the ice on which you are camped—all of these noises heard through the floor, as described below.

TO PREVENT HOUSE MELTING

If the weather outdoors grows warmer than the temperature in which you made the camp, your body heat may be too great or the cooking heat may raise the temperature high, so that the roof will commence to melt. This is not so much a sign that the house is too warm as that the roof is too thick; so you send a man out with a knife to shave it thinner, perhaps from 4 down to 2 inches, giving the outside cold a chance to penetrate and neutralize the heat from within.

METHODS OF DEALING WITH DRIPPING

We have said that during the thawing which precedes the glazing of a new house the thaw water is soaked up into the dry snow, blotter-fashion. After the freezing has changed this slush to ice a further melting will not result in dripping if the dome is nearly perfect in its curvature and free of downward projections; for the water, instead of dripping, will trickle down the sides. But, as also explained above, the temperature of the house decreases rapidly as you approach the floor. Accordingly, the water, as it trickles, will first reach snow that has not been glazed, producing by congealing there a new, somewhat irregular glazing. If there is enough water so it continues running still farther down, it will either just freeze a certain distance above the floor or else it will trickle all the way down to the snow of the floor, where it will certainly freeze.

Because of this possible trickling, and also because snow might crumble down, the bedding usually should not go nearer the wall than about 6 inches, leaving an open space between.

If unevennesses in the roof produce dripping, in spite of shaving the roof thin as explained above, there are two other remedies. The first and better is to shave or chisel away the unevenness, restoring this part of the roof to an approximately perfect curvature. When that is impossible (as, for instance, when a cave-in has begun) you apply a temporary remedy by providing blocks of snow of shape and size anything between that of a house-building brick and that of a half-pound cake of soap. Press one up against the roof where it drips. The water will immediately freeze, causing the snow to adhere to the roof. Even without freezing (as in weather near the freezing point) snow will adhere to a wet surface. As water now gathers in toward the dripping point it is soaked by this chunk of snow blotter. You have to keep a watchful eye; when the blocks are soaked nearly to capacity, and are about to drop, you replace them with others.

The snow block blotters are indicated when you know that the house is going to be at an extreme heat for only a little while. For instance, a thaw during cooking will usually stop when the cooking is over.

TO PREVENT HOARFROST

It may happen that the weather turns enough colder than the temperature in which you made camp so that hoarfrost begins to form on the inside of the roof and to drop like snowflakes. On this sign that the roof is too thin, a man goes out with a shovel and spreads on soft snow enough to blanket it suitably.

LIGHTING

One ordinary commercial candle gives more, or better, light in a snowhouse than a 50-candle-power electric bulb would give in a drab room. For the dome is practically a hemisphere of diamonds, every facet reflecting light, multiplying and diffusing it uniformly. This light is comfortable, easy on the eyes. The diffusion is so effective that if the single candle that lights the dome is behind you your body throws only a scarce noticeable shadow on the book you are reading.

When a snowhouse is heavily banked only 2 or 3 feet up and when, therefore, a good part of the dome is only 3 to 6 inches thick, you get enough light from outdoors, even on a densely overcast day, so that there is no need for a candle. You do not, in fact, need a candle for some time after sundown or before sunrise; a full moon in a clear sky will give you enough light for dressing and even for handling cooking utensils (but, of course, not enough for reading). When a house stands on sea or lake ice there may be considerable light in

184

daytime coming up through the floor in front of the bed platform.

The coming in of light from several or all sides has its drawbacks. The chief is that it may produce snowblindness. Similarly there may be too much light when you are recovering from this eye trouble. In such cases you sometimes throw canvas over the house. This has the disadvantage that it blankets the snow so as to produce melting of the roof from the indoors heat.

WINDOWS

Especially when a snowhouse is intended for long residence, window panes of ice are sometimes used. In addition to admitting more light, these panes have the advantage that they melt less easily than snow, being good conductors of the outside cold. A sample use of an ice window is to furnish bright light where you want it for cooking and at the same time to prevent the cooking apparatus from melting the wall in its immediate vicinity. (We have described in connection with earth-and-wood houses the ways of securing and shaping ice window panes.)

The snowhouse is practically soundproof, most so if the blocks have been cut from new or fairly soft snow; they are increasingly soundproof with heavy banking. The soundproofness is less if a house is unbanked or if the snow it is made of is granular or so hard packed as to approach ice.

But sounds come into a house through the floor. When you are camping on sea ice the crunching of snow under the tread of a polar bear can be heard several hundred yards away if your ear is near the floor. Since polar bears are dangerous to sleeping dogs, and also because their flesh and fat may be needed for food and fuel, sea travelers always have "polar bear on the brain," and with most of them this works while they sleep. A man obsessed either with the fear or the value of bears will hear their tread through deep slumber, apparently farther away than the dogs do. Undoubtedly dogs have better hearing, and their ears are equally near the snow; but they are not as keenly on watch for that particular sound. Doubtless a chief reason why the occupant of a snowhouse hears through the floor is that otherwise the house is absolutely silent; a dog, out of doors, may be distracted by various noises.

A frequent evidence of the soundproofness of snowhouses and of the transmission of sound through the floor is that when there is a dog fight you hear them spurning the snow and tumbling about but don't hear the growls, barks, and yelps.

That occupants seldom hear through the snowhouse door, although this is usually open, seems to show that the sound is deadened on the principle of mechanical silencers.

One of the great comforts of a snowhouse is that you are not disturbed by a howling gale, so long as it merely howls; but you are instantly disturbed if the ice on which you are camped begins to break up under the stress of wind or current. The sounds of this will come to you through the floor from miles away in the quiet of a snowhouse but cannot be heard a few feet away in the din of a flapping tent. Still the reason you can't hear breaking ice in a tent is partly that the flapping blends with the general roar of ice breakage in such a way that exceptional sounds do not impress you.

A snowhouse settles rapidly if built of soft, new, spongy snow. The other extreme is when you build of snow that has practically turned to ice through lashing by a gale and through long rest in its drift. That material is sometimes chosen if you don't care for warmth and need a house that will stand up a long time, as, for instance, if it is a storehouse or perhaps intended for the sleeping quarters of well-furred dogs that need shelter from the wind rather than warmth. Such structures will stand for months without losing their shape; but even they do settle a bit.

A house settling with intermediate or normal rapidity gets too small for its occupants in 2 to 4 weeks. A dwelling which at first has a clearance of about 2 feet above the heads of the occupants when they sit on the bed platform may have a foot clearance in 3 weeks. By that time, also, the walls have turned to ice and the house is no longer warm. There may have been a few times when a seal oil lamp has smoked or the roof may have been darkened by tobacco smoke, in which case you no longer have the uniform soft effects produced by reflection of candle or seal oil light from crystal surfaces.

For several reasons, then, the house is no longer as good as new, and Eskimos customarily make fresh camps in anything between 2 and 5 weeks.

The process of building the new house, shifting the few belongings of an Eskimo family or of a traveling party, and setting up full housekeeping in the new quarters, need not take more than 3 hours, and seldom takes more than 4.

If you think of the shifting of quarters as equivalent to housecleaning and mentally split up the 4 hours among, say, 20 days, you see that the average time for housekeeping and tidying is not great.

Housekeeping in snowhouses offers many chances for simplification. When you want to hang up something, you drive a peg in the wall. If you want a shelf, you drive in two pegs and put a board on them. If your pillow is not high enough, you just put a block of snow at the right place under the bedding—the bedding insulation will keep an ice pillow from melting, as it does the rest of the snow beneath the skins. If you want to look out, you make a hole in the wall; then you plug it with snow when you are through looking. Similarly, if you want to move some object in or out, you cut a hole in the wall, do your shifting, and then close the aperture with a block of the right size, or with several blocks.

If dogs have no access, you can put down low in front of the bed platform anything you want to freeze and preserve, as, for instance, meat or baked beans. When you want them you just reach down and get them. If dogs have access, you can freeze things similarly and then preserve them safe from dogs and unthawed beneath your bedding. When you throw down into the alleyway anything that is not greasy, you have a perfect disposal. For instance, if it were half a bowlful of oatmeal, you could half an hour later step on it down there in your stocking feet without a sign of stain on your socks, even if they were pure white.

VISIBILITY OF SNOWHOUSE CAMPS

In direct light of sun or moon, a snowhouse is clear to see because of shadows. But when there are no shadows because sunlight is uniformly diffused through an overcast sky, you cannot see one at all unless perhaps if you are wearing amber glasses. You may walk right into it as you would a snowbank. When moonlight is similarly diffused through clouds, the house, unless lighted, is similarly invisible. But with a candle burning inside, the house will show up in darkness, and to a less extent in moonlight, as a dome glowing softly pink, brightest at the top because it is there thinnest, the light not visible in the lower parts if there is banking. This soft glow is not likely to be visible, however, at more than half a mile or a mile. When there is an ice window the pane is visible considerably farther, probably several miles.

But a snow camp will be visible as a whole in diffused light even when a snowhouse is not. For there practically always is something dark—dogs, sledges, piles of meat, skins that are drying, and so on. Dark things are visible in diffused light at long distances, though not as far as on a clear day.

From the air a snow camp would be visible in diffused light through its dark objects and discolorations. But an airman particularly needs to remember that temporarily, during, or immediately after a heavy and quiet fall of snow, everything may be white, even the dogs sleeping each under his snow blanket. Then a snow camp may well be unobserved when you are passing over it.

A snowhouse may be lined for any of several reasons. At low temperatures the purpose is likeliest to be to make the house warmer or to save fuel. When the temperature outdoors rises toward the freezing point, a lining may be put in to keep the interior heat from melting the roof. If you are afraid of snowblindness, or if you are recovering from it, you would line to secure darkness.

White men sometimes line snowhouses because they are afraid of rubbing against snow. This is really a sign that they do not yet understand how to use a snowhouse, for the blocks cannot crumble on touch after the glazing of the upper part of the dome, and there is seldom occasion to touch the lower part of the wall. Again, white men seem to line snowhouses for psychological reasons—the idea-association of snow and cold is so strong with them that they don't feel comfortable. However, a thermometer will usually serve even better than a lining to convince a tenderfoot that he is not necessarily cold just because he is close to snow. Stefansson reports that he found it advisable if not necessary to make this demonstration with new men, and Harold Noice says in *With Stefansson in the Arctic* that his own feeling of comfort increased sharply when he had been convinced by the thermometer that the interior of the house was really warm.

ESKIMO CUSTOM

Before whites came, some Eskimos used skins to line snowhouses. Around Coronation Gulf, the heart of the snowhouse district, the principle of using linings was known by hearsay but was seldom if ever applied—then probably only in case of fuel shortage. In Baffin Island, on the contrary, lining appears to have been frequent. The conscious motive was doubtless the increase of warmth rather than the saving of fuel, for temperatures of from 80° to 100° were desired as an accompaniment to sitting naked. (Coronation Gulf people usually were dressed in their unlined snowhouses, although they sometimes sat stripped to the waist upon the bed platform, the children sometimes playing on the furs completely naked.)

GLAZING PREFERABLE

It is desirable that a lined snowhouse, like any other, should be glazed. As already stated or implied, a snowhouse that has just been built from blocks of medium hardness would crumble under the weight of a child. When, however, over the upper half of the dome the inner portions of each block have first been allowed to freeze, the resulting eggshell of glazing makes the house so strong that, although the lower tiers are still nothing but snow, the structure as a whole will nevertheless support several men and probably would support about as many as could stand on it. Dogs at play on occasion break down an unglazed house, though when it has been set with glazing a thousand-pound polar bear would not break through by merely scrambling over. There are, in fact, numerous records of polar bears climbing upon glazed houses but few, if any, accounts of the houses having broken. What does break them are sharp blows, as when a man stamps with his heel. A bear will gash a roof with a scratching blow from his forepaw.

CLOTH LINING PREFERRED

When cloth lining is available, it is preferable to skins. It should be both thin and nearly airproof. It could be cut and sewed into dome shape but seldom is, for then it would fit only one size of house. Ordinarily you have a piece that is square, or even irregular, in shape, with tie strings sewed or otherwise fastened in numerous places.

METHOD OF LINING

If the house is strong enough, as when glazed, a man climbs up on it outside, sticks a knife down through and makes a hole say 2 inches in diameter. Someone inside then shoves up through the hole the central tie string of the cloth. The man outside ties this to the middle of a cross-piece of wood so that the cloth hangs an inch or two below the snow roof. He then fills in the hole around the string with snow. Similar arrangements are made at other points of the dome until the cloth is suspended so as to be on the average 2 or 3 inches from the snow everywhere—perhaps a little more at the lower parts of the wall where it hangs slack.

If, for want of fuel, you are unable to glaze a snowhouse, the whole job of suspending the lining is done from inside. The operator makes holes in the dome from inside, pushes out the tie strings with their cross sticks, and fills the holes by tamping with soft snow from inside.

VENTILATION

There is usually a hole in the cloth corresponding to the ventilator hole in the snow dome. Because the cloth has been suspended from the center, the ventilator is usually a little off center in a lined house.

c. Tents

CHOICE OF TENT CAMP SITES

It is everywhere important to choose house sites carefully; in the Arctic this is doubly important with tents, for reasons which will appear. We therefore discuss under Tents the general subject of camp location, referring mainly to winds and their effects, for these are the chief foes of comfort, convenience, and safety.

In matters other than winds and their effect, temperate zone experience, and forethought based on it, are in the main suitable guides for Arctic camp location.

DO NOT CAMP IN A LEE

The first instinct of Europeans when they go to cold lands is to build or camp in a shelter. But lees gather snow in an open country. You should not build a house in a lee, for it may get covered and that will be a nuisance. You must not pitch a tent in a lee, for, weaker than a house, it collapses under the pressure when snow buries it. Well before collapse the snow covering may bring serious results. Carbon dioxide gathers through decrease in ventilation so that lamps will not burn and breathing grows difficult; carbon monoxide may gather, and then there can be tragedy. (For further discussion of monoxide poisoning, see Chapter 10.)

LONG HISTORY OF MONOXIDE TROUBLES

There is a series of recorded difficulties with carbon monoxide from the Barents expedition of 1596 to the Byrd expedition of 1929. In a good percentage of the cases the trouble was in one way or another connected with tents or camps becoming snow-covered because of a lee. Three out of four of the Andrée expedition of 1898 died of monoxide poisoning, apparently because they had camped in a lee.[6] Their bodies were discovered in 1930.

A white man's desire for what might be called natural protection for his camp sometimes takes very special forms. The 1933–34 expedition which the U. S. S. R. sent out on the *Chelyuskin,* under Professor Otto Schmidt, consisted of a hand-picked personnel. Yet on page 142 of *The Voyage of the Chelyuskin,* New York and London, 1935, we find:

" * * * A number of tents * * * were let down a good meter into the ice so as to present less area to the wind.

---

[6] For causes of deaths in the Andrée party, see Stefansson, *Unsolved Mysteries of the Arctic,* New York, 1939.

As soon as the cold decreased a little, water began to soak into the pit and swamp it. Those 'experimental' tents had to be completely rebuilt in another place."

By this procedure the ice found itself between two warmths—from below the warmth of the unfrozen sea and from above the heat of the tent's interior. Therefore it melted. You can never safely use ice or snow for wall, floor, or roof except when inner heat is counterweighed by outer cold.

If in winter a camp is on land in −50° weather, the snow in the floor is at first −50° and the earth just below −50° at the surface, though it gets less cold gradually as you go down. The sea water below the *Chelyuskin* tents was at 27° or 28° F. Under such conditions you should camp on ice as thick as possible, to get away from the comparative warmth of the water. You should, if you can, have snow on your floor for further insulation. You should build up a platform of snow (skin-covered, as in a snowhouse) to sit on so that you may be sufficiently warm up there without having it get so warm lower down that the floor tends to melt. In fact, you should keep a specially watchful eye on the laws of physics when you camp on sea ice that is only a few feet thick.

IN A FOREST

Naturally in a forest you always pitch camp in a lee, for in woods the snow does not pile up by drifting. It would be silly to hunt for an open space and pitch camp there just to fit in with principles that apply in treeless country.

IN MOUNTAINOUS COUNTRY

Where you are a stranger, a forest, then, or very extensive patch of willows is the only terrain where you would camp in a lee. But if you know the country, you can sometimes find lees extensive enough to be safe among hills or mountains.

Strong winds passing overhead, giving you an extensive lee near a mountain, are reported chiefly from Greenland but are not unknown in northwestern Alaska back of Cape Lisburne, and may be found, no doubt, here and there in all mountainous areas. The difficulty is you seldom can tell in the summer that there is going to be a safe lee in a given place the following winter. In midwinter you can, of course, determine it from the character of the snow which already lies on the ground.

In mechanics this overhead lee resembles the dry space behind certain waterfalls, due to the water having such speed that it shoots over the edge of the cliff and descends in a curve. A wind from inland blowing 50 miles per hour might not strike the ground for one or even several miles after passing the edge of a cliff or very steep slope that is a mile high.

HOW CAMPS GET BURIED

In a forest or any other big lee you can leave sledges, baggages, etc., to windward of your camp; but you cannot safely do so if the tent is in the open, for these obstructions will produce their own lee, forming drifts to and upon the tent. Neither should things be left in the lee of the tent, for they will get covered up.

No obstruction can produce in any one storm a snowdrift deeper than its own height, so that it does not matter for a single night's camp if the tent is in the lee of your sledge; but it does matter a whole lot whether the sledge, being lower, is in the lee of the tent—it may get so deeply buried that you will have difficulty in digging it out next morning. But if you are going to live in a tent for several weeks, the sledge, which has doubtless been moved meantime, will produce in the second blizzard another drift of the same height as the first, though perhaps at a different angle. Eventually various drifts from various obstructions will be so superimposed that your whole camp site is a hill in which your tent gets buried. In short, if a camp is to be occupied several weeks, and if you are not in a "trade wind" area, you should see to it if possible that no drifts at all are formed near enough to the tent to start the burial process.

WHERE WINDS ARE REGULAR

There are places where winds of only a few directions occur, behaving almost like trade winds though usually locally produced by land configuration. Stefansson reports a coast, the north Alaska shore from Barrow, or at least from the Colville, to near the International Boundary, where for several score miles only three winds occurred that were strong enough to form bad snowdrifts—S. W., N. E., and E. N. E. In that district they felt free to leave a sledge standing only a few yards from the tent if it was to the northwest or southeast of it. Similarly, two or more houses or tents could there stand close together without danger of getting each other covered up by snowdrifts, if they were placed approximately on a N. W.-S. E. line.

CONTROLLING DRIFTS

An example of the possible great commercial or military importance of realizing that any obstruction will produce a snowdrift in its lee was furnished during the construction of the Hudson Bay Railway through the last one or two hundred miles before reaching Churchill. The first winter of building, the crews of men cleared the track after a storm by shoveling in both directions, thus making a trench which had the railway track at its bottom. In the next storm the trench filled level with the windward embankment, whereupon the track was shoveled clear again, heightening each embankment. Before spring the track was buried so deep on the open prairie that a freight train passing between the ramparts was nearly invisible from a distance. This method of snow shoveling cost thousands of extra dollars in wages and slowed up construction to an extent for which the wages were not an adequate measure.

Next winter the work and expense were reduced to a small fraction. The engineers had noted that all the strong, and therefore drift-forming, winds were from one direction. Accordingly, such snow as gathered on the track was always shoveled off to leeward. The snowdrift produced by that rampart was directed away from instead of across the track.

WINDBREAKS FOR TENTS

If you pitch your tent on an open prairie, it can have, and in most cases should have, a windbreak of snow blocks. It is windbreaks at intermediate distances that bury a camp; those far enough or close enough protect it. A far windbreak is usually beyond one's resources—it has to be something as big and effective as a range of hills or low mountains. A windbreak right up against a tent is therefore indicated.

If it is a one-night camp, a tent should, then, be protected by a wall of snow or ice blocks that forms a segment of a circle to windward, and a few feet away. Even a wall only 2 feet high is of considerable value for a 7-foot tent. A 5-foot windbreak for a 7-foot tent is about all that is worth building, for it matters hardly at all even in the most violent gale if the peak of your tent is exposed to the wind, so long as the sides and bottom of the tent are not exposed.

MANNER OF BUILDING

A windbreak wall can be built after European sod-wall fashion; but, if the campers have the necessary skill, it is usually much quicker, and is in some other ways better, to build Eskimo-style, curving in just enough so that the wall segment will stand on dome principles. In such case the windbreak is just far enough from your tent so that a man can work comfortably between.

FOR PERMANENT CAMP

If you are going to spend several days, or think there is danger of the wind changing direction in the night, you might build a windbreak in a circle completely around the tent.

Usually such things as building windbreaks are not a waste of time. For instance, after six men have cooperated in the pitching of the tent, two would be occupied with cooking, two staking out and feeding dogs, while the remaining two could build the windbreak and have it done by the time the others finish their jobs. Besides, activity is sometimes necessary for keeping warm.

REINFORCED WINDBREAKS

If you think that a particularly violent gale may come up (for instance, if you are encamped in a known "blow hole"), it might be well, if water can be obtained, to pour a few bucketsful over the windbreak wall, whether this is made of snow blocks or of ice. In the case of snow blocks this watering is not to hold them together—they will stick to each other anyhow. It is to make a glazing on the windward side of the snow so that the gale shall not cut it away. In winds of 50 to 70 m. p. h. even fairly hard snow blocks are gradually cut, perhaps not so much by the wind itself as by drifting grains of snow acting in the manner of a sand blast.

Another way of protecting a snow wall from breaking is to cover the windward side with some fabric, or with skins.

TENTS, GENERAL

While the warmth of a tent, like that of clothes, depends on air spaces, it is not practical with fabric tents to have enough of these air spaces within the fabrics themselves. The equivalent must be obtained by using a double tent.

Skin tents, like skin garments, derive their warmth largely from air spaces, those between the hairs where the fur is so twined that the interstices amount to nearly the same as air cells. Or, as in the case of caribou, the warmth is partly secured on the above fur principle and partly through the hairs themselves being hollow and filled with air.

However, even with skin, it is frequently advisable to have a double covering so as to get a layer of air, say an inch thick, to separate the outer and inner covers. This is easily attained with furs—place the fur sides toward each other and the hairs hold the skins apart. To keep an air space between two cloth covers you stretch the tent tightly so that bagging shall not obliterate the space, or else you have to stuff something, as grass or feathers, in between the layers.

With skin tents it is usually best in summer (when you need only one layer) to keep the hair side out. The same is true in winter when you have only a single layer; but if you have two layers the hair is out on your inner covering and in on the outer.

SHAPE OF TENT

To save material and economize on heat, there should be little waste space in a tent. This means that a tipi form, or any with a sharp peak, is undesirable—the peak requires extra material and greatly increases the necessary fuel consumption in that the warmest air gathers where occupants get no direct use from it. If your tent does have a peak, however, you can get some indirect use by hanging there things that need drying. This by no means justifies the peak, for a dome-shaped tent (most economical because of the law of spheres) is so much more easily kept warm that garments will dry better suspended from its roof than from the peak of a tipi or A-shaped tent.

Translucence of a tent promotes interior warmth when there is sunshine; it enables you to utilize daylight; even at night you can make indoor use of moonlight and other natural night light. You can light the interior from a bon-fire which is near it outside. A white tent is least easily detected on snow background, but this is rarely of much value, even when you want to hide, for there are likely to be many dark, easily visible objects around, such as dogs, sledges, people. A disadvantage is that in a translucent tent you must bandage your eyes when trying to make a quick recovery from snow blindness. Indeed, snow blindness may develop inside the tent—a person whose eyes are in perfect condition at the beginning of a 3-day blizzard has, in more than one reported case, become snow-blind on the second or third day of confinement. Snow blindness may come on, or be aggravated, during sleep; so that it may be advisable, even for those whose eyes are perfectly well, to sleep with them bandaged. Whenever awake during the day, and if you have reason to fear snow blindness, you would in a translucent tent, or in a snow house, use amber glasses as if you were out of doors.

OPAQUE TENTS

A dark tent cuts down the utilization of outdoor light, naturally. Its chief advantage is that it prevents snow blindness from developing indoors and helps to cure that which has resulted from out-of-doors exposure.

TENT FORMS

There are current numerous bright ideas which work badly, indifferently, or at least have drawbacks not ordinarily men-tioned by their proponents. For instance, the door which ties shut like the mouth of a dufflebag works only while the material is either not frozen or else frozen and dry. When moisture gets in at below-zero temperatures, which is soon, the mouth of the bag becomes increasingly difficult to tie, and finally impossible. That you do not find more accounts of this trouble in the books of explorers is mainly for the reason which Peary gave frankly—that the things he had learned from experience were trade secrets and should be kept for his own advantage or that of the country and flag he represented. Other travelers have been reluctant to describe defects of equipment because the inventions were their own, those of friends, or of famous men whom they did not want to seem to criticize.

ONE-PIECE FLOORED TENTS

An idea usually found in connection with the dufflebag door is having a floor sewed into one piece with the rest of the tent, the theory being that the snow cannot then get in. The troubles with this are numerous. You don't always succeed in brushing from your clothes all snow before crawling in through the door; a swish of wind may bring in snow while you are entering; moisture from the breath will condense on the roof and sides of the tent, to drop practically in the form of snow. Some of the snow, however it enters, will get under you when you sit down or lie down. Then it melts and turns to ice which permeates or clings to the flooring.

If one has a floor, it should be separate from the rest of the tent.

MONOXIDE DANGER

An aggravated danger of the completely enclosed tent—an attached floor and a dufflebag door—is that of monoxide poisoning, which we discuss elsewhere. For if a tent is capable of being made airtight you are likely to take a chance on making it so when you feel very cold, or you may by accident close the door tighter than intended.

The conical tent with central pole is in most places easiest to pitch and it stands up pretty well, but not nearly so well as the hexagonal or octagonal tent with bamboo ribs hereafter described.

Bell tents, wall and center pole, are not so very hard to pitch. For special method of pitching see below.

198

The A-tent is undesirable in windy weather, for the rectangular surfaces will belly in and hold wind like the square sails of a ship, making a terrific strain in case of a gale.

An A-tent with walls is worse for stormy countries than the simple A-tent in that the wind catches still more, and holds.

UMBRELLA TENT

Perhaps on the whole the most successful European invention of a tent for windy and cold countries is the umbrella type. These are in shape cones of four, six, or eight sides, constructed on the umbrella principle as to ribs, these, however, being straight, unbendable, of bamboo. Such four-sided tents were used by the British in the Antarctic and by some others. But each side of a four-sided tent is so big that it bellies in before a strong wind and the tent is likely to blow away or break down. Six bamboo ribs are, on the whole, most advantageous—one-sixth of the circumference is then the most that fully bellies in to hold the wind. The two adjoining sectors, though bellying in somewhat, nevertheless spill the wind. Eight sides would be best of all if it were not that you then have a larger bundle to carry on your sledge.

The only structural problem with this tent is to devise a good cap into which the upper ends of the ribs fit at the apex. So far as I know, this detail has never been satisfactorily handled by a polar expedition. It is, therefore, a problem that should be tackled in a laboratory manner.

The four-, six-, or eight-sided umbrella tent is made double by having a slightly smaller tent of the same construction suspended from the inside. It is tied to each rib with tape at two or three points between floor and apex, and, of course, the apex fastened similarly. This gives, when the tent is well stretched, an air space of about 1 inch everywhere. The space will lessen somewhat, or may disappear, when the tent bellies in under a strong wind; but it disappears at most only for a portion of two of the sides of a four-sided tent (if the wind blows right on a corner) and correspondingly for tents of six or eight sides.

The outer covering of a double-fabric tent should be windproof. There is some question as to whether the inner cover-

199

ing, or lining, should be similarly wind proofed. Probably it should. However, there is force in the argument that if the inner tent lets air through easily, then a considerable part of the steam from cooking and from the breath of the occupants will pass through and condense between the two tents. Then the hoarfrost dislodged by flapping will not fall on the beds but will slide down to ground level between the two coverings.

The best material which Stefansson has actually tried for a double tent is Burberry. This used to be a great deal better than any form of silk on the market, no matter how treated. There may have been developments since that would give a material surpassing Burberry. But no material will work which depends for windproofing on some such filler as paraffin, which at low temperatures makes the fabric stiff. Paraffin also cracks, especially at low temperatures, and drops out where the fabric bends.

EASY TO CARRY

The straight-ribbed type of tent folds into a long bundle and carries well on top of a sledge. The corresponding Eskimo invention, below, does not transport so well; but in most other respects it is better.

The Eskimo dome tent has little except portability to distinguish it from the Eskimo dome house already described. We add here, therefore, only a few points.

The dome house was assumed in our description to have a frame of willows that were of local growth. They might be somewhat crooked and they might be heavy and knotted. But tent framing which you are going to carry with you should be of slender, sapling willows, if you depend on Arctic materials. If you bring the material with you, as on a ship, it could well be of steamed hickory or other pliable and strong wood.

ROOF

In the house description we rather insisted that the shape be approximately hemispherical, for then a frame of minimum strength supports a reasonably heavy roof. In a tent you are going to have only light roofing and the willows can, therefore, be not only slender but also bent in a way that produces marked wall curvature and a roof that may be nearly flat, especially if the tent is large. A strictly hemispherical tent would always have to be of the same size; you can vary the size if the willows are bent for the walls and straight, or nearly so, for the roof.

One great advantage of this type of tent is that in emergencies you can make it of several small pieces of cloth—torn sail, for example. As said, you can make it practically any size—if you want it large, you lash the hoops so they overlap very little; if you want it small, you have them overlap a lot.

Eskimos sometimes carry a cover sewn in just the right size and shape to fit the frame when put up in a set way. That probably is a new adaptation—either borrowed from whites or a result of using cloth in place of skins.

POSSIBLE NEW STYLE TENT

The best two tents ever developed for cold weather are the dome-Eskimo and the straight-ribbed-umbrella type worked out by the British Antarctic explorers. It seems possible that our ingenuity and range of materials might enable us to develop a new tent combining the two ideas into a form superior to either. Suggestions are:

A tent might be made strictly like our umbrellas. The umbrella handle would then be the center pole of the tent, the ribs would hold it out into hemispherical shape, and the braces would not be useless, since you could put things up there to dry. Obvious difficulties are that, if the ribs were of steel, they might lose their resilience at very low temperatures—might break in bending—and that steel, in any case, is heavy. More hopeful, it seems, would be to find some wood like hickory which, perhaps through some form of reinforcing, would bend just right each time the tent is put up and would straighten out again for packing.

Another possibility is that curved ribs must be carried loose on the sledge during the day, as willows are by the Eskimos, and fitted in at camp time. They could then have the required curvature but would, of course, be unhandy on the sledge, as the Eskimo bent willows always are.

The Eskimo dome tent dispenses wholly with guy ropes; the British Antarctic straight-rib-umbrella type does also. Guy ropes would, therefore, probably be unnecessary, unless when in fear of a terrific gale you might want to run one rope to windward from the peak.

PITCHING TENTS OF VARIOUS TYPES ON ICE

On glare ice, the worst of all locations for a tent, it can be fastened down by any number of devices, each suggested by conditions. In extreme emergencies you can freeze down the edges by getting water through a hole in the ice a little distance off and sloshing it on to the edges of the tent, holding them down during the freezing. The difficulty is that when you break camp it is hard to avoid tearing the tent or carrying off with it (when you chop it loose) a considerable weight of ice.

ANCHORING WITH ICE OR SNOW

When ice is thin, you can cut through it, as when a New Englander puts up in winter ice intended for summer use. Blocks so obtained can then be put on the edge of the tent to weigh it down, the ice beneath previously roughened so as to give the weighting blocks a chance to hold. Perhaps an actual trench will need to be dug.

When snow is available, you first put enough blocks of it on the edges of the tent to hold it temporarily. Then you shovel up some loose snow for additional weight and to cement the blocks together. When you have enough weight on the tent flaps you pull them outward (with the snow load on them) till the tent is set to your liking.

If snow has a chance to set for half an hour during cold weather it becomes almost as hard as concrete and will hold the tent if a storm blows up later. If the storm is already blowing when the tent is being pitched, the same principles apply, though the pitching is more difficult. One or two men may have to hold the windward side of the tent while the snow is being piled on and for some time thereafter. Often the holding up is best done from the inside.

When you have a sledge, you can tuck the windward edge of the tent under one of its runners, weighting the sledge

down, if necessary, with blocks of snow. It is explained elsewhere that a sledge must not be left to the windward of a
tent, but this refers to one at a moderate distance. A sledge
standing right on the edge of a tent will hardly accumulate
a snowdrift.

TOGGLES FOR BELL AND OTHER TENTS

With a bell or other such tent, on glare ice, there would
be a wooden or other toggle at the end of each guy rope.
Dig a circular trench in the ice at a considerable distance
from the tent or dig a separate hole for each guy rope; put
the toggle, at right angles, down into the hole or trench and
pack in snow if a little is available, or finely chopped ice;
perhaps pour on a little water, if that seems necessary. If
the tent is pitched on snow, the toggles would be buried in
the snow and tamped down—as said, such packed snow sets
in the manner of concrete, not, of course, nearly so hard but
usually hard enough to hold a rope in a gale if the toggle is,
say, the length of a policeman's billy and strong enough.
The wall is banked and otherwise fastened down in the manner of a single cone tent.

One of the best ways to fasten the end of a tent rope on
ice is by "ice toggles." You cut parallel trenches (with ice
pick, pickaxe, hatchet, or whatever) 3 or 4 inches apart and
6 or 8 inches deep. Perforate the dividing wall, pass a rope
through, and tie.

A tent has to be carried on the sledge but the snow awaits
you at camp time. Over rough sea ice, the bulk of a load
is sometimes more serious than its weight, and even a dry
tent has some bulk. When ice from the breath of the occupants, cooking, etc., gathers in a tent through use, it not only
becomes heavier but also stiffer and therefore bulkier. The
tools you need for building a snow house are, practically speak-

---

[7] This is, of course, a comparison of tents with unlined snowhouses. However, a lining does not necessarily accumulate ice; in
cold weather a tent inevitably does, unless you can superheat it
and thus dry it occasionally (which practically means having a
wood stove and plenty of dry wood to burn).

Nares, in his *Voyage to the Polar Sea,* states that his tent weighed
31 lbs. 14 oz. before starting and 55 lbs. on return. In his *Farthest
North,* Nansen gives a similar result for his long sledge journey.

ing, none. For your snow knives are used for other purposes and your shovel is also a tool of general utility—you want it as badly for a tent as for a snowhouse.

While it takes longer to build a snowhouse than to pitch a tent, this is partly cancelled next morning; for you have to pack up a tent and load it on your sled, but you just walk away from a snow house.

When your breath and the steam from cooking rise to the roof of a snowhouse, they congeal and stay. In a tent they rise to the roof and congeal but do not long remain, for the flapping of even a slight wind will dislodge flakes that flutter down upon bedding and clothes, eventually melting. Not even in a perfect calm are you free from this snowfall; the flakes will loosen and begin to drop when the hoarfrost on the roof gets thick enough. However, some of your breath and the other moisture will remain on or in the tent fabric as icing.

While it takes a good deal of heat for an hour or more to neutralize the cold of snow walls at low temperatures, you do not thereafter need any heat except that from the occupants to keep a snow house comfortably warm; the temperatures, at least toward the roof, will continue to run well above freezing indefinitely. A tent, on the other hand, heats quickly when you light a fire but cools as quickly when the fire goes out. It has been found in an ordinary single wall tent of, say, 10-ounce duck, that when the temperature at night is −50° outside it is likely to be −10° or −20° indoors.

DRYING CLOTHES

Because snowhouses stay warm, you can dry wet clothes in them to some extent by merely hanging them up, and better by wearing them. In a tent you can similarly dry clothes while the fire is going. Clothes dried in snowhouses stay dry; if dried in tents, say during the cooking, they are likely to get wet again in the night. For instance, you might, in either snow house or tent, dry a wet sleeping bag by crawling into it. After the fire goes out the drying process would continue in a snow house; for, as said, the room is warm. But a tent gets so cold that hoarfrost would begin to gather in the bag; probably it would be at least as wet again next morning.

In good weather both tents and snowhouses are quiet. In a storm a tent (with the partial exception of the umbrella tent) makes a racket through flapping. A snowhouse in a gale is not only immobile but completely silent except, as mentioned, for sounds that may be transmitted through the floor and for the soft buzzing of granular snow that drifts over the roof.

VENTILATION

There is temptation for bad ventilation in a tent—you close up everything for warmth. When ice fills the pores of the cloth, and if the tent is well banked, you court monoxide poisoning. With a snowhouse there is every inducement to good ventilation—the building is designed for it and is comfortably warm even when well ventilated. (See chapter 10 for discussion of monoxide poisoning.)

Lights and cooking apparatus work better in a snowhouse. The flapping of a tent makes a primus or other flame flicker, reducing effectiveness and perhaps making smoke and soot. A candle gutters in a tent but burns decorously in a snowhouse. Besides, as explained, one candle will give more light in a snow dome than several even in a white tent—and a tent never stays white very long.

Those who have camped in tents have memories of inconvenience and discomfort, except, of course, under conditions where you burn in suitable equipment all the fuel you want. To snow camps the traveler looks back with memories of quiet, cosy well-being. This is even true where no fuel is available that can be satisfactorily burned in a snowhouse. For instance, David Hanbury tells in his *Sport and Travel in the Northland of Canada* that, although the midwinter temperature of the snowhouses near Back's River were always below freezing, and sometimes below zero, the occupants were nevertheless comfortable. Doubtless Hanbury's saying this harks back to his memories of tent camping among the forest Indians of the Bear and Slave Lake districts.

WINTER TENTS

For camping in a northern forest during summer practically any standard tent is suitable, if you remember that special devices have to be used against mosquitoes and sand-flies—you have to have tents that close tight except where there are windows or ventilating devices of fly netting.

Also for winter camping in a forest tents of standard make are suitable, with few exceptions. They should not be particularly high, for it is wasteful to heat air within a tent higher up than the occupant reaches when standing erect.

USE OF DOUBLE TENTS

Because there is little wind in a forest, you find it easy there to apply the air space principle. Take, for instance, two A-tents, or two of these with walls added. Have one of them slightly smaller than the other, the smaller being suspended from the ridge pole of the bigger and being inside the uprights that support each end of the larger tent's ridge pole. The two tents are then fastened together by tapes that are at all points where there are guy ropes on the outer tent. You then have a double structure, with an air space three or four inches, that heats up so readily that the fire in your camp stove is no more than well started when the interior is as warm as anybody wants it to be.

CONTROL OF HOARFROST

For a winter camp it is probably not worth while to use special material—drilling or light canvas will do very well. During the day, or whenever the fire is going, no hoarfrost will form inside the inner tent. A tremendous amount of hoarfrost will form in the space between the two tents; but that does not do any harm. If so much forms that you begin to notice the inner tent sagging under the weight, then you just slap the bulge with your hand and the frost, now the equivalent of snow, will slide down to the ground in between the two tents. A little rime may form on the inside of your inner tent during the night, when the fire is out, but not enough to cause serious inconvenience. For if a little does drop on the bedding, the tent is going to be so warm the next morning, as soon as the campfire is started, that any damp-ness will soon dry away.

DANGER FROM SPARKS

For a camp in a forest one percaution is crucial, although no more than of slight importance on the prairie. You must guard the tent against sparks from the stovepipe. You do this with a cap of wire gauze that you put on top of your stovepipe.

On the prairie there is nearly always a breeze, and sparks will be carried clear of the tent; however, in a very calm night you are likely to burn holes in your tent roof, even on a sea coast. In a forest you would have holes within a few hours, if not within a few minutes, unless precautions were taken.

It may be practical to fireproof the material out of which are made tents intended for winter camping, whether in a forest or on a prairie where firewood is abundant. Then you would not have to bother with a wire gauze cap for your stovepipe.

WINTER FOREST CAMPS

For northern emergency housing we have discussed types suitable to forest, to prairie, and to sea or lake ice. Tents we have discussed thus far only with reference to prairie and to ice, except that the dome Eskimo tent has been treated as a marginal forest-prairie type. We now discuss the two main camping methods that are used by the Indians of the northerly spruce forest, the tipi (tepee, teepee), and the open camp.

TIPI CAMPS

The tipi sort of winter camp used by the forest Indians just south of the Eskimos in Canada is one sign of the profound adaptational differences between these two peoples. The Eskimos—in their clothing, housing, and use of fuel—have come so near perfection that even those white men who have lived among them many years have succeeded only in making negligible improvements; the winter use of the tipi, common though not universal in the northern edge of the forest, is an example of flying almost directly in the face of nature.

ERECTING THE TIPI

You start the northern tipi by cutting down a number of slender spruce trees, 10 to 14 feet long. You fasten two of these together a foot or two below their tops by a rope, withe, or strip of bark so that they make a crotch; you lean a third into this crotch, the three having their butts standing in what is going to be the circular base of the tent. Hereafter you lean more and more poles up against this tripod, until with 10, 12, 14, or more, according to the size of the tent, you have a complete circle (cone). Next you wrap a big robe of skins or big piece of canvas around the tent so that it overlaps considerably; but you leave a wide opening at the top.

During summer, when this type of camp is unexcelled, you see that none of the tent covering touches the ground—either you have a clear air space all around or you pile brush so that the lower margin of your robe or canvas rests on a pile of twigs instead of on the ground, the air then filtering in through the brush. You start your fire and this creates such a draft all around that even on a hot day it is not uncomfortable to sit in a tipi around a big fire. The front of your body may be overheated but there is a cool current up your back. And one of the best points is that the draft sucks in mosquitoes and sends them up with the smoke—likely scorched but at any rate expelled.

In winter no arrangement could be much worse than this. At a minimum you will need a draft coming in under the tent edge at three places, equal distance from each other, otherwise the tent fills with smoke. Let us say the temperature outside is 60° or 70° below zero, and that may well be in the northern forest, where the lowest known temperatures of earth are registered. If the blaze indoors produces a high temperature there is a reinforcement of the summer draft mechanism; because of the now more pronounced gravitational differences between the outer and inner air, the draft is much accentuated. You are then in a position where, if dressed in wool, you feel instantly an insistent chill on your back when the front of your body is scorched by the fire. If you turn around, with your back to the flame, you can see hoarfrost forming on the front of your coat and trousers. If you hang up a wet pair of woolen mittens they will dry on one side while hoarfrost develops on the other; turn them around, and while the hoarfrost is melting a similar rime will form on the side that was recently dried. If fur clothes are worn you do not have quite the trouble with rime but you are likely to injure your garments by scorching them.

It is not quite impossible, however, to dry wet garments in a tipi camp. For instance, a mitten of cotton or wool, of any material not readily spoiled by scorching, may be fastened to a board which you stick up at a suitable distance from the source of heat. That way you can dry one side without hoarfrosting the other. The first side dry, you turn the mitten over; when that side has dried you put the garment somewhere away from the heat—under your bedding or out of doors.

Damp clothes will dry on your body if you wear them in a tipi near the fire, except for the outer layers. This means that if you have three or four layers of woolen cloth you can dry all of them on that side which faces the fire and all but the outer one or two on the side away from the fire. For while the fire is going the air in the tipi is a good deal warmer than out of doors except just in the three or four places where it enters under the tent flaps.

In the Great Bear Lake woods it is common during midwinter that two men sitting 3 or 4 feet apart cannot see each other for the steam that is being created by the mingling of the intensely cold outer air with the air heated by the fire.

When bedtime comes in a winter tipi camp you are in a dilemma. If you keep the fire going you also keep going the intense draft. If you let the fire die down the warmth of the earth on which it was burning will continue to heat the air, continuing the draft to a point where the interior of the tent is practically as cold as outside. This will mean 50° below zero inside if it is 60° below zero outside.

The above may seem exaggerated; but it is really an incomplete and inadequate description of the discomforts of a tipi camp. Therefore it is the preference of many whites of the northern forest and of some natives to sleep in the open.

Winds are of course never strong in the woods, but there may be a breeze. You then make a windbreak against this out of logs and evergreen boughs. Even if there is no breeze you still put up the equivalent of a windbreak for it acts as a reflector against the fire that you are going to build. Between this windbreak and the fire you cover the snow with spruce boughs to keep your blankets away from the snow. In front you build a long and narrow fire, parallel to the windbreak and 6, 8, or 10 feet away from it, according to circumstances. This fire is best made by laying whole logs parallel to each other. To keep such a fire going there must be a minimum of three logs at a given time—two will not burn. You can, of course, use shorter pieces of wood if logs are not available; and you use short pieces as kindling or to revive the fire.

This type of fire can be built in a way to last 2 or 3 hours. If one or another of the campers will replenish it three or four times during the night, the party will sleep in fair comfort. At any rate, you escape the draft that is unavoidable in a tipi.

The marginal forest Indians, as, for instance, the Loucheux at the head of the Mackenzie delta and on the Peel River, had winter tents or winter camps that were a sort of incomplete adaptation of Eskimo shelters. They were not as simple or comfortable as those Eskimo tents and houses of which they were imitations and are, therefore, not worth discussion in a practical manual, although of considerable scientific interest for those who want a grasp of the cultural history of the two peoples. That the Indians borrowed, or tried to borrow, from the Eskimos, and that the Eskimos did not borrow from the Indians, seems logical to those who have lived among both peoples. For practically every forest Indian method or device was less well adapted to its purpose than the corresponding Eskimo feature.

Section III

ARCTIC FUEL AND HOW TO USE IT

STRIKING A LIGHT

Intimately connected with the problem of emergency fuels is the question of emergency ways of striking a light. The best is the use of iron pyrite. This is found on a good many of the Arctic islands and on many parts of the mainland coast. If you watch for it as you travel, you will likely find some in a day or two.

In summer you just carry along two chunks, each your idea of a right size to handle. The standard Eskimo size is about the shape and dimensions of a lemon. For cold weather use these should be about two-thirds covered (best with rawhide, for that shrinks into snug position after you have sewed it on).

When a fire is to be lighted you spread out any kind of tinder, preferably in a place where it can be reached by wind but not by rain or snow. Best is a large pad, say the size of an ordinary correspondence envelope. The tinder may be anything that catches fire easily, such as rotten dry wood or pussy willow fuzz. Strike the stones together and a shower of sparks falls on the pad, dozens of them probably catching. If the wind is right, it fans the sparks into a glow. If there is no wind, you or your helper must keep blowing. When sufficient of the tinder is lighted, you pick it out of the pad, transfer it to the vicinity of the dry kindling and let the wind blow on it some more or else blow on it yourself.

This method is so well adapted to stormy weather that Stefansson found on his second expedition when parties of civilized Eskimos, using matches, and uncivilized Eskimos, using pyrites, were traveling together, the uncivilized usually got their fire started with less trouble.

BOW-DRILL

With a bow-drill or something similar you can twirl the rounded end of a fairly hard stick in a socket in a piece of softer dry wood and get a fire if you work hard and are skillful. Many Eskimos know this method, but few use it—none when pyrites is available.

STOVES AND FIREPLACES

In such case as the wreck of a ship or the arrival of a sledge party at a coast, there is usually something available (perhaps gasoline tins) out of which a stove and stovepipe can be constructed. If wood is to be burned, a stove is much better than an open fireplace. (See description of fireplaces *ante*.) The difference is still greater if you are to burn coal, and that may well happen; for if a ship has been crushed between floes or against a beach you would normally have coal. Or a sledge party may discover a coal outcrop—as the Stefansson expeditions did at several places during various years.

COAL

Across the entire Arctic from Canada through Siberia, coal of satisfactory quality for use (though sometimes scarcely of commercial saleability) is found in almost every other river valley. In some creek mouths pieces of coal-float indicate that there are veins inland. This coal usually lends itself to surface mining and is commonly a fair quality lignite. You will occasionally find a sort of pitch which can be used for kindling. It burns with a flame like that of sealing wax, with a very black smoke and an odor resembling asphalt. Other coal has much the appearance of wood compressed into bricks and irregular fragments. On sea beaches in some places, as between Barrow and Icy Cape, you find coal sometimes in windrows. This has been scooped from the sea bottom and piled up there by ice that was pressed toward the coast by wind or current.

Coal was used extensively by a Stefansson wintering party at Cape Grassy, in northwestern Melville Island, near 76° N. Lat. They also found coal on Lougheed Island, considerably farther north.

If coal is to be burned, starting the fire is sometimes difficult. At Grassy, asphalt was found which served for kindling. You might happen to have a little wood to start coal fires or you might start them with animal fat burning on some kind of wick, such as broken-up dried bones or a piece of rag. It may be necessary, if kindling is scarce and coal abundant, to keep fires going day and night, perhaps standing watch-and-watch for that purpose.

You will occasionally come upon wood partly turned to coal, reddish in color. Sometimes this burns with such an agreeable smoke that you will stand in its way to sniff it—an incense effect, from tree gum that has been preserved.

Driftwood, which was once piled high on northern beaches. has grown scarcer every year since the custom of burning wood in stoves instead of animal fat in lamps spread far among the natives. In northern Alaska and northwestern Canada driftwood is usually found in great abundance, though sometimes exclusively on westward-facing beaches. This is because low waters occur with easterly winds and high with westerly; the westerly wind with its high water lodges the driftwood well above the reach of the most violent easterly gale, the while it carries away whatever the easterly wind may have brought.

There are similar regularities on other coasts, depending on the prevailing strong winds. This dependence of driftwood on certain winds in most of the Arctic is because of the insignificant tides there—see Chapter 2.

Willows (not only true willows but alders and other species) and small resinous plants are the most widely distributed fuel sources of the inland Arctic. Willows found on many of the Arctic islands are of considerable value for fuel if you take the roots along with the stems. Sandy ground where "heather" either does not grow or does not burn well seems specially adapted to a certain kind of willow, the dead and bleaching roots of which will there be found in sufficient quantity for cooking.

As an Arctic fuel, the resinous plant *Cassiope tetragona* (a sort of white heather) is far more valuable than willows. We repeat here what we said in Chapter 6 that an important element in what might be called polarcraft is to learn during summer to recognize locations where this heather will grow. Then during the winter you can go with some confidence to places covered with several feet of snow, dig down, and likely to find your fuel.

This heather is in winter always dry and in ideal condition for burning. In summer it is likely to be damp with a rain or a fog. Even if soaking wet, it burns if you once get a fire started with something else for kindling and with a breeze

213

blowing for a good draft. Therefore, you usually have to do your cooking in a particularly open spot, as on top of a hill. You can arrange for some increase of the draft by putting up flat stones or pieces of sod that will focus the wind.

KINDLING

Traveling in rainy weather across an Arctic prairie where you fuel is going to be *cassiope*, it is well to carry along kindling or to pick up some if you happen to find it on the march. For instance, a little heather may be discovered growing in such shelter that it is dry even on a rainy day. Pick it up and carry it underneath your coat, if there is no better place, and use it for kindling at camp time.

When you are crossing gravel bars and are in any way of the opinion that fuel will be insufficient for your camp, pick up as you go along any little sticks and thrust them under the rope lashings of your sledge.

WOOD AND FAT

In traveling on islands in spring you will occasionally find one where there are no resinous plants and no mosses dry enough for burning. In this case you may be able to spare for fuel some wood you have with you, using it together with animal fat. Stefansson found that a piece of half-inch board 3 inches wide and 18 inches long, whittled or split, and burned with one-quarter of a pound of caribou suet is sufficient to cook at one time meat to last three men all day. When meat is cut into pieces about the size of sugar cubes and put on in cold water, it is cooked even before the water boils.

You can also cook with the hair and wool of a musk ox or of a grizzly bear. One hide will probably cook two or three pots holding 8 quarts each.

WHEN NOT TO BURN FAT AND HIDES

Of course, you do not burn skins for warmth or cooking if you need or may need them for clothes or bedding; nor do you burn animal fat if there is a chance of running out of food. It is much better to eat your food raw and to get your warmth from food eaten and clothes worn than to burn them for heat. This may seem an unnecessary statement to put into a book; but members of the Franklin expeditions did continue to burn some of their food to cook the rest of their food even after they were on small rations and getting weak from hunger. Some of them starved to death as a directly traceable result.

SEAL OIL

For parties living by hunting, traveling over the sea ice, the great fuel is seal oil or blubber.

Under such conditions the seal furnishes food, clothing, heat, and light. The blubber of the animal is, if anything, even more important than the meat, for it must furnish heat and light as well as food.

OUTDOOR COOKING

Stoves for cooking outdoors with seal oil or blubber have been rigged by using a cylindrical galvanized sheet-iron tank, the sides and bottom of which were clinched as well as soldered so that it could not come to pieces upon application of heat. On leaving the base the tank was filled with kerosene; when this had been used the top of the tank was removed and a draft hole cut near the bottom; then halfway up the stove two or three heavy wires were run across for the cooking pot to stand on. To be suitable for cooking purposes these cylindrical tanks should have a diameter a little larger than your largest cooking pots and a height of about 15 inches.

WICK

In burning seal oil or blubber, as in burning tallow, you must have a wick. It has been said that asbestos might serve, since it could be used over and over again; but probably this would not work permanently, for the fibers would become so clogged with the incombustible residue of oil that its usefulness as a wick would be destroyed. Besides, there is a simpler method.

After your meals, save the clean-picked bones. When next the fire is to be built use a little piece of rag for kindling, not necessarily more than an inch square, soaked in grease and put on the bottom of the stove. On top of it make a little heap of the bones and on top of the heap lay several strips of blubber, resembling so many strips of fat bacon. A match is touched to the rag and it burns like the wick of a candle, with the flame playing up between the bones and striking the blubber, which begins to try out so that the oil trickles down on the bones, making a film on their outside. Upon sufficient heating this film blazes up, and thereafter your fire burns with a furious heat so long as strips of blubber continue to be placed upon it.

You now stand your cooking pot, filled with meat and water, upon the cross wires within the stove 6 or 8 inches above the bottom. The flame first strikes the bottom of the pot and then spreads and comes up all around it, since the diameter of the stove is an inch or two larger than that of the pot. This brings the pot to a boil as quickly as would the large wood fire.

The disadvantage of this method of cooking is that the smoke of seal oil burned in this manner is thick and black and exceedingly sticky. It is, in fact, the best quality of lampblack and clings to everything. The Stefansson parties were careful not to have the tent or the sledges in the path of the smoke, and the man who was doing the cooking used to stand asidle, once his fire was started, and keep out of the smoke. White dogs that lay in the path of the smoke were nearly black after the cooking of one meal.

Eskimo stone lamps, which are used both for cooking and for heating, are large half-moon-shaped bowls that have been dazed or scraped out of blocks of native soapstone. The wick is a ridge of powder, of one of the materials described below, lying along the straight edge of the lamp.

Members of traveling parties should know what makes a good wick for an Eskimo-type oil lamp. The best answer is that almost anything serves if it is dry and you know how to handle it, which comes from practice. Thoroughly decayed soft wood is fair, hardwood sawdust is excellent, soft wood sawdust is medium. The Eskimos sometimes use scraped walrus ivory, dried moss that has been rubbed into powder between the hands, or the fuzz of pussy willow. Occasionally, if other materials give out, "civilized" Eskimos will take small pieces of manila rope and hack the fibers into lengths of one-twentieth of an inch or less, thus practically converting the fibers into powder. Stefansson reports seeing commercial smoking tobacco used with good results and without causing an appreciable tobacco smell in the house. He once tried using ordinary commercial lamp wicks but they were difficult to keep burning so they did not smoke.

For ideal burning, the bowl of the lamp must always be almost full of oil but never quite full. This may be regulated automatically. A slab of polar bear or seal fat is hung almost over the flame. If the oil in the lamp gets a little too low, there is more of the lamp wick exposed and the flame becomes larger; the increased heat of the flame tries out the fat hanging over it and makes the oil trickle down more rapidly. This gradually raises the level of the oil in the bowl until it floods part of the wick and decreases in that way the size of the flame, which in turn cools off the vicinity of the lamp enough so that the slab of blubber stops dripping. Then the flame gradually increases in size as the oil lowers in the lamp until a second flaring-up again brings streams of oil down from the slab of fat.

An Eskimo oil lamp that is kept properly trimmed produces no smoke and will burn with regular fluctuations 6 or 8 hours at a time. Ordinarily lamps that are trimmed when you go to bed in the evening are still burning brightly the next morning, unless you have forgotten to put a large enough piece of blubber on the hook above the lamp.

All Eskimos, but particularly those who live in snow houses, are meticulous that a lamp shall not smoke. Their sense of smell (though perhaps not their other senses) seems keener than ours and there is nothing disturbs them so quickly as the least bit of that odor which goes with the formation of lampblack. Accordingly, there is instant attention from the first person who smells a lamp smoking— he fixes it himself or warns someone who is nearer. Stefansson reports that, as a result, he has seen snow houses of Eskimos (who did not use tobacco) where, after 2 or 3 weeks of lamps burning day and night, there was less stain on the ceiling than would have been produced by one evening of moderate cigarette or pipe smoking. The likeliest time for a lamp to smoke is at night when people are sleeping. Lamps will, as said, burn without smoke unattended for long periods; even the least smoke will awaken somebody who promptly attends to the lamp.

LIGHT

In houses of earth-and-wood, or in lined snow houses, the pot swung over the lamp so obscures the light during cooking periods that other lamps are burned exclusively for lighting. In snow houses, however, the back and forth reflection of light from the spotless snow walls sees to it that the same lamp which does the cooking also furnishes enough light.

SUPERIORITY OF IMPORTED FUELS

The foregoing are fuels indigenous to the Arctic and, as indicated, are satisfactory when commercial fuels are not available. When circumstances permit, however, kerosene should be carried. We repeat here what we point out in Chapter 11, that hauling fuel along with you is more important than hauling food and that the kind of fuel is more important than the kind of food. Better light and more convenient heat are derived from kerosene burned in lamps and in blue-flame stoves than are to be had from seal blubber burned by any method so far devised.

We do not describe kerosene lamps and stoves; for better ones designed for travel use are constantly being developed and invented.

CHAPTER 8

FOOD AND DRINK

Whatever rations a party starts with are fairly sure to be all right, particularly if they are from Army stores. We devote ourselves chiefly, then, to discussing foods which may be picked up along the way, prefacing, however, with a brief discussion of special methods and special foods for cold weather travelers.

Section I

SPECIAL METHODS

If weight is of no consequence because the journey is short, or because the transportation facilities are unlimited, you take with you whatever food you like, except, of course, nothing that is going to spoil. What foods will spoil in hot weather, and how this can be avoided, is so well known that it needs no discussion. There are not many foods spoilt by cold, or at least not materially. Potatoes, if frozen once for all (if not intermittently frozen and thawed) are almost as good as if they had not frozen. The same is true with eggs, apples, and the like. Meats are so little affected that it takes discriminating if not expert judgment to tell the difference between those that have been frozen and those that have not.

There is, of course, a great deal of prejudice against frozen foods. But this is probably in the main just a lot of folk beliefs. Certainly it is on the whole more advantageous for a traveling party that everything should remain frozen than that everything should remain unfrozen; for when things are unfrozen it is frequently difficult to keep them from souring, decaying, or being otherwise spoiled—it is almost impossible to spoil a food while it is frozen.

Under permanent conditions of thaw, or conditions of intermittent thawing and freezing, you have to be very careful about how things are packed; under permanent frost practically no care is required. Milk can be frozen into bricks and handled like bricks. Meat can be cut into separate steaks or roasts before freezing and then handled like chunks of wood. You can carry your meat in large pieces if you like, as an entire ham or even a carcass. Then, when meals are to be cooked, you cut up the piece with saws or axes. Saws are generally better, for with intense cold an axe will splinter meat and some of the splinters may be lost. Sawing does, of course, waste a bit of the meat if you are not careful; but you can always gather the sawdust together and save it.

All foods can be carried frozen and handled with freedom except those that are greasy. Even greases freeze "clean" when it is cold enough. Some of them like tallow, may be freely handled, without much staining of mittens, at temperatures only a little below freezing. Butter is clean to handle at zero. Lard will not grease you up much at temperatures of 20° or 30° below. At 50° below zero any fat can be handled in chunks except a few of the oils, such as whale and seal. These are in a semiliquid state, and behave as we are used to think of grease as behaving.

A food much carried in the North, if weight does not count, is baked beans. Most people have them frozen into bricks. However, they are more convenient if you bake them dry and let them freeze in separate kernels so you can handle them like a bag of peanuts. For warming up, whether the beans are in bricks or separate, you have a little water in the pot or a little grease in the pan when you start the cooking.

If fuel is likely to be scarce, certain foods are to be avoided. If you have plenty of fuel and plenty of time you would naturally carry uncooked things, like beans and rice. Beans are among the slowest things to cook, requiring leisure

220

and much fuel. Rice and oatmeal, although usually avoided because said to require a lot of fuel, can be cooked with a minimum. What you do is to put them into the cooking pot on top of the snow, if you are going to cook with snow water, or on top of cracked ice if that is going to be your source of liquid. You must be careful, of course, that cereals and things of that sort are not right on the bottom of your pot before the snow or ice begins to melt, for then they will burn.

If cereals are in the pot when the snow is being melted or are put in with the cold water, and if the fire is slow as a seal oil lamp will be, then they are nearly cooked when the water comes to a boil. It was standard practice on the Stefansson expeditions when rice had to be used to take the pot off the fire 1 or 2 minutes after it came to a boil and to stand it on a piece of wood or other nonconductor, the pot being also wrapped up in a blanket or placed under a skin—a fireless cooker effect. Twenty or thirty minutes after being taken from the fire the rice would be adequately cooked. Oatmeal cooks still more easily.

A good way to use beans, peas, or lentils is to have them ground up into coarse flour. They cook, then, with hardly more difficulty or time than oatmeal.

Traveling parties that are self-supporting, of course, live on whatever game there is in their district. We discuss elsewhere cooking and housekeeping under those conditions.

SECTION II

SPECIAL FOODS

FAT IN THE DIET

We shall see as we go along why fat is the most important ingredient of an Arctic ration. We begin with considering some beliefs in regard to this food which do not appear to be well founded.

It is a common view that people like fat in cold weather, dislike it in hot. A variant is to say that fat is good for you in winter and bad for you in summer. It is difficult to guess what may have been the origin of this belief for, although widely held, it is contradicted by universal experience. For

221

instance, it is a common objection of North Americans to Latin American food that it is greasy. Northerners within the United States who go to the southern states find that a lot of fat is eaten—fat pork and corn bread is a standard diet at least among certain classes. Few animals are greasier than the opossum; yet this is a delicacy in our South with negroes and apparently with many of those whites who have tried it. Carl Akeley reported from Africa and Carl Lumholtz from Australia that natives there would gorge with fat. The early Australian sheep men (English), according to Sir Hubert Wilkins, roasted the fattest mutton and dipped it in drippings— which was, of course, in the early days before sugar was abundant. When Homer is trying to bring out that the gods had more delicious food and lived more sumptuously than mortals he did it in part by saying that they were able to command meats that had more fat on them than available to mortals. Dr. Edgar Johnson Goodspeed, one of the foremost of our biblical scholars, has given it as both his view and that of several colleagues whom he consulted that the Jews in "Biblical times" were extremely fond of fat mutton.

However, this must not be taken to overstate the case to the effect that people in hot countries are more fond of fat than in cold. They do *seem* to be more fond; but this is no doubt because, on the average, fats are harder to secure the warmer the country. This is for complex reasons which we have not space to discuss. We just state the fact, which anyone can prove to himself if he stops to think, that on the average the animals of the coldest countries are the fattest. Insofar as man is a hunter he lives on fat animals in cold countries and animals comparatively deficient in fat in hot countries. Thus it is in hot countries we are likeliest to find people who are fat hungry. This is why fat animals, like the opossum and pig, are delicacies in tropical and sub-tropical lands.

The fact is, apparently, that the normal human craving for fat is, in ratio to other foods eaten, just about the same in all climates. You eat more in winter than you do in summer; to that extent only do you eat more fat in winter than in summer. One of the many cases where this has been proved is that of Stefansson and Anderson when in 1928–29 they lived, under

222

the supervision of the Russell Sage Institute of Pathology for 12 months and some weeks on an exclusive meat (lean and fat) diet in New York City. They ate more in winter than in summer, but the proportion of fat to lean remained about the same.

Another seemingly unwarranted belief concerning fat is that it is a better heating food, produces more heat in the human body, than any other. This is probably not true in any sense except that of containing more calories per ounce. You probably get just as much heat, and get it quite as easily, out of 9 ounces of sugar as out of 4 ounces of fat. Fat then, is the best of heat producers only in the sense that it is the most condensed of known foods—has the most calories per unit of weight.

There are a great many people who tell you that they "cannot eat fat." Among a hundred of these there may be one or two that really cannot—these may be "sensitive" too fat, allergic. The other 98 or 99 are merely describing to you a state of mind. If they happen to be for a number of days where the fat equivalents, sugar and starch, are lacking they will develop a taste for fat. There are cases on record where a man "never ate fat in his life" and acquired a preference for fat over sugar in half a year on an exclusive lean and fat diet.

It must be remembered, too, that a man's declaring he eats no fat may have a linguistic explanation—he may not speak of as fat what the rest of us call fat. Perhaps he will be found eating things like butter, gravy, hard sauce, and cream.

It is claimed on behalf of fat, and perhaps rightly, that it is the only food in which lies no danger of overeating, or at least no danger if you eat slowly. The contention is that with sugar at your elbow, or any food of which you are fond other than fat, you may eat a good deal more than you need and even possibly enough to hurt you. For an illustration of how this would not be so with fat, take cream, for this is to many a palatable form.

Get somebody who is extremely fond of cream, place before him a dish of it with a teaspoon and see that he does not eat faster than 2 teaspoonfuls per minute. After the first 10 or 15 spoons he will begin to notice that each tastes a little less well than the one before. Presently, he will have no desire to eat. If he continues he will finally gag—either his will power will not enable him to swallow more or if he does swallow he will throw it up.

It is, of course, true that in eating any sort of food you do eventually get enough; however, the reaction against too much of other foods which are palatable is not so reliable or strong as in the case of fat.

Fat is, in calories, the most condensed of foods. An ounce of fat (butter, bacon fat, tallow) is more than twice as nourishing in the caloric sense as an ounce of sugar or an ounce of dried lean. If portability of a ration is being considered, it is then essential that it shall contain as much fat as the consumer can take without beginning to turn against it; the rest of his requirements will be supplied from other sources.

It is considered that the human body cannot repair itself without protein. Theoretically, then, the ideal condensed or portable ratio is as much fat as you need for calories and as much protein as you need for body repair.

The question of vitamins is discussed hereafter. We mention, however, that pemmican, the food towards a discussion of which we are working, contains an adequate amount of all the currently known vitamins, except Vitamin C. If your body is thoroughly stocked with C by a good diet previous to a journey, you will probably stay at optimum health on the journey, so far as you or anyone else can notice, for several weeks eating just pemmican and water. Thereafter will begin to develop slowly symptoms we shall discuss later in connection with scurvy, but likely you will still be able to report yourself in pretty good health after 2 months. It is somewhere between 6 weeks and 12 that you will develop pronounced Vitamin C deficiency symptoms—recognizable scurvy. (See Section IV, Chapter 10.)

Pemmican is, then, an ideal emergency food for a journey up to 6 weeks, after which it will have to be supplemented by other foods, or else the Vitamin C will have to be supplied as a drug, probably in capsule form.

Both the word and the idea, "pemmican," are from Indian sources. The essential ingredients are the two chief components of meat, lean and fat.

Many Indians who do not make pemmican carry with them on journeys whatever dried lean meat they have and carry fat separately. This may be, on the whole, better than using pemmican. The human digestive apparatus, and the associated feelings and "instincts," do not automatically prevent overeating of lean; they do prevent overeating of fat. For, as said, when you eat slowly something fat, the goodness of the taste decreases so that it is almost if not quite possible to notice decreased palatability with successive mouthfuls. If fat and other food elements are mixed, as fat and lean are in pemmican, you are either tempted to overeat of fat in order to get enough lean or else you may become improperly nourished in that the excessive fat begins to nauseate you before you have had quite enough of the lean.

The theoretically ideal ration, then, from the caloric angle, is a predetermined adequate weight of lean, supplemented each day by all the fat you want. The addition of other ingredients, such as sugar, raisins, meal, though some of them are possibly useful in themselves, go against what is the main idea with pemmican—to secure a maximum of nourishment with minimum of both weight and bulk.

The danger of too much lean against fat in pemmican is not solely one of faulty economy. If the excess of lean over fat is sufficiently marked, the men eating it may develop protein poisoning—nephritis. This was undoubtedly the cause of at least one death in the Bartlett party of the third Stefansson expedition.

What is probably a good standard for pemmican was determined at the Russell Sage Institute of Pathology of New York when Stefansson and Andersen lived a year exclusively on meat and water. It proved that on the average their requirements were supplied by about 1⅓ lb. of lean and ½ lb. of fat. No salt is necessary. Should the Army decide to make pemmican, or have it made from specifications, this would be a reliable guide—probably better than anything else now available. (The weights given are for steak and suet before either was cooked.)

DANISH PEMMICAN SATISFACTORY

Pemmican has in the past been made by guess and rule of thumb. What seemed to be the best ever tried by the author was made by the Beauvais firm of Copenhagen, and was approximately half powdered lean meat and half tallow. This pemmican was made in blocks somewhat the shape and size of house-building bricks. The bricks were wrapped in tinfoil, which may have been of some help for keeping the food in good condition but was a nuisance to the users, for the foil stuck. Perhaps the blocks of pemmican might be wrapped in some form of oiled paper. The wrapped Beauvais bricks were packed in a 10- to 14-inch cubical tin. Such pemmican has been found in good condition after half a dozen years, at least one summer of which had been under temperate zone conditions.

AMERICAN PEMMICAN NOT SATISFACTORY

Pemmican thus far commercially made in the United States has been of only partly dry meat. In the pemmican of the third Stefansson expedition, excessive salting was used by Underwood for extra safety along with the canning; Armour seemed to depend mainly on the cans and the canning process for preservation. The Underwood pemmican contained far too high a percentage of lean, and the Armour product contained an unnecessary and uneconomical admixture of vegetable matter.

If the meat is thoroughly dry when ground, and if the only other ingredient is beef or mutton tallow, no canning of the individual pieces is necessary in the Arctic and the above-described Danish method of packing is advisable.

If pemmican is bought canned, the tins can be removed just before a winter journey starts—they always should be, for they are extra weight and in winter have no value for anything, unless it be as protection from dogs.

The first reason why pemmican should not be salted is that whoever wants salt ought to be allowed to use it to his taste. A further reason is that salt increases thirst; and, although it is safe enough to quench this by eating snow as you walk along, it is a nuisance to have to be reaching for snow all the time. Besides, salt appears to have a particularly bad effect on dogs—the above-mentioned Underwood pemmican made dogs sick.

Additions to pemmican have included fish meal among Scandinavians, and chocolate among various nationalities. These have been put in either according to some theory or to "improve the taste."

There is no need to improve the taste of pemmican. All who have used it in its fundamental or nearly fundamental forms have liked it. (True enough, many also have liked the variants.) Peary says, for instance, that his standard daily ration of 1 pound pemmican, 1 pound biscuit, and tea with a very little sugar for sweetening, was satisfactory both in keeping up the strength of the party and in that nobody got tired of it. (This ration, however, would not do for more than, say, three months, as appears in what we say about scurvy in Chapter 10.)

Peary used hard bread (pilot bread) with pemmican because he thought it was needed to supply bulk, and possibly for other reasons. Members of various Stefansson parties lived for as long periods on dried lean and dried fat, the ingredients of pemmican, eaten separately, as any of the Peary detachments ever lived on the pemmican and biscuit. The results were equally good in both cases—the biscuits did not prove disadvantageous, except perhaps in being bulkier on the sledges and then in supplying less nourishment per pound; neither did they prove themselves advantageous, since the results were also perfect without them.

The fundamental reason why there is no cause to flavor, disguise, or in any way "improve" the taste of pemmican is that men who work hard have such good appetites anyway that it is enough of a strain on their will power to keep to a ration even when it is not particularly appetizing. Besides, it is true with pemmican, as probably with most or all foods that are complete in all the dietal requirements, that the longer you eat them the better you like them.

Pemmican can be eaten as if it were chocolate. That is how Peary used it. Tea was the liquid they had with their biscuits and pemmican. Some expeditions have preferred to do without the tea and to get their liquid by making a thin soup of the pemmican. In that case, usually each man would break his individual ration of biscuit into his ration of pemmican soup; or some of the biscuits might be pooled and put into the pemmican stew just before it was ready to serve.

CHOCOLATE AND RICE GOOD CONDENSED RATIONS

Although not nearly as rich in calories, pound for pound, chocolate is usually looked upon as good condensed rations. Rice is another. On the third Stefansson expedition, where fuel did not have to be economized because it was secured along the way through killing seals, one of the favorite rations was a stew made by boiling rice in a lot of water to which were added chocolate and lumps of chopped-up suet— in that instance caribou fat.

Peary never got full satisfaction for men working hard under much less than 2 pounds per day of his pemmican-biscuit-tea-sugar ration; the Stefansson party got results which appeared satisfactory, at least for a week or two at a time, from something like half a pound of rice, half a pound of suet and a quarter pound of chocolate. However, the Stefansson parties depended so largely on hunting that they seldom had occasion to use substitutes for very long— chiefly in the midwinter period of inadequate hunting light; and even then they used to secure game occasionally.

DRIED FISH

For men and dogs dried fish is a good as well as a cheap ration. Along the Yukon River, and elsewhere in Alaska, dried salmon are put up by the ton, and an expedition planning to go into the sea north of Alaska could, especially by a year's advance arrangement, secure great quantities of this excellent food to take along. It needs no preservative even on a ship's deck, except against the sea washing over it or against rain. The Stefansson experience was that the men became very fond of these dried salmon, in some cases retaining the fondness after they had returned to civilization, but at any rate greedily eating quantities when in the field, winter or summer. The salmon, dried native style, are not salted.

Section III

LIVING OFF THE COUNTRY

a. Food Sources

In much of the Arctic, about the only food you can pick up along the way is derived from animals you secure. (See Chapter 6 for Arctic vegetable sources.) Our main discussion, therefore, relates to a meat diet, which we define as one from which all matter directly from the vegetable kingdom is absent. Here we deal only with the types of meat that are likely to be secured in the North, with the preferences as to parts of the animal, and with cooking methods. In chapter 10 we discuss at length the relation of a meat diet to health, both physical and psychological.

b. Palatability

FAVORITE NORTHERN MEATS

The usual view of northern meat eaters is that caribou is the best land animal and seal best at sea. White newcomers are likely to prefer the musk ox. This is because it is practically identical with beef, while caribou has individuality.

MUSK OXEN

Some travelers have stated that the flesh of musk oxen is strong—that it tastes of musk, from which the animal is supposed to have received its name. Observers who have lived on these animals for long periods say, however, that the strong taste is found chiefly in old males and that it is no stronger than the corresponding taste with old seals, old caribou, or with old domestic sheep.

A strong taste in old caribou is seldom reported because animals are killed by wolves before they get old—few people, Eskimo or white, have ever had an opportunity to taste an old bull caribou. Seals, musk oxen, and mountain sheep live much longer, especially musk oxen, which apparently either die of old age or are killed by wolves only when they have become decrepit.

Peary said that musk ox was better than domestic beef, but he probably meant only that his appetite was better when he was eating it, since the two seem almost indistinguishable. In color and flavor the fat of the musk ox is similar to that of beef, though not practically identical as is the case with the lean. Stefansson's companions agreed they preferred musk ox fat to beef fat; and further agreed that there is more range of flavors as between fats from different parts of the body. The largest accumulation is on the neck, and this is especially delicious.

MILK

No northern wild animal gives a large amount of milk, not even the huge moose. Domestic cattle, when allowed to run wild on the range, give only from 3 to 5 pints of milk where the same cow would give four times that much under dairying conditions. Under the circumstances musk oxen give surprisingly much. In flavor the milk is about like that of the Jersey cow, though somewhat richer, for the "whole milk" is about the consistency of commercial light cream. Probably the percentage of fat in the undiluted milk is not as high as in city cream, but the consistency does give a creamlike impression.

POLAR BEAR

Europeans commonly like the taste of bear meat, saying it is like pork. But it is stringy, gets between the teeth, and makes the gums sore. After you have been on bear for a week or two you are likely to begin cutting it in small pieces and swallowing them before you are through chewing. This applies to cooked meat, not to raw. Cooking increases toughness and brings out the stringiness. Chewing frozen raw bear meat is like eating raw oysters; half-frozen it has, like other raw meats, the consistency of hard ice cream.

It is commonly said by whalers that Eskimos have told them polar bear liver is poisonous. What the Eskimos have said is that if you eat bear liver you will get sick. When Stefansson became familiar with their language and their manner of thinking, he learned that what they meant was that bear liver is taboo and if you eat it punishment in the form of sickness or death will follow. But this did not seem like a rational belief, for the illness or death were supposed to afflict members of a family irrespective of which had eaten the liver. On his third expedition he therefore conducted a series of liver-eating experiments. They found the taste pleasant, about like that of calf liver. On about 90 percent of the tests there were no ill effects; on the remaining 10 percent the experimenters became temporarily ill, recovering in a day or so. The only conclusion they could draw was that certain livers of bears may be slightly poisonous while others are not.

SEALS

With seals there is little preference between parts. Most people like the liver boiled, or frozen and raw. The heart is liked and the kidneys. Practically all parts of the body, except the entrails, are much on a level.

CARIBOU

With caribou, the other great food animal of the North, there is a scale of choices and there are marked preferences. The best is the head. Next come brisket, ribs, backbone, and pelvis. The brisket is too fat at certain times of year and in that case you peel much of the fat and nearly all the lean away before boiling the bones. Ribs are seldom considered too fat, but some of the ribs have too much meat on them, which is removed before cooking. Similarly a considerable part of the meat is cut from the backbone before cooking. For Eskimos and all other meat eaters agree with the Elizabethans that the sweetest meat is nearest the bone.

The halfway parts of a caribou in dividing the food between men and dogs are the neck and shoulders. The men usually get them while the dogs get the hind quarters.

Most Eskimos are very fond of their dogs and so are many whites, but they agree on keeping the best parts of animals for human use. Accordingly, you begin the dog-meat classification from the opposite end of the scale. They get first what we think worst—the entrails and lungs. Usually the humans get the heart and kidneys but the dogs get the liver, sweetbreads, and all other internal organs and glands. As said, the dogs get the hams, unless the men are so much more numerous that they need them.

231

The great particular delicacies of the caribou eater are the various fats. Except perhaps some of the marrows, the best is that behind the eyes. There is also some very good fat under the lower jaw. When caribou are skinny the tongue is much fancied, for it usually contains some agreeable fat. Another good fat is around the kidneys.

The least favored is the slab of fat which lies along the back. In the case of a very fat full-grown bull the layer may be half an inch thick at the front of the shoulders, just where it goes over on the neck, and at which point it is usually severed from the neck fat. Back on the shoulders it thickens, particularly in two ovals, one each side of the ridge of the back, just behind the shoulder blades. Then it gets perhaps a litle thinner but rapidly thickens again until just in front of the tail it may be (some say) 3 inches thick. A slab of this fat peeled from a bull of 300 pounds live-weight may weigh 30 or 40 pounds.

In the economy of both caribou Eskimos and northern Indians the back fat is important. It is always separated from the body.

Among the Indians it may be smoke-dried, while the Eskimos usually dry it by just hanging it up, though a few also smoke it. As said, it is valued because of its massiveness, not for its quality. Most people prefer many of the other fats.

One thing dogs never get is the marrow bones. The meat is peeled from them, sometimes to be cooked, sometimes to be given to the dogs. The bones are then broken for marrow in the fashion of Stone Age man. The only marrow bones that are customarily boiled or roasted by Eskimos are the humerus and femur, which are cooked with a certain amount of meat still adhering. The rest of the marrow is eaten raw.

When you take them at "room temperatures," the marrows farthest from the hoofs are hardest. At the head of the femur and humerus it is approximately as hard as reindeer or beef tallow; at the lower end of the same bones it is softer and the top of the next bone is softer still; it continues in that way until finally toward the toes the marrow is liquid and almost the color of water.

Meat is a complete diet only when the animal you eat is fat. It is therefore easiest for the most northerly men of the northern hemisphere to secure an adequate diet by hunting, for it is there that the animals are fattest. The whales, the walrus, and the seals are so fat that if you secure enough of them to furnish the protein necessary for the health of men and dogs you at the same time secure so much fat that even when all cooking, househeating, and lighting are done with oil, there is still a surplus. Stefansson found when traveling over the sea ice and living exclusively on seals that when the fat of animals secured had been put to all its uses he still had to throw away about a third.

But these are the only northern animals that have an excess of fat.

A polar bear may be either skinny or rolling at any time of year, according to his individual luck in hunting. If you were to live exclusively on polar bears you would be hard put to it—you would have to eat as much lean as your health permitted, always being careful of the fat.

Grizzly bears are fattest in the autumn just before hibernation. There may be nearly a hundred pounds of fat on a 500-pound bear. They awake from the hibernation in the spring practically as fat as when they retired in the autumn; but these vegetarians awake in April and are not able to dig roots until the ground thaws, which may be 6 weeks later. During this fast they lose fat rapidly and are fatless when the thaws begin. Hunting man would find it difficult to manage a normal diet on that kind of animal.

We have already dealt with the fat cycles of the musk oxen and caribou. The moose has a like cycle. You cannot therefore have a balanced diet on these animals any more than you can on the grizzly bear, if you kill each month those that you eat that month. The only way to manage with beasts of seasonal fatness is to kill a large number at the top of the fat cycle and to preserve the fat.

Some animals are never fat. The only one of these important in northern economy is the rabbit. It is recognized that you cannot live on them exclusively. The expression "rabbit starvation," common in the North, sounds as if you were talking about there being no rabbits. What the phrase means is that the people have been reduced to living on nothing but rabbit.

RABBIT STARVATION

If you are transferred suddenly from a diet normal in fat to one consisting wholly of rabbit you eat bigger and bigger meals for the first few days until at the end of about a week you are eating in pounds three or four times as much as you were at the beginning of the week. By that time you are showing both signs of starvation and of protein poisoning. You eat numerous meals; you feel hungry at the end of each; you are in discomfort through distention of the stomach with much food and you begin to feel a vague restlessness. Diarrhoea will start in from a week to 10 days and will not be relieved unless you secure fat. Death will result after several weeks.

Some Arctic birds are well supplied with fat, but only those that migrate. Geese and ducks are fat in the spring and never quite without fat during the summer, fattening again somewhat in the autumn. Swans have a good deal of fat but cranes do not. By common northern opinion, Eskimo and white, the owl is one of the best of the food birds, but it has inadequate fat. Ravens are not considered good, because they are skinny. The ptarmigan has little fat. These three are the chief birds that spend the whole year in the farthest north, the owl, the raven, and the ptarmigan—some of them go south but some stay.

On the average, fish have enough fat in them for food but little or nothing over for lighting, cooking, and heating purposes.

There are only two things out of the ordinary to be said about the palatability of fish.

All Eskimos and northern Indians seem to agree that in the case of most fishes, as with caribou, the head is the best part of the animal. The Eskimos, who are extremely fond of their children, usually reserve fish heads for them, and thereafter for visitors. Unlike the caribou head, which may be either boiled or roasted, fish heads should always be boiled. The northern general attitude towards fish heads is, then, what the New England attitude is towards them for chowder. Nor is it unknown in Europe that fish heads are a delicacy—people are very fond of them in certain parts of Norway and in other countries.

COD LIVERS A DELICACY

A thing known to some Europeans is a commonplace in the North, that cod liver is the most delicious form of fat. The greatest of all delicacies is the liver of the fresh-water cod, the ling. These are eaten boiled.

SKIN CLOTHING AND BOATS IN CASE OF STARVATION

In discussions of skin boats and skin clothing, we have pointed out that, before the extremity of cannibalism is reached, all articles made out of rawhide or hide not commercially tanned can be used as food. They have considerable food value and there is no substance in them that tends to make you ill.

c. Cooking Methods

BOILING BEST METHOD OF COOKING

The easiest method of cooking, and the one best liked in the long run, is boiling.

On shore or at sea you will have fresh water for cooking in summer and autumn—on shore this is from lakes and rivers, at sea it is from rain or thaw water on top of the ice. But, in winter, sometimes on land and always at sea, you are dependent on snow or ice. Typically you begin cooking with your pot three-quarters filled with cracked ice; on top of that you pile chunks of meat, a few of them as small as your closed fist but the average size perhaps that of both fists held together—except, of course, the parts which are thin, like ribs. As the ice melts the meat sinks down. While the water is gradually warming up the meat thaws. When the pot comes to a boil, or perhaps 2 to 5 minutes later, you take it off the fire and set it on some nonconductor such as a piece of wood, for the cooking to proceed fireless-cooker style. It is a good thing to have something special along for this purpose. You may have with you a wooden box which contains pots and other things when you are traveling; this box can be used as a fireless cooker at mealtimes.

The reason for taking the meat off as soon as it comes to a boil may be any one of several, or a combination of them. You may be saving fuel; you may need heat for the warmth of the room, in which case you want it direct and dry rather than indirect by way of the steam from the boiling pot. It may be the nuisance of the steam itself is your chief reason, for perhaps it is condensing on the roof of a tent, thence to drop later in snow form on your bedding to make it wet.

In any case, the meal is sufficiently cooked, for in the long run you find it best to boil meat about as rare as we roast beef. Our typical roast is well done only for a small fraction on the outside; inside there is a layer that is medium done, and innermost what we call rare, which is really raw. The eaters of boiled meat like the same to be the case, having the inside of each piece rare or medium. This practice has developed, no doubt, in response to taste or, shall we say, instinct. Scientifically speaking, oxidation destroys or weakens vitamin C in those outer layers of the meat which are well- or over-cooked. There is little oxidation on the middle layers and practically none on the raw (rare) central portion. Therefore, you are always protected from scurvy so long as your meat is cooked in approved Eskimo fashion. (See also Chapter 10.)

Meat eaters do not, properly speaking, have soups, but it is customary with some of them that when meat has been boiled it is removed from the broth and then a little blood poured in, the whole stirred meantime. This produces, with the right proportions, a broth of the consistency of pea soup.

Frying, besides being a method of cooking unknown to most if not all of the "native" races, is least likely to be convenient. If it is convenient, and if you like fried things, there is no argument against it. Whites, no matter how long they have been on meat, are likely to get the notion occasionally that they might like fried liver. Even in this case, however, the general preference, growing stronger with the years, is for the liver either boiled or, if raw, frozen. Generally, as explained elsewhere, it is only seal livers that are used as human food—caribou liver is usually dog feed and bear liver is thrown away.

It happens frequently on land, though seldom if ever at sea, that roasting is more convenient than boiling. Perhaps you have killed a caribou and have no cooking gear. Then you make a fire and hang the meat at the right distance from it; or else you hold it toward the fire on a stick. There are various methods, and all of them are so familiar to whites who have done any camping that they are not worth describing in detail—except for one part, the head of caribou or moose.

METHOD FOR CARIBOU OR MOOSE HEAD

As said, most or all meat eaters believe that with caribou, moose, and with most of those fish which have large heads, the head is the best part of the animal. Usually these are eaten boiled; but many, and particularly the Indians of the northern woods, consider that either caribou or moose head should be roasted.

You do nothing to the head except skin it and remove the tongue—in some cases the brain may be removed, but not ordinarily. A head is so big that about the only suitable way of roasting it is to suspend it by the nostrils with a fairly long string, one that allows a good deal of spinning. You start the head spinning in one direction and keep it going for some time, then you stop it and it spins back again, and then back and forth for several minutes. When it is about to stop you are there to get it well started on the second cycle.

It takes between 1 and 2 hours to roast a head. In any case, there are few experts who can tell offhand when a head is done. So if you think that it may be nearly done, you just pull it away from the fire occasionally long enough to examine it.

FISH USUALLY BOILED

Even more decidedly than with meat, boiling is the preferred cooking method with fish. We have mentioned that heads are always boiled; the same is usually true of the rest of the fish, if it is fresh. The chief exceptions are with fish that is high or that has been dried.

Even high meat is usually eaten boiled. When fish are high they are seldom or never boiled. Eskimos are not fond of gamey fish if they are unfrozen, and they are usually kept for dog feed unless there is an emergency. But after the freeze-up in autumn, fish that were caught at various times of summer, and which therefore are now in various stages of decay, are looked upon as a delicacy, somewhat in the manner of our cheeses.

If not intended for drying, fish caught in midsummer are piled in windrows and covered with logs to protect them from dogs, ravens, foxes, and other thieving animals. On the north coast of Alaska, where the freeze-up is typically in September, July fish is pretty well decayed by then, August fish is moderately high, while a late August or early September fish is practically or wholly fresh.

High fish are eaten for a snack, corresponding to a tea, a forenoon lunch, or a supper; but they may be eaten sort of as a desert in one of the regular meals. Eskimos and northern Indians do not generally have the desert eating habit; the Eskimo use of high fish comes nearest to it. Otherwise the northerly peoples eat more small boy style—they eat first what they like best and make a whole meal of it if there is enough. If there is not enough, they finish up on the next best.

DRIED FISH

The other exception to fish being boiled, is as said, that they may be dried. Whether for decaying or for drying, fish are cleaned (all entrails removed) immediately after being caught. For the decaying nothing else is done to them. For the drying, they are split and the backbone removed. Usually the backbone and head are dried together, the rest of the fish being split in halves and hanging together at the tail. Dried backbones and heads are intended for dog feed—this is almost the only case where dogs get a chance to eat heads.

d. Preservation of Food

The use of cold, both intense and moderate, for preserving food and the like is discussed elsewhere, but we here mention some points.

If animals are properly butchered, the meat without cover is perfect after 6 or 8 months of winter, except that, for instance, a ham may develop a sort of skin by drying on the outside—this if it is exposed to the air but not if it is buried. Beans baked with pork will similarly be perfect for several months, although there may develop eventually a slight rancid taste in the pork. If you bake beans with fresh seal or whale fat, as whites in the North sometimes do, they will go rancid in a few days or weeks. The sea mammal fats become rancid even at the lowest temperatures if air gets at them.

If you are going to spend several years in a given place, you can store meat in underground chambers for years with only the precaution of avoiding certain molds that flourish at ground temperatures at least down to 20° below freezing. If these molds get into your storehouse you have to empty it of meat and destroy the mold either chemically or by peeling an inch or two of earth from floor, walls, and ceiling.

If an animal is buried so that the body is protected from air at average Arctic ground temperatures (from 0° to 10° F.), the flesh remains apparently practically unspoiled for thousands and perhaps tens of thousands of years, as shown by the remains of the now extinct mammoth which have been uncovered in the Arctic.

It has been reported by the Lomen Commercial Company and others that both reindeer meat and domestic beef have been preserved in perfect condition 4 years in galleries utilizing the natural underground temperatures of Alaska, as said, about 10° above.

Directly the best food preservative known, frost is indirectly valuable, too. For instance, if you want to dry fish or meat in summer you have to take some pains about keeping maggots out of them. If the season is rainy it may be difficult or impossible to produce good dried meat or dried fish beyond what facilities you can manage for smoke-drying. In winter, however, there is no trouble. True enough, drying then is very slow—it is said to take about a week in calm air at 50° below zero to dry a wet cotton handkerchief. But if it is several months before spring, you can split up your meat thick and spread it out on anything—on the snow, on a piece of wood, on stones—and it will be dry before spring, with no possibility of contamination except, as said, that even in cold weather seal, walrus, and whale blubbers become rancid when exposed to the air. In view of that you must be careful to remove all fat from any pieces of these meats you are drying.

Section IV

SOURCES OF WATER

At sea far from land the experienced Arctic traveler uses for drinking and cooking last year's ice, or older.

It can be distinguished from this year's by the rounded corners which are due to the rains and thaws of one or more summers, by looking bluish in comparison with salt ice, which is grayer, and by being glare while salt ice, even a snag sticking upward, is milky in appearance. A further difference, which you learn by experience how to judge, is in the way it splinters when you peck at it with your hunting knife. Salt ice is tougher, splinters less easily.

Ice of last year hardly ever has noticeable saltiness; ice which is 2 years old is probably fresher than average river or spring water. (See discussion in Chapter 2, Section III.)

In summer you are always sure of perfectly fresh water at sea by dipping it up from the hollows in old ice—you are safe unless the pond you are using is so near the edge that spray has dashed into it. Even on this year's ice, which itself is salty, you find in midsummer water plenty fresh enough for drinking—usually so fresh that it will do even for tea.

When the winds are unable to produce much wave action, because the surface where you are is mostly ice, you will find fresh water on top of leads in summer. Stefansson has reported 10 feet or more of perfectly fresh water in a lead resting upon the salt water underneath. These leads keep fresh into autumn so that even a month after the freeze-up you can chisel a hole in the ice, now a foot or 18 inches thick, and get fresh water.

As winter advances, however, the drifting of the ice churns up the ocean enough so that there probably are no fresh leads by November or at most Christmas.

However, the ice that formed in autumn on such leads is naturally still fresh.

In the early fall, fresh water is sometimes found by noting where there is a deep snowdrift covering a hollow in that paleocrystic ice—which we have described elsewhere and which looks like a rolling prairie. If the snow is 2 or 3 feet deep, you may find, even 2 or 3 months after the freeze-up, that the ice on the pond underneath is only a foot or so thick with quantities of fresh water underneath.

If there is no fresh ice around when you are far out at sea, you may have considerable trouble in getting perfectly fresh drinking water by melting snow. For the crust of salt on top of sea ice gets mixed with the snow in blizzards and drifts with it. However, the slight taint of brackishness is not likely to bother you—it would not be as bad as alkali water common in certain western states to which you are used.

If you are on ice so young that as yet it has little snow on it, then it is almost academic in most cases where you can find drinking water; for you are in so much danger that you are too scared to camp or even to stop for cooking a meal. Such stretches are not likely to be wide, and you will just keep going till you get on firmer ice where there is at least reasonably fresh snow.

On land the Arctic winter traveler will by preference chisel down through the surface of a lake or river till he gets fresh water. It saves a lot of time at camp, and it is a convenience when you are traveling. However, few like to cut through more than 5 or 6 feet. After that you prefer to melt ice.

It is perfectly safe to eat snow when you are thirsty, but most travelers find it pleasanter to drink water. If no water is obtainable, you eat snow or cracked ice during the day to quench your thirst and at camptime you bring indoors chunks of ice which are cut up for the pot as needed.

There are places where you cannot find fresh water or fresh ice. Usually these are on a coast where the ice to seaward is solid and where there is perhaps brackish water in a lagoon on the land side, your camp likely being on an intervening spit, for that is where the driftwood, which you may be using for fuel, is likely to be found. In this case you look around for snow that is granular. The more granular the snow the greater its water content per cubic unit of snow block. The best snow of all is so granular that it will not even cut into blocks. You bring this snow to the house in buckets or wrapped in a piece of cloth or skin.

There is no trouble about using new, spongy snow except that a lot of bulk makes very little water and also that, because of the air chambers, it takes a little more fuel to do the melting.

Here a caution is worth while. If the snow is extremely spongy and you have a hot fire under the pot, the snow will suck up, blotter fashion, the water which forms immediately over the flame, leaving a cavity there which permits the flame to play for awhile on metal which has no liquid on the other side of it. This is not dangerous with ordinary cooking utensils, but trouble will result if you are using, as Peary sometimes did, a 5-gallon kerosene can for a kettle. In that case the heat may spread out to the corners where they are soldered, melting the solder and ruining the pot.

The thing to do if you are using very spongy snow over a very hot flame is to put only a tiny bit of snow into the pot at first, just covering the bottom. You stand over it with a chunk of snow and a knife in your hand, and as you see melting what is on the pot's bottom you whittle more snow in to keep pace. When you have a quarter inch of water or so, there is no further need to be careful. Then you drop in chunks, but not too large. Only when you have several inches of water is it safe to fill the pot to its rim with the spongy snow.

During the summer there are innumerable sources of pure, fresh water. As explained elsewhere, it is in very few parts of the Arctic, and only in mountains, that you are likely to be at any time several miles from a lake. And in mountains, during the summer, you come upon a river or rivulet every little while. They are numerous though lakes are few.

CHAPTER 9

CLOTHING AND PERSONAL EQUIPMENT

Section I

GENERAL

As protection against the weather of their various seasons, the Eskimos have developed on the whole better garments than probably any people in history.

Completely dressed for winter in reindeer (caribou) skin, Eskimo style, you have a suit that weighs less than 10 pounds, all garments counted, inner and outer from head to heel. There are various degrees of softness in the garments according to the age of the animals, but, approximately speaking, every garment except the boots is as pliable as velvet. Nothing feels so good against the skin—not even silk—as underwear of the skin of a young caribou. With these garments you can sit outdoors at —50° and be practically unaware of the temperature, if no wind is blowing. It is commonplace, for instance, even with whites who have never worn such clothes before, to be so comfortable that, quite naturally, they will take off their mittens, pull out a pipe, light up and smoke with no thought as to whether they are doing it in cold or warm weather.

ARCTIC COSTUME

When typically dressed for cold weather in Eskimo clothes, an Arctic traveler wears fawnskin undergarments with the fur in—socks, drawers, shirt, and mittens. The outer garments—trousers, coat, boots, mittens—are made with the fur out, except that the hair side is in on boot soles always and on the palms of mittens usually. The coat goes over the head like a sweater—has no buttons or anything of the sort at the neck.

Of recent years Eskimos in western Alaska, and perhaps elsewhere, have started using zippers. This adoption is probably on a fashion basis, chiefly—the Eskimos see the whites using zippers and want them too. It is Stefansson's opinion, after wearing fur garments every day for 10 winters, that the zipper is no advantage. Whether there is a disadvantage is a mechanical problem that should perhaps be investigated—whether such things as caribou hair and ice from the breath, or a combination of them, can get into the zipper mechanism so as either to prevent its opening or, what would be more serious, prevent its closing again.

Since one of the advantages of the Eskimo style coat is in its being tailored loose, there can hardly be much advantage in the zipper, for nothing can come off more easily than the properly designed coat. There is, true enough, the slight advantage that when overheated you can open up the front of your coat; but, as hereinafter described, most people used to the Eskimo garment will prefer to take it off entirely, for a 2-pound fawnskin undershirt will keep you warm at the lowest calm weather temperatures as long as you are walking or otherwise exercising.

The hood of the coat should not come close around the face. The typical Eskimo style merely covers the ears and leaves the whole forward half of the head unprotected. The first "improvement" that a white man usually tries to make is that of having the hood fit snug about the face. The result, if the hood comes out to the cheekbones and to the point of the chin, is that a circle of hoarfrost forms on the face along the edge of the trimming of the hood, and presently the skin under the hoarfrost ring begins to freeze—or, at least, there is a tendency that way. If the face is completely bare there is sufficient distance between the nose or mouth and the trimming so that the breath, in very cold weather, freezes in the air on its way to the trimming and settles upon it in the form of hoarfrost, which is dry and can be brushed off.

An important feature of the Eskimo coat and shirt is that the sleeve is cut more like a trouser leg, so that you can slip your arm inside the coat. Then, if one of your hands gets cold, you pull that arm out of the sleeve and tuck the empty sleeve in your belt, carrying your bare hand against your bare breast. If you have to sleep outdoors without shelter, you remove both arms from the sleeves and sleep with them against your breast. You then have all possible body warmth imprisoned inside of your garments.

Both the shirt and outer coat are made so that they hang loosely outside of the trousers and come down about halfway to the knee.

WEIGHT

The entire caribou suit, when made of skins that are ideal as to the age and sex of the animals which contribute (see below), should weigh below 9 and 10 pounds. Outside the furs you may want to wear what are called snow pants and snow shirt, which are made of drilling or of some light and more windproof cloth such as burberry. A "filled" silk or other filled cloth should not be used—it will become stiff in the cold and the filling will crumble out where the garment wrinkles. These snow clothes combined should not weigh more than a pound. They are the only improvement so far suggested by whites that is more of a nuisance than it is worth. On a stormy day they keep the snow from being beaten by the wind into the roots of the hair of the outer furs. Also they contribute materially to warmth. For to the extent that they are windproof they imprison air and, of course, air is the nonconductor upon which we chiefly rely for conserving body heat.

WATER BOOTS UNEXCELLED

It is, however, only the winter clothes of the Eskimos that are near perfection. For the rains and heat of summer they are on the whole not so well clad as we. Still there is no invention of the white man that approaches their water

245

boots. The sole, though stiff and durable, weighs only an ounce or two; the upper to the knee is as thin and soft as the arm of a woman's evening glove. Yet they are practically as waterproof—the sole, the seams and the legs—as if they were of heavy seamless commercial rubber.

SECTION II

SKINS FOR CLOTHING

We discuss first skins which are obtainable in the Arctic and sub-Arctic, whether on purchase from natives or as the product of your own hunting.

POLAR BEAR

The skin of the polar bear is used of necessity in some parts of the Arctic and by choice elsewhere. For rough use, trousers of the skin, with the hair out, are perhaps about the best possible. They are not warm for the weight, but they are strong (will last many years if properly cared for), they shed snow, or rather, snow beats out of them easily; and they are to an extent waterproof—what would be called showerproof if they were being advertised by a dealer. They are made knee-length and almost necessarily so, for long trousers of this material would not bend easily enough to permit free movement of the legs.

FOX

A coat or shirt of fox, either blue or white, is certainly very warm for the weight. But, while they keep the hair longer than caribou, the skin proper is so fragile that the clothes need meticulous care. The fur mats, does not stand wetting, and gathers snow. Fox skins are much used by the Cape York Eskimos, probably because caribou is scarce. However, since they are much used, the people know exactly how to handle them and they like these skins because they are used to them.

WOLF

Wolf is stronger than fox and garments made of wolf are nearly as warm for their weight. The objections are the same as to fox—the matting, the sogginess when they are wet, and the difficulty of beating snow out of them.

WOLVERINE

Wolverine is used by the Eskimos who have access to the skins of these animals chiefly as a trimming material. Hoods are often edged with a band of wolverine fur. The skins are strong and may be about as good as domestic dog for clothing. But northern people have no experience of this, for wolverine is too costly—is used only for trimmings.

BEAVER

Beaver makes a very good coat. The natives use it un-plucked, for the long hairs aid in keeping snow from caking, and they shed rain to some extent. A beaver coat will last three or four times as long as caribou, but is heavy—not warm for its weight.

MUSKRAT

Muskrat coats are between good and medium in desira-bility. They are stronger than rabbit (see below). If you have skins enough for two coats, it would be better to make one out of the bellies and the other out of the backs than to make each coat out of whole skins. The hair is longer on the backs and the skin is stronger. Thus you would use the belly skins for a shirt and the backs for an outside coat. The skins are not as warm as beaver per coat, but they are probably warmer per pound.

SQUIRREL

The Arctic squirrel, or marmot, would come in for about the same remarks as muskrat.

HARE

The skin of the polar hare is so fragile (that of the bush rabbit still more so) that it is to be used only when you can-not get better things. Still, it makes very good slippers, not next to the foot, but in between the first and third layer of footgear. You can manage hare for a shirt if you handle it very gingerly.

OTHER FURS

Coats and other garments may be made out of almost any of the other fur animals, such as otter, marten, and mink. It is most unlikely that you would use marten or mink, for you know their commercial value and, if you had skins, you would, except in dire necessity, save them to bring home because of their market value.

BIRDS

The feathered breasts of certain birds, among them loons and some ducks, as well as sea-birds, make very good slippers to use like hareskin slippers—they are warmer and last longer than hare. Coats are sometimes made of birdskins, but only by those Eskimos who are hard put to it.

CARIBOU

Caribou is the best of all native Arctic materials for winter clothes, and so we discuss this skin more in detail than others.

UNDERWEAR

Underwear—shirts and drawers—should be made of calves anything from a few weeks to a few months old, or yearling females killed before September. Eskimos like underwear of newborn and even unborn fawn. But unborn or very young fawn is so delicate that you should not choose them for yourself until you have had considerable experience in the use of sturdier fur underwear.

For outer garments, coats and trousers, you want fawn from 4 to 6 months old or yearlings, male or female, killed between early July and early September, according to what part of the Arctic you are in—the earlier the spring the earlier the month in which skins are best for clothing. If they are later than September they are even warmer, pound for pound; the chief reason they are not favored is that the hair is then getting brittle. October to December skins are almost too warm for ordinary use; in spite of the coat shedding you may want to use them if you expect to travel as a passenger in a sleigh or in the open cockpit of an airplane. The reasons for the increased warmth per pound are two: As the season

248

advances the skin, which is the heavier part but not so warmth-giving, grows thinner, while the hair, the chiefly insulating portion but very light, grows longer.

MITTENS

For inner mittens you should have the summer skin of yearlings, though fawn is good if you do not work hard and if your hands don't perspire freely. The hair is inside for the entire hand. Outer mittens should ideally be of the leg skins of yearling or two-year-old caribou; the hair is outside except on the palm and on the inner side of the thumb.

The inner mitten should be to the wrist; the outer mitten may be either to the wrist or with a gauntlet, depending largely on what kind of coat you wear. There is no point in having a gauntlet mitten unless it fits snugly around a somewhat puffy sleeve and the puffiness usually results mainly from the length of the hair on your coat. If the gauntlet does not fit closely, snow gets inside and is a nuisance. Drawstrings are sometimes tried for gauntlet mittens, and are all right if you don't have to take them off frequently.

SOCKS

The socks, with the fur in, should usually be of summer yearling. Slippers to wear outside the innermost socks may well be of fawn skin. They may be of hare, bird, or other skin, but (in this one case in the entire suit) blanketing (duffle) is probably an improvement over any skin.

BOOTS

There is more variety in northern boots than in any other article of clothing.

BOOTS FOR USE ON LAND

A boot much in favor is of caribou leg and comes to just below the knee (as does the sock) where it fastens with a drawstring. Usually the breeches are something like two inches more than knee-length and you tuck them into the top of the boot which grips them by means of the drawstring. But some Eskimos prefer to have no drawstring in the boot, having it in the breeches instead, the breeches then coming outside the boots. The sole, shoepac type as always, is of August or September bull caribou, and from the back skin. October hides are sometimes used; but, as said, the skins get thinner as the season advances, so that in October they are not quite as strong.

An August or early September bootsole is so durable that on snow exclusively, or on snow and grassland, one pair of soles will carry you a thousand miles at least. However, you need a second pair to change into in order to keep both dry and thus prevent the hair from falling out, as later described.

BOOTS FOR WEAR ON ICE

If you expect to go out on the sea occasionally, where there is slush on top of the young ice, you have a boot as above except that the sole is bearded seal (ugrug) or beluga (white whale)—in emergency you would use the skin of a small seal but it would not keep its shape, be strong enough, or be really waterproof against brine. You may have to use walrus. This would not keep its shape so well as bearded seal or beluga, but is considered fairly good if your soles are cut from a skin that has been used a season in the cover of an umiak—the large Eskimo boat.

If you have a sealskin sole instead of caribou, you will necessarily have to wear more footgear inside. Normally, for a boot wholly of caribou, your entire foot equipment is in two pieces, only the boot itself and a sock of yearling skin. With a seal sole you should have, between the sock and the boot, at least two pairs of slippers—and preferably the outer of these should be of blanket, the inner of fawn or yearling skin. The outermost blanket slipper is advocated both to take up any brine that may enter (possible especially if the sole is from the small seal) and to take up moisture which forms from the condensation of the invisible perspiration (discussed later in this chapter) of the foot against the sole leather.

For winter the Eskimos of interior Alaska prefer a boot of caribou with the hair everywhere inwards. This boot is soled exactly as above described, but the leg, instead of being

250

made of caribou leg skin, is made of skin from almost any part of the body.

Other boots are described under Seal.

MOUNTAIN SHEEP

The nearest competitor to caribou among the native Arctic skins is the mountain sheep. The warmth-to-weight ratio may be even more favorable than that for the best caribou. However, the skins will then not be quite so durable nor is it quite so easy to beat snow out of them. The preparation and care are the same as with caribou—except that the care is somewhat more difficult.

SEAL

Seal is the most used skin if you take the whole Eskimo world, but in many cases this is from necessity rather than choice. For certain things, however, the skin of the small hair seal (several species) is unsurpassed.

Raincoats are usually made, as later described, of other materials, but sometimes they are of seal. If the garment is purely a raincoat, the tanning (see below) is the same as for water boots. A seal coat with the hair out and not specially prepared is merely showerproof.

OUTER COATS

The hair seal is not suitable for underwear at any season. For an outer coat with the hair out, the skin is good for weather that is not extremely cold. This garment is less warm for its weight than any we have so far described, but makes up for this partly by being the strongest of all materials, by being water-resisting, by the ease with which it sheds snow, and because it stands most kinds of rough treatment better than any other skin. This includes getting wet and staying wet, although no skin is really proof against much of that—the hair of all of them begins to drop off.

TROUSERS

For trousers, worn hair out, the seal has the same advantages and disadvantages as for a coat.

ALL-SEAL WINTER BOOTS

A very good all-round winter boot is of seal skin, hair out for the leg, and bearded seal or beluga sole. If the sole is bearded seal it may or may not have hair against the foot, usually not; if whale is used there is, of course, no hair. If all materials are available, this is the type usually chosen by hunters who cultivate the sea and frequently have to deal with the slush on young ice.

SUMMER WATER BOOTS

The ideal material for summer water boots is: for the sole a piece of bearded seal skin that has been in use for 1 or 2 years as part of an umiak cover; for the upper, the skin of one of the smaller species of the small seals—in northern Alaska and northwest Canada the *Phoca hispida*. This is black or dark brown in color, having been prepared merely by removing blubber and hair (as described later) and then by simple drying.

Substitutes for the ideal bearded seal sole, in descending order, are white whale, walrus and the skin of a very old male of one of the small seal species. In emergency you will use the hide of the back of the neck of a full-grown caribou bull or some thick part of musk ox hide. With the last two greasing is required, for those skins are more porous.

The thickness of the upper is controlled partly by choosing the age of your animal and partly by using back or belly. There are effective water boots made with upers so thin that when you hold them up against the light you can see clearly the outline of your hand pressed against from the other side. When slightly damp, as they must be before you put them on, the uppers of these boots are as soft as the finest kidskin. The sole is stiff and keeps its shape even after many weeks of wearing—especially, as said, if it comes from an old umiak cover, and if it has been well crimped (see below).

The reasons for the waterproofness of Eskimo boots and directions for the care and use of such boots are set forth later in this chapter.

COMMERCIAL BOOTS

For certain kinds of rough work, as around mines or in digging ditches, commercial water boots are better than the Eskimo. These will be in Alaska of the kind tried and tested by prospectors and miners. Representatives of the Army should try these out on the ground, at some such place as Fairbanks. We do not, therefore, attempt either a description or suggestions here.

There are possible a number of temperate zone substitutes for Arctic skins.

DOMESTIC SHEEP

Doubtless the most important southern competitor of the reindeer (caribou) in northern clothing is the domestic sheep. The advantages are abundance of supply, cheapness, durability, and comparative resistance to grease, the last making them specially suitable for use of mechanics. The chief disadvantage is that sheep is not nearly as warm as caribou for its weight. A further drawback, until better tanning processes are developed, is that sheepskin stiffens in cold weather.

Since lightness and pliability are not very important except for those who have to walk long distances, or who may have to do so, it would seem likely that in the beginning at least most skin clothes used by the Army for Arctic and sub-Arctic work will be made of sheep. We withdraw from application to them our possible objection to zippers, above; for sheepskins are likely to be worn chiefly in a forest where fires can be made and where icing of zippers would not be so serious.

Eventually there will perhaps be a seasonal issue of clothing so that even those who, in the long run, are best served by caribou skins for midwinter will use sheep in spring and autumn. However, the economy of doing this is lessened in that caribou skins, although they keep their hair well for a single year and with good care are suitable for two years, will not keep it satisfactorily for much more.

FUR SEAL

A commercial skin worth considering for winter clothing is that of the fur seal. Its advantages and disadvantages

253

are probably about the same as those of beaver, discussed above. Like beaver it should be used unplucked.

SECTION III

ESKIMO CLOTHING

a. Procurement

The perfection of Eskimo garments comes through the skill of the maker rather than through special processes. It is, therefore, difficult to give helpful instructions in a Manual. There are, accordingly, only four ways in which to provide yourself with Eskimo clothes.

The ideal way is to discover a family in which there is on hand, already made for one of its members, the garment you want and of the size you need. This is not so difficult as it might seem, for these clothes are all loose fitting—they must not be too small but it does little harm if they are a bit on the large side. Were it the plan to make them in lots of thousands (for the difficulty of which, see below) they would not need to be in more than three sizes, except for the boots which should perhaps be in almost though not quite as many sizes as the ordinary Army footgear.

The reason why it is best to purchase a garment which was intended for a member of the family is that the best are made only under two stresses—loving care and the knowledge that the maker is going to be criticized if defects appear.

The only way to secure a near approach to the same care in the making of clothing as a member of the family gets is to employ the requisite number of Eskimo families by the year, giving each seamstress the job of clothing a certain number of men and of looking after their clothes while they are within reach or of repairing the clothes when the wearer returns from a journey. They will look upon the men assigned them to clothe more or less as if they were members of their families. Very good results can be secured in this way, especially after some years when you have had a chance to coach for awhile those seamstresses who have not given the best satisfaction and to discharge any who may prove incurably careless or incompetent.

It is possible that tolerable results can be got in places where there are large Eskimo communities near you by having a certain number of your men assigned as regular customers to a given seamstress. She then knows they will come to her with complaints and that she will have to keep in repair the suits she makes.

The fourth method is the one that most white men have used in the Arctic, particularly in Alaska—just to buy clothes that have been made to sell. The results here are best when you inspect carefully each garment as it is brought in for sale. They are worst when you let it be known that you want a certain number of suits by a certain time.

The inadequacy of the fourth method, from the Army's point of view, is increased by the difficulty there would be in finding local white men to give advice on what clothes were up to a reasonable standard. For not many white men in Alaska (the exceptions being perhaps a third of those who have Eskimo wives) know what a good garment is. They have never had any good ones themselves, although they have been using Eskimo clothes for years, and they have never noticed the difference between the inadequate clothes which they have been wearing and the good ones that were being worn by some Eskimos.

The badness of the best clothes that Nome Eskimos make for sale results from the following main things: The skins are not of the right age and sex for the intended garment; the animals were not killed at the right time of year; the skins have been hastily and poorly sewn.

We must not overstate the case against clothes secured by the fourth of our plans. Polar expeditions, notably those of Admiral Byrd, have been outfitted by this method. It seems to explorers used to better clothing that being so dressed must be a handicap, if not a hardship. But men of the Byrd expeditions seem to have complained very little. They did good work in what to them evidently seemed reasonable comfort.

Garments like those supplied to Byrd have been worn since 1900 by an aggregate of thousands of different white men and white women around Nome, and generally on the Bering Sea coast of Alaska, usually with satisfaction to the wearers.

While the clothes have fallen below Eskimo standards, they nevertheless proved on the average beyond, or at least up to, the expectations of the white purchasers.

With all its drawbacks our fourth plan will probably have to be used if the Army wants large quantities of Eskimo style clothing. It will be necessary, then, to have for adviser to each purchasing agent a white man who, from having worn them through several years, knows what it is that makes good Eskimo clothes. The Eskimos themselves are, of course, even more competent judges; but it is difficult to find one of them who is willing to act as arbiter and to give, when called for, adverse opinions on the handiwork of his people. The next step will be to impress upon all Eskimos planning to submit garments for sale that they are going to be inspected by an expert and that clothes will not be accepted unless they pass his scrutiny. Alternatively, the Eskimos could be informed that garments will be graded into first, second and third class; that there will be a considerable price difference between the grades, and that whatever is offered for sale will be inexorably graded by the said competent expert. If some such procedure is rigidly followed it ought not to take many years until there have been developed in Alaska several hundred competent preparers of skins and cutters and sewers of garments.

b. *Preparation of Skins*

The following description of the preparation of skins is intended to give an understanding of the processes rather than facility in their use. However, preparing skins is not a fine art comparable to the making of the garments.

It is a loose expression, or a result of careless observation, to say that Eskimos "tan" caribou skins intended for winter clothes. True, certain processes which are fairly called tanning have crept into Eskimo territory from here and there—from the forest Indians chiefly, although in places from whites. Most if not all of these result in one or both of the drawbacks that the skins are stiffer and that they smell stronger.

The steps in the best preparation of caribou for garments are only three or four.

PRELIMINARY STEPS

Immediately after the animal is skinned, you spread the hide on the ground, flesh side up, or you hang it similarly over a pole. The drying preserves the skin until you want to use it.

For the first stage of preparation you work on a skin which either happens to be bone dry or which you have just dried by suspending it far from a fire—about twice as far as an inexperienced man would consider safe, for caribou skins spoil with ease difficult to believe. They should hang where the direct heat from the fire is just barely perceptible on your hand or cheek.

FIRST STAGE

Taking the dry skin, you sit so as to hold it conveniently over your leg above the knee. Another thing you can do is to spread the skin out on your caribou bedding or on any fairly level soft and reasonably flat surface. With a resilient softness underneath, you scrape the flesh side with any dull scraper. Those of flintlike stone are very good but of recent years Eskimos have preferred scrapers of brass, iron, or steel. One kind they like, is made of a short section of a 10-gauge shotgun barrel, the edges sharpened but not to razor keenness. A portion of a brass shotgun shell will do. An iron piping somewhat larger than 10-gauge is better. Sometimes they split the pipe so as to use only half, and there are other scrapers of various curvatures. In other words, practically anything will do.

When all the facia has been scraped from the hide, you dampen the skin slightly and hang it up, again remote from the fire, till it is thoroughly dry. Then you scrape again.

SECOND AND SUBSEQUENT STAGES

The process of scraping, dampening, and drying is repeated until you think the skin sufficiently soft. In the case of young fawns one scraping is usually enough. With yearlings two scrapings usually suffice, the first rough one and the second after the skin has been once dampened and then dried.

It is customary with Eskimos after the first scraping to dampen the skin, roll it up, and let it stay overnight in some

257

place where it will not freeze but is nevertheless fairly cool. Whether this is necessary is doubtful. The dampening must be so light; the hair must not get soaked when you roll up the skin—in that case it might rot loose from the hide.

RESULTS

A caribou skin that has been prepared with nothing but scraping, as above, is white in color and practically odorless. If you want to change the color and give as well what most whites think is an agreeable odor, you smoke the skin. The woods Indians do it by merely hanging it far enough from the fire in the place where they do their cooking, letting it stay there for a few days. Doubtless the same result can be attained more quickly in a smokehouse built and used in the style of farmers smoking meat—again with caution against overheating.

The smell of Eskimo caribou clothing, though frequently objected to when they are brought into city homes, is not necessarily disagreeable to everybody, even at first. For instance, both Colonel and Mrs. Lindbergh said they liked the smell the first time they used or handled Eskimo clothes, and Mr. and Mrs. Rockwell Kent gave the same testimony. Those who object to the smell, at least in some cases, do so apparently from a preconception—they seem to feel it is expected of them.

COMMERCIAL PROCESSES

There may be commercial processes now which produce skins as good for clothing as the scraped Eskimo, but none could be found between 1889 and 1906 during the heyday of the American whaling fleet in the western Arctic, when whaling captains went so far as sending skins to Europe for tanning. However, the best of the processes had only one serious defect—that the commercial tanned skins, although soft as Eskimo style in warm weather, stiffened with the cold. The Eskimo preparation keeps them as soft at −50° as they are at 50°.

FOREST INDIAN PROCESSES

Woods Indian ideas, such as rubbing decayed caribou brains or decayed liver on the skins (a process adopted by some

Eskimos) results in a strong odor, unpleasant to many whites, and, what is more serious, produces the same sort of stiffening with cold weather that resulted from commercial tanning.

SKIN FOR BOOT TOPS, GAUNTLETS

As described, one type of winter boot has the uppers from the leg-skin of caribou, and long mittens may have leg-skins for the gauntlets. Stiffness is here a merit and so leg-skins are scraped only enough to take out all the wrinkles that may have resulted from drying. If the piece is intended for socks, it is scraped as soft as any other part of the hide.

SKIN FOR BOOT SOLES

Also for the sole of a winter boot you scrape just enough to take out the wrinkles. The skin you want for this is from the back of the neck of a bull caribou killed when the hair in that part is about ½ or ¾ inch long, which might mean anything between early August and late September, according to where in the Arctic the animal is killed.

BULL HIDES FOR BEDDING

Commonly it is not wasteful to take the necks off your caribou hides for this purpose, since doing so makes them a better shape for bedding, and that is the chief role of bull hides. For that use they are either scraped merely to remove wrinkles or left quite unscraped.

If you are short of the right kind of skins for boot soles, you may get other pairs from the hide along the back, the next best being from the shoulders and possibly even from the rump.

If the hair is more than ¾ of an inch long, you can, so far as the hair itself is concerned, deal with the situation by clipping. But what you cannot help is that as the hair lengthens the skin gets thinner, so that if your bull has hair 2 inches long on the back of his neck, his hide is no longer ideal for boot soles.

It is sometimes said that Eskimo women chew these soles to make them soft so they can be given the shoepac shape. It is more correct to say merely that the soles are crimped into the required shape by biting with the front teeth. (This is not the beautifully regular full crimping of the soles of water boots; it is, in fact, more a wrinkling or puckering of the edge of the sole.)   Certainly the bootmaker has no conscious object of softening the leather—the stiffer it is the better, for what you desire is that the boot shall keep its shape, which is attained partly through the stiffness of the leather itself though partly by designing the boot so that the upper tends to hold the sole in position.

Sometimes, for want of hide that is stiff enough to need crimping, the soles of your caribou-leg boots are just bent by hand into approximate shoepac shape.

INLAND TYPE OF BOOT

The inland type boot never has a crimped sole. Either just from custom or because footgear wears out less quickly in most places inland, the back country Eskimos use thinner skin for their boot soles. If they know they are going to have to travel over rocky ground they use underneath the heel and the ball of the foot round patches of some heavy leather, frequently sealskin which they have bought from coastal people—otherwise neck skin of bull caribou from which the hair has been scraped. This sewing is with stitches that do not, or at least preferably should not, go all the way through the sole leather.

PREPARATION OF SMALL SEALSKINS

The preparation of the skins of the small seal (any of the ordinary northern seals except the bearded) for coats, trousers or uppers of boots is essentially the same as with caribou. What you have sticking to the flesh side of the skin, however, is not fragments of lean, as with caribou, but a little blubber. For that reason you begin by wetting the skin and then, holding it over your knee, shaving off the blubber with a very sharp knife. Next you dry and remove the last vestiges of fat by rubbing with something like sand or ashes. Now you stretch the skin to dry, preferably out of doors—it will dry in a day in summer or in a week in winter. Eskimos frequently peg out the skins on the southward face of a snow wall, in some cases a wall erected for that purpose.

When the skin is thoroughly dry, you scrape as with the first caribou scraping.

REMOVING HAIR

In dressing seal and walrus for use where no hair is wanted, as for waterproof boots or for boat covers, you first remove particles of flesh and fat as above. The skin is then rolled into a bundle with the hair side inward and kept in a warm place until sour and the hair loose. Small seal skins are sometimes dipped in hot water to hasten the loosening of the hair.

When loose, the hair is scraped off and the skin is stretched on a wooden frame, made from sticks of driftwood, by stout cords passed through slits around the edges and over the side bars of the frame.

WHITE TAN

The beautifully white, parchmentlike leather used for dress boots and ornamental work is made of small seal skins from which the hair has been removed. The skin is then soaked in urine to free it from the oil, stretched upon the drying frame and exposed in the open air during the coldest months of winter; the intense cold and the beating of the dry snow upon the surface of the skin bleach it to a satiny whiteness.

c. *Use and Care*

No grease should ever be rubbed on the upper of a well-made sealskin water boot or into any seam—the only greasing theoretically permissible is for the outside of the boot-sole, in case the material is second-rate and inclined to be porous.

Among Eskimos there are two reasons why you must not grease a seam. If the woman who made the boot, her friends or relatives, see you doing it they take it for an insult— a sign that you do not have confidence in the workmanship. The second reason is that, in Eskimo belief at any rate, greasing shortens the life of the boot. Almost certainly it is true, as they say, that you need even more care in drying a boot after it has been greased than before. There is a further difficulty if the boot has been greased: Some of the oil will get into the sinew and will prevent it from expanding properly, a necessity for making and keeping the seams watertight.

However, it is usually necessary to grease these water boots that have been made to sell—ones, for instance, you purchase in a shop at Nome. The "civilized" local Eskimos do not mind seeing you greasing those; they don't take seriously garments which have been made to sell and they are getting used to white men's views and ways. It is hard to restrain a white man from greasing a boot.

A SPECIAL TYPE OF SEAL BOOT NEEDS GREASE

We have seen that seal boots well made out of stock rightly prepared should not be greased; that if shoddily made from good stock they have to be greased at the seams. But sometimes water boots are made of sealskin not originally intended for water use. Then not only all seams but the entire boot have to be greased.

For certain uses a boot of this last type is best. The Eskimos do not have any way of so preparing sealskin that it retains the hair and is also water excluding. But there is warmth in the hair; during spring and autumn you need warmth in your boots as well as power to keep your feet dry. To meet that condition a boot is made with a sole of waterproof bearded seal, or one of the substitutes, and an upper of the fairly heavy skin of a mature small seal. The hair is turned in; the outward facing skin side is greased at least twice. After the first greasing the boot is hung up to dry for a day or two, preferably outdoors in the shade. A second greasing is applied just before the first time the boot is worn.

CARIBOU WATER BOOTS MUST BE GREASED

In spring and autumn waterproof boots are needed inland and it may be that the only material available is caribou. The uppers are then greased just as we have described for the seal boots that have a hair side in towards the leg. It is hard luck if you have to make the sole of the inland water boot also of caribou. If you must, you use the thickest skin you can find, no doubt from the back of the neck of an August- or September-killed bull caribou, and grease it again and again with the best fat available.

262

It is considered that the best oil for greasing leather which is not otherwise waterproof is seal, and new seal oil is considered better than rancid—it is stickier, forms a better waterproofing. Whale and walrus oil are next best. If you are inland you use as a substitute the fat from hoof bones and those just above the hoofs of caribou, mountain sheep or moose, the equivalent of our neat's-foot oil. Tallow of the northern herbivorous animals, or our beef and mutton tallows, are passable waterproofing in warm weather; but they are not good in winter for the grease coating breaks and the ingredients fall away where the boot creases. Lard is medium good—it is much better than tallow but not as good as an oil.

A makeshift waterboot can be made of canvas with sole of bearded seal or one of the substitutes. The canvas must be fairly heavy. The best greasing here is lard—if you grease a canvas upper with seal, the oil will keep working through into your socks; whereupon they cease to be nonconductors and your feet are in danger of freezing.

CARE OF LEATHER USED IN WATER

The main principles in the care of all water gear made of skin—among them clothes, boats, leather water buckets—are: Be careful they are kept dry when not in use; dampen them a little while (say, ten minutes to half an hour) before use; don't let them stay wet continuously long enough for bacterial breakdown (not more than two or at most three days); dry them carefully.

The technique of drying and dampening of water boots needs special description because they are the most delicate and special conditions apply.

The rate of bacterial action upon rawhide depends on degree of warmth and uniformity of warmth; it may depend also on salt in the water. It would appear to be for both chemical and physical reasons that a water boot will last longer if you use it in salt than fresh water—the salt water is likely to be colder, inhibiting bacterial action, and the salt itself kills many bacteria. A boot used in fresh water, then, decays more rapidly because it is warmer and because the bacteria which flourish only on the inside of a boot used in sea water flourish on both sides of the leather with fresh water use.

263

The warmth which promotes decay in a boat is furnished by the weather and the water. In the case of a boot there is an additional source of heat, the warmth of your foot.

ON JOURNEYS CARRY SPARE BOOTS

You start a journey with boots which are either new or which have been so dry since they were made that you know there can have been no bacterial action. You are very careful to keep dry all spare boots. For the pair you are going to wear tomorrow you do one of two things: If you expect to have to start traveling the moment after you awaken, you dampen your boots in the evening. This is best done by taking each boot separately, holding the mouth of it tight so no water can enter, and thrusting it completely below the surface of water. Pull it out after a moment's immersion, let it hang till dripping from it ceases, then roll it up and put it where it will be reasonably cool, as, for instance, underneath your bedding. If you do not expect to travel until half an hour or more after you wake up, you dampen the boot, as above, the first thing in the morning. You can put it on immediately, if you like; or else lay it aside while you are breakfasting. In either case, the sinew thread swells so that the seams of the boot will be waterproof when you start to travel.

EMERGENCY DAMPENING

If, through emergency, you are compelled to put on dry boots, then you watch for your first opportunity and thrust your foot for a fraction of a second into water almost to the top of your boot, pulling your foot out before an appreciable amount of water has had time to trickle through the seams. If, after this, you can walk 15 minutes to half an hour before beginning to wade, you will find the boots giving you full protection.

In summer the best way to dry boots is to hang them in the air, whether sun or shade does not matter except that sun dries them quicker. Take the boot down when it is dry rather than shrivelled. They may be packed either by folding the upper round and round the sole or, better still, by folding the leg, accordion-fashion, so that it fits inside the sole of the boots.

If you dry by use of a fire, you must be even more careful with water boots than with winter clothing to have them far enough from the source of heat. Take as a rough standard a kitchen where cooking is being done on an ordinary old-fashioned range. Winter skin clothes should not be closer than 6 feet from such a stove, and water boots should be at least 10 feet away.

On the third Stefansson expedition a lot of water boots were ruined by sailors who hung them 3 or 4 feet away from a stovepipe. Their excuse was afterwards that they had noticed hardly any appreciable heat from the pipe.

These directions should not be misunderstood to mean that it is almost impossible to keep skin boots in good condition. All we mean is that you must be very careful. This care becomes second nature after awhile—you take the right precautions almost without thinking.

It follows from the above that you must have two or three pairs of water boots for summer travel. When the weather is dry two would be ample; the third is a precaution against rainy spells. Our statement that each pair can be worn a maximum of 3 days at a time without drying is on the assumption that you always take them off when you camp. If you sleep with them on, or have to wear them day and night for any reason, the maximum period between dryings will be reduced to 2 days or even less.

The period during which a boot remains dry need not be long—just long enough to kill the bacteria by desiccation.

With proper alternation and care, the uppers will last longer than the soles, for there is practically no wear on them. The soles will last through a 4-months' summer if you do not walk much on stony ground. As explained for winter boots, you take precautions against stones when necessary by sewing large roundish patches under heel and ball of foot, these to be replaced when worn out. Approximately speaking, then, an outfit of two or three pairs lasts you through a season—even with continuous use, as, for instance, if you are the caribou hunter of a party and average 20 miles of walking per day throughout the summer.

The waterproofness of the best Eskimo sealskin boots depends on two things, the skill of the sewer and the use of a sinew thread that swells enough on being dampened to fill all needle holes.

TESTING A BOOT FOR WATERPROOFNESS

If you are compelled to use water boots not made by someone practically a member of your family, you should before purchase test them as good seamstresses do when they are making them. The shopkeeper naturally shows you a dry pair. Before accepting it, dampen as above, and wait at least half an hour. Then take the soft top of the boot in your hand, somewhat as you might a paper bag, blow until you have completely inflated the boot, and then give a twist so as to confine the air. Press and increase the pressure steadily till the boot is smoothly inflated at every point, then pass each seam along near your cheek so as to try to detect the escape of air. A more delicate way is to have a candle burning steadily and pass the seams of your boot near the flame—being careful, however, not to hold any spot very long near the flame; for we repeat, it is incredible to most people how a little heat will injure this type of leather. A still more conclusive and a simple way is to hold the inflated boot under water and see if any bubbles arise.

If the least bit of air does escape from a boot that seems to be of good workmanship, you might give it a second break. Dampen additionally the seam where the air has been escaping, wait a quarter of an hour and try again. If the air still escapes, the seam needs resewing at this point. If that is not attainable, you dry the boot, and grease the untrustworthy seam before you wet it again preparatory to wearing.

Short water boots, or slippers coming a little above the ankle, may be of use around camp, sort of as bedroom slippers, in damp surroundings. For other use you want a boot which comes at least to just below the knee. There it grips your leg tight with a drawstring. Ordinarily this is just tight enough so that if you were to slip casually into water for a moment a little above the boot top no appreciable amount would get in.

TIGHT DRAWSTRING MAY PRODUCE VERICOSE VEINS

But it may be that you have to wade all day in water that comes above the knee. Here a difficulty arises—there certainly appears to be at least a small danger of the development of varicose veins through such extremely tight lashing as is necessary if you want to keep all water from entering during an all-day wade. That you will have to take this small chance is not to be taken as granted, for you cannot in any case keep your feet dry all day, no matter what footgear you use. In the angle we are just going to present, your feet get wet even sooner in a sound rubber boot than in a well made skin boot.

NO FOOTGEAR WILL KEEP FEET DRY IN SUMMER WADING

There is ice water outside your boot and your foot and leg are inside of it. From every part of your skin there is emerging the invisible perspiration (discussed later). This is bound to condense against the chilled material. For some time your woolen or other fabric socks will absorb this; but long before evening your feet are going to be distinctly wet. We said this condition was even worse in a rubber boot. This is because that material is a better conductor than leather of the chill from the water. (In cases where feet are actually kept dry inside rubber boots, if such occur, this must be because they are open at the top, allowing the escape of moisture, which would not serve if the water in which you travel is over your boot tops.)

On the Stefansson expeditions the men were given their choice about tight lashing of boot tops, the risk having been impressed upon them. Some excluded all water the whole time with tight lashing. Others lashed so that the water trickled in very slowly. The difference between this and having it come in fast is that your foot warms up the confined water so that you are in effect wading in warm water all day. In cases where water was permitted to enter, the boot, of course, had to fit rather tightly against foot and leg. Otherwise the man would have had to lift a considerable weight at each step.

267

There were from the various Stefansson expeditions only one or two cases of the development of slight varicose troubles. It is even possible that these may have had another origin, although the men did blame them on the tight lashing.

Though you walk all day across a swampy northern prairie in Eskimo boots your feet will keep dry unless they perspire. For the water you step into is more or less warm and the immersions are only occasional, so little or no inside condensation need occur. It is only during summer travel on sea ice that you have to wade say two-thirds of your traveling day through water ranging from ankle to knee-deep. That you do seldom have to wade through deeper water is because of the standard thickness of sea ice. When the puddles on top of it begin averaging more than eighteen inches deep the ice is no longer safe for travel. As elsewhere explained, you must be ashore before the thaw proceeds that far, or else you must select a good heavy floe on which to camp and spend the summer, resuming your travel in the autumn.

SEMIWATERPROOF BOOTS FOR SEA ICE TRAVEL

In dealing with slush ice you should be wearing preferably boots with soles of bearded seal and legs of small seal with the hair in. (Regular summer water boots are too cold; full deerskin winter boots will get wet through.)

Or, also very suitably, you could use the intermediate form which has a bearded seal sole with an upper of oiled caribou skin with the hair in.

HIP-LENGTH WATER BOOTS

Seal water boots are sometimes made to the hip by Eskimos for their own use, and frequently for whites. They are best for such semisedentary occupations as duck-shooting or fishing. They did not win favor on the Stefansson expeditions, for in most cases such boots remain dry up around the knee and are therefore stiff enough to interfere appreciably with knee action.

INSOLES OF MOSSES AND GRASS

If your socks are insufficient, especially if your boots are large and with thin soles, you can do well putting moss into the sole as a pad. Dry grass is used for this, too, and good results can be had with no socks at all—with your feet bare inside of the boots and with enough grass or moss between them and the sole.

The chief disadvantage of feet bare except for moss or grass is that you cannot then deal with hoarfrost very well by the methods outlined in Section IV of this chapter. A compensating advantage is, however, that you can throw the grass or moss away when it gets full of hoarfrost, or soggy, and use new material. This applies more or less even if the journey is across sea ice, for you can provide yourself with a bag of moss or grass before leaving shore. On an Arctic prairie you can find as you go along grass that will do for insoles.

The advocates of grass as an adjunct to Arctic footwear sometimes claim that it keeps your feet warm by bacterial action—by the heat of fermentation.

WATERPROOF COATS

Waterproof coats are sometimes made of skins prepared as those for uppers of water boots. More often they are made of the dried intestines of large animals, slit lengthwise, the strips arranged vertically in the garment. For waterproofness the sewing thread used ought to be sinew.

KAYAKER'S COAT

A special variant of the waterproof coat is used by kayakers, chiefly in Greenland and Alaska. The garment is hooded, with a drawstring pulling it close around the face so that very little water can get in. It is also tightened at the neck, so that, if any water does get by around the face, it will not go farther down. Tight lashing at the wrists prevents water entering there, and the bottom of the coat is lashed around the mouth of the kayak. Man and kayak are thus in one water-excluding piece. (See Chapter 12 for discussion of kayaks and their use.)

So far we have dealt chiefly with ways of caring for skin boots; we now turn to the other garments which constitute an Arctic costume.

A first essential in the care of garments to be worn in cold weather is that they shall be kept free of grease. On the well-known principle which we have mentioned several times, that the warmth of a garment depends on air chambers, it follows that if grease fills the chambers the insulating qualities of the material are greatly decreased; for grease is a good conductor of heat.

At the time of the mishap it is equally bad to get the air chambers of your garments filled with water or with grease. But getting wet is less serious in the long run; for the water can be removed by a simple process of drying, while removing grease is not simple under the best of conditions and may be in practice impossible when you are on a journey.

All northern travelers should, therefore, acquire the point of view of the Eskimos with regard to grease. Those of them who are not sedentary, and whose culture has not been too much influenced by whites, are as careful to see that no grease gets onto a winter garment as a meticulous housekeeper is with us to see there is no dust on the furniture. There is a difference between dust with us and grease with them— dust in a house need not be more than a sign of untidiness; grease in winter clothing can be a matter of life and death.

It follows from what we have said that nothing can be more silly than what we hear occasionally about Eskimos keeping warm in winter by greasing their bodies.

We mentioned the idea of some whites that frostbite may possibly be retarded by heavy vaseline greasing of the face. We pointed out there and repeat here that even if vaseline did serve as a face protector, it ought not to be used, nevertheless, for it would be nearly impossible to keep some of it from getting into some part of your clothing.

Other suggestions for the care of both the outer and inner garments of a skin suit, and for the care of skin sleeping bags, have chiefly to do with preventing moisture from getting into them, not only the moisture that may come from contact with snow, ice, and water, but that which results from visible and invisible perspiration. This is a special northern problem, requiring special explanation. We therefore treat in the following section the further precautions involved.

270

PROTECTION FROM VISIBLE AND INVISIBLE PERSPIRATION

a. Statement of Problem

The problem and technique of how to keep winter clothes dry hinge upon there always being an "invisible perspiration" coming out of the human body—a vapor invisible at ordinary temperatures but visible even around $-30°$ or $-40°$ and becoming rapidly more conspicuous as temperatures drop towards $-70°$, $-80°$, and $-90°$. If you hold out a dry hand at $-50°$ or colder you will see a cloud of steam rising from the palm and wisps of steam from the fingers. Added to this as a source of moisture is, of course, the ordinary, visible perspiration caused by exertion and too-warm clothing. The combined moisture of the two perspirations condenses somewhere in the garments in the form of hoarfrost.

In cold weather the dew point, or point of condensation, is reached in the second or third layer of clothing where the cold from the outside meets the warm "steam" and turns it into hoarfrost. If only two layers of clothing are worn, it may be at $-20°$ that the dewpoint is reached outside of the second layer and that all frost will either float away on the air as a fog or gather exclusively on the outside of the outer garments, where most of it can be brushed off. But if the temperature drops another 20° or 30°, the condensation will begin to take place between the two layers. Then, unless necessary precautions, as outlined below, are taken, there will be a melting if the temperature later moderates or in the warmth of a camp. Later, on being exposed to the cold, the dampness turns to ice.

To illustrate: If, wearing three-ply mittens, you walk in cold weather with your hand unclenched for several hours and then clench it into a fist, you will soon feel dampness against your palm and between your fingers, while the back of your hand still feels dry. You have melted the rime which had gathered between the layers in the palm of your mittens, while on the back of your hand the hoarfrost is still hoarfrost. Now open your hand; presently the palm of your mitten will be stiff while the back remains flexible. Take off the three-ply mitten, separate the layers, and you will find that you can shake or beat the hoarfrost out of every part except the palm. There a shaking or beating process is of no use because the dry and powdery hoarfrost has first been liquefied and has later had a chance to freeze into ice.

b. *Procedure in Camp*

The problem of garments thus becoming damp from visible and invisible perspiration, and of growing constantly more wet during travel at low temperatures, was stated by Nansen as being insoluble. The dangers and inconvenience which result from a failure to follow the proper procedure when in camp can be illustrated by his experience.

Nansen and his one companion, Johansen, traveled during the cold days dressed in several layers of clothing, with hoarfrost forming in one layer or another. They camped at evening by pitching a tent, inside of which the temperature would possibly be $-10°$ against say $-40°$ outside. None of their clothing was removed. The change of temperature between outdoors and camp was enough to shift the melting point in the garments—the hoarfrost lodged in the middle of the three layers would melt, making that layer damp, some of the moisture reevaporating and condensing over again in the outside layer. If any passed through the outermost layer without condensation it would rise and condense against the canvas of the tent, where would condense also the breath of the campers and the steam from cooking.

The Nansen-Johansen sleeping bags were of several layers. When, fully clad, they crawled inside these bags they began to get wet. A very little of the moisture was from snow which had adhered to their clothing accidentally; most of it was from hoarfrost which now melted in various garments.

What reevaporation there was during the night condensed in some layers of the sleeping bag, to remain as hoarfrost only till the sleeper turned over so that what had been above him was now underneath his body. Then the hoarfrost became liquid.

The first morning Nansen crawled out of his bag with damp rather than wet clothes. Little of that moisture

272

evaporated during the day, while he was accumulating as much again in the form of new hoarfrost. After the second night in his sleeping bag he was nearly twice as wet; after the third nearly three times, and so on until, after some weeks, the bags weighed several times as much as they had in the beginning, the difference being ice.

Because of the melting due to his body heat, Nansen slept, he says, in the equivalent of an ice-water bath every night. When he got up in the morning he did not dare to permit the sleeping bag to freeze crumpled up. So that he might be able to get into it at evening it had to be kept straight to freeze rather like a barrel. He was forced to be even more careful with his own clothing. He took hold of the sleeves and stretched them while they froze, being similarly careful with his trousers. He kept bending his body, elbows, knees, and hips, so that there would be joints to permit movement. When the freezing was complete the clothes worked somewhat like medieval plate armor. They were almost as hard as metal. Nansen tells that the edge of his frozen sleeve cut his wrist so that he would carry the scar to his dying day.

The Nansen type of difficulty becomes serious only on long cold journeys where there is no chance to dry your clothes by a fire. During such weather it is advisable to use snowhouse camps, which Stefansson's parties normally did. Their clothes, as said, were caribou—underwear with fur in; outer garments with fur out; outside of these the snow shirts and snow pants of drilling, khaki, or gabardine.

To outline the procedure, take for example an extremely cold day, of fairly light work, when the members of the party are wearing three suits (total weight, furs and outer cloth garments, 11 pounds).

PREPARATION OF BEDDING

With the snowhouse erected, the cook of that day goes inside and the bedding is handed in to him. The first skins are to be the lowest and they are laid fur-side down on the snow. It does not matter how much snow clings to the fur side of these bottom skins, for it is never going to have a chance to melt. All the housekeeper does, then, with the first layer is to brush the snow from the top or skin side.

273

The second or top layer of bedding will be skins placed with the hair up. At low temperatures snow and hoarfrost are as dry as the dryest dust. The housekeeper beats off the fur side and brushes off the skin side before putting the top skins in position.

The snow platform underneath the bedding is now covered with a double insulation so effective that, even if you bring the temperature of the dwelling later to 50° or 60°, there will be no chance for the lower layer of skins to get wet by the melting of the snow underneath.

The third stage is to bring in the sleeping bags—of one thickness and with the fur short, for a reason which will appear.

Standing in the low part of the house in front of the bed platform, the housekeeper now peels off his outer garments. He gives each a perfunctory shake as he takes it off and then puts it down on the floor or into the alleyway. For, as said, no amount of hoarfrost or snow can make a garment wet unless it melts, and the temperature in front of a bed platform will remain far below freezing.

The housekeeper is now dressed in one layer of clothing, his light reindeer skin underwear. There may be a little hoarfrost on the outside of this, which he brushes off. There can not be any inside the underwear, for the body warmth during the day has prevented invisible moisture from condensing that close to the source of heat.

The housekeeper has entered a cold house which he later warms up with a fire—hence the above procedure. The rest of the party will enter a house already warm. Accordingly, they take off their outer clothes either outdoors or in the alleyway. They handle them carefully if they want to bring them into the house (beating off all hoarfrost and snow), or shake them casually if they are going to leave them in the alleyway.

The frost can be removed by beating with a stick if the hair side is involved; the frost that is on the skin side of a garment is usually removed by scraping with a knife.

As said, about the only improvement on Eskimo clothing has been the snow shirt (snow coat) and trousers. The only considerable improvement on technique is that you might carry a whiskbroom which would remove more easily than a knife the frost that gathers on smooth surfaces. A broom is also pretty good for removing frost that is in hair or fur, although beating with a stick is best—the snow flies out as dust flies when you beat a carpet.

A little hoarfrost may remain on the skin side and the hair side of your outer garments. The best thing, then, is to see to it that they do not thaw out during the night. You can do that by leaving them outside, which is best if there is no danger such as from dogs; if you feel you have to take them into the house for safety, then you slip them underneath your bedding, which must be so thick that it completely insulates the snow beneath from what is going to be the considerable warmth of the interior of your tent or snowhouse.

PROCEDURE WITH SLEEPING BAG

This description of technique is based on Eskimo methods as practiced on the Stefansson expeditions. Had his men slept in their clothes, as did Nansen and Johansen, they, too, would have had trouble. For if there are, say, 10° of frost on the bed platform and if you are dressed in fur underwear inside the sleeping bag, the invisible perspiration will condense either on the outside of your underwear or on the inside of the bag. In either case, when you turn over in your sleep, you will melt some of this hoarfrost and that will make you wet. Accordingly, the way to keep dry is to sleep naked.

Stefansson's men tried very light pajamas in the sleeping bags and found they added nothing to comfort under the best of conditions, while under the worst conditions they imprisoned enough body heat so that the condensation point for invisible perspiration was reached inside the bag, resulting in hoarfrost, followed by liquid moisture and stiff freezing in their turn.

We now come to the above-mentioned point, that the fur on the inside of a sleeping bag must be short. If the hair is a half inch long or more there are two bad results—the sleeping bag is too warm, so that liquid perspiration (sweating) is produced; and the invisible perspiration condenses in the roots of the hair.

If you sleep in a thin reindeer bag, most of the invisible perspiration does not become visible until after it has actually left the bag, so that it ascends as a kind of steam to the roof and condenses against the snow, where it sticks. A little may form on the outside of the bag and this will melt if you turn over in your sleep, but there is at all temperatures a certain amount of evaporation and this occasional slight dampening does not aggregate enough to make and keep the bag wet.

It will happen that a portion of the sleeping bag becomes slightly wet. If you see to it that the section frozen stiff is on top of you when you go to sleep, it nearly always dries so that next day there is no stiffness. If the wetting is more than ordinary, take off your clothes soon after camping, get into your bag, and spend that many more hours in it. After a few campings the bag will be dry.

SOLUTION 2

The preceding solution depends upon the careful removal of more than 90 percent of the hoarfrost when you undress at each camping, and an arrangement to make the remaining 10 percent evaporate. Peary developed a solution which relies on making all the hoarfrosts first melt and then evaporate.

Practically every man who traveled with Stefansson has testified that he enjoyed himself from day to day and never had any hardships. Peary's men, of similar caliber, have nearly or quite all said or intimated that their journeys were unpleasant. The chief answer is that Peary's solution, though simple and nearly foolproof, leads to much discomfort.

Peary carried no sleeping gear except bedding, the men sleeping on top of it in full wearing apparel. The only modification was that sometimes they had night socks—they took off their boots and stockings, most or all layers of which had become wet, wore the bedsocks, and dried the day socks by putting them next to their skin inside their clothes for the night.

If you wear the same clothes day and night it seems, from Peary's experience, that you can more or less balance the hoarfrost accumulation by drying. You have, then, the advantage of carrying no sleeping bags. But there are disadvantages: the loss of strength from unsound sleep and from discomfort is considerable; men have to eat more food to counterbalance physiologically the loss through chill; outer garments will always contain a certain amount of hoarfrost, so that they are both heavier and less warm.

The saving in weight by the Peary method is, therefore, apparent only. The saving in bulk is real, and the saving in handling. The main advantage, as said, is that the plan is nearly foolproof.

c. Procedure When Traveling

On the road you keep the formation of hoarfrost in the clothes to a minimum through preventing the ordinary visible perspiration that results from physical activity and warm clothing. The method, as practised by Stefansson and his men during thousands of miles of travel in cold weather, is one of regulation of temperature by adjustment of clothing:

On a very cold morning, when breaking camp, the traveler will wear the full outfit of three layers, except that occasionally a man will work with one or both hands bare for a few minutes at a time, the mittens, or the one not in use, hanging by a string that passes over his shoulders.

STANDARD ARRANGEMENT OF CLOTHING

As explained earlier, the coat and shirt are not tucked into the top of the trousers; they hang loose except that they are kept in at the waist by a belt which probably is outside the outer fur coat, leaving the snow shirt unrestrained. The shirt, coat, and snow shirt come about halfway to the knee.

On the road, after half an hour of rapid going, the traveler begins to feel too warm, no matter how cold the weather. The first adjustment for coolness, and to prevent wetting by perspiration, will be to remove the belt so that a certain amount of chill can come up around his body, naked from the waist. So far as this chill comes up it is agreeable; but it does not come up much because of cold air being heavier than warm.

The coat and shirt are loose at the neck. Therefore the next cooling step may be to pull the coat forward at the neck to make an air channel all the way down from the throat. Cold air will then begin to flow down over the front of the body, which again feels most agreeable if you are overheated. By now you are probably walking barehanded, both mittens hanging suspended by their cord.

On growing still warmer, you stop the sledge to take off your outer skin pants, wearing now just the drawers and snow pants. The next step (not necessitating a stop for you can manage while walking) is to remove your outer skin coat, wearing now the shirt and snow shirt. If this is a little cool, as it may be, you put on your belt again.

If in a little you begin to feel warm even so lightened, you take off the snow pants and snow shirt, walking now in just your underwear. It does occur at even −40° and −50°, with no wind blowing, that you wear nothing but underwear much of the day, putting on outer clothing, however, any time you stop to rest or when you stop to camp.

You must never decrease the amount of foot protection, for several reasons. Your feet are particularly liable to freeze; or, rather, freezing of the feet is particularly serious. You can always tell when any other part of your body approaches the freezing point, but you may not be able to tell with your feet because they are so encased. It would, moreover, be particularly disastrous to lose foot garments which you had taken off, for they are much more difficult to replace than other garments. For instance, if you lose a mitten you can wrap something around your hand or walk with your hand inside your shirt; if you lose footgear, you are up against it.

RE-CLOTHE IMMEDIATELY AT CAMPTIME

Important, if the day is very cold, is to put on the moment you stop most or all the garments you have shed during the day. There have been cases of travelers who allowed themselves to get so chilled that, through numbness, they finally needed help to put on their outer clothing. This is carelessness; for, of course, the chill and numbness come on very gradually.

There are several dodges for cooling which may be applied at any stage of the above adjustment. One important thing to remember is that, if you chill any part of the body, the coolness extends to other parts and more or less all over you. Cooling on this principle is started in the morning when you first begin to walk with one or both hands bare. Even while your hands are warm enough to be supple and free from numbness, they are still chilled enough so that the effect passes up your arms and apparently affects the temperature of the whole upper part of your body—perhaps the temperature of the whole body, through a slight cooling of the blood, which no doubt takes place chiefly near the surface.

Your next step on the "cool a part and you cool the whole" principle is to throw your hood back, letting it rest so that it still covers your ears, giving the effect of a high fur collar. (Ears are so susceptible to frost that they must never be left uncovered for long on a cold day, no matter how warm you feel.) Hoarfrost will form in your hair from invisible perspiration of the scalp, but you can shake most of it out if you want to resume your hood or if you are about to go indoors.

A very effective and convenient way of cooling off is to walk bare-kneed, something like a Scot in kilts. The chief reason for preferring long boots and short trousers to short boots and long trousers is that if you separate boots and trousers at the ankle you get snow on your bare skin, but under ordinary conditions you can separate them at the knee without this trouble. Usually you walk with just an inch or two of space between trousers and footgear, but if necessary you can widen this space by folding down the upper part of the footgear or by turning up a cuff on your breeches.

Ordinarily none of these adjustments are made perfectly—you are likely to have perspired a little before making them unless you are very watchful and have little else to occupy you. Undergarments that become slightly damp from perspiration will very likely dry during the day; if not, they will dry in the evening while you are in camp sitting around and waiting for supper.

WET GARMENTS

If a garment gets very wet from excessive perspiration, you must dry it practically as described for drying a coat after you have fallen into water. You just have to sit with it on in camp until it is dry, devoting yourself to that as long as necessary, perhaps through two or three successive evenings.

CHAPTER 10

HEALTH, ACCIDENT AND DISEASE

SECTION I

DIET

There are few regions of earth that produce as much meat in proportion to area as the northern polar districts, both land and water. There are few that produce so little of plants that are used for human food. Therefore the only diet locally procurable is 100 percent meat, or nearly that.

Our definition of a meat diet as one from which all matter directly from the vegetable kingdom is absent, would permit, in addition to meat and fish, the inclusion of milk and its products as well as eggs. But that is academic in the Arctic— you can hardly ever secure milk from animals that you hunt, and eggs can be secured only in spring and, even then, only in a few localities.

FAT ESSENTIAL IN MEAT DIET

We state here briefly what has been more fully developed in Section II, Chapter 8: If you are on a meat diet you must have fat with your lean, the fat taking the place of the butter, cream, vegetable oils, sugar, and starches that are present in ordinary mixed diets.

No hard-and-fast rule can be given for the proportions of lean and fat. The basic procedure is to eat by palate—at each meal eat along with your lean as much fat as tastes good to you. At first the fat will taste delicious. Presently, as you approach the point of satiation, it will seem less and less desirable, just as lovers of sweet cream have found that

281

each succeeding spoonful is a little less delicious than the one before. One of the safety factors in getting your calories from animal fat is that you cannot overeat of it, as can so easily be the case with sugars and starches.

In the previously mentioned controlled experiment under the supervision of the Russell Sage Institute of Pathology, when Stefansson and Andersen lived on an exclusively meat diet for 1 year in New York City, it was found that they averaged about a pound and a third of lean per day and a half pound of fat—which is about like eating a 2-pound broiled sirloin with all the fat such a steak usually has on it.

Within the body of any single animal, land, sea, or air, is found a complete human diet, with the exception that skinny animals, such as rabbits and some birds, need supplementary fat. You could, so far as we know, live 3 score years and 10 on geese, for they have enough fat to counterbalance the lean. You could live equally long on rabbits if supplemented with bacon. On rabbit alone you would be ill in a few days.

It is probably true that if one man has nothing but water and another has rabbit and water, they are likely to die in about the same length of time, from 3 to 8 weeks. The one who has just water dies of outright starvation; the other from diarrhoea and kidney afflictions.

As said, any beast from the animal kingdom, fish, flesh or fowl, is satisfactory for a meat diet, if it contains sufficient fat or if you have a stock of supplementary fat to make up a possible deficiency. The kind of meat eaten will, therefore, depend largely on the part of the country in which you find yourself. Where caribou are abundant, their meat will be your chief food supply; at sea you will depend chiefly on seals, with an occasional polar bear; along the coast and in the vicinity of rivers you may for periods live mainly or entirely on fish. (For the manner of cooking, preserving, and handling meat and fish see Chapter 8.)

AVOID POLAR BEAR LIVER

There is perhaps a single part of one of the Arctic animals that should be avoided—the liver of the polar bear. Stefansson reports having eaten a dozen bear livers before suffering any ill effect; but he and several of his companions finally became violently ill from one liver. He has studied the evidence critically, both through literature and by interviewing large numbers of Eskimos, and concludes that once in 2 or 3 dozen cases polar bear livers contain something that makes you ill. The symptoms are excruciating headache and vomiting, lasting from a few hours to as much as 2 days.

Apparently all people everywhere in the world who live mainly or solely on meat dislike and avoid salt. It has been reported occasionally that Eskimos boil meat in salt water. This report must be the result of careless observation or, more likely, invented to fit a theory, unless, indeed, it was an observation on Eskimos who had adopted salt-using from whites, along with other European ways.

It was found on the Stefansson expeditions, by trial with more than 20 persons of European, African, and South Sea descent, that there is no racial difference in adaptability to an all-meat diet. Apart from the possibility of "sensitivity" in rare cases, the individual differences are psychological, depending on what the man believes and what his dietetic experiences have been. Generally speaking, the difficulty of breaking a man to a new diet is small if he is young and adaptable, but it may be considerable if he is older and set in his ways. Probably the difficulty with the older man is not physiological but rather psychological—older persons are likely to be more conservative.

Novices on the Stefansson expeditions were usually broken to meat when traveling over the sea ice and therefore living on seal. Speaking generally and roughly, they got along very well for the first day or two, eating square meals, for they were already as fond of that meat as the average American is of beef. On the second or third day the appetite would begin to fail, and in from 3 to 5 days, especially with those who believed or feared the diet was going to hurt them, appetite would almost or quite cease. Then there might be nausea at the name, sight, and thought of meat. Some would nibble a little every day. Others would go without food for 2 or 3 days, but then they, too, began to nibble. In 2 or 3 weeks from the last tasting of a vegetable element the whole party, of whatever size, was eating square meals, though in some cases under a good deal of protest.

In from 2 to 6 months on exclusively meat and water there is left only such hankering for vegetables and fruits as is parallel to the hankering you have in almost any foreign country for the diet of your home or of your native land.

It was found on these expeditions that when men who had never previously lived on meat were returning to the base camp they talked about what they would like to eat when they got there. It was standard practice to tell them that the steward would have orders to cook separately for each man all he wanted of anything he chose. The commonest things looked forward to were: bread and butter with coffee; mashed potatoes with gravy; hot cakes with syrup.

But there were some who hankered for corned beef, ham, bacon, or sausages. One of the men, who had been a sailor for a number of years, would frequently remark, both on the homeward journey and at other times, that he would give anything to be able to trade the fresh caribou or seal meat he was eating for "a good hunk of salt horse." No other dish was so frequently wished for aloud by anyone else as salt beef was by this man. That he was not expressing a longing for salt, as such, was brought out by questions; besides, wistfulness for corned beef was sometimes expressed when salt for seasoning native meat was available.

When you are new to the meat diet you are likely for several months to have a desire to vary the cooking. You want to fry, roast, and stew, as well as boil. You also desire a variety. You like to change from seal to caribou and from caribou to goose. These hankerings disappear some time during the first year, at latest during the second.

Most often the change in point of view takes place after men have returned from their first long exclusive meat journey. Getting back to the ship or other base camp each stuffs himself with what he has been hankering for, overeats, gets indigestion, and feels rotten. Thereupon he is ready to go back to the meat again, ceases to talk of variety in cooking or in kinds of meat, and will not do much anticipatory talking about food when returning to the base from a later journey.

GENERAL HEALTH ON A MEAT DIET

The broad conclusion to be drawn from study of reports on the lives and health of meat-eating peoples such as the Eskimos, northern travelers who have adopted an exclusive meat diet, and from the controlled experiment of Stefansson and Andersen, is that such a diet affords comfort, enjoyment, and all-around well-being. Another way of stating it is that apparently you can be healthy on meat without vegetables, on vegetables without meat, or on a mixed diet.

There are several beliefs concerning a meat diet that appear on scrutiny to be without foundation but are so common that they should be discussed. Among these are chief that meat is more wholesome for you (or that you like it better) in winter than in summer; that it is best for the Arctic, intermediate for the temperate zone, and worst for the tropics; that it is better for active than for sedentary life; and that it is deficient in needed food elements such as calcium and Vitamin C.

About the heaviest meat eaters of English speech that have been reported were the sheepmen of Australia, in a subtropical environment. Even today it is claimed for Australians that they eat a higher percentage of meat than any part of the British Empire; but during the early nineteenth century, the first 2 or 3 decades of British-Australian colonization, little was eaten except mutton, unless it were beef or game like kangaroo. Sir Hubert Wilkins, whose father was the first white child born in the state of Victoria, reports from information of his family not only what we have said about how they ate the fattest mutton dipped in grease, but also that they relish this food equally in summer and in winter. Carl Lumholtz has reported from the aborigines of tropical Australia that they never ate anything else during a meal if the meat did not run out.

The heaviest meat eaters of the New World are, or were until recently, the cattlemen of northwestern Argentina where summers are long and hot, with the standard food beef and maté.

In the United States few tables groan so with numerous meats on heaping platters as those of old-fashioned country inns, and of certain families, in States like Alabama, Georgia, and Mississippi.

In 1928–29 when Stefansson and Andersen lived for a year exclusively on meat and water in New York City, they found no disinclination to eat steaks and chops or boiled meats that would not have applied equally to other diets—they ate less in hot weather than in cold, as all people do on any diet; the decrease was proportionate to that on other diets. They simply did not need as many calories in summer as they did in winter.

The Stefansson-Andersen experiment was on men who were more sedentary than common in a city. Andersen does take walks for exercise occasionally. Stefansson never takes exercise, whatever his diet. He has reported that on one occasion in the Arctic, the winter of 1910–11, he spent 3 or 4 months that were the most sedentary of his whole life. During this time he seldom went out of doors, or on those occasions more than one or two hundred yards from the house. He did no manual work of any kind, devoting himself to linguistic study, which meant writing and listening all day long. During this period the diet was exclusively meat; his appetite remained normal, and his health excellent.

It appears true that views concerning a meat diet have changed rapidly since 1920. The beliefs discarded since then are, among others, the supposition that meat produces hardening of the arteries and high blood pressure, that it is hard on the kidneys and that it lacks certain dietetic elements, among them calcium and vitamin C. We discuss the vitamin C deficiency idea in section IV of this chapter under Scurvy, but need a separate paragraph here for the calcium.

MEAT DIET CONTAINS SUFFICIENT CALCIUM

It appeared to the chemists who were part of the scrutinizing staff of the Russell Sage Institute while that body was supervising the exclusive meat year of Stefansson and Andersen, that they were not eating enough calcium. No signs of calcium deficiency had appeared toward the end of the year and it was supposed that perhaps one year was not long enough for these evidences to show themselves. Accordingly the department of physical anthropology at Harvard was commissioned to study whether there was indication of calcium lack in the diet of exclusively meat eaters whose skeletons were available in museums. Under the supervision of Professor E. A. Hooton, extensive studies were made of the bones of wholly carnivorous people in the Peabody Museum of Harvard and elsewhere. Dr. Hooten reported no sign of deficiency; he reported, on the contrary, every sign that there had been an abundance of calcium in the food of these people.

That an all-meat diet gives people like the Eskimos sufficient calcium has been said to be due to their eating bones. This argument looks sound if you consider it only with relation to people who live on fish and on land animals; it appears to be without support when you consider those groups which live exclusively, or nearly so, on sea mammals.

When you eat fish, caribou, birds, rabbits, and the like, you will find upon trial that nothing tastes quite so good as the soft ends of bones. Indeed, all bones that are chewable taste good; so that an Eskimo would go farther than Shakespeare, saying not merely that the sweetest meat is nearest the bone but that the bone itself is even sweeter than the meat.

The eating of considerable amounts of bone would seem, then, to explain the calcium situation. The argument, as implied, disappears when you turn to the eaters of water mammals.

There are Eskimo groups who for most of the year, through entire generations, live exclusively on sea mammals—the whale, the walrus, the seal, and perhaps an occasional polar bear. None of these have ordinary marrow in their bones—the fat of their bodies accumulates mainly on the outside, between the skin and the musculature. You learn by observation that people who live on these animals do not chew bones, and you learn by trial why they do not—your attempt to eat the bones will show them hard to chew and, insofar as you can chew them, they do not taste particularly good.

The studies of Professor Hooton, to which we have referred, were in part on the bones of people who had lived on land animals and fish, in part on sea mammal eaters. Neither this investigator nor apparently anyone else has found evidence of a calcium lack in either group—one appears as well supplied as the other.

Nor does there seem to be trouble on the score of wanting bulk. Constipation is rare or absent among those exclusive meat eaters who chew large quantities of the bones of land animals, birds, and fish; but it appears to be just as rare among the meateaters who live on sea mammals. Equally in the case of the bone chewers and those who do not chew bones, constipation becomes troublesome upon the introduction of "civilized" diets—where the first elements introduced in quantity are usually flour, hardbread, rice, beans, dried and canned fruits, canned and desiccated vegetables. For instance, in Coronation Gulf, where among several hundred people no constipation was observed by Stefansson during 1910–11 and little or none by Jenness during 1914–16, constipation is now so developed that one of the chief groups of trade articles with the Hudson's Bay Company and other traders are cathartics and laxatives, ranging from the mildest to castor and croton oils.

In short, it would appear that a diet consisting exclusively of meat is a complete diet even when bones are not chewed— that it contains all the stuffs necessary for health, including calcium and all the vitamins

Section II

EXERCISE

No specific rules for exercise need be given, except those implied in the directions for various aspects of Arctic life. When you are clad in comfortable Eskimo-type clothing, with its nearly perfect insulation from cold and wind, the bracing Arctic winter air will make you enjoy activity of any kind. The best rule, then, for rest periods or other times when duties do not require activity, is to take as much exercise or as little as you feel like.

However, we repeat a few warnings:

WARNINGS

1. If exercising "for the fun of it" or as a matter of routine, keep in mind the suggestions outlined in Chapter 9 for pre-

venting excessive perspiration and the consequent formation of hoarfrost in your clothing.

2. You should probably refrain from violent exercise when temperatures are below —50°, since the rapid breathing might produce either actual freezing of the inside of the breathing apparatus or congestion from over-chill.

Whether it is possible to freeze the inside of trachea and bronchial tubes by rapid breathing of very cold air is one of the debated questions. It is frequently asserted, particularly in the Yukon, that both horses and people die with pneumonia symptoms which are alleged to have resulted from the heavy breathing that accompanies violent exercise. But there are other people in the Yukon who maintain that this has never happened—that the deaths with pneumonia symptoms were from other causes than freezing of pulmonary membranes. Perhaps we should take here the attitude of "better be safe than sorry." In any case, few people breath through the nose when weather is extremely cold—they find by experience that they are more comfortable breathing through the mouth; which has at least one further advantage, that your nose is less likely to freeze when there is cold air merely outside of it instead of both inside and out.

3. If lost in a blizzard, bear in mind the warning given in Chapter 11 against over-exertion, resulting in dampening and freezing of the clothes through perspiration, and in physical exhaustion.

4. Should you, through carelessness or through circumstances over which you have no control, develop scurvy, remember that exercise is of no value in retarding or curing the disease. As developed later in this chapter, the treatment of scurvy is wholly a matter of diet, and whatever energy is expended should be used toward securing fresh food.

Section III

FIRST AID

First-aid problems connected with the Arctic summer are the same as those for other climates, so that no special instructions need be given for dealing with them. In case of immersion or heat stroke (and heat strokes do occur in the Arctic), you would follow the procedure that is in general use elsewhere.

Special first-aid problems do arise under the conditions created by low temperatures. Here it is important to have first a grasp of the underlying principles and then a knowledge of how to deal with the effects of cold.

It is ordinary north Alaska and northern Canada Eskimo practice to jump naked out of bed to stop an outdoor dog fight in any weather. Several members of the Stefansson expedition did the same. Since the dogs do not choose particular weather for their fights, they have to be stopped at all temperatures. No one is known to have suffered ill effect, or even discomfort that lasted more than a moment or two after getting back into bed.

When cold is unaccompanied by wind, the human body does not feel it immediately. The most striking testimony is that furnished unconsciously by children. A naked baby against its mother's back inside her fur coat may begin to cry from overheating or difficulty in breathing. If she is on the march, the mother will simply open wider at the top the breathing and ventilating channel between the coat and her back. But if she has time, she will, if there is no wind, spread a caribou skin out on the snow and place the child upon it naked on its back. The child will at first smile in the most pleased and comfortable way. It may be anything between half a minute and two minutes before the youngster begins to pucker its face and show signs that it perceives a growing discomfort. Before it starts crying the mother slips it up her back inside her coat.

Apparently the most intense possible nervous shock from chill is through a shower of cold water. The coldest, without laboratory manipulation, is a sea water shower at about 28°. It is doubtful whether the shock of this is appreciably greater than that of an ordinary city water shower at around 40°. The shock from water at 50° or even 60° is many times greater than from air at —50° or —60°. In fact, there is no shock at all from going from a warm bed into still air outdoors at —50°.

The preceding detail on exposure of the whole body is to emphasize that there is neither danger nor discomfort through short exposure of parts of the body at intensely low temperatures, so long as the snow is not drifting. If the snow drifts, discomfort comes mainly from what of it gets inside the clothing, to melt later. Snow driving before anything like a 30-mile wind at —30° would bounce off your naked body before melting and would, therefore, produce the sensation of drifting sand rather than that of something clammy.

CARE NEEDED IN EMERGENCIES

We do not mean to discount the advisability of speed and precision when extensive, though partial, body exposure is necessary, as when a man who has fallen into water changes his clothes out of doors. The water in which he has been drenched will produce such a preliminary chilling that almost certainly he could not change completely from one suit to another without assistance—his hands would become numb and unusable before the change was complete. (It follows that a man who is alone when he falls into water should not try to change to dry garments without first making some sort of camp—and by then he cannot change anyway, unless he has a fire, for his clothes will have frozen stiff.)

When the right snow is available, the first thing to do after falling into water is to roll in a deep, soft bank. The snow acts as a blotter, abstracting some of the water from the clothing. The colder the snow the better it works.

A minor change outdoors, as from wet socks to dry, is really no bother at all, whatever the temperature, if the rest of your body was warm at the time you got your feet wet.

A full change of suits in the open can usually be managed, but only with assistance; for, as said, you might get numb and helpless. If there is a wind you will certainly have to find or build a windbreak as a preliminary, and during that time the soaked clothes will freeze. In case of a full soaking it is probably best to do as Wilkins and Eielson did, when Wilkins fell in and got soaked to his armpits, on their way ashore when they had abandoned a fuelless airplane 100

291

miles north of Alaska. The temperature was —10° and the outside of Wilkins' clothes froze almost instantly. They proceeded to a natural windbreak which they happened to see. During that time the actual running water had soaked downward from the coat and trousers, and they squeezed downward some of the moisture with their hands. When sure that not much would later soak downward, Wilkins, with Eielson's assistance, took off boots and socks, replacing them with dry.

There is a partial compensation in soaked clothes. While they are heavier, better conductors and stiff, they are more windproof than before, giving you a sort of rebate.

DRYING A SOAKED SUIT

When a suit is fully soaked and fuel is scarce, you can dry it successfully in 1 or 2 days only on your body. The best way, if you have time, is to stay in camp for at least a day, devoting yourself to the drying. This would mean you would spend most of your time standing up, occasionally varying by sitting down or kneeling. The change of position is because not much drying would take place between your body and anything on which it rests. (It would probably take 2 or 3 weeks in winter for a wet suit to dry if hung up out of doors.)

FROSTBITE

It is not possible to prevent frostbite entirely, but it is possible to go through winter after winter without suffering any serious consequences, if suitable clothing is worn and the right procedure followed. The frostbites that do occur need be no more serious than a mild sunburn, if you thaw the part promptly.

Assuming proper clothing, only the face is apt to be frostbitten, and the face is the easiest to treat. When the face is frozen you almost necessarily thaw it with your own hand or get someone else to thaw it for you. In moderately cold weather, the point is to keep your hands warm and to run a hand over your face every few minutes to see if any part of it is frozen. You can also keep informed by making grimaces, when a stiff spot is easily detected. All you then have to do is to take your warm hand out of your mitten and press it to the frozen spot a few moments, until the whiteness and stiffness are gone.

In the very coldest weather the method is a little different. When you are properly dressed for winter your coat is loose-fitting and with the sleeves cut so that any time you like you can pull your arm out of the sleeve and carry your hand on your naked breast inside the coat. Whenever any part of the face refuses to wrinkle, you push your hand up through the loose-fitting neck of the coat and press it for a moment on the stiffened portion of the face. As soon as the frozen spot thaws, you pull your hand in upon your breast again. In this way one can walk all day facing a steady breeze at —35° or —40° F., which is the worst kind of weather one ever gets in the Arctic. For when the temperature falls to —50° or below, there is usually a calm.

BE CLEAN SHAVEN

You should always be clean shaven. If you wear a beard, the moisture of your breath congeals on it and makes for you a face mask that is separated by an air space of a sixth or eighth of an inch from your skin. If then you begin to freeze underneath the ice mask you cannot get at your cheek or chin to thaw it out with the warm palm of your hand, as you could do immediately if you were smooth-shaven. If you try to thaw such an ice mask with your hands, you soon find that you have to choose between a frozen face and frozen fingers. There is no choice. Your hands and feet you must protect at all costs.

FACE MASKS

Most travelers conclude after trial that a face mask of skin or cloth is of no avail. It protects you for half an hour or so, but then ice forms on it. The comforting and protective velvet of morning is crusted with ice long before noon. However, there are people of great experience who use velvet masks that cover the whole face, with openings for eyes, nostrils and mouth. One of these is Wilkins.

293

WRISTS

Next after the face the likeliest part to freeze is the skin of your wrists. If a wrist is frozen, because coat and mitten do not meet, you very likely thaw it by grasping with the other hand, but you may thaw by holding the wrist against your face or, better, slipping it inside your clothes.

PROTECTING HANDS AND FEET

Keeping hands and feet from freezing is primarily a matter of proper clothing, which is described in Chapter 9.

THAWING HANDS

If a hand does begin to freeze, the procedure is as explained for warming the hand to thaw the face—pull the arm out of the sleeve of the coat and carry the hand on the naked breast until it is warmed.

There are conditions where special dodges may be practiced. On a windy day when your hands are cold with two pairs of woolen mittens, you may perhaps soak the outer pair to advantage, provided you can get it back on again before it freezes too stiff. You now have an outer mitten that sheds the wind whereas formerly, when it was dry, the wind came through.

When you are taking fish out of a net with bare hands at −30° to −50°, you will find it advisable every half minute to stick your hands deep into the water. The like is so, for a greater reason, when you are skinning a large animal. You can then usually get adequate warmth by putting your bare hands for a few moments in between skin and flesh. Except that it makes your hands slippery, it may be better to stick them into blood, for instance, when you are cutting up an animal after skinning.

THAWING FEET

If a foot is frozen, the situation is the most difficult possible. When you are alone in the open it is hard to say what to do. If you happen to have warmer or more footgear available, you will put that on. Perhaps your foot can be thawed by wrapping a skin around it. If a dog is available, you might in some way get him to help you, say putting your toes in between his thigh and belly. In some cases you can thaw by running. That is dangerous, as elsewhere pointed out, for it may lead to perspiration and exhaustion, which in turn may cause freezing to death. Of course, if there is a camp at a reasonable distance the thing is to run toward it as fast as possible—thereby you may produce a certain thawing while you are on the way and you have, at any rate, shortened the period of freezing.

If you have a human companion, the best way ordinarily is to take off all your footgear and to have him put your foot between his coat and abdomen, or wherever else on his body seems most convenient.

WHEN LOST IN A BLIZZARD

The above precautions to avoid freezing face, hands and feet apply, of course, if you become lost in a blizzard. The larger aspect, that of avoiding freezing to death in such circumstances, is a matter of travel technique. It is, therefore, discussed in this Manual in the section dealing with travel procedure—see Chapter 11, Section II.

TREATMENT OF FROSTBITE

Authorities differ on the procedure to be followed in treating severe frostbite. Because of the difference of opinion, we state the opposing theories and the reasons given for each.

It has been claimed by some Canadian and other physicians that they have secured good results by thawing a frozen part with water heated to just short of scalding. The motives given are: (1) that you want to keep the frostbite from getting deeper, and (2) that you believe the injury to tissues is greater the longer they remain frozen. Stefansson is inclined to agree that the frozen part should be thawed with the warmest thing available, feeling that there is apparently no merit in a slowness of thawing to counterbalance the demerit of long freezing. But, although the above method appears logical, he is prepared to modify his stand if experience supports the gradual application of heat (described below). For in his 10 winters north of the Arctic Circle he associated almost exclusively with people who understood so well how to dress and how to take care of themselves that his experience with severe frostbite is very limited.

THAWING GRADUALLY

The opposing view, that of thawing the frozen part gradually, we quote from a pamphlet issued by the United States Coast Guard, "Directions for Restoring the Apparently Drowned * * * and for the Treatment of Frostbites," Washington, 1939. Under the heading of Third Degree (severe) frostbite, the pamphlet says:

"* * * if the part is dead no reaction takes place upon the application of heat; the dead portion turns black and a line of demarcation appears between it and the living tissue. If the heat is applied suddenly to a badly frozen part of the body, the liability to gangrene (death of the tissue) is increased on account of the intense reaction that takes place in the tissue that is still living."

The topic being at once important and debated we sought the opinion of the Harvard Fatigue Laboratory, submitting to them the opposed views given above. Professor John H. Talbott, that member of their staff who has most devoted himself to problems of freezing, replied that so far as he knew "* * * no particular harm comes from the rapid thawing of tissue * * *" and added his belief that "* * * theoretically certain advantages may be gained by this treatment [rapid thawing]."

DON'T RUB WITH SNOW

The belief in the efficacy of rubbing snow on a frostbite, probably derived from ancient doctrines of sympathetic magic, has been so long and so widely held that it is a part ⌐f almost everyone's "knowledge."

Such treatment of frostbite, however, is contrary to the laws of physics that relate to heat and cold. No less is snow application contrary to common sense. For if we stop to think, we must realize that if a cold body is brought in contact with a warm body the warm one is cooled down; and that, if one cold body is brought in contact with another still colder there is a similar lowering of temperature of the body that is less cold. Consider, then, what would be the effect if snow at $-50°$ were applied to a frozen part of the human body. The flesh that had suffered the freezing would then be only a little below the freezing point, while the snow would be $80°$ colder than freezing. The result must necessarily be a deeper and more solid freezing of the part affected.

Because of the danger involved, we repeat: Never rub snow on a frostbite. Always apply something that is warmer than the affected part.

Don't try to warm frostbite by friction. Heat is generated by friction but slowly, and in the rubbing you are likely to break the skin; for the part that is being rubbed has already become stiff. You may have a mechanical injury to deal with in addition to the frostbite.

SNOW AS AN ANESTHETIC

After the thaw has been completed you may find cold a good local anesthetic, and perhaps the only one available. Indoors, when the thaw is well completed, it is good if you are in considerable pain to use slushy snow, or any cold application. But if you have thawed outdoors, perhaps with your warm hand, a facial frostbite which is deep enough to cause pain, you automatically have an anesthetic application in the cold air which previously froze you. In the case of such frostbite you may notice little pain during the day, because of the said anesthesia produced by the air, and the paining may start after camp time. Then you may safely use slushy snow.

Even for use in a warm camp we have specified slushy snow. Of course it need not be warmed to the slush point before use if you know that the temperature which it brings in with it from out of doors is only a few degrees below freezing. It must always be remembered that, the snow and the air outdoors are about the same temperature—if the air is exactly $-50°$ then the snow is approximately $-50°$. Now that temperature, $80°$ below freezing, is so low that you could produce with it in a warm room almost the effects that can be produced by liquid air in a laboratory. There is no doubt that in ordinary room temperature you could freeze a man's entire face by rubbing it with snow, if fresh snow is brought in from outdoors every few minutes.

DANGER OF USING COLD KEROSENE TO "THAW" FROSTBITE

A related belief quite as dangerous as that about snow and frostbite, except perhaps not so widespread, is that a thing is not frozen if it is liquid—that you can thaw a frozen part of the human body in any material which itself has not been stiffened or hardened by cold. There was a horrible illustration of this belief in an Alaska mining camp during the Gold Rush. A man came into camp suspecting that one of his feet might be frostbitten. When shoes and stockings were removed it turned out that the toes of one foot were more or less frozen. Someone then went out of doors, secured a five-gallon tin of kerosene, brought it in, poured kerosene in a bucket and told the man to step into it. He did, and kept his foot there until it was frozen solid. Instead of losing perhaps a few toes, he lost his leg half way to the knee.

GREASE AS FROST PREVENTIVE

There is a debate about greasing the face to prevent frostbite. Some believe that a thick coating of vaseline is a useful protection. This has, however, two dangers which we have mentioned once or oftener. First it is bad practice to have grease around you anywhere, for it is liable to get into your clothes, destroying their insulating quality. Then it is bad to have anything on your face (we referred previously to an ice mask) which prevents the ready application of a warm hand to neutralize a frostbite. If you have tried the vaseline method and are nevertheless freezing you will have to rub off most of the grease, with some grass, moss, or the like, before applying the warm hand for thawing purposes.

AFTER EFFECTS

There is little danger that a wound from frostbite will fester, since the micro-organisms involved are rare in the polar regions and, no doubt, particularly so in winter. You would proceed as with any other wound, except for the said omission of antiseptics. If the frostbite merely produces peeling, like that of sunburn, you treat as for sunburn. Most likely you would do nothing, or you might use lanolin. With such applications, as in every other respect, you must be careful not to get your clothes involved. The gradual accumulation of fats in them, whether mineral or organic, will progressively decrease their value as protection against cold.

SUSCEPTIBILITY TO FROSTBITE

There is no racial immunity or racial susceptibility to frostbite. Norwegians and Spaniards, Negroes, South Sea Islanders, Eskimos, and Indians of the northern woods have been found on observation to be about equally susceptible. A man susceptible to frostbite is not necessarily unsuited for cold-weather service, for he is not of necessity correspondingly susceptible to other effects of cold.

The best Eskimo traveling companion Stefansson ever had, Natkusiak, froze his face more easily than any other of his men, of whatever race, although his hands seemed to stand as much cold as those of the rest of the expedition. But to him frostbites were minor annoyances. He handled them almost subconsciously—thawing out his face at short intervals without this interfering appreciably with his work.

Susceptibility to frostbite is, then, though not racial, highly individual. It may be true as commonly believed that it depends on circulation, then perhaps on the capillaries in the skin. It depends to some extent on facial contours—sharply angular chins and thin noses are apparently predisposed to freezing, although this effect is at times obscured by other qualities, perhaps those of circulation.

Hands that grow numb easily should rule a man out from Arctic service. The third Stefansson expedition had one member whose fingers were not properly nimble except in summer. He reported that his hands used to become numb when he washed them in city water in Seattle, Wash. At temperatures when other men were working barehanded he had to wear two or three pairs of mittens and was able to use his hands only as if they were stumps.

SNOWBLINDNESS

Since snowblindness is not a real disease, we deal with it in this section rather than in the following one on diseases.

For reasons not fully agreed upon, sunlight on snow does not usually produce snowblindness before March or April in those parts of the Arctic where the sun first becomes visible some time in January. Clear sun in spring produces snow-blindness, but not so quickly as diffused light. When the snowblindness season has arrived, exposure to any kind of light may bring on and aggravate the difficulty—instances of snowblindness have been reported as developing toward the end of a period of several days during which the party had been confined to camp, the light having come in either through the roof of a snowhouse or through the fabric of a white tent.

CAUSES

Snowblindness is, as said, most apt to occur on days when the clouds are thick enough to hide the sun but not thick enough to produce heavily overcast weather. Light is then evenly diffused and there are no shadows anywhere. You may collide with a snow-covered ice cake as high as your waist and, if anything more easily, you may trip over snow-drifts a foot or so in height; for, wanting the help of shadows, everything that is pure white seems to be level. The eye, therefore, is continually straining to detect obstacles.

SYMPTOMS

Signs of trouble develop slowly. It may be after a long day's march that when you enter camp in the evening your eyes feel as if there were small grains of sand in them. Such things as tobacco smoke will make them water excessively. Gradually they become more uncomfortable and sore, and during the night shooting pains (resembling those of earache or toothache) will start. The period of considerable pain seldom extends over more than 3 days.

If the vision of the eyes is unequal, the weaker eye may be attacked first, for the reason that the glare appears stronger to the stronger eye and you naturally protect it first, as by shading it or keeping it shut. When once you have begun to shield an eye it becomes increasingly difficult to keep it open, for when an eye has been in darkness it is blinded by a light which does not blind an eye that has been exposed to it. Those who become snowblind in both eyes simultaneously have either used great will power to keep both eyes open or have eyes of nearly equal quality.

It is probably true that if one man has keener eyesight than another then he is the one to go snowblind first. If this be so, it would no doubt follow that with eyes of unequal vision the better eye would be blinded first, if both were kept open and used equally.

Another belief is that each snowblindness you suffer predisposes you to the next one. This is considered true not merely during a given season but also from season to season. It is also believed that recurrent snowblindness gradually weakens your eyesight and tends to produce blindness. If this be true it will follow that one snowblindness does not necessarily lead to another except at first—later on, when the eyesight has begun to be dulled, there will develop that partial immunity to snowblindness of which we have spoken.

After complete recovery a second attack is not likely to come in less than a week but careless persons will have attacks every week or 10 days. No immunity is developed—the more attacks you have suffered the more you are predisposed to the next. It is probably for this reason that Eskimos usually become snowblind more readily than whites.

Since snowblindness is not a real blindness, it is only in fiction that it looks like actual blindness and that people can simulate it for days. During severe snowblindness, for one thing, tears flow as rapidly as in violent weeping.

TREATMENT

The only treatment is to take whatever steps you can to shield the eyes from light—to remain in a darkened place or, if you must be on the march, to wear smoked or amber glasses. Bandages shutting out all light should be used in severe cases, even if you have to travel. (You can then cling to the sledge and stumble along, unless the load is so small that you can ride; or you can get somebody to lead you.)

For ameliorants it may be worth while to use the prescription of an oculist, such as morphine drops, or wash with boracic solution.

AFTER EFFECTS

During convalescence you gradually become better and better able to endure light. On first use of the eyes you will see double—they do not focus. On perhaps the second day (maybe the fifth or sixth day from the onset of a severe attack) your eyes are all right for such things as traveling and camp-making but will not yet serve for purposes such as reading a fine scale on an instrument or taking sure aim with a rifle.

PREVENTION

The constant use of amber glasses will prevent snow blindness. Unevennesses imperceptible to the naked eye can frequently be seen by the aid of these light filters. Smoked glasses are poorest of all. Chlorophyll green is good when the sun is shining but cuts out too much light and on cloudy days interferes with clearness of vision.

Glasses frost over from eye moisture and from moisture of the face. This frosting is not a serious annoyance on a windy day, especially if one keeps the face sidewise to the wind; but on a calm day, if one walks fast enough or works hard enough to perspire, they cannot be worn at all. In such circumstances, keeping the eyes on a dark object is a valuable preventive—for instance, the dogs or the cover of a sledge. It is said that blackening the nose helps, especially if it is a high nose. You can rest eyes by using them alternately, and save them by looking through half-closed lids, through your eyelashes.

Eskimo goggles, made of wood with slits about large enough for half a dollar, have the advantage of not frosting over, but the disadvantage of a field of vision so limited that you cannot, without stooping over, see what lies at your feet.

Section IV

DISEASE

The problems of infection are the same in the Arctic as in the tropics and temperate zone, except that the dangers are fewer in the Arctic and that in most cases those present are less serious.

INFECTION OF WOUNDS

It seems to be a general tropical experience, particularly in the humid districts, that every scratch festers, even small wounds are dangerous, and that antiseptics must be the central part of your emergency medical equipment. In the polar regions you have the opposite extreme. Step on a nail, clean or rusty, and there is no danger or any difficulty except from the mere surgically clean wound. Antiseptics are perhaps the least necessary part of an Arctic medical kit. It is reported that the hospital at Barrow, Alaska, uses considerable less asepsis procedure than would be required in the temperate zone.

As mentioned already, cases of blood poisoning from "stepping on a rusty nail" and things of that sort have been reported from polar expeditions in recent years but the statement has usually or always been accompanied by the theoretical explanation that the micro-organisms involved must have been brought by the expedition itself from tropic or temperate-zone lands.

TUBERCULOSIS

Diseases which require person-to-person contact or near association spread in the Arctic as elsewhere. For instance, there is the same danger from sputum in tuberculosis that you have farther south except that in winter the spit is likely to freeze when it is voided. Apart from whether this kills the germs, it does restrict their distribution.

THEORIES TO EXPLAIN HIGH DEATH RATE

It was formerly common in books about the Arctic to say or assume tacitly that the Eskimos had some tuberculosis among them before white influences began to operate and that the heavy death rate from this disease among communities in the process of being "civilized" was due to a weakening of the power of resistance by several factors. The more thoughtful observers, as, for instance, medical missionaries and whaling captains, usually put the heaviest blame upon the introduction of white men's house types and housekeeping methods.

For places like northern Alaska they would argue, for instance, that because the roofs of the native houses were not rainproof the families had to move out of them in the spring. They would shift into tent encampments which they occupied during the summer, moving from place to place and having an automatically clean site each time they moved. After the freeze-up the houses were reoccupied.

A reoccupied house was a clean house, the cleaning process having consisted of chopping out the floor with pickaxes and getting rid of several inches of frozen mud by throwing it outdoors. Any germs not killed by frost were cast out with the debris.

There were supposed to be various contributory reasons for the development of tuberculosis among Eskimos who were adopting white men's ways. The people were no longer as healthy, notably constipation had developed and this was assumed to lessen resistance to other diseases. The natives might catch other white men's diseases which would further lessen their ability to fight off tuberculosis. These and other things were used to explain the terrifying mortality which, in some cases, was believed to have reduced Arctic communities by half in as little as ten years.

But a reexamination of the evidence has brought most students to a different conclusion. The main explanation of the high tuberculosis mortality is now considered to be that the Eskimos did not have the disease until it was introduced by whites. Since their ancestors had not been exposed to it, the present generation does not have what we call inherited immunity. This, by the current reasoning, is the main explanation of the appalling death rate; it is still said that white men's houses, housekeeping and, diet have been injurious, but these are now looked upon as subsidiary factors.

In Greenland, where more scientific thought and care have been put on the welfare of the Eskimos than in any other section, it has been recommended during the last few years, notably by a physiological expedition from the University of Oslo which studied conditions in East Greenland, that natives should be encouraged to eat more meat. With the Greenland Eskimos, as with all Eskimos and perhaps with all people, fashions are powerful. They have seen the Danes eating foods brought from Denmark which they know are costly and which they desire in proportion. They eat as much Danish food as their financial resources permit. The scientists of the Oslo group consider they have established that the prognosis of tuberculosis is much better if the invalid can be put back on his native diet, chiefly seal and fish. For a like reason the chance of catching the disease is said to be less among those who live mainly or solely on meat.

This argument does not of course mean to advance a diet of meat as a panacea. Demonstrably it is no panacea. You see that in districts like Coronation Gulf where as yet there is little departure from native housing practice. By Stefansson's observation there was no tuberculosis in that district among 500 to 700 people in 1911. Diamond Jenness of the third Stefansson expedition, who spent in this neighborhood the years 1914–16, feels that tuberculosis has been introduced to Coronation Gulf since then. By the reports of Richard Finnie, as of about 1939, the tubercular death rate in Coronation Gulf had been through the preceding decade much heavier than anywhere else in Canadian Eskimo territories. The explanation is that other parts of the Arctic went through their heavy death rate cycle anything from several hundred to several score years ago.

POPULATIONS REDUCED BUT NOT EXTERMINATED

A broad statement, covering tuberculosis and the other new factors of destruction, is that the white man's influence, in chief his diseases, reduce Eskimo communities to a half, a quarter, or possibly even a tenth of their former population, but that extinction does not result. At some point the new influences have killed off so many of the susceptibles, and left among the remnants such a high percentage of the partly or wholly immune, that the birthrate begins to compensate for the death rate and finally gains upon it. Today there may not be any part of the Arctic, except northern Canada from Coronation Gulf to King William Island, that is seeing a marked decrease of population. There are small increases in other parts of Arctic Canada and in Arctic Alaska, with a high rate of increase both in Danish Greenland and in the Soviet territories of Arctic Siberia.

TYPHOID

Typhoid is spread by carriers in the Arctic as elsewhere. For instance, there is no reasonable doubt that in 1917 Stefansson contracted typhoid at Herschel Island from a member of the Royal Canadian Mounted Police, or possibly from some other white man there who was a carrier. Of three cases that winter two died, a constable and an Eskimo.

Typhoid is also spread in the Arctic as elsewhere by contaminated water. An approximately conclusive example is from Barrow, Alaska. People who had died of typhoid were buried Eskimo-style (in boxes on top of the ground) on a hill near the pond which is the main water supply of the village. The next year there was an epidemic which cost several lives. The disease came under control when the water supply was changed.

MEASLES AND INFLUENZA

Measles and influenza spread in the Arctic as elsewhere. The first known measles epidemic, around the beginning of the present century, killed as high as 75 percent in some villages and it is not known to have killed less than 25 percent in any village. There is one statement, from the Kuskokwim, that of 99 in a village, 98 died, the only survivor being a half-grown child.

That this heavy death rate is due to lack of immunity and not to a special virulence of the disease appears to be demonstrated by the comparative immunity of Europeans living in the Arctic. Stefansson has been unable to find a single case of an adult European dying there of measles. Except that the recorded cases are as yet perhaps too few for generalization, it seems clear that the children of white fathers and Eskimo mothers have a considerably higher immunity than the full Eskimos.

ITCH AND VENEREAL DISEASES

The spread of itch and the venereal diseases is not affected by the climate. Most or all Eskimos have been exposed to these diseases, which are all apparently of European introduction. Native immunity seems lower than that of whites.

306

EYE DISEASES

Eye diseases, itch, and some other troubles were greatly accelerated in their spread among Eskimos by the introduction of bathing and face-washing, involving the promiscuous use of towels.

COMMON COLDS

Head colds, though doubtless they obey the same laws as elsewhere, have a superficial difference in the Arctic which has attracted much attention.

When small parties are isolated from all other human beings, their members eventually recover from whatever head colds they may have. After that they do not catch more, no matter how warm or cold they are or how suddenly they change from cold to warm. Neither do any of the other things commonly supposed to produce colds take effect. You can't catch cold unless there is someone or something to catch it from.

The one thing, other than a new person, which has apparently on some occasions started colds on Arctic expeditions is the opening up of packages that date from countries and times where there were colds.

When two previously isolated groups meet, members of both will come down with colds and very likely everybody will catch them. This seems to mean that the disease organisms were present in both parties but each lot had been deprived of the power to make its own community sick, while retaining the power to infect the new community.

Certain travelers have reported that head colds are particularly numerous among Arctic Eskimos in spring and fall and have connected this with the weather as such. In Stefansson's opinion no isolated party will develop colds either spring or fall. The reason for the spread and prevalence of colds at those seasons is that they are the times of most general traveling, yielding the best facility for the transfer of germs between groups.

COLD-AND-FEVER EPIDEMICS

In addition to the epidemics of measles and influenza, which can always be connected definitely with epidemics or other spread of those diseases among neighboring whites or Indians, there are milder but nevertheless serious epidemics with the symptoms of severe head colds and fever, which spread among Eskimos from community to community, not every year but still at rather frequent intervals. These epidemics seldom kill directly, but they are the usual start of a famine.

For instance, a party of fifty or a hundred people may have arrived from inland at a sealing locality on the shore of Victoria Island. They come with their food nearly exhausted and it takes a little while to get camp established and the proper scouting done for the seal localities—which vary from year to year. If a severe epidemic of head colds strikes just then, confining most of the hunters and other workers to houses for a week, and if then there should be a spell of bad weather, you have a combination which first results in the killing of the dogs for food and then in the inability of the people to find seals because they have no dogs to guide them. For, under the conditions given, the mauttok is the only tenable sealing method, and that method rests on the cooperation of dogs (as described in Chapter 13).

The main point, as said, about Arctic diseases is that those you find are never other than the ones with which you are familiar in a more severe form farther south. Many of them have been brought in by Europeans remotely or recently. A number of ailments are still wholly absent from uncivilized or little changed Eskimo districts. Among these are the entire group of deficiency diseases, as well as tooth decay (caries). In a community that still keeps to its native wholly carnivorous diet you never have scurvy, rickets, pelagra, or beri-beri. There is not one decayed tooth in a thousand heads among people who are wholly meat-eaters. Pyorrhea is rare or absent. Alveolar abcess seldom occurs.

CANCER

Cancer has not yet been reported from uncivilized Eskimos. One death from cancer has been reported at Barrow of a man who had been working for or with Mr. Charles D. Brower for nearly 40 years and living to a considerable extent on European food. However, an inquiry from Dr. Greist, medical missionary at Barrow, brings an answer which casts doubt upon the diagnosis.

ARCTIC HYSTERIA

There appear to be no mental symptoms which result from darkness as such—during the more or less prolonged period when the sun is below the horizon. There is, however, the possibility that through powerful suggestion, either just your own belief or your own supplemented by that of your comrades, mental difficulties may result.

The most striking reports of mental trouble that is said to be caused by "the midwinter darkness" are from Yukon Territory and interior Alaska, where the sun is visible at midday during midwinter from 1 to 3 or 4 hours and where people are gathered together in small villages that are comparatively inactive during the midwinter period. On whaling ships that wintered at Herschel Island, where the sun is below the horizon for a month or so, far less mental difficulty was reported; and generally what there was afflicted those who were spending their first winter.

That the "darkness" has more effect in Yukon towns where the sun never wholly disappears than at Herschel where it disappears for a month or two, seems most readily explained on a suggestion basis. In a Yukon camp of 1897 or 1898 very likely the whole village consisted of people who were spending their first winter, who all were afraid of the darkness, and who "knew" that they would be depressed by it. This was an ideal set-up for mass hypnosis. By contrast you saw at Herschel Island on every hand natives who were jolly continually; many of the whalers were veterans who were about as jolly as the natives. The Eskimos would not be able to tell the newcomer anything about the terrors of the darkness, that idea being to them unknown. The most any white veteran was likely to say was that he had been depressed the first year but that he got over it. The chances would then be, on the suggestion hypothesis, that the newcomer would only be mildly depressed, having the belief that it was a condition he would get through all right.

Stefansson has established at least to his own satisfaction that no depressing effect is felt by Europeans during the first Arctic winter if it is explained to them that the cause of the depression, if any, will be their own imagination—and if the newcomer is willing to believe this explanation. There are always people who cannot be induced to believe, and they usually or always succeed in producing, at least during their first winter, enough depression to prove to themselves that they were right.

As to his own case, Stefansson reports that the first winter he spent in the Arctic he wrote a joyous entry in his diary when the sun came back after an absence of a few weeks. At that time he thought himself to have been depressed and to have been released from the depression by the sun; he still knows that he was depressed but thinks the cause was probably his own imagination.

Among people who live in the North, white or native, the midwinter is usually the season of most enjoyment. This is not because the absence of the sun, as such, makes it a preferable time of year. The northerners' attitude to January is in fact about like the common American attitude to August, to which month we look forward not because of its weather but because it is vacation time. Perhaps, then, it may be right to say that August in Missouri and January at Point Barrow are of themselves the least attractive months of the year, but that people in both places find them attractive because it is the vacation time. That it is vacation time results in Missouri from the difficulty of working in the heat of August; at Point Barrow it results from the difficulty of working in the twilight of January.

Arctic hysteria being probably auto-suggestion or mass hypnosis, it is real only in the sense that any trouble based upon imagination may be real. We turn back to diseases that are real in a different sense.

TAPEWORM

Becoming infested with tapeworm is, of course, a serious matter, but the chances for that appear to be small anywhere in the Arctic. There was a scare in northwestern Alaska a few years ago that whites would be getting tapeworm from the reindeer, but this was probably a rumor which started through ignorance, or it may have been propaganda against the reindeer industry.

Certainly there is a chance of getting tapeworm wherever dogs are handled, since they are the chief hosts.

DISEASE FROM SNOW UNLIKELY

Stefansson has heard of no instance connected with Arctic exploration, or with European pioneer life in the Arctic, where diseases have been contracted from the use of snow for water. However, since it has apparently been determined that some germs are not killed by freezing, and since the like may possibly be true with such eggs as those of the tapeworm, it is no doubt best, especially if you are catering to large numbers of men, to take precaution and boil your drinking water.

However, we should insist that the danger of this type of infection from snow in the Arctic is not as great as from the indiscriminate drinking of water from village and city water systems when you travel about. Once more—the dangers in the Arctic are the same as farther south, only with a smaller percentage of risk.

WATER FROM RIVERS AND LAKES IN SUMMER

There are few Arctic rivers which have cities or other communities located anywhere except at the mouth. Accordingly, most of these rivers are safer to drink from than almost any stream in thickly settled temperate zone countries. The same applies to lakes. Again, where numbers of men are involved, it may be a worth while precaution to boil the drinking water.

SCURVY

We now discuss in detail the disease which, of all others, has had the most serious consequences in connection with Europeans in the Arctic—consequences which have ranged from discomfort and reduced efficiency to numerous fatalities among the members of exploratory expeditions, ships' crews, Alaska miners, etc. Some expeditions have lost half and three quarters of their men. In one case, that of Sir John Franklin, every one of 129 men was lost, and the main cause likely was scurvy.

311

Scurvy is a deficiency disease and is considered to appear when Vitamin C is absent from the diet or is insufficient.

It seems clear from an analysis of polar literature and of corresponding records elsewhere that preventives of scurvy are originally present in most foods, whether they are derived from the animal or vegetable kingdom, and that these preventives are weakened or destroyed by storage and by cooking.

No doubt antiscorbutics vary from one vegetable or animal material to another in quantity and efficiency; seemingly, too, they vary in the tenacity by which they retain their virtues against storage and cooking. Generally speaking, it is felt that what destroys the antiscorbutic value of a food is oxidation. This is naturally greater the longer the time through which the food is stored and the more intense and protracted the heat to which it is subjected. Chemistry of media with which it comes in contact no doubt has its effect, too. It seems pretty clear, at any rate, that salted or dried meats and vegetables lose their antiscorbutic power partly because of the salt.

FRESHNESS IN FOODS ESSENTIAL

Not a single case of scurvy has been reported from natives living wholly on meat, and there has been no scurvy reported from any polar expedition which ate a considerable amount of fresh meat that was not over-cooked. There is no doubt, as the quantitative studies have shown, that the percentage of vitamin C, the scurvy-preventing factor, is higher in certain vegetal foods than in meats. But it is equally true that the human body needs only such a small amount of vitamin C that, if you have some fresh meat in your diet every day, and if you don't overcook it, there will be enough C from that source alone to prevent scurvy. Since freshness is the essential element, the thing to do is to find your antiscorbutics where you are, pick them up as you go. In the Arctic fresh foods are almost necessarily of animal derivation.

It is not necessary in order to avoid scurvy to select particular sections of an animal, such as the liver or marrow. For there is ample experience to show that fresh meat from any part of a healthy, normal, well-fed animal, if that forms the main part of your diet, is an adequate protection from scurvy. It is also an adequate protection from all the other deficiency diseases. Children, who appear to be more prone to rickets than adults, are always wholly free from rickets among meat-eating people.

One of the things which show that you do not have to select parts of animals to avoid scurvy is that most meat-eaters give the parts said to be richest in vitamin C to their dogs. Other parts rich in vitamin C are reserved for children; some are taboo and therefore eaten neither by people nor dogs. Thus there are thousands of meat eaters every year who go for long periods (plenty long enough to develop scurvy) on diets from which nearly or quite all the parts specially rich in vitamin C are absent. Yet no scurvy develops—showing that the parts which are eaten are amply supplied with the element to protect health.

BLOOD RICH IN VITAMIN C

There is, of course, the point that if vitamin C is found in milk it should be found in blood, for milk is, approximately speaking, modified blood. Few, if any, hunting people bleed animals deliberately, so that most of the animal's blood remains in the meat. If some blood escapes into the body cavity, as by the cutting of one of the large vessels, then the hunter, be he white or Eskimo, will usually save the blood which he finds accumulated. He will carry it away in a bag made from a part of the entrails and will use it as a thickening for blood soup.

The preceding paragraph was written not so much to state a fact as in reply to an argument; for it has been contended that Eskimo immunity to scurvy when on a diet of nothing but animal tissue may be due to their not following our practice of letting an animal bleed in such a way that most of the blood is removed from the flesh parts that are to be eaten—the assumption here being that white men would get scurvy on a meat diet. But we know through the experience of scores of Hudson Bay Company traders in northern Canada during the last hundred years, that white men no more than the forest Indians or the Eskimos, developed scurvy from a meat diet. The fact is no doubt that there is a higher percentage of vitamin C in the flesh than

313

in the blood of an average animal so that a person who gets, say, 10 percent of his nourishment from blood is not so well off from the vitamin point of view as another who gets only 5 percent of his vitamin C from the blood.

ALL-MEAT DIET HAS AMPLE VITAMIN C

Dr. Arne Høygaard, of the University of Oslo physiological expedition to East Greenland, considers that the people there who still live on the native diet—seal supplemented with fish—receive from these flesh foods about twice the quantity of vitamin C that is required for optimum health.

It seems to take anything from 1 to 3 months on the least desirable diet to produce marked symptoms of scurvy. Probably the lag is due to there being stored in the body a considerable amount of antiscorbutic substance at any given time.

SYMPTOMS

Probably, on careful check by the victim and his companions, the first observed symptom of scurvy would be mental—he becomes less optimistic, more irritable and inclined to gloom, quarrelsome. The next symptom, on close observation, would probably be dizziness—he would fall back into his seat after being startled and jumping up suddenly. Then, perhaps, comes a pain in some joint, which may be taken for rheumatism. The joints first affected are those which in that individual are under the most strain—the ankles or some leg joint if he walks much, an arm joint if he is a blacksmith. Then would appear a light bleeding of the gums, detected perhaps when he bites into a piece of white bread, and likely to be taken for pyorrhea.

The development so far sketched may take between a week and a month from the appearance of the first mental symptoms. These are by now more pronounced, the irritability having become proportionately less noticeable and the gloom more so. The progress hereafter is more rapid, or at least more noticeable. Pain invests every joint. The gums bleed at every touch, they grow purple in color and soften, finally to the consistency of cheese. A man picking his teeth with a wooden toothpick will likely bring out a piece of gum, thinking it a chunk of food. The teeth grow so loose that the patient, feeling of them to see how they are, may pull one out without quite realizing he is doing it.

Some time before the gums turn cheesy there appears a symptom from which the disease gets its vulgar name, "blackleg." The smaller blood vessels break under the skin; often this is noticed first on the calf of the leg where there now are black patches. The same fragility of small blood vessels causes bleeding from the nose and throat. Death, no doubt, usually if not always comes from internal hemorrhage.

Well toward the later stages of the disease the patient maintains a good appetite, good digestion, and for a sick person presents a pleasing appearance. It is, therefore, difficult to see why the name of the disease should have such a particularly disagreeable connotation.

The appetite, as said, is normal, unless perhaps it be slightly excessive. It is claimed by some that patients have a strong desire for the very things that hurt them most. One longing frequently cited is for salt beef, boiled. But those who long for this dish are usually sailors who are accustomed to it and the longing may be no more than the sign of that appetite which we have said is normal if not excessive.

Regular elimination accompanies good digestion for the stages observed by the author, which are all but the very last stages.

CURE

The only treatment is to bring the patient back to health by the use of fresh and not overcooked foods. Since this is a manual for Arctic use, we consider in detail a treatment involving fresh meat, but the same rules apply for other fresh foods. The treatment here outlined proved successful in curing two scurvy patients who were under Stefansson's direct observation. (They were members of his expedition who became ill through thoughtlessness in eating canned, salted, and dried foods although fresh meat was available.)

At the time the treatment was begun the patients were so weak that one could not walk at all, while the other could barely stumble along holding on for support. One of the men had pulled out a tooth without realizing it until he saw it between his fingers. Their gloom, despondency, was profound. They had pain in every joint.

The treatment was staying in bed on a diet exclusively of fresh caribou (any other kind of meat or fish will do equally well). The morning meal was boiled to an underdone stage in a lot of water, and the weak broth from this was used for drinking all day, supplemented when necessary by water. The other two and sometimes three meals each day were raw meat, slightly frozen (the freezing through circumstance and because the patients were used to it). They were not fed with those parts of the animal which are said to be rich in Vitamin C; they did not get the liver or internal organs, for, Eskimo style, those were fed to dogs. They may have had an occasional kidney or heart.

The parts eaten cooked were boiled caribou head, briskets, ribs, and pelvis; those eaten raw were chiefly hams and shoulders. Since the animals were killed with rifle bullets, they had not bled appreciably and there must have been a good deal of blood in the various tissues.

The only thing given these persons which is now supposed to be particularly rich in vitamin C was marrow from the long bones. They got a larger share than the other two members of the party who were well, not for therapeutic reasons but merely because you give preferred food to invalids.

The meat was boiled as described in Chapter 8. By this method it is considered sufficiently cooked when it is about as rare as our ordinary roast beef—the outside layer well done, the layer next under it medium done, and the center rare. The theory will be that in the center portion the vitamin C content has not been weakened by the oxidation that has taken place in the outer layers of the meat. Broiling or roasting, so long as the center portion is rare, would do equally well.

On the third or fourth day of this diet all pain had disappeared from every joint of both patients and optimism had replaced gloom. But they were still very weak, their gums as yet soft and their teeth loose. In two weeks they were able to begin traveling in easy stages; in four weeks they were completely recovered, except that the gums which had receded from the teeth did not fully regain their position.

Stefansson ascertained later in New York, by comparing notes verbally with Dr. Alfred F. Hess, probably then the leading specialist on scurvy in the United States, that Dr. Hess, using raw crushed fruits and vegetables, had, with patients in about the same stage of the disease, attained approximately the same mental and physical curative results in the same length of time—so far as the two could judge, by practically identical stages.

FORMER THEORIES AND TREATMENT

There was for centuries a firm belief that "lime juice will prevent and cure scurvy." This belief is sometimes said to have originated with Captain James Cook, but it is demonstrably much older. Throughout several centuries expedition after expedition (including the Scott Antarctic Expeditions of 1901–04 and 1910–13) failed to prevent the disease through the most liberal use of lime juice, but these failures were explained away by whatever argument came to hand. The main concern seemed to be to preserve undamaged the faith in lime juice. So it was claimed that the merits of it in the given cases had been counteracted by lack of cleanliness, fresh air or sunshine; it was said that food had been decayed, that the men had not had enough exercise, that the gloom induced by darkness had affected them.

During the same centuries that witnessed the lime juice failures, meat as a preventive of scurvy was discovered, forgotten and rediscovered any number of times, as shown by the narratives of numerous explorers whose expeditions were free of the disease. The more general idea, that the antiscorbutic qualities of food depend on the freshness of the food, entirely apart from whether it is vegetable or animal, has had the same history. None of these discoveries made enough impression upon medicine to become incorporated in the literature and tradition of the science.

We know now that there is no reason to carry fresh lemon or lime juice as an antiscorbutic into a meat country. Neither is there any reason against carrying it except the bother of doing so.

317

On ships and in a large establishment it may be well to provide lemon juice, fresh as possible, against the eventuality that fresh meat may not be obtainable. Since vegetables cost less than meats, it is cheaper to protect yourself against scurvy by vegetables if you are in a place where you can buy them. If you are a vegetarian you will insist on that method in any case. But, even if you are a vegetarian, you had better swallow some meat if you get into a place where for several months you are unable to secure fresh vegetable elements.

DANGERS OF OVERCOOKING

Nor has scurvy been the nemesis of explorers only. In the war of 1914–18 the British Army in the Near East was seriously handicapped by it. Upon investigation, it was found that the cooks were boiling most or all foods excessively. It was with difficulty that they were induced to obey orders to cook things only moderately or slightly.

VITAMIN C AS A COMMERCIAL PRODUCT

The preceding is based on the idea that you prevent or cure scurvy by eating the right food and handling it the right way. During the last few years the manufacturing chemists have been putting on the market concentrates of a number of the vitamins, including vitamin C. The belief is at present both that these products are effective and that, except in the possible case of vitamin D, there is no great danger from overdosage. So it is now possible to outfit an expedition, whether civil or military, with prepared concentrates that will keep you free from scurvy, irrespective of the diet. This has obvious advantages. The most apparent disadvantages are two: that you may lose your stock of medicines; and that, in any case, you may secure advantages other than vitamin C by having a considerable element of fresh food in your diet. It would seem best, then, to plan a diet which does not require the taking of vitamin C as a medicine, but to supply a party nevertheless with vitamin C concentrates for use in an emergency.

Summing up: To avoid scurvy by diet you must eat some fresh food, either meat or vegetable, and it must not be

318

overcooked. To cure scurvy, increase the amount of fresh food, at the same time increasing the amount that is eaten rare or raw. Like results can be obtained by vitamin concentrates taken as drugs, but a diet containing the needed vitamin C is preferable.

Section V

MONOXIDE POISONING

The dangers of camping in a lee and of poisoning by monoxide are twins—but not Siamese twins, for although they are usually found together they are not inseparable. If you consider them as being one, they are probably responsible for more deaths in the polar regions and more narrow escapes from death than any other single cause. They are the trickiest or dangers and more likely to take toll among the experienced than perhaps any of the other causes.

The chief inconveniences and dangers of Arctic winter camping in a lee on a generally open plain are discussed in Chapter 7. As said there, things outside of your camp are likely to get buried and lost, for instance, snowshoes and such gear, and even a sledge. Dogs sometimes get killed this way, for their fur may freeze to the ground and then when the snow drifts over them they are stifled. Worst of all, the same lee that catches snow enough to bury a sledge and dogs will very likely bury your tent, cutting off ventilation and causing the formation of carbon monoxide.

It is now generally agreed that the death of Andree and at least one of his two companions on White Island of the Svalbard group, in 1897, and the death of the four men of the Anderson party from the *Karluk* (Captain Robert A. Bartlett, commanding) of Stefansson's third expedition, on Herald Island in 1914, were caused by a combination of the two difficulties.

These parties through lack of understanding pitched their camps in lees, the snow settled on both tents so as to stop that ventilation which is through the fabric of the tent. Both were cooking with primus stoves and in both cases (we have no doubt) death came without warning—almost certainly none of these men ever knew what was happening to them, or about to happen.

319

Inexperienced men, particularly if they are from a forest country, will always want to pitch their winter Arctic camps in shelter; they will try to keep warm by curtailing ventilation. Since this is, as said, one of the chief causes of death in the Arctic we think it worth while to make the basic facts clearer than otherwise through narratives of special cases. We take first a modern one.

In 1910 Stefansson had his first experience with the insistence of a forest dweller for a lee camp. He and his old traveling companion, the Alaska Eskimo Natkusiak, were making a sledge journey northwest from the mouth of the Dease River, northeastern Great Bear Lake, to Langton Bay, at the foot of Cape Parry. They had with them a Bear Lake Indian, named Johnny Sanderson, who was impressed with how much superior his own camping technique was to that of white men, and who was proud of his experience in having been several times a considerable way beyond the margin of the Bear Lake woods out upon the prairies to the north (which, because of the lack of trees, are locally called barrens).

Johnny's technique was undoubtedly good for the woods to which he was used; but it was scarcely better than that of a man fresh from a lifetime in a big city in relation to the plainscraft needed for the Arctic prairie.

When, during a blizzard, Stefansson selected an open place as a camp site, Johnny was displeased, saying that he had seen a cutbank half a mile back, under the shelter of which the tent could have been pitched. Or, said he, only a little way ahead he could see a round hill with a steep slope to leeward that would be a fine place under which to camp, for the hill would break the wind.

Stefansson's and Natkusiak's ideas did not coincide with Johnny's. To them it seemed obvious that if they camped in a lee the drifting snow would in the night cover the tent and place them in danger of being smothered, even were the tent not to cave in with the weight of the snow. Johnny's ideas had all been gained in the forested country, where it really is wise to choose the most sheltered spots; and it seemed to him that his companions were little better than insane. It was only after his sledge was taken away from him by a show of force that Johnny was restrained from pitching the tent in the shelter of the hill.

POOR VENTILATION AND MONOXIDE POISONING

Even when the camp is not in a lee, monoxide may form through faulty construction of the dwelling or through carelessness of the occupants. There is a chain of tragedies and near tragedies connected with such monoxide poisoning from the first of modern expeditions which wintered in the Arctic, that of William Barents in 1596–97, to the 1928–30 and 1933–35 Byrd expeditions of the Antarctic.

The narrative of the Barents (Heemskerck) expedition gives, in an Elizabethan diction that now seems quaint, the account of modern polar exploration's first encounter with monoxide:

BARENTS' EXPERIENCE

"The 7 of December [1596] it was still foule weather, and we had a great storme with a north-east wind, which brought an extreme cold with it; at which time we knew not what to do, and while we sate consulting together what were best for vs to do, one of our companions gaue vs counsell to burne some of the sea-coles that we had brought out of the ship, which would cast a great heat and continue long; and so at euening we made a great fire thereof, which cast a great heat. At which time we were very carefull to keepe it in, for that the heat being so great a comfort vnto vs, we tooke care how to make it continue long; whereupon we agreed to stop vp all the doores and the chimney, thereby to keepe in the heate, and so went into our cabans to sleepe, well comforted with the heat, and so lay a great while talking together; but at last we were taken with a great swounding and daseling in our heads, yet some more then other some, which we first perceiued by a sick man and therefore the lesse able to beare it, and found our selues to be very ill at ease, so that some of vs that were strongest start out of their cabans, and first opened the chimney and than the doores, but he that opened the doore fell downe in a swound

321

[with much groaning] vppon the snow; which I hearing, as lying in my caban next to the doore, start vp [and there saw him lying in a swoon], and casting vinegar in his face recouered him againe, and so he rose vp. And when the doores were open, we all recouered our healthes againe by reason of the cold aire; and so the cold, which before had beene so great an enemy vnto vs, was then the onely reliefe that we had, otherwise without doubt we had [all] died in a sodaine swound."

STEFANSSON'S EXPERIENCE

The danger of poor ventilation in a camp where fire is burning was first and dramatically impressed on Stefansson in March 1911, when, with Dr. R. M. Anderson and the Eskimos Natkusiak and Tannaumirk, he was traveling east along the ice of Coronation Gulf in clear, calm, intensely cold weather. To save the trouble of building, they camped late one evening in a commodious and clean-looking snow house which had evidently been abandoned by a party of Eskimos not more than 2 days before. A new camp is warmer than an old camp, for a new snow house is a snow house, but an old one is partly an ice house. The walls of this one had been melted and then frozen into solid, glistening ice.

In their hurry to get the camp heated up, the Stefansson party closed the door tightly. There was just room for three of the men to sit on the bed platform; the fourth, Natkusiak, sat below them on the floor. Stefansson was cooking, with the primus stove placed on a block of snow while he knelt beside it on the bed platform cutting up snow into the kettle for water.

Suddenly, in the midst of telling a funny story, Tannaumirk fell backward on the bed with a sort of gurgling noise. When Dr. Anderson turned to see what Tannaumirk was up to, he fell face forward on top of the Eskimo.

Stefansson now realized that they were being poisoned by carbon monoxide and extinguished the primus stove. He instructed Natkusiak to hurry and break a hole in the snow wall behind him. But when the Eskimo tried to rise he was powerless to do so. That scared him so that with his last strength he threw himself back against the wall and broke away the loose block of snow by which the door had been closed. He then crawled outside on all fours, but was too weak to stand up. Stefansson followed him out, stood for a moment, and then fell down beside Natkusiak. Both were too weak to get back into the house and drag Anderson and Tannaumirk out.

It must have been 15 minutes that they lay flat outside before Anderson's face appeared at the door. His mind was clear, apparently, but he had no realization of what had happened. When the situation dawned on him he crawled out and started walking about and drawing deep breaths. But he soon found, as Stefansson had, that the deep breathing seemed to make things worse. He finally had to stretch himself out flat on the ground like the others.

It must have been another 10 minutes before Tannaumirk also came to his senses and crawled out. By that time Stefansson, who had been less affected than any of the others, had strength enough to fetch the sleeping bags from the house and to assist Anderson and Natkusiak to crawl into theirs. Tannaumirk, who had been most affected, was unable to think clearly; so he was unwilling to crawl into his bag and began wandering around in circles. Eventually Stefansson forced him into the sleeping bag and then went indoors, lit the primus stove again and started preparing a warm drink. An hour later Anderson, Natkusiak, and Stefansson were feeling comparatively fit again, and the next morning they noticed no ill effects. But Tannaumirk was ill not only that night but also the next day.

In his account of this experience in *My Life with the Eskimo,* Stefansson concludes:

"Of course our trouble had been from closing the house too tightly. Looking back upon our various experiences with primus stoves in the past, I can now see that we must have been near a similar outcome frequently before. We had escaped this time by a narrow margin. Had I gone off my head simultaneously with Tannaumirk and Anderson there would have been no salvation, for the stove would have kept on burning, generating fresh quantities of poison.

"It seemed to us the next day, and it seems so to me still, that this not very romantic adventure was the narrowest escape we had on our whole expedition."

It was under similar circumstances of a fire burning in a poorly ventilated room that one of the men of the first Byrd expedition to the Antarctic (1928–30) was overcome in the room used as a photographic laboratory. And there is indication of monoxide poisoning in Admiral Byrd's own experience during the "vigil" of his second expedition. Thus has the peril of monoxide poisoning dogged polar explorers at least from Barents in 1596 to Byrd in our time.

Some of the points with regard to monoxide poisoning are:

1. It is unfortunate that the word "fumes" is so often used in describing monoxide poisoning. If there are any smelly and disagreeable fumes they are from another cause; and, while a nuisance, are really a good thing, for they constitute a warning. Frequently there is no such warning.

2. It is equally unfortunate that many associate monoxide with dioxide and believe that, particularly if they are watchful, they are going to notice a warning difficulty with their breathing. There are many, too, who believe that by lighting a match or burning a candle you can get advance notice of how the gas accumulates. Such warning, if any, is indirect and connected with the, from our present point of view, not dangerous dioxide.

3. Even among those who, from automobile experience, understand that monoxide does not smell or give much warning, there is a failure to be suspicious of many common sources. Monoxide, for instance, is produced by charcoal fires and there is danger when, as explained in Chapter 7, you use the inland Eskimo style of making a roaring fire, throwing out the smoking embers, and covering up your smoke hole. Eskimos, when they do this, usually have a door open; but white men, especially those new in the country and afraid of the cold, are likely to close the door.

4. It is not sufficiently realized that carbon monoxide will pass through iron. Apparently it begins to pass right through the sides of a stove out into a room when the iron is at red heat. If and when it gets to white heat the dioxide is said

to pass out through sheet iron, and probably cast iron, almost as readily as if it were air seeping through canvas.

SYMPTOMS

Stefansson feels, in thinking back to his experience described above, that in many cases, if you watch carefully, a feeling as of pressure on the temples can be detected for some little while, perhaps only a few moments, before you keel over. In some cases, particularly if the poisoning is slow, there are auditory symptoms. You hear what may seem like a slow drum or a measured tread but what is really the beating of your pulse.

A DEBATED PROCEDURE

It was the experience of Stefansson and three companions, when two of them "passed out" and two were barely able to move, that when they came out into fresh air and began to breathe it as deeply as they could there was an acceleration or increase of the monoxide effect so that (it seemed to them) the deep breathing produced a collapse—they had been barely able to stand and were now forced to lie down. From this they thought that perhaps the deep breathing had forced the monoxide farther out into the lungs and should be avoided accordingly. However, this does not appear to be sound, in view of recent studies.

Professor Yandell Henderson of Yale has recently done extensive work on the symptoms and effects of carbon monoxide poisoning, as well as in the treatment of this type of asphyxiation.

HENDERSON'S TREATMENT OF MINOR CASES

The treatment which Henderson suggests for cases in which the victim is still conscious and able to take certain precautionary steps is:

"Lie still, keep warm and, if it is available, drink either a bottle of some carbonated water or a cup of coffee. The carbon dioxide in the carbonated water will stimulate deeper, fuller breaths, and thus hasten the ventilation of carbon monoxide from the blood."

325

For acute carbon monoxide asphyxia, Henderson has introduced a treatment which is now standard with doctors and hospitals. This is:

Administer an inhalation of CO_2+O_2 for the purpose of increasing pulmonary ventilation and thus expediting the elimination of CO from the blood.

On the basis of his own experience and the results of Professor Henderson, Stefansson believes the order of procedure when you realize you are being poisoned should be:

1. Remove the cause; as, for instance, turn the spigot of a primus stove to relieve the pressure, whereupon it goes out instantly.

2. Go outdoors, if you are able, walking slowly or perhaps crawling with a minimum of exertion.

3. If some occupants cannot walk out, the important thing naturally is to do whatever is necessary to secure ventilation.

4. So far as possible follow the treatment outlined by Henderson—lie still, keep warm, draw deep breaths to help elimination of carbon monoxide from the blood.

5. As soon as possible after you get into the open air, crawl into a sleeping bag to avoid danger of freezing—also to comply with the second rule of Henderson's treatment, to keep warm.

CHAPTER 11

TRAVEL

Section I

GENERAL CONSIDERATIONS

Many things bearing on travel are discussed elsewhere in this Manual—for instance, in the sections on camps, hunting, dogs, sledges, etc. Here we deal with the general principles and the basic technique of Arctic travel.

MAPS

Besides being inaccurate, most Arctic maps carry only the names of explorers, patrons of exploration, or friends of the map makers. Therefore the places and names on such maps are unidentifiable through information from natives, and commonly even from resident whites. To have full value to the traveler, a map of any given district should carry local names as a supplement to the others. Such maps need frequent amending, since most native settlements are temporary in character and shift in locality from year to year.

CHRONOMETERS

No matter how small the party, three chronometers should be the minimum number carried, for if you have only two and one goes wrong you will not know which one is wrong.

WATCHES

Watches where the dial is numbered to 24 instead of 12 hours are a great convenience and almost a necessity because, in summer when the sun never sets, and when at times there is thick foggy weather for many days in succession, it is often a matter of doubt, if you carry an ordinary watch, whether it shows 12 o'clock midnight or 12 o'clock noon.

It may seem incredible carelessness to lose track of time so far that you are in doubt which of the 12-hour periods you are in; but it happens frequently. Under special conditions you may travel 15 or 20 hours continuously. At the end you may happen to get a blizzard which induces you to rest in camp a while, free to sleep as long as you need or desire. In summer, when there is no darkness, one's irregularity of habits become marked. You may not feel any special inconvenience from staying awake 20 or 30 hours (Eskimo children do it frequently) and you are equally likely to sleep for 15 or 18 hours. Such things may put you 12 hours out of your reckoning, not so likely 24 hours.

CLOCKS

If you are taking sextant observations, you will find few things more useful than an alarm clock. In summer, when most traveling is done at night, you will, without an alarm clock, either have to sit up past camping time and wait for noon or you will neglect your observation because you will not be awake for it. Similarly you may need a midforenoon or midafternoon awakening for a longitude sight.

MAPPING AND SURVEY

If the conditions of visibility are favorable and the coast line pronounced enough so that one can see at a distance the distinction between land and sea, fairly good mapping can be done, on some such scale as an inch to the mile, at the rate of 10 miles a day.

Those unfamiliar with low Arctic coasts will scarcely realize how difficult it is, when you are traveling along offshore, to decide on looking toward land whether you see an island or part of the mainland. An example is the north coast of Alaska. Suppose yourself traveling along, by sledge in winter or boat in summer, and using the best map available to 1940, that made by E. deK. Leffingwell and published by the U. S. Geological Survey. Some of the islands will give you no trouble, being far from the mainland. For instance when you look toward Cross Island, 10 or 12 miles from the shore, you see no mainland beyond and there is nothing to confuse you. It is quite different with an island like Flaxman which is only 3 miles from the mainland. If you are a traveler passing by in summer by boat or in winter by sledge, and if you are 2 or 3 miles outside Flaxman, you will have to depend on your dead reckoning or upon a longitude sight, rather than upon your eyes, to be sure that you are passing an island and not an outward projecting section of the mainland.

The first of travel principles is "Do in Rome as the Romans do." In the Arctic this means using methods of travel which the forces of evolution have taught to the dwellers of northern lands, instead of methods which Europeans, some of them ingenious and energetic, have evolved from their inner consciousness and from the limited experience of half a dozen years.

John Rae and John Franklin probably seemed about equally resourceful in London, England; but in Repulse Bay, Arctic North America, John Rae wintered his party in health and comfort; a few years earlier, in the same locality and with the same resources, John Franklin's entire company of able-bodied Englishmen starved helplessly and died to the last man.

"Better be safe than sorry." A thing that is showy, that looks daring and sportsmanlike, has a strong appeal but frequently leads to distressing results. Equally distressing results, however, follow the too conservative course. The idea, then, is to take such risks as come but do not go out of your way to invite them.

You cannot keep anything secret in the North. This was true even before the days of radio; if a Hudson's Bay agent stubbed his toe in January, everyone for hundreds of miles had heard about it by March. If you want to keep operations secret, you must give them a logical explanation other than the true one.

This disposes of the fiction that is written about criminals hiding successfully in the North. It cannot be done; for people are so few that every newcomer is thoroughly scrutinized and discussed, and his path from one village to another is as clear as if it were studded with torches.

TRAVELING SEASONS

Spring is the worst of all seasons for Arctic travel. The total snowfall of the year among the Arctic islands north of Canada is equivalent to only a few inches of water; but half of this falls in the form of snow, mist, or fog between late April and late June, when the rains commence. On the ground during these spring months visibility is frequently for several days at a time always less than half a mile. Diffused light is continuous for many days at a time. Sledges stick in slush far worse than they do in the soft snow of winter, and much of the time you wade as you walk. Mush ice will ruin a sledgeboat (described elsewhere) after two or three trips.

SPRING CAMPING DETAILS

In spring, travel platforms of some sort are needed at camp time to keep bedding from contact with the ice which, when the sun shines, is wet from thaw water, and in rain even wetter if that be possible. For so keeping bedding off ice you use what you have—box boards, willows, pieces of rope.

ICE TRAVEL SHOULD NOT BE PLANNED AFTER MAY 1

If ice travel is planned, if not the result of emergency, you should not leave shore after May 1. (For the dangers and difficulties of travel at this season, see discussion in Section III of this chapter.)

SUMMER

In summer travel overland, pack dogs are used. As described in Chapter 12, the pack-saddles consist essentially of two big pouches that nearly reach to the ground on either side of the animal when the pack is in place. However, as pointed out there, if the dog is small the mere fact that he has to wade will get your pack wet. Any dog is liable to lie down in water deliberately, to cool off. In Section II of this chapter we tell of the difficulties of summer travel—the number of lakes, the

330

mosquitoes, the swamps, the rocky areas that wear out your boots.

AUTUMN

Autumn is the harvest season on the Arctic tundra. Caribou are still short-haired and their skins suitable for clothing; they are still fat and their meat therefore good eating.

But autumn is a transition period. In travel you are not comfortable for the snow is as yet not hard enough for snow houses but the temperature already too low for comfort in a tent. During a week or two after the equinox you still have more daylight than if you were at the equator; but thereafter darkness comes on with giant strides. Particularly if you are on a small and northerly island, or out at sea north of Alaska or Siberia, fog, fine mist, and snow fill the air continuously for days and even weeks in the period September–October. As will appear in the discussion on winter (below), sea ice travel should not be planned for autumn.

WINTER

Snow and ice are your best friends in the north, for they make travel easy in cold weather. Winter travel and its conditions are dealt with later in this chapter, under Sections II and III. However, the following applies to both sea and land travel.

In midwinter it is cold in the Arctic, but when you are properly dressed you don't mind it. Fifty or sixty below is a little too cold, for if you run or exert yourself violently and take the air rapidly into your lungs in consequence, it has a sort of burning and half-stifling effect. Moreover sledges, unless shod with ice, drag heavy, almost as if the snow were sand.

Forty below is about right. Your first morning in that kind of weather is a marvelous experience. The air is so clear that you can see 3 or 4 times as far as you can in any lowland in the south (mountain air is clear in all parts of the world, though not quite equal to polar air). But if your seeing is improved 2 or 3 times over, your hearing is aided 10 times more—the sounds carry 10 times farther. You can hear distinctly at a mile the footfall of caribou walking quietly through slightly crusted snow. (See also Chapter 3.) From Christmas to April most days have these clear Arctic skies, with help to sight and sound.

Assuming that no emergency is involved, you should not leave land for sledge travel over the sea until after the first part of February. Before this the nights are so long that the probability of getting involved during darkness in ice movement is very high. Attempting to travel without daylight with sea ice breaking under you is almost as dangerous as it would be for a blind man to cross streets in heavy traffic.

TEST OF WINTER TRAVELING WEATHER

Whether your dogs will or will not face the wind is the test of fit and unfit traveling weather in the Arctic, for a properly dressed man will face a wind that is too much for the Eskimo dog.

There is nothing you can do to force a dog to travel into a wind or a snowstorm that he feels is beyond him. He will simply curl up, nose in tail, and try to go to sleep. If you insist on forcing your dogs, you will end by having to go ahead of them and drag the team as well as the sledge.

HEALTH

It seems to be a law of human nature that when you are in good health, relief from discomfort becomes so keen a pleasure that it compensates for whatever has gone before. Even in the discomforts of spring travel, you will find that there is no connection between such ills as rheumatism and being continually soaked with cold water, getting dry in between times. Common respiratory infections (the common cold, for instance) are found in travel only under special conditions that seem unrelated to weather or comfort. For this and other related subjects see Chapter 10.

SORE FEET

It seems to be the general experience of long-distance walkers that you give out through sore feet rather than weariness of the whole body. The best remedy, next to a rest, is to change socks and boots. The new footgear presses on different spots and rests the chafing parts. If your footgear is of the Eskimo type, with no difference of shape between left and right boots, it will be better than nothing to shift boots and socks from one foot to the other.

EMERGENCY DIETS

On a diet of fats alone you gradually lose strength but this symptom of malnutrition is not so conspicuous as a sleepiness and a mental inability to call quickly into action such strength as you have.

The symptoms that result from a diet of lean alone are practically those of starvation. You eat so much that your stomach is actually distended, but you feel continually hungry. See Chapters 8 and 10 for detailed discussion of diet.

In emergency the best practice is to feed your dogs as long as you feed yourself, for the speed of the party depends on the strength of the dogs. Aside from humane considerations, hoarding food to their disadvantage eventually means losing speed to your disadvantage.

RIDING ON SLEDGES

We have said elsewhere (Chapter 12) that no man should undertake Arctic work who cannot walk as many miles a day as his dogs are able to haul his sledge and camp gear. This, naturally, does not apply to a man who is invalided for one reason or another, though the best procedure is, if possible, to stop and camp.

LOADS CARRIED

In cases where it is necessary for a man to pack his own load, it is worth noting that in the early days of the Hudson Bay Company, goods used to be made into 90-pound packages, each of which was known as a "piece." Some men could carry two of these. The Company's rule was to employ no man in portaging who could not make 80 miles in 4 days, carrying, in addition to the 90-pound piece, whatever he needed in the way of food and bedding.

HAULING FOOD

The weakness in a system of travel which takes with you all the food you think you can possibly need on a journey and makes no preparation for gathering more from the country when stores are exhausted, is that when unlooked-for circumstances stretch the time beyond the reckoned limit, supplies run out, dogs are eaten, skin, clothing, and harness follow, and then death comes from cold and starvation.

So long as you are traveling in a country supplied with game, you are safer to start with a rifle and with the resolution to find food (but, if the compensating is required, without a pound of food on your sledge) than you would be in starting with a sledge heavily loaded with food and with no provision made for getting more when the load has been eaten up.

HAULING FUEL

In Chapter 7 of this Manual we discuss the materials that will serve you as fuel. However, we repeat here what we say there: Hauling fuel is more important than hauling food and the kind of fuel more important than the kind of food. You get better results from kerosene burned in a blue-flame stove than from seal blubber burned by any method so far devised—a primus stove cooks more rapidly than a seal-oil lamp, and is more cleanly than an outdoor fire of seal blubber.

ERRORS IN JUDGMENT DUE TO DIFFUSED LIGHT OR FOG

If you are in foggy country in winter, you must be continually on guard. The daylight is negligible; the moonlight, if it comes to you first through clouds that are high in the sky and later through an enveloping fog, is a light which enables you to see your dog-team distinctly enough, or even a black rock a hundred yards away, but is scarcely better than no light at all upon the snow at your feet. In mountainous terrain, for instance, your eyes cannot tell whether you are going to step on a bank of snow or into an abyss.

PROCEDURE

Under such conditions you would ordinarily stay in camp unless you could follow a valley where, without great danger of falling, you would be merely inconvenienced by walking now and then against the face of a cliff.

334

But if you have to travel where there is possibility of walking into a crevasse or over the brim of a precipice, you can at least use some fairly effective precautions. For instance, you could carry two or three dark mittens or boots that you would be able to do without if you lost one of them. With these in your hands or in your pockets you walk ahead of the team. Throw one mitten about 10 yards ahead, keep your eye on it until you get within 3 or 4 yards of it and then throw a second mitten. Keep doing this so that most of the time you can see two black spots on the snow ahead of you separated by 5 or 6 yards of whiteness. You are not safe in throwing one mitten only and walking up to it; for, being light in weight, it may be lying on the snow overhang at the edge of a cliff, an overhang that would break under your weight. (See chapter 4 for a more detailed discussion of diffused light.)

EQUIPMENT FOR TWO OR THREE MEN TO LIVE BY HUNTING AT SEA OR ASHORE FOR 2 YEARS

In keeping with the main purpose of this Manual as a guide in emergency, we give a sample list of equipment by which two or three men can find their way about, supporting themselves, living and traveling in comfort for 2 years, whether on the Arctic pack, on an Arctic shore, or inland in an Arctic country. Substantially this is the outfit used on the third Stefansson expedition when planning a 2-year journey for three men and six dogs.

With the general aviation slant of the Manual, we point out that this is also the emergency outfit that might be carried in an airplane by three men making a flight across the Arctic Sea by any of its diameters. If they make a safe forced landing and can neither fly again nor summon help, if they are in good health at the start, use reasonable judgment, and have reasonable luck, they ought to be able to make their way to some native or white settlement in 2 years, or less, through the use of this equipment.

SLEDGE

For an airplane we recommend a sledge of the type made by Anthony Fiala for Charles A. Lindbergh, in consultation with Stefansson, when Lindbergh was preparing for his survey of Greenland and of the lands east and west of it in 1933. For description see Section IV of this chapter. For description of sledges to be used on a planned journey from a base camp, see Section II, Chapter 12.

DOGS

For a long journey from a base we recommend five large dogs of weights from 80 to 120 pounds, hitched tandem; second choice would be seven smaller dogs driven Nome style—three pairs on either side of a central trace and the seventh dog at the end of the trace as a leader. For methods of hitching see Chapter 12, Section IV.

We make no recommendation as to whether an airplane should take one dog or none. This would depend chiefly on the character of the flyers and on their opinions. If the dog is taken, he is for three chief uses: (1) to help get seals by the mautok method described in Chapter 13, Section II; (2) to give warning of polar bears that may approach camp (not so much because the bear is dangerous as because you want to be waked up or warned so you can go out and shoot him for food; and (3) to help in securing a bear that is fleeing—see Chapter 13, Section II for discussion of dogs in bear hunting.

WILKINS ON EQUIPMENT

Wilkins, who formed his ideas of northern travel during 3 years on the third Stefansson expedition, differs from Stefansson only upon minor points as to equipment for a party planning to live by hunting while making its way ashore from a forced landing. As he has unequaled experience with flying over the northern pack, we give next the actual list of things he took with him in 1928 on the first (and up to 1937 the only) flight by airplane across the Arctic—from Point Barrow to Spitsbergen by a course which took him past Greenland between 100 and 200 miles north from its north coast. This outfit he looked upon as adequate for supporting himself and Ben Eielson for 2 years. They had no dog, so did not expect to use mautok hunting. They carried no sled because they expected to construct one if it were needed from certain parts of the airplane.

As basis for comment on the list we insert numerals within parentheses:

EQUIPMENT FOR TWO MEN FOR 2 YEARS

Combined seal spear and ice chisel (1), an axe, a small alpine axe, an apparatus for securing seals from the water (2), two rifles (3), 350 cartridges (4), 3 snow knives (5), a saw (6), two pairs of snowshoes, two half sleeping bags with waterproof covers, strips of deerskin to place beneath the bags, a wind-proof and waterproof tent with a waterproof flooring (7), straps for making packs of sleeping bags, a duraluminum-shod runner which we could fix to the upper part of the fuselage and so construct a sled-canoe (8), a Primus stove, two cooking pots, cups, plates, and spoons, four half-gallon containers for fuel, one of them filled with alcohol, another filled with ether to be used either for starting the engine in cold weather or in case surgical operations following an accident were necessary, bandages, medicines, a complete field surgical outfit, a small quantity of tobacco and some coca leaves to be used for alleviating hunger (9), two canvas covers for the engine and special stoves for heating them, fishhooks, fish nets, and sinkers. A piece of the fish net could also be used on the end of the seal spear for netting small auks and other birds should we find ourselves marooned on one of the Arctic islands (10). Our spare clothing, with what we wore, provided for each man two fur shirts, two pairs of fur socks, fur breeches, sealskin breeches, one pair of cloth breeches, four pairs of Angora woolen socks, two pairs of sealskin winter boots, two pairs of sealskin summer waterproof boots, two pairs of fur mittens, one pair of waterproof mittens, silk snow shirts and silk snow trousers (11), tooth brushes, tooth paste, hair clippers, safety razors and shaving cream, soap and a towel (12), a small mirror, a small pocket compass, sheath knives and small files for sharpening them, a magnifying glass, a waterproof box for matches, handkerchiefs, a sewing kit, silk and sinew for repairing boots and skin clothing, two pairs of snow glasses (13), and a thermos bottle. For food we carried 5 pounds of sweet chocolate, 20 pounds of biscuits, 20 pounds of pemmican, 24 pounds of malted milk in tablet form, and 5 pounds of raisins (14).

1. An ice chisel should have a hardwood handle, 1¼-inch diameter, 7 or 8 feet long, or should be made of two segments to total that length, for you may have to chisel through 6 or more feet of ice. The chisel itself should be of steel about ¾ inch wide and 1 inch thick. The seal "spear" is a harpoon — an actual spear would be of no value.

2. This is the manak described in Chapter 13, Section II.

3. For economy, and because of the kind of game there is in the Arctic, the rifles should not be of larger caliber than .256 (possibly .22 would be as good). There are special reasons for a very flat trajectory, given in our Chapter 13, Section I.

4. Wilkins allowed 350 cartridges for two men for two years. Stefansson cons ders this an adequate allowance for three men and six dogs for two years.

5. The snow knives should be butcher knives of rather soft steel. You might have them different lengths, 14-, 16- and 18-inch blades.

6. This would be a carpenter saw with, say, 2-foot or 2½-foot blade, and would be used for cutting snow blocks when the snow was very hard; apart from that it would serve any other purpose of a saw.

7. Wilkins is probably wrong in preferring that a tent shall be self-contained—floor in one piece with the rest. It is not possible to keep snow out of that kind of a tent; and once you have snow in, getting it out is difficult. Better have flooring in a separate piece.

8. Wilkins plans to make a combined sled and canoe out of his fuselage. He had no sled. We recommend carrying a sled and a tarpaulin. You can then construct a sled-boat, as described in Chapter 12, Section II. This tarpaulin will serve also a number of other uses.

9. The tobacco and coca leaves would be intended for use during the same period as the emergency rations listed below. In the long run there is no point in carrying either tobacco or stimulants.

10. Use of such nets is described in our Chapter 13, Section III.

11. The silk must not be of the waterproof type that is filled. What you need is some densely woven unfilled cloth.

12. In the list "tooth brushes, tooth paste, hair clippers, safety razors, and shaving cream, soap and a towel," the only thing necessary is the clippers. They should be beard clippers that will give you the nearest thing to a shave. In summer you can afford to let beards grow; in winter you must always keep them so short that ice does not cling, which means that you use beard clippers about once every 3 days. (Wilkins no doubt carried the toilet equipment because at the end of his journey from Barrow he wanted to make a good impression on the Norwegian colony in Spitzbergen—which he did, having shaved and cleaned up in a camp in their neighborhood before coming into the first settlement.)

13. The glasses Wilkins carried were amber; this color protects the eyes as well as any other and is better than other colors for aiding vision in diffused light.

14. If you add up the weight of all these food articles and divide by two you have 74, the number of days for which Wilkins carried rations. His idea was to use them while getting ashore, if his plane came down near land; alternatively, they were to be used while getting equipment ready, as, for instance, while building a sled canoe out of the fuselage of the plane. There are more than 700 days in 2 years. Obviously you cannot carry food for that length of time whether for two or three men. You could perhaps carry it in the plane, but the men could not haul it with them when they started toward shore—would have to leave most of it behind.

The Wilkins outfitting is on the basis of not using a radio for SOS purposes and then waiting for help. If one relies on a radio and a rescue one should take as much food as the plane will carry in addition to the things it must carry, as gasoline.

As we have explained in the sections on Hunting and on Animal Life, if you camp on a floe waiting for rescue, bears are sure to walk in every now and then, each giving you on the average more than 400 pounds of actual food, for they would run at least 800 pounds live weight. The ice would crack near you now and then and in the leads you could get seals. You could dip up shrimps out of the leads with a net made from a handkerchief.

Important things not mentioned by Wilkins are sextant, field glasses, and miner's pickaxe. He had a sextant and simply forgot to mention it when he made up the list. He also had field glasses. These, if not of too high a power, are, as we have dwelt on elsewhere, next in importance to the rifle itself when it comes to living by hunting. He probably had a miner's pickaxe, for he is a believer in this instrument. It should have a head weighing between 2 and $3\frac{1}{2}$ pounds. Perhaps you might carry a 2-pound pick and a $3\frac{1}{2}$-pound pick, whether there are two men or three in your party.

If the party is three you would want three rifles; as said, the 350 cartridges would be enough for three men whether they have two or three rifles.

Section II

ON LAND

LANDMARKS

When a group sets out for a day's land travel, they may need to be found at evening, perhaps in darkness, by some other person, such as a man who hunts to supply them with food. They should, then, agree in advance that the camp will be made near some landmark, preferably of a linear nature. Pitching camp near the foot of a conspicuous round hill would be of little use, for whenever the weather became thick, or the night dark, you would be unable to see the hill from any distance. A lantern hung on a tent is sometimes of use but is frequently taken to be a star. Besides, you could not see it far in thick weather. The landmark of most use, then, is a long, fairly straight ridge or a cutbank conspicuous enough and characteristic enough not to be overlooked or mistaken for another.

Likewise the group should agree in advance that if one member is separated—whether through accident or through the deliberate purpose of hunting—the trail of the party following a coast by sea ice should go close in at every prominent headland so that the one following will have less difficulty in picking it up. If he loses it, he can make for the next headland and pick it up again there.

LEAVING CAMP TO LOOK FOR GAME IN THICK WEATHER

If you are in a country new to you and if there are no river courses or landmarks that can be followed with the assurance that you can also follow them back again, it is, in thick weather, a matter of the closest observation and the most careful reckoning to find your way home to camp.

NOTE WALKING SPEED AND WIND DIRECTION

As you advance, you must notice the speed at which you are walking and the time you walk on any given course, and you must know exactly at what angle to the wind you are traveling. Furthermore, you must check the wind occasionally, either by a pocket compass or a snowdrift, to see that it isn't changing, for an unnoticed change would throw any reckoning out of gear.

MEMORIZE TOPOGRAPHY NEAR CAMP

Before leaving camp, walk around it, study each aspect of any landmark, until you feel sure that if you strike any point within half a mile of home you will recognize it on the return.

TRAVELING PROCEDURE

When the topography of the half-mile square or so surrounding the camp has been memorized, you strike out perhaps into the wind or perhaps at an angle of 45° or 90° to it and travel straight for an hour or two hours, according to the degree of confidence you have in your ability to get back. If no game has been found, you turn at some angle, commonly a right angle, to your original course, and walk in that direction an estimated distance, perhaps as far as in the first direction. If nothing has been found, you turn again. If this time also you make a right-angle turn in the same direction, it is easy to calculate at what time you are opposite camp and 1 hour or 2 hours' walk away from it. Turning a third right-angle will face you directly for camp. If you have been careful, you will come within half a mile of your mark, or within the area memorized before starting. But should you miss it, you will know at any rate at what time you are close to camp. By thinking the matter out you will see how to walk around in circles or in squares of continually increasing size until you find a place you recognize.

PROCEDURE WHEN GAME IS SIGHTED

If in the course of your walk you do see game, your first thought must be to take the time by the watch or make some similar observation to assure yourself of the direction of your camp at that moment. If you can kill the game on the spot, the matter is simple. But if you have to follow your quarry about a good deal, or if it is a trail you have come upon rather than the game itself and you follow the trail, then it is not so easy to lay down rules for getting back.

341

Everything can, however, be summarized by saying that you must continually memorize your course; if you do this, angles and distances will determine approximately the course you must eventually take when you start for home.

This outline of procedure in a storm, or at any time when direct vision will not serve, shows at once why it is that a white man of trained mind can find his way home so frequently when a native gets lost and has to camp and wait for clear weather.

FINDING CAMP IN THICK WEATHER OR DARKNESS

If you want to try to find a camp in darkness or thick weather, the first rule is not to try making a straight shot toward it. For if you do and miss, you will not know which side to turn to look for it, will flounder, get confused. The thing, then, is deliberately to set your course to the right or to the left of where you know the camp to be.

PROCEDURE WHEN LOST

In the sentence just above, the important word is *know*. If you don't know where the camp is, the first principle is to stop quietly where you are and wait for daylight. Every time impatience whispers to you, "Make a shot at it, you might hit it," let discretion answer, "Yes, but if I miss once I'll never know if the camp lies to the right or left, ahead of me or behind. Now I know it is ahead of me and that I will inevitably find it when I begin to be able to see clearly."

Even when your instincts amount to conviction, you should remember that a night's camping out will do you no harm, but wandering around hopelessly lost will exhaust your energy and endanger your life.

The suggestion here made, that instead of aiming straight for camp you should aim deliberately for a point to the right of it or to the left of it, is applicable to flying. Two flyers who have been particularly successful in supplementing navigational technique by common sense are the American Lindbergh and the British Cobham. They have both said that when flying across an ocean toward a coast they head either for the right or the left of their target so that when

342

they strike the coastline there will be no vacillation—they will know which way to turn and will never have a doubt that after turning they should continue in the chosen direction until their goal is reached.

There are on record many failures due to attempting a direct hit on your target. One of these was the flight of the Americans Bert Hassell and Parker Cramer in 1928, when they took a departure from Labrador and were aiming for the University of Michigan base, Camp Evans, in the Holsteinsborg district of Greenland. When they struck the coast they were disappointed not to recognize the topography. Having attempted a direct hit, they did not have any conviction as to which way to turn, but decided on turning right and flew south along the coast for 100 or 200 miles. They found no camp and were eventually convinced that they should have turned left. Reversing their course, they flew north; but their gasoline gave out before they got as far as the point where they had originally struck Greenland. Obeying an elementary rule, not to descend upon snow-free land if a glacier is available, they flew east, had gas enough to get 20 miles beyond the ice margin, made a safe descent on the Greenlandic Inland Ice, abandoned their plane, and walked back to the coast. It turned out that they had originally struck Greenland only a few miles to the right of their target, Camp Evans. If they had made sure by striking 50 or 100 miles to the right and had then turned left, they would have had ample gas to find the University of Michigan camp.

This is, then, a general principle, applicable whether you are walking, sledging, or flying: If your target is on a coastline, along a river, or along any linear feature that is at an approximate right angle to your course, then never aim direct for the target. Aim farther to one side or the other, so that when you strike your landmark you will be without qualms of doubt on whether you should turn right or left.

TO FIND A CAMP OR DEPOT ON A COASTLINE

When, afoot and in darkness, you get near a place you want to find which is on the coastline, or along some more or less linear topographic feature, you begin a zigzag search—except, of course, if the linear mark is something abrupt and unmistakable, like a river cutbank or a cliff along a sea-shore. Suppose, for instance, you have been told that a camp you have never seen is on the coast 15 miles ahead of you. Remembering the uncertainties of an estimate based on time and distance, you should not go more than what you think is 10 miles before you start your zigzag.

We have explained elsewhere that it is never pitch dark in the Arctic; so that a camp, even if it be snowhouses invisible in themselves, is certain to have dark markings (like sledges or dogs) that you can see a hundred feet away. You may not know whether the camp is on the sea ice a little way from the shore or on the land some distance from the beach. Accordingly, you will walk as far as you think necessary out to sea; then you turn and walk toward the land so as to strike it not more than 200 feet ahead of where you left the shore (the hundred-foot visibility being your standard). You now continue in the same direction inland. A camp, in ordinary northern practice, whether white or Eskimo, would not be more than a hundred yards from the beach; more likely 25 or 50 yards. Finding nothing, you zigzag back down to the coast and out to sea, repeating until you are sure you have gone well beyond the 15-mile distance. Then you stop and wait for daylight, moonlight, or a mere clearing of the sky that will extend your range of vision. You camp if you think necessary. But it may be that even in daylight it is not easy to tell just where the land meets the sea; numerous travelers have reported that they were half a mile or a mile inland before they realized that they were ashore. If that is the sort of coastline with which you are dealing you must kneel down every now and then and, with your hunting knife, dig through the snow and do some chipping. Probably you can tell from the consistency whether you are driving your knife point into ice or into frozen muck. If not, you should take very small pieces and melt them in your mouth. Don't try a large piece, for you might freeze your lips or tongue, even perhaps losing a piece of skin that stuck to the chunk of ice or mud.

344

CAMPING OUT

One of the hardest to eradicate of false beliefs is: "When lost in a blizzard you must keep moving; you must not go to sleep, for if you do you will never wake again."

This has led to the deaths of many men, the deaths themselves seeming to furnish corroborative evidence. However, analysis has proved, as will appear below, that these men died not because they were lost in a blizzard but because they kept moving while lost.

By pinching and punching yourself, by forcing yourself to keep awake, you use up energy that is needed to keep you warm. Through exercise and through panic your sweat glands start working and perspiration makes your clothing wet. When you are so worn out that you cannot keep awake any longer, exhausted and wet, you drop in your tracks and then you may never wake again.

It happens fairly often with Eskimos that they are caught in blizzards and that they return to camp when the weather clears, no worse for their adventure. In fact, to their way of thinking, it has not been an adventure at all.

EXAMPLE OF CORRECT PROCEDURE

The winter 1908–09, Stefansson, traveling along the coast west of Herschel Island, came to an Eskimo camp and found there an old woman who had just reached home after being out in a 3-day blizzard. When half a mile from her house, she realized she could not reach it and sat down on a hummock with her back to the wind. But the temperature was well above zero, as it usually is especially at the beginning of a gale, so her body heat melted the snow under her and she noticed dampness. Blaming herself, as she said afterwards, for not having foreseen this, she took off her mittens, laid them one on top of the other, and sat on them, which gave sufficient insulation between her body and the snow. She slipped her arms out of the sleeves of her coat, tucked the sleeve openings under her belt, and sat with her bare arms crossed on her bare body inside the clothes. Leaning forward, she was soon asleep.

But during sleep your "vitality" is lowered and you are chilled more quickly than if you were awake. This chill woke up the old lady, just as a corresponding chill would awaken you if your bedroom window was open and your blankets were too few. Not having a window to close or blankets to put on, the old lady stuck her arms back into the sleeves again, put on her mittens, and walked about until the stiffness from her cramped position was gone, as well as the chill. Then she sat down on her mittens and did exactly as before, including the sleeping.

By alternating procedures, she passed approximately 70 hours, the weather getting much colder toward the end and finally clearing with intense frost. When the drift lessened she saw the house and returned to it. She said the time had not seemed particularly long because she slept a great deal, and that she had not been very hungry except toward the end of the first day.

The principles to remember, then, are:

Don't keep moving—keep still.

Keep your clothing dry.

Sleep as much as you can—because it both saves energy and passes time.

In temperatures of $-10°$ or lower, a makeshift snowhouse, such as described in Chapter 7, or a snow wall will be of advantage. In higher temperatures your clothes are sufficient protection and a snowhouse will make you soaking wet. For snowhouses are dry and really useful only in very cold weather.

If you have a sledge and dogs, you should not, as explained elsewhere, trust them to bring you into camp. They are likelier to lose their way than you are. The exception is that if your camp is up the wind the dogs will take you home, their lead being the sense of smell.

Well-furred dogs need no protection from snow and wind. Just unharness them and let them lie where they want to. In very cold weather, take them into your emergency snowhouse—in your own interest, not theirs, to warm up the house. They are company, too.

When you have a sledge but don't build an emergency house, do whichever you find most comfortable—sit in the snow with your back to the wind (in the lee of the sledge) or lie on the sledge with your head to the wind.

TELLING DIRECTION BY WIND

If you know the country, the wind is an aid in determining direction. Take, for example, a region like that east of the Colville delta, Alaska, where commonly only three winds blow—southwest the strongest, northeast next, and east-northeast third. Ordinarily you will know as a matter of recent history which wind it was that blew last, but in any event an examination of the ground will easily show.

TELLING DIRECTION BY SNOWDRIFTS

You should have learned the traits of drifts by studying the snow repeatedly after storms. The force, duration, and other characteristics you know. Failing that, common sense (if you don't get into a panic) will tell you a lot. Some elementary rules are that drifts made by the strongest winds are hardest, and that drifts are harder the longer ago the storm which made them. Furthermore you can tell the direction of the wind by the fact that the drift is lower and narrower to windward and gets higher and wider to leeward before finally dropping down abruptly to the general level.

You may find, by seeing it or by feeling of it with your feet or your hands in darkness, that there is an overhang at what, by the rest of the signs, you think should be the leeward end of a drift; this means there has been a strong wind after the drift was formed which blew in approximately the opposite direction. This shows the drift you are studying is not from the last blizzard, perhaps from the second-last or third-last. If you were within a hundred miles (or at least within the same wind area) during the preceding few days or weeks, your memory of recent storms will aid in these interpretations and will help to give you your bearings.

As implied, if there is diffused light so there are no shadows, or if it is so dark that you can't see the drifts, you stop and feel them carefully with your feet or drop on all fours and examine them with your hands. Then, having determined either the northeast or the southwest drifts, you may decide to cross every such drift at an angle of about 45°, ignoring all the other drifts. You are then traveling the compass course east or west, and you probably know which of the two it is because you know from memory or otherwise, surely, the direction of at least one of the last two or three storms. If you don't know that, you may find a natural sign to guide you. For instance, east of the Colville, the coast generally runs southeast. An east course will, therefore, take you out to sea and you soon check that by the rough ice. For you cannot go far to seaward on that coast without meeting crushed ice.

On landfast ice you treat the snowdrift compass as if you were on land. To use it out at sea you must call upon knowledge that falls into another group. Floes of ice do not merely drift, in a general way, with the currents and before the winds; they are also pushed around in such a way that they rotate, one turning from left to right, another from right to left, depending on how other floes shove them. If you are within 15 or 20 miles of land, floes are small and they will have moved around a great deal so that the direction of snowdrifts is of very little use to you. The farther you are from shore the less the rotating motion, because of a less active moment and greater size of the floes which, in some cases, are 15 or 20 miles across. Anything more than a hundred miles from shore you can safely put a good deal of faith in the drifts, at least those that were made only a few days ago.

In properly mountainous countries the topography has such control over the drifts that they are of little value, unless you are a local man and know the topography thoroughly. In an Arctic forest there are no drifts that suffice for guidance— you will there have to fall back on woodcraft principles, which are the same as in the forests of the temperate zone.

SNOWDRIFTS ON GREENLAND ICE CAP

On the ice cap of Greenland the snow drift case is special. Toward the center of the cap, and perhaps more along a line running northerly and southerly a little east of the center, is region of comparatively few winds where the snow is soft and drifts not pronounced. Moving from central Greenland

348

toward either east or west coast you have mainly drifts that go the same way you are going, that point downhill or point toward the nearest open sea; for, as explained elsewhere, the winds that produce these drifts are mainly of gravitational nature—the cold air flowing downhill toward the sea.

However, there are naturally gales of broad scope that sweep Greenland, ones not of local gravitational origin. In using for guides the drifts these make, you have to fall back on what we said earlier—your own knowledge of how long ago each of these gales blew, what its direction was and what its strength was.

PROCEDURE FOR CROSSING RIVER ICE

When the course of autumn travel takes you across rivers, a man should walk ahead of the leading sledge with an ice spear. This he jabs methodically into the snow ahead of him every three or four steps.

TESTING THE ICE

It may seem unnecessary to test ice when you have had continuous frosts for more than a month and the temperature is 20° or 30° below zero, but an understanding of the condition will show that this test is indeed necessary.

In the autumn when the river is still open, the falling snow melts in the running water and disappears. Later you may have a sharp frost for 2 or 3 days when there is no snow falling, and ice 2 or 3 inches or even a foot thick may form on the river. Then comes a heavy fall of snow. This blanket, like an eiderdown quilt or a fur robe, keeps the chill away from the river ice.

It now makes little difference how cold the air is above the snow. If the running water is a little above the freezing point, the current will gradually eat away the ice that was formed until there remains only a scum to support the snow above it. In some cases even this scum is eaten away and snow drops into the open water, leaving a gaping hole which can be seen and avoided. However, when an actual hole appears, the frost gets another chance so that it will not be many hours until clear ice, perfectly safe to walk upon, forms over that particular patch. The danger places, therefore, are not where any danger sign is visible but where the snow in front of you lies white and apparently safe.

FLOOD WATER ON RIVERS

In rivers so shallow that there is little danger of drowning there may be special danger of getting your feet wet, for such streams quickly freeze to the bottom in some rapid. The water upstream from the frozen obstruction will then be held back until finally it will burst through the ice somewhere upstream and flood the surface for hundreds of yards or perhaps even for a mile or two.

There are perhaps on the river's surface snowdrifts that lie clean across the stream in ridges, forming obstructions that dam the overflow water back, so that you may have 10, 15, or 20 inches of water on top of the previous ice.

If this flooding has taken place a few hours before you come to that stretch of river, there are only two courses open. Either you must scramble up the hillside and travel parallel to the river till you get beyond the flooded place, or else you must camp and wait till the surface water has frozen over. In winter this is seldom a long wait. The general rule is that if you come to one in the afternoon you camp overnight and expect the ice to carry you next morning.

IF YOU BREAK THROUGH

If for any reason you must travel over thin ice on a river, you are bound to break through several times. As soon as you do, jump instantly out of the water into a snowbank and rub snow over your wet footgear. Dry snow at low temperature acts like the best kind of blotter, soaking up all moisture. If you have on several thicknesses of woolen socks, for instance, you may slip to your ankle into water and jerk your foot into the snow so quickly that this blotter sucks the moisture out before it gets through all the different layers to your skin.

PREVENTIVE MEASURES

If you know in advance that you are going to get into water anyway, and if you are not wearing waterproof boots, go some place where you can stand firmly on one foot while you stick

350

the other quickly into water and then into a snowbank. This will form a coating of frost in your outer stockings which will later on be waterproof and keep out further wettings almost as well as a sealskin boot.

The significant part of the above procedure is that it must be done quickly. It is best, therefore, to practice it at a base camp before you set out on a journey, for if you are inexpert your footgear will get wet through and frostbitten heels and toes may result. (See Chapter 10 for instructions as to what to do if you get wet all over.)

PROCEDURE FOR CROSSING LAKE ICE

In big northern lakes, strong currents are occasionally developed. Far from shore these are not dangerous, but in the vicinity of a point of land in a strait between islands the traveler should be exceedingly careful. Though the ice may be 10 feet thick in places, there are other places where men and sledges will disappear suddenly through the snow because the ice that formed before the snow fell there has since been eaten away.

Not merely proper waterfalls but very strong rapids will remain open all winter. In such cases there is usually an ice foot along either or both shores wide enough for dog sledges and men to pass. This is the case, for instance, with Bloody Falls on the Coppermine, which is a violent rapid rather than a fall. This ice shelf may possibly develop to a width that would accommodate a tractor but would probably not be of the requisite strength. Using an ice foot of this type is, in any case, likely to be dangerous, for it will probably slope towards the water giving the sledge a tendency to slide in sideways. The current being strong, the team would probably be dragged in after the sled and everything would disappear in under the ice at the lower end of the rapids.

A place likely to be open is the head of a river that comes out of a big lake. To travelers this is not a very dangerous situation. For one thing, under practically any condition, you will know that you are where a river is coming from a lake; then it is usually true that the ice is fairly thick right up to the open water. These ice-free places are a blessing to natives and to whites who are living off the country; for the fishing is usually pretty good in that sort of location and you can set your nets in the open water all winter.

DIFFICULTIES OF SUMMER TRAVEL

Unless it be spring travel along a coast, summer travel is the most disagreeable and difficult.

In Chapter 2, Section I, we have brought out in connection with ground frost that in about half of Canada, two-thirds of Alaska and an area in the Soviet Union as large as the whole of the continental United States, there is permanent frost in the ground; which, toward the end of no matter how hot a summer, is on the northern edge of the forest only a few inches below the surface, while near the southern limit of permanent frost the distance down is only of the order of 10 feet.

INNUMERABLE LAKES

The permanent frost, and the more so the nearer it is to the surface, creates innumerable lakes, ranging in size, let us say, from that of a silver dollar to that of Lake Erie. The tiny lakelets are a chief source of trouble in that they breed mosquitoes and other insects. When the lakes get bigger they are a nuisance to the summer traveler in that he must avoid them. When they are of considerable size in an unknown country you frequently are unable to tell when you strike one of them whether you should turn to right or left. You make your best guess and may win through between lakes; or you may find yourself on a peninsula, so that you have to retreat. When out on the tip of the peninsula, however, you have very likely had a good chance to study the lake and may have a clear idea which way to turn for the circumvention.

WADING ACROSS LAKES

If a lake is on flat country it may be worth while, even when the water ahead of you is a mile or two wide, to see whether you cannot wade across. There are cases where you can wade more than a mile at a practically uniform depth of four feet or less—so that, by carrying your baggage high on your shoulders, you can keep it dry. On such wading it frequently proves that you sink a foot or more into ooze at each step; for the tendency is for a thaw to go deeper under a small lake than where there is no water. It is probable that under most or all of the big lakes that do not freeze to the bottom the thaw goes indefinitely down— that there is no ground frost below them.

LAND BETWEEN LAKES MOSTLY SWAMP

On flat terrain lakes a hundred yards or more in diameter will occupy 60 percent of the area. The land between these lakes is mostly swamp, unless you are in rocky country. Accordingly, you sink more or less at every step. There are, true enough, large areas where this sinking is only slight and really agreeable to the feet—it gives a certain springiness to your walk. In other large areas you sink in a good deal and the mud may be sticky, clinging to your boots. There are parts of Banks Island, for instance, where you are likely to be carrying several pounds of mud on each foot except when you are on top of hills.

We have said that where there is ground frost there is no underground drainage. While true, this must not be given too extreme an interpretation—you must remember that where there is a considerable slope there will be surface drainage such that when it is a number of days between rains the ground will be fairly dry. What we just said about areas in Banks Island where you carry a pound or more of mud on each foot has broad application only following a rain.

NIGGERHEADS

A particular nuisance in the North is the niggerhead. These are about the worst at the northern limit of the forest, getting less of a nuisance as you pass from the American mainland out upon the Canadian islands. The formation somewhat resembles a mushroom—it is a knob of earth wholly covered with a grass pad which seems to act as a sort of umbrella against the rain, so that the foundation of earth upon which it rests is less in diameter than the head of the knoll. In between the knolls are cracks of mud. Typically, the knobs are of such size that a man with a good stride will step from the first to the third—stepping over one without touching it.

A perennial unsolved problem is which to do, to try to step upon the center of the niggerheads and slip off every second or third time, or whether to step in between them every time, straight down into the mud. Usually the slip downward, when your foot slides off a niggerhead, is something between 6 and 10 inches—seldom as much as halfway to the knee. It is a considerable jar, particularly when you are carrying a heavy back load.

As long as the ground is mud, grass or sand it is easy on your footgear. If you have the best type of Eskimo water boot, with an upper of small seal and a sole of bearded seal, two pairs will last you all summer—for as much as a thousand miles of walking. On stony ground, however, these soles will go in two or three days. There are known regions in the Arctic, as, for instance, east and southeast of Darnley Bay, where the broken rock is so sharp that your boots will go in 20 miles. For a party of Europeans it is best, if possible, to carry as spares for that sort of ground hobnailed boots of the heaviest type. If you do not have them, you use patches underneath your Eskimo boot soles, in the manner described in Chapter 9. The wear comes mostly on the heel and toe; so that, if the patches are renewed every morning, you can go on indefinitely. It is best, of course, that they shall be of the same leather as the boot sole, but if you don't have that anything else will do. You are probably living on caribou; you then save the fresh hide from the back of the neck of the largest bulls and use it for patches.

Section III

ON SEA ICE

a. Along Shore

A glossary of ice terms, together with brief explanation and description, is found in Chapter 2 of this Manual.

One of the ways in which coastal travel is transitional as to conditions and methods is in the ice. Ice that formed from water of brine saltness may be flush against the shore or, as in the mouth of a river, you may have near the land fresh water ice that extends many miles out to sea, even beyond sight of the land. So we discuss here interrelated qualities and behaviors of ice which was formed from salt water and ice derived from fresh water.

YOUNG ICE

The expression "young ice" is seldom used for fresh water ice, constantly for salt. The reasons will appear.

When fresh water freezes beyond the slush stage it has that glasslike quality with which we are familiar and which remains substantially unchanged as the ice thickens. The situation is quite other with salt water. The freezing does begin with a slush stage, as in fresh water; but this continues as the ice thickens. You may have fresh ice of glasslike quality only a quarter of an inch thick that is strong enough so you can handle it almost like a pane of window glass. You cannot so handle a piece of sea ice a foot square until it is more than 2 inches thick, perhaps 3. Sea ice as much as 3 inches in thickness will splash out rather than break if you drop a piece of it from a 6-foot height on to a hard surface.

It is because of this consistency of young ice that a man does not venture to walk upright on 4-inch ice, even in a lead only a few yards wide. If he has to cross he will crawl, or walk on snowshoes, or, best of all, on skis. Young ice has to be 5 or, better, 6 inches thick before you dare to cross a lead with dog sledges and men. This ice is stronger the colder the weather; 8-inch ice that has formed in 2 days at —30° and —40° is probably as strong as 10-inch ice that has formed in a week or more at temperatures around 10° and 20°.

After the 6-inch or perhaps 8-inch thickness is attained there appears to be a change if not a reversal of strength ratios. Ten inches of sea ice will probably support as much as 10 inches of fresh ice. It is believed, but not known, that salt ice more than a foot thick supports more than would the same thickness of fresh ice.

Certainly the nature of salt and fresh water ice seems to have undergone a reciprocal change before the beginning of the spring thaw. As we describe below under needle ice, fresh ice crumbles during the thawing stage, even when of a considerable thickness. Salt ice appears to have the opposite nature. We have said that 4 inches of young salt ice would not support your foot if you put on it your full body weight. Experiments have been made where there is a narrow isthmus of salt ice between two water holes, the isthmus perhaps not as wide as your foot is long and only an inch or two in thickness. Upon such an isthmus you can support the full weight of your body on one foot, although perhaps you might break through if you jumped on it with your full body weight. Fresh ice under the same conditions would break for a child if not for a dog.

(Laboratory experiments to check some of the above points would be desirable.)

NEEDLE ICE

This expression is used solely with reference to ice that is thawing and occurs, then, only in fresh-water ice. Seemingly ice that has once been salty and has become fresh through elimination of the salt is, nevertheless, of different structure from ice that was originally fresh, for it does not seem to break down into the needle structure. (This is belief rather than knowledge.)

Needle ice is found at sea but probably only in one of two conditions. It may be ice from water that was "normally" fresh, as in the mouth of a river—the sea is fresh enough for drinking perhaps 40 miles offshore abreast of the delta of the Mackenzie and for less but considerable distances in the case of smaller rivers. Then, out on the paleocrystic ice, far within the pack, you get a lot of needle ice. This may be from the fresh water that has stood on top of the salt water in leads at the end of summer or from lakes of fresh water that have been on top of the ice.

The most striking description of the needle condition has come from river banks where huge chunks of fresh-water ice are left aground by spring floods. Stefansson reports having walked past a boulder of this ice in the morning when going out to hunt from a bank of the Coppermine River, and having found no ice at all in the evening. On this clue he began to examine the ice boulders. When he struck one a smart blow with a stick it crumbled into a heap of pencils—

long crystals, apparently each the length of the vertical thickness the ice had as it lay on the river.

On lakes of the Parry peninsula in the spring thaws the experiment was repeatedly made of driving a stick about the size and shape of a broom handle vertically down through ice that was more than 3 feet thick. The crystals or needles separated to let the stick all the way through. On one of the same lakes a dog that had gone into open water to cool off tried to climb up on the edge of ice that was more than 2 feet thick. The ice crumbled under the paws of the dog and he made a sort of tunnel or bay into it for several feet before he could get enough support to haul himself out.

It appears that ice does not break into needle formation when it is covered with snow, even though the snow is soaked with slush water. It may be, then, that the action of direct sunlight is required to produce separation into needles.

That needle ice is "treacherous" is shown by frequent reports of Indian drownings in northern Canadian lakes in the spring. That Eskimo drownings seldom occur may not be due to their taking better precautions but may be rather because the Eskimos in spring are usually on the seacoast and have little occasion for crossing lakes.

PROTECTING DOGS

The upward points of the needle ice during the spring thaw are so sharp that they lacerate the feet of dogs, no matter how sound their pads are. If you have to sledge in this situation during spring, which is the only time needle ice occurs, you will have to use boots on your dogs. These are best made of some skinlike smoke-tanned moose; they are about the size and shape of the thumb of a large mitten and are tied with a string around the dog's ankle. Rawhide must not be used, for it smells like food to the dog and is eaten. Commercially tanned leather would be good. Canvas may be used. Under conditions where a moose-hide boot lasts 2 days a canvas boot may last a day. Drivers watch the boots on their dogs and when they wear on one side they are turned around, which doubles the life of each boot. It is a bigger chore than you at first realize to make these boots for your dog team—each dog has four feet!

b. *Far from land*

In planning for operations likely to take you out on sea ice, it is well to remember that Alaskan and Canadian Eskimos are in great and irrational fear of going far from land. In winter these Eskimos make their living upon the ice in the vicinity of land, and they are there competent, confident, and at ease. But they and their ancestors have seldom ventured more than 5 miles from shore, and never willingly more than 10—which is why they fear the region beyond. You are likely to find local seamen, traders, and the rest of any white population agreeing with the Eskimos—on the theory that an Eskimo knows all about ice.

LANDFAST ICE

There are in the Arctic a few headlands—among them Cape Lisburne, northwestern Alaska, and Nelson Head at the south tip of Banks Island—where deep water comes so close inshore, and where strong winds and currents are so frequent, that very little ice clings to the land. Usually even in these places there is, however, an ice foot similar to that which we have described for river shores along an unfreezable rapid. Indeed, the shelf at Lisburne or Nelson Head is likely to be a good deal wider, several yards if not several dozen; but, in the case of Nelson Head at least and probably in the case of Lisburne, there are occasions when the pack tears along the cliff with such force that the ice foot is practically or wholly removed. This is an awkward situation, for it is most likely to occur at the tips of promontories so that a party sledging along the coast would have to climb a mountain to get around to where the ice is wide enough again for travel. The situation is the more difficult in that the mountain configuration produces violent local gales, after a manner already described.

The Arctic rule is that in winter the ice frozen fast to the beach runs out to sea one to several miles. That nearest the land is usually grounded solidly upon a shallow bottom. But as you proceed from the land you come to the flaw, or floe, the place where the edge of the shelf frozen fast to the land meets the moving pack.

RELATION OF PACK TO FLAW

When the pack is in rapid motion, as after a severe gale, its speed on the north coast of Alaska may be as much as 2 miles an hour, rarely a little more. The ice masses are of all sizes and all thicknesses. When a heavy floe moves along the edge of the land ice in such a way as to rub against it, we say that the pack is grinding.

This grinding of the floes against the landfast ice and against each other makes much ice, which may be a soft slush or may consist of fragments the size of your fist, the size of a kitchen range, or of a house. As the floes spin about, open patches of water of all shapes and sizes will form, to close again when the floes continue their revolution.

EFFECT OF GALE ON PACK

After a heavy gale pieces more than a dozen acres in area are rare at the flaw or beyond it for several miles to seaward. The farther from land the larger the pieces; and fifty miles out the hardest gale will leave most of the ice still in the form of big coherent masses, miles in diameter. Naturally, when the edges of such floes meet, a certain amount of mush ice is formed, no matter what the distance from shore.

DANGER ZONE

The handicaps to sledge or foot travel over the pack, then, are usually greater the nearer you are to the flaw. The dangerous edge of the danger zone is the mush belt immediately against the flaw where the pack grinds itself into fragments against the edge of the landfast ice.

SLUSH ICE

As described in Chapter 2, slush ice is a special form of ice from which brine is being eliminated and which, if blanketed with snow, may preserves its slushy character even when air temperatures are at or near winter lows. In travel over this kind of ice, wear the semiwaterproof boots described in chapter 9; for even after a long cold spell you may step without warning into brine that will soak through the sole and upper of ordinary winter footgear.

TELLING AGE OF SEA ICE

Ice which has weathered one or more summers is easy to distinguish from that of the current winter by sight and by taste. This is useful for several reasons, among them to judge its strength for safety in camping upon it and to tell in advance if water formed by melting it is going to be fresh. (See explanation in Chapter 2, Section III.)

During the melting of summer, the pressure ridges and the projecting snags of broken ice change in outline. When the ice has been freshly broken it may well be compared with the masses of rock in a quarry just after the blast; or, if it is thinner, with the broken-bottle glass on top of a stone wall. But during thaw periods all the sharp outlines are softened so that at the end of the first summer they are no more jagged than a typical mountain range. At the end of 2 or 3 years they resemble the rolling hills of a western prairie.

Old ice is easily recognizable at a distance by its outlines, and on closer approach by the fact that the hummocks are frequently glare. That can never be the case with salty ice, which is sticky and therefore always has snow adhering to it. Being glare, the old ice gives poor footing for men and dogs, yet it is commonly preferred by travelers as being smoother than newly broken floes. For young ice is frequently heaped up in indescribable confusion, the jagged ridges sometimes 50 or 60 feet above water level. This sort of broken ice is in rare cases so chaotic that an unhampered dog is not able to make his way over it.

When you come to bad pressure ridges you have to make a road with pickaxes. Progress may be less than a hundred yards per hour. Cases are on record where half a dozen men equipped with pickaxes were unable to advance three- or four-dog teams and sledges no more than 400 yards in 10 hours of hard labor.

LET GO OF SLEDGE IF IT DROPS

As described above, the ice of the northern seas, especially just beyond the flaw, is during winter in surface character and appearance something between a system of miniature mountain ranges and the interior of a granite quarry. In traveling over such ice, you must steer sledges as best you can but let them go when they begin to drop. Otherwise they will pull you with them, and cuts and bruises will result. One of Stefansson's men, an old Alaska sourdough named Captain Peter Bernard, was nearly killed through keeping hold of the steering bars of a sledge and falling upon a crossbar. He had to be invalided from the party and sent ashore, causing besides a time loss of several days to the entire party.

As explained in section I of this chapter you should not start out from land for an ice journey later than May 1, nor should you start earlier than the last of January or the first of February. The spring start is inadvisable because thaws and rainstorms are producing the difficult ice conditions. You should not start when the daylight is less than a third of the 24 hours because of the danger that you may not be able to find during daylight a camping area that is safe from that tumbling pandemonium of rearing, crashing, and splashing blocks that results when the pack, in a storm or driven by a current, meets the unyielded shore ice. Whatever the time of winter it is bound to be a tense experience to get your sledges across the first 30, 40, or 50 miles which, in different parts of the marginal area of the Arctic Sea, make up the worst pressure belt—which, as we said a few pages back, is most dangerous at the flaw and gets less and less dangerous as you progress farther from shore.

SAFE AND DANGEROUS DISTRICTS

The danger in crossing the pressure belt is not so great if the base from which you start is on land in some region of sluggish ice movement, such as northern Prince Patrick Island, Ellef Ringnes Island, or Peary's starting point, Cape Columbia, Ellesmere Island. But anyone beginning a journey from a region of violent ice movement, such as the north coast of Alaska or the northeastern coast of Siberia, is taking serious chances if he starts out before the full moon of February.

In taking the chance of starting on a polar ice journey late in January or early in February, the encouraging factor is that your great danger zone is a narrow one in the vicinity of land. If you have a week or so of calm and intensely frosty weather the turbulent shore belt may be quiescent; so that by a "dash" of 3 or 4 days you may be able to get 40 or 50 miles offshore before the first gale strikes. Beyond that distance from shore midwinter travel is reasonably safe no matter how little the daylight.

DIFFICULTIES OF SPRING TRAVEL

After the first warm days of spring the thaw water sinks to the bottom of the snowdrifts and begins to trickle along the ice, gradually eroding little water courses which grow deeper and wider day by day. The snow itself will presently disappear from the ice, except where it is drifted deep in lees. By midsummer year-old ice will be cut into a network of channels a few inches or several feet deep and separating ice islands, analogous to those of a river delta, of all shapes and sizes. Upon old ice the tiniest of these islands resembles mushrooms, a narrow stem with a wide table top. Progress is a continual climbing up on islands of this or other types and plunging into the water beyond. Frequently the dogs have to swim and sledges must be buoyed so that dogs can tow them.

When the sledge is actually in the water there is little danger of upsetting; therefore your task is to keep dogs and sledges in the water as much as possible, climbing upon the "islands" only occasionally. The danger is when the sledge is crossing one of the islands, especially if there are rounded hummocks upon them, for it is then likely to slide sidewise into the water and upset. When a sledge starts to slide, it is the steersman's task to lessen the chance of an upset by so directing the sled that it slips into the water bow foremost.

This condition of ice is not only bad for traveling but also for seal hunting. A basking seal will likely hear some splash you make; the least splash will send him into the water.

NO CAMP ON ICE IS EVER ENTIRELY SAFE

It is evident that no camp on sea ice is ever entirely safe. Even a hundred miles from shore a crack may open in the middle of the floor of your snowhouse or tent, though the chances of this decrease with the distance from land.

You may also be in danger from a crack originally several hundred yards from camp; for when two floes begin to grind past each other the edges of both tend to break up and the disintegration may soon get to where you are. The danger is greatest when the lines of motion of the adjacent floe and of your floe intersect at some such small angle as 10° to 30°. Huge pieces are then torn rapidly off the edges of both floes if they are of similar thickness, or off the edge of the weaker. If you happen to be camped on the weaker one, it behooves you to move quickly. Pieces of your floe the size of a city lot will rise on edge, tower up and crumble toward you. The ice around camp and under it will begin to groan and buckle and bend. Where it bends down, little rivers of sea water come rushing in; where it buckles up, small pressure ridges form.

FLEEING FROM BREAK-UP

Since the relative speed of the floes can never differ by much more than 2 miles, the rate at which you have to flee is never more than 2 miles an hour and commonly much less. Still, if the breaking up begins when you are sleeping, the awakening is abrupt and something has to be done in a hurry. As described in chapter 7, one important aid to safety is that the tremors of breaking floes are transmitted for miles through the ice, where they might not be audible at all through the air.

PROCEDURE OF BREAKING CAMP

If men camped on ice feel the quivers of approaching pressure, or hear by way of the ice the detonations of the breaking, or the high-pitched squealing as heavy flat pieces of ice slide over each other, one man should run outside to spy out the situation while the others begin to dress. Unless his report is most reassuring, you all dress as quickly as firemen upon the ringing of an alarm bell. The sledges have been kept loaded—except for bedding and cooking gear, and these can be transferred rapidly from camp to sled. Harnessing the dogs takes but a few moments—each man can harness about two dogs per minute.

The need for fleeing precipitately, as above described, does not often occur, since you have been particular to camp on a safe floe. But during the day's march a situation quite as dangerous, though not so startling, may develop. This is most likely when you are traveling across ice that has been grinding and is still under pressure, crossing from one cake to another by the corners where they touch. If you find yourself upon a weak cake a few acres in area that is surrounded on all sides by stronger cakes, its edges crumple up if the pressure is steady, and a ring of ice ridges begins to form around you. As the pressure continues, the ridges get higher, and the level central area of your cake gets smaller. It is not comfortable to have these ridges marching toward you from all sides, with a noise that is anything between a slight rumble and a deafening roar and the ice shivering where you stand. Worst of all, your dogs may get paralyzed with fear and useless.

The thing to do is to select some rather low place in one of the advancing ridges, where the motion is slower and where you think the floe beyond comparatively strong. To find such a place is difficult, more difficult because the weight of the forming ridge depresses the edge of your floe and causes a moat of sea water to separate it from you.

In cold weather dogs are even more afraid of putting their feet in water than of putting them on moving ice. So you may have to drag both teams and sledges by manpower. If you have four or five men and two sledges, you will drag the teams one at a time over the ridge, for the tumbling motion of the cakes is slow enough to cause a sure-footed man no great trouble. A party of three with a single sledge has the advantage that only one trip is necessary but the disadvantage that, with one man at the handlebars to keep the sledge from upsetting, the other two are scarcely stronger than the six dogs. You are, however, able to move them, for they do not balk in unison.

When the first team is beyond a ridge, you have less trouble with the others—they will, apparently, sense that their colleagues are safe and will strive to join them.

JUDGE ICE BEFORE CAMPING

When ice breaks in the dark of night the danger is greater, more complicated. For this reason it is advisable, particularly in those months when the nights are without daylight around their middle, to camp an hour or two early if you come upon an exceptionally firm cake that promises a night without a break-up, or to travel 3 or 4 hours longer when you fail to discover one firm enough for a campsite—in fact, you travel either till you find safe camping or else till you get so tired (you or your dogs) that you simply have to stop.

Bright moonlight gives the most help, after sunlight, in ice travel. Cloudy days and nights hold danger, for a reason special to Arctic latitudes which we have described under the head of diffused light.

Sea ice is seldom in reality smooth, but when sun or moon is behind clouds it will appear smooth through absence of shadow. On any landscape color except white, the hole out of which you have just pried a stone looks distinctly different from the stone lying beside it, no matter what the conditions of light (so long as you can see at all). But in the frozen sea a boulder of ice and a hole beside it are just about the same shade of white, and you cannot see either of them unless in the relief produced by shadows.

Either sun or moon in a clear sky will cast shadows, but neither will do so when obscured by clouds, though either may give diffused light enough to reveal a man or a stone at half a mile or a mountain at 20 miles.

On the rough sea ice, you may on an unshadowed day, without any warning from the keenest eyes, fall over a chunk of ice that is knee-high. You may step into a crack that just admits your foot or into a hole big enough to be your grave. And, bad as the cloudy day is, the cloudy night is worse. (For other discussion of diffused light see section II of this chapter, also chapter 4.)

UTILIZING LEADS

When the temperature is −20° or −40°, as in February or March, the opening of a lead is not a serious matter. It may stop you one day but the next it has been bridged and you can cross it if it happens to lie athwart your course. Occasionally luck is such that it lies almost in the direction you are going. In that case the ice traveler can have no better fortune than to meet with a lead. If he finds it already frozen over, it is as if he had come out of the woods upon a paved road; if it is still open he knows that a little wait and a night's encampment will convert it into a boulevard for fast and easy traveling the next day.

WHEN NOT TO USE FROZEN LEADS

But at the end of April, even though the lead may be running in your direction, and though it may be a week old and the ice 6 or 10 inches thick, still it is so soft from the mildness of the frost that it does not form a safe road, and a bridge of older ice must be discovered for crossing it.

The first precaution on thin or rotten ice is to spread the legs and slide the feet along as evenly and rapidly as possible without lifting them from the ice. If this is not enough, get down on all fours with arms and legs spread wide and shuffle along without lifting hands or feet. In extremity, lie flat with arms and legs extended and squirm and wriggle slowly along. If snowshoes or (still better) skis are available to increase further the bearing area and distribute the weight, it is possible to negotiate surprisingly thin ice.

STRENGTH OF ICE

For a statement on the thicknesses of ice, salt and fresh, that will bear a load, see earlier in this chapter.

UTILIZING SKY MAP

In Chapter 4, Section II, we have described in detail how a map of your surroundings may be reflected in the clouds when you are far at sea on a day completely and uniformly overcast; the higher the clouds the greater the area of the sea which will be shown in the map. Looking into the sky, the experienced traveler will see the types of ice which he wants to avoid as well as those which are most desirable. For instance, he may notice early in the morning on a day when he wants to travel north that if he were to go east about 3 miles he would strike an old and smooth lead running 15° west of north. A simple calculation and a view of the sky straight ahead will decide him whether he had better go 3 miles out of his way to secure good travel in a direction that does not quite suit him or whether he had better work doggedly straight ahead, taking good and bad as it comes— and as it is represented in the sky.

See Chapter 4, Section II, for descriptions of Land Sky.

UTILIZING SLEDGE-BOATS

Two of the most important things in travel over pack ice, the retrieving of seals that are shot far off in open water and the crossing of leads, are both managed with a sledge-boat, which essentially is an empty sledge wrapped in a piece of waterproofed canvas. A description of this is given in Chapter 12.

Section IV

OVER INLAND ICE

THE GREENLAND INLAND ICE

The occasion for travel afoot over inland ice, from the point of view of this Manual, seems most likely to arise in connection with a forced landing while flying across Greenland.

To a flyer the salient and unique points of Greenland are two:

1. Excepting the snowfree coastal districts and the crevassed regions where the ice flows down toward the sea, Greenland is practically one continuous and nearly perfect landing field for a plane equipped with skis. Most of the inland ice is good for wheels, too, except that near the center the snow might be so soft that you would find it hard to take-off again.

AIR CIRCULATION

2. Because Greenland is a turtlebacked mass of snow with comparatively warm, open oceans on both east and west, it has a local air circulation of its own. Pictorially you are not far wrong if you think of the cold and heavy air behaving like water that is being poured down on the middle of Green-

land to flow off in every direction. A line north and south somewhat east of the middle is the divide. East of this the air generally flows east, and west of it generally west. These local flows are, however, upset at times by storms of wide area. Generally speaking, you can rely on it for the middle of Greenland that if, after a forced landing, you start walking toward either coast you will have a fair wind most of the way, growing stronger as you approach the edge, until you may have a gale at your back on your last 50 or a hundred miles. (See Chapter 2 for further discussion of the characteristics of Greenland.)

Assuming a forced landing on the inland ice, the eventualities are four: You may repair and fly again; you may send an SOS and wait for help; you may try to get your plane to the coast; you may abandon your plane and walk to the coast.

FIRST, REPAIRING

If you succeed in repairing, no comment is needed except to repeat that you may have difficulty in taking off if on wheels and near the comparatively calm center. Likely enough, however, a wind of broad scope will come along in a few days and harden things up.

SECOND, CALLING FOR HELP

If you call for help, you have several advantages. Most days you see the sun and can therefore report your latitude and longitude correctly. The weather is on the average clear when looking down from above, although it may be hazy when you look horizontally, so that rescue planes should pick you up easily; for you are conspicuous in that you and your equipment are the only dark things on a vast white expanse. The temperatures are such that you can build a snow house and make use of the regular Arctic technique for living in comfort—except, as below, that the only food and fuel will be whatever you have with you.

THIRD, TAKING PLANE WITH YOU

With either the third or the fourth eventuality you will travel west unless you are markedly near the east coast;

for there are only two main settlements to head for on the east, Scoresby Sound and Angmagssalik, while on the west coast there are any number of settlements.

The only advantage of the third procedure is to make it more convenient to salvage the plane. Except for the peculiar conditions of Greenland, it might seem absurd to speak of two or three men taking the plane away with them. But part of your preparations should have been to provide sails against this emergency. If you are right at the calm part of Greenland, at the so-called wind center, it may not be possible for your crew to push or drag the plane along on its skis, the snow being soft and the slope negligible. But if you are anywhere well off center you will have harder snow and more frequent and stronger fair winds, even though the slope is not appreciably greater. With something for a sail, or even merely the wind blowing on the plane, the crew may be able to work toward the coast. Eventually the wind may do most of the work.

This has been written on the assumption your engine does not work, through mechanical injury or want of gas. With engine working you may have power enough for taxiing though not enough for taking off. Then, naturally, you taxi toward one of the coasts.

There may, of course, be head winds as you approach the eastern or western sea. Those will, then, be of broad cyclonic nature and will pass. In a few days you are likely to get your local winds back again helping you.

You cannot, naturally, take the plane all the way down. The winds get too violent, the slope is too steep, in places there are crevasses, and in any case the plane would be more difficult to salvage if you did get it down than if you left it at the right place at the edge of the inland ice. For down near the coast it would be in a rough spot and the salvage plane could not land near it nor could that plane and yours take off after repairs. Up on the inland ice there are perfect conditions for landing and take-off.

CORRECT PLACE TO LEAVE PLANE

The correct place to leave your plane is just before you come to the crevassed slope, the location of which you know approximately from your map. You face the plane into the prevailing wind, dig trenches for the skis, anchor with ropes fastened to deadmen, and build a sheltering snow wall.

In view of the comparatively regular direction of the most violent winds when you approach the edge of the Greenland inland ice, a better scheme than facing the plane into the wind may be to put it broadside to. It is more difficult then to protect it by a snow wall, but you avoid the difficulty of having a wind strike effectively surfaces designed for lifting.

After anchoring the plane you walk to the coast and report where the plane is. Somebody flies in with the necessities for bringing it to a coastal base.

DANGER FROM CREVASSES

The dangerous part of the journey comes where the coastward flow of the inland ice begins to speed up, producing crevasses. Many of these, especially in late winter, are likely to be so strongly roofed over with snow that, particularly if you have snowshoes or skis, you will pass over them without knowing it. However, if there are two or three men, they should be roped together and should travel alpine fashion, just in case one breaks through into a crevasse. (See below for needed equipment.)

When the thaws of spring begin, the snow roofs of the crevasses cave in, showing trenches which gape. This is an advantage in that you now see where they are, but a disadvantage in that no snow bridges are available and everything is very slippery. There will be small and large water courses, some digging deep channels and tunnels, and they increase the difficulty. It is now that the length of your sledge becomes important (see below). You can often maneuver so as to make of it a bridge across a crevasse.

CHOICE OF ROUTE WITH RELATION TO FJORDS

For safety's sake you should descend to the coast, unless you have local knowledge to the contrary, at some point about halfway between adjoining fjords, since the ice usually flows more rapidly toward the fjord heads and is there more crevassed and dangerous.

When you are down past the worst crevasses, you naturally head for whichever fjord you feel likeliest to have a reachable settlement. For Greenland, information on this and other local matters will be found in the Greenland Guide Book of this series.

FOURTH, ABANDONING PLANE AND WALKING TO COAST

If you abandon the plane and walk to the coast, a sledge is important. We describe here one that was made specially for use in Greenland by the well-known polar explorer Anthony Fiala for the use of Lindbergh on his flights of 1933. This is now on exhibition at the American Museum of Natural History of New York. It was made by Fiala in consultation with Lindbergh and Stefansson.

The sledge is of the double-ender Nansen type (described in Section II, Chapter 12) but somewhat higher. It is in three pieces, the end sections 4 feet, the middle section 3 feet. It is easily knocked down and set up again. The ends are identical so that separately the two 4-foot sections will make two sledges if it is desired temporarily to carry the middle section as part of a sledge load or to discard it. At one end of the completely set-up sledge is a hoop to guard against breakage in rough ice. The material is ash or hickory; the runners are polished like skis so that no shoeing is needed, but is nevertheless bored for shoeing; the strength is so that with a 250-pound distributed load a man weighing 200 pounds can crawl across it when the seldge is supported by its two ends. (This is important in using a sledge to bridge a crevasse.) Steel shoeing, capable of being rolled into a hoop of not more than 2 feet diameter, is furnished already bored so that it can be applied to the seldge in either the 8-foot or 11-foot set-up described.

ALPINE EQUIPMENT

Where the route of a flyer includes a crevassed area such as Greenland, alpine equipment should be taken.

Hassell reports that when he and Cramer landed on the inland ice and had to make their way across the crevasses, they had to follow a more tortuous route simply for lack of this equipment, but particularly for lack of crampons or of hobnails on their boots.

Whether you use the third or the fourth eventuality, it will be worth while to carry six-power binoculars to find your way about after you get down to the coast, to see houses and people at great distances. The rest of the equipment, as said, is that of an alpinist—crampons, alpine axes, alpine ropes.

GLASSES

For mere protection of the eyes you carry along any kind of smoked or colored spectacles (not goggles). For flying across the most flatly white surface in the northern hemisphere, the inland ice, you need amber spectacles—they bring out a sharp and clear horizon when bare eyes or smoked glasses give no idea where snow and sky meet.

Amber glasses are similarly a necessity when you descend from the inland ice to the coast, particularly if the light is diffused. For light filtered through amber will bring out the inconspicuous inequalities of the snow, the subtle danger signs of crevasses, when you would otherwise have no warning.

SUNBURN PROTECTION

The snow on the ice cap is likely to give you a quick and severe sunburn so that it might be well to have a dark veil, either a real one brought with you or something you improvise.

CLOTHING

It may get pretty cold on the inland ice, though probably not quite so cold as it is on certain Arctic lowlands. Nevertheless the flyers would be provided with Arctic winter clothing, except, as implied, that their footgear might be somewhat different, to provide for the use of crampons. However, a good kind of footgear, not unsuited to this travel, is the semi-waterproof winter boot which we described in Chapter 9.

TENT

You will carry some light tent, but it must be capable of standing up against terrific winds; therefore the 6- or 8-sided

Antarctic conical is probably best, if you can carry such long bamboos in the plane. Should that be difficult, carry one of the standard types of mountaineering tents obtainable from any outfitter. It is one advantage of getting ready for Greenland that much of what you want is standard alpine equipment.

BEDDING

The bedding will be substantially the same as that described for Arctic winter travel. Your trip to the coast will, however, be so short that you do not have to take all the precautions for keeping your gear in first-rate condition that are required if you have a journey of several months ahead of you.

FOOD

All food has to be carried, for there are no game animals till you descend from the inland ice to either the west or east coast. Both coasts are inhabited at known points, so that it is doubtful whether to carry a rifle on such flights. Perhaps each plane should have one of the kind elsewhere described, with, say, 50 rounds of ammunition.

The journey will be so short that no antiscorbutic or other dietetic precautions need be taken. Use the most condensed food, requiring little fuel—therefore pemmican, hard bread, chocolate, probably dispensing with tea and sugar.

COOKING EQUIPMENT

Cooking equipment should doubtless be a primus stove and some aluminum gear. There is an obvious advantage in having a stove that burns the same fuel which your plane uses. Some travelers have preferred, however, to carry along a little kerosene in a special container. If you do, you should have alcohol for priming, which is not needed if you burn gasoline.

TRAVEL DIRECTIONS

Directions for making your way to the coast under the fourth eventuality are the same as for the third. If your sledge is equipped with a sail, or if you can devise one, you take advantage of the down-slope winds just as you would with a plane fitted with sail. As you move away from the center of Greenland toward either coast the wind does more and more of the work. It is, in fact, possible that you might ride on the sledge and steer.

When you get nearer the coast the winds may grow to such strength that you actually have to dispense with the sail—the wind may push you and the sledge along quite enough without it.

SECTION V

ON WATER

BOATS FOR SUMMER TRAVEL

Until the coming of the airplane, boats were the chief means of coastal summer travel and of reaching the interior—by rivers or by lakes and portages. Our chief discussion of boat travel is in Chapter 12, but we place here a few generalizations.

For inshore travel by sea and for river, lake, and portage travel, native Arctic boats are not merely better than ordinary white men's boats but also better than any "patent" ones yet devised, such as those of collapsible rubber.

An umiak that will carry two or more tons is so light that two strong men can carry it across country; four men carry it with ease. Being flat-bottomed, umiaks draw only a few inches; of dory-type, they have the great seaworthiness of that design so that if you come to a wide lake where high waves are possible you are still suitably equipped. For camping or for taking shelter in a storm they are also good, for you pull them ashore, unload them and prop them up so as to form a combination of a roof and a windbreak. The hide that covers the boat is so tough that you can land on a stony beach in a moderate surf without danger to the cover. If you break a few ribs against boulders it is scarcely more than a pastime to repair these while you are storm-bound or in connection with a night encampment If the boat is partly stove, a number of ribs broken, and if you still have to continue the voyage without repairs you can do that. Your craft will merely be slightly less handy to manage and of course loses cargo capacity in proportion to how much it bulges in; but water does not enter unless the skin has been cut by a rock that was practically as sharp as a knife. A mere bruise against a round boulder is not going to let in water.

Second in merit to the Eskimo umiak for white men's pioneering use is the kayak. Except in Bering Sea, where this canoe sometimes accommodates two or even three, the kayak is a one-man boat, built approximately on the lines of a racing shell but covered over so that not only can the waves dash about without entering but, as already described in connection with waterproof clothing, the kayaker can so dress himself and so lash himself to the boat that capsizing only means righting himself again. A good kayaker will not capsize more than a few times an hour, even in the roughest sea, and it is considered that a strong man who is skillful can right himself 30 or 40 times before becoming so exhausted that drowning results. There are few lakes in the Arctic, perhaps none, so large that you would expect waves which could upset a good kayaker who was not absent-minded.

The kayak has no unmotorized competitor for speed except the racing shell. The Iroquois and certain Algonquins were considered the best canoeists when Europeans first reached the St. Lawrence and Great Lakes regions. In their bark canoes these Indians could paddle away from any crew of European rowers. But when the early explorers, employing these Indian canoeists, met the Eskimos in northern Canada they found that the Eskimos could paddle away from the Algonquins even more easily than the Algonquins could from Europeans.

PURPOSES OF THE UMIAK

The umiak is a traveling boat for considerable numbers of men and a cargo boat. A 40-foot umiak will take ashore 50 unencumbered men from a ship that is being lightered, if the waves are no more than a foot or two high; a 40-foot boat should carry on a river perhaps 30 men with infantry equipment and camping gear.

PURPOSES OF THE KAYAK

The kayak is a boat for hunting, setting fish nets, for scouting and carrying messages. One man carries it with complete ease, except perhaps in a high wind.

SKIN BOATS ARE FOOD IN CASE OF STARVATION

It is no mere crudity of humor to say that one of the advantages of a skin boat over wood or rubber is that the skins can be eaten. For it has been found among all nationalities and all social grades that a starving party will eat anything even supposed to contain food value and is finally driven to cannibalism.

CANNIBALISM

It is rare, except in fiction, that men are killed to be eaten. There are cases where a member of a party becomes so unsocial in his conduct towards the rest that by agreement he is killed; but if his body then is eaten it is not logically correct to say that he was killed for food. What does happen constantly is that those who have died of hunger, or of another cause, will be eaten.

SKIN BOATS STAVE OFF CANNIBALISM

But long before cannibalism develops the party has eaten whatever is edible. It is probable that leathers tanned by ordinary commercial processes have little food value; or, what is much the same, that the chemicals in these leathers will hurt enough to at least partly cancel the food value. But rawhide has no injurious chemicals and does have a large percentage of protein. It is not likely to be disagreeable in taste—rather it is tasteless. If you have plenty of fuel you boil it; when cooked you find that it has a jelly-like consistency, familiar to most of us through having eaten the skin on pig's feet or pig's knuckles. If cooking is not possible, you cut rawhide into small pieces and swallow them. Cooked or not, there is considerable emergency food value in an umiak; there is some in the smaller kayak.

It is elementary that a boat must not be eaten while it is still valuable for its natural use in transportation. It may be doubtful whether it should be eaten later even by men who are starving; they will have to balance in their minds its value as food and its value for bedding and shelter. This seems almost too obvious for mentioning; but the fact is that mistakes of this sort are on record. It is also true that members of a party have differed as to when a leather article should be converted from its original purpose to food. The commonest instance is with leather footgear and body clothing, which has sometimes been devoured from mere animal instincts of hunger when one would think the man would have realized that the value as protection from cold was greater. For if you are cold you need more food. Wearing a garment is a cheaper and better way of securing body warmth than eating it and getting the warmth through the digestive processes.

SCATTERED ICE KEEPS DOWN WAVES

For sea navigation, scattered ice will have more advantages than disadvantages. However rough the ocean where it is open, as soon as you get in among the ice you have no more trouble with the waves. The floes near shore are usually scattered. Few of them are bigger than a city block in area and there likely are between them half-mile open patches where you can sail through water that is smooth even with a stiff breeze.

In the course of such travel you are able to go up to an ice cake and dip fresh water off its surface—as described in Chapter 8.

ICE ALONG SUMMER COASTS DEPENDS ON WINDS ONLY

There are few Arctic coasts where the amount of ice visible from land in summer depends upon the warmth of the season. It is theoretically possible that observations taken through coming years may eventually show a slight relation between local air temperature and amount of ice near land; but, so far as observations have yet gone, all sailors and "practical" men of the North agree that the wind is the only factor that needs consideration. At Point Barrow, for instance, there have been cases where nearly or quite the chilliest season on record had nearly or quite the least ice—the ice went away early in spring, went far off and stayed away long.

However, the wind that controls the ice is not necessarily blowing locally. A gale at a considerable distance may set up special (temporary) currents that move the ice in your locality. As explained in Chapter 12, a striking region for the demonstration of this is the Alaska coast for several hundred miles east from Point Barrow, where ice behavior is profoundly and frequently affected by gales that blow around and north of Bering Strait.

WARM CURRENTS KNOWN TO DESTROY WINTER ICE

It may be gales, perhaps in the North Pacific, that control warm waters which arrive now and then at Barrow, having come, no doubt, from the Pacific via Bering Strait.

It may happen at Point Barrow in winter that seal hunters go 10 or 15 miles out on perfectly safe ice a good many feet thick and come back 6 or 8 hours later to find that, especially beneath snowdrifts, the ice has been eaten away from below by a warm current so that men and sledges may break through into the water below.

As yet this condition has not been observed at Barrow except in winter; but that is no doubt because adequate studies have not been made. We should, therefore, modify our concept on the relation of warmth to absence of ice from the Barrow region in summer by adding a corollary: While there is probably seldom if ever a material relation between the warmth of the air at a given place and the amount of ice offshore, there may be, and probably is, a relation between the amount of ice and the warmth of the sea water—this warmth deriving from accessions of North Pacific water which was perhaps driven north by a gale.

CHAPTER 12

TRANSPORTATION

SECTION I:

SHIPS AND BOATS

ICE MOVEMENTS OFF ALASKA COAST

For a discussion of the underlying principles of tides and currents, and of the differences between Atlantic and Pacific Ocean influences upon the Arctic, see Chapter 2.

It seems illogical when you look at the map, but it is a fact attested by many witnesses between Point Barrow and Herschel Island, that although a west wind there blows off the land, it brings the ice into the land; and although an east wind blows toward land, still it commonly carries the ice away from shore enough to leave handsome room for ships to pass east and west along the coast.

As said, with easterly winds the ice on the northeast coast of Alaska will move away from the land. This is true, however, only with mild winds, and is not true even with these if they persist for a long time. A gale, or a strong breeze of long duration, will bring the ice back in, and cause pressure likely to crush ships that are beset on that shore.

A west wind, although blowing off the land between Barrow and Herschel, will bring the ice landward and set the pack grinding eastward along the edge of the landfast ice.

BASIC IDEA OF ALASKA NORTH COAST NAVIGATION

One of the basic ideas of navigation along the north coast of Alaska, and along the north coast of western Canada, rests on the ocean being shallow inshore, with a number of rivers in the spring bringing warm water from the land to melt away the inshore ice. It happens frequently that while heavy ice still lies offshore too strong for any icebreaker yet constructed to get through, there will be a lane of thaw water along the land through which a ship of small draft can worm her way.

It is told by New England sea captains that when they first navigated the Alaskan north coast they lost ship after ship by following the Atlantic rule of keeping 20 miles from land. Their experience northward from the Atlantic, in Greenland and Spitsbergen waters, had been that if ships got stuck among the ice they were very likely to be let loose again eventually; for in most of these places the current runs south into freer waters where the ice slackens out. But north of Alaska a ship that gets into ice and starts moving with it is not likely ever to get out, or at least not for years, since the pack sets tighter instead of loosening, and the drift is not southward but northward to the more ice-infested regions. As developed in Chapter 2, the movement is really that of a spiral curving north and west, farther and farther offshore, deeper and deeper into the pack—till you finally work out again in the region to the north of Iceland and Norway.

When Yankee whaling ships were wrecked far from land north of Alaska, the men could with difficulty make their escape by boats or sledges. Cargoes were then invariably lost. If a ship was squeezed against the land, or sunk by pressure near shore, the crews were not in serious danger. In some cases entire cargoes were saved, and the more valuable parts in others. These things were so well known that, in olden days, whenever a whaler sank near shore without saving cargo the gossip in the whaling fleet was that the gain from the insurance policy would explain the loss of the vessel.

If a ship is crushed by rapidly moving and tumbling ice floes in summer, a retreat from her with any equipment may become dangerous. But if she is broken in winter, then the process of breaking up is fairly sure to be slow, giving ample time to place on reasonably stable ice in the vicinity the stores and equipment one cares to save.

TYPES OF SHIPS FOR POLAR WORK

Since this is a Manual chiefly for emergency use, we do not attempt to describe ice breakers and other ships made specially for Arctic use. But for the possible use of parties organized in a hurry who may have a chance to secure medium and small ships of various types, the following points are mentioned:

For navigation of icy seas a single propeller vessel is to be preferred to one with twin propellers. The reason is that double propellers are usually placed so that they stick out at angles and are likely to be snapped off by the ice. When a single propeller is in the center, aft, the bulge of the ship in her passage so pushes ice to the sides that none touches the screw.

At least this has been the view of most authorities. The summer of 1939 the Soviet Government exhibited at the New York World's Fair a model of their then new ice breaker, *Josef Stalin*. To the astonishment of American sailors familiar with the Arctic this ship had two propellers and had no device (at least had none on the model) which would keep these propellers from striking ice that would be flowing back along the side of a ship that was forcing her way through heavy ice. Since then has come much news of the success of the *Stalin* in what must have been difficult ice, as, for instance, when around the holidays of 1939–40 she struggled far to the northwest of the Spitzbergen Islands to meet the southward drifting *Sedov*. The report said nothing about her propeller striking ice or about any damage suffered by the vessel.

Until a real explanation is available, we shall have to assume one of two things, that the *Stalin* as actually built had cages or other protective devices to shield her propellers from ice contact; or that her propellers, and the shafts and other things connected with them, were so strong that they could safely hit ice—breaking it instead of being themselves broken.

A vessel of shallow draft (drawing, loaded, say not over 4 feet) is frequently to be preferred to a more powerful ship of deep draft. In the spring, when the rivers open and thaw water begins to flow in little and big streams off all parts of the coast, the sea ice is melted by this comparatively warm land water and an open lane is formed along the beach, while the heavier grounded ice is still continuous along the coast a few hundred yards farther to sea and the pack is still heavy in the offing. A boat with a draft of 4 feet can make good progress along such a lane, when no matter how powerful, a ship of deeper draft could make no progress at all.

Besides, the rivers of Canada, Alaska, and Siberia are open to shallow-draft boats. A chief reason why so many northern ships are flat-bottomed, have centerboards instead of keels, and draw only 4, 5, or 6 feet, is that vessels of small draft can carry their ocean cargoes up into rivers—in some cases even 1,000 or 2,000 miles upstream.

SPECIALLY CONSTRUCTED FLAT-BOTTOMED BOAT

An example of what can be done with small boats was the *North Star,* used on the third Stefansson expedition. She had been built to take advantage of inshore thaw waters. She drew 4 feet 2 inches, loaded; in place of a keel there was a centerboard that could be withdrawn into the body of the ship. Her designer, Matt Andreasen, had made no attempt to build her strong, for he had a special method, of which he may have been the inventor, of dealing with the closing in of the ice around her.

The *Star* was only about 50 feet long and could turn around almost in her own length. When her commander saw the ice closing in, where there seemed to be no chance of getting out of the way entirely, he would select in the neighborhood some big ice cake that sloped to the water's edge on one side. He would then steam full speed against this floe.

The bow of the *North Star* was so shaped that, instead of hitting the ice a hard blow she would slide up on it, standing level because she had a flat bottom. Thus, by her own power, she was able to put herself halfway on top of the ice. The crew were prepared to jump out, fasten an anchor into the ice, and with blocks and tackle to haul the ship entirely up on the floe, so that when the other floes closed in and began to crowd each other their pressure did not come upon the ship but merely upon the ice on which she was standing. If this was a solid piece, it was not likely to break; if it broke, the *Star* was no worse off than she was before—had, in fact, escaped at least one squeeze.

On the several occasions when the *Star* was hauled upon a floe the ice under her did not break. She therefore had to be launched again. Accordingly, when the ice slackened out and there was a chance to continue navigation, a small charge of powder was placed in an augur hole in the ice. On exploding this would shatter the cake and let the ship down into the water.

ESKIMO SKIN BOATS

Among Eskimo devices which have not been equalled by other Indians, or by whites, for certain types of work are the two skin boats, the open large umiak and the decked small kayak. They belong to the group of boats which have for chief elements a wicker frame and a membrane cover. These include such well-known examples as the Irish curragh and the Iroquois bark canoe.

According to Irish folklore, which until recently has been considered fantastic by most historians of navigation, the Irish curragh was capable of long ocean voyages and would carry 60 people. There has been ingrained, however, in the belief of the Irish people themselves the conviction that curraghs were the most seaworthy boats possible. For instance, a ballad as recent as from the sixteenth century tells of a number of people who were drowned in a gale that came up when they were on their way to church in a wooden boat. It is a refrain of this ballad that if the boat had been of leather instead of wood the tragedy would not have occurred.

If we assume that the seaworthiness of the curragh was at all comparable to that of the umiak then Irish faith in the skin boat is being justified. For it is the view of many if not most officers of the United States Coast Guard, good sailors themselves and familiar with the storms of Bering Sea, that there are few if any boats more seaworthy than an umiak they have seen in use there. It would seem from what these officers, and others, can tell us from Bering Sea skin boat navigation that the Irish stories are reasonable which tell about long North Atlantic voyages in curraghs. Nor is the reported size of the ancient curragh absurd when given as ability to carry 60 people; for the early Russians tell from Bering Sea that they saw umiaks carrying 70 passengers.

Judging from a model of the second century B. C., discovered in Ireland, the curragh did not change in design between that time and the sixteenth century. Its lines and general appearance were those of the Iroquois bark canoe, not those of the umiak which is essentially a modified dory form. Since the dory is looked upon as about the safest boat model ever devised, it may be that the umiak is even more seaworthy than the curragh.

Securing Eskimo boats differs from securing Eskimo clothes in a very important way. You cannot buy really good clothes except those which you find already in existence as part of a wardrobe; but Eskimos will make good boats for you—perhaps not quite as good as for themselves, but nearly. This is perhaps because boats have "always" been among them an article of commerce; clothes were made by each family for its own use.

SIZE OF UMIAKS

The largest umiaks dependably reported were 44 feet in length. Those seen by E. W. Nelson, both east and west of Bering Sea and Bering Strait, between 1877 and 1881, were from 15 to 40 feet. He felt that the average length was 30 feet but 36- and 38-foot boats are common. Like the dory the umiak is a double-ender. The keel piece is flat, a plank split and adzed from driftwood (usually spruce). The rim or railing piece is also of spruce, is round and obtained from a driftwood log by splitting and adzing. The ribs, too, are from drift spruce, and so are the one or two strips parallel to the gunwale that are lashed across the ribs to hold them in position. The lashing is preferably of whalebone, but rawhide may be used.

The best of both the umiaks and kayaks are found at the two extremes of Eskimo culture—around Greenland in the east and around Alaska in the west.

From southwestern Alaska northward and eastward to

the Mackenzie River the umiak was used for travel in large parties, for transport of goods, for whaling and walrusing. In modern times the umiak did not extend eastward beyond the eastern limit of the Mackenzie Eskimos, somewhere near Cape Lyon, and was not found again until around Hudson Bay, Labrador, Baffin Island, and especially Greenland. Here the uses were the same as in the west, with one exception. In the west the rowers or paddlers and the steerer might be either men or women—usually both men and women paddled and some man steered. In Greenland it was not good form for men to do any work in an umiak except steering. For that reason the umiak is spoken of around Greenland as a woman's boat.

From southwestern Alaska north, and then east beyond Barrow, the kayak is used for journeys by single individuals or by two or three. Men are the ordinary users, but it is permissible for women to use them. They are hunting boats for sea mammals up to walrus and white whale in size, and are used for setting fish nets. (The net, however, is not a primitive Eskimo device; has come into their culture during recent times.)

East of Barrow the kayak changes rapidly in function, becoming largely a boat for caribou hunting—for spearing them when they are swimming lakes or rivers. The kayak is so used in the interior of Alaska; there is practically no other use of the kayak than for spearing caribou when you get east toward Coronation Gulf, and this remains true until you get toward Hudson Bay, Baffin Island, and Greenland, where the uses are similar to those of Bering Sea. Particularly in Greenland, the kayak is a device for hunting seals.

No doubt the similarity of Bering and of Greenland use of the two skin boats is due to the absence of ice from the water, so that the people are water hunters. In the region between, water hunting is practiced in some districts, but generally the hunting technique is more adapted to land and to sea ice.

SKINS FOR BOAT COVERS

When the skins of seals, small or big, are intended for boat covers they are put into tubs and kept in a warm place while the hair rots loose from one side and the blubber more or less loose from the other. When the rotting has gone far enough, both the hair side and the flesh side are scraped, sand, ashes, or other material being used to remove the last traces of blubber. The skins are then sewed together while wet, overlapping seams, with stitching as fine as that needed for water boots. As in the boots, the thread has to be sinew, or some material that swells on getting wet.

While still pliable through being soaking wet, the sewed skins are stretched over the frame of the boat. In the case of the enclosed one, the kayak, the two sides have to be held together by hand while the last seam is being sewn. The wet skin covering is then reasonably tight and becomes as tight as a drumhead upon shrinkage with drying. In the case of the big open boats, umiaks, which are covered with the skins of bearded seals, walrus, or white whale, a great deal of strength is used in stretching the skins. This is possible, for their edges are passed over the gunwale all around and overlap on the inside a little where they are lashed to the ribs or railing by thongs passed through perforations in the edges of the boat cover.

Like a dry water boot, a dry skin boat may leak a little. You dampen them, accordingly, before putting them in the water. An ideal dampening is to have rain fall on them while they are lying bottom side up. If you have to launch a boat that is very dry, you count on it leaking a little and figure on paddling ashore after a while and turning it upside down, spilling the water. After that the seams are water-tight.

Neither the big nor small boat should be permitted to remain constantly wet for more than 2 or at the most 3 days if the weather is hot and they are being used in warm fresh water, as on rivers. On the third, fourth, or fifth day of such use the seams begin to go with the decay of the sinew. It is customary to pull boats out of the water whenever you expect to stay several hours, as over night. The kayak is placed upside down, resting on stones or sticks; the umiak is propped on edge, leaning over in such a way that it forms a good camp shelter from rain or wind. Even when tents are pitched, it is customary for traveling parties to work in the shelter of the umiak. They dance in its shelter, too, or sit around telling stories.

It has been stated, as an extreme, that an umiak of bearded seal can stand a continuous 10-day voyage in the ocean without injury—that you could make a protracted coastal voyage if you gave the boat a thorough drying every 10 days. It is considered that the factors which stretch the 3- or 4-day river voyage interval between dryings to 8 or 10 days between dryings on sea voyages are two: Decay of rawhide and of sinew is slower when temperatures are low; Arctic sea water usually runs from 2° or 3° above freezing to 2° or 3° below it, say from 29° to 35° F., while river water may be 10°, 15°, or 20° warmer. The second factor making for slow decay is that salt (NaCl) and perhaps other chemicals in the sea water retard bacterial growth.

Umiak covers are sometimes of walrus hide or of white whale. Some think white whale as good as bearded seal; few think the walrus so good—it is heavier and the cover does not remain so long in good condition.

Kayaks are sometimes made of caribou skin, which has been rotted and in other ways treated as the skin of small seals, which is the usual material.

LIFE OF SKIN BOATS

The average life of an umiak is 3 years. It may be less than that in fresh water, a good deal more than that in salt. The life of a kayak with equal use and equal care is perhaps less. However, a kayak is easier to care for. With hard luck or poor management an umiak may go bad on you the first year.

Greasing the seams of kayaks and umiaks is not ordinarily necessary, but it is not such bad form among Eskimos as greasing the seams of water boots. You see it done every now and then, especially with umiaks. For extreme cases, as when a umiak has either been badly constructed or is in its last year of use, tallow may be employed to fill seams which would otherwise leak. In most cases lard is here better than the native caribou or similar tallows, for they get too hard and may crack out of the seams at temperatures under which the lard would be soft and flexible.

There are districts where umiaks were greased in what might be called white man's style, apparently before the influence of white men began to control. E. W. Nelson describes from Bering Sea a process where a new boat is placed upside down and greased all over, as if it were being painted. The oil, preferably seal, is allowed to dry for 2 or 3 days, which makes it a little sticky. A second coat is applied and allowed to dry; perhaps even a third.

The advantages of the umiak over the wooden New England type whale boat of approximately equal length are: The umiak carries more cargo because of its higher sides and lighter weight—it weighs between one-quarter and one-half as much as a whale boat. It can go in shallower water because of its flat bottom. Most important of all, it is stronger.

A New Bedford whale boat going 5 to 7 miles an hour under sail may be stove by a chunk of ice the size of a bushel basket, or smaller, practically invisible through being awash; an umiak pays no attention how it bunts into ice of such or even considerably larger size. Going full speed into practically any obstruction, it is either uninjured or a rib or two are broken. Only a sharp cutting edge like that on a fractured rock would pierce a hole.

Whether in whale boat or umiak the first emergency repair when pierced would be to pull something, as a piece of skin, outside of the boat over the hole. When you get the two boats "ashore," either on land or ice, you have a big and difficult job with a whale boat; but with the umiak you just get out needles and sinew thread and, in half an hour, either Eskimos or white sailors used to a needle will have a patch on that is either completely waterproof or which allows water to come in so slowly that it scarcely matters.

You can run an umiak ashore in a surf the way you would a dory. It is easier to pull upon a beach than a dory because of its lighter weight—two strong men can carry a umiak of three or four thousand-pound cargo capacity while four men carrying it can walk along at a good swinging gait. It would take at least eight men to carry similarly a dory of equal capacity.

In both Greenland and Alaska a square sail has been in use for centuries. Fore-and-aft sails have been introduced

recently, following whites, and are considered dangerous—
these boats capsize easily if they carry a big spread of canvas.

Paddling, sailing, or drifting in a river you can have a
considerable load with a 4-inch draft, and, because of the
combined light weight of the craft and its flat bottom, you
can half carry boat and cargo over patches of very shallow
water. On the second Stefansson expedition they sometimes
worked through with a considerable load where the draft was
only 3 inches, the men walking alongside, partly lifting and
partly towing the boat.

No craft is better for tracking upstream than the umiak.
Preferably there is a mast, and the tracking line runs from
three or four feet up it to the dog team ashore or to the men
who are pulling. It is seldom easy to track with less than 50
feet of rope. Under special conditions, as rocks or shallows
near shore, you might well use two or three times that much
line. If things are too unfavorable on your side of a river,
you climb into the boat, paddle across and begin tracking on
the other side. The dogs will swim over. Toward fall, when
rivers are icy, you had better carry the team across in your
boat.

The umiak has certain drawbacks which go with its virtues.
Being flat-bottomed and with much higher sides than a whale
boat it sticks far out of the water unless heavy-laden, takes
on a lot of wind and is therefore difficult to paddle against
the wind. For the same reasons, you cannot tack it into the
wind; while even with a beam wind it makes considerable
leeway.

When dealing with rough waters the Eskimos use a number
of inflated seal skins tied outboard on both sides, a little back
of the bow and front of the stern. Sometimes an inflated
seal skin is put crosswise of bow or stern. According to the
size of the seal these bags have a buoyancy of 150 to 300
pounds each. (An umiak being made chiefly of rawhide,
with only a little wood, will sink on being swamped unless
provided with floats.)

A device for rough weather which in 1877 Nelson took to
be of pre-white use was what our sailors call a weather cloth,
which to the Eskimos would be a weather skin. Flaps of
seal, not more than 2 feet wide, were attached to the rail of

the boat all around and were folded down inside during smooth weather. When there began to seem danger that the boat would take water during a rough sea these flaps were raised and held in place by sticks lashed to the framework, thus practically giving it that much more freeboard.

It is generally believed that the square sail was borrowed by Eskimos from Europeans, perhaps by Greenlanders from the old Norsemen of the colony which occupied Greenland from 986 to after 1500 A. D. Where Eskimos use oars, rather than paddles, that idea is also considered to be borrowed from Europeans.

KAYAK

The superiority of the kayak over all similar inventions of Europeans or North American Indians has been recognized everywhere at all times. The earliest European explorers found that with oars they could never overtake an Eskimo in a kayak and it was only under the rarest conditions, with oars and sails combined, that one of their boats could equal the paddled speed of a kayak. Even then, the Eskimo could always get away just by refusing to be pursued straight down the wind. Similarly, as noted earlier, the best Algonquin canoe men fell far short in speed as well as in ability to face rough water.

The nearest thing in lines to an Eskimo kayak is the modern racing shell, which is also the only man-propelled boat that can equal the kayak in speed. For practical use there is, however, no comparison. A shell can be used only on placid water; a kayak faces the roughest sea and goes through breakers.

The kayak is a completely enclosed vessel except for the mouth into which the voyager inserts himself carefully while he is alongside of a steep shore, a floe of ice, a log or an improvised dock. He sits with his body flexed at right angles, the legs stretched straight out before him.

Usually in Greenland, occasionally in Alaska, you wear a waterproof coat tied around the mouth of the kayak and around your wrists and neck so as to make your garments and your kayak one piece, water-excluding.

Where water-excluding garments are used, tumbling in

kayaks is a recognized sport, whether with double or single paddle, usually double. The kayaker upsets himself and maneuvers around underneath to come up on the other side, righting himself and the kayak with a dexterous twist and shove of the paddle blade.

The sport of kayak rolling leads to practical results, especially in Greenland. In the southern two-thirds of that country most of their food is secured by natives in kayaks, sometimes at considerable distances from land. Indeed, in parts of Greenland kayak hunting is done practically throughout the year.

The use of a kayak is a fine art, but not even the greatest expert can remain stationary in it—comparison is to walking a tightrope, where you are all right as long as you keep a certain amount of motion but where you cannot possibly remain quite still. When an Eskimo stops he has to have the blade of his paddle in the water. When he throws a spear he does it with one hand, the other on his paddle. To fire a gun where both hands are used, boat and man must be facing directly toward the target; the hunter must have the paddle so in hand or so within reach that he controls himself by it almost simultaneously with the recoil of the gun.

The above applies to the kayak of very fine lines. There are kayaks of fairly broad beam which are not so skittish.

When learning to use a kayak, the main thing is skill in getting out of it. You can practice this first on shore, the object being to be able to wriggle free if you capsize. Only after this is thoroughly mastered should you undertake the second step, paddling about. Then you learn such ticklish operations as firing a gun. Finally, with the use of a waterproof suit, you learn to right yourself after capsizing.

Journeys of several hundred miles by kayak are on record, particularly from the Aleutian Islands and southwestern Alaska. When traveling along a hostile coast, or for other reason not wanting to go ashore, two or more kayaks will use cross beams and lash their boats together, side by side. It is then possible for the men of even just two kayaks to sleep, although more or less in a sitting-up position. If three or four kayaks are lashed into a single raft, they can be decked over in such a way that kayakers can emerge from their manholes and sit or lie around. Kayaks are sometimes rafted to prevent capsizing; but in that case there would have to be more than two, or else the two kayaks must be some distance from each other with a bridge holding them together.

Kayaks are sometimes rafted for freighting. A raft of two kayaks kept well apart by a bridge, or of three and more, will be towed by a single kayaker; as when ferrying across a river, or (in modern times) when lightering a ship.

Formerly it was customary both in Alaska and Greenland waters for parties to travel that consisted in part of umiaks and in part of kayaks. Women, children, decrepit old men, and sometimes others, would ride in the umiak; most of those men who owned kayaks would paddle along in them. One reason was that the kayakers could go faster than the umiak and could scout around, as for game. They made detours to secure game, either bringing it to the umiak or signalling the umiak for a detour. In this sort of travel the kayakers would take turns climbing on the umiak to rest and perhaps to sleep. The empty kayak would be ballasted sufficiently, with a stone or something else heavy for its size, and would be towed; or the kayak might be carried aboard the umiak for a while.

Converting sledges into rafts or sledge-boats is described in the following section.

Section II

SLEDGES

In outfitting a sledge, essentials are rifles, ammunition and other hunting gear, scientific instruments, cameras and photographic supplies, diaries, spare clothing, bedding, and cooking utensils, snow knives, axe, pickaxe, shovel, etc. Equipment provided, take on as much food and fuel as can be hauled without making the load too heavy. As stated earlier, hauling fuel is more important than hauling food and the kind of fuel is more important than the kind of food. For game is to be found nearly everywhere on the polar sea if you know how and where to look for it and how to secure it.

The scientific equipment might be: two sextants with

necessary tables for computing latitude and longitude, three good watches (not pocket chronometers), two thermometers, aneroid barometer, several prismatic compasses. On a journey over sea ice, if you want to pick up a little geographic information (and also for guiding you to land by giving the slope of the sea bottom), you might carry a sounding machine with several leads and about 10,000 feet of wire. The watches, or at least one of them, should (for reasons given elsewhere) have a 24-hour dial numbering.

We said that watches should be preferred to pocket chronometers. For it has been the experience afoot that with a chronometer escapement a jar is much more likely than with a watch escapement to make your timepiece lose a beat.

Every article carried on a sledge should be as immune as possible to breakage or other injury and, of course, should be as light in weight as compatible with other needed qualities. Scientific instruments are protected from jolting by being wrapped in the bedding or in spare clothes. The camera should be protected likewise, for jolting may put it out of order.

SPEED

In Alaska, where you can buy dog feed at roadhouses and where businessmen travel fast because of the value of time, speed driving is useful. But in survey and exploratory work, in country where land and ice are as rough as in most places in the North, you cannot drive fast with a loaded sledge without breaking it—you collide with things every now and then, and the shock of impact varies with the square of the speed.

Cold weather increases the hauling weight of loads. At —50° or —60°, the grains of snow seem to act upon steel shoeing as would grains of sand on a beach. It has not been determined but it seems likely that a drop in temperature from 10° above zero to 50° below will increase at least by three the strain put on dogs in pulling a given load. A popular explanation is that the increased friction is because the snow crystals get so hard that they begin to scratch the sledge runners like sand.

The resistance to the sliding of metals over snow varies with

393

the kind of metal; it also varies with the condition of a given metal. For instance, copper slides better than iron and soft iron slips along more easily than hard at low temperatures, or at least soft iron glides better than steel.

A slight increase of friction on steel sledge runners may begin right from the melting point of snow, increasing cold-wards; but in practice we think of it as beginning somewhere between 10° and −10° F. It increases in some growing ratio, perhaps even geometric, so that there is a very big difference between −40° and −50°. The difference is believed by most travelers to be greater between −50° and −60° than between −40° and −50°.

ICE SHOEING

With ice shoeing, as discussed elsewhere in this section, the hauling weight is probably only a quarter or a fifth as much as with steel shoeing. In cases where ice shoeing cannot be applied, the way to minimize the drag, in months when the sun is above the horizon, is to travel only in the daylight, and consequently warmer, hours.

In cold weather, sledges pull very hard, especially if they are metal shod, when crossing leads on new ice. As described in Section III, Chapter 2, this is because the elimination of salt by freezing has already begun and there is a crust of salt on top of the ice.

SLEDGE CONSTRUCTION

The making of good sledges requires so much skill and practice that an apprenticeship is necessary. However, a general discussion will help for the choice and understanding of sledges and also for making them, if you have to in an emergency, We begin with the emergency type.

EMERGENCY SLEDGE FROM HIDE

In country where little wood is available, Eskimos have made runners out of skins and ice. You fold several thicknesses of wet skin, such as musk ox or caribou, into long slabs resembling planks. The skins are soggy, the water having penetrated to the cells in the hide as well as filling in between the hairs. You lay the wet skins out on a very flat surface, as on the ice of a lake, to build up your plank. (Likely wet sail cloth, blankets, and other fabrics would serve as well as hides.)

When the skins have frozen, you adze the plank down into the right shape. This does not have to be a fine job, for there is to be shoeing.

The greatest difficulty with these emergency sledges is to make of skins the crosspieces needed for holding the runners together and holding them on edge. These crosspieces practically have to be of wood.

Approximately speaking, you make the sledge, with its two runners and cross pieces, about as if you were making a ladder out of two planks, with the crosspieces for rungs.

You fasten the crosspieces by countersinking them into the runners and by boring holes through the runners and lashing with rawhide thongs.

When everything has been made as tight as possible you reinforce by freezing. You pour in water that will fill the holes and then you plaster on mushy snow of ice cream consistency. This snow should be mixed with something to make the ice tougher, as grass or the long hair of some animal.

There are various ways of shoeing this type of sledge. One way, the commonest, is to use sods. If the plank of which your runners are made are 3 inches thick, then cut the sod so that it is about 6 inches wide and say 3 inches thick. Along one of the flat sides of the sod you cut a trench into which the plank will fit. When you have enough sods cut to shoe both your runners, you place them in position, set the sledge on top so the runners stand in the grooves of your shoeing where it lies on the level lake ice, pour in water along the edges, and fill in with mushy snow.

When the shoeing is frozen solidly to your runners, you turn the sledge upside down and adze, hack, or scrape away the bumps and ridges. Insofar as there are indentations or cracks you fill these with mushy snow, mixed as before with hair or grass.

When the lower side of the shoeing has been whittled down to approximate smoothness, you take a bucket of water and a swab made of long-haired skin, dip it into the water and swab the bottoms of the shoeing. This should be done on a very cold day, the colder the better; for if the temperature is near freezing the water may erode your runners, getting them out of shape.

This description may seem difficult to follow, but you will find the process easy; for it is all a matter of common sense, and trial and error, when you once get the broad idea.

Sledges such as just described can be used only in cold weather. They will, of course, collapse and disintegrate in the thaws. However, you can use them pretty well into spring by making sure that every time you stop it is on snow rather than on ice or earth. When the sun is warm you carry some kind of awning on the sunward side of your sledge to shade the runners; at camp time you see to it that the sledge is so shaded as to prevent the sun reaching the runners at all. In some cases the best way is to bury them in so much snow that you know it cannot all get melted while you are in camp. You prolong the use in the spring by traveling at night and protecting the runners as indicated while you sleep during the day.

If you have wooden planks, or can make them out of logs, a sledge will be made on the principles above described for hides, the shoeing also similarly applied. In this case, however, you might want to use nails, if you have them, in place of lashings for the crossbars. Lashings are better, on the whole, if the job is well done.

Sledges of the above types that are fairly rigid are sometimes shod by Eskimos with fossil elephant ivory, walrus ivory, caribou antler, the jawbone (not the baleen) of whales, or even with small pieces of rib or leg bone of other mammals. The pieces must either fit very snugly against each other or else they should overlap so that the piece in front goes a little way back on the one next behind. Ivory is perhaps the smoothest gliding of these materials. When the thermometer is in the vicinity of freezing they don't glide more easily than metals, but they do glide more easily at low temperatures. They are usually fastened on to the runners with pegs but occasionally with lashing, in which latter case the shoeing has to be thick enough to permit holes to be bored. Naturally the lashings must not project, so you will have to countersink them both into the edge of the shoeing and into the edge of the runner.

If you kill a seal while on the march you pass a rope through its nostrils, turn it on its back and drag it that way behind the sledge. The hair is smooth, turned backward, and slides very well. A polar bear, unskinned, will not drag similarly, because of his angular shoulders and because he will not stay on his back. But you can make a temporary sledge out of the front portion of his skin. You butcher the animal, remove as much of the hide as seems necessary, put the parts of the meat you want to carry into this, and lash it up in some way so that it takes more or less the shape of a toboggan. On the Stefansson expeditions, improvised sledges of this sort were sometimes used for days at a time—until the meat was all gone.

Caribou and many other skins slide so badly that they cannot well be used for this type of emergency sledge.

NANSEN SLEDGE

It is generally agreed that for travel over such smooth surfaces as the Inland Ice of Greenland or of Antarctica you want sledges to be as light as possible. The Lapp type, as developed by Nansen and borrowed by later explorers, consists of runners which are much like skis, with a light body superadded, all the attachments by lashing. These are easily strong enough for 10 pounds of sledge to carry 100 pounds of load; in some cases 5 pounds of sledge have carried 100 pounds (a 30-lb. sledge carrying 600 lbs.).

Most travelers agree that the Nansen sledge is unsuited to work on rough sea ice. Nansen used them and did not complain, but he knew no other kind and had become fond of them during his previous work on the Greenland Inland Ice. Amundsen approved them for work on the Arctic Sea, but a study of his record will show that he had negligible personal experience with rough ice. Fiala tried them and did not violently disapprove, though he recognized the need for much strengthening and modifying. Mikkelsen and Leffingwell came to northern Alaska fully convinced of the superiorities of Nansen sledges but were undeceived during the first few months of their experience when they had a chance to compare them with the Nome type in properly rough sea ice.

PEARY SLEDGE

If you want a sledge where the main qualifications are lightness combined with strength, probably the native Eskimo type as modified by Peary is best. However, these sledges have serious drawbacks, among them that they are too low when passing over ice snags, and that they are hard to steer and otherwise manage.

BASKET SLEDGES

Basket sledges are of two main types, that developed by the Yankee whalers in northwestern Canada and northern Alaska, and that developed by the gold miners, trappers, and traders of western Alaska—called the Nome sled. They are so springy that an ice-and-earth shoeing, as above described, cannot be used—it would peel off. The Nome design is the springier—which is probably an advantage if you permit springiness at all.

The Nome sledge will be about twice the weight of the Nansen sledge for handling a given load, but it has so many advantages over both the Nansen and Peary types that, especially when equipped with a toboggan bottom (see below), it should be preferred in outfitting an expedition. In real emergencies you are not likely to have available material to make Nome sledges. Moreover, they are so much more difficult to build than the Peary type (though no more difficult than the Nansen type) that the thing to do is to outfit an expedition or a party with enough of these sledges, purchased from northern makers or from firms in cities like Seattle which supply Northerners. If you have tools and a supply of materials, good carpenters or other handymen can learn how to build this type on the basis of a few samples.

A valuable attachment for the Nome sledge was developed by the third Stefansson expedition. The problem was that in soft snow, and particularly in the spring, a loaded sledge will sink down into a drift until the crossbars act as brakes in the snow. The new idea was to put a toboggan bottom underneath the crossbars of the sledges so that when they sank in they would be automatically converted into toboggans. The toboggan boards (of $\frac{1}{4}$- to $\frac{1}{3}$-inch hickory) added 20 to 40 pounds to the weight of the sledges, but this was amply compensated for not merely because of the above toboggan action in snowdrifts but also because the toboggan bottom protected the crossbars against sharp blows from snags of ice—the sledge would ride over ice pinnacles somewhat as it did over snowdrifts.

In previous chapters we have described two sets of conditions from which it will be inferred that sledges sink deeper into snow during spring than at other seasons. The first explanation is that more snow falls during this season than any other and that it is particularly fluffy because of falling in a temperature that is only a little below freezing. Being sticky, too, from this fluffiness and the comparative warmth, it is not swept along the ground by the wind and powdered up as it might be in colder weather. The second cause, and the one which chiefly drives us to this restatement of certain spring conditions, is that old snow which has been in hard drifts will turn granular in the thaw weather and under the light rains of early spring so that you no longer step upon a drift but rather into one, as if it were a bin of wheat. Sledges act similarly. If you have the Nansen type, with runners four or even more inches wide, they may keep on top; but if you have the Nome type, with runners somewhere between an inch and a half and two and a half inches in width, your sledge will sink in—again somewhat as if you were dragging through rather than over a bin of wheat.

It is, then, more against the old granular snow than against the new-fallen soft snow that you need toboggan bottoms in your Nome sledges. The need is greater out at sea than on shore; for, through reasons not well understood, the sort of granulation described is comparatively not troublesome on land.

SLEDGES FOR FOREST USE

With the partial exception of the Nome sledge with the toboggan bottom attachment, all the above sledges are worthless in a forest. They sink down and drag like a snowplow, besides snagging on stumps, bushes, and trees. The only kind there useful is some variety of toboggan, a vehicle so familiar that it needs no description.

A 2-inch width seems about right for steel sledge shoeing and about ⅛ inch the right thickness. If runners are narrower than 2 inches, they cut into the snow more or less like a knife. If they are wider than 2¼ inches, then the increase of drag becomes very noticeable at low temperatures. If you have wide shoeing, the width, for instance, of a ski, the dragging surface must either be polished wood (unless it is ice) or else one of the soft metals, such as nickel. Nickel, however, is so weak that it has never yet stood up under hard usage.

It is said that other metals run more easily than steel over snow at low temperatures, and Nansen had good luck with german silver. However, the experiences of Sverdrup, Mikkelsen, and others with german silver leads to the opinion that, even if steel drags harder, it is better in the long run. For, unless you get tangled in rocky ground, it will last half a dozen years, while german silver gives out promptly in rough ice.

Peary and Stefansson advocate cold-sheared steel with edges sharp as a skate, soft enough to be drilled in the field and hard enough so that it does not wear out quickly. One advantage of this skate-like edge is that when there is an inclination to slide, it "bites" into the ice.

The only shoeing that is really practical besides steel is ice, and this cannot be used on sledges of the Nome or Nansen type, for both are pliable and the ice pulls off when the runner bends. To keep ice shoeing, the sledge runner must be a stout plank on edge, as in the Peary and Eskimo sledges. These are rigid, and ice shoeing will stay on them indefinitely. It needs to be repaired every morning; but swabbing them to provide new icing is only a few minutes' job with each sledge.

Ice shoeing glides so much more easily than any other Eskimo or European invention that rigid sledges of no matter what make have therein a great advantage. Even if the runners themselves weigh an aggregate of hundreds of pounds, as when made of sod, it will be amply compensated for by the smooth gliding qualities—unless, indeed, your journey is a protracted one uphill, as when proceeding from a seacoast toward the interior.

The chief disadvantage to ice shoeing is that, like german silver or copper, it has nothing to keep it from sliding sidewise on an incline.

When spring comes, the ice shoeings melt off. But sledges can be made with steel shoeing underneath the ice, so that one has it to fall back on when the weather gets warm.

SLEDGE COVERS

The Eskimos, before whites came, apparently saw to it that each parcel they put on their sledges was self-contained and protected from snow. Whites have found, and the Eskimos have readily adopted the idea, that a better plan is to have what is called a sledge cover. This may be just a rectangular piece of canvas which you put over the sledge (or inside the basket if it is that type). You load up and the last step is to wrap the edges up on the side and over the load. This cover is held in place with cross lashings that go under the crossbars of an Eskimo-type sledge or under the rail of the Nome type. For midwinter use you require nothing very heavy—8-ounce duck is usually considered to be on the heavy side and drilling is preferred. In spring travel it may be advisable to have something in the nature of a tarpaulin that will cover the load and shed rain. For, especially at sea you may travel for weeks after the spring rains begin. Besides, the snow will melt on your load and it is well that the resulting water should run off.

ARTICLES FOR EMERGENCY USE SHOULD BE OUTSIDE COVER

As mentioned elsewhere, it is important that things which you may need in emergencies (your rifle, for instance, and your camera) shall not be inside the load, ordinarily not even under the last-mentioned rain-shedding cover. Each such article must have its own waterproof covering.

SLEDGE WITH SAIL

It helps when traveling to leeward just to have the wind pushing on the sledge itself, and on its load. When this does not give enough of a push, square sails are rigged. They can be made out of most anything—a single caribou hide will help a lot, or you might use a blanket. Ordinarily it pays, however, to take with you special equipment. This would consist of two bamboo or other light poles to be erected at the sides of the sledge with anything at all for a crossbar between them at the top. On this you rig the sail. Sometimes a single mast is used, in which case you have some sort of stick for a yard at the top. At the bottom no yard is needed, the corners of the sail being attached to the sledge at either side.

SLEDGE-BOAT

The making of a needed and simple invention, by which a sledge is converted into a boat, was delayed through apparently logical though really incorrect reasoning. Obviously you could make a boat by setting a sledge on a waterproof fabric and wrapping it up on the sides. But it was said this would help you to cross only one lead if the temperature were low; for hundreds, if not thousands, of pounds of water would be converted to ice that would cling to the canvas and compel you to leave it behind. Since you could not possibly afford to carry a separate canvas for each crossing of a lead, the idea was dropped. Sometimes the plan was mentioned, to be dismissed, in books on exploration.

But Ernest deKoven Leffingwell, then joint commander of the Anglo-American Polar Expedition wintering at Flaxman Island, conceived in 1906 an easy solution. If you greased the canvas the ice would peel off like candle grease from the back of your hand. Seal oil was too messy, beef or similar tallows were so hard they would crack off. Lard might be a happy medium. Leffingwell tried it and found that it worked perfectly.

This invention of Leffingwell's was first put to extensive use on the third Stefansson expedition during a journey of five or seven hundred miles (according to which way you figure it) north from Alaska and then east to northern Banks Island.

You must have properly open water. Forcing a canvas boat through young ice chafes it along the water line; half a dozen crossings will probably wear a hole in the cover. But leads can be several hours old and still without ice at $-40°$

if there is a fairly strong wind. Then they are as crossable as an ordinary river in the summertime.

A tarpaulin for this purpose is No. 2 canvas, treated with lard or otherwise waterproofed. It is about 18 feet long and 10 feet wide. Unload the sledge; spread the cover on the ground and place the sledge upon the middle of it. Take two sticks, about 6 feet long (carried for the purpose) and lash one crosswise of the sledge near the back end, another near the front end. Between the ends of these sticks lash one ski on each side. Or a second pair of skis may take the place of the special cross-sticks—they may prove handy to have along even on travel over sea ice.

The described frame gives the boat a beam of 6 feet instead of only 25 or 30 inches. The frame constructed, the tarpaulin is lashed up on the sides of the sledge. The whole is now a boat which carries about a thousand pounds. For propulsion, use a paddle, or, if you haven't one, a shovel or a ski.

Sometimes at low temperatures a great deal of ice will form on the canvas while you are crossing; but as all the interstices are filled with lard or similar material the tarpaulin cannot possibly become water-soaked. The grease makes a surface to which ice cannot adhere tenaciously, and can be removed by rolling the tarpaulin about, walking on it, or beating it with a stick.

The tarpaulin with its waterproofing weighs about 40 pounds. Its weight is seldom increased as much as 5 pounds by the ice that still adheres when you roll it in a bundle and put it back on your sledge. The bundle resembles a bolt of flannel as you see it in a dry goods store and is loaded in the bottom of the sledge, conveniently and with no danger of injury during travel.

The advantage of this system of crossing a lead is manifest to anyone, but especially to those who have read, for instance, the account of Nansen's use of boats for crossing open water. These were of fragile canvas; and, as he carried them on the sledges with the canvas stretched tightly over their frames, they were easily punctured when the loads happened to upset or to collide with broken ice. Nansen, accordingly, found that, besides the disadvantage of the great care they required, the canvas canoes were so badly damaged, their covers so full of holes, when open water was reached that it took several days of repairs to make them seaworthy.

SLEDGE-RAFT

For crossing leads Peary used sledges supported by inflated seal skins. These would have to be lashed, on his type of sledge, to the outside of the runners, so as to give more beam. Additional buoyancy could be secured by an inflated skin set between the runners. As said elsewhere, the buoyancy of these skins will range from 150 to 300 pounds, so that it would not take many to transport a considerable load.

The disadvantage of this method is that ice forms on the sledge itself and has to be chipped off. The main advantages are that the skins are not heavy, that they fold flat when uninflated, and that toward the end of their usefulness they can be fed to dogs, cut up into patches for clothing, or used in some other way.

Section III

SKIS AND SNOWSHOES

Where the ice is smooth or the land flat, skis are useful especially before a fair wind when one can glide almost without effort and at a higher speed than is attainable on snowshoes. But among jaggedly broken ice of the open ocean skis are almost as out of place as in a thick forest. Their main use on the third Stefansson expedition, several members of which were originally prejudiced in favor of skis, proved to be for occasional crossing of leads on thin young ice and, as said, for use in constructing the frame of a sled-boat.

KAMCHATKA SKI

Bergman reports that the ski as developed in Kamchatka has points of superiority over that developed in Sweden. The Kamchatka skis are about 2 yards long and 8 inches wide. Undernenath they are covered with sealskin with the hair lying back. Their advantage is that they do not slip backward when going up hill even if one is not using staffs. They have the further advantage that they do not get clammy in a thaw and are particularly effective making a road for dogs in loose snow. If, however, it is merely a question of getting from one place to another, he agrees the Swedish (Norwegian) skis are better.

SNOWSHOES

Wilkins reports that the submarine *Nautilus* carried both skis and snowshoes. When there was hauling to be done, the Norwegians used skis while he wore snowshoes. When the Norwegians saw how much better he got on they began to use snowshoes themselves. Eventually his greatest difficulty was trying to keep a pair for his own use. Stefansson had earlier met a like situation with Norwegians on his third expedition, of which Wilkins was a member.

INDIAN AND ESKIMO TYPES

The hunting snowshoe of one of several Indian models is useful in any Arctic work except on the roughest ice. The type used by the Eskimos on the north coast of Alaska— with a length of between 3 and 4 feet and a greatest width of about 10 inches—is most convenient.

PEARY TYPE

Peary carried two sizes of snowshoes, both made in Maine. Those furnished his white men were 6 foot by 1 foot; those furnished his Eskimos 5 foot by 1 foot. The shoes were made with raised toe, as were those used by Stefansson, and with a ski curve in the middle.

SIBERIAN TYPE

Vanderlip reports of Sibebria that two sizes of snowshoes are in use, one for soft snow 5 feet 10 inches long and 8 inches wide, pointed and curved up in front and gathered to a point at the back, and one for use in hard snow, 3 feet long and 8 inches wide. These were shod with reindeer skin with the hair pointing back, which prevented slipping.

ALASKAN TYPE

In the softest and deepest snows on earth, found in certain parts of central and southern Alaska, snowshoes of great size are used—almost as long as Norwegian skis and, of course, much wider.

Wherever snows are soft and deep, which includes all forested Arctic and sub-Arctic lands, at least two kinds of snowshoes should be carried by each party—large ones for hunting and ordinary travel, small ones for walking ahead of the dogs, breaking trail. These should not be particularly wide. The trail-breaker should use short steps so placed that the two shoes together make a trail the width of the toboggan which is to follow. Two or even several men should walk ahead to break and tamp down the trail. It is a good plan at camp time, if there are extra men, to send one or more ahead to break next morning's trail for some miles. A trail well tamped down in the evening will be hard enough next day to support the feet of dogs, which is not so if the team immediately follows the trail-breaker.

COMMERCIAL TYPE

Commercial makers often sell and stoutly recommend snowshoes of size and design not suitable for northern work. But when it comes to strength (resistance to breakage) and wearing qualities, the commercial product from Maine and elsewhere is better than anything made by the natives of northern North America, either Eskimos or Athapaskans. The thing, then, in outfitting an expedition, is to get commercial makers to adopt a proper style and weight and then secure from them all the snowshoes you think you are going to need.

MAKESHIFTS

A man who has used or even merely examined attentively a pair of snowshoes can, under most conditions, construct makeshifts for himself. Steamed hickory and woods like it are best for the frame, but you can use the Arctic willow rather effectively, and even driftwood spruce.

406

The thongs that support the foot can be cut from any heavy leather there is on hand, either rawhide or tanned. Rope can be used, but it stretches more than rawhide in cold weather and is then comparatively undesirable. On the other hand, rawhide stretches badly when wetted by slushy snow.

For the meshing of the snowshoe, other than beneath the foot, you also use leather thongs—fine (*babiche*), preferably of rawhide.

ALL-METAL TYPE

All-metal snowshoes have been considered but perhaps never made. They could easily prove most desirable. For instance, the frame might be of duralumin or similar tubing, with the equivalent of the fine mesh perhaps on aluminum sheet perforated with numerous holes. Or you could have (copper?) wire replacing the *babiche*. Under the foot probably you would still want thongs, even in an otherwise metal shoe.

For attaching the snowshoe to the foot you might, under certain conditions, find an elaborate gear useful—such as employed on skis. But snow is liable to pack in these, especially in warmer weather, and perhaps a thong fastening such as used by the natives is, on the average, the best.

SECTION IV

DOGS

We have discussed in chapter 5 the origin and characteristics of northern dogs, the best types for cross-breeding, etc. Here we deal with their care and use in Arctic work.

WEIGHT

Large, heavy dogs, weighing about 120 pounds, are more satisfactory than lighter dogs, say those weighing 50 to 70 pounds. It is obvious that there is an advantage in having six heavy dogs pull a sledge which would require nine light ones—not so much in the amount of food consumed, since heavy dogs need more than light ones, but in such things as harnessing, unharnessing, etc. In addition, when sledges are cached at the end of the snow season and dogs are used as pack animals, not only will the bigger dog carry a heavier back load but he carries it higher above the ground. A small dog may drag his pack through water where a bigger dog carries it high and dry.

One of the reasons to prefer big dogs is that, although you have to feed them more than smaller dogs, you do not have to increase the food quite in proportion to the dog's weight and strength. More nearly you increase it in proportion to his greater body surface, though probably somewhat more than that. It was Stefansson's experience that when an 80-pound dog did well on a pound of food a day, a 120-pound dog would manage with a pound and a quarter.

Dogs must be well furred. A poorly furred dog needs more food because he has to use some of it as fuel to keep himself warm. (Travelers usually put it that you can't keep a dog fat unless his fur is good.) A short-haired dog may freeze, particularly on the flanks, as discussed below. He needs a windbreak when others do not; he may need housing.

A dog in cold weather requires fur so thick that the snow does not melt under him when he curls up to sleep or rest. When a dog is thinly furred he gets wet. Chunks of ice will then freeze to him, or, worse still, he may freeze fast to the ground if he has been sleeping on a thin covering of snow. In such cases a dog is prisoner until he dies, if a man does not liberate him.

If big dogs and small ones have to be used with tandem harness (the kind described below as most efficient and as the only one suited to wooded country), the smallest should be in the lead, the size increasing toward the sled; alternatively, the biggest dog should be in front and the smallest near the sled. The reason is that if a small dog is between two big ones the tandem harness will, through its nature, give an upward pull which, although it may not lift the small dog clean off his feet, will decrease his traction power— the firmness of his step on the ground. Or if you have a big dog between two small ones he has to more or less carry them so that in addition to pulling he is also burdened.

Another disadvantage of having dogs of various sizes in a team with tandem harness is that, if it becomes necessary at any time for them to swim, the rear dogs, if large and therefore faster swimmers, will overtake and bunch up with the ones ahead. (The occasion for swimming is chiefly in spring when you sledge over sea ice.)

RATIONS

Fresh meat of any kind is the best food for dogs. They will eat parts of an animal that men do not—entrails, for instance, and bones.

It is the best practice to feed the dogs as long as you feed yourself, for the speed of a sledging party depends on the strength of the dogs. If you are not motivated by feelings of humanity, you should at least be aware of the poor economy of hoarding food to the disadvantage of your team when speed is the thing to be desired.

EMERGENCY RATIONS

In an emergency, dogs can be fed worn skin boots, skin clothing and hides.

PEMMICAN

Dog pemmican requires careful supervision in the packing, since the packers, who do not know the conditions under which it is used, are not always careful to stick to specifications. Often they put in too high a percentage of lean and of salt. Dogs fed on such pemmican suffer from excessive thirst, develop symptoms of starvation, and in some cases become pronouncedly ill, doubtless either from "protein poisoning" or as a result of the saltiness.

In Peary's view the proper composition of dog pemmican is one-half dried lean meat and one-half fat. Stefansson believes that, if they receive it every day, dogs will not overeat of fat any more than a man will, so he prefers one-third of a pound of lean and all the fat (e. g., seal blubber) the dog wants. This, he believes, will come to less than a pound per day total for a 60- or 70-pound well-furred dog—the kind of dog Peary used. No salt or other ingredient should be added.

TIME OF FEEDING

Opinions differ as to how often a dog should be fed, but probably once a day is best—in the evening, not when you stop but after the dogs have been tied (if they are going to be) and when you are yourself ready to call it a day. The dogs will then curl up and go to sleep. They have, true enough, done this when you stopped to camp and have slept till you are ready to unhitch them; but if you feed them at that time they sort of resent being disturbed when you come to the unhitching. (It may be partly imagination, but many drivers agree that the procedure just outlined is psychologically and physiologically advantageous.)

There are drivers who give a small feed in the morning and a big one in the evening, and there are others who give a snack every few hours; but all agree that a big feed in the morning or during the day decreases a dog's efficiency—makes him lazy.

FOOD PREJUDICES; HOW AND WHEN TO OVERCOME THEM

Dogs brought up around ships and used to foraging in slop pails will eat any food that is offered them. The conclusion is that a dog already used to many sorts of food does not mind eating one sort more.

Dogs brought up on a diet restricted to two or three articles will, if they are more than a year old, always at first refuse when an entirely new food is offered to them. This prejudice is stronger the older the dog, and probably stronger in females than in males.

A dog's objection to new food is apparently based on the sense of smell—if a strange meat offered is high enough so that the putrefaction smell completely hides the native smell, then the dog will eat it. In other words, all rotten meats smell substantially alike and are, therefore, recognized as a familiar diet; while any new kind of fresh meat offends the dog through its strange smell.

New litters of pups should be fed many varieties of meat so that they will not acquire food prejudices. Older dogs should be broken of their prejudices as quickly as possible so that your whole team shall consist of animals that will eat whatever food is available.

The first procedure is to offer the unfamiliar meat again and again, feeding no other. You may have to do this for 3 or 4 days before any of your dogs touch it. They will then start eating, in the order of their age, the youngest being the first to give in. The oldest dog may fast as much as 2 weeks. (Stefansson reports one old dog which apparently would have died on hunger strike rather than eat fresh goose.) The procedure can be shortened by feeding decayed pieces of the strange meat at first, and later pieces that are fresher and fresher. It is also possible, if time is not ample for breaking in, to induce dogs to eat a new meat by dipping the pieces in seal oil—the smell of the oil hiding that of the meat.

METHODS OF HARNESSING

On hitching dogs to sledges there is historically little reason to follow Eskimos. For there are few if any parts of their territories where they had large dog teams until after white men began to influence them, so they do not have in this respect the advantage of a weeding out of mistakes through long-continued processes of trial and error.

GREENLAND OR FAN METHOD

The Greenland or fan method of hitching dogs to a sledge seems to have developed when people who were used to attaching one or two dogs to a sled almost any old way found themselves using many dogs. They would then at haphazard attach them each with a separate trace. Later, no doubt, came the development of having a longer trace on the best trained dog so that he would become the leader.

ADVANTAGE

The chief advantage of the fan method, as usually given, is freedom of movement. This would seem to be an advantage chiefly from the dog's point of view.

411

DISADVANTAGE

The disadvantages of the fan method are that the traces become tangled, that the dogs get in each other's way and start fighting, that the dogs may go on opposite sides of an obstruction, snagging the sledge, and that they pull at various angles, the efficiency being decreased as the angle increases.

HITCHING TO A SINGLE TOW LINE

The method of hitching alternately to a single tow line was developed at the Mackenzie River and some other places. This gives considerable freedom but has the disadvantage that all dogs except the leader pull at some angle from the straight ahead, so that force is wasted. Another disadvantage is that when there are many dogs in the team, say nine or over, they are strung out excessively far ahead, making it bad when you turn a corner.

The method of hitching in pairs, with a single dog out ahead, seems to have been developed chiefly in western Alaska, and no doubt by whites or under their influence. Their analogy was from pairs of horses. In some cases whiffle trees were used as on horse wagons, in others the dogs were attached to the tow line by shorter individual lines. The advantage over the Mackenzie method is that large teams do not string out so far. The disadvantage is that in each pair the dogs pull away from each other, to a certain extent wasting their strength.

THESE THREE METHODS WORTHLESS IN FOREST OR BRUSH

All these three methods are bad at sea among very rough ice and worthless in a forest or among bushes. For the dogs are continually snagged. In a forest the only method to use is tandem, the dogs working one ahead of the other between traces that extend the full length of the team. Each dog's harness is fastened to the traces by or in the vicinity of the collar.

The disadvantages are that freedom is interfered with in such a way as to decrease speed (but this is hardly significant except in racing) and that the rear dogs of the team are thrown out of line or jammed against obstructions when you turn a corner. Also, if there is a long team and they go over a ridge, a downward strain from the front dogs will press those toward the rear down to the ground or compel them to carry a heavy back load at the same time as they pull. Conversely, if they cross a hollow, the dogs in the middle and aft portion of the team will be lifted up, sometimes completely off their feet. These latter difficulties are significant only in long teams. Tandem teams should therefore be short. Some notable journeys have been made with as many as six or seven dogs tandem, but four or five should usually be the limit. In a forest three big dogs make a good team on a toboggan.

The tandem method, with teams of not more than five dogs, is well suited to rough sea ice where the danger of snagging is next after that of a forest. For sea ice journeys big dogs should be hitched tandem and small ones either Mackenzie or western Alaska style. One of Stefansson's tandem teams, averaging well over a hundred pounds in weight and running up to 140 pounds per dog, hauled an average of more than 240 pounds per dog more than 20 miles per day. With other methods of hitching and smaller dogs, few expeditions over broken sea ice have averaged 100 pounds. Some have averaged around 60.

HARNESS

Harness for all methods but the tandem are simple to make and sort of logical. You will develop them from your own common sense when the need arises. Supplies for harness making should include webbing of several widths of the standard types carried by wholesalers who trade with Alaska.

The harness should be tailor-made for each dog. The essential is the collar which must not be small enough to choke him or big enough to slip back on his shoulders. Roughly it is shaped like the collar of a man's ordinary business suit, where the top coat buttons corresponds to a place between the dog's forelegs. From that point there should be a single strap far enough to clear the forelegs; then two straps will come up to meet about the middle of the dog's back. There they connect with a single strap that comes from the collar at the back of his neck and continues backward to somewhere near his croup where it fastens on to the individual trace by which he is attached to the tow line. That is the simplest and more or less Eskimo style. Whites perhaps secure somewhat more efficiency by not having one strap running along the back but rather two straps along the sides of the dog—the idea no doubt borrowed from horse harness.

Dog harness for tandem use is almost necessarily a great deal like horse harness. There is a round, stiff but padded collar. The two traces run from the sides of the collar to back of the dog's forelegs where there is a band around his body, again as in horse harness. The belly band is fastened with buckle or toggle. At side points of the back-and-belly band the individual harness is attached to the two main traces.

When you are outfitting you will buy your supplies from those dealers who professionally outfit dog drivers and you will get things more or less made up. You will be justified in taking the dealer's advice, at least to a certain extent. In emergencies you will make up this type of harness, like the other types, out of whatever you have.

Raw skins are well enough for harness as long as they keep dry. Such harness, if not eaten during the winter, will rot in the spring unless you dry it carefully after each use. Dogs when hungry may chew anything and those not so very hungry may eat not only rawhide as rawhide but also canvas harness if it smells like food through being greasy. Then you lose not only the harness but also the dog, for canvas in pieces of any considerable size will stick in his entrails. Tanned leather has several advantages: It does not rot easily, it does not seem like food to dogs, and does not kill dogs if they do eat it.

CHAIN HARNESS

You can protect your harness and the towline by having them of light chain wound or sewn in with lampwick or canvas. Chains naturally cannot be used for the collar or any part of the harness that presses hard on the dog, for they would bruise and chafe him.

414

If you figure on making tandem harness, you should have along with you for stiffening the collars iron rods a little less thick than a lead pencil. Wood is lighter, perhaps hickory which by steaming or otherwise can be bent into bows.

BELLS

The use of bells on dog harness is for ornament, sentiment and swank. The only time dogs pull better under the influence of bells is when they hear them from another team, and then only under conditions of surprise or other keen interest.

PACKS

On summer hunts the dogs are equipped with pack saddles, consisting essentially of two big pouches that reach about to the knee on either side of the animal when the pack is in place. These pack saddles are loaded with the heaviest and least bulky things. A fifty-pound dog will carry a thirty-pound pack or even heavier and he will carry it all day, although his walking gait is rather slow, perhaps not much over 2 miles an hour. The people of the party carry on their backs the bulky things, such as bedding, tents, and cooking utensils.

In some cases the dogs can carry at least a part of the bedding. It is tolerably safe when the packs are heavily ballasted with meat or some such thing, in which case the bedding can be tied in small bundles on top of the dogs' backs.

In traveling with pack dogs in summer, however, it must be remembered that they often lie down deliberately in water to cool themselves off, in which case the entire load gets wet.

LOADS CARRIED

As said, a team of big dogs, hitched tandem, can haul an average of more than 240 pounds per dog more than 20 miles a day. The Nome (pair) hitching and the Mackenzie will give intermediate results. Dogs hitched fanwise may pull no more than 150 pounds each.

In figuring on the load for a team you remember that intense cold will increase the hauling strain or weight. At

415

—50° or —60° the grains of snow have (or some think they have) angles sharp and hard enough to act on the steel shoeing of the sledges somewhat as grains of sand would. No laboratory experiments have been conducted, but, as said elsewhere, it is likely that a drop in temperature from 10° above zero to 50° below increases by at least three times the strain put on the dogs in pulling a given load.

It is unfair to the dogs and unwise policy to ride on a sledge. If they can haul you on top of the rest of the load 25 miles a day, they can perhaps haul the load without you 30 or 35 miles. No man should be engaged in Arctic work who is unable to walk as many miles a day as his dogs are able to haul his sledge and camp gear.

REST PERIODS

On journeys the Indians of the northern Canadian woods stop to smoke pipes at regular intervals, say, 2 hours apart. Then the dogs curl up to rest. In sea travel you frequently come to ridges of ice where you have to make a road with pickaxes, or at least have to search about for a way, and that gives the team a rest. Opinions differ as to how frequently you should stop on purpose to rest dogs. In the Alaska races teams have gone 2 or 3 days without a single stop, day or night. On the Stefansson expedition, when dogs were making 3 or 4 miles an hour pulling more than 200 pounds each, they seemed to be indifferent to rest, went steadily ahead for any number of hours, say, 4, 5, or 6. When this team stopped, it showed no particular fatigue. The dogs would either stand around or lie in alert positions.

WHEN NOT TO REST DOGS

It can hardly be amiss, however, to rest a team under ordinary conditions for a few minutes every 2 or 3 hours. But under one condition, resting a team is dangerous—when you know they are tired but when you nevertheless feel bound to reach a certain place before camping. If you let tired dogs lie down they apparently become stiff, really; certainly they hate to pull. So don't rest a very tired team unless you are prepared to stop long enough to give them a chance to recover from fatigue. Two or three hours might do this, but 20 or 30 minutes would not.

TEST OF TRAVELING WEATHER

As stated earlier, whether your dogs will or will not face the wind is the test of fit and unfit traveling weather in the Arctic. If you try to force them on, they will curl up with their noses in their tails, in spite of anything you can do. In a snowstorm their eyes fill with snow, and you will either have to keep freeing their eyes from it, or else you will have to go ahead dragging the dogs. Your sledge will upset, and the dogs will curl up; the process must be started all over once the sledge is righted.

USE OF DOGS IN HUNTING

Seals.—If the mauttok method of hunting seals is used, the help of dogs is indispensable. This method is described in Chapter 13.

Bears.—If, from yelping of dogs or otherwise, you have reason to believe that a bear is approaching, your first concern should be to see that your dogs are securely tied. It is the nature of dogs to set upon the bear, and it frequently happens that dogs are injured or killed by stray shots while the bear has walked away unscathed. (The use of dogs for bears is described in the section on Hunting, Chapter 13.)

Caribou.—Dogs will fly after caribou whenever they see or smell them. You will need to keep a firm grip on your sledge. Dogs carrying packs have been known to dash off, pack and all, sometimes returning after days but more often not returning; for a pack may come off in such a way as to drag on the ground while still fast to the dog's neck. Some dogs will then bite themselves loose; others do not, and remain tethered until they starve to death. Remember, in this connection, that northern dogs are not, as a rule, as good as ours in finding their own way home. This is no doubt because their owners are continually on the move and the dog does not get used to a permanent home.

Wolves.—It is not safe to leave a camp without a man on guard. So long as it is unguarded it is at the mercy of wolves, whether there are dogs or not. Dogs do not have the sense to stay in the camp and attempt to protect it, but will give chase to wolves. In a fight there can be no doubt of the outcome. Dogs may be of the same size as the wolves but they have neither the swiftness nor the cunning. Wolves do not allow themselves to be overtaken by dogs unless they are numerous enough to get the best of the fight.

TRUSTING TO DOGS FOR DIRECTION

A corollary to the above statement, that most northern dogs are not used to permanent homes, is that it is futile to give a dog his head and expect him to bring you to camp. It may be fatal, for it has been recorded that parties following dogs (which they thought were guides) have passed within a hundred yards of a camp without noticing it. By the time you realize the dog is not bringing you home, you may not be able to form any idea yourself of what direction to take.

The exceptions to the above rule are two: A dog may take you to camp along a trail he can smell (but he has an even chance to go wrong each time the trail forks), and a dog will take you home up the wind (but this applies only if you know you are directly to leeward, if the wind does not change on your way home, and if no trail he crosses interests him more—such as a fresh animal spoor).

Dogs, like bears, have been known to smell a camp 10 to 12 miles. They take you there, then, equally whether it is your own camp or some other.

As said above, dogs will follow trails. It is not safe to unhitch them near the place where you bought them, for they are apt to get homesick and to follow their own trails back.

METHOR OF HANDLING DOGS ON MOVING SEA ICE

It happens occasionally that a camp will be endangered through break-up of the floe on which it stands, and the campers must move to another floe. The shivering and crashing of ice may so paralyze the dogs with fear as to make them worse than useless. (See Section III, Chapter 11.)

In emergencies of this sort, the tandem system of harnessing is especially valuable. In the Nome type the dogs have too much freedom and are able to turn completely around and face the sledge. The fan system is even worse, for there each dog has complete freedom and can pull in any direction he likes.

HOUSING

There is no point, ordinarily, in housing dogs if they are well-furred and well-fed. To illustrate:

It was the custom of the Stefansson parties when traveling over sea ice to make on very cold days individual windbreaks for the dogs. Those which gratefully slept behind them were really too thin-furred—under ideal conditions you would not take that kind of dog with you at all. Most of the dogs were indifferent to the shelters and some used to climb on top of the (intendedly) sheltering wall and sleep there. Some dogs would do this even in the most trying weather that ever comes to the polar sea, temperatures of −20° or −30° with a fairly strong wind. (If the weather is colder than that you hardly ever have wind.)

Some dogs when loose will come voluntarily to sleep in the alleyway of your house but the motive is more likely to be a desire for companionship or the hope of food than a search for warmth.

However, at least a small saving in food can be effected, even with a well-furred dog, by housing him. The barn should not be warm, for if it is, filth will develop and contagious diseases, should there be any, will spread more rapidly. A dog barn should be almost as cold as outside, protecting the animals merely from wind. But that in itself is a good deal of protection. In a barn, each dog should have a separate stall, or at least they should be tied as described below.

METHODS OF TYING DOGS

Dogs have to be restrained to prevent fighting. It is probable that they seldom mean to start a fight but in the exuberance of play one will bite another too hard and then there is a scrap. The worst thing is that the whole bunch will pile on the under dog, perhaps injuring him so severely in less than a minute that he may need several days to recover. In another minute they perhaps would kill him.

Ordinarily, even at permanent camps, dogs are accordingly tied either to separate stakes or at intervals along a tie rope. Because some dogs will bite rope you use chains, and for the tie rope either a wire or a chain. The chains are long enough to give each dog individual freedom of movement, and not long enough so he can reach the next dog. There should be a swivel in the dog's individual rope; otherwise he will kink it up, even to the point of choking himself—better have two swivels at opposite ends of his rope for he may lie on one and get it so iced up from melted snow that it will not work.

If there is nothing permanent available for fastening, the ends of the tie rope are usually anchored with deadmen in the snow. On ice you can fasten the ends by digging two parallel trenches a few inches apart and then perforating the ice partition. Such toggles are very strong. They are used by Eskimos, for instance, in hauling a whale out of water onto level ice. A toggle in a partition no more than 4 inches thick will therefore stand a strain of several hundred pounds, and probably several thousand.

NOISE OF FIGHTING TRANSMITTED THROUGH ICE

As described in the section on snow houses, a snow camp on ice is so soundproof that the barking and snarling of fighting dogs outside can seldom be heard. Their spurning of the snow and tumbling about, however, is plainly audible, especially if you are lying in bed with your ear not far from the ice. Such fights must be stopped promptly, as said above, and can be stopped in from 30 seconds to 2 minutes. For such (very necessary) promptness you must dash out unclad if you have been sleeping naked, and you should do this *via* a door that is never shut—both these things are discussed elsewhere in this Manual.

Healthy mongrel dogs have a great deal of resilience. If, in emergencies, they are thin and weak from long-endured hunger, they recover quickly when you are able to feed them fresh meat. As outlined under food prejudices, it is important that your team is broken so that they will eat this fresh meat, whatever kind it happens to be.

FROSTBITE

A frozen flank may incapacitate a dog. It is difficult there to heal a sore, for the skin stretches with every step the dog takes. The only chance after a severe frost injury is to give the animal a rest for several days, preferably to confine him, best of all inside your own house. This is certainly no more difficult or objectionable in many cases up North than it is to keep a house dog in a city.

If the dog's own flanks are insufficiently protected with fur, a piece of skin (say caribou) is suspended under the belly, cut to fit, and tied with strings over the dog's back. This must be taken off at camp time and, preferably, should be taken off during the day every time the team stops to rest, for a dog never freezes his flanks except when walking. When at rest he curls up.

The reasons for removing the blanketing skin when you make even a short halt are two: The dog may eat the skin if you are not watching him—he may not be starving but his appetite is good. If he does not eat the skin he will lie on it, melting the snow and making it wet. The snow that melts may be chiefly what is between the protecting skin and his body.

PROTECTION OF FEET

Under some conditions (as, for instance, when a thin film of ice has formed over snow, whether or not snow has again fallen on this shell of ice) dogs break through the snow and get sharp angular pieces between their toes. The toes will bleed and the pads will be sore and raw. In such case it is the practice to use boots on the dogs. These are made preferably of canvas, without much shape (somewhat like a mitten without a thumb) and will serve 1 day, if this is spring travel over needle ice (q. v.) or several days if it is winter travel on snow. If the dog wears a hole in one side in the forenoon, you change the boot so that the use comes on the

421

other side in the afternoon. Seal and caribou skin boots have the advantage of longer wear but the disadvantage that the dogs will eat them unless constantly watched.

HYDROPHOBIA

Hydrophobia is practically absent from the Arctic. However, there are other diseases the nature and origin of which are obscure.

ARCTIC DISEASES

It is impossible to count on the length of a polar dog's life. Peary's dogs worked hard on almost nothing to eat, withstood exposure to the worst storms, and then, with plenty to eat and little to do, would be suddenly taken with a malady which he calls *piblokto*. The victim of this disease refuses all nourishment and howls and snaps, biting any other dog it comes in contact with, dies in convulsion frequently the same day it is attacked.

In Kane's second expedition, only 6 dogs survived (of 44) a disease which ended in lockjaw. Kane describes the malady as "clearly mental." The dogs, unlike Peary's, ate voraciously, retained their strength, and slept well, but "They bark frenziedly at nothing and walk in straight and curved lines with anxious and unwearying perseverance. They fawn on you, but without seeming to appreciate the notice you give them in turn; pushing their heads against your person or oscillating with a strange pantomime of fear. * * * Sometimes they remain for long hours in moody silence, and then start off howling as if pursued."

At Cape Kellett, Stefansson's dogs began to die one by one. In some cases it was the fattest and youngest, in others the oldest and most decrepit. Stefansson isolated the dogs and this may have helped, but one or two died that apparently never had any contact with those that were diseased.

CONCLUSIONS ABOUT DISEASE

Peary made no conclusion about the cause of the disease, but in buying dogs he allowed for 60 percent probably dying from accident or illness. Kane made the conclusion that absence of light accounted for the malady by which his dogs died. Stefansson noted that his expeditions never lost any dogs that had been living on caribou or other land game, but only dogs that had been living on seal.

J. Baashuus-Jessen, after a study of the published accounts of polar explorers, believes that what resembles rabies is not true rabies because he can find no instance where the disease was transmitted by bite to man or beast. He concludes that the trouble is caused by a deficiency of fat in the diet. He adds that apparently all fats are not alike as preventatives, for Peary had bad results from feeding his dogs on pork, whereas he attained good results when they were fed walrus meat. (This conclusion is the opposite of Stefansson's; for caribou-fed dogs get little fat and there is plenty of fat available whenever men or dogs are living on seals—as explained, earlier, when you secure enough seals to give you all the lean you need you have fat to throw away.)

DANGER IN CAMP FROM OILY RAGS

There is one usually little-considered danger to a dog in camp, that he will in some manner get hold of a piece of rag which you have been using in connection with animal fat or other food. Getting the food smell he will bolt the rag; it cannot pass through his intestines and he will die. You must therefore be careful to keep well out of a dog's reach any cloth, cotton waste, or the like, which has animal fat or other food smell on it.

WHIPS

It is probably true, though debated, that Eskimos had no whips until they were introduced by Europeans. The use of the whip among Eskimos first developed in Greenland where they have associated with Europeans for nearly a thousand years. Indeed they began intermarrying with Europeans nearly that long ago.

In the Mackenzie River delta there were as late as 1906 only a few young men who used whips. The practice met the disapproval of the older generation; it was considered one of the signs that the young people were a degenerate lot.

423

Around Coronation Gulf in 1910 whips were unusued and appeared unknown. By 1918 they were in nearly universal use around the mouth of the Mackenzie; they had been in use earlier, back to varying dates, in different parts of Alaska. In Coronation Gulf their use did not become usual until perhaps 1925.

A good many of the best white Alaska drivers use no whips and on some expeditions, such as those of Stefansson, they were not used except for stopping dog fights. For this they were always carried, however; for you are more likely to stop a fight without injury to the dog if you use a whip than if you use a club.

COMMON TREATMENT OF DOGS

One of the things to which a person of any feeling or imagination does not soon grow callous is the cruelty and thoughtlessness with which dogs are treated by the northern forest Indians and by many whites—also increasingly by civilized Eskimos. It is a common thing that they are not fed all summer; some therefore die of starvation, while most of them survive only as living skeletons until the approach of fall makes it necessary to feed them up for their winter's work. On the Mackenzie River some white men treat dogs better than the average native, but a dog used to uniform kindness is seldom found. Expecting a kick, they will receive your approach with a snarl. Stefansson bought some of these dogs and found that, even after this sort of upbringing, most of them quickly became under kind treatment as friendly as our usual house dogs. One of them, 4 years old, did require half a year before he became reasonably gentle.

If you are fond of house dogs you will like good northern dogs even more. They have the same loyalty; in addition they work for you uncomplainingly even when they are tired and hungry.

COMPARISON OF PONIES WITH DOGS

Peary argues that even if a pony is equivalent in tractive force and weight to a team of 10 dogs, you should still use dogs. His reasons are: Fewer ponies required but each dead one is a greater percentage loss; ponies break through ice where the dispersed weight of 10 dogs will enable them to cross; dogs live on meat, bulky food must be carried for ponies; dogs need no assistance on the march, no care or shelter at camps. Stefansson comments, without disagreeing with Peary, that there is more to the story. Ponies can live on meat (do so in Iceland); on land they will scrape away snow and find grass underneath, being in that nearly equal to reindeer.

Section V

REINDEER

In Section II, Chapter 5, we have dealt with the reindeer as an important source of food supply and as a source of material for clothing for civil or military establishments in Alaska. Here we discuss their value as draft and pack animals.

Reindeer are the gentlest of all domestic animals—do not become vicious or pugnacious after the manner of rams and bulls. The danger of stampede is about the same as with horses, probably somewhat less. In good reindeer country— most any part of the prairie, or in clear and semiclear patches of wood—a large number of pack reindeer would require about as much grazing area per head as horses would in nonmeadow portions of a Montana range.

USE BY ALASKANS

As stated earlier, in Alaska there is at present little utilization of reindeer as draft and pack animals, although 2 decades ago considerable use was made of them. However, as colonization advances and defense operations are increased in the Territory, more and more reindeer will no doubt be used for draft purposes. They will do work corresponding to that of mules, winter or summer—they are adapted to the terrain; large deer, such as some of those in Alaska, can carry from 100 to 150 pounds each; they graze and browse where they go, so there is no need to carry feed for them.

In the Finnish-Russian campaign the Finns demonstrated their value in Arctic and sub-Arctic military operations. In addition to transporting supplies, reindeer were found useful in ambulance work. One beast, attached by a single trace to a toboggan sort of sled, could transport a wounded soldier through a pathless forest with comparatively great speed.

Although the breeding stock which established the Alaska reindeer industry came from Siberia, the methods of handling came from Norway. For the U. S. Government imported a number of Norwegian Lapp families to instruct the Eskimos of Alaska in herding and other utilization, including the technique of driving. We describe the Lapp technique as practiced both in the Old World and, with some modification, in Alaska. In the main we depend on a manuscript by Arnold Haverlee who has made several journeys in Lapland, traveling and living with reindeer Lapps.

HARNESS

The most common harness is a simple leather collar resting on the shoulders and running around the neck of the deer. A rope tied to the lower part of this collar passes between the legs and under the belly of the deer to the sleigh where it is fastened to the bow. The rein is a single line fastened to the left antler, its other end is wound around the right arm and hand of the driver, so that if the harness should break the driver is still able to hold on to the deer. To check the speed of the sleigh the Lapps sometimes have another deer tied to the back of it. This is especially effective when going down hill where the sleigh has a tendency to exceed the speed of the deer that is pulling it. On long trips this second deer may be put in the lead for relief. Ordinary distances covered on long journeys are said in Norway to be 30 or 40 miles daily when 1 passenger uses 2 reindeer alternately. There is an apparently reliable report that a distance of 112 English miles was covered in 26 hours.

SLEIGHS

The sleigh most popular among the Lapps is called the *akja* (pronounced akya), a Gothic word; in pure Lappish it is *kerres*. This is an open sleigh made of thin planks, shaped a bit like an Indian canoe. It is approximately 5 feet long,

1 foot deep, and 18 inches wide, with a sharp bow and a square stern. The driver, on a reindeer skin at the bottom of the sleigh, sits in an upright position, his back resting against the sternboard, his legs stretched out along the bottom of the sleigh.

PULKA TYPE

While the kerres is the most common sleigh for transporting goods and people, several other types, of Finnish inspiration, may be found among the Lapp tribes. Of these the *pulka* is the most popular and is used only for human transportation. It is built on the same principle as the kerres but shows much finer workmanship and sometimes is adorned with designs. The front part is often covered with sealskin. This sleigh is used by families for special occasions, such as going to church or other formal functions. The harness used, though on the same simple principle, may be highly adorned, i. e., made of white reindeer skin onto which have been sewn red, green, and yellow strips of cloth and in some cases bells and silver buttons. To climax the effect a white reindeer is used for pulling.

The word pulka or pulk is Finnish but has been widely adopted among the Lapps who often use it in describing any type of sleigh.

LAKKEK TYPE

A characteristic and also most purely Lappish sleigh is called the *lakkek*. It is used only for the transportation of goods and provisions. It is a covered sleigh made of thin planks slightly curved, approximately the same length and width as the kerres but somewhat deeper. A square or oval opening is cut in the center of the top and through this the load, among natives frequently frozen or salted meat, is tightly packed. A lid fits the opening snugly.

CARAVAN TRAVEL

The lakkek and the kerres are the two sleighs which are most characteristic in the making of a *raid* (caravan). A raid may consist of just a few sleighs or dozens of them, according to the size of the family and distance they are moving. The raid moves slowly, led by a Lapp on skis. The other Lapps walk alongside. Only women and children ride. The daily distance covered is seldom over 12 miles. If two or more raids are moving in the same direction the custom is to overlap, so that the last one to start will pass the camp site of the preceding raid, stop for a short rest and continue on ahead to pitch camp. On the following move the raid now left behind will pass the camp site of the other, stop for a rest and in turn proceed ahead for another camp, and so on till the destination is reached. In this way each party has its fair share of breaking trail, if the snow is soft and deep. When stopping for the night the deer are let loose to shift for themselves and feed. In the morning they are rounded up and the trip continues.

PACKS

The reindeer is also used for transportation in summer. The Lapps have not adopted the idea of the wheel and carriages are unknown among them, even in terrain where fairly level ground might have made them of value. The transportation of goods during summer is therefore by pack animals. Babies are carried in baskets strapped to the sides of the deer. Great care is taken that weights are evenly balanced on the two sides of the deer. Sometimes a broad strap is used around the body holding a reindeer skin or blanket in position over the back and down both sides. Lapp reindeer are perhaps the smallest of any of the domestic deer, so that 80 pounds in all, 40 on each side, is considered a maximum load.

Haverlee described a journey which gives an idea of the small Lapp reindeer as a pack animal. They were traveling in very mountainous country, each beast carrying 80 pounds. On a 25-mile march they stopped only once and then for only half an hour. In spite of some steep climbing the reindeer showed no signs of fatigue, during the journey or at its end. (Alaska reindeer, being partly of the large Tungus stock and having interbred somewhat with the large Alaska caribou, may be expected to do somewhat better.)

Alaska and northwestern Arctic Canada are the only reindeer countries where driving them is not extensively practiced. Across Bering Strait in Siberia, whether you follow southwest toward Kamchatka or west along the Arctic shore toward and beyond the Kolyma, you will find everywhere people used to driving reindeer, and many animals that have been trained.

USE OF THE PACK REINDEER BY PROSPECTORS

An effective use of reindeer has been made in Alaska by prospectors, especially those searching for gold in the Brooks Range or to the north of it. Formerly, these prospectors carried their own packs, in some cases using dogs. There were prospectors, too, who used horses as pack animals. These did well, except that they were driven crazy by the mosquitoes and other biting insects.

The reindeer were not as much troubled by the mosquitoes as the horses, and were taller than the dogs and thus able to keep their pack loads out of water and mud. They had the great superiority over dogs that they secured their own food; in this they were to a degree superior to the horses also, especially in the high mountains where (although not in the low country) lichens and mosses were sometimes found to be the chief vegetation.

Thawed Arctic ground is always a swamp. The feet of the reindeer did not sink in as deep as those of the horses. However, neither horse nor reindeer would be in danger of being properly mired in an Arctic country, except perhaps right along the shore of a river, for elsewhere the ground frost would usually be only a few inches, and at most 2 feet, below the surface.

EMERGENCY USE OF UNTRAINED ANIMALS

If you should find yourself in a community of reindeer-owning Eskimos, even though they are not accustomed to the use of reindeer as pack or draft animals, you should with no great difficulty be able to adapt one or another of the Lapp methods to your needs. From canvas or skins you can rig up some sort of harness and sleigh. Breaking a reindeer to pull a sleigh, or to carry a load, would not compare in difficulty or in the time required to breaking a Western bronco. For, as said, reindeer are naturally gentle animals. With patience in accustoming them to their new function and with ingenuity in putting together a makeshift harness and toboggan-like sleigh, or the even simpler pack harness, it should not be more than a few days before you can set out on a journey.

CHAPTER 13

HUNTING AND FISHING

SECTION I

GENERAL

a. Introductory

It is a safer emergency plan now than ever before to live in the Arctic by hunting; under certain circumstances it may be as necessary to do so now as it ever has been.

Wilkins has said that there is no point on the ice-covered surface of the Polar Sea from which he does not believe he could walk out to the nearest settlement if he had one good companion, good clothes, an adequate hunting outfit, and a sled or the means of constructing a sled—as, for instance, from portions of an airplane in which he had made a safe landing. This is probably right, especially if you postulate that there should be one dog—not a trained dog necessarily—but one with a keen sense of smell for use in the mauttok hunting method, described below in this chapter.

The journey to a settlement from a descent in a central region of the Arctic pack might require 2 years, or two winter seasons with an intervening idle summer. The danger would be greatest if the descent were made somewhere between

Greenland and the Franz Josef Islands, for it might be difficult to move rapidly enough to west or east to reach land before the ice was carried south into the warm waters to the north of Iceland, melting from under the travelers.

There seems little doubt that, for men skilled in hunting and properly equipped, the Arctic sea is safer than most Arctic lands, so far as securing food and fuel is concerned. However, it averages farther from a sea landing to a settlement; besides, you might have to cross some Arctic lands after having managed the journey ashore.

Although there are more European settlements now in Arctic lands than there were a hundred years ago, there is probably a less total number of people, at least in the Canadian and Alaskan sectors, for white men's diseases have killed off many of the natives that used to live here and there on the northern lands, and many of the rest have been drawn to rivers and seacoasts by the influence of whites, so that the lessened chance of finding encampments of natives more than cancels the greater chance of finding whites. This is, of course, assuming that lack of radio, or radio failure, has made it impossible to send out information on the position of a stranded party so as to arrange for relief.

Game is on the polar sea about what it "always" has been. On the polar lands it seems likely that game is more abundant now than it was a hundred years ago, for the diseases and other white man influences which have depopulated large sections of Arctic territory have thereby removed the hunters that used to kill thousands and tens of thousands of caribou and other game animals. The second enemy of the caribou, the wolf, has probably decreased in numbers, also; the primitive caribou hunter was not much of a wolf hunter, but trappers of recent years have been killing a great many wolves, particularly in the northern edge of the forest. With fewer wolves, there are more caribou.

We said it was easier now to make a living by hunting than it used to be. This is partly because on the average game is more abundant; but a greater reason is that hunting appliances are constantly being improved. The musket was better than the bow and arrow, if the user was an equally good hunter. The breech-loading black-powder rifle was better

432

than the musket. The modern rifle using .22, .25 or .30 caliber bullets, with a muzzle velocity of perhaps 3,000 feet per second, is a great improvement on the 45–70 or 40–82 Winchesters that were standard at the turn of the century. Then there has been an improvement in field glasses, and they are second only to the rifle in the equipment of a caribou hunter—important, too, in the equipment of a seal hunter.

LONG RANGE MILITARY CRAFT SHOULD CARRY HUNTING EQUIPMENT AND CAMP GEAR

In the event of a war on a grand scale, involving the polar sea and the Arctic lands, there are bound to be every now and then cases of an airplane that comes down for want of gas or through engine trouble; cases, too, of men who bail out. As many as possible of these should have, to begin with, the necessary information and skill; and then some practical minimum equipment that will enable them to live indefinitely in a given locality without travel, waiting in that case for rescue; or that will enable them to subsist while they travel in the direction of some possible or probable source of help. (See also Chapter 14.)

b. Principles

ON SEA ICE PARTIES SHOULD KEEP TOGETHER

On sea ice that is not landfast, parties of no matter what size must always keep together unless numbers and policy indicate that they ought to separate into two or more groups permanently or semipermanently. For not even the strongest paleocrystic floe is immune to cracking and the formation of a lead. If this forms between different members of a party they will of course attempt crossing so as to reunite, using any of the methods we have described for that purpose or others which they devise. But it can be that no methods will suffice and that the parties will not find each other again, even if both survive.

ON LAND PARTIES SHOULD NOT KEEP TOGETHER

On land the contrary principle applies—the rule is that parties should separate, or spread out, for greater probability of success in finding game. If all men are carrying packs there is no reason why each should not take his own way to an agreed-upon rendezvous; if there is a sledge, or other reason why some of the men have to cooperate in transportation, then one or more free men can hunt parallel to the course. There should be, of course, arrangements for communication by signal. What these will be depends on circumstances; men of sufficient ingenuity to have a chance for survival at all will devise communication methods that are suitable for each day or situation.

Living by hunting was practiced more extensively on the third Stefansson expedition than has otherwise been the case in the entire history of Arctic journeys by white men. For an estimated 20,000 miles of his own travel afoot, whether accompanied by sledges or not, at least half the distance covered both on sea and land depended exclusively on hunting for the food and fuel of men and dogs when at sea, and for food though not fuel when on land. Then there were many separate parties, as, for instance, when a dozen people made a living while resident most of a year in Melville Island and again when four men drifted for 6 months in a floe encampment at varying distances of 200 and 300 miles north of Alaska, depending for themselves and about 20 dogs exclusively on game.

Accordingly, we shall in the following discussion depend most exclusively upon the experience of the said expedition, and upon the views therefrom developed; but we shall mention the experience and views of others now and then to illustrate or to bring out disagreements.

We discuss first travel on land or along a coast.

On a journey dependent upon hunting it is standard practice for the men engaged in transport to travel as direct as possible toward a destination, and by the easiest routes possible. Arrangements should be made each morning for the probable location of the camp. During that length of winter day which permits the hunter about 20 miles of walking at three miles per hour, the transportation members of the party should travel perhaps 10 or 12 miles. It may be that during the day the hunter can see the sledging party, once or oftener; they will be more conspicuous than he. But the main thing is that camp shall be made in some such location that it can be found even in a blizzard, in a thick fog, or in the dark of a cloudy night. Instructions for finding camp under such conditions, and alternatively for passing a night in the open, have been given in Chapter 11. However, we stress here some elementary precautions.

ELEMENTARY PRECAUTIONS

Camping in a place easily found means, among other things, that camp must not be where there is any difficulty in distinguishing the meeting place of the sea ice and the land; nor may the camp be in toward the bottom of a deep bay.

On a coast the trail must close in to very prominent headland but should cut across the mouth of a bay as direct as convenient.

The hunter has a rough idea whether the sledges are ahead of him or behind. He goes to some promontory they should pass and picks up the trail; or determines from its absence that they have not passed. The campers, after dark, put a lantern outside, if they have one; if not, they burn tallow or oil dip within the camp so that the flame will show through. In foggy weather and in blizzards the camp cannot be seen more than a few yards, but even then it can usually be found; if it cannot be found, you merely have the tedium of passing a night in the open or in an unheated snowhouse which you build for yourself.

NUMBER OF HUNTERS TO A PARTY

For a journey of dependence on hunting, there ought to be at least two good hunters in a party of three. On many occasions two men will have to travel where the sledge can go while the third takes a different route to find game. In that case, and in all cases except emergencies, the best hunter, rather than the senior officer as such, should do the hunting. Nor can you afford to alternate men just from a sense of fairness, or to break the monotony; the journey is not sport but a serious undertaking where success, if not life and death, may be at issue. Several Arctic journeys have been made

435

where it was necessary to secure for food practically every animal seen. A slight increase in the percentage of failures would have been disastrous.

We said two good hunters out of three, which is because in most cases one man has to be at camp anyhow, doing such things as protecting the dogs in case a polar bear arrives or preventing fights where a dog may get maimed or killed. If there are no dogs, you need protection for the camp anyway, though not so badly. Anybody, whether a hunter or not, can kill a polar bear that is walking into camp, or stop a dog fight. It is, of course, best that all members should be good hunters; but from the angle just presented it is not essential.

That one good hunter for a party of three is not enough depends on the chance that he may be lost or disabled. For instance, on one of Stefansson's journeys he sprained a leg so that he could not walk for several weeks. At this time the party was depending exclusively on hunting. Had there not been a second hunter, the three travelers would have had to turn toward home and probably would not have made it, at least not without killing and eating most or all their dogs. Because all three were hunters they were able to continue the journey, traveling steadily away from home instead of retreating homeward. The sprained ankle did cause a loss of speed, since one of the three now had to ride on the sledge. But it did not otherwise interfere with safety or success.

CHOOSING MEN FOR HUNTERS

You choose comrades for a hunting journey both for physical and mental fitness, but the mental is the more important. For there are in the literature reports on men whose physical equipment was approximately perfect, who were both of athlete and sharpshooter rank, but who were unsuited for living by hunting because of a tendency to assume that game would not be found ahead and that the only safe and sensible thing was to retreat.

The man who thinks there is probably game beyond the first range of hills, or, if not there, then beyond the second or third, is the right one for your work. The man who knows that it would be a waste of time to go and look is wrong for this particular job, no matter how well he could do if he would try. The justified deduction from hunting retreat experience is that it averages as safe to advance as to retreat.

On the average, white hunters are better than natives. Where both know the country, both are good. In a strange land a white man has several resources which are missing from the native's equipment. For instance, an Eskimo is more likely than a white to decide there is no use hunting because game is certainly not going to be found. If safety is your main concern, the native is all right, for he will induce you to turn back in time; but if success is paramount, the white on the average is better.

With men equally qualified otherwise, patience should be a deciding factor in choosing hunters. Here the native is likely to excel, but there is no reason why an exceptional white man may not develop the same quality.

Perhaps the chief superiority of a white hunter over a native is in ability to find his way about. By timing himself carefully, by making either a written or mental record of all distances and angles of travel, the white man will frequently know just what direction to turn for home when the native is completely muddled.

The only important superiority of the native is that he is familiar with local conditions and not afraid of them; but this familiarity can be acquired by the white man, and fear will diminish as knowledge grows. Besides, you cannot make a very long journey without passing beyond your native guide's familiar ground.

c. Equipment and Its Care

RIFLES AND AMMUNITION

When you plan a long journey where men and dogs, or men without dogs, are to live by hunting, you must of necessity rely on big game. A cartridge weighing half an ounce fired from a rifle weighing 7 pounds may give you a thousand pounds of food by killing a polar bear; a 10-gauge shotgun shell weighing two ounces fired from a gun weighing about the same as the rifle would give you only a pound or two of food by killing a ptarmigan or a duck. Though never, except in emergencies, firing at an animal smaller than a wolf, the various Stefansson expeditions were able to average 100 pounds live-weight of animals per cartridge. These cartridges (6.5 mm. Mannlicher-Schoenauer) ran more than 30 to the pound. There has never been an actual competition of the man-miles and dog-miles involved, but a conservative estimate might be 50,000 man-miles, which would mean several hundred thousand dog-miles, perhaps one-quarter or one-fifth of all this on ice drifting above the sea out of sight of land, sometimes several hundred miles from shore.

The food average per cartridge was considerably better at sea than on land; and all those who took part in the expedition's various deep sea sledge journeys appeared in agreement that living by hunting is both easier when you are successful and more likely to be successful at sea than on shore.

The first principle of living by hunting is, then: Depend on big game.

The second principle is: Use one arm, though perhaps with varied ammunition. The main points of arming the whole party with a single type of weapon are, of course, that ammunition and spare parts are interchangeable, and that a damaged weapon can be dismembered into parts that will be useful for others.

TYPE OF RIFLE

In 1912 when the third Stefansson expedition was being outfitted, a study was made of rifles in the United States, Canada, and abroad. The one selected was Mannlicher-Schoenauer 6.5 mm., of Austrian manufacture but rechambered by Gibbs of London. The muzzle velocity claimed was 2,860 feet per second. The carbines weighed 6¼ pounds; with full rifle length a pound or so more. The carbines were full wood, to protect the hand from iron at low temperatures. For midwinter use such other parts as experience suggested were bound with adhesive tape to keep the hand from metal. Both ordinary and set triggers, for instance, were taped.

BULLETS—THREE TYPES

The three bullets carried by the Stefansson expedition were ordinary soft nose, hollow point, and full jacket. Experience showed that a thousand rounds would be ample for supporting a sledge party of three men and six dogs for 2 years. Of the 1,000, 800 were soft nose, 150 hollow point, and 50 full jacket. The full jackets were intended by the expedition for two purposes: to shoot a small animal in an emergency with something that would not mess it up too much, and to kill without too much mutilation animals the skins of which were wanted for scientific purposes.

VALUE OF DUMDUM QUESTIONABLE

The advisability of the 150 hollow points should not be insisted upon. They were carried in the belief that if you wanted to be extra sure of killing a medium-sized animal, such as a caribou, they would serve. Experience seemed to confirm this, for on caribou, at any rate, the hollow points had an explosive effect. Experience also appeared to show that for very large animals, if struck in certain parts, the hollow point bullet did not have sufficient penetration.

FLAT TRAJECTORY

A flat trajectory has a special importance under Arctic winter conditions; for, as explained elsewhere, it is difficult to judge distance even for those experienced, while an inexperienced man is nearly helpless.

We have dealt elsewhere with the general problem of diffused light; here we note some of the confusions that may result from it, and that are made somewhat less of a problem to a hunter if he carries a gun with a flat trajectory.

RELATION OF DIFFUSED LIGHT TO TRAJECTORY

It may seem incredible that in daylight so intense that the eyes have to be protected against it, objects not of a dark color are frequently invisible. McClintock points out that a snowclad hill with thawed ground on top does not

439

appear as a white hill with a black top, but only as a black horizontal line apparently suspended in the sky. This is because the daylight on cloudy days is so evenly diffused that no shadows are cast. When, in diffused light, a man is seen to walk behind a snowclad hill, his legs disappear without visible cause of eclipse and then his whole body. You infer the hill conceals him, but you cannot see it doing so. A snag of ice will be equally invisible until you stub your toe against it, though it may show then by contrast with your feet.

It sometimes happens, even on clear days, that things may be easily misidentified. Nordenskiold tells of mistaking a walrus for an island and of identifying the white tusks with two extensive glaciers coming down between mountain ranges to the coast. Hanbury tells of mistaking a mouse for a polar bear. On Stefansson's first expedition, officers and passengers on the Hudson Bay Company's boat *Wrigley* steamed toward what they thought was a stranded steamer but which proved to be a small log lying on a sand bar. He also records mistaking a marmot for a grizzly bear.

However, while diffused light may cause you to waste a rifle bullet on a mouse or squirrel when you think them polar bears or grizzly bears, and while you may waste other bullets that fall short of your target when you mistake a grizzly for a wolverine, your chief light difficulty in shooting, or the chief thing which makes a flat trajectory of paramount importance, is what we also dwelt on before and here recapitulate briefly—the "incredible" clearness of northern air, particularly at low temperatures.

If you do not know the size of your object, and have nothing for scale, you judge distance by clearness of outline and by what fine details you can see. We have described how an experienced traveler mistook a jagged peak 2,000 feet high for a broken ice hummock of 20 or 30 feet. You cannot make quite that much of a mistake with animals, for not even in the clear air we are describing can you see a bear or musk ox at 20 miles. But you can be sufficiently deceived by noting details of antlers and other fine markings or small parts of a caribou to conclude that an animal which is really 300 yards away is only 100. You are then a lot better off if your rifle drops a few inches in 300 yards and not two or three feet.

SIGHTS

Several types of extra sights were provided for each gun so that they might be varied according to the preference of each user and according to experience as it is accumulated in the field. In the main three sights turned out to be used—a bead front sight, a leaf sight on the barrel, and a peep sight back on the stock which folded out of the way and was seldom used. However, this was very convenient to have, for under certain conditions a hunter could take several aims at an animal, comparing the peep-sight effectiveness with that of the leaf sight before pulling the trigger.

It is difficult and perhaps impossible to lay down for choosing sights valuable directions beyond the above, for the variation is not merely in the kind of light and your angle to it but is also in the color of the animal, color of the terrain and in the varying conditions of the user's eyes. For instance, incipient snowblindness or an incomplete convalesence from it may give you a better effect now with one sight and now with another.

TELESCOPE SIGHTS

The rifles were also provided with telescope sights of 2.5 magnification. These were particularly useful when the sun was below the horizon for that power makes an excellent night glass. The telescopes were used at other times but the only occasions upon which they were practically indispensable were during the midwinter absence of the sun.

Where hunting is to supply all the food (at sea, all the fuel as well), you cannot afford to carry any arms but rifles if the journey is to be longer than 3 months. For a party of three or more there should be a rifle per man, while a party of two should carry three rifles in case one goes wrong or gets lost. A revolver is not worth carrying from the food provision point of view.

For a journey of less than 3 months, you can more or less carry what you like, a shotgun, for instance, or an extra rifle

441

which you think may have special use because of its caliber being either notably larger or smaller than that of the standard weapon.

FISHHOOKS AND FISH NETS

For long overland journeys you might perhaps carry some fishhooks, since they weight practically nothing, and a fish net or two. If nets are carried there must be extreme care both in keeping them dry before they are used and in drying them after each use. Otherwise they drop to pieces. There are examples in travel literature of difficulty and tragedy through the rotting of nets.

CARE OF HUNTING EQUIPMENT

For the summer period the care of northern hunting equipment needs little discussion, for precautions and methods are those to which we are used. In midwinter the treatment has to be very special on certain points.

IN WINTER DO NOT TAKE RIFLE INDOORS

You should never bring your rifle into house, tent, or camp of any kind. If through carelessness a rifle has been carried indoors, you must not rush it out again immediately, for the harm has been done in the first few seconds. In that case, take the rifle fairly near whatever heating arrangement you have. It will first get covered in every metal part with icing. This melts into water and you facilitate the drainage by suspending the gun upside down. If you can't do any better, dry the rifle thoroughly and then carry it out. Best of all, take it to pieces and wipe every part before putting it out again.

At the beginning of steady cold in the fall remove all grease. Take down your rifle, wipe every part carefully. Should you fear that you haven't quite the skill for this, use gasoline to eat up the oil; but doing so appears to have the drawback that it produces a tendency to rust. However, that need not worry you much, for it is scarcely possible that appreciable rust will take place, at least during the midwinter period of fairly steady and pronounced cold.

442

KEEP RIFLE IN CASE

Keep snow out of your rifle. You should always carry it in a case or else wrap something around the muzzle that is bulky enough so you are sure to notice it and take it off before firing.

Ordinary stiff commercial leather or canvas rifle covers are not good, for snow is liable to sift in. One of the best covers is that used by many northern Indians and Eskimos, a buckskin sack of the right shape into which you slide the rifle and then tie at the bottom. A case on similar principles can be made out of any cloth you have available.

METHODS OF CARRYING RIFLE

Be careful how you carry the rifle. You may have to use it in an emergency, either because of attack by an animal or because you have a fleeting glimpse of one you need to get and time is important. If you carry the rifle crosswise on your back, Eskimo and northern Indian fashion, you can (unless in a blizzard) have the end of the case open, whether it is buckle or drawstring, and the gun will come without a hitch when you need it. If the rifle is carried diagonally across the back, European style, then its position should be the reverse of what we are used to; for if you carry it muzzle down you can have the case open at the butt end.

If it seems necessary to carry a rifle without its case, as when you are crawling up on an animal, you must be very careful not to let snow get in. An ordinary precaution in such cases is to slip a mitten over the front end of the barrel.

When rifles are carried on the sledge they should be on top of the load, in positions where you can get them out quickly.

Whether you have buckle fastenings or drawstrings, you must be sure that these are always clear.

IMPORTANCE OF RIFLE

Particularly in sea travel, you must remember that you are not going to survive many days the loss of your last rifle. For that reason, where travel is particularly dangerous, the man

443

who walks ahead to break trail should carry a rifle and 20 or 30 rounds of ammunition. For the sledge may sink through young ice and disappear.

Should two or three men find themselves well dressed but with everything gone except one rifle and some ammunition, they could very likely get ashore safely even a distance of one or two hundred miles, and perhaps farther. The main determinant would be that footgear should last, for in an emergency you can eat raw the animals you kill. Fortunately boots do not wear out quickly on snow—a pair of soles may take you 1,000 miles. The same pair, however, may wear out in a day on stony ground; the brine of slushy young sea ice will shorten the life of a bootsole, though not to less than 500 miles.

FIELD GLASSES

For Arctic hunting, field glasses are second in importance to rifles. Each member of the party should have one. The best all-round power is probably 6. It is a fair night glass, it is good in dull daylight, and it is not seriously affected by the pulse in your wrist. Eight-power, which sounds like a happy medium, is usually voted unsatisfactory on trial. It is worth while in a party of three to have at least one 12-power glass, which you use lying down or resting it on something—or perhaps you mount it on a snag of ice, a camera tripod, or the like. The 12-power is particularly valuable for identification of things you pick up with the 6-power. Glasses of 4-power are excellent for twilight or for use in a forest. They are doubtless good from an airplane. (For the use of binoculars in hunting, see Section II of this chapter.)

Field glasses, like all metal instruments, should be kept outdoors all winter.

EFFECTS OF COLD

In cold most things shrink and many become harder and more brittle. A green spruce log may break an axe blade, both because the steel becomes brittle and because the log has been hardened. Formerly, and perhaps still, steel bits were welded on to soft iron axe bodies; the break might be either by notching the cutting edge or by having the bit separate from the body of the axe at the line where the two are joined.

Knives intended for outdoor use have to be of different temper and character for cold weather. For instance, there is said to be general preference for Rogers over Wilson (Sheffield) knives in Africa, but the reverse is true for the Arctic, where, both from experience and hearsay, Rogers knives are (or at least were) reported to break almost like glass, while Wilson knives stood up under practically any use. For a long time—several decades—no hunting knives but Wilson were sold on the lower Mackenzie by the Hudson Bay Company. Natives learned to look for the diamond brand and "refused all substitutes"—or at least paid more and more cheerfully if they found the diamond.

There seems no doubt that rifles frequently become ineffective at low temperatures, but there is doubt as to the cause. It seems possible that a proportionately greater shrinkage of the rifle barrel than of the bullet may so tighten the gun that much of the bullet's velocity is taken up by friction; or it may be the reverse, that the bullet shrinks so much that a lot of gas escapes.

Rifle springs and other parts may break; the hardening of springs may change their action and force; the hardening of lubricants may retard or block moving parts.

Moisture from a dry face or dry hands will, particularly at temperatures in the $-40°$ to $-80°$ range, cloud spectacles, field glasses, and sextants. The moist eye produces more pronounced clouding and frosting of instruments; the breath is still worse. Such clouding of surfaces can be avoided, or lessened, in various common-sense ways: You wear mittens, you hold field glasses a little way from the eyes instead of close up to them, you wear spectacles a little farther from the eyes than usual, you try to have the wind at right angles when you use field glasses or instruments so that it may blow the moisture away before it reaches a surface to condense upon.

Section II

METHODS OF HUNTING

a. At Sea, Along Shore

SEALS AND BEARS

At sea in winter there are two main animals, the polar bear and the seal. We consider the methods of hunting them.

The hunting of seals does not call for original methods. The best are those borrowed from the Eskimos, unchanged except for the omission of a number of superstitious practices.

Where seals exist, they are found in one of three situations: on top of the sea ice, under it, or in open water between the floes. Accordingly, there are three branches to the method of the hunter.

IN OPEN WATER

The simplest case is when you hunt seals in open water. On arriving at the edge of a lead or other body of water you may find dozens of seals swimming about within gunshot. You shoot through the head, commonly, because a seal is more likely to sink with a body wound, especially one that lets blood or water into the lungs. In all seasons except summer, 9 killed seals out of 10 will float if shot through the head and perhaps 7 out of 10 even with a body wound. The sinking of a large percentage in summer is probably due not so much to the seals then being less fat, with resulting higher specific gravity, as to the comparative freshness and diminished specific gravity of the surface of the sea, the fresh water of the rains and thaws forming in the quiet spaces among the floes a top layer through which the seals sink to the heavier, saltier water below.

RETRIEVING BY MANAK

If the killed seal floats, and is not more than 20 to 30 yards away, he is secured by the *manak*. This is a ball of wood the size of a grapefruit but pear-shaped. At its equator are

446

three sharp recurved steel hooks and at the small end is a ring to which is attached a long cod line or slender thong. The hunter holds the coiled line cowboy fashion in his left hand and with a fathom of free rope he swings the manak about his head till it whizzes, then throwing it somewhat as the South Americans are said to do the bolas. You throw beyond the seal where he floats like a short log in the water. Before pulling in you try to flip the line over so that as you haul toward you it will drag over the seal. As the manak is about to slide over his back you give a sharp jerk, one of the hooks catches, and you pull the seal to you.

If the seal is too far off to be reached by the manak you convert a tarpaulin and a sledge into a sledboat (as described in Chapter 11) and paddle out to him.

When you come to open water you may see dozens of seals swimming about; another time you may have to wait a day or 2 days before you see the first one. It never happened on the Stefansson expeditions that a seal was not secured within 4 days of watching; but anyway you continue waiting till a seal comes if you need the meat and have no other way of getting it.

If you are on a "water hole," surrounded on all sides by ice that is not broken, you should not wait more than a few hours; for without means of safe travel (opportunity to breathe) no seal may come at all. But if you are on a lead of considerable length it is merely a question of a few days at most till they arrive, for the great leads are their highways. From your camp by a lead you may see no seal Monday and Tuesday where a hundred may pass you Wednesday and Thursday.

UNDER ICE

Each successive summer gale breaks the ice more, and there are no frosts to cement the fragments together before autumn. There is now enough water between the floes so seals can travel freely in all directions; and they do, rising in water patches to breathe. Then comes the autumn with its light frosts, mushy young ice forming everywhere. The seals are reluctant to stop their wanderings and are indeed free to continue them awhile, for a sharp upward bunt of their heads will break ice up to 4 inches thick (young salt water ice is mushy) and give them a chance to breathe.

When a seal travels along a lead covered with young ice he leaves behind a trail of circular fracture spots from a dozen to several dozen yards apart.

Months later, and up to next summer, these fracture spots are your game signs, your index to the former presence of seals. Most of the fracture spots are hidden by the snow in winter, but if you watch as you travel, all day and every day, you will eventually be rewarded by seeing an ice patch swept bare by some wind eddy where there happens to be the characteristic round spot.

THE SEAL'S WINTER RESIDENCE

When the ice thickens beyond 4 inches, and hardens, the seals must stop traveling and take up residence. Here, by industrious gnawing, they keep breathing holes open all winter. At the surface these holes have openings only an inch or two in diameter, but underneath they are enlarged continually until, as the ice thickens to 2 or 4 or even the maximum of 7 feet, they are vertical cigar-shaped chambers of diameter large enough for the seal's body. Each seal may have a half-dozen of these chambers leading to breathing holes that are covered with a few inches or a few feet of snow and thus hidden from the observation of man and from the eye of an animal.

A bear can discover a seal hole by the sense of smell. On young ice as well as in open water they know how to get seals. But far from land the pressures are mild and the ice less often broken by it, so that there are large areas where the skill and strength of the bears do not suffice to get them any seals. Accordingly, bears are rare or absent, which is one of the reasons for the view which was universally held till recently that seals are nonexistent in the deep polar ocean far from land. Actually, when bears are absent it is usually because they lack the ability to get seals rather than because seals are absent.

448

Man alone would not succeed any better than the bear in securing seals on the large areas of fairly level ice at sea; but man and dog in partnership combine the needed abilities.

The breathing holes of seals are sometimes found on patches of ice swept bare of snow by the wind, but these holes have usually been abandoned. The ones in actual use are generally covered with snow so no eye can see them and no faculty of man detect, and only bear or dog can find them by the sense of smell.

If a man who has no interest in seals, or to whom it has never occurred that any might be near, drives a dog team over snow-covered ice and finds the dogs wanting to stop and sniff the snow, he urges them on impatiently. But if you believe that seals are found here and there all over the polar ocean, you will infer when a dog wants to pause and sniff the snow that a seal's breathing hole is concealed underneath.

DOG RETIRES WHEN SEAL HAS BEEN DISCOVERED

If you allow, the dogs may begin to dig in the snow. You must not permit that, for daylight or a strange smell in the breathing hole will scare the seal. The dogs' usefulness is over when they have scented out the holes. You lead or drive them to a distance of a few score yards where they lie down and sleep while your part of the work is on.

After quieting the dogs you go back, take a long rod like a slender cane and with it poke and prod the snow till the rod slips through into water. Now the hole is exactly located. You withdraw the cane and fill the hole made by it with soft snow to prevent daylight from entering. Then, by scraping with your hunting knife or by cutting blocks, you remove most of the snow from over the hole, leaving a layer of only a few inches. Next you take an ivory "indicator" that much resembles a coarse knitting-needle and stick it down through the snow so that its lower end passes through the breathing hole and is immersed in the water. When the seal rises to breathe his nose will strike this indicator and shove it upwards.

You are now standing motionless above the hole (and perhaps have been for hours, for this hunting method, like most other primitive ways of getting game, requires patience). Your eye should not leave the indicator where it stands upright like a peg in the snow. When the seal rises to breathe you cannot hear him, you cannot see him, and you have no warning till the indicator quivers or moves up. Then you drive your harpoon down alongside the indicator. If you hit the one- or two-inch hole you hit the seal, for his nose is in the hole. He is now harpooned and you hold him by the harpoon line twisted around one leg, or around your waist, while with an ice chisel you enlarge the hole enough to drag him out. One man can do this easily with a common seal (*Phoca hispida*) weighing 150 or 175 pounds, but with a bearded seal (*Erignathus barbatus*) weighing 600 or 800 pounds it is no easy job for two men.

WINTERING HABITS OF SEALS

The reason why you may have to wait for hours and even days for your seal to come up in the breathing hole (though he needs to breathe five or eight times an hour) is that he may have a dozen other breathing holes scattered through several acres of snow-covered ice, and he may be using one of the others temporarily. It is therefore best for several men to work together. When one hole has been located and a hunter stationed there, other hunters should take dogs in leash and lead them around in circles until as many holes have been located as there are available hunters. This greatly increases the chances of getting the seal promptly. Any clumsiness of method at one hole will, furthermore, merely drive the seal to another hole watched by a better hunter.

No one should aim to live by hunting on the sea ice without understanding this manner of sealing, called by the Eskimos the "mauttok" or waiting method; but in actual practice you want it mainly as another string to your bow. Seals are usually secured either by the (among the Eskimos) nameless way first described where a seal is shot in open water, or by the procedure about to be described, called by the Eskimos the "auktok" or crawling method.

450

At any season of year seals may come up on the ice to lie there and sleep; but they do it chiefly in the spring and summer, from March when it still goes down to —30° or —40° F. to midsummer when much of the surface of the ice is covered with pools of water.

At no time of year is the northern seal unguarded about coming out on the ice from his hole (enlarged by his teeth, or by the thaw, till it will let him up) or from the lead in which he has been swimming. He is always fearful of polar bears. Therefore, when he wants to come up and bask, he spies out the situation by bobbing up from the water as high as he can, lifting his head a foot, two, or even three, above the general level. This he does at intervals for some time—perhaps for hours—until he concludes there are no bears around and ventures to hitch himself out on the ice.

SEALS SLEEP IN SHORT NAPS

Here follows another period of extreme vigilance during which the seal lies beside his hole, ready to dive in again at the slightest alarm. Eventually, however, he begins to take the naps that seemingly were his desire in coming out of the water. But his sleep is restless, through fear of bears. He takes a nap of 30, 40, or 50 seconds or perhaps a minute. Then he raises his head 10 or 15 inches from the ice and spends 5 to 20 seconds in making a complete survey of the horizon before taking another nap. Three minutes is protracted slumber for a seal; although far away from land or in other regions where bears are few or absent, they have been observed to sleep for 5 and 6 minutes.

In rare cases basking seals will be found lying within rifle shot from an ice hummock and can be shot from cover. Ordinarily, however, they select a level expanse of ice. In that case they will see the hunter long before he gets near enough to shoot. An essential of a successful hunt is therefore to convince the seal that you are something that is not dangerous. He may see you move and so you must convince him that you are some harmless animal.

THE HUNTER PLAYS SEAL

There are only three animals with which seals are familiar—bears, white foxes, and other seals. It would not serve the hunter to pretend he is a bear, for that is the one thing the seal fears. This consideration shows you must not wear white clothes "for the advantage of protective coloration" on the white ice. For if the seal sees a thing both suspicious and white he will think of a bear and dive instantly. You cannot very well pretend to be a fox, for they are not much larger than cats, are very agile and continually keep hopping around. But if you are dressed in dark clothing and are lying flat on the ice you look at a distance much like a seal, and you will find by trying it that you can imitate his actions closely.

You can learn the auktok method of sealing from an Eskimo if you are among some group who practice it, but there are several groups among whom it is not in use. In any case, you can learn from the seals themselves, for your task is but to imitate them. Take your field glasses with you and spend a few hours or days in watching basking seals from a safe distance, which is 400 or 500 yards. A seal is not likely to see you at much over 300 yards.

Your cue, then, is to begin playing seal when you are about 300 yards away. Up to that point you advance by walking bent while the seal sleeps and dropping on your knees to wait motionless while he is awake. But at less than 300 yards he might notice you bent over or on all fours. Those are not seal-like postures and you must begin to wriggle ahead flat. You must not crawl head-on, for a man in that position is not so convincingly like a seal as he would be in a side view or quartering. You crawl more or less side-on, crawfish style.

You advance while the seal sleeps and you lie motionless while he is awake. Had you been upright or on all fours he might have noticed you near 300 yards but now he does not till you are perhaps 200 yards away. When he first sees you he becomes tense, raises his head a little higher, crawls a foot or two closer to the water to be ready to dive, and then watches you, intent and suspicious. If you remain motionless

452

his suspicions increase at the end of the first minute, and before the third or fourth minute is over he plunges into the water, for he knows that no real seal lies motionless that long. Therefore, before the first minute of his watching is over, you should do something seal-like. You are lying flat on the ice like a boy sleeping on a lawn. The easiest seal-like thing to do is lift your head 10 or 15 inches, spend 10 or 15 seconds looking around, then drop your head on the ice again. By doing this half a dozen times, at irregular intervals each less than a minute, you very likely convince him that you are another seal.

But some seals are skeptical. If yours seems restive and suspicious it is well to increase the verisimilitude of your acting by not only lifting your head at varying intervals but also going through whatever seal-like antics you have observed while watching the real seals through your field glasses.

Seals are lousy—not with our graybacks, of course, but with a variety of their own. Being thus infested, they itch; itching, they are continually rubbing and scratching themselves. They use hind flippers, which are long and flexible and armed with claws admirable for scratching. It is advisable, then, for the hunter to roll about and to flex his legs from the knees frequently, as if scratching with hind flippers. These actions make an impression. In 8 cases out of 10 a good hunter is accepted as a fellow seal that has just come out of his hole to bask and sleep.

Seals that refuse to be convinced may have had a narrow escape from a polar bear recently, or may be hungry and taking occasion for going down to have a feed. That this motive frequently influences seals we judge from the fact that toward midnight a seal usually goes down soon after noticing us. They normally come up on the ice in the early morning or forenoon and go down to feed toward midnight.

If you once get your seal convinced he stays convinced. There is nothing fickle about a seal. He not only does not fear you but even appears to rely on you. It is as if he said to himself: "Over there is a brother seal, and if a bear approaches from that side he will get him before he gets me.

453

So I can afford to leave that quarter unwatched." As if he held this view, the seal will give you only a casual glance now and then and you can approach with great confidence. You crawl ahead while he sleeps and stop when he wakes up. If he watches you for more than a few moments you reassure him of your sealship by raising and dropping your head, rolling and wriggling as if itchy, and by flexing your legs from the knees as if scratching with hind flippers—all this lying flat on the ice with your side or quarter toward the seal and never allowing him to see your long arms, for a seal's front flippers are short. If you are careful, if the snow is not hard so it crunches, if a moderate wind from the direction of the seal covers any noises there may be, you can crawl as near as you like. Ordinarily an Eskimo throws his harpoon from a distance of from 10 to 20 feet. A man with a rifle would shoot from a distance of 25 to 75 yards.

HARPOONING OR SHOOTING BASKING SEAL

An Eskimo, using his native gear, holds the harpooned seal by the harpoon line. With a rifle only a brain shot will serve; you do not fire at 100 yards because the seal is lying on an incline of ice beside the hole or lead. There are few things so slippery as wet ice and the mere shock of instant death may start him sliding. The seal in most cases has buoyancy enough to float, but in sliding toward the water he acquires momentum enough to take him down diagonally 10 or 20 feet. He then comes up diagonally under the thick ice and you can't get him.

So you drop your rifle the moment you fire and run as hard as you can toward the seal. In some cases he does not slide at all and you slacken speed on getting nearer; in others he is slipping toward the hole, gradually gaining headway, and you slide for him like a player stealing a base. In some cases you will catch the seal by a flipper just as he is disappearing; in others you will be too late and the beast, though stone dead, is lost.

You are a good hunter if you get 60 or 70 percent of the seals you go after. The approach takes, on the average, about 2 hours.

454

AUKTOK METHOD CONSIDERED BY SEASONS

In the fall, hunting by the auktok method is often dangerous, for the seals are lying on ice so thin and treacherous that you may break through, especially while trying to get the seal after he is killed. In midwinter seals can seldom be secured in this way because they do not come out on the ice. From April to June we kill most of our seals by this approach. From June to September there is so much water on top of the ice that the auktok necessitates wriggling snake-fashion through pools of ice water from a few inches to a foot or more deep. This is disagreeable; the almost unavoidable splashing may scare the seals. Auktok is, therefore, essentially a springtime method.

Basking seals are usually spied first with glasses from some high hummock. The hunter gets them while his companions are making camp; or else there is a pause in the day's march. In that case, the men usually cook a hot lunch for the hunter while waiting. The animal, when secured, is dragged behind the sledge till camp time and then cut up, part fed to the dogs, part cooked for the men, and the rest stowed in the sledge. Three men and six dogs need about two seals a week. Forced wintering on ice means that fat is more necessary than lean, for you will have to depend on it for light and fuel as well as food. Seal blubber at any temperature, even at 30° or 40° below zero, will lessen in weight day by day, the oil trickling out perceptibly. It is therefore necessary to preserve the blubber in bags. This you do by skinning the seal through the mouth, or "casing" his skin, to use the language of the furrier. The skinning is commenced at the lips, the hide is turned back and, as the skinning proceeds, pulled backwards over the head and then back over the neck and body, as one might turn a sock inside out. When the skinning is done in this fashion there are no openings in the hide except the natural ones, which are closed by tying them up. The bag may be used for a seal oil container, or as a float.

HUNTING POLAR BEARS

During some Beaufort Sea off-shore sledge journeys about 10 percent of the food secured was bears. Most of these came to camp, probably not exactly to attack but rather thinking they were going to plunder. It appears that these bears have a sense of fear when on land, doubtless chiefly from their experience with men. At sea they have met but three animals, the seals on which they feed, the foxes which follow them around to pick up leavings, and the seagulls. It seemed, in conformity with this, that whenever a bear identified man or dog as a seal he would stalk or move to attack. When men were shouting and dogs barking, sometimes half a dozen men and 20 or 30 dogs, the bears would walk unconcernedly right toward them, apparently thinking they were yapping foxes that would run or squawking gulls that would fly away.

Bears find a camp on sea ice in one of four ways, which we mention in order of rising frequency. The first requires no discussion—they may hit the camp by pure accident. This accounts for surely less than 1 percent of all cases.

A bear may cross a sledge trail and follow it. Cases have been recorded where a bear has followed a trail through several encampments, these being perhaps 8 to 15 miles apart. At each encampment he has found something that he has eaten—the story being told by post-mortems. There have been instances of glass bottles, tin cans, cartridge shells, paper, bits of rope and other things that have been found when the animal was cut up, whereby is raised an interesting problem which we no more than mention.

There are many known cases where a bear on land has walked by a depot of caribou meat, passing it on the leeward side and necessarily smelling it but without paying any attention. This seems to indicate that he does not recognize the smell of fresh caribou meat as the smell of food. How can that be reconciled with his eating plugs of tobacco, medicine bottles, tin cans, and pieces of rope? It is also possible, of course, that some of these might have had about them a smell of seal oil, or of something recognized by the bear as food; but that can hardly account for all the cases.

When a party is living by hunting they necessarily secure, as we have explained, more blubber than they can use, and must discard some every now and then. The bear naturally cleans up these leavings as he follows the trail.

A bear's third way of finding your camp depends on what we have explained, that he does not succeed in catching seals except along the edge of open water, or through very thin ice that can be broken by a stroke of a bear's paw. It is true, also, that seals may haul out on ice from any open water, and thus become huntable. Obviously, then, a bear finds seals most readily by traveling along the edge of a lead. But sledging parties frequently camp at leads, for several reasons. They may stop there to take a sounding; they may have been delayed by inability to cross the lead; they may have stopped there because it gives them a chance to kill seals for their own food. This intersection of the hunting technique of the bear with the traveling methods of a sledging party brings about frequent meetings at leads. But perhaps half of all the bears that arrive in camp are brought by the sense of smell. It has been established that they can scent a camp 10 miles; likely enough they can detect it even farther. They arrive traveling upwind.

A bear that comes in following a trail or up the wind, guided by his sense of smell in either case, will pause every now and then. If he is a trail-follower, he finds occasion to examine some peculiarity in the trail every now and then. If he is coming up the wind there will apparently be, at least during the final half mile, changes in the scent that interest the bear, perhaps through a slight fluctuation of the wind, make him stop and sniff. One that is traveling along a lead discovers fewer things to distract him; he does not know about the camp until he hears or sees it. Such a bear is probably traveling a good deal faster than either of the other two. It may be that the average rate of walking along a lead is 3 miles per hour, and that the averages up the wind or along a trail are 2 miles.

A bear approaching a camp upwind on ice will smell seal meat. He ought to know the difference between dead and live seal; what he smells is dead. He therefore walks toward it without precaution. If he sees motionless dogs outside the camp, he apparently considers them dead seals, for he does not change his approach. However, if a dog stirs, the bear, apparently, begins thinking of the dog as a live seal. He makes himself unbelievably flat on the ice and, with neck and snout touching the snow, advances almost toboggan fashion toward the dogs, stopping dead if one of them moves, advancing again when they become quiet. If there is any unevenness in the ice, he will take cover and advance in its shelter.

The eyesight of polar bears is such that you are not apt to be visible to one until he is within 250 to 300 yards.

In twilight, their yellowish white outlines against white ice are so indistinct that, except for their shiny black noses, they cannot be seen unless they are moving. When bears are on the alert, they move their necks and their whole bodies to peer about, in a peculiar snaky way—giving somewhat the effect of railway men's signal lights being swung on a dark night.

If your dogs notice the bear they start barking. He then loses interest in them, apparently now identifying them as foxes, which he knows he can't catch. However, there is still the dead seal (i. e., seal meat) which he has originally smelled and he therefore resumes his walk toward camp. By that time a shot provides you with bear meat.

AIM FOR THE HEART

For many reasons, one of them to economize ammunition on a long journey, any animal you shoot ought to be killed with one bullet. When a polar bear is walking into camp he is, as said, usually moving ahead as if window shopping, turning this way and that to sniff and look and examine. Wait, then, until he gives you a broadside view and place a soft nose bullet just behind the shoulder in the vicinity of the heart. Don't use hard nose bullets on a polar bear if you have anything else. A beast that large and tenacious of life can carry a half dozen hard bullet wounds, so long as the heart or one of the very large blood vessels is not penetrated or the brain or spinal cord struck.

If a polar bear is charging, the procedure, as with all charging animals, is to aim for the center of your target—for the main consideration is to be sure that every bullet hits somewhere. Taking the center of this target is more important than otherwise because, unless the conditions of light are perfect, you do not perhaps have a clear outline of the body that is moving toward you. For, as explained elsewhere, it is only in the best light that the difference between the yellowish white of the bear and the pure white of the snow is enough to give you a distinct outline of him.

Here, as in all cases that require discriminating sight, you should either wear no glasses or amber glasses. Bare eyes are indicated if the sun is below the horizon. If the sun is above the horizon in a clear sky then any sort of glasses worn for protecting the eyes against snowblindness will do although none of them help you much except the amber ones, which clarify even the clear outline furnished by the perfect lighting. Under diffused light the amber glasses show up to the fullest advantage, giving you sometimes a clear view of the whole bear, including leg movements, when he would be little more than a blur to you without the help of the amber.

In extremely cold weather it may happen that until some moment of excitement, such as a charge of a bear, you have protected your glasses from frosting (as elsewhere described) but that now you forget the precautions and all of a sudden find your sight obscured by a haze on the glasses. The only thing to do, then, is to snatch them off and work with bare eyes till the emergency is over. (Such possible need for casting away glasses is a further reason why each man should carry two or three pairs.)

Do not shoot a large polar bear while he is in the water, as you will find him extremely difficult to haul out. Remember, he may weigh nearly a ton.

If your shot wounds but does not kill a bear, he will likely make for the water. Do not attempt to forestall this by standing between him and the water, for he will then do the only thing left to him—spring at you—and only luck or most effective action can save you.

DO NOT USE DOGS UNLESS YOU HAVE TO

Although Eskimos and some whites permit their dogs to set upon a bear, dogs are too useful to risk in this fashion.

One blow from a bear's paw can injure a dog fatally, or crush his skull, killing him instantly. Your first concern should be to have your dogs tied, for it has frequently happened that if not hurt by the bear they have been injured or killed by stray shots, the bear in some cases walking away unscathed.

If you are in desperate need of food and the bear seems likely to get away you may have to use dogs. In that case, and if you have several dogs, you release first the one that in your opinion will be (scaredest) of the bear—one that will go up to him and bark but keep out of reach. If this first dog does not stop the bear, you will have to release a second. Two dogs together sort of get courage from each other and will both go up closer, increasing the risk of injury but also giving a better chance of stopping or delaying the bear. You may have to release a third or fourth dog. How many you release will always have to be a matter of your judgment—you balance the risk of losing the dogs against the need of getting the bear.

When there are several dogs around a bear you have to shoot very carefully. Ordinarily, however, the bear will every now and then more or less rise on his hind feet; that gives you the chance for a well-placed shot.

When traveling along and in need of a bear you ought to stop every hour or so, climb a prominent hummock and sweep the horizon slowly several times with your binoculars. Doing it once or even twice is not good enough, for if the ice is at all rough even a traveling bear may be obscured by a hummock just when your glasses are passing over his segment of the horizon.

Having located a traveling bear, you watch him a while to get the direction of his movement. He may be following a lead that is not visible to you, although he is. The thing to do, then, is to reach that lead a good long way ahead of him and lie in wait.

A method worth trying—which is the likelier to work the farther you are from land—is to drive your sledge in such a way that the smell from it will strike the bear at a distance of half a mile or a mile. It will depend on that bear's past experience, or perhaps on his temperament, whether he flees

460

or comes up the wind. (The reason why this works better far from land has been explained—that bears have no enemies at sea, but do have land enemies and therefore feel the more at ease the farther they are from shore.)

OTHER SEA ANIMALS, BIRDS, FISH, ETC.

The only animal besides the bear and seal which may be worth considering, from the subsistence point of view, on a journey out on the deep sea northern ice, is the white whale, beluga. The experience of the third Stefansson expedition showed that in spring and summer (and perhaps also in autumn) beluga, singly or in schools, may be seen occasionally even at hundreds of miles from shore, hundreds of miles, too, from where any ship can sail. But there is no use killing them unless you can harpoon them either before or just after the killing, for they sink like stones.

Far out in the pack the belugas travel along leads. You become aware of them, while encamped at a lead, through hearing the noise of their blowing—most commonly through the barking of dogs that have been aroused by the blowing. Like other whales, they usually travel on the surface but a short distance, then go under and come up a little farther ahead. The rate of speed is such that when the ice along the lead is fairly level a man can easily run faster and thus wait for a given beluga. However, since they usually travel in schools this is not necessary—you let the first ones pass and try to get those that come later.

Belugas pass you far out at sea chiefly during the season when seals are numerous, basking here and there on the ice; so that securing one of these whales means no more than your not having to secure at most two or three seals. For if you are traveling you cannot load upon your sledge more meat from even the largest whale than at most the equivalent of two seals—unless, of course, you have a party of several sledges, whereupon an entire beluga could perhaps be utilized. Accordingly, the suggestion is that a small party, say up to 5 men with 2 or 3 sledges and 10 to 15 dogs, are not justified in burdening themselves with a special harpoon equipment for beluga hunting.

About the only thing that would justify carrying beluga equipment is a plan for a large party to camp for a year or more on a drifting floe. If that is contemplated you should take along Eskimo whaling harpoons, or their equivalent, and two or three hundred feet of perhaps quarter-inch braided cotton rope, of the clothesline or window-cord type. Any floats thought necessary for harpoon hunting can be made in the field of sealskins that have been removed by the casing method, which we have described.

Extensive sledge travel on sea ice is seldom practical where there is much open water, so that it is nearly axiomatic that where you do go you don't find walrus. However, if you find them, the killing is so simple that it hardly needs describing. If they are sleeping on ice, you sneak up from behind cover and shoot in a vulnerable spot, that spot determined by your view of each particular beast. Shooting at the base of the skull is preferred if you are using a shotgun, revolver or weak rifle; a powerful modern rifle will reach the brain through any aspect of the skull. You may be able to rush up and kill a walrus with a spear. Certainly you can combine harpooning with shooting, using the harpoon that you carry for getting seals through the ice.

When walrus are swimming you are unlikely to be able to kill one profitably unless you have a boat so that you can harpoon in connection with the shooting. Naturally you cannot carry a boat on a sledge journey. (Nansen tried it and from the hunting point of view it was a failure although the boat served in another connection.) You can, however, convert a sledge into a boat, as described in Chapter 12.

Foxes prowl widely and their tracks will follow those of the bears; for they are parasites, feeding on the leavings when a bear has killed a seal. A fox is intermediate in size between a bush rabbit and a hare, is usually skinny and difficult to secure, so that it does not pay to make any provision for securing them to eat; you cannot afford to loiter for skins (furs) if you have serious objectives.

SEAGULLS

There are seagulls all over the polar sea in summer, but it does not pay to carry a shotgun for them nor would it be sane to use up on them your rifle ammunition. Gulls apparently feed mainly on shrimps but no doubt get some fish. They join the fox in cleaning up after polar bears during that part of the spring season when both are out at sea. For details of this see Chapter 5, Section I.

SHRIMPS

In some leads, whether near land or far from it, you will notice shrimps drifting in the water. They were reported by the Papanin expedition from the North Pole's immediate vicinity. They are the food of the seal and usually it pays you better to confine your diet to seal. But you could pick up shrimps by making an emergency dip net, perhaps with a handkerchief.

FISH

There are fish in the sea—we know that from theory, from the occasional appearance of fish remains in seal stomachs along with their main diet of shrimps, and from now and then finding a dead fish on top of the ice. Perhaps it may be all right to do a little fishing with hooks when something prevents you from traveling; certainly it is all right if you have scientific purposes—to find out what kinds of fish there are in the sea. From the subsistence point of view, it is not worth the bother to carry with you fishhooks, nets, or other fishing gear for a journey over sea ice. Even when you get ashore you will probably have no need for fishing equipment.

b. On Land

For Arctic land journeys you place your main dependence on caribou. We therefore consider the technique of finding and securing them. We then discuss the other animals and birds which form supplementary food supply for the land hunter.

ESKIMO METHODS OF HUNTING

Eskimos who have no rifles hunt caribou with bow and arrow. When a band is seen grazing, a council is held and an ambush determined upon toward which the caribou shall be driven. If natural features, such as lakes, will not fully serve, the ambush may be at the angle of two long convergent lines of monuments, *inuksuk* (plural, *inuksuit*), that have been set up from 50 to 150 yards apart, according to the topography. In rocky country the inuksuk (likeness of a man; substitute for a man) is made by putting two or three stones one on top of the other to a height of 1 or 2 feet. If the herd is large and the drive is looked upon as important, the two lines of monuments may be run out each a distance of 5, 6, or even 10 miles, although lines of 2 or 3 miles are more common. The angle between them may be anything from 15° to 45°.

At intervals of perhaps half a mile, men, women, or even children are stationed; there must be at least one person at each extreme of the lines where they are farthest apart. The Eskimos rely on suggestion in having a person every half mile standing in line with the low monuments but moving about (jumping, waving arms, stepping forward and stepping back). Apparently when you convince the caribou that some of the visible uprights are people you get them to believe that they all are people.

The hunters with bows and arrows lie in ambush at the angle of the V while the rest of the men and women form a crescent curve beyond the caribou so as to drive them toward the ambush. A drive is started by men giving long howls, in imitation of wolves, or by inducing leashed dogs to howl. It may happen, too, that the caribou get the wind of the drivers, which has the same effect, starting them to leeward. The drivers gradually close in and the caribou enter the V-shaped area through which they are driven at a speed of from 5 to 8 miles per hour toward the ambush where several of them are shot.

The greatest slaughters of caribou by North American natives, whether forest Indians or Eskimos, are by spearing when they swim rivers or when they cross lakes at narrows. Sometimes the animals are deliberately driven; at other times people can judge from the way the herds are moving where they are likely to cross. In canoes, if they are Athapaskans, in kayaks, if they are Eskimos, the hunters wait out of sight behind a bend or in a clump of willows, being careful that the wind is right so the caribou do not get human or dog scent—or smoke scent, as from a camp fire. The wider the river or the lake, the greater the slaughter, the hunters cannily waiting till the maximum number of animals are swimming. They use spears, of course, though travelers sometimes miscall them harpoons. The dead animals float high in the water, partly or mainly through the buoyancy of the hollow hairs. In rivers they drift downstream, and the hunters follow to pull them ashore one by one, or to pick them up where they have been stranded.

If there are more hunters than boats, perhaps because women share in the hunting, there is a second kill where the caribou survivors scramble out. This is most effective when there are willows or trees. But few wild animals recognize human beings as such when they are motionless, and sometimes the hunters have no other concealment than to stand perfectly still until the caribou are about to pass them.

In a few places in the North it is customary to try to drive caribou to their death over a cliff.

A method of near approach to caribou, used more by the northerly Athapaskans but known to the Eskimos, is for a man to walk hunched forward, as if on all fours, and to carry strapped to his head or shoulders the antlers of a caribou—the hunter thus pretending to be a caribou. A close approach can sometimes be made in this way, the hunter of course moving upwind.

There is only one ordinary trap for caribou, used chiefly by Eskimos of northeastern Canada. This is a deadfall, the animal being speared after it tumbles into a pit. These are made chiefly of snow, but usually have something for reinforcement, perhaps wood or large bull caribou antlers.

HUNTING FOR A LIVING

When a man hunts seriously for a living in the autumn months, say 200 or 300 miles north of the Arctic Circle, he gets up in the dark of night. By dawn at the latest he leaves camp and is 8 or 10 miles away, beyond the area from which game can have been scared by the barking of dogs or the smoke or smell of the camp, by the time that daylight enough for good shooting comes into the southern sky. He then uses to the best advantage the 4 or 5 hours of hunting light, going from high hilltop to high hilltop and examining with his field glasses every exposed hillside or valley. If he does not see game the first day, he hunts similarly the second; and if he finds none the first week, he continues the second week. For it is an essential of hunting that, although game may be abundant in the country as a whole, it may at any time be absent from a given small specific section.

HUNTING INLAND

If on a continental mainland in the fall you decide that caribou have left the coast and that you should go inland for them, the best procedure is to ascend a river as far as possible. The reasons for doing this, instead of striking across country, are mainly two: first, a boat of shallow draft, which you can perhaps improvise if you don't have one, may be taken up-stream a considerable distance along most Arctic rivers; second, you expect a river valley to be stocked with a heavy growth of willow suitable for fuel, even in places where spruce trees are not to be found.

HUNTING IN A BLIZZARD

Generally it is only in times of extreme need that one hunts caribou in a blizzard. Not that nine-tenths of the blizzards in the Arctic need keep a healthy man indoors; it is rather that the drifting snow (even when you can see as far as 200 yards) diminishes many times over the chance of your finding game. If you do find it, however, the stronger the gale the better your chance of close approach without being seen; for these animals, though they double their watchfulness in foggy weather, seem to relax it in a blizzard.

STALKING

The main thing in stalking caribou that are not moving is the ability to keep in mind their location accurately while you are circling and winding about so as to approach them from a new direction behind cover of irregular hills and ridges that are unfamiliar to you.

USE OF FIELD GLASSES

Binoculars and a knowledge of their use are about as important as the quality of your rifle and the pair of legs that carry you. It is a difficult thing to teach newcomers the proper use of field glasses. The green man stands erect with his heels together, lifts the glasses jauntily to his eyes and spins slowly around on one heel, taking from half a minute to a minute for a complete survey of the horizon. Then he announces there is no game in sight. The experienced hunter will take some pains to find the best place to sit down, will bring out a piece of flannel that is clean, no matter how dirty he himself and every other item of his outfit may be, and wipe every exposed lens till he is sure there isn't a speck or smudge anywhere. If the landscape is well within the power of his glasses he will probably rest his elbows on his knees. But, if the distance is great or the wind blowing, he will lie down flat with elbows on the ground, or will build up out of stones or any available material a rest for the glasses that cannot be shaken by the wind. If the wind is blowing hard, he may even place a 15- or 20-pound stone on top of his glasses to keep them steady. There is never any pivoting or swinging motion as he brings them to bear upon successive fields of view. If the angle of vision is 6°, as it may be with 6-power glasses, or 3° with 12-power, he examines thoroughly the field disclosed by their first position and then moves them a less number of degrees than they cover, so that the second field of view shall slightly overlap the first.

In calm weather and with an ordinary landscape it takes about 15 minutes for one good look around from a hilltop;

under special conditions it may take twice that long. If, for instance, somewhere near the limit of the power of the glasses is seen a patch that may be a caribou but which may be a stone or a wolf, it can take half an hour of study to make sure. For example:

When there is in the atmosphere that quivering wavy motion which is due to the sun shining on areas of different nature, causing air currents to rise that differ in temperature and humidity, all things have blurred outlines and shapes may appear fantastic. Small stones, round or flat, may look like tall pillars and may even seem to move. If stones or the like simulate motion they will appear to be moving in the same direction, although perhaps reversing it. This may be the case with caribou; but they will hardly keep their relative positions, as immovable bodies seen through a mirage would do.

If you notice six specks, then, they may be caribou or they may be stones. Under conditions when you cannot estimate distance (as, for instance, when you are looking across a range of hills over invisible ice beyond to a second land), they might be white geese. It may take half an hour of watchfulness before one of the bodies moves with reference to the other five. They are then not stones, since one has moved; and not geese, because six geese would not retain their positions unchanged for half an hour. By a process of elimination you will decide they were caribou which had all been lying down until one got up and moved about.

On the third Stefansson expedition the sea north of Alaska was explored through several years by sledge parties which, after the first 2 months or so of each journey, depended for food and fuel solely on water game, 90 percent of it seals. Information gained on these journeys has been used in various parts of this Manual. Coming ashore on northern islands, some of which were discoveries of the expedition, the parties changed their dependence to grazing animals, mainly caribou, but in some islands also musk oxen. A statement giving information on caribou and on the manner of hunting them is here taken from Stefansson's *Hunters of the Great North,* pages 250–260:

"When you consider that an experienced hunter is an expert in a very simple task, you will not think it remarkable that we

468

count on being able to secure at least three out of every four caribou we try to get. The same proportion applies to seals and polar bears. This is why we feel no hesitancy in making journeys of hundreds and even thousands of miles in the Arctic regions, depending on hunting entirely for our food. If you read of travelers starving to death up there it will be through some special misfortune, or else because they either did not try to hunt or else did not know well the technique of finding and securing game.

"A common mistake about caribou is to suppose that they are more difficult to hunt in districts where they are frequently hunted by people than in countries where they are never hunted at all. I find there is no such difference. The reason is simple. They have one great enemy, the wolf. On the prairies in the northern half of Canada and on the islands to the north of Canada there are many millions of caribou. Some say there are 10 million all together and some say there are 30 million. In these great herds there must be born every year anything from 2 million to 6 million calves. The number of caribou killed by human beings in all of northern Canada is far less than 1 million per year. Accordingly, the caribou would increase very rapidly were it not for the wolves which kill several times as many as do the human hunters— Indian, Eskimo, and white. Wolves are found wherever caribou are found and the caribou are in continual dread of them. They are, therefore, almost equally harried in countries that are uninhabited by men as in countries that are inhabited. I have, accordingly, found that even in the remote new islands which we discovered in 1915 caribou are about as difficult to approach as in northern Alaska or on the Canadian mainland where they are continually hunted by Eskimos.

"Apart from the islands actually discovered by my expedition there is no known country in the northern hemisphere that has been so little visited as Isachsen Land in north latitude 79°, west longitude 103°. We feel sure that no Eskimos ever saw that island. From the beginning of the world to our time it had been visited only once—by Captain Isachsen in 1901. Isachsen made a hurried sledge trip around the island. The journey took him about a week. In one place

469

he saw some caribou tracks and I think he may have seen some caribou at a distance, but he did not try to hunt them. The next visitors were my sledge party in 1916 and on that occasion we saw no caribou and had to feed ourselves and our dogs entirely on seals.

"My second visit, and the third visit of human beings to the island, was in 1917. We were then on the most dangerous adventure that has ever fallen to our lot. By the road we had to travel we were some 500 miles away from the nearest Eskimos and 600 miles away from our own base camp. Four of us had been on a long journey out on the moving sea ice to the northwest. When we were more than a hundred miles northwest from Isachsen Land, two of my three companions were taken seriously ill. We turned toward shore immediately and it was a hard fight to make land. When we got there after a struggle of 2 weeks we found ourselves with one man so sick that he could not walk, another who could barely walk but was of no use otherwise, and with two teams of dogs that were exhausted with hard work and so thin from short rations during the forced march toward shore that they were little more than skeletons. It had been my pride through many years never to lose a dog. Furthermore, I was exceedingly fond of every one of these dogs for they had worked for me faithfully for years. I was concerned for their safety, and still more concerned for the safety of the sick men. By that time, however, my confidence in our ability to make a living in the Arctic had become so strong through 8 years of experience that I felt more worry for the lives of the men on the score of illness than for fear they might actually die of hunger.

"But the first day on Isachsen Land was a depressing contradiction to my hopes and expectations. The one man in good health and the two men who were sick had to make their way as best they could along the coast while I hunted inland parallel to their course. I walked that day 20 miles across one of the very few stretches of entirely barren land that I have seen in the Arctic. Under foot was gravel without a blade of grass. Much of the land was lightly covered with snow as in other typical arctic lands in winter, and I looked in vain in the snow for track or other sign of any living thing.

"That evening my men were depressed partly because of their illness and also because it looked as if we had at last come into a region as barren as many people think the polar countries generally are. It was clear that if we saw game the next day we would simply have to have it. Where game is plentiful, you may lose one chance and soon get another; but where it is scarce, you must not allow any opportunity to slip through your fingers.

"I am telling this particular hunting story rather than any other to illustrate the principle of how you must hunt caribou in the polar regions if it is essential that you shall get every animal you see. It certainly was essential in this case, for I wanted not only to stave off immediate hunger but to secure meat enough so we could camp in one place for several weeks to give the sick men a chance to become well.

"Our second day on Isachsen Land the men again followed the coast line with the sledges, cutting across the shortest distance from point to point while I walked a much longer course inland. I had gone but a few miles when I came upon the tracks of a band of caribou. You can seldom be sure of the minimum number in a band from the tracks if there are more than 10 animals, for caribou have a way of stepping in each other's footprints. There are always likely to be more animals in a band than you have been able to make out from the tracks.

"The trail showed that these caribou were traveling into the wind as they usually do. There were only light airs and the snow had on it a crust that broke underfoot with a crunching noise. Under such conditions the band were likely to hear me 4 or 5 hundred yards away. The country now was a rolling prairie—not barren gravel as yesterday. It was impossible to tell which ridge might hide the caribou from me, so instead of following the trail ahead I went back along it for about half a mile studying the tracks to see just how fast they had been moving. They had been traveling in a leisurely way and feeding here and there. I estimated their average rate of progress would not be more than 3 or 4 miles per day. I could not rely on this, however, for a wolf may turn up any time and begin a pursuit which takes a band 25 or 50 miles away. Should a wolf pass to windward of them so that they got his smell without his knowing about them, they would be likely to run from 5 to 10 miles.

"When I had made up my mind that these caribou were moving slowly, I went to the top of a nearby hill and through my glasses studied the landscape carefully. With good luck I might have seen some of them on top of some hill and the problem would have become definite. But I watched for half an hour and saw nothing. Clearly they were either feeding in some low place or else they were lying down, for caribou are like cattle in their habit of lying down for long periods. I now commenced a cautious advance, not along the actual trail but crisscrossing it from high hilltop to high hilltop, hoping to get a view of the animals while they were at least half a mile from me and while I was beyond the range of their eyesight, for they cannot see a man under even the most favorable conditions farther off than half a mile. Under ordinary conditions they would not see you much beyond a quarter of a mile.

"Finally I saw the band lying quietly on some flat land. There was no cover to enable me to approach safely within 500 yards and that is too far for good shooting. I thought these might be the only caribou in the whole country. We had 13 hungry dogs and 2 sick men, and now that I had a large band before me it was my business to get enough food at one time to enable us to spend at that place 2 or 3 weeks while the men had a chance to regain their health and the dogs to regain their flesh and strength.

"On a calm day when caribou can hear you farther than you can shoot, there is only one method of hunting. You must study their movements from afar until you make up your mind which direction they are going. Then you must walk in a wide curve around them until you are in the locality toward which they are moving and well beyond earshot. This takes judgment, for they usually travel nearly or quite into the wind and you must not allow them to scent you. You, therefore, have to choose a place which you think is near enough to their course so that they will pass within shooting distance, and still not directly enough in front so that they can smell you.

"On this occasion the glaring light on the snow had been so hard on my eyes that I did not feel they were in perfect condition, and no one can shoot well if his eyes are not right. Unless there is a change of wind caribou are not likely to turn their course back along the trail by which they have come. I accordingly selected a hill across which they had walked that morning and half a mile away from where they now were. On the top of this hill where I could see them, although they could not see me (because my eyes were better than theirs) I lay down, covered my head with a canvas hunting bag to keep the sun away, and went to sleep. Sleeping is the best possible way of passing time, but my object now was not only to pass the time until the caribou began moving but also to get my eyes into perfect condition.

"When you go to sleep at 20 below zero you have in the temperature an automatic alarm clock. My clothes were amply warm enough to keep me comfortable while I was awake, but I knew that when I went to sleep my circulation would slow down. This reduces the body temperature and the same weather that will not chill you when you are awake will chill you enough to wake you from a sleep.

"In this case the chill woke me in about half an hour to an unpleasant situation. A fog had set in and I could not see the caribou, nor had I any means of knowing whether they were still lying down or whether they had started to move. If this had been a good game country, I might have taken chances on advancing through the fog a little, but I was so impressed with the possibility that these were the only animals within a hundred miles that carelessness was not to be considered. At this time of year we had 24 hours of daylight. The fog was bound to lift sooner or later and whenever it did I would commence the hunt over again.

"The fog did lift in about 2 hours and I did have to commence the hunt all over again, for the caribou were gone. I was to the north of them and I felt sure that they had not gone by near me; so they must have gone east, west, or south. I was probably so near them that I could not with safety go on top of any of the adjoining hills, so I went back north half a mile and climbed a high hill there. From that hill I saw nothing and went half a mile to one side to another hill. Then I saw the caribou. They were now feeding half a mile south of where they had been when the fog covered them up. In the meantime the breeze had stiffened enough so that now there was no longer danger of my being heard. I did not, therefore, have to circle them and lie in wait in front but could follow up directly behind.

"Eventually I got within about 300 yards. But I wanted to get within 200, so I lay still and waited for them to move into a more favorable locality. During my wait an exceedingly thick fog bank rolled up, but with it the wind did not slacken. Under cover of this fog I felt safe in crawling ahead a hundred yards, for I knew that I could see through the fog quite as well as the animals and that they could not hear me because of the wind. The reason I had not approached them in the previous fog was that the weather then had been nearly calm and they would have heard me.

"At 200 yards I was just able to make out the outline of the nearest caribou. I did not dare to go closer and, of course, I could not begin shooting with only one or two animals in sight where I wanted to get them all. I had before now counted them carefully. There were 21, which I estimated would be enough to feed our men and dogs between 2 and 3 weeks, giving them a chance to recuperate.

"After about half an hour the fog began gradually to clear and in another half hour I could see all the animals. I was near the top of a hill and they were in a hollow, the nearest of them about 150 yards away and the farthest about 300.

"In winter the ground in any cold country will split in what we call frost cracks. These are cracks in the frozen surface of what in summer is mud. They are ordinarily only half an inch or so wide but I have seen cracks 4 or 5 inches wide. These cracks form when the mercury is dropping and with a noise that resembles a rifle shot. Under the same conditions the ice on the small lakes cracks similarly. These loud noises are so familiar to the caribou and the report of a rifle is so similar that the mere sound of a rifle does not scare them. Of course, we have smokeless powder so they cannot see where the shots come from. What does scare them is the whistle of the bullet and the thud as it strikes the ground. It is instinctive with all animals to run directly away from the source of any noise that frightens them. It is another instinct of caribou when they are alarmed to run towards the center of the herd. A band that has been scattered feeding will bunch up when they take fright. When you know these two principles, it is obvious that the first caribou to kill is the one farthest away from you. On some occasions when I have been unable to get within good shooting distance of a band, I have commenced by firing a few shots into a hill on the other side of them, hoping that the noise of the striking bullets would scare them towards me. Frequently it works. On this occasion, however, I merely took careful aim at an animal about 300 yards away. It dropped so instantaneously that, although the sound of the bullet striking it induced the other caribou to look up, they recognized no sign of real danger. They were, however, alert and when they saw the second caribou fall they ran together into a group and moved somewhat towards me. I now shot animals on the outer margin of the group and as each fell, the others would run a little way from that one. Their retreat in any direction was stopped by killing the foremost animal in the retreat, whereupon the band would turn in the opposite direction.

"It would not have been difficult for me to kill the whole band alone, but I was not shooting alone. From a point somewhat above and behind me I could hear other shots, and some animals I was not aiming at were dropping. Without looking around I knew what this meant. My companions traveling along shore on the ice had seen the caribou and had waited for some time until they began to fear that I might have missed the band. The two sick men had then been left behind in camp while their Eskimo companion had come inland to try to get the caribou. When he got near he saw that I was approaching them and very wisely did not interfere. There is nothing so likely to spoil a caribou hunt as two hunters whose plans conflict. Even when they have a chance to consult at the beginning of the hunt, two men are less likely to be successful than one. For one thing, caribou may see a black dot on the landscape and take no warning from it, but if they see two black dots and later notice that they are either closer together or farther apart than they were a moment before, this makes a danger signal which they understand. That is the main reason why I always hunt alone. If there are two hunters to go out from the same camp on any given day, they should go in opposite directions. That way they double the chance of finding game and each has a fair chance of getting the animals he does find.

"On our journeys we never kill more animals than we need, but in this case we needed the whole twenty-one."

MUSK OXEN

Wild musk oxen are found chiefly on certain islands and then in a small section of the northeastern Canadian mainland—for details see Chapter 5, Section I.

RANGES AND GAME LAWS

There is supposed to be a permanent closed season on all musk oxen under Canadian jurisdiction, whether on mainland or islands; except that naturally anyone, white or native, would be expected to kill a few if it were a matter of life and death. Some of those on the Canadian mainland are in an actual game reserve, on and near the Thelon River. Here the restrictions are theoretically even stricter, but still matters of life and death would control.

The rest of the wild musk oxen are in Greenland. There they have been exterminated from all the west coast, and from all the east coast north to the Scoresby Sound vicinity. From Scoresby they run north along the east coast and around the north coast westward to and through Peary Land. The Danish Government has wanted to discourage killing in this whole region. What they have succeeded in doing is to restrict wanton destruction, which some years ago was almost like the well-known slaughter of the buffalo on the western prairie. Hunters and explorers who go to the region are now supposed not to kill musk oxen except in extreme need.

Peary says: "Presence of musk oxen can be detected very quickly by the patches of luxuriant grass which mark all their rendezvous. * * * A careful examination of these places will soon show whether they have been about, bits of wool and hair shed from their shaggy coats being scattered here and there on the ground, while their tracks show how recent has been their visit." It is only in rugged country, however, that (in Stefansson's experience) you find recent traces without usually being able also to see the herd from some nearby hill.

In clear weather these huge bison or black animals can be seen, whether on a snow field in winter or against a green hillside in summer, as far away with the naked eye as caribou with the best six-power glasses—probably for six or eight miles in summer and ten or twelve in winter. Even in a snowstorm they can be seen three or four times as far as caribou. When seen by hunters they seldom escape.

ESKIMO HUNTING METHOD

The common Eskimo method is to set a few dogs on the herd to hold them in defense formation and then to stab with spears. (See Chapter 5 for description of defense formation of musk oxen.)

A white man's modification is to have men form a circle around the herd at fifty to a hundred yards, shooting at the largest animals first and finishing up with the calves. However, this method is wasteful of ammunition and rarely has workmanlike results. The anatomy of the animal is so well concealed by the tremendous mass of wool on the shoulders that most men do not soon learn how to hit the hearts, and the brain and spinal cord are small targets. As a result, it commonly takes five or more bullets per animal, the wounds are anywhere in the body, and, especially when a shot passes through the intestines, it is hard to make a clean job of butchering.

A better method is to get as close to the animal as possible (approximately ten yards). He will stand with lowered head and the bullet can be placed in the back of the neck at the base of the horns, resulting in instant death and clean butchering.

There is nothing about the killing of musk oxen which has any of the savor of sport. It is about as exciting as killing domestic cattle in a pasture.

If you need a large amount of meat, as for a party spending some months or the winter, it is best to kill an entire herd rather than several out of several herds. The reasons are:

1. The animals stand in such close formation that you can rarely be sure of killing one without wounding others. These would probably later die or become a prey to wolves.

2. If the big animals are killed, the calves and yearlings would probably be unable to defend themselves against wolves.

3. Wolves and bears are continually prowling about and if you have meat depots in many places they cannot all be guarded from theft. But when a large number of musk oxen are killed in one place you can have a man stand on guard until all the meat has been hauled home.

4. You want for your diet animals of different ages because of the varying qualities of the meat. The biggest animals have the best fat, and fat is precious; but their lean is often tough. Yearlings are preferred for beef, or two-year olds. Small calves are about like bob veal and are seldom preferred, but there is no advantage in letting them go and be killed by wolves.

Musk oxen are usually found in bands of from 10 to 40. Stefansson's party of about 15 people and 4 dogs wintering in Melville Island 1916–17 exclusively by hunting, killed as many as 30 musk oxen from a single herd. The number killed depended on the number that could be cut up in a few hours by all hands working together.

BUTCHERING

It is necessary to clean a carcass at once; for, because of the thick skin and deep hair, musk oxen appear to have a fast putrefaction rate even in the coldest weather.

WOLVES

Wolves are found wherever there are caribou. They run to 100 pounds in weight and even beyond. At certain times they are fatter than caribou and therefore more desirable as food. The taste is excellent—like young pig.

It was a rule in the North to shoot wolves because they destroy caribou and because they are good eating. Still, few are secured by parties that live on game—probably not more than one for each hundred caribou. This was because they were so wary and because they move so rapidly and constantly that they cannot be stalked. Trapping is the best way to secure them.

FOXES

As stated earlier in this chapter, it does not pay to shoot foxes for food, nor should you stop to try to secure the skins when making an Arctic journey. However, if you are stationed in a permanent or semi-permanent camp in a locality where foxes are numerous, and if it does not interfere with other work, there is no reason for not trapping them.

TRAPPING

Seton describes one Eskimo method of trapping foxes: "Eskimos use the pitfall. It consists of a circular arched hut, built of stones, with a square opening at the top. Over this opening some thin blades of whalebone are set firmly in the wall at the near end, so as to form an apparently secure footing; at the far end is bait. A sprinkling of snow adds a final deceptive touch. When the animal attempts to get the bait, the whalebone slats over which he must pass bend downward and drop him into the pit below which is deep enough to prevent him from jumping out. The whalebone immediately springs back, and the trap is ready for another victim."

Another method is to cut a shallow hole in the snow, just deep enough for an open steel trap to lie below the level of the surrounding snow. Then a slab of lightly packed snow, just hard enough to lift without cracking, is cut to cover the trap. This slab is laid carefully over the trap, and then shaved and smoothed with great care. The snow slab should be just thick enough to support its own weight, brittle enough to be easily broken when an animal steps on it. A few chips of blubber, fish or meat are shaved off and scattered loosely and carelessly over and around the vicinity of the trap—just enough to give a scent and cause the fox to hunt around until the trap is sprung.

Sometimes a little box-like snowhouse is built over a trap, usually of four blocks of snow, three sides and a roof, leaving one side open to leeward. The bait is placed at the farther end of the house so that the fox must step directly over the trap to get it.

There is no humane way of killing foxes by steel traps and the only thing is to visit the trap lines often. A fox will frequently gnaw one leg off to get free. If two feet are caught, he may be frozen to death by morning.

DEADFALL TRAPS

The nearest thing to a humane trap is a deadfall. You lift up one end of a heavy log, or one end of a long slab of stone, and prop it up with a stick which supports it so insecurely that a little tugging or pushing will displace it and permit the weight to drop. If around the log or slab you build a kind of house of sticks or stones that is shaped just the right way you can probably arrange it so that the heaviest pressure of the weight will strike the fox just back of the shoulders, whereupon death may come almost instantly.

BIRDS

It is probably never worth while to take a shotgun on a long journey, and birds should be hunted with a rifle only in extreme emergencies (because you get so little food for each shot, because you are so likely to miss, and because of the mutilation of a small animal by a high-power bullet). But it is worth while to keep in mind that birds can be used in certain localities and under certain conditions.

There are large sections of the Arctic, including most or all of the islands in the first tier north of Canada, where geese moult by the tens of thousands. The Eskimos at the moulting season make a camp in one of the moulting districts and go out, different days in different directions, round up the geese, perhaps several hundred at a time, drive them slowly to camp and butcher them there, cutting them up immediately so as to hang up or spread out the meat to dry.

The moulting districts may or may not be nesting districts—sometimes the moulting geese are exclusively males.

Where you have nesting regions the geese may be of some consequence as food.

It is one of the curious facts of the Arctic that in some of the best nesting regions eggs were not eaten by the natives. An example is the Richardson Island section of the Mackenzie delta, which apparently was one of the greatest nesting districts of Arctic Canada. The local people made no use of the eggs until after the American whalers began to winter at Herschel Island, following 1889. They brought with them Alaska Eskimos used to feeding on eggs who introduced the custom. However, even as late as 1912 little use was made of the eggs. When an egging party went out to Richard Island it was even then usual that the foray was led by or instigated by an Alaska Eskimo.

STRATEGIC SPOTS FOR SECURING MIGRATING BIRDS

There is in the Arctic here and there strategic topography for the killing of ducks and geese, particularly ducks. Ordinarily these birds migrate along river courses or along a coast line. While great multitudes come down the Mackenzie River, there is apparently no place of the sort we have in mind on that stream, so that most or all are on seacoasts. A typical place is the Shooting Station, one of the best known, about halfway between Barrow Post Office and Point Barrow, Alaska. The ducks are migrating along the coast. When they come to the narrow land and the lagoons at Shooting Station they apparently realize that they have arrived at a turn in the coast and they cross the isthmus, practically speaking all of them in one place, all in a belt half a mile or a mile in width. Nowadays people wait at the Shooting Station with shotguns and kill the ducks by the hundreds.

But it is possible for those who do not have shotguns to utilize the migration controls of the topography by using a hunting device on the principle of the South American bolas, with the differences that the Eskimos use six or more balls instead of two and that they do not hold on to it by a line but let go as if, in using a slingshot, you were to throw the sling as well as the shot.

The bird bolas is of six, seven or eight balls, each the size of a walnut but more almond-shaped or pear-shaped, and made by the Eskimos of bone or ivory. The string on each is from 30 to 40 incres long and there is a handle of feathers or of a bundle of the strings where they come together. Grasping this handle you swing the bolas around your head, lasso fashion, and let fly towards a coming flock of birds, perhaps at an upward angle of 45°. The strings spread out like the ribs of an umbrella. The balls are probably visible to the keen-eyed ducks; but not the strings, or perhaps the strings are not understood by the ducks—at any rate, they sometimes fly into the bolas when you would think they had a chance to avoid it. If strings get properly obstructed by the bird, they and the rest wrap themselves around and bring her to the ground, usually so tangled that she cannot move fast. It happens, however, that either in the air or on the ground she gets so freed that she can fly, with the bolas trailing. For that and other reasons it is well for each hunter to provide himself with half a dozen sets each morning.

There are not many places in the Arctic where there are bird cliffs. Some are found in northeastern Siberia and a great many around Greenland. The birds, of the little auk or puffin type, may there be secured with the bolas or, as is the local custom in Greenland, with a net on a pole used on the principle of a butterfly net.

There are certain Arctic birds, notably the ptarmigan, that can be netted in large numbers by an ordinary fish net or by a net that you make up, no matter how carelessly, out of any sort of string. You prop up the net on edge in any place frequented by ptarmigan. Then you watch until a flock is in the neighborhood, go round to the proper side and approach very slowly. Upon a man's slow approach these birds usually run away instead of flying. They will then walk into the net, which should be tilted in their direction in such a way and so loosely that it falls on top of them.

Ptarmigan as well as rabbits can be snared in brush. You will find almost anywhere in the northern fringe of the Arctic forest, but more especially among the thick willows of the river flats that both ptarmigan and rabbits have trails along which they walk or run. By watching a few birds you soon discover the proper height at which to suspend snares. This is somewhat lower for ptarmigan than for rabbits, except in places where a rabbit has to sort of stoop down to go under a bough or a fallen tree.

SECTION III

FISHING METHODS

We have said that on journeys over the polar sea it is probably not worth while to carry any sort of fishing gear, even though you may be expecting to spend some time on an uninhabited land after coming ashore. For when you are doing two things at the same time, traveling and living by hunting, you cannot afford either the time required for small game or the carrying of the paraphernalia that would enable you to utilize these minor resources.

The argument changes, however, if your plan is to spend a long time in a given place, and particularly if there is a considerable number of men. Even so, fishing would not pay from a camp on a drifting floe, but it may very well pay on any of several of the larger Arctic islands, and it will pay handsomely in certain districts of the mainland.

For a permanent or long-continued establishment in Alaska, or in a similar country, all you need to know with regard to fishing is that the natives are experts at it, that they will sell you quantities of fish if you provide them with a market, and that they will show you their technique if you want to learn from them. We consider, therefore, chiefly methods to be used where there are few natives or where there are natives not expert in or well equipped for fishing.

Fish nets are on the whole the best of human inventions in this field. White men are the world's greatest experts in the making and the use of nets. Most of the forest Indians of North America did have nets before the Europeans came, and nets seem old, too, in Siberia. Eskimos did not have them till recently, when they were introduced either by whites or by non-Eskimo natives. It may be 300 years ago since the net was first used on Bering Sea; it is not much more than a hundred since it reached Point Barrow; it

483

reached the Mackenzie district so late that there were still living in 1906 a number of people who remembered when they had seen the first fish net. The practice of using nets did not get east beyond Cape Parry until following 1910. At that time nets were not in use from Parry to somewhere near King William Island, but east and south of that they were again found. Today they are in use in all Eskimo countries.

In an emergency a net has to be made almost necessarily from twine, although this can be secured by unraveling cloth if no netting twine is obtainable. Of native materials, only two have been found moderately good for nets—whale bone (baleen) and the bark of certain trees. There may not now be living anyone who knows how to make bark nets, although the practice was continued on the lower Mackenzie into the present century—one bark net was secured near Slave Lake in 1906 for the American Museum of Natural History of New York. There may be Eskimos living around Point Barrow or Point Hope who have made whale-bone nets, but this is unlikely. However, baleen can be split by anyone by just common-sense methods and can be knotted as a cord.

The thing to do is to take nets with you. If you do not know the country you expect to traverse, you might perhaps carry meshes of 2-inch, 3-inch, and 4-inch stretch.

There are two most important things about the use of fish nets on journeys, one of these peculiar to the Arctic.

You must be very careful to keep your fish net dry when it is not in use—you must never let it stay wet long enough to decay. This would appear so elementary as not to need stating; but it is a fact (or is commonly believed to be) that an editor of an American sportsmen's journal, who had been giving advice to sportsmen for years on matters of hunting, fishing, and travel, lost his life on a journey he made in Labrador because he neglected drying his nets when they got wet from rain or from canoe upsets. When, through a combination of accident and other circumstances, it became important for him to use the nets for fishing they were already so rotten as not to hold the fish.

The special thing about the use of nets in the Arctic is setting them through ice. If you are spending the winter in a set place you will naturally begin fishing soon after the ice is strong enough to bear a man—when it is, say, 4 or 5 inches thick (although it will bear a man when somewhat thinner). You make holes in the ice, perhaps 10 feet from each other, for a distance equal to the full length of your net. You take a pole that is more than 10 feet long, fasten a string to one end of it, push the pole all the way down through the hole and let go of it so that its buoyancy will bring it up flush against the ice. Then you maneuver it so that it is visible to a man looking down through your second hole. From that it is shoved along to the third, fourth, and other holes, until at the last it is brought up out of the water.

Now you fasten each end of your net to an end of the string, so as to have an endless-chain effect, and then pull through so that the net is all in the water and the string all on top of the ice. You must weight your net so that nowhere does it touch the ice. It will probably be best to suspend it so that it is at approximately the same depth through its whole length, say ten or fifteen inches below the under surface of the ice. You manage this by fishing down through your holes, get hold of the upper edge of the net and attach a string which suspends it at that point. The reason why your net must not touch the ice is that the ice is growing thicker by freezing at its lower side. If the net touches the ice its upper edge will be embedded in the ice tomorrow morning and you will not be able to get it out except by chopping up all the ice.

If you have to chop your net out, do not try by careful chiseling to free it from the hundreds of pounds of ice that will be clinging to it. Make a large round hole in the ice somewhere and lower your net, ice and all, into the water. If you stand by a while, gently working the ice and net around by poking with a pole, the chunks will thaw off and the net will be free—there will be no damage unless you have cut some threads when you were chopping the net loose in the first place. For it is only water immediately in touch with the ice and in process of freezing that is at the freezing point of fresh water—all the rest, farther down, is a little above freezing.

In winter there are places where you can set a net in water that is open no matter how cold the weather. The best of such places are where rivers originate in large lakes. There your method of fishing during winter is just the same as it would be in open water during summer.

When you are taking fish out of a net at temperatures well below zero you will probably want to work with bare hands—most northern fishermen do. The water in the hole from which you have pulled the net is, of course, unfrozen. If the air is 40 below zero it is more than 70 degrees colder than the water. The best way, therefore, to warm your hand is to stick it every now and then down into the water. This warming in ice water ought to be enough to enable you to take the fish out of one net at a time. If you find your hand growing numb, the best way is to shake the water off it as best you can and then stick it somewhere inside of your clothes. Handiest is to wear a coat and shirt wholly of fur and cut Eskimo style as described in this Manual's section on clothing. Then you can slip both arms, if desired, out of the sleeves and hold them on your bare breast until they are warm.

Taking fish out of a net with bare hands at 50 below zero demonstrates what we said in the clothing discussion, that if the rest of your body is warm as toast you can stand almost any amount of cold on your hands. It is men who are badly clad whose hands get numb under such conditions.

It is possible to use waterproof mittens in taking fish out of nets although among northern fishers, at least among the Eskimos, you are considered rather a sissy if you do—or else the excuse is made for you that naturally your hands get numb because your clothes are so poor. The mittens, when used, are of seal skin, the same material and sewing as for the upper of a seal skin water boot, and they are cut gauntlet style. It may be that rubber gloves or mittens would be good, perhaps the kind used by surgeons. However, there is not much protection from cold in the surgeon type of rubber glove; there would be more from a rubber mitt, since all four fingers would be touching and warming each other, and you could slip your thumb cccasionally into your bare palm to warm it.

It is important when taking fish out of a net in very cold

weather to do you handling on top of snow, not on top of glare ice. For if a wet piece of the net touches glare ice it will freeze fast and there will be danger of breaking the threads. However, if this occurs, you chip the net loose with your hunting knife or a pickaxe, not minding if chunks of ice cling to the netting. For they will melt and drop off when you put the net back into the water again and set it.

FISHING FROM THE BEACH

Along certain Arctic coasts people are more successful than you would believe in setting nets from the beach. West of the Mackenzie at Shingle Point, for instance, Stefansson took part in fishing with two-inch mesh, the nets about 30 feet long and 18 inches wide. Logs were split and the splinters lashed together so as to make poles 60 or 70 feet long. With these the nets were shoved out from the beach, buoyed so as to float just below the surface. Half a dozen people could be kept busy with four nets. You shove out all four from the beach, about 100 yards apart. After pushing the last out you go back to the first, pull it in, and find anything from 10 to 30 or 40 fish. Shove that net out and take in your second net, and so on, rotating all day or until you are tired.

LENGTH OF RUNS

Fishing of this kind could in some cases go on for a week or ten days at a time when there was a run. Even when there was no run you would probably get something, although in that case you might not find it worth while to pull in the nets more than three or four times a day.

USE OF SWEEP NETS

Fishing from shore with sweep nets depends on local knowledge although you may discover a shoal of fish by accident any time. You must have at a minimum one boat. Your net should be fairly long and wide and of a rather small mesh. When you know there is a run you fasten one end of the net to the shore by a long line, go out with the other end, attach it to your boat and paddle around in a semi-circle, coming back to shore. In this way great quantities of "herring" are captured at various points on the north coast of Canada, particularly at the Baillie Islands (near Cape Bathurst). Some of these are real herring similar to the Norwegian. On August 3, 1911 (August being there the month of runs—especially late August) Dr. R. M. Anderson drew in about 3,000 California herring (*Clupea pallasi*) with one sweep of a 200-foot net that had an end fastened to the beach at the Cape Bathurst sandspit.

The Eskimos have a way of using hooks which at least in cold weather is a great deal better than our method. The body of the hook is made of ivory or bone, and shaped like a small fish so as to be its own bait. A very good material for a point to this sort of hook is a shingle nail, or for larger fish a 6-penny or 8-penny nail, which you pass through a hole bored in the head of your ivory fish at right angles to the long axis of its body and then bend up L-fashion, or a little more, perhaps U-shape.

To use these hooks you make a hole in the ice 12 to 18 inches in diameter, so that it will let in a good deal of light. You sit beside the hole and keep jiggling the ivory fish at various depths, always being ready to pull in the moment you feel something on the hook. You pull in straight and fast; then your fish will not get off the hook. As he comes out of the water you throw him, with a continuation of the same motion, upon the snow beside you—you have no bother taking him off the hook as you would if it had been barbed.

It was the experience of a party using this method in the delta of the Mackenzie River that an ivory fish the size of your index finger and with an 8-penny nail was rather on the big side. More likely it should be the size of your little finger or somewhere in between the two. With an ivory or bone body of this intermediate size they caught fish of many species and ranging in weight from less than a pound to connies that weighed more than 50 pounds.

LAKE FISHING

It is not easy for a stranger to tell in advance what are going to be the better fishing localities in a lake. You might try setting your net off a promontory. If you have several nets you better set them in different parts of the lake under different conditions. After some of this experience you will be a better judge than any wise fisherman, white or native, who does not know that particular lake.

There are perhaps only two important northern ways of using hooks that are different from the ordinary. The Dogrib and other Athapaskans who travel on Great Bear Lake carry hooks of the codhook type. These they bait by wrapping a piece of fish, a piece of bacon, or something of that sort, around the shank and drop them into the water so weighted that there is a noticeable strain on the line as you pay it out. You keep on letting out the line until you feel the hooks strike bottom. Then you pull it back so that the hook will be suspended a foot or two feet from the bottom. This is said to be the best way to catch the Bear Lake trout, a fish numerous in the 15 to 20-pound weights, not very rare up to 35 pounds and said to attain top sizes of 50 or more pounds.

SPEARING FISH

At the foot of a waterfall there may be an opportunity nearly throughout the year for spearing fish, although the best opportunities are when there is a run, or an attempted run. Bloody Falls on the Coppermine is an instance. Eskimos will crouch around on rock ledges with fish forks that have handles which are short at 10 feet and may run to 20 feet or more. They hold the spear motionless, or nearly so, in the water, until a fish swims within reach, when they give a little push. These are two-pronged spears with a barb on either side.

In shoal water Eskimos use very short fishing spears with a handle only three or four feet long and usually with three prongs. You just wait around till you see a fish near you and jab at him.

FISH TRAPS

When fish are running up or down a stream, or when for any reason they are numerous, you can sometimes divert and catch them with fences where the water is shallow. Eskimos build these more or less like the caribou drives we have been describing, except the boulders have to be close together to form a wall. Sometimes a number of people beating the water will drive fish along one of these walls into a pound which usually is not of rocks but of sticks that have been driven into the river bottom. There are also indiscriminate ways of building what are practically mazes for the fish, consisting of any number of separate compartments—square, triangular or any other shape. When a lot of fish have been tangled in these mazes the Eskimos go wading around and spearing them, usually with the three-pointed spear.

SECTION IV

GAME LAWS

ALASKA AND CANADA

Each person who intends to hunt land animals, apart from emergencies of the trail, should be provided with a copy of the game and hunting laws and regulations published by the Alaska Game Commission, U. S. Department of Agriculture, and of the corresponding laws and regulations for Canada obtainable from the Department of Mines and Resources, Ottawa. There is no point in trying to summarize these laws and regulations, for they change from time to time.

GREENLAND

By Danish law, Greenland is a closed country, more so than Tibet. If you get there at all it will be either with permission to hunt or in such extreme emergency that you would take the law into your own hands.

Your application to visit Greenland, as a private person, should be transmitted by the State Department of the U. S. to the Danish Government through its representative at Copenhagen. The American Minister will make an attempt to secure your permit from the administration of Greenland (Grönlands Styrelse). He will have to make a case that you are not a tourist. It is theoretically impossible for a mere tourist to visit Greenland. However, the Greenland administration will accept most any "serious" plan. You are a musician and you want to study the music of the Eskimos. You are a painter and specialize in glaciers or mountain scenery. You are a botanist and desire first-hand experience with Greenland vegetation. In all such cases it is better to be able to show that you are connected with some organization, or at least that your findings and collections are to be used by a learned society or at least a public institution— your music will be studied by a specialist on primitive music at Yale; your botanical collections are going into the Gray Herbarium at Harvard, or something of the sort.

SVALBARD

Norwegians have not been so strict and formal about the Spitsbergen group and Bear Island as the Danes have been about Greenland. The basic reason for this is considered to be that the Danish regulations are intended in the main for quarantine—to protect Greenland Eskimos against white men's epidemic and other diseases. The population of the Svalbard Islands is wholly either Norwegian or Russian and therefore possessed of about the same immunities as the rest of us; so that our diseases are no more dangerous to them in Svalbard than they would be in Oslo or Moscow.

There is a permanently closed season on reindeer, which are native, and on musk oxen, which have been introduced and which are really domestic animals. There are no restrictions on sea game, including polar bear.

U. S. S. R.

Things are very special in the U. S. S. R.; but they have been appreciative of and readily helpful to travelers and explorers in peacetime. In 1940 scientists of the U. S. Government (Smithsonian Institution) and of American universities were welcomed and given every facility—consult, for instance, Dr. Ales Hrdlička of the National Museum, who has much recent experience of travel off the beaten tourist track in the U. S. S. R. Permits have to be secured in advance for private travelers, whether scientists or not. The arrangements would be made either through the Soviet Embassy in Washington or the American Embassy in Moscow.

491

Section V

CACHES, DEPOTS, AND BEACONS

On the polar sea, caches and depots of all sorts are out of the question unless for a very few days. To leave something behind on the pack during an outward journey and expect to pick it up on your return would be like detaching a dory on an eastward voyage across the Atlantic and expecting to pick it up coming back. Besides, there is no known emergency way of caching things to be safe from the first two of the three serious things which may occur—the floe may tip on edge and spill your belongings into the water; the floe may crumble and bury them under a mountain of broken ice; a polar bear may come along.

On landfast ice, one sort of depot may be bear-proof. You sink a pit into the thick shore ice, as if you were digging a grave so large that it would contain what you desire and still be filled only to within three or four feet of the surface. You now cover your belongings with something waterproof, perhaps the hides of animals. Then you shovel in a little snow and pour in some sea water. Before the mush has hardened you drop in chunks of ice so that they will freeze as in a matrix. Putting in more snow, more ice, more water, you obtain a conglomerate through which you can work easily with pickaxes when you want to open the cache but through which even a polar bear would find it difficult to penetrate.

More valuable than knowledge of how to cache things from polar bears is an understanding of what it is they recognize as food and will eat. Fresh seal is their staff of life. They can smell it from 10 to 12 miles to leeward and they will get at it in spite of practically anything. All decayed meats apparently smell alike to all carnivorous animals so that caribou, musk ox, or the meat of a fellow bear will be just as much like food as if it were seal. But in his whole experience the bear has never eaten bear and he has never eaten caribou. If these meats are fresh, the smell of them apparently means nothing in the way of food. Travelers have reported bears so hungry that they followed a sledge trail to pick up refuse but nevertheless walked a few yards to leeward of a depot of caribou meat and paid no attention to it.

Polar bears get to be very old and they travel far. There is, accordingly, no guarantee that an old and experienced bear may not have learned through some accident that caribou is food, so you cannot swear they would never touch that sort of depot. Certainly the rule is that they will not. But, remember, if there is even a slight decaying smell, caribou, like any other meat becomes food to their nostrils.

TRAPS ARE DANGEROUS

Against bears, as other animals, you can employ such devices as a loaded gun which shoots when a bait is pulled. This is so dangerous that it should be used only in extreme need. Even one of your own men, through forgetfulness or accident, might be the victim, let alone strange men or your own dogs. The same objection applies to the setting of very powerful steel traps. Anything strong enough to hold a bear is likely to break a man's leg if he steps into it, and will certainly ruin a dog.

With the grizzly bear you have about the same trouble as with the polar, since they, too, are powerful. However, they are largely vegetarian, are few even where they are found, and are absent from large portions of the Arctic territory. We need not discuss caches against grizzlies except as some which are developed in other connections may happen to be more or less effective against them, too.

Protection from wolves and foxes is easy. Pile up stones around a heap of meat and, if they are heavy, these beasts will not disturb. If the stones are small, you can fix them in a matrix of slushy snow. Logs piled over meat are similarly effective and so are box caches built log-cabin style.

But there is one animal hard to outwit or repel, the wolverine. He is clever in his depredations; he is mischievous as well, for he will carry off things that are of no possible use to him—such as watches or scientific instruments.

By the ancient Greek principle of natural history, that an animal has intelligence in proportion to the physical organs it possesses for dealing with the outside world, the wolverine ought to be intelligent. His paws, next after apes and their near relations, are most like human hands. His teeth are powerful. He is indefatigable, and he has either intelligence or a persistence which frequently amounts to the same thing. We give some examples:

Climb a tree and hang a bundle of meat from a limb by a rope. Any animal might bite this line if it were rawhide or if it smelt like food, as through being greasy. A wolverine will bite the line whatever it is and however it smells.

If you suspend by a wire which the wolverine cannot bite, he grasps the wire as if with arms and slides down it to the bundle. This author has never seen a wolverine actually doing that, but he has numerous testimonials that they do somehow arrive at the bundle and cling to it while they tear it to pieces, perhaps eating some of its contents there and the rest after they fall to the ground.

Through a cache of log cabin type, wolverines will eat their way no matter how big the logs. Apparently time means nothing to them. If they don't get through in a day of gnawing, they will get through in a week.

What seems to be the most ingenious of possible animal stories about cache rifling is vouched for by Stefansson through his own observation and that of his companions. A pit was made for caribou meat; on top of it were placed round stones, the biggest about the size of your head, and these were fixed in a matrix of ice derived from snow slush. The ground was hard as concrete so the beast could not burrow through it. It could not chew through the stones. What the wolverine did was to lie on the stones until the body heat melted one loose from its matrix, whereupon he rolled it out. He then gnawed away what ice he could, and lay down again to do some more melting. Finally, doubtless after several days, he got to the meat.

It has been suggested that this story shows no real intelligence—that what happened was merely that the beast knew where the meat was located, wanted to be as near as he could be, and so lay down on top of it. Every little while, moved by blind instinct, he would try to get nearer the meat.

At last he would find that a stone was loose which he then rolled away.

Some of the best arguments for the intelligence of a wolverine are not from his cache-breaking but from his direct stealing. The biggest of them, proportioned like skunks, will not run over 40 pounds. Stefansson had killed and butchered a caribou in such a way that most of its body was still in one piece. This was unwieldy, several times bigger than the wolverine as well as heavier, yet he carried it off as a man will drag a log through snow—lifting and carrying one end on his back, dragging the other.

A man on guard is the only real protection against the rifling of caches by wolverines. However, if you smoke-dry your meat, it has the advantage that you can leave it for a few days with tolerable safety (or you can cache anything else you like in the smoke house) for the smoke smell, while fresh, will keep beasts of prey at a distance. Eventually, of course (in about a fortnight) some wolverine will become contemptuous of the fire smell, which he at first dreaded, and venture into the deserted house.

DEPOTS

Hunters take advantage of frozen ground for temporary storage of meat. If you kill a caribou and leave the meat exposed to the sun it will be fly-blown in no time, for blue bottles are numerous even in islands well north of the continental limit of America. So when you butcher an animal you scoop out a hollow in the ground, protect the meat by skins under and over, and then cover with earth. These excavations are down to frost, which may be anything from a few inches in a swamp to say two feet on a sandy southward slope. The meat is safe from flies and decay is slowed.

Sometimes large depots require little or no protection from animals by the nature of what they contain. For instance, when Captain Kellett left 288 days' provisions for 66 men on the south shore of Melville Island, he deposited such things as flour in barrels, bread in casks, sugar and currants in kegs,

495

chocolate in cartwheels resembling grindstones, quantities of woolen clothes, tools, etc. These supplies Stefansson found more than half a century later to be some of them in good condition and few if any of them disturbed by animals, though polar bears, wolves, and foxes must have visited the locality frequently.

Certain of the things most important to cache in the Arctic are by their nature perfectly safe, as, for instance, gasoline in large drums, ammunition in factory packing. Biscuits are safe from anything but mice, for they would not be recognized as food by the Arctic animals even when the packages are open.

The Stone Age Eskimos did not recognize such things as food either. For instance, those Victoria Islanders who found on Banks Island McClure's abandoned ship and the considerable stores of food, both on it and ashore, used none of the European edibles but did use the packing cases and other related materials, such as nails, hoops, and wires.

So far as the Eskimo people are concerned, depots in the Arctic are safer than they would be in most other countries. If it is known whose property they are and what they are intended for, they are likely to be respected unless there is a special enmity with the group involved. This respect for caches is a matter of honor and custom. In addition, it may happen that an Eskimo is afraid to touch a depot for reasons of taboo.

There are, however, no sure ways of instilling effective taboo dread by any sign which you can put on a cache or place near it. Most often an Eskimo taboo, if applied, will be the idea of some shaman or will be connected with a folklore story which is current locally (as gospel). In a few places special things might work; as, for instance, putting a human skull on top of the depot. You would have to know your locality before trying this dodge, or take a chance on it. For there is diametric variance among uncivilized Eskimos as to their attitude toward human remains. In some districts anybody would be frightened by a skull, or would have a taboo feeling, while in another place a man equally free from European influence might pick up the skull and hand it to his children to play with.

496

BEACONS

Where records are being deposited, the best way is that which has been commonest in polar exploration, to erect, out of things of no value to the Eskimos, a beacon which will be seen from a distance. Then at a prearranged distance and direction from this, and in a prearranged manner, you bury or otherwise hide the record. You will have to be pretty ingenious about hiding traces of your burial, but that would be accomplished exactly as if you were hiding something from European inquisitiveness.

It is probably not true anywhere of the Eskimos of Canada or Alaska, but in the U. S. S. R. the icebreaker *Sibiriakov* found on her 1932 voyage that identification marks on the Chukchi shore had been destroyed by the Chukchis because they believe such marks scare away seals.

PRESERVATION OF RECORDS

How to preserve a record for years or centuries is everywhere a problem, but not quite so much in the Arctic as elsewhere. For instance, Stefansson found in an open cylinder which had been filled with wet sand for more than half a century, thawing every summer and freezing every winter, the record of McClure's discovery of the Northwest Passage. It was written on ordinary paper and still legible except in a few spots that had "rotted" away.

In old records that have been recovered in the North, the preservation of pencil writing has usually been better than that of ink. In some records where both were used, nearly all the pencilling was legible, nearly all the pen writing undecipherable.

The early explorers usually put records into whatever they happened to have with them, though some carried special contrivances. Since rust is slow in the Arctic, an ordinary water-tight tin can, such as those which hold casein or malted milk, is likely to keep a record safe for a quarter or half century. Within their natural limits bottles are excellent, or glass jars with screw tops. A brass shotgun shell, corked, would be good (except that this Manual counsels against shotguns being carried at all on long and difficult journeys).

CHAPTER 14

MECHANIZED TRANSPORT

Section I

DIRIGIBLES

This chapter on the use of dirigibles, airplanes and motorized land vehicles does not aim to be a complete discussion of the problems but merely an application to them of certain geographic, oceanographic, and meteorological peculiarities of the Arctic. We are discussing the application of certain elements of polarcraft to mechanized transport.

The voyages of the *Norge, Italia,* and *Graf Zeppelin* brought no surprises except that there is still a mystery, and seemingly always will be, as to why the *Italia* crashed.

As brought out in our discussion of climate, the weather is on the average stable and the winds on the average not strong when you get into the Arctic basin away from the shores of the polar sea. The only condition seriously hostile is the formation of ice upon the envelope and other parts of the craft. This may be less serious with a dirigible than an airplane when the cause is of the nature of spicule fog (discussed in Chapter 3, Section V). It is quite as serious as with planes when the cause is damp snow or sleet.

We summarize what is developed in our climate discussion about the seasonal distribution of Arctic fogs and sleet:

FOG

Except near the margins of the pack, fogs that might form ice are practically absent during four months, December to March, inclusive. They are rare in November and April;

498

well within the pack they are rare also in May. In May near the edges of the pack, and anywhere in the polar basin during June, July, and August, fogs are bad. Near the center of the pack September becomes a clear month; but fogs are prevalent through October out by the margins of the ice and along the continental Arctic shore.

SLEET

The seasons for sleet and snow soft enough to cling are similar to but not identical with those of the fogs.

The records of polar expeditions show that there is no winter month anywhere in the Arctic, except perhaps on the Greenland ice cap, when a sleet storm may not strike. However, it is not likely to happen in any one year that sleet occurs near the center of the Arctic pack during the four-month space December–March; nor is sleet likely even towards the margins of the pack in November or April. The month of May will have little soft snow near the center of the pack but may have it occasionally near the margins. June, July, and August are the sleet months. However, it is not probable that even on the Arctic fringes, except perhaps where the Gulf Stream waters intrude to the north and northeast of the Atlantic, that sleet would be as bad during the worst four months as it is during the worst four over the Newfoundland Banks.

One difficulty with icing peculiar to the dirigible is that when it forms on struts and wires, and continues forming, there will come a time when it begins to break off in chunks. Some of these will get into the slip stream and hit the propeller, which bats them so they fly almost like bullets, some of them striking the envelope. This came near being serious with the *Norge*. Once appreciated, the difficulty can be avoided, as by a suitable placing of wire netting. (This statement, derived chiefly from the experience of the *Norge*, is not so applicable to later dirigibles which avoid exposed struts and wires.)

As with airplanes, dirigibles have found in the Arctic that they can usually control the formation of ice by rising and dropping to levels of different temperatures.

499

We mentioned under climate the average lowness of Arctic fogs, pointing out as a commonplace of the Yankee whaling fleet to the north of Alaska in summer that when the men on the decks could see no indication of neighboring ships the captains at the mastheads could see each other clearly, the blanket of fog being then a hundred feet or less in thickness.

There are not over the polar sea, although there may be over polar lands, those sudden down drafts that are so risky for a dirigible flying low in rugged or mountainous country.

CASE HISTORY OF ITALIA

A case history may bring out certain things about northern aviation clearly and with more force than possible in an abstract statement. We use that of the *Italia.*

Umberto Nobile had built the airship with which Amundsen and Ellsworth crossed the Arctic in 1926, and had been its navigator. In 1928 he was in the Arctic again, with the dirigible *Italia,* operating from a hangar at King's Bay, Spitsbergen. He had already made a good exploratory voyage to the east when, on May 24, he flew from Spitsbergen westerly to the northeast corner of Greenland, crossing an unexplored part of the sea. Then he continued from Greenland to the North Pole by a route unexplored because it was far more easterly than the Peary journeys.

From the Pole, Nobile was returning to Spitsbergen, and was a little to the northeast of that island group, when, on May 25, he was overtaken by a cataclysm that has many explanations, each conflicting with one or more of the others, and none conclusive. All we can state beyond argument is that suddenly the airship was found to be dropping rapidly.

It seems that by a quick change of rudders, or in some other way, Nobile had tilted the ship upward before she struck the ice, so that her tail dragged. Two of the three gondolas were torn away. Ten men, with goods and wreckage, were dumped on the ice. Freed of their weight and that of the gondolas and cargo, the dirigible rose swiftly and drifted off before the wind. Men who had not been stunned by the shock got to their feet and watched it soar away.

They are in reasonable agreement that when the *Italia* was something like 5 miles off she exploded. The six men aboard her in the forward gondola must have been lost.

One of the marooned men, Pomella, was killed as the gondola was being torn loose from the airship; two had broken hips and legs, Nobile and Cecioni; Malmgren suffered a fractured shoulder and, as it proved later, his kidneys had been torn loose so that he eventually died from this cause.

RELIANCE UPON RADIO

If there had been no radio, the Nobile party would have started moving toward shore. Such a 20- or 30-mile walk would have been a mere commonplace in the history of exploration—in fact, several exploring parties have walked ashore on this and near-by groups of islands during the last few centuries, some of them covering several hundred miles. Even with the cripples, the Nobile party could have double-tripped ashore, probably in a week or two.

RADIO SUCCEEDS IN 9 DAYS

But, since they had a radio, Nobile was correct in staying where he was. It took them some days to get the radio in proper working order and it was not until after 9 days (June 3) that an operator in Archangel got and properly interpreted their signals. Days more elapsed before, on June 7, they were in contact with their base ship, the *Città di Milano*. Ten days later they saw the first two planes, Norwegian, piloted by Riiser-Larsen and Lützow Holm, which turned back because of engine trouble shortly before reaching the party. In succeeding days an Italian plane circled near them, and the Norwegians twice approached and then disappeared from view, each time without sighting the Nobile camp.

Finally, on June 20, an Italian plane, working from the base ship, sighted the party, but did not land. It dropped equipment, much of which was broken in the fall. Two days later Italian planes dropped provisions and further supplies. June 22 two Swedish planes flew over, dropping provisions and a note with instructions for marking out a landing place on the ice.

The next day, June 23, almost a month after the disaster, Lieutenant Einar Paal Lundborg descended with his Swedish plane on the pack about 500 feet from the camp. Hopping from cake to cake, he and his mechanic arrived at the camp to find Nobile demanding, in the best grand-opera tradition, that all others should be saved first and he himself be removed last. Lundborg replied (personal communication to Stefansson; see also his book narrative) that this was no grand opera; that he was in command, and that the rescue would be conducted as seemed best to him and his associates.

Nobile was skin and bones from worry, and he is small-boned to begin with. Cecioni, the other cripple, was always large and had put on an extra 50 pounds lying there in the tent, eating much and worrying little since the accident. Lundborg, glancing at the two men, decided that the plane could not carry Cecioni in addition to himself and his mechanic, but that it would carry Nobile. So, taking Nobile under one arm, he and the mechanic hopped from cake to cake again, returned to the plane and flew to the Swedish base on Foyne Island. A few hours later another Swedish plane delivered Nobile to the Città di Milano.

LAST OF MEN RESCUED IN 49 DAYS

Meantime, leaving the mechanic behind at the Swedish base so as to be able to carry the big and fat Cecioni, Lundborg returned alone. Engine failure compelled him to glide for a landing. He fell short by a yard or two, so that his skis, instead of planting themselves on the floe, stubbed their toes against the edge of it and the plane turned on its back, without, however, injuring the pilot. So the fat man had to remain to get still fatter until the Soviet steamer *Krassin* arrived to pick up the entire party of seven on July 12, a month and a half after their descent. (Lundborg had been taken off the floe a few days earlier by a small Swedish plane.)

This case history of Nobile has brought out things both applicable to dirigibles and airplanes. We mention some points not touched upon that concern the dirigible.

One of the difficulties of dirigible operation in tropics or temperate zone is that its gas tends to expand in the daytime when the sun shines and then to contract at night, giving unequal carrying power and tending to the waste of gas. During summer there are in the Arctic long periods of continuous sunshine so that, if you are able to keep above the usually low fog, you have a uniformity of gas buoyancy for weeks and even months at a time—since for weeks near the margin of the polar area and for months near its center the sun is constantly above the horizon. There are similar reciprocal periods of uniform buoyancy in winter due to the absence of the sun.

THUNDERSTORMS RARE

If it be true that the *Hindenburg* and similar disasters resulted from accumulation of electricity under a thunderstorm condition, then in this respect the Arctic is one of the safest of flying regions. There are thunderstorms in the Arctic, but they are extremely rare and probably occur chiefly on its margins. (It seems, by the way, that lightning in the Arctic, and in some other northerly lands, is more likely to occur in winter than in summer. In Iceland, for instance, it is recognized that the severest thunderstorms come in winter.)

SUMMARY

Generally speaking, then, the dirigible is well adapted to Arctic work. Its safest time begins for the main area of the pack in September and ends in May. For the margin of the pack it begins in October and ends in April. For half the year conditions are about the best in the world; for no month of the year are they worse than the worst month on the Newfoundland Banks.

SECTION II

AIRPLANES

Before considering the more specific points we take up the comparative safeties of airplane operation over liquid and ice-clad seas. We turn first to how they compare for safety in forced landing:

Most early flyers who came down on liquid seas far from land and beyond sight of a vessel were lost. All were lost who made forced descents beyond sight of rescuers in a gale.

Before 1937 there had been perhaps a dozen forced landings on the frozen sea. Some were in good weather, some in falling snow, some in blizzards, and one in a combination of gale and the darkness of night. All these had been safe descents—no lives had been lost and there had been only minor injuries to planes. The flyers were always saved in one of three ways: they made repairs and flew again; they were rescued, by plane or ship; or they abandoned their plane and walked ashore.

Take specifically for the North Atlantic the entire period from its first crossing by the United States Navy airplanes in 1919 to the beginning of survey flights by Pan American Airways and Imperial Airways in 1937. During this period at least 19 ocean descents were made in all weathers from calm to gale. Nine planes were lost. The people saved were mostly those who had specially good luck, as coming down in fairly good weather either within sight of a ship or after being able to communicate to a nearby ship through radio the approximate position where they were about to descend.

During the same period more than 90,000 miles were flown over the polar sea. There were at least 56 voluntary and forced descents in all weather from calm to gale (not all Soviet figures are available). No lives were lost from any of these descents.

The safety of the polar sea, as compared with the deadliness of the North Atlantic, is the result of frost. If water is liquid, the best you can hope for is to swim awhile before sinking. When water is solid you behave upon it as if it were land. You are warmer on the ice at −50° than you are in the water at 50°, for water gets to your skin but cold air is held at bay by your clothing. In a 50-mile storm on a liquid sea the waves break over your plane and toss it about until it sinks. In a 50-mile wind on the pack ice you can lash down your plane as if it were on land. Then you can construct a windbreak of snow blocks and tent behind it. You can build a dwelling of snow in which, by Eskimo technique, you can have a warmth of 50° when the thermometer outside reads −50°. If your airplane is beyond repair your radio may not be, and you have time and comfort for getting it into shape.

We can focus the broad contrasts between liquid and frozen seas best with case histories. We need not describe those of the liquid oceans, for they are so clearly in mind; all we need to do is refer to them. There was, for instance, the loss of Charles Kingsford-Smith, Australian, in 1935, and of Amelia Earhart, American, in 1937—these are remembered not merely in themselves but as typical of what so often happens with tropical or temperate zone ocean descents, whether in stormy weather as with Kingsford-Smith, or in good weather as with Miss Earhart. Our need is for the case histories of those who have descended on frozen seas.

FROZEN SEA CASES

The first land plane descent upon sea ice far from shore was made with a ski plane on March 29, 1927, by Hubert Wilkins and Ben Eielson. They took off from Point Barrow, Alaska, with the thermometer around −40°. They planned to fly northwestward for about 6 hours, to the vicinity of latitude 80° north, longitude 180° west, where they would descend and take soundings. They would then fly south for 2 or 3 hours, and thence return to Barrow on a southeasterly course.

A hundred miles from shore the plane was already beyond the previously known region, for they had crossed the track of the *Karluk*, a ship with which Wilkins had once been connected temporarily. They continued for 400 miles beyond the *Karluk* exploration, when they had engine trouble, which necessitated not only a forced descent but also the first ski or wheel descent ever attempted on the pack far from shore.

Wilkins selected a landing spot he thought favorable, depending, as he has said, on the experience he had gained when traveling over pack ice afoot during the years 1913–16 when he was a member of the Canadian Arctic Expedition of 1913–18. Eielson, schooled by North Dakotan and Alaskan winters, brought the plane down to a perfect landing. This was in clear and nearly calm weather 500 miles from shore. A sounding, which Wilkins took while Eielson was repairing the engine, gave more than 16,000 feet, so that they were above the deepest place yet found in the polar sea. During the repairs, the sky had clouded over and snow was beginning to fall.

After a take-off from pack that was made difficult by the softness and depth of new-fallen snow, they flew eastward a little way, had engine trouble again, and made their second descent in a snowstorm. They were still approximately 500 miles from land.

Upon the second take-off the plane headed back toward Alaska and fought this wind through the afternoon. Planes were not so fast in 1927 as they are now, and speed was cut to something like 50 or 60 miles. They continued through the daylight of the late afternoon. In this latitude at this time of year, and with clouds in the sky, it is practically dark at seven o'clock. At nine o'clock, flying a mile high, the plane's engine stopped for the third time, now for want of gas.

The only thing to do was to keep straight against the wind and to bring the plane down as gradually as possible.

Here was a test of a theory in practice. During a previous expedition Wilkins had arrived at the belief that you seldom have to go more than 5 miles, and probably never more than 25, on the northern sea in winter before you find a patch of ice level enough and large enough for an airplane descent and take-off. These patches, then, are scattered; certainly 80 percent of the ice is too rough for a plane, perhaps 95 percent. Even in the coldest weather there is open water here and there; for the ice is continually breaking under the stress of the currents. The chances were, then, at least 10 to 1 that in the darkness and blinding storm the plane would be injured; perhaps 1 chance in 20 that it would come down in open water. What happened, however, was that it descended on a fairly level patch. There was not even a severe jolt. Only the fabric of one wing was slightly injured, torn by a snag of ice. This last, however, was immaterial; for the plane, lacking gas, would have to be abandoned. (There were not in 1927 such facilities as now for rescue operations from the shores of the polar sea.)

In the blizzard and darkness, Wilkins and Eielson, able to get only a limited idea of where they were and how situated, went to sleep in the cabin of the plane and had a fairly good night. Morning found them drifting on a floe some square miles in area, surrounded by leads and patches of open water. The weather was still cloudy and there was not much frost, so that new ice did not form rapidly upon the open water and the floes were comparatively free to move in a drift which appeared to be southeastward, parallel to the north coast of Alaska. An astronomical observation later showed that they were about 75 miles northwest of Point Barrow.

In 7 days the floe, with the camp on it, drifted about 200 miles in an easterly direction. Then the skies cleared and the weather became cold so that new ice formed, binding the floes together. Wilkins and Eielson now took their bedding, camp gear, rifles and ammunition on their backs and started walking toward shore. They averaged 10 miles a day and made it in 10 days.

In the Wilkins story everything went according to plan— they had counted on the possibility of forced landing, on perhaps having to leave their plane, and they had figured the chance that they might have to walk as much as 500 miles to shore. Since it is not possible for men to carry on their backs food enough for that much of a walk over drifting ice, Wilkins had provisions only for about 20 days—in other words, emergency rations. The main plan for subsistence was through hunting equipment which would provide food and fuel in the manner to which Wilkins had become accustomed between 1913 and 1916 on the third Stefansson expedition.

An even more striking contrast between safeties of liquid and ice-clad seas we have from two forced descents where one man was the central character of both. For Roald Amundsen had two forced landings, the first on the pack to the north of the Franz Josef Islands, the second in the never-frozen Gulf Stream (warm North Atlantic drift) just north of Norway.

CASE OF AMUNDSEN

Amundsen and Ellsworth, with four companions, flew north in two airplanes, pontoon-equipped. They started from Spitsbergen May 21, 1925, and were within 100 miles of the North Pole when engine trouble forced both planes down within 3 miles of each other. Pontoons can in an emergency serve as skis upon snow or upon level earth, but the Amundsen planes found open water and descended into leads. These leads soon closed through ice movement, but the party saved one of the planes from being crushed between the floes by hauling it up on the ice.

PONTOON TAKE-OFF FROM ICE

The ice surface was rough, as it usually is in the vicinity of leads, and the men had to work for days to smooth out a runway—a particularly difficult task because they had not brought along tools suitable for this work. With makeshift gear they did level off a runway. One plane was able to carry the men of both, and, using the pontoons for skis, they took off on June 15, flying back to Spitsbergen.

We have discussed the Nobile predicament of 1928. Amundsen was one of those who wanted to come to his help. As a passenger in a French seaplane piloted by a French naval officer, Captain Guilbaud, Amundsen flew from Tromsö, Norway, June 18th, bound for King's Bay, Spitsbergen. There was also a French crew of three and Dietrichson, a Norwegian who had piloted one of Amundsen's planes during the 1925 work. The weather was neither calm nor stormy but halfway between.

The world listened to the plane's radio. When the signals stopped, we knew there had been a forced landing. Ships began to cruise back and forth over the vicinity where the party must have descended but only wreckage of the plane was found—eventually.

Because Amundsen perished several hundred miles north of the Arctic Circle, it was repeated through the press frequently and with variations that he, the great conqueror of the Arctic, had finally been conquered by the Arctic; that the temporary master of the ice and snow had been mastered permanently by these inexorable forces. But not during thousands of years, probably not since the last Scandinavian Ice Age, has there been a floe or any piece of ice in the waters where Amundsen was lost.

Amundsen's descent was several hundred miles short of that ice pack which, at the very moment of his death, was keeping safe Nobile and the rest of the men whom the famous Norwegian explorer meant to help.

The contrast between a frozen and a liquid sea is basic. The pack gives you the amenities of land. You do not sink because ice is firm; you do not thirst, for sea ice is fresh if it is more than 9 months old and there is fresh snow on much of it in any case (or fresh rain and thaw water in summer); your clothes keep you warm and dry, for they have been designed to repel air and rain; there are no waves and spray, for the hard surface is not stirred by the wind.

It is of course ideal that a pilot should have both a theoretical and practical knowledge of the various kinds of Arctic ice described in this Manual before coming down upon any of them for the first time. However, he can take courage from remembering what we have said elsewhere, that on the first 50 descents made upon the northern pack no life was lost and no pilot suffered serious injury; and surely at least a third of these landings must have been the first upon sea ice for the pilot concerned.

COMMON SENSE WAY TO JUDGE ICE

Common sense does the trick. No matter how inexperienced you are you can tell water from ice. With an almost elementary knowledge you realize that the youngest ice looks darkest, almost as dark as water, in comparison with the whiteness of the snow and of the level and strong this year's ice; and that if it looks green, blue, or anything darker than a rather light grey, you must not come down upon it if you can possibly help yourself. You will see, like rivers turned boulevards, the winding and forking ramifications of the leads, most of which were as level as a floor when the ice was formed and some of which are still practically that level even when the ice has become many times stronger than required for the biggest airplane that is coming down for a proper landing.

JUDGING ICE SAFETY FROM AIR

Previous weather must always be taken into consideration in judging landing conditions from the air. However, color is, as we have said, the main thing. Not only is black ice (blue or green under certain light conditions and angles) unsafe, but so are the various shades of grey—the safer the lighter the grey. If it has not been snowing since the pressure that broke the ice and produced the lead upon which you want to land, then the lead may be strong enough though greyish in color.

Here we should keep in mind what was said about young ice in Chapter 11, Section III, particularly the discussion of comparative strength at different temperatures. We said there that 8-inch ice with an air temperature of $-40°$ might be as strong as 10-inch ice at $20°$. That was probably an understatement, if we think of both the 8-inch ice and the 10-inch ice subject to a blow, as if a man were to jump on it from a height; likely, the 10-inch ice at $20°$ would give way more easily than the 8-inch ice at $-40°$.

Another thing the flyer must keep in mind about ice of the 8- to 14-inch range of thickness is what we said in Chapter 2, Section III, about slush. The essence of it is, from the point of view of judging ice strength, that even with no snow blanketing its surface a thaw is taking place at an air chill of $20°$; for that temperature is not low enough for freezing brine of such concentration as you get on top of young ice through the elimination of (shoving upward of) salt that was farther down. The slush formation will produce a darkening of the ice, so that a true appreciation of the color of the surface really gives a better indication of the strength than you would receive from a thickness measurement.

An important thing to remember about salt water ice, in comparing it with experience you may have had with fresh ice, is that salt ice bends more readily than fresh. If on a lake your plane gradually comes to a half and finally stops, without any sign thus far that the ice is going to break, you are all right permanently, but you are not necessarily all right at sea. If there is any doubt, keep your engine turning and lean out, or somehow manage to see the ice around your skis. If you notice it beginning to change color, becoming a little darker, and, of course, if you see that a saucer hollow is gradually forming either around each ski or around the plane as a whole, then you better start moving. You need not necessarily take off, for you have already found that the ice is strong enough to support your plane while in motion. Taxi to an ice area that for one reason or another looks to you safer, and try again standing still.

We describe later a risky but sometimes advisable experiment, flying along ice and letting your skis touch it occasionally, an observer watching the marks both to see how black they are immediately and also to detect a gradual later darkening, during the next second or two. A part of the observer's background for interpreting these signs is that there are two things, or if you like three, that are involved in the darkening. It may be that your ski bent the ice and that the darkening noticed is produced by a seepage of sea water from below. Or it may be that you have merely pressed down into a slush on top of the ice a white covering which has one or two origins: It may be a very thin layer of hoarfrost produced by a condensation of that fog from young ice which we discussed under the head of "water smoke" in Chapter 3, Section V; or it may be that you have pressed down into slush a snow covering.

If the edges of the heavy ice bordering the lead are rounded off (filled in) with old snowdrifts, then the lead should be considered safe. You may happen to know how long ago it was the wind blew that made these drifts, and how cold it has been in the interval, which knowledge is most important if there is only one direction of drift. If you see that drifts are in two or more directions, you have additional evidence that the ice is not so very new—it has been there through as many different strong blows as there are different directions of drifts.

Whether the strength of comparatively thin ice is going to be sufficient depends, of course, on other factors besides its own strength, among them the weight of your plane, the length and width of your skis, and the angle and speed at which the skis hit the ice.

You may be down on a lead that is surrounded by comparatively thin older ice (for instance, you are on 10-inch lead ice with 4-foot ice forming either shore). In that case the difference in level between the lead and the older ice is so small that you can without difficulty taxi up on the old ice and rest there till the lead is safe, knowing pretty well that ice which bends only slightly under your weight now will be strong enough not to bend at all a few hours hence. Or if there has been a wind since the lead froze over, there are drifts from the old ice out upon the new, and you can perhaps use one of them in taxiing off the lead for safety— if the difference in level between the lead and its shore is too much for your skis to take otherwise.

Again assuming that your lead ice is bending only slightly under your plane, there is the third possibility, that a man who is with you in the plane can jump out with a miner's pickax and go along to some place where, with a few dozen blows, he is able to slope off the edge of the old ice so that you can climb onto it from the new.

If you are planning to stop so long that your engine will cool off it is well not to have your plane standing on a lead even though the ice may be 2 or 3 feet thick and a hundred times the necessary strength for your plane. For you can never tell anywhere in the Arctic (although the danger is greater the nearer you are to land) when ice pressure may start. Under stress at the right angle and of the required power any ice will crack, even that which has been brought to a thickness of more than a hundred feet by crushing, overlapping and freezing. Still, the chances of breakage are greatest with the thinnest ice. So if you are going to spend the night, or longer, you had better move your plane to the heaviest ice you can practicably reach by taxiing from the lead.

So far as ice breakage is concerned, there is no need for a man to stand watch over a plane while the others sleep, if they make camp on the ice and sleep with their ears close to the ice or snow. For even if your ear is separated from the

512

floor of your camp by 2 or 3 thicknesses of caribou skins and then by something you are using for a pillow—even so you will hear through the ice the sound of ice breaking though it be miles off. However, if the men sleep in the cabin of the plane it may be necessary to stand watch; for apparently there is no testimony available as to whether the sound of breaking ice is transmitted through the structure of the machine to the interior of the cabin—probably it is not. Or at least it would probably not be loud enough there to wake an ordinary sleeper.

However, we must qualify this by what is said in our Chapter 7 on the difference between snow-house camps and tent camps. In a tent you hear the noise of breaking ice only when there is no wind, for a flapping of the canvas or other fabric may drown out the noise; in a snow house you hear the noise of breaking ice equally far whether there is a gale or a calm. Indeed, men inside of a snow house will hear noises transmitted through the ice that would not be heard by a sentry standing guard outside.

PROCEDURE WHEN ICE IS BREAKING

Upon finding out that ice is breaking not many miles away, you prepare for taxiing rather than for a take-off—unless, indeed, you have served the purpose of your stop and are ready to travel. While you warm up the engine you station men on hummocks, perhaps with field glasses, looking for signs as to where the ice is breaking. This can perhaps be seen by the gradual elevation of a snag of ice against the horizon. For it is likely to happen, especially near the start of a crush, that individual flat cakes of some dimension are gradually tilted, one edge down in the water and the other up in the air. Sometimes you see them rising 10, 20 or more feet before they topple over, broken either by their own weight or by a thrust.

Possibly at the start, but more likely after half an hour or so of pressure, you see ridges building up here and there. It was Stefansson's practice with dog sledges, and the like could be done with airplanes, to get everything ready for the start and to move, if there is pressure all around you, into the center of the floe that you are on.

With dogs you might wait till the level piece around you is but a few square acres before you begin trying to cross a ridge and escape, as described in Chapter 11, Section III. With an airplane you would noturally want to take off while your runway is long enough. It may, then, be the safest—when you are good and ready and are convinced that your neighborhood is really in for a bad pressure—to take the air and circle around for a while till you have determined upon an area that is not being crushed; whereupon you would land again and make a second camp.

A description of ice crushing may over-impress a reader; those used to it do not ordinarily get excited by it, nor worry much. It will not be, whether with dogs or airplanes, nearly as dangerous as a lot of other situations to which you are so used that they do not worry you.

The circumstances under which pressure is dangerous is that of darkness or really thick weather. There are no rules; you have to rely upon your own judgment or upon a hunch, which is perhaps the same thing. It may be that if you remain still the pressure will cease before anything happens in your immediate neighborhood. On the other hand your neighborhood may break up, and then a take-off is no longer possible. However, the crushing that destroys or immobilizes your plane is probably not otherwise dangerous to the men. If your plane radio is still functioning you can send an SOS; if not, you take your portable radio equipment to a place of safety and send out messages at leisure.

It is possible that ice may not only crush but also bury a plane; for slabs that resemble brick walls three or four stories high may tumble upon it. Much more likely, however, your damaged plane will still serve a number of purposes, such as use of radio or employment as living quarters. Likely, too, there will be ample time for dismembering it and taking away anything you need if you have to retreat.

CASE HISTORIES OF CRUSHED PLANES

Of all the scores of planes that have stood for longer or shorter periods on the Arctic ice none, so far as we know, have yet been crushed in the manner described. The nearest thing was that during one of the Ellsworth-Wilkins Antarctic expeditions a machine was standing on level ice when a crack opened so as to let down one ski, the ice thereupon closing and pinching the ski and its fastenings enough so that the plane had to be brought out for repairs. This was a winter type of situation. A like thing happened in summer during the Levanevsky search when a pontoon craft belonging to the Soviet Government came down alongside an ice breaker in the sea to the north of Alaska. Some time later drift ice closed in and broke up the plane before it was possible to hoist it aboard the ship.

TESTING WEAK ICE

Under a number of conditions, among them rescue operations, it may be necessary for you to descend in a given locality where the indications for a safe descent are few. There may be, for instance, a lead with ice of such color that you feel pretty sure it is not safe. A skillful flyer can make a preliminary test that is valuable if he has with him an observer who is a sound judge of conditions. The operation we are about to describe is so risky that it should be attempted only with a powerful motive and good visibility conditions, as well as the skillful pilot and competent observer.

You come down with the machine in full control, touch the ice lightly with your skis and rise again. Your observer watches the color of the marks that are made on the ice. If the ice is too weak they will not only be dark at first but they will continue darkening for a few moments. This is a darkening possibility of snow that was on the lead; if not proper snow it is a darkening of snow-like rime that has accumulated on the surface of the young ice through its "sweating"—the condition we described when discussing water smoke in Chapter 3.

The hypothetical situation of desire to land within a small radius of a given spot may occur where there is not merely an absence of all good types of landing places which you would ordinarily use but also not even a dangerous looking lead. That situation fortunately is not likely to be found in winter except in a region of paleocrystic ice. The description of this ice in Chapter 2, Section III, and elsewhere, will indicate that it is not desirable for ski landings, and even worse for wheels. Superficially the unevenness may not be greater than that of the snowdrifts among which Canadians land in their winter prairie flying. But the situation is nevertheless worse, for the snow is likely to be soft in the hollows between the rounded hummocks of glare ice. However it is the opinion of Wilkins, the only really expert flyer who has as yet traveled on foot extensively over the Arctic pack, that where there is a large field of paleocrystic ice you can almost always find a level area of considerable size which was a fresh water lake the previous summer and upon which you descend and accomplish such a slowing up of your speed that by the time you have slid across the level patch into the hummocky district the jars need not be enough to break or upset your machine.

A serious difficulty with this type of paleocrystic ice landing is in taking off. Almost certainly you could not make it. However, it is likely that you could taxi from where you came down to some old lead or other level field and take off there. The taxiing may of course require stopping occasionally and getting out with pickaxes to cut away snags of ice; for even among the heavy paleocrystic floes breakage and crushing take place, particularly in summer. You may find 20 successive miles of this kind of ice without snags; but it is not likely you can leave your paleocrystic field for a level one adjoining without crossing either a low pressure ridge or an area that has snags sticking up here and there.

ESTABLISHING A LARGE "PERMANENT" CAMP WITH FREIGHTING PLANES

A situation the opposite of a rescue, which demands your coming down right by, is one that requires you to scout a broad region to find a good spot where it is intended that a number of planes shall come down later; as for instance, to establish a scientific base camp on drifting floes. Such a camp was established at 90° North by the Administration of the Northern Sea Route when they delivered to that locality a Soviet scientific expedition with its four members and 10 tons of supplies. But while the case we have in mind is like theirs we cannot use their actual procedure for a guide; rather we would do what they planned to do but did not. They sent one or more observers who did visit the immediate North Pole vicinity but who had such bad luck with the weather that no observations of value could be made. These weather difficulties were due to the lateness of the season. It was already May, and the 4- or 5-month season of practically no fogs comes to an end during April. As May advanced the weather was constantly getting thicker and foggier so that delay was not permissible.

What the Northern Sea Route planes did, therefor, was to arrive in a group of four the third week of May. A pilot, considered to be their best judge of sea conditions as viewed from the air, circled a likely spot two or three times and then came down. The others stayed aloft. The crew of the first plane scampered around the neighborhood, picked out the best landing field and made their customery T-symbol to indicate the direction of wind and the one in which the other three planes were to land.

BEST SEASON TO ESTABLISH CAMP IS MARCH

If parties are to be landed on sea ice, and if you can choose your time for doing it, then the preferred month is March. Your scouting party should arrive at the desired locality either early in the morning or later than midafternoon; for although the Arctic sun is never high still it is higher at noon (except right at the North Pole) than at other times and consequently the shadows will not be so conspicuous and clear. Probably you should travel at first at 3,000 or 3,500 feet until you have picked out two or three likely spots. You will give each of these a more thorough examination by flying around them at an elevation of 200 or 300 feet.

ANCHORING PLANES IN SNOW

Since men can camp anywhere, with a few exceptions as outlined elsewhere in this Manual, the first consideration of a survey party landing away from a base is for the plane. The camp site should be selected in the relation of obstructions in the terrain to the prevailing wind—you want a lee for your plane though you do not want a lee for your camp otherwise. The direction of the prevailing winds, or at least that of the last strong wind, can be determined from aloft by the furrows in the snow (sastrugi) which are parallel with the direction of the wind, with the wider and more rounded ends to leeward.

If your camp site looks as good to you after you have landed as it did from aloft, you next choose a place where it is possible to dig a trench into which the plane can be taxied and secured, facing into the prevailing wind. (See below for exception to facing the plane into the wind.) Secure the plane by digging the trench wide enough for the skis, and about 2 or 3 feet deep, according to the size of the plane. It will stay with tail high and wings nearly parallel with the ground. For a low-wing monoplane a snow wall could be built around wings and fuselage, thereby preventing the wind from getting any lifting hold under the plane. Deadmen should be put in front and under each wing tip, buried about 3 feet deep, and snow packed hard on top. If these don't break loose the first half hour while the snow is setting, they will not come out later; for, as we explained in relation to snow house building, snow, after being packed in, sets and hardens in a way that reminds one of concrete (of course a soft concrete).

When it is necessary to tie down an airplane for short periods on ice a satisfactory method is to dig two holes in the ice at locations near the end of each wing, connecting the two holes under the ice by means of a tunnel. A line is then tied to one wing, passed down through the tunnel and made fast to the end of the other wing.

When an airplane is left in the open where it may be subject to high winds, it is important to tie the controls so that the flippers and rudder will not lash back and forth. There are wooden gadgets made on the order of a clamp which can be fastened on to the flippers and the rudder to prevent movement in highest winds.

In connection with making a plane fast it has been learned that a plane faced into a strong wind will be harder to keep fast than one which is broadside to the wind. A 60-mile wind blowing against the plane when it is facing the wind causes tremendous lift, as the wing design intended. Apparently this is an important rule to keep in mind whenever the trench and wind-break method, described above, is not employed. However, winds over 50 m. p. h. seldom if ever blow on the Arctic pack if you are more than 50 miles from land, at least in winter—or so have testified De Long, Nansen, and Stefansson, among others. Gales of 60 m. p. h. therefore occur only on or near land in the Arctic—but possibly farther within the pack north of Iceland and north of western Europe where the warm currents from the Gulf Stream may create a special condition.

A difficulty in operating with skis is that the skis "freeze" to the ice or snow if the plane is left standing for any length of time. If timber is available, it is a good thing to put one small log in front of each ski and then taxi the plane up on the logs, thus preventing the skis from sticking to the snow or ice.

The preceding is, of course, a rule for all ski landings on snow anywhere. That a ski "freezes" to the snow is a special application of a general principle we have mentioned several times. But perhaps we had better make it doubly clear in this connection.

When snow falls gently upon the ground and remains there, it settles or subsides gradually, being perhaps eventually subject to the transformation into granular snow, a form we discuss under several relations; but never does snow that lies undisturbed where it fell undergo the process spoken of as resembling the hardening of concrete.

When snow is pounded into drifts by a strong wind there is an intermediate result. This snow is hard enough to cut into blocks, as for snow houses, but still (at least superficially) the process is not the one we think of as turning to concrete.

The concrete-like process will result if you take soft new-fallen snow, or the powdered results from crushing a block of drifted snow, and subjected to pressure. When you are building a snow house, for instance, you rub the originally soft or the pulverized snow into a crevice in the wall. If you test it immediately it is still soft. Test it in 5 minutes and it has undergone a noticeable hardening. Test it in half an hour and it is much harder than even snow that has been pounded into a drift by a gale. This is the process spoken of as hardening like concrete.

Now when a heavy thing, like a loaded sledge or an airplane on skis, stands with a plane surface heavily pressed down on snow the "concrete" process takes place. Accordingly, when you land an airplane the first thing to do, or at least a thing to be done within 5 minutes, is to place blocks of wood, blocks of ice, or something of that sort, underneath the skis so as to keep them off the snow.

If skis have been allowed to "freeze" to the snow you will have to loosen the plane first by some such process as shaking it or by prying up the skis with levers. Then you will have to raise the skis so that you can get at their under sides and scrape them free of the snow that sticks to them.

Snow will stick in this fashion apparently to any ski or runner. Certainly it sticks to steel, iron, and wood. There is, probably, a difference in how tenaciously it sticks. For instance, it is said to rub very easily off ivory sledge runners.

So it may be worth while to make experiments with soft metals, such as german silver or copper, to see if they have a special value in "concrete" snow sticking less to them.

We have suggested that the age of a lead can be inferred from snowdrifts that extend out upon it in the lee of hummocks that are on the old ice at its margins, and that you can be still more certain the lead is strong if you note drifts crossing each other that have been made by successive winds. This brings up a discussion of snowdrifts both as a help and as a hindrance.

The snowdrifts are an obvious hindrance in that they constitute a roughening of the surface. This will not be worse than what Canadian flyers deal with constantly on their prairies.

In discussing snowdrifts as a compass, we explained that in diffused light, when they are not visible, the man on foot can still use them through the sense of touch. Obviously a flyer cannot use them that way—cannot use them in diffused daylight or in twilight. But if the sun is clear, and low in the sky, as it is bound to be, since it is the Arctic, the shadows cast by the drifts will be clear and a pilot can use them not only to indicate how rough the surface is but also, within the limitations discussed in Chapter 11, Section II, he can make some use of them as a compass.

DETERIORATION OF ICE LANDING FIELDS IN SUMMER

But all this discussion has been on the assumption that you are flying in winter, or at least not during the season of thaws. We have dwelt on the summer being the worst time of year for sleet and fog, conditions that may produce emergency landings; it is also the worst for making safe descents upon the sea ice.

It was with reference to winter we quoted Wilkins as saying that usually there is a fit landing spot every 5 miles and almost certainly at least one in 25. In saying that he counts not only upon the leads that are flat, and upon certain fields of ice that formed level in the autumn and have never been crushed, but also upon the paleocrystic ice where the surface of rounded hummocks is like a miniature rolling prairie and where snow has filled in most of the hollows so that the glare knobs do not constitute much more of an unevenness that snowdrifts frequently do.

All this is different in summer. A lead or stretch of other flat ice that might accommodate a thousand planes in April, or even in May, will begin in late May or early June a slow deterioration. First the snowdrifts become so soft and granular that you will have to be very careful when you come down not to nose over—your skis may sink where you expect them to slide. A little later there is slush pretty well all over the level field. This is not quite so bad a stage as the granular snow one just before; but the next that follows is worse.

JULY AND AUGUST ICE CUT BY CHANNELS AND PITTED WITH LAKES

For somewhere in the neighborhood, perhaps half a mile or 2 miles away, there is a crack in the ice made through pressure or a hole cut by a seal. The buoyancy of ice is greater than that of water and the thaw water flows off into these openings. Gradually here and there currents develop, and they cut channels for themselves. By early June near the margin of the pack, and late in June towards its center, you have the ice crisscrossed by these channels that have become ditches, some of them 2, 3, and even 4 feet in depth, with perpendicular or overhanging sides and of a width ranging from 1 to several yards. The channels connect lakes, some of an area of a few square yards, others as big as several acres; lakes that are from 1 foot to 3 or 4 feet deep.

PALEOCRYSTIC ICE NOW WORST OF ALL

If this is perhaps a slight overstatement for an ice field that was perfectly level it is an understatement for those fields that had unevenness here and there. In particular it is now suicide to come down on paleocrystic ice, where the lakes are everywhere, with some at least of the formerly rounded hummocks now shaped more like anvils or mushrooms.

If you have to come down with a land plane under these conditions the situation is, however, not quite hopeless. You try to find some open lead and come down parallel to it. Perhaps you can find on the shore of one of the leads a stretch as much as half a mile or a mile long and a score or more of yards in width that has no big channels, water courses, emptying into the lead—the only channels may be tiny ones that your skis would hardly notice as you cross them at right angles, sliding along parallel to the lead and as near to it as you can trust yourself to steer safely.

When the freeze-up starts you are not at once through with these difficulties. Some of the lakes and water courses will be more or less empty and they will fill with such soft snow that there will be a deceptive levelness of the surface—you come gliding along after your skis are on the ice and may strike one of these soft patches that will either stop you and nose you over through the mere softness of the snow or, more likely, will permit the skis to sink in so much that they stub their toes against the far side. Then it also happens that the lakes we have described, some of which are nearly or quite large enough for a landing, will be covered with soft snow. For some time after the freeze-up this blanket of snow may keep the ice from thickening so long that even when you feel sure that everything must be frozen solid you find you have come down upon snow-covered ice so weak that it lets you through into the water.

Assuming the quoted estimate right, that there is a landing place on an average every 5 miles for the best time of winter (which, from the landing point of view, would be March or April) we might say that the good landing spots are in October only one-tenth that many and in December only half that many. When we consider also the poor light of October—the short days, the prevalent cloudiness, and occasional fogs—it appears that the fewest possible sea landings should be attempted before November. Thereafter with the light of moon, stars, and aurora, with the absence of fog and the rareness of clouds, you have a much improved condition.

There is no time of year when a descent upon the Arctic pack does not give you a better chance of safety than do the other oceans on the average.

WATER DESCENTS POSSIBLE IN WINTER

In summer, pontoons and flying boats are preferable over the Arctic pack to landplanes. It is probable that even in February, the coldest month of the year, you would find open water of sufficient extent for coming down with water gear on an average once every two or three hundred miles—probably oftener. You might make the descent safely, but you could hardly take off again; for the very splash as you strike the water will fasten a lot of ice on your craft. You should be able to taxi up to the edge of the lead and, with block and tackle, to haul the plane up so that it does not freeze fast. Here pontoons are better than a flying boat; for, as said, you can use them as skis on the ice and take off with them.

In summer you will find a great deal of open water at the North Pole (Lat. 90° N.) and even at the center of the pack, which is reckoned to be about 400 miles from the Pole in the direction towards Bering Strait. However, it is difficult to see from aloft whether there are floating around small chunks of ice. Ones plenty big enough to puncture your hull will be almost the same color as the water and practically flush with it. Still it would be at least a 50-50 gamble, and perhaps with the odds as much as 4 or 5 to 1 in your favor, that you would make a safe landing followed by a safe take-off after repairs.

AUTUMN CHANGE FROM SEAPLANE TO LANDPLANE

In the 1937 search for Levanevsky, Wilkins used a civilian model of the Consolidated flying boat then in use for long-range bombers by the Navy, and flew in it about 10,000 miles over the pack before the middle of September. By that time he considered that the formation of young ice on most of the open water had made flying boats more dangerous than a landplane. This statement is, however, for the central pack only; seaplane operation could have been carried out along the Alaska and Canada shores some 2 weeks longer.

When Wilkins resumed flying in October with a Lockheed, operation by landplane was still hazardous, for the season of sticky snow was not quite over and landing conditions were bad. However, there was in practice no difficulty; he never had to land for he was able to get rid of icing by changing his levels of flight. Operating conditions improved rapidly and were good by late November. As mentioned elsewhere the total flying of this landplane was about 10,000 miles before the middle of March, the longest flights (up to 2,700 miles) by moonlight.

In our discussion of ground ice we have brought out that over half of Canada, two-thirds of Alaska, and an area in the Soviet Union as big as the United States, lakes account for 50 percent to 60 percent of the surface, except in districts which are mountainous. These lakes are a great safety factor. In summer you use pontoons or a flying boat and come down on the liquid water. In winter you use skis and wheels and come down on the level ice. When flying a mile high you usually have within gliding range a choice between several good emergency landing places.

There is, however, a transition period during which in the autumn a given lake has too much of a skin of new ice upon it to permit descents with flying boat or pontoons and not enough of an ice-platform to allow ski or wheel landings.

If you assume that you cannot fly over a given region with water gear unless all waters are liquid nor with land gear unless there is safe ice on all the lakes, then planes would have to be idle over vast areas of the Soviet Union and considerable ones in Canada and Alaska for perhaps 6 weeks in fall and another 6 in spring. However, it is usually possible to play the lakes off one against the other so that this transition period is nearly or quite eliminated.

In the fall two lakes perhaps only a mile apart may freeze a good 6 weeks apart. There are a number of such cases around Great Bear Lake, where shallow ponds will usually freeze before the end of September, while bays of the lake itself may not freeze until November. You use the frozen or the open lake according to the landing gear that you carry.

In the spring the situation is reversed. The small lakes thaw much sooner than the large and deep ones, so that you can find on the same day, near a good many places in the North, safe ice for ski or wheel descents and safe and perfectly clear water for pontoons or flying boats. Sometimes you can even get these conditions on different arms of the same lake. A well-known instance of this from Great Bear Lake is that landings have been made around the 7th and 10th of June with pontoons on Cameron Bay while tractors were still operating on the larger Echo Bay, of which Cameron is a branch.

A frequent northern situation gives you both ice and water facilities on the same spring day even in a small lake if it is deep. Because there is such a large quantity of cold water in the lake, and because so much of the sun's light has been reflected from the lake's surface without being converted into heat, three-quarters of its surface will still be firm enough for airplane landings when several square miles of wholly ice-free water have developed at one side, where enters the current of a river that has gathered warmth from hundreds or thousands of square miles of snow-free land which it drains.

As we described in Chapter 11, Section II, there is, or may be, open water throughout the winter where a river leaves

525

a large lake. This, however, will be used during cold weather only in an extreme emergency, for you will get your plane all iced up.

In taxiing or landing on frozen surfaces of rivers or lakes, particularly during the transition period, precautions should be observed for special conditions: In lakes, for instance in the Liard section of northwestern Canada and in some parts of Alaska there are occasional soft spots caused by hot springs. In rivers, the ice is frequently very thin in certain locations when that nearby may be several feet thick. It is a local northern belief that this is sometimes caused by whirlpools in the river which wear the ice thin, due to the sand in the bottom of the river being constantly thrown against the under side of the ice. More likely it is caused as described in Chapter 11, Section II.

As described in the Chapter 11 section just cited, rivers may flood at any time of winter. There is an obvious danger hardly needing comment in descending either upon snow that is seen to be wet or upon a watery section of the ice surface. A danger not obvious is that sometimes the ice of a river is covered with 1, 2, or even 3 feet of very soft snow when the flooding starts, and the water may seep along for a mile or two, soaking the lower few inches of this snow but seldom or never coming to the surface so as to show a dark spot. It is hard to tell a flyer how to guard against the danger of coming down on this kind of snow, except that he should look as far as he can ahead (upstream) and not come down on snow, no matter how white it looks, if half a mile or so ahead he can see a darkening that indicates water.

The trouble is that if your plane sinks through snow into slush you will get ice frozen on your skis in such a way that the situation is going to be very difficult to manage. Most likely you will freeze in right where you are and have to chop your plane out eventually. This can be done the sooner by beating or tramping down the snow in the vicinity of your plane, so that it will all have a chance to freeze quickly.

526

DANGER SPOTS IN WINTER LAKE ICE

On lakes there are the dangers for planes which will be inferred from our description of the danger to men on foot and in sledging parties described in Section II, Chapter 11, where we tell about how ice may be eaten away from under snow, leaving either a surface consisting exclusively of snow or of snow with only a skin of ice underneath.

In connection with what was said above about coming down on lake ice during the spring transition period, one should have in mind the discussion of needle ice in Section III, Chapter 11. The main things from that discussion for the aviator to remember are that he better not come down near the meeting place of the lake's ice with its open water; and that he should come down, if possible, where there is a certain amount of snow on top of the ice, for there it is not likely to have disintegrated yet into the needle formation.

DESCENTS ON GLASSY WATER

A problem not special to the North but more serious there than the average is that of descents on glassy water.

When you are doing salt water flying, whether deep sea or coastal, you have the water glassy much oftener than in other latitudes because floating ice prevents wave action. Even if less than a quarter of the surface has ice upon it the water will be without a ripple in a way that seems strange to southerners. The coastal lagoons, in the early spring, also have cakes of ice floating about.

The small ice fragments detached from larger ones are a danger which we have discussed already. What we deal with here is the glassiness which results from their presence.

Arctic lakes are frequently glassy although after a manner not differing from what you find in more southerly districts.

If you have a shore line by which to judge height, there is no danger in landing on glassy water. Come as close to the shore line as practical, bring the machine to an ordinary glide, 100 or 200 feet in the air, place it in landing position and allow it to sink until it bounces—i. e., come down in a power glide in normal landing position.

You will be reluctant to use these tactics among ice, for detached chunks are more likely to injure your plane if you come down near a considerable floe. It may be well, then, to throw overboard such things as cushions (whatever you have that will float) and strike the water close to them.

SEASONAL AND GEOGRAPHIC VARIATION OF ARCTIC FLYING

We have said that generally speaking Arctic flying weather is best in winter and next best in summer. Of the two bad seasons, it is debatable whether spring or fall is the worse. Spring has the drawbacks of most fogs and most sticky snow and sleet; but it has daylight for nearly or quite all the 24 hours. The autumn has a good deal of fog and sticky snow, though not nearly as much as spring; but autumn daylight is limited and moon, stars, and aurora do not cooperate with the flyer very well when skies are cloudy.

Such exceptions as there are to the above rules occur where the conditions are special. The most special region is to the north and northeast of the Atlantic, where Gulf Stream and iced waters meet. Next most special is the vicinity of Greenland, because of the relation of a high and chill plateau to surrounding open seas. The third and perhaps least important group of exceptions is around Bering Strait and Bering Sea. The Strait is, or may be, kept open by a strong current. The ice is mobile in Bering Sea and there is some interference by warm Pacific waters. These and similar things which make flying conditions worse have been discussed elsewhere and are merely referred to here, as a résumé.

But it seems worth while to bring out, more fully than was done in our discussion of climate, certain weather features that have a special relation to flying.

With the exception of the Gulf Stream waters, the Greenland neighborhood, and Bering Strait and Sea, it is generally true for Arctic and sub-Arctic that you can pass from the good flying conditions on the continental lands to the good flying conditions of the interior pack ice without having much trouble with the bad coastal weather if you cross between land and pack at right angles to the coast, thus spending the least possible time in the worst belt. However, coastal weather does not differ much from pack and inland weathers during winter or early spring.

AVOID COASTWISE FLYING

From late spring through the summer and into the hard freezing of the autumn you get, on the whole, the worst possible flying conditions if you follow a coast line. Airways should therefore be so laid out, and sporadic flying should be so planned, that if you have to fly in the same direction as the coast runs then you do so parallel to the coast, preferably 50 to 100 miles inland. All approaches to a coast from the interior of the continents, or from the central region of the pack ice, should be as nearly as possible at right angles to the coast.

Two sub-Arctic lines of flight are, from the weather point of view, through much of the year extremely bad, about the worst in the northern hemisphere. They are following or approximately following the Aleutian chain in the Pacific and following in the North Atlantic the line or belt where the south and southwest flowing East Greenland and Labrador currents brush against the northward and northeastward flowing Gulf Stream.

SAMPLE CASE OF AIRLINE ROUTING

We illustrate through the geographically and climatologically best all-the-year route from New York to some such point in Asia as Peking or Irkutsk. This would keep at least 100 miles west of Hudson Bay, would cross the Rocky Mountains where they practically disappear abreast of Fort Macpherson (between latitudes 67° and 68° N.), and proceed down the Yukon to what should be the most northwesterly important base of this line, near Nulato.

Taking off from Nulato, the plane should acquire a considerable height, whereupon it can pass over without being troubled by most of the weather that makes the Bering coastal areas of Alaska and Siberia, and the sea between them, so bad in winter.

According to Soviet reports, Bering Sea weather extends somewhat farther inland in Siberia than Alaska, so that Anadir is perhaps a little too easterly for the Siberian main base of the suggested line. It should probably be at Krasnino, which is about 100 miles upstream from Anadir, or at some intermediate point.

An extensive correspondence with Canadian and Alaskan Arctic and sub-Arctic flyers has brought out some further points which we summarize:

WINTER FLYING

It is the experience of northern flyers that "you can't hurry the weather." If you take your time, camp in case of blizzards or too much ground drifting, it is not more dangerous to fly in the Canadian Arctic and sub-Arctic, or in central and northern Alaska, than farther south.

In northern Canadian flying little time is lost in winter because of weather—not more than 4 or 5 days a season. Conditions of visibility are usually good, in the interior, and snow doesn't freeze on the wings. Interior Alaska estimates for time lost are higher—about 25 percent of the days are considered unsuitable for flying. This difference in favor of Canada may well be not personal with flyers or due to equipment but due to the weather, and other natural flying conditions, really averaging better in Canada than Alaska.

SUMMER AND WINTER FLYING

An important factor in Arctic commercial aviation is the distribution of light and darkness—short periods of daylight each day in the winter and long periods of daylight in summer. (We have discussed this under Light in the Polar Regions.)

NIGHT FLYING

In connection with night flying a situation has developed which makes Canadian Arctic flyers nervous about giving out information. Government regulations say that you may fly only from half an hour before sunrise to half an hour after sunset; but no provision covers the period (several weeks in certain active flying districts) in winter when the sun does not rise. These Canadian flyers have mail contracts which they must carry through, and yet they cannot get a ruling which will permit them to do it legally. The testimony of some of the best Canadian aviators is, therefore, elaborately hedged around with qualifications, such as "I don't do it myself because it is against the regulations, but I know that * * *."

If a flyer knows the country, Arctic night flying with a moon in a clear sky is less dangerous than flying on a dull day (day of diffused light); you get, on the average, better flying weather at night. Full moon flying, and some say down to half moon, is perfectly safe. There is no glare on the snow in moonlight and the shadows are clean cut.

When several Alaskan and several northern Canadian flyers were consulted on the adequacy of moonlight for night landings on snow, and when the results were tabulated, it was found that the Canadians average a considerable more favorable attitude toward relying on the moon than did the Alaskans. In some cases of approximately equal ability and experience, Canadian testimony would give almost twice as many days as the Alaskan, per lunar month, for the time during which night landings by moon and stars are safe. Almost certainly this marked difference between the two groups is not in any large part of the result of personal equation or of equipment, but is in chief due to the greater reflection of moonlight by snow in northern Canada.

For the Canadian flyers were thinking mainly of the section north of Great Bear Lake, and of the northern treeless plains in general, while the Alaska flyers were doubtless thinking of the middle third of their territory, the Yukon basin. The Canadians were, then, speaking of a terrain that is mainly prairie or lakes and is from 90 percent to 100 percent covered by a snow blanket that reflects whatever light comes to it, while the Alaskans were thinking of land that is half, three-quarters, or in some cases seven-eighths covered with forest. Also, in the part of Alaska most familiar to these flyers are mountains so high, valleys so steep, and precipices so abrupt that they cast extensive shadows. Such topography is rare in Arctic Canada (except in the Yukon,

531

with which district many of the Canadian flyers questioned had little familiarity).

Doubtless because of considerations such as these, the Alaska estimates for safe landings at night by natural light on snow range from 4 to 8 days per month; the Canadian estimates were nearly double that—as high as 16 nights of the 28-day lunar month.

GLACIER LANDINGS IN SUMMER

During both winter and summer, places for emergency landings are few in Arctic mountains; but they are even fewer in summer, for snow fields that can be used in winter are now gone. However, there are some Arctic mountain glaciers, with great glaciers in sub-Arctic mountains, as in those of southern Alaska.

All flyers new to the Arctic who may have occasion for crossing mountains should be instructed that most glaciers will furnish a safe landing. Their seaward ends, the ones downward in the valleys, will be heavily crevassed, and so dangerous. Follow a glacier up its slope and, a long time before you reach its head, you may come to a stretch where crevasses are few. In any case, there is pretty certain to be a snow area near the very head where there are few or no crevasses.

GLACIER LANDINGS IN WINTER

Although, as said, winter landing places in Arctic mountains are more numerous than those of summer, still you may need to use glaciers even then. You can, of course; but with this difference of conditions: Crevasses are fewer in winter, and in that sense the glacier is more serviceable. But such crevasses as there are will be camouflaged by snow, so that you cannot be so sure from aloft whether you are coming down in a good place. However, the very head of the glacier is pretty safe at any season.

Apart from the great number of lakes in all nonmountainous Arctic and sub-Arctic countries, there appears little about northerly summer flying in lowlands that requires further special comment. On the continents of both New and Old Worlds are found June, July, and August temperatures that

resemble those of the States, running up to and even above
100° in the shade. They have thunderstorms, but no worse
than those of the States; and so on for various other com-
parisons.

SECTION III

TRACTORS

We discuss the northern geographic setting for the use of
tractors and then sketch their recent development in Alaska.

In connection with ground frost we have given in chapter 2,
section I, the reason why half or more of the surface of
northern flat lands is covered with lakes and we have discussed these lakes from the point of view of the aviator in
the present chapter. For mechanized ground operation, dependent on tractors and other motor vehicles, the "eternal"
frost is at least as important as it is for aviation.

SUMMER USE OF TRACTORS HANDICAPPED BY LAKES AND SWAMPS

Lakes on flat land are likely to be connected by sluggish
streams. In rolling and hilly country northern lakes are
somewhat more likely to be connected by streams than those
farther south, because of the lack of underground drainage.
In summer, even if the ground were hard between the lakes,
this network of them and their connecting streams would
prevent the use of tractors. Summer use of them is doubly
impractical because the ground between the lakes is mostly
swamp.

WINTER USE FACILITATED

But in autumn the situation changes. The swamp becomes
as hard as concrete; every lake and every sluggish stream gets
a hard and smooth surface which, 3 or 4 weeks after the beginning of the freeze-up, will support tractors of practically
any burden, giving them boulevard conditions for travel.

ARCTIC AND SUB-ARCTIC HAVE OVER 5,000,000 SQUARE MILES NEARLY IDEAL FOR WINTER TRACTOR OPERATIONS

Accordingly, there are few natural terrains in the world
across which a mechanized land force could move so readily

as across the northern prairie—traversing the lakes, following the winding streams, crossing the isthmuses between lakes that are usually low. In those parts where the land is forested the advantage to the tractor is similar, except that now and then it will be necessary to chop down trees that grow on the isthmuses between lakes that are not connected by suitable rivers. The ground being as hard as concrete, all you need to do is cut the trees off flush with surface. That gives you a hard and nearly level road.

In advancing, a force will be directed in one of three ways, by local guides, by maps, or by airplanes circling above and telephoning directions to the ground.

RIVERS ARE WINTER BOULEVARDS TO THE HEART OF A COUNTRY

Not only does practically all of the nonmountainous Arctic and sub-Arctic, a total area equal to nearly double that of the forty-eight States, become a ready highway for tractors in winter through the lakes; every river is also a boulevard reaching from the sea toward the heart of a country. The Yukon penetrates Alaska, and the Mackenzie Canada, each for 2,000 miles. There are at least three equally large Siberian rivers, each giving a road 2,000 miles toward the center of Asia. There are three or four other Soviet rivers comparable in size to the Missouri, each giving a thousand miles of access. There is a still greater number of sizes like the Kushkokwim, Kowak, Noatak, and Colville of Alaska, rivers that furnish roads of several hundred miles.

DEFENSE FACILITATED BY THE NATURE OF ARCTIC LANDS

This is not a work on military procedure. Still we point out that while an Arctic territory is perhaps more easily invaded than any other by a mechanized army of combined land and air forces, it is also nearly or quite the easiest, terrain in the world to defend. Through the very fact of mechanization, the advancing land force must follow lakes and rivers. It has to cross isthmuses between lakes where they are low and narrow. Therefore, you can forecast more easily than in most countries just about what way the invading army will have to take through an Arctic land.

534

Even where there is prairie this gives considerable advantage to the defenders. But remember that of the land covered by lakes because the subsoil is frozen more than 3,000,000 square miles is an evergreen forest, with trees in many places growing close together and 50, 80, or even 100 feet high. They come down nearly or quite to the water's edge both on lakes and rivers. These forests are often so dense that even a scouting plane cannot see down through between the trees to determine with even fair accuracy the force that may be there. Machine guns and other guns will find admirable willow and evergreen cover all around most lakes and along most stretches of river bank.

An invading army knows that there will be ambush here and there and may try to advance in snowstorms and during the dark of night. Here, too, there is advantage to the defense forces in being on lake or river shores; for guns can be sighted in daylight to be much more effective during darkness on those even surfaces than they could possibly be if the land were rolling or in any degree uneven.

The most striking difference between the utilization of the results of ground frost by plane and tractor is that the planes can use the resulting lakes the year round. The tractors are blocked by them in summer and aided by them in winter.

Because tractors operate only in winter in such countries as northern Finland, the northern third of the Soviet Union, and large sections of northern Canada and Alaska, movements that depend on tractors are of necessity winter operations.

In Alaska, Canada, and the Soviet Union, there has been in recent years a rapid growth in the use of tractors for commercial purposes.

ALASKA USE OF TRACTORS

Crawler or track-type tractors became popular in placer mining with the development of the bulldozer, and they now take a considerable part in this industry. During the operating season tractors equipped with bulldozers are used principally for stripping off the overburden—shoving the waste gravel to one side of the cut, pushing the gravel up to the sluice box, and also for stacking tailings at the end of the sluice box.

Previous to their use in placer mining, tractors were used primarily for winter freighting, when the marshes and rivers are frozen over, and for the building of such roads as the Alaska Road Commission has constructed throughout the Territory. There is also a limited number used in farming, both in clearing land and in pulling farm equipment. Their Alaska use for this purpose was up to 1940 chiefly confined to the Matanuska Colony and to the Tanana valley around Fairbanks.

Due to the saving in fuel, it is estimated that at least 95 percent of the tractors operated in the Territory during the last few years have been powered with diesel engines.

Since the price of gold increased, following 1932, and more modern methods were developed in placer mining, the Alaska use of the crawler tractor has no doubt increased 300 percent to 400 percent. It is estimated that in 1940 there were between 400 and 600 crawler tractors in the Territory, between 60 and 75 per year having been shipped in during the period 1937–40.

○

THE BUILDING OF SNOW CAMPS

DRAWINGS AND PHOTOGRAPHS

STRUCTURAL DRAWINGS

Seven drawings, illustrating the construction of a snow-house, were made at my request and under my direction by the well known frontiersman and artist, Belmore Browne. They were done at Camp Buckley, Colorado, where Mr. Browne is civilian adviser to the Arctic Training Division, and are based in part on photographs of a snowhouse which was set up by me for the Board of Winter Warfare, Camp Hale, Colorado, in late March, 1943.*

One of the hurdles of the beginner is the mistaken notion that because the snowhouse relies on dome principles the blocks should be cut and fitted together with the meticulous care we see when looking upward in domed temples. For this reason I asked Mr. Browne to emphasize the permissible irregularity; and this he has done throughout, particularly in the seventh drawing. An expert, working with blocks of nearly ideal snow, could build a house quite as irregularly as suggested by these drawings; but he probably would not do so, unless to illustrate to students, as Mr. Browne is doing, how greatly a snow dome can be made to differ in detail (though not in principle) from the usual masonry dome.

When a good builder is working with good snow the result, as indeed brought out by our photographs, is somewhere between the geometric regularity of a Greek temple and the extreme irregularity shown in the drawings. In a slap-dash job like drawing VII you have to chink the larger gaps with blocks that are roughly triangular, for if you try to fill with soft snow you will just be shoving that much snow into the house.

The main blocks set up by the builder do not fit snugly, except at corners, and neither do the triangle blocks used by the chinker for the crevices, meaning that in either case the final step is to rub soft snow into every crack with a mittened hand. The snow used may be any sort, except that it must not be granular. It can well be new fallen, still soft because it is new; or it may be blocks that have been chopped up with some tool, stamped under the heel and crushed. In the

---

* These drawings and some of the photographs are used in this book by courtesy of the Commanding Generals of Camp Hale and of Camp Buckley. Permission has also been granted by the Bureau of Public Relations of the United States Army.

latter case there will be a lot of angular fragments mixed with the soft snow, which does no appreciable harm.

But an interesting and really important thing to remember is that when the crevices have been filled with snow, reasonably pressed in, and have had a few hours to set, then the house will be stronger in the parts represented by the crevices and the formerly soft snow than in those represented by the original blocks.

In the first drawing (the ground plan) the wind is indicated as blowing at right angles to the door, which is customary. But a wind may change, and when it does you will make at the end of the tunnel (which has been housed in with a porch structure of snow blocks) a transverse addition like the cross bar of a capital T, and you build this so it opens on one end of the T crossbar, either roughly at right angles to the wind or in a lee position. If the wind changes again, you close that end of the T cross bar which was previously open and you open the end that was previously closed. With blocks of snow, such alterations are made in a few minutes and by a few snips of the knife.

It is important to keep in mind for a snowhouse that the door should always be open, for the free passage of men in and out. Therefore some such arrangement as the proposed T alteration must be used whenever the wind changes, for the wind must never blow into the house—the substitution of cold outdoors air for the warm air of indoors would be too rapid; besides, the gusts would bring snow drifting into the house.

As we have explained in our text, there is never any real reason for closing the door of a properly constructed snowhouse; for right construction means that the top of the door is at least eighteen inches lower than the bottom level of the bed platform, so that gravity prevents the cold air from rising up into the house (except through slight diffusion of gases) any faster than the warm air escapes through the ventilator. The ventilating chimney is not shown in Mr. Browne's drawings but is shown in one of our photographs.

Another feature not shown in the drawings, but in some of the photographs, is the banking of the house with soft snow. This banking should not be more than half way up the sides. If it were much higher than that the roof blocks would melt while you were cooking supper and you would find yourself living in the equivalent of a snow cave, such as boys dig into snowbanks, whereupon you could not keep your room dry and would have difficulty in keeping your clothing dry.

In drawings VI and VII we find illustrated the valuable principle that there is no great advantage in blocks uniform in width or length. As to thickness, blocks up to six inches thick may well be used in the lowest tier, as shown in drawing III, or perhaps in both first and second tiers. The blocks in the higher tiers should be thinner than that, the ones at the top of the dome seldom thicker than four inches when you put them in place. The thawing or glazing process, which we have described in our text, thins down the roof blocks to perhaps two inches, producing the most thinning at the highest places, less and less as you come down the wall. The thinning produced by this intentional preliminary thawing of the interior should stop about two tiers from the ground.

In drawing VI is indicated the temporary door, through which blocks are shoved in to the builder. There is no rule as to where this door should be placed, but usually the temporary door will be at some point other than the one where you are going to have the permanent door. More important, you will cut the temporary door at a place in the wall where the blocks are particularly sound; for if you are building with poor snow, and then cut a door where the blocks are specially poor, your house may cave in on you.

THE ARMY TEACHES SNOWHOUSE BUILDING AT
ECHO LAKE, CAMP BUCKLEY, COLORADO

Drawings by Belmore Browne, civilian, adviser on
cold-weather camping.

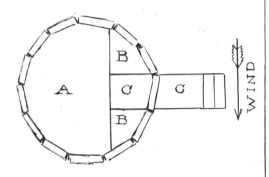

FIG. I. GROUND PLAN
A. SLEEPING PLATFORM.
B. STORAGE PLATFORMS.
C. PASSAGE THROUGH DOOR.

B

A

C

C

B

WIND

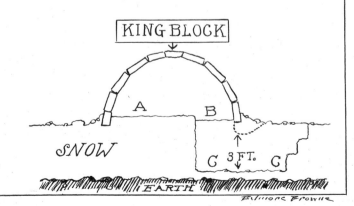

FIG. II. SIDE ELEVATION.
A. 1 FT ABOVE LEVEL OF SNOW.
B. 6 IN ABOVE LEVEL OF SNOW.
C. DOOR PASSAGE.

KING BLOCK

A

B

SNOW

C   3 FT.   C

EARTH

Belmore Browne

FIG. III. CONSTRUCTION OF SNOW HOUSE.

1ST TIER BLOCKS PLACED NEARLY PERPENDICULAR.
DIMENSIONS OF BLOCKS ABOUT 36IN LONG, 18IN WIDE
& 6IN THICK.

FIG. IV. FIRST TIER COMPLETED, SHOWING 3 BLOCKS CUT TO FORM INCLINED PLANE.

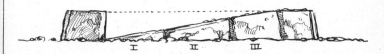

FIG. V. SECOND TIER SHOWING SPIRAL FORMED BY INCLINED PLANE

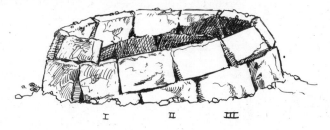

FIG. VI. NEARLY COMPLETED. DOOR FOR
PASSING IN SNOW BLOCKS SHOWN AT RIGHT.

I   II   III

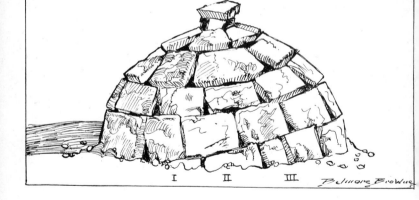

FIG. VII. FITTING THE LAST BLOCK, FILLING
IN DOOR AND SHOVELING OUT MAIN ENTRANCE,
(FIG. I & II), COMPLETES STRUCTURE.

I   II   III

Belmore Browne

TEACHING THE ARMY TO BUILD SNOWHOUSES

At eleven thousand feet in the mountains
at Camp Hale, Colorado.

Building with crumbly snow on a warm spring day. The first tier.

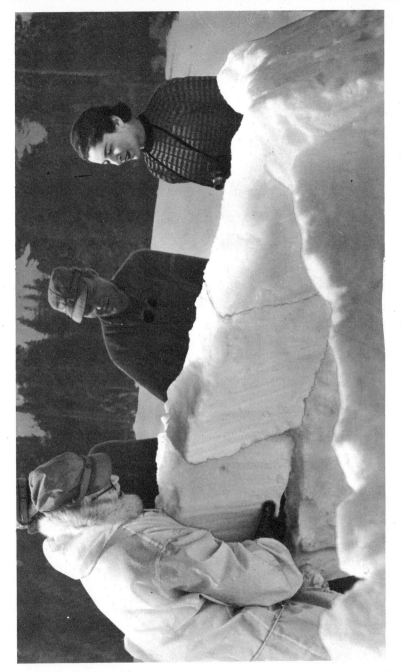

Placing a block in the second tier.

Making repairs where blocks have crumbled under their own weight.

1. Receiving a block for the third tier.
2. The block has been placed.

1. A snow flurry has coated the first three tiers, hiding the crevices.
2. Placing a fourth-tier block that came in through the temporary door.

Demonstrating irregular placing of upper blocks when speed of construction is desired.

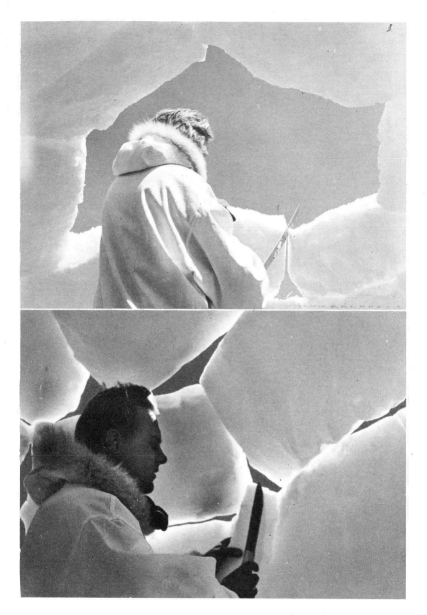

1. The camera is pointed upward from the floor as the house nears completion.
2. Looking upward again: the dome is complete except for the chinking.

1. Roof removed to show the permanent door and the well in front of the bed platform.
2. Cooking on bed platform.

BUILDING A SNOW CAMP

On the moving pack ice of the Arctic Mediterranean.

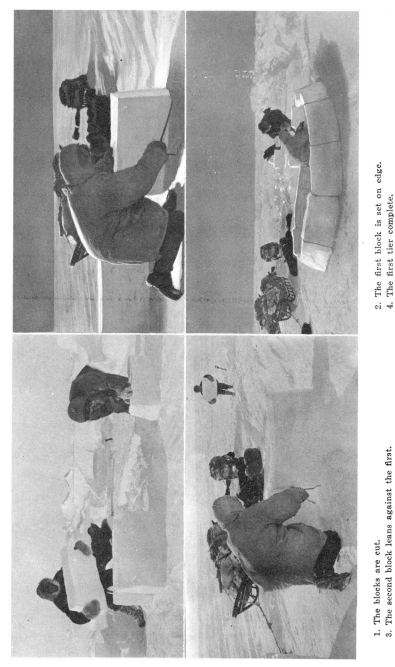

1. The blocks are cut.
2. The first block is set on edge.
3. The second block leans against the first.
4. The first tier complete.

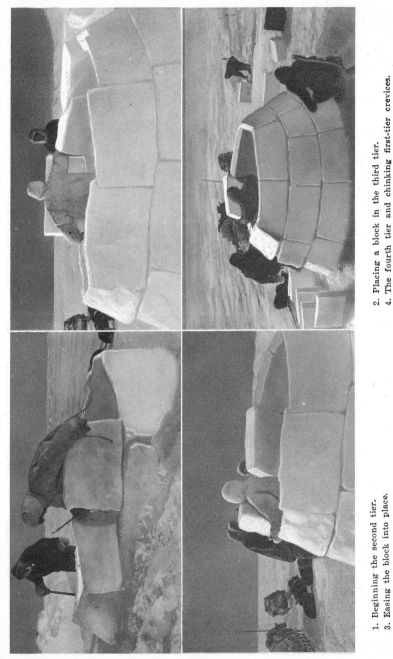

1. Beginning the second tier.
2. Placing a block in the third tier.
3. Easing the block into place.
4. The fourth tier and chinking first-tier crevices.

1. Lifting a roof block.
2. The roof block is shaped and adjusted.
3. The roof block in place.
4. The last block.

1. Shoving blocks in through temporary door.   2. Shoveling snow into crevices.
3. Banking the lower tiers.   4. Finished camp with porch and ventilator chimney.

1. The dogs sleep in harness while the men work.
2. When once glazed, a snowhouse will support almost any weight.

INDEX

Airline routing, 529

Airplanes, anchorage of, in snow, 517-519; Arctic use of, 503-533; first descent on Polar Sea of, 505-507; forced landings of, on Inland Ice, 367-370; icing of, 48-49; judging safety of ice from, 511; landings of, on glaciers, 532-533; landings of, on sea ice, 26; types best for different seasons, 523, 524

Akeley, Carl, on fat hunger in tropics, 222

Alaska, 27, 162, 163, 193, 228, 269; brown bear, 98-99; caribou in, 76, 81; coastal prairie, 14; driftwood in northern, 213; fishing in, 118-119; first Arctic airplane tragedy in, vii-x; first U. S. airmail in, vii; Game Laws, 104, 490; glaciers in, 13-14, 20; ground frost in, 21, 143; musk oxen, domestication in, 114-115; night flying in 70; topography of, 13-14; type of emergency snow-house used in, 165-66; use of tractors in, 535-536

Alaska, north coast, fog off, 500; ice movement off, 379; navigation, 379-380; precipitation, 55; sinking, 14

Alaska Peninsula, 98, 112

Alaska Road Commission, 536

Alazeya Plateau, 15

Albinism, in reindeer, 110

Aleutian Islands, 28, 69, 112

Alexandra Land, 17

American Museum of Natural History, 484

Ammunition, rifle, 437-438

Amund Ringnes Island, 12

Amundsen-Ellsworth Expedition, x; sounding obtained by, 24

Amundsen, Roald, 500; forced landings in ice pack, by, 507-509; on absence of lice among Eskimos, 126

Andersen, Karsten, on exclusive meat diet, 222-223, 225, 282, 285-286

Anderson, Rudolph Martin, experience with monoxide poisoning, 322; on fish and fishing, 119-123, 488; on musk oxen, 85; on whaling, 106

Anderson Valley, 113

Andreasen, Matt, 382

Anesthetic, use of cold as, 297-298

Angmagssalik, 369

Antiscorbutics, *see* Scurvy

Archangel, 501

Arctic Circle, 15, 137; full moon at, 71; snow-free land within, 41; temperatures recorded within, 40

Arctic, classic view of, 1-3; continental shelf, 24; historical background, 1-7; hysteria, 309-310; physical geography of, 8-37; snow-free land in summer in, 41; summer temperatures in, 40-44; invasion and defense of, 534-535

Arctic Institute of the U.S.S.R., 138

Arctic Ocean (Arctic Mediterranean), 13. *See also* Polar Sea

Arnold, General Henry H., xii

Athapaskan method of caribou hunting, 465; type of fish hooks, 489

Aurora borealis, 71

Aviation Corporation Eielson-Borland Relief Expedition, x

Aviation problems, in Arctic fog, 61-64; at low temperatures, 48-50

Azizia, 38

Baashuss-Jessen, J., on dog diseases, 423

Back's River, 205

Badigin, Constantine, 28; on temperature records of *Sedov*, 43-44

Baffin Bay, 24

Baffin Island, 12, 136, 164

Baikal, Lake, 22

Baillie Islands, 65, 106, 120, 122, 488

Baird Mountains, 13

Balaena, 106

Banks Island, 12, 28, 60, 93, 107, 496; caribou on, 78, 80; musk ox on, 84

Barents Island, 17

Barents Sea, 24, 27

Barents, William, Expedition, 321-322

Barometric pressures, 65-67

Barren Ground caribou, *see* Caribou

Barren Ground grizzly, *see* Grizzly bear

Barrow, *see* Point Barrow

Bartlett, Robert Abram, 225, 319

Bathurst Cape, 93, 107, 120, 121, 123, 164

Bathurst Island, 12